Conceptual Revolutions in Twentieth-Century Art

From Picasso's Cubism and Duchamp's readymades to Warhol's silk-screens and Smithson's earthworks, the art of the twentieth century broke completely with earlier artistic traditions. A basic change in the market for advanced art produced a heightened demand for innovation, and young conceptual innovators – from Picasso and Duchamp to Rauschenberg and Warhol to Cindy Sherman and Damien Hirst – responded not only by creating dozens of new forms of art, but also by behaving in ways that would have been incomprehensible to their predecessors. *Conceptual Revolutions in Twentieth-Century Art* presents the first systematic analysis of the reasons for this discontinuity. David W. Galenson, whose earlier research has changed our understanding of creativity, combines social scientific methods with qualitative analysis to produce a fundamentally new interpretation of modern art that will give readers a far deeper appreciation of the art of the past century, and of today, than is available elsewhere.

David W. Galenson is Professor of Economics at the University of Chicago and Research Associate at the National Bureau of Economic Research. His other published works include *Painting Outside the Lines* (2001) and *Old Masters and Young Geniuses* (2006).

D1282333

Conceptual Revolutions in Twentieth-Century Art

DAVID W. GALENSON
The University of Chicago

NBER

CAMBRIDGE
UNIVERSITY PRESS

CAMBRIDGE UNIVERSITY PRESS
Cambridge, New York, Melbourne, Madrid, Cape Town, Singapore,
São Paulo, Delhi, Dubai, Tokyo

Cambridge University Press
32 Avenue of the Americas, New York, NY 10013-2473, USA

www.cambridge.org
Information on this title: www.cambridge.org/9780521129091

First published 2009

Printed in the United States of America

A catalog record for this publication is available from the British Library.

Library of Congress Cataloging in Publication data
Galenson, David W.
Conceptual revolutions in twentieth-century art / David W. Galenson. – 1st ed.
p.   cm.
Includes bibliographical references and index.
ISBN 978-0-521-11232-1 (hardback) – ISBN 978-0-521-12909-1 (pbk.)
1. Art, Modern – 20th century.   2. Art and society – History – 20th century.   3. Creation
(Literary, artistic, etc.)   I. Title.
N6490.G225   2009
709.04 – dc22   2009012050

ISBN   978-0-521-11232-1 Hardback
ISBN   978-0-521-12909-1 Paperback

Relation of the Directors to the Work and Publications of the NBER

1. The object of the NBER is to ascertain and present to the economics profession, and to the public more generally, important economic facts and their interpretation in a scientific manner without policy recommendations. The Board of Directors is charged with the responsibility of ensuring that the work of the NBER is carried on in strict conformity with this object.

2. The President shall establish an internal review process to ensure that book manuscripts proposed for publication DO NOT contain policy recommendations. This shall apply both to the proceedings of conferences and to manuscripts by a single author or by one or more co-authors but shall not apply to authors of comments at NBER conferences who are not NBER affiliates.

3. No book manuscript reporting research shall be published by the NBER until the President has sent to each member of the Board a notice that a manuscript is recommended for publication and that in the President's opinion it is suitable for publication in accordance with the above principles of the NBER. Such notification will include a table of contents and an abstract or summary of the manuscript's content, a list of contributors if applicable, and a response form for use by Directors who desire a copy of the manuscript for review. Each manuscript shall contain a summary drawing attention to the nature and treatment of the problem studied and the main conclusions reached.

4. No volume shall be published until forty-five days have elapsed from the above notification of intention to publish it. During this period a copy shall be sent to any Director requesting it, and if any Director objects to publication on the grounds that the manuscript contains policy recommendations, the objection will be presented to the author(s) or editor(s). In case of dispute, all members of the Board shall be notified, and the President shall appoint an ad hoc committee of the Board to decide the matter; thirty days additional shall be granted for this purpose.

5. The President shall present annually to the Board a report describing the internal manuscript review process, any objections made by Directors before publication or by anyone after publication, any disputes about such matters, and how they were handled.

6. Publications of the NBER issued for informational purposes concerning the work of the Bureau, or issued to inform the public of the activities at the Bureau, including but not limited to the NBER Digest and Reporter, shall be consistent with the object stated in paragraph 1. They shall contain a specific disclaimer noting that they have not passed through the review procedures required in this resolution. The Executive Committee of the Board is charged with the review of all such publications from time to time.

7. NBER working papers and manuscripts distributed on the Bureau's web site are not deemed to be publications for the purpose of this resolution, but they shall be consistent with the object stated in paragraph 1. Working papers shall contain a specific disclaimer noting that they have not passed through the review procedures required in this resolution. The NBER's web site shall contain a similar disclaimer. The President shall establish an internal review process to ensure that the working papers and the web site do not contain policy recommendations, and shall report annually to the Board on this process and any concerns raised in connection with it.

8. Unless otherwise determined by the Board or exempted by the terms of paragraphs 6 and 7, a copy of this resolution shall be printed in each NBER publication as described in paragraph 2 above.

To Stan Engerman
Lance Davis
Clayne Pope
And the memory of Bob Gallman

Contents

List of Tables

Preface

During my last semester in college, I took a course on the history of modern art. I loved it; what I learned has increased the pleasure I have gotten ever since from visiting museums and art galleries. When I took that course, however, I never imagined that more than three decades later I would write a book that would provide a very different analysis of the art of the twentieth century.

I still have the textbook from my college course, George Heard Hamilton's excellent *Painting and Sculpture in Europe, 1880–1940*. It began with a clear statement of the problem to be explored, which I dutifully underlined:

In the half-century between 1886, the date of the last Impressionist exhibition, and the beginning of the Second World War, a change took place in the theory and practice of art which was as radical and momentous as any that had occurred in human history. It was based on the belief that works of art need not imitate or represent natural objects and events.

The book's cover illustrated what Hamilton called the "watershed between the old pictorial world and the new," Picasso's jarring painting of 1907, *Les Demoiselles d'Avignon*.

Hamilton's book, and the professor's lectures, provided a detailed narrative of the shift from an art that represented the natural world to one that recorded the artist's ideas and emotions. Yet neither Hamilton nor the professor offered any explanation of why this radical change had occurred when it did: their narratives described the ideas and styles of a series of artists and movements, without offering any analysis of why this sequence occurred at this particular time. The description of the rapid succession of styles was so absorbing, however, that I did not think of the underlying issue of causation. I simply concentrated on understanding the narrative on its own terms, as an explanation of the formal concerns that had led one artist after another to make a series of dramatic innovations.

In 1997, I began studying the question of why some modern artists have done their most important work early in their careers, and others late in theirs. This research eventually led to a new understanding of individual creativity in general, based on a recognition of the fundamental differences in the processes followed, and the work produced, by conceptual and experimental innovators. This analysis placed the history of modern art in a new light: I could now see that the radical change that Hamilton had described was initiated and carried out almost exclusively by conceptual innovators. Intrigued by this discovery, I began studying the new patterns of behavior that conceptual artists had devised in the course of the twentieth century. As I catalogued these surprising new practices, it became increasingly clear to me how the art of the twentieth century as a whole was dramatically and systematically different from that of all earlier periods. And as a result of a separate research project, I realized that the underlying reason for this was economic.

In the course of my research on the life cycles of modern artists, I had gotten to know Robert Jensen, an art historian who had written a book about the early development of the market for modern art. In 2002, we wrote a paper that presented an economic analysis of the changes that occurred in the market for advanced art in the late nineteenth century. We showed that the Impressionists' group exhibitions of 1874–86 had the effect of eliminating the monopoly the government-sponsored Salon had previously exercised over artists' ability to present their work for serious evaluation by critics, and purchase by collectors. The Impressionists' exhibitions, and others that were established following their example, constituted a legitimate alternative means for artists to present their work to both critics and collectors, and this created a competitive market where there had previously been a monopoly.

Our paper dealt only with the late nineteenth century, but when I considered the extension of this analysis to the early twentieth century, I found another important institutional development. As Monet and the other Impressionists began to gain success in the market, increasing numbers of private dealers became willing to sponsor and exhibit the work of artists who, like them, had not gained recognition in the traditional way, by exhibiting in the official Salon. By the early twentieth century, there were enough of these enterprising dealers to create real economic opportunities for young artists. The first young artist who appears to have recognized this, and set out in systematic fashion to create competition among dealers for his art, was Pablo Picasso – the same young artist who made the most dramatic break with traditional painting, with *Les Demoiselles d'Avignon*.

Combining the economic analysis of the development of competition in the market for advanced art with Hamilton's narrative of the dramatic change in modern painting, I realized that Picasso and other conceptual innovators who followed him were profoundly affected by the new market structure. In modern art, as in many activities, a competitive market allowed innovators greater freedom of action than monopoly: Picasso and his successors did not have to satisfy a jury controlled by the conservative Academy of Fine Arts, but instead needed only to find a dealer who would exhibit their paintings, and a few collectors who would consistently buy their work. This change in market structure explains why artists in the twentieth century behaved so differently from their predecessors of the nineteenth century. This book examines some of the most novel forms of behavior they created. Thirty-five years after I learned the traditional view of the history of modern art, I believe this book presents the first real explanation of *why* modern art changed so radically in the early twentieth century, and of why it has continued to change so rapidly ever since.

This book is dedicated to Lance Davis, Stanley Engerman, the late Robert Gallman, and Clayne Pope, four economic historians who have been my friends since I first entered the profession. In spite of the fact that none was ever paid for the job, they have also all been my teachers. And thanks to the National Bureau of Economic Research, for a number of years they were formally my colleagues, as fellow research associates of the Bureau. All four are wonderful economic historians; together they taught me the fine art of doing quantitative history and showed me the pleasures of doing it well. I will always be grateful for the interest they took in my research in economic history, and for the extraordinary education they gave me.

Immediately before I began to study the life cycles of artists, Clayne Pope and I collaborated on a research project on the life cycles of immigrants in the nineteenth-century United States. Clayne's interest in my work survived my radical change of subject matter, and I am grateful to him for many valuable conversations on a subject that was far from his own professional interests.

Throughout my work on this book, Robert Jensen provided active encouragement and unlimited access to his vast knowledge of modern art. Discussions with Rob improved my understanding of nearly every topic treated in this book, and made the process of writing it much more enjoyable.

I am grateful for Morgan Kousser's continuing enthusiasm for my research on artistic creativity, and for Joshua Kotin's interest in this work outside his own field of study. Conversations with Josh Schonwald helped me solve problems of both substance and style. I appreciate the encouraging reactions to my research of a number of my Chicago colleagues, particularly the generous comments of Robert Lucas and Richard Posner. At the NBER, I thank Marty Feldstein for his interest in my research.

At Cambridge University Press, I thank Frank Smith and Jeanie Lee for their interest and efficiency.

I am grateful to Julio Elias for arranging for me to present my work at three extraordinary forums in Argentina. I have benefited from the opportunity to present portions of this research at the American Federation of Arts Conference, "Art Matters," in New York, 2005; at the Skoll Forum on Social Entrepreneurship, Oxford, 2007; at the Annual Meeting of the Canadian Museums Association, Ottawa, 2007; at the Civic Ventures Purpose Prize Summit, Palo Alto, 2007; at the NESTA Conference on the Creative Economy in the 21st Century, London, 2008; at the SYFR Conference on Creativity, Vail, 2008; at symposia on creativity at the Universidad del CEMA, Buenos Aires, 2008, and at the Universidad Nacional de Tucuman, 2008; at a forum on contemporary art at the Museo de Arte Latinoamericano de Buenos Aires (MALBA), 2008; and at the Annual Social Entrepreneurship Summit, Toronto, 2008. I am grateful to many of the participants at these conferences for their comments, as well as participants at seminars and lectures I gave at the Ecole des Hautes Etudes en Sciences Sociales, Paris; the American University of Paris; SUNY Buffalo; Queen's University, Belfast; Trinity College, Hartford; and the University of Chicago.

I thank the John Simon Guggenheim Memorial Foundation for a fellowship that gave me time to finish this book. Earlier versions of Chapters 4, 5, and 7 were published in *Historical Methods* and *Historically Speaking*; I thank them for permission to reprint some material here.

Shirley Ogrodowski, Amanda Edwards, and Saerome Parish all learned firsthand the trials of experimental research, as each typed a series of revised versions of the chapters of this book. Their feelings toward this process may be evidenced by the fact that none of the three still works for me, but I am grateful for the efficiency and unfailing good cheer with which they worked on the manuscript.

Introduction: And Now for Something Completely Different

WE DECLARE:...
That the name of "madman" with which it is attempted to gag all innova-
tors should be looked upon as a title of honor.
Umberto Boccioni, Carlo Carrà, Luigi Russolo, Giacomo Balla, and
Gino Severini, *Futurist Painting: Technical Manifesto*, 1910[1]

The title immortalized by Monty Python has three distinct meanings in the
present context. Most generally, it is a remarkably apt description of the
history of visual art in the twentieth century. Innovation has always been
the distinguishing feature of important art, but the need for innovation to
be conspicuous is a particular hallmark of the modern era, and the pace
of change has accelerated within that era. For example the critic Clement
Greenberg observed in 1968 that "Until the middle of the last century
innovation in Western art had not had to be startling or upsetting; since
then... it has had to be that."[2] Only a year earlier, a critic of very different
sensibility, Lucy Lippard, wrote that "Today movements are just that;
they have no time to stagnate before they are replaced... Younger critics
and artists have matured in a period accustomed to rapid change."[3] The
twentieth century witnessed artistic changes that had no precedent in the
history of our civilization, and it is now time to recognize the century as
the Age of Something Completely Different.

The Monty Python effect also neatly characterizes a new model of
artistic behavior that was invented early in the twentieth century, and
went on to thrive over time. Fittingly, it was the century's greatest artist,
Pablo Picasso, who first devised the practice of changing styles at will,
and he was followed by a number of other key figures. The eminent critic

David Sylvester observed that this was a kind of behavior that could not have existed before the twentieth century, for no artist who produced art in a variety of styles would have been taken seriously in an earlier time. That stylistic promiscuity was practiced by some of the greatest artists of the twentieth century clearly sets it apart from all earlier artistic eras.[4]

Finally, the Monty Python formula describes the nature of the present book. That this is true has come as a surprise to me. I began studying art history a decade ago, after doing research on economic and social history for nearly 25 years, as a member of both economics and history departments. It seemed natural to approach art history with the same blend of quantitative and qualitative techniques that I had learned and used in my earlier research. What surprised me, however, was the hostility I encountered from art historians, who almost unanimously refused to acknowledge the value that quantitative methods could have in their field, and who equally blindly refused to look past these methods to my conclusions. Unlike in the other fields of history I had encountered in my earlier research – not only economic, but also social, demographic, and urban history – quantification has been almost totally absent from art history. On the one hand, this meant that there were questions I could study, and large bodies of evidence I could use, that had effectively not been touched by earlier scholars, and this produced enormous intellectual gains: I have learned fascinating things about modern art that art historians do not know. On the other hand, I had to recognize that I would be treated as a hostile interloper by art scholars, simply because my work didn't look like theirs. I persevered in spite of their unfortunate lack of intellectual curiosity, and it is, therefore, with some residual surprise that I can point out that the use of measurement and systematic generalization in a study of twentieth-century art makes this study something completely different.

I

The Back Story of Twentieth-Century Art

Making it New

What modern art means is that you have to keep finding new ways to express yourself, to express the problems, that there are no settled ways, no fixed approach. This is a painful situation, and modern art is about this painful situation of having no absolutely definite way of expressing yourself.

Louise Bourgeois, 1988[1]

It has long been recognized that innovation is the core value of modern art. In 1952, for example, the critic Harold Rosenberg could remark that "the only thing that counts for Modern Art is that a work shall be NEW."[2] The recognition of this association first arose roughly a century earlier. In 1855, Charles Baudelaire, the poet and critic who was one of the earliest prophets of modern art, observed that the growing acceptance of change in nineteenth-century society would inevitably have an impact on artists' practices. He reasoned that the widespread appreciation of the great economic benefits of technological change in industry would lead to a demand for visible progress in all spheres, including art.[3] In a celebrated essay published in 1863, "The Painter of Modern Life," Baudelaire proposed no less than a new "rational and historical theory of beauty," that explained why artistic change must occur. He posited that although beauty did have "an eternal, invariant element," it also had a "relative, circumstantial element," that represented the contemporary – "the age, its fashions, its morals, its emotions." The ambitious painter could not simply study the art of the Old Masters, but also had to seek to represent "modernity," which consisted of "the ephemeral, the fugitive,

3

the contingent." And artists must be concerned not only to choose new contemporary subjects, but to represent them with new techniques, for in the accelerated pace of modern life "there is a rapidity of movement which calls for an equal speed of execution from the artist."[4]

Paris became a battleground for advanced art during the late nineteenth century, as artists and the critics who championed them debated the merits of a rapid succession of new movements, from Impressionism and its challengers onward. For example the philosopher and critic Arthur Danto recently compared the Paris art world of the 1880s to the New York art world of the 1980s – "competitive, aggressive, swept by the demand that artists come up with something new or perish."[5] Yet throughout these debates, the artists who played the leading roles implicitly accepted Baudelaire's formulation of the two elements of beauty, recognizing that they must learn from the best art of the past, but that they also must add new developments of their own making. It was with both of these elements in mind, for example, that in 1905 the aged Paul Cézanne explained to a critic that "To my mind one does not put oneself in place of the past, one only adds a new link."[6] And as advanced art spread out from Paris into other European capitals, the need for progress was always clearly understood. Thus in Moscow in 1919, the logic of Kazimir Malevich's declaration of the value of new artistic methods and means echoed Baudelaire's argument about the origin of the demand for the new in modern art: "Life develops with new forms; a new art, medium and experience are necessary for every epoch. To strive towards the old classical art would be the same as for a modern economic state to strive towards the economy of ancient states."[7]

Valuing Innovation

Well, thank God, art tends to be less what critics write than what artists make.

Jasper Johns, 1959[8]

Important artists are innovators whose work changes the practices of their successors. The greater the changes, the greater the artist. It is those artists who have the greatest influence on their peers – and the artists of later generations – whose work hangs in major museums, becomes the subject of study by scholars, and sells for the highest prices.

There is a persistent belief, not only among the general public but even among many art scholars, that artistic importance can be manufactured, deliberately and artificially, by powerful critics, dealers, or curators. In the short run, prominent critics and dealers can unquestionably gain considerable attention for an artist's work. Yet unless this attention is transformed into influence on other artists, it cannot give that artist an important place in art history. Thus in 1965, Harold Rosenberg, who was himself a leading critic, conceded that "Manipulated fame exists, of course, in the art world." Yet he emphasized that this fame was fleeting: "The sum of it is that no dealer, curator, buyer, critic or any existing combination of these, can be depended upon to produce a reputation that is more than a momentary flurry." Real power in the art world came from only one source: "the single most potent force in the art world is still, in the last analysis, the artist... A painter with prestige among painters is bound to be discovered sooner or later by the tastes of those who determine when an artist deserves to be bought, hired, or chosen as one of the four or fourteen Americans currently entitled to museum fanfare."[9]

In 1989, Sir Alan Bowness, the former director of the Tate Gallery, presented a more formal version of this argument in a lecture titled "The Conditions of Success: How the Modern Artist Rises to Fame." Bowness explained that, contrary to the general supposition that artistic success is arbitrary or due to chance, there are in fact specific conditions of success, which can be precisely described, so that "Artistic fame is predictable." Bowness contended that there are four successive stages on the exceptional artist's path to fame: "peer recognition, critical recognition, patronage by dealers and collectors, and finally public acclaim." The key was the first stage, of peer recognition – "the young artist's equals, his exact artist contemporaries, and then the wider circle of practicing artists." Once artists gave a peer their respect, the other stages would invariably follow: "it is always the artists themselves who are first to recognize exceptional talent."[10]

Rosenberg and Bowness both spoke from substantial art world experience – one from years of writing critical assessments of art, the other from years of acquiring and exhibiting art for a great public museum. Thus for example in support of his contention that the artist was the key force in the art world, Rosenberg explained that "It is to him that dealers and collectors, curators and art department heads turn for recommendations. It is his judgments of his colleagues that reviewers listen in on before committing themselves in their columns."[11] But long before either Rosenberg or Bowness wrote the words quoted here, it was an artist who identified the most important reason why it is artists who are the key judges of artistic success. In 1910 the English painter Walter Sickert, who moonlighted as a critic, explained to an ambivalent London art world that there could no longer be any question as to the importance of the French Impressionists. Sickert analyzed two specific contributions of the group, in composition and the use of color, that led to a clear conclusion: "They have changed the language of painting." This definitively settled the question of their importance, because of a simple criterion: "Perhaps the importance that we must attach to the achievement of an artist or a group of artists may properly be measured by the answer to the following question: Have they so wrought that it will be impossible henceforth, for those who follow, ever again to act as if they had not existed?"[12] Important artists are those whose work changes the practices of other artists.

Alan Bowness contended that there had been no major change during the modern era in the process he described, and he was correct with respect to its structure – the sequence in which the artist was first recognized by other artists, then by other members of the art world, and finally by the public. Yet one important change did occur involving the speed with which the process took place, as over time a series of critics, dealers, and collectors learned from the successes – and failures – of their predecessors. Each time a modern artist became famous, from Monet, Cézanne, van Gogh, and Gauguin on, one element of the retrospective narratives of their careers that always gained considerable public attention was the early, extended neglect of their work. For all those involved in the art market, whether critics who sought fame by becoming early champions of great artists, or dealers and collectors who sought riches by becoming early agents or patrons, each such episode carried a powerful lesson about unexploited profit opportunities. As time went on it became clear that advanced art was producing a steady stream of important innovators, each of whom was passing through the sequence of stages that Bowness described. As the awareness of this process spread, the search for new and unrecognized innovators intensified. In 1968 the poet John Ashbery, who also moonlighted as an art critic, remarked on the result: "Looking back only as far as the beginning of this century we see that the period of neglect for an avant-garde artist has shrunk for each generation. Picasso was painting mature masterpieces for at least ten years before he became known to even a handful of collectors. Pollock's incubation period was a little shorter. But since then the period has grown shorter each year so that it now seems to be something like a minute.

It is no longer possible, or it seems no longer possible, for an important avant-garde artist to go unrecognized."[13]

Generation Gaps, Part 1

People who were formerly considered revolutionaries have now turned out to be counter-revolutionaries: the same thing happens in art.
Kazimir Malevich, 1920[14]

Significant artistic innovators are of course not simply initially unappreciated: they are vigorously attacked. Any innovative new art form necessarily involves the rejection of older values. For practitioners and admirers of those older values, this causes "a sense of loss, of sudden exile, of something willfully denied... a feeling that one's accumulated culture or experience is hopelessly devalued."[15] It is hardly surprising that those committed to established forms refuse to accept innovations that would make those forms obsolete, and thus cause a devaluation of their own knowledge and skills. This phenomenon is not unique to art, but in scholarship is known as Planck's principle, named for the physicist Max Planck, who observed that "a new scientific truth does not triumph by convincing its opponents and making them see the light, but rather because its opponents eventually die, and a new generation grows up that is familiar with it."[16]

Examples of great artists who evolved from youthful revolutionaries into aging reactionaries are not difficult to find. In spite of the fact that some of the most important abstract painters were deeply influenced by his own innovation of Cubism, Pablo Picasso never accepted the validity of abstract art.[17] Picasso's companion Françoise Gilot reported a remarkable conversation between Picasso and Henri Matisse that occurred in the early 1950s, when the two great painters had both passed the age of 70. After looking at some catalogues Matisse had received from his son Pierre, an art dealer in New York, that reproduced recent paintings by the American Abstract Expressionists, Picasso categorically rejected the work: "As far as these new painters are concerned, I think it is a mistake to let oneself go completely and lose oneself in the gesture. Giving oneself up entirely to the action of painting – there's something in that which displeases me enormously." His old rival and friend was more circumspect. Matisse contended that artists couldn't understand the innovations of their successors, and therefore couldn't judge them: "One is always unable to judge fairly what follows one's own work." He explained that "One can judge what has happened before [one's own work] and what comes along at the same time. And even when a painter hasn't completely forgotten me I understand him a little bit, even though he goes beyond me. But when he gets to the point where he no longer makes any reference to what for me is painting, I can no longer understand him. I can't judge him either. It's completely over my head." Unmoved by Matisse's caution, Picasso dismissed it, together with Jackson Pollock's art, declaring: "I don't agree with you at all. And I don't *care* whether I'm in a good position to judge what comes after me. I'm against that sort of stuff."[18]

Others in the art world, including great dealers, are subject to the same forces. Leo Castelli opened an art gallery in New York in 1957, and only a year later presented Jasper Johns' first one-man exhibition, which was an immediate sensation in the art world. Castelli became the leading art dealer of the 1960s and 1970s, representing Johns, Robert Rauschenberg, the major Pop artists – notably Andy Warhol, Roy Lichtenstein, and Claes Oldenburg – as well as such younger stars as Frank Stella, Richard Serra, and Bruce Nauman. In an interview in 1994, Castelli recalled his dismay when the 1993 Whitney Biennial exhibition had forced him to recognize the impact of new developments that had been occurring in advanced art, with the increased use of new media, including video, and the prominence of younger German and Italian painters: "I had to accept the fact that the wonderful days of the era I had participated in, and in which I had played a substantial role, were over." He initially could not accept the legitimacy of the newer art: "I felt that what had been there before, during the great era of the sixties, was unbeatable, and that nothing of that kind could succeed the heroic times that we had had here in New York." On reflection, however, he realized that he had to accept the new art, so that he would not repeat the universal error of aging art experts: "There was a certain sadness that I felt about it, but well, with the Whitney show, I realized that I had to change my attitude, and not be rejecting – as people generally are, as you know. Someone like Kahnweiler, for instance, after Picasso and the Cubists felt that there was no good art anymore. I would say that there is a span, a relatively short span, in which somebody really lives seriously with a period of art and after that, all those people – whether it be dealers or art historians or museum directors – after that they don't see what's going on anymore. They reject whatever comes after that. I didn't want to be one of those." In spite of this recognition, however, in 1994 the 87-year-old Castelli confessed that he could not find any artist under the age of 50 whom he could consider genuinely important: "So for me, Nauman was really the last groundbreaking artist."[19]

Significant innovations inevitably impose losses on those who cherish the values the new innovations reject, but of course they also offer gains. The artistic innovators who are faced with attacks on their new methods understand this. For example, Kazimir Malevich remarked in 1919 that "People always demand that art be comprehensible, but they never demand of themselves that they adapt themselves to comprehension."[20] When artists create significant new forms of art, they almost invariably see their innovations denounced by critics who are judging their new methods by the rules or conventions of earlier art, which the innovators have intentionally discarded. Thus in 1914, Wassily Kandinsky warned against critics who claimed to have found flaws in new art: "one should never trust a theoretician (art historian, critic, etc.) who asserts that he has discovered some objective mistake in a work." Kandinsky explained that, in ignorance of the purpose of the new work, the detractor was invariably applying outmoded criteria: "*The only thing* a theoretician is justified in asserting is that he does not yet know this or that method. If in praising or condemning a work theoreticians start from an analysis of already existing forms, they are most dangerously misleading." Ideally a critic would take care to understand the new methods of the innovative new work, then explain it to a wider audience: "he would try to feel how this or that form works internally, and then he would convey his total experience vividly to the public."[21]

Yet the difficulty of understanding innovative new art has increased over the course of the modern era, because of the increasing prominence of highly conceptual art. Harold Rosenberg argued that a shift occurred with the innovation of Cubism, because it substituted intellectual for aesthetic values: "Cubism changed the relation of art to the public, and, in so doing, changed the nature of the art public itself. It excluded those who merely responded to pictures and replaced them with spectators who knew what made pictures important."[22] Understanding advanced art would subsequently be primarily intellectual rather than visual: "An advanced painting of this century inevitably gives rise in the spectator to a conflict between his eye and his mind; as Thomas Hess has pointed out, the fable of the emperor's new clothes is echoed at the birth of every modernist art movement. If work in a new mode is to be accepted, the eye/mind conflict must be resolved in favor of the mind; that is, of the language absorbed into the work."[23] It is perhaps not surprising that Picasso had earlier defended Cubism in almost precisely these terms. Thus in 1923 he told his friend Marius de Zayas that "The fact that for a long time cubism has not been understood and that even today there are people who cannot see anything in it, means nothing. I do not read English, an English book is a blank book to me. This does not mean that the English language does not exist, and why should I blame anybody else but myself if I cannot understand what I know nothing about?"[24]

In part, the difficulty at issue here is simply that of assimilating innovative new art in a period of rapid change. Thus Kirk Varnedoe recently reflected that "Early modern society created – and we have inherited – that paradoxical thing: a tradition of radical innovation," and much earlier, in 1855, Charles Baudelaire's sardonic sensibility had led him to ponder the bittersweet nature of indefinite progress, wondering "whether proceeding as it does by a stubborn negation of itself, it would not turn out to be a perpetually renewed form of suicide, and whether . . . it would not be like the scorpion which stings itself with its own terrible tail – progress, that eternal desideratum which is its own eternal despair!"[25] Yet as the specific terms used by Rosenberg and Picasso suggest, there is something more at stake here, involving the particular qualities of the art in question. This can be highlighted through the introduction of the analytical framework that will provide the theoretical basis for this study as a whole.

The Language of Analysis

Does creation reside in the idea or in the action?
Sir Alan Bowness[26]

There are two very different types of artistic innovators. These two types are not distinguished by their importance, for both are prominently represented among the very greatest artists. They are distinguished instead by their conception of art – the goals they have for their work – and by the methods they use to produce that work.[27]

Experimental innovators are motivated by aesthetic criteria: their goal is to present visual perceptions. They are uncertain how to do this, so they proceed tentatively and incrementally. The imprecision of their goals means that experimental artists rarely believe they have succeeded, and their careers are consequently often dominated by the pursuit of a single objective. These artists repeat themselves, returning to the same motif many times, gradually changing their treatment of it in an experimental process of trial and error. Each work leads to the next, and none is intended to be definitive, so experimental painters rarely make preparatory sketches or other plans for a painting. They consider the production of a painting as a process of exploring, in which they want to discover the image in the course of working, and they typically believe that learning is more important than creating finished works. Experimental artists build their skills gradually, improving their work slowly over the course of their careers. Many are perfectionists who are plagued by frustration at their inability to achieve what they can consider satisfactory results. Their innovations appear gradually over extended periods: they are rarely declared in any single work, but instead appear piecemeal in a large body of work.

In contrast, *conceptual* innovators want to express ideas or emotions. Their goals for individual works can usually be stated precisely, in advance, either as a desired image or as a specific process for the work's execution. As a result they often plan their works carefully, with detailed preparatory sketches or other instructions. Their execution of their works is often systematic because many think of it as merely recording an image that has already been fully conceived. Conceptual innovations appear suddenly, as the realization of a new idea immediately produces a result distinctly different not only from other artists' work, but also from the artist's own previous work. Because it is the idea that is the real contribution, conceptual innovations can usually be implemented immediately and completely, and therefore are often fully embodied in individual breakthrough works that can be clearly recognized as the first statement of the innovation.

The suddenness of conceptual innovations often makes them shocking, and this effect is magnified by the fact that they are often intentionally conspicuous and transgressive. Many important conceptual innovations have been denounced as tasteless jokes before they have changed the way art is made. Conceptual innovations consist of unexpected syntheses of earlier art, that paradoxically have the effect of violating basic conventions of that art.

The clarity of their goals allows conceptual artists to be satisfied that they have made specific works that achieve a particular goal. Unlike experimental artists, whose inability to achieve their goals can tie them to a single problem for decades, the conceptual artist's ability to consider a problem solved can free the artist to pursue new goals. The careers of some conceptual artists have consequently been marked by a series of innovations, each very different from the others. Thus whereas over time an experimental artist usually produces many works that are closely related to each other, the career of the conceptual innovator is often marked by discontinuity.

Generation Gaps, Part 2

You're a killer of art, you're a killer of beauty, and you're even a killer of laughter. I can't bear your work!
Willem de Kooning to Andy Warhol, 1969[28]

As noted earlier, artistic innovations always create a sense of loss for those who are committed to the values they reject. But the intensity of the clashes new innovations create can be magnified when experimental values are rejected by young conceptual innovators. In the modern era the shifts in values can be so abrupt and extreme that aging experimental artists may have trouble accepting that young conceptual innovators are in fact serious artists at all.

One such shift occurred in New York in the late 1950s, as a series of young conceptual artists successfully challenged the dominance of the experimental art of the Abstract Expressionists. The older artists, who had spent decades working to develop new forms of art that would make profound statements about beauty and truth, could not accept the ready-made images of the young artists, who appeared to have no respect for the art of the past. After seeing the paintings of targets and flags at Jasper Johns' first one-man show in 1958, Mark Rothko commented, "We worked for years to get rid of all that."[29] When Robert Motherwell first saw Frank Stella's early paintings of parallel black lines a year later, he remarked, "It's very interesting, but it's not painting."[30] Motherwell considered Pop art to be unrelated to fine art: "It's not possible to have an allegiance to painting and to pop art at the same time ... As for the pop artists whom I've met, their detachment from aesthetic problems is incomprehensible to me. It fills me with a sort of horror."[31] To Motherwell, the Pop artists could not be serious artists, for they had no interest in the masters of the past: "The pop artists couldn't care less about Picasso or Rembrandt."[32] A fellow painter explained why Rothko was so depressed in the early 1960s: "the problem was not just being replaced, but *what* was replacing him."[33]

The critic Calvin Tomkins observed that it was not difficult to understand the Abstract Expressionists' anger at the rise of Pop art: "They had struggled for many years in total obscurity, their achievements recognized only by one another ... The recognition that they had so recently and so arduously won was now being usurped, or so they believed, by a new generation of brash youngsters who had become 'artists overnight,' who had not earned anything the hard way, and whose most apparent common bond seemed to be mockery and rejection of all serious art, especially Abstract Expressionism. Pollock and de Kooning and Rothko and Newman had not repudiated Picasso, Mondrian, and Léger. They had worshiped the European masters, while striving heroically to go beyond them. Now, suddenly, heroism and high art were out of style."[34]

The Abstract Expressionists were separated from their chronological successors not merely by differences of style, but by differences in their very conception of art. Experimental artists who had spent their entire careers, and lives, working toward vague and elusive aesthetic goals could not accept new forms of art that not only rejected their particular goals, but that rejected aesthetic criteria altogether. The inability of these older experimental artists to respect the conceptual art of the younger painters meant that they could not accept them as successors, because they could not consider their conception of art to be valid. Transitions like this one, when an experimental art is replaced by conceptual innovations, can therefore produce conflicts even deeper than those that occur when one style replaces another: the conceptual revolution of the late 1950s and early 1960s produced such a vast change in values that the very survival of painting as a fine art seemed in doubt to the older experimental artists.

Age and Innovation

> When we look at the late works of Titian or Rembrandt we cannot help feeling the pressure of a massive and rich experience which leaks out, as it were, through the ostensible image presented to us, whatever it may be. There are artists, and perhaps Titian and Rembrandt are good examples, who seem to require a very long period of activity before this unconscious element finds its way completely through into the work of art. In other cases, particularly in artists whose gift lies in a lyrical direction, the exaltation and passion of youth transmits itself directly into everything they touch and then sometimes, when this flame dies down, their work becomes relatively cold and uninspired.
>
> Roger Fry, 1933[35]

The distinction between experimental and conceptual innovators will provide a basis for understanding a succession of novel practices of artists in the twentieth century. A number of implications of this analysis will be considered in the course of surveying these practices. Yet one implication involves an issue that is so basic, and that has been so completely neglected by art scholars ever since it was raised by the eminent critic Roger Fry more than seven decades ago, that it is worth spelling it out before beginning the examination of twentieth-century art and artists.

The two types of innovators have very different life cycles of creativity. The long periods of trial and error often required for important experimental innovations means that they tend to occur late in an artist's career. In contrast, conceptual innovators are generally best early in their careers. Major conceptual innovations require the ability to see old problems in radically new ways, and this ability declines with experience, as artists become accustomed to thinking and working in particular ways. Some conceptual artists make a series of distinct innovations over the course of their careers, but the most important of these will normally be the earliest, when they are least constrained by habits of thought.

These differing patterns of creativity over the life cycle reflect the very different attitudes and processes that affect the creative ability of the two types of artists. Experimental innovators' approach to their art is dominated by uncertainty, concerning both methods and goals. This leads them to proceed cautiously, in the belief that progress can only occur slowly. In many cases they in fact progress so slowly that for long periods their progress is imperceptible not only to others, but to the artists themselves; even the greatest experimental innovators often suffer from doubt over whether they have accomplished anything at all. They stress the need for patience, with the gradual accumulation of knowledge over time, and they trust their own experience more than any other sources of knowledge. In time great experimental innovators acquire better judgment of their own work, as they develop a personal aesthetic that becomes a consistent basis for their art, and for the new departures that emerge in the course of their research.

Conceptual innovators have a very different understanding of creativity: they believe that discoveries can occur suddenly, in flashes of insight, and that they can arrive fully formed, in discrete leaps of comprehension. Conceptual innovators are typically precocious young practitioners who quickly assimilate the art of the past, then deliberately violate basic conventions of that art. They are iconoclasts whose self-confidence and lack of respect for established practices allows them to discard those practices at will. Because conceptual innovators value pronounced change, in many cases their work may display no consistent aesthetic. The diminution of their creativity over time is a product of the increasing rigidity that tends to set in as specific habits of thought and assumptions about what constitute proper artistic practices and products become fixed in their minds.

Roger Fry spoke the words quoted at the beginning of this section in 1933, on the occasion of his inaugural lecture as Slade Professor of Fine Art at Cambridge University. After stating this proposition, he immediately conceded that "I fear a great deal of this must appear to you to be rather wildly speculative and hazardous." The stated task of his lecture was to outline a systematic approach to art "where at all events the scientific attitude may be fostered and the sentimental attitude discouraged."[36] It might normally be expected that the bold hypotheses of an inaugural lecture would become the subject of a new professor's research agenda in the years that follow. Unfortunately, however, Fry was elected to the Slade Professorship at the end of his career rather than the beginning, and his death the next year prevented any effort to document his hypothesis.[37] In the event, no other art historian took up the challenge to pursue Fry's hypothesis of the life cycles of artistic creativity. Yet now, more than seven decades later, systematic research has provided a firm empirical basis for Fry's remarkable generalization, and many of the gains from this research will be seen throughout the course of this study.

Measuring Artistic Importance

> There is, it seems, a graph of creativity which can be plotted through an artist's career.
>
> Sir Alan Bowness[38]

Wassily Kandinsky believed that the judgment of the artist was critical to the creation of art, and that true art could not be made mechanically, through the use of mathematical calculation or any other system.[39] In an essay of 1936, he extended this position, claiming not only that measurement could not be used to make art, but that measurement equally could not be used to judge the quality of art: "There has never been a 'thermometer' for measuring the level of art, and there never will be one."[40] This meant, for example, that it was impossible to determine when in an artist's career he had done his best work: "in the case of generally and rightly acknowledged artists, some 'specialists' constantly rate their 'early' period far higher than their 'later' works, while other 'experts' maintain the opposite. Thus, there exist not simply individual works, but whole 'periods,' made up in turn of numerous individual works, for which no one has yet devised any 'yardstick of quality' either."[41]

Kandinsky did not deny the existence of quality in art. In fact, two years later, in 1938, he devoted an essay to the problem of judging artistic value. The discussion again dealt with the irrelevance of calculation in assessing artistic quality, and the consequent impossibility of creating scientific standards. Yet at the end of the essay he offered a specific criterion to those who sought standards of value: "Ask yourselves, if you like, whether the work of art has made you free of a world unknown to you before."[42]

Kandinsky thus recognized that innovation was the key standard for artistic importance: he simply did not see how this could be identified systematically. Yet since he wrote, art historians have devoted vast amounts of study to identifying the most innovative artists, and analyzing their most innovative contributions. And many other art historians have devoted considerable effort to surveying the results of these many studies of individual artists, and weaving them into summary narratives of the history of art. Each of these narratives describes a canon of important artists – those artists who, in the opinion of the author, should be considered in explaining the development of modern art. The most important artists, whose contributions are essential to a coherent narrative, will be discussed in every textbook. Other artists will be included only in some of the books; by omitting them, some authors signal their opinion that these artists are not necessary for their narratives. Measuring how often particular artists are included or omitted in textbooks therefore effectively allows us to survey art historians' judgments on the centrality of selected artists to the development of modern art. This can be done systematically by counting the illustrations of individual artists' works included in the textbooks. This will not only reveal which artists are deemed most important – greater artists receive more illustrations – but can also indicate which of their works are considered their major contributions – greater paintings or sculptures are more often illustrated.

Many quantitative studies of this kind have now been carried out, and they have shown that the method is a very useful one. One reason for this is that, contrary to Kandinsky's belief, there is in fact very little disagreement among art experts over which artists, and which periods of those artists' careers, are most important.[43] The development of this method has made it possible to use systematic generalization in the study of art history, by effectively surveying the opinions of large numbers of experts on the art historical issues at hand. This method will provide an empirical basis for many issues treated by the present study.

Approaching the Twentieth Century: The Market for Advanced Art

You see that an era of a new art is opening, you feel it coming.
Paul Cézanne to Charles Camoin, 1902[44]

The Impressionists have killed many things, among others the exhibition
picture and the exhibition picture system.
Walter Sickert, 1910[45]

Painting has lost a lot of the functions that once used to provide discipline
and continuity. I mean commissioned art, from portraiture to whatever,
which only incidentally gave painters the chance to make art. Nowadays
they can't do anything *but* make art. That alters a lot.
Gerhard Richter, 1977[46]

During the late nineteenth century, momentous changes in both markets
and technology set the stage for an unprecedented era of revolutionary
change in art. As a consequence of these changes, in a number of respects,
advanced artists in the twentieth century enjoyed dramatically greater
creative freedom than their predecessors. The single most important cause
of this was a fundamental change in the economic structure of the market
for advanced art.

Although the story of the Impressionists' challenge to the official Salon
has long been a staple in narratives of art history, art scholars have never
fully appreciated the significance of the changes it initiated. The problem
is that art scholars have generally not understood the connection between
markets and the production of art; they have typically considered art
markets as if they involved only dealers and collectors, who buy and
sell works that have been made by artists who are unaware of, and
uninterested in, the transactions to which their works are subjected after
they have produced them. This conception is wrong: it is not only bad
economics, but also bad art history. In this instance, it has prevented
art scholars from understanding how the changes that occurred in the
market for advanced art in the late nineteenth century gave artists an
almost unprecedented degree of freedom in producing their art.

Since the Renaissance, most artists had faced markets for their work
that were dominated by powerful institutions or individuals. In Paris,
immediately prior to the emergence of modern painting, the market for
fine art was dominated by the government.[47] The central institution in
the art world was the Salon, an annual or biennial exhibition that was

operated by the official Academy of Fine Arts. A painter's work could not be widely reviewed by critics, or considered for purchase by important dealers or collectors, until the painter had proven himself by having his work admitted to the exhibition by the Salon's jury. The most important artists were those who were deemed worthy of prizes by the jury, or were elected by the jury to honorary positions. The Salon held an effective monopoly of the legitimate presentation of new art to the public throughout most of the nineteenth century: until the 1870s, no aspiring artist could have a successful career without the jury's acceptance of his work. The work of important artists was sold by private galleries, but only after those artists had effectively been certified as important by having their work exhibited at the Salon, and in general the most valuable paintings were those that had actually been displayed at the Salon. The control of the official Salon over artistic success was so great that the sociologist Pierre Bourdieu observed that under this regime "the artist is a high-level civil servant," who had a highly structured "*career*, a well-defined succession of honors . . . by way of the hierarchy of awards given at the Salon exhibitions."[48]

This situation began to change in 1874, when Claude Monet and a group of his friends organized an independent exhibition that included paintings by twenty-nine artists. Although its initial impact was limited, and its full significance would not be recognized until considerably later, the first Impressionist group exhibition in 1874 began a new era, in which the reputations of advanced artists would no longer be created in the Salon, but instead in independent group exhibitions. The most important of these would be the eight Impressionist exhibitions held during 1874–86, and the Salon des Indépendants, which was held annually from 1884 on. Analytically, the critical change that the Impressionists initiated in 1874 was the elimination of the official Salon's monopoly of the ability to present fine art in a setting that critics and the public would accept as legitimate. The jury of the Salon would no longer be able to determine whether an aspiring artist could have a successful professional career. Monet and his fellow Impressionists were the first nineteenth-century painters to become leaders in Paris' art world without having received medals or other honors from the official Salon, but after 1874 this became the rule, as none of the later artists whom we now consider important made their reputations through the Salon, in the traditional manner. In 1902, one of the Impressionists' most important successors paid tribute to their achievement, as Paul Gauguin described their independent exhibitions as "one of the most influential efforts ever made in

France, only a handful of men, with only one weapon, their talent, successfully doing battle against a fearsome power made up of Officialdom, the Press, and Money."[49]

The Impressionist exhibitions gained considerable attention from critics from the very beginning, and this was sustained over time: the first show, in 1874, received fifty-one published reviews or notices, and no later Impressionist group exhibition received less than forty-four separate reviews.[50] The Salon's control of artists' ability to have their work publicly assessed and debated was therefore eliminated by these new group exhibitions. The problem of selling their work was more difficult, however. The value of fine art had traditionally been certified by the imprimatur of the salon jury, and collectors were not sure that the innovative new art would be a good investment. The caution of collectors meant that the demand for the work of young artists who had not exhibited extensively in the Salon lagged behind critical debates of its merit.

The lack of demand for the new art, in turn, made private galleries reluctant to stock it. So, for example, Vincent van Gogh reported on the situation in Paris in 1887, complaining that "Trade is slow here. The great dealers sell Millet, Delacroix, Corot, Daubigny, Dupré, a few other masters at exorbitant prices. They do little or nothing for young artists. The second class dealers contrariwise sell those at very low prices."[51] Four of the five artists van Gogh named were dead, and the fifth, Dupré, was 76 years old. All five had established their reputations at the official Salon. A few dealers became known for selling the work of younger artists – Paul Durand-Ruel, for example, began buying paintings from the Impressionists in the early 1870s, and Theo van Gogh, the artist's brother, bought paintings by Monet and other younger painters when he became the business manager of a branch of the Boussod and Valadon gallery in the 1880s. Yet sluggish demand by collectors prevented these galleries from competing actively for the work of most of the younger artists. Thus Camille Pissarro wrote to his son Lucien in 1891 that "What I need is a good exhibition, but where? At Durand's, I get all sorts of propositions, I get offers without even asking – but they don't buy a thing . . . At Boussod & Valadon's, they soft-soap me and talk against Durand . . . [I]n short: neither will buy my work. If anyone else were available, I would unhesitatingly turn to him, but there is nobody." Pissarro was frustrated that Durand-Ruel could stockpile paintings by all the Impressionists, buying them at very low prices in the expectation that they would rise in value later, but he understood the underlying problem: "If I could find some base of support, I would certainly frustrate his hyena-like calculations – but my work is not understood."[52]

Gradually, however, during the 1880s and 1890s the demand for the work of some of the younger advanced artists began to increase. A small network of French collectors, many of them friends of the Impressionists, began to buy their work in modest quantities. The painter Mary Cassatt, who was also a friend of the Impressionists, was instrumental in bringing a number of her American friends, several of whom were important collectors, to the Impressionists' art. The prices of Monet's paintings began to rise during the 1880s, and Cézanne's prices began to increase during the 1890s.[53] The rising prices for the art of these earlier innovators began to convince more dealers and collectors of the potential gains to be made from the work of a new generation of younger artists who, like the Impressionists, had not achieved success in the traditional way, through the Salon. Thus the art historian Michael Fitzgerald observed that "Although the basic model for an entrepreneurial avant-garde was created by the Impressionists, it was the artists of the next century who truly reaped the benefits," in the form of "critical acclaim and financial independence far earlier in their careers."[54]

In the early years of the twentieth century, the number of independent entrepreneurial art dealers who were willing to exhibit the work of younger artists who had not achieved success at the Salon began to grow, as the improving market for the work of the Impressionists and the leading Post-Impressionists demonstrated the potential profitability of innovative contemporary art. This opened the way for another important transition in the market for advanced art. Although group exhibitions continued to proliferate, and a growing number of independent societies sponsored salons that might display thousands of paintings, private galleries became increasingly important in presenting new art to the public. Thus for example by 1910 the leading critic of the advanced art world, the poet Guillaume Apollinaire, observed that "The plethora of individual exhibitions tends to weaken the effect of the large annual salons. The curiosity of the public is less keen, since many painters have already shown in the galleries the most important, if not the best, examples of their work during the year."[55] Over time, private galleries would replace group exhibitions altogether as the key exhibition spaces for new advanced art, and this would remain true not only in Paris, but also in most other art centers, for the balance of the twentieth century. Interestingly Pablo Picasso, who first arrived in Paris from his native Spain in 1900, would become the first important modern artist who established himself by exhibiting exclusively in private galleries rather than large group exhibitions. In this he set an example that would be followed by nearly every important artist for the remainder of the twentieth century.

Private galleries held several advantages over group exhibitions for artists. Dealers could offer an artist more highly concentrated attention, in the form of a one-person exhibition, and dealers could actively promote the artist's work. Both of these devices could increase in value when an artist and dealer had a continuing relationship, for a dealer's exhibitions and other promotional efforts could help to find collectors who would consistently buy the artist's work. When a painter had both a regular dealer and a group of loyal collectors, he had a degree of freedom in making his art that few artists had ever enjoyed in earlier times.

Michael Fitzgerald wrote that "Whatever one's opinion of Picasso's achievement may be, there is little doubt that during the first half of [the twentieth] century he quickly became the most famous artist of his time and a model for success – with critics and curators as well as dealers and collectors – that other artists sought to emulate."[56] In 1901, the 20-year-old Picasso was given his first exhibition in Paris by Ambroise Vollard, who was respected in the advanced art world as the dealer of Cézanne and Gauguin. In 1905, Gertrude Stein began to buy Picasso's work, and in 1906 the Russian merchant Sergei Shchukin followed suit: both would continue to purchase Picasso's paintings for many years. Early in 1906, Vollard bought twenty paintings from Picasso. At 25, Picasso thus had the support of two important collectors, and the prestige and financial windfall of a large sale to a prestigious dealer. The impact – economic and psychological – was clearly considerable: Fitzgerald speculated that "The financial security these sales afforded may . . . have contributed to his manifest self-confidence in creating *Les Demoiselles d'Avignon*," which he began in late 1906 and completed the following year.[57] Picasso's realization of success in the market may therefore have led directly to his creation of what would prove to be the most important artistic innovation of the twentieth century. Yet Picasso still had no regular dealer, and before long he clearly began working on this, as during 1909–10 he painted portraits of no less than four important dealers, including Vollard. When the Italian painter Umberto Boccioni visited Paris in 1911, he reported to a friend that "The young man ruling the roost here now is Picasso. There is much talk about him . . . [T]he painter scarcely finishes a work before it is carted off and paid for by the dealers in competition with each other."[58] In 1912, Picasso signed a formal contract with Daniel-Henry Kahnweiler, who had already bought more than 60 canvases from him. Kahnweiler became Picasso's exclusive dealer, at fixed rates per painting that put Picasso "on his way to becoming a wealthy man."[59]

The Impressionists thus set in motion the process that eventually transformed the market for fine art from a monopoly, to which artists' entry was controlled by the French government and its institutions, into a highly competitive market. Unlike most of their predecessors since the Renaissance, advanced artists of the twentieth century would rarely produce commissions for wealthy and powerful patrons, and would rarely if ever be in the position of having to produce works that were subject to the approval of any official judge or jury. The elimination of official gatekeepers has meant that artists of the past century have had greater freedom to work, and to innovate, as they have pleased. The only constraint on their ability to do this has been that discussed earlier, namely the lag in recognition of important new art by critics, dealers, and collectors. And here too there is a relevant process that originated in the nineteenth century and has continued over time, namely the growing awareness in the art world that early investments in the work of innovative artists can yield handsome financial returns. The collectors who have captured these returns have most often done so as a result of advice from artists, who are the first to recognize other talented artists. The growing recognition that innovative art will increase in value consequently produced a result that has sustained the early careers of many innovative artists, as Alan Bowness observed that "Almost every major talent attracts one or two collectors at an early stage in his career, and these collectors almost always appear on the scene because of their friendships with artists, whose advice they take."[60] This is a key feature of the existence of a competitive art market: innovative artists do not have to make work that appeals to the public at large, or even to large numbers of collectors, but need simply find a few consistent purchasers of their work among the hundreds, or thousands, who see their work in exhibitions. If these few collectors support the innovator long enough for his influence on other artists to become apparent, many other collectors will invariably discover their own admiration for the artist's work.

An early landmark in the demonstration of the investment value of innovative contemporary art occurred in 1914, at a public auction in Paris. Ten years earlier, a young businessman named André Level had organized a consortium of collectors, as he and twelve other partners each contributed to a collective fund that allowed Level to spend 2,750 francs a year on art. The group was named La Peau de l'Ours (the Bear

Skin), after a La Fontaine fable in which two trappers sold a furrier the skin of a great bear before they had tried – and failed – to catch it. Level bought paintings by earlier artists, including Gauguin and van Gogh, but invested most heavily in the work of younger artists, particularly Matisse and Picasso. When the accumulated paintings were sold at the end of ten years, the auction realized 116,545 francs, or more than four times the group's total investment. Paintings by Matisse and Picasso brought the highest prices, and a major early work by Picasso, *The Family of Saltimbanques* (now in the National Gallery in Washington) sold for 12,650 francs, more than twelve times the price Level had paid for it in 1905. The auction's results were seen as a great success for Fauvism and Cubism, and news reports of this victory spread the fame of Picasso and Matisse not only throughout France, but also abroad, including the United States. The Peau de l'Ours sale was the first time an important group of works by the leading artists of the day had come to auction, and its public success helped to convince many people that contemporary innovative art could be a good investment.[61] This laid the foundation for a new era of artistic freedom that allowed artists to follow their own interests rather than those of patrons.[62]

Approaching the Twentieth Century: Photography

From today painting is dead.
French painter Paul Delaroche, upon learning of the invention of the daguerrotype, 1839[63]

The camera cannot compete with brush and palette – as long as it cannot be used in Heaven or Hell.
Edvard Munch, 1904[64]

Technological changes also had an important impact on the course of modern art. Most notably, the improvement of photography from the 1840s on affected painters in a number of ways.

By the early twentieth century, conceptual painters could use the availability of photography as an argument for a new division of labor. For example in an interview in 1909, Matisse contended that it was time for painting to break decisively with the realistic goals of Impressionism. He declared that it was no longer necessary for painting to be concerned with objectivity, because this could be provided by photography: "The painter no longer has to preoccupy himself with details. The photograph is there to render the multitude of details a hundred times better and more quickly." The painter was now free to pursue expression: "Plastic form will present emotion as directly as possible and by the simplest means."[65] Nor is it surprising that Picasso agreed. In 1939, while looking at photographs of Parisian street life taken by his friend Brassaï, Picasso remarked that "When one sees what you express through photography, one realizes everything that can no longer be the concern of painting. Why would the artist stubbornly persist in rendering what the lens can capture so well? That would be crazy, don't you think? Photography came along at a particular moment to liberate painting from literature of all sorts, from the anecdote, and even from the subject. In any case, a certain aspect of the subject now belongs to the realm of photography. Shouldn't painters take advantage of their new-found freedom, and do something else?"[66]

Yet photography also directly complemented the artistic practice of Matisse and Picasso, and other later conceptual artists, in several important ways. One of these was to stand in for a model. Conceptual painters generally plan the images in their works, and one way to do this is through the use of photographs. For example John Richardson noted that Picasso's 1908 portrait of Clovis Sagot was based on a photograph Picasso took of the dealer, "a practice he would resort to ever more frequently."[67] Matisse had begun using the same practice, basing sculptures as well as paintings on photographs, a few years earlier.[68] Over the course of the twentieth century, photographs would become increasingly important for the work of many conceptual painters.

Another conceptual function of photography was to provide convenient access to the history of art. Conceptual artists typically innovate by creating syntheses of specific elements drawn from earlier art: Picasso is again a prime example. Thus his early masterpiece, *Les Demoiselles d'Avignon*, contains references to, or quotations from, the paintings of Cézanne and Gauguin, Egyptian and pre-Roman Iberian sculpture, and African carvings.[69] This art was available to him not only in Paris' museums, but even more conveniently in photographs. Thus William Rubin observed that "The growth of museums since the early nineteenth century and, even more, the documentary use of photography have made available a world of images that earlier artists could never have seen... This simultaneous accessibility of all historical sources, which sets the modern period off from any other, is encapsulated in the oeuvre of Picasso."[70] Throughout the twentieth century, conceptual artists could draw on the entire history of art without having to travel, or even go to their local museums, through the medium of photography, and this availability would have a major impact on the appearance of fine art.

The Growing Audience for Art

Art's popular. That's my generation. It wasn't before.
Damien Hirst, 2000[71]

A few changes in the environment of advanced art that occurred during the twentieth century are so central to an appreciation of the context of the century's art history that they demand at least brief preliminary mention. One is a very substantial increase over the course of the century in public interest in art in general, and in modern art in particular.

An obvious manifestation of this trend is the growing importance of museums. A milestone early in the twentieth century was the opening of New York's Museum of Modern Art in 1929. Not only was it the first American museum dedicated to modern art, but it defined its mission broadly, to include collections and displays devoted to photography, architecture, film, and design, as well as painting and sculpture.[72]

Attendance at museums became a topic of increasing economic importance after mid-century, as greater prosperity and rising levels of tourism contributed to steady increases in the volume of museum visits, with an accelerating rate of increase in the final decades of the century.[73] A key contribution to this trend was made by Thomas Hoving, who served as director of New York's Metropolitan Museum during 1967–77. Hoving envisioned museums as places of mass entertainment, and he is considered the originator of the blockbuster exhibition, aimed at attracting both large public audiences, who often pay substantial admission fees, and lucrative corporate sponsorships. As attendance rose, and museums competed more actively for the public's patronage, many museums established marketing departments for the first time.[74]

Growing attendance at existing museums was complemented by the establishment of new museums, and many of these focused on modern art. One important instance occurred in 1977, when the opening of the Centre Pompidou gave Paris a major museum devoted exclusively to twentieth-century art. In 2000, Tate Modern gave London its first major museum of the art of the century just completed. Tate Modern quickly became the world's most popular museum of modern art, as for example during 2007 more than 5 million people visited the museum.

Another new museum that immediately became a major attraction to tourists when it opened in 1997 was the Guggenheim Museum in Bilbao, in northern Spain. Designed by Frank Gehry, the Guggenheim Bilbao has widely been recognized as the most important new museum architecturally since the New York Guggenheim, designed by Frank Lloyd Wright, opened in 1959. The spectacular Guggenheim Bilbao was the most successful to date of a series of satellite institutions created and planned by the New York-based Guggenheim in an attempt to become the first global museum.[75]

As museums multiplied and expanded, their attention to recent art increased: many small museums of contemporary art were opened, and larger museums of modern art began to devote greater attention to the work of living artists. One notable manifestation of this new interest was the Turner Prize, established by London's Tate Gallery in 1984 with the intention of giving contemporary English visual art a status comparable to that afforded English novels by the Booker Prize. From 1991, the Turner Prize was restricted to artists under the age of 50, and the focus on younger artists increased the attention given to the prize. Attendance at the Tate's Turner Prize exhibition rose sharply during the 1990s, and media attention expanded accordingly; heated controversies now regularly erupt over the nominees and winners of the prize, not only in broadsheet newspapers, but equally in the English tabloids.[76]

Artists as Celebrities

Picasso is now wealthier and more famous than any other artist who has ever lived.

John Berger, 1965[77]

With the growing public interest in modern art came a new public status for important modern artists. Since the Renaissance, gifted artists had often been accorded great respect by their patrons. So for example in 1506 the pope was willing "to forgo his claims to reverential submission from an artist whose genius he fully appreciated," as Julius II "met Michelangelo as an equal" in order to gain the artist's agreement to paint the ceiling of the Sistine Chapel.[78] Similarly, in the seventeenth century, Philip IV of Spain granted Velázquez honors normally reserved for men of noble descent, and was devastated by the painter's death.[79] In 1667, when the young Prince Cosimo, the future Archduke of Tuscany, traveled to Amsterdam, one of the artists whose studios he visited was described in the official logbook of his journey as "Rembrandt the famous painter."[80]

These and other master painters were honored by kings, popes, and aristocrats. Yet it was only in the modern era that living artists would gain fame among a much wider public. As the audience for art expanded during the modern period, some artists became genuine celebrities. New forms of artistic behavior became possible as these artists responded to the opportunities their new status presented. Many of these behaviors will be examined in the course of this study. Here it is useful to point out a few of the most prominent cases of twentieth-century artists as celebrities.

A biographer remarked that Pablo Picasso "mastered the publicity game before the world knew that such a game existed."[81] Early in his career Picasso created not only a startlingly new style of art, but also cultivated a colorful persona to match it. Thus one art scholar observed that by 1914, "Picasso had established the character of his genius: an amalgam of alchemist, Shakespearean fool, and satyr that placed his creative imagination at the center of his art."[82] His Cubist fragmentation of the human figure, which could readily be caricatured by cartoonists, and his many love affairs combined to make Picasso "the archetypal modern artist as far as lay people were concerned."[83] Considerable mystery surrounded Picasso, for he rarely granted interviews, but he nonetheless played an active role in fostering the spread of his fame through the press. For example in 1939, photographs of Picasso taken by his friend Brassaï were featured in *Life* magazine. It was a time of considerable stress for the artist, for Picasso was busy moving his accumulated paintings and drawings into bank vaults to protect them from possible German bombing of Paris. Yet Brassaï noted that for the *Life* assignment, "Nonetheless, he was prepared to devote an entire day to me."[84]

Jackson Pollock became the prototype of the American artist as celebrity: an art historian observed that "while his career peaked before modern media saturation was achieved, he was the first modern artist to be given wide publicity in the popular press even before his avant-garde reputation had been secured."[85] Pollock's fame was established in 1949, when *Life* magazine published a story titled "Jackson Pollock: Is He the Greatest Living Painter in the United States?," which described him as "the shining new phenomenon of American art," and "a fine candidate to become 'the greatest American painter of the 20th Century.'"[86] During the next few years Pollock's public image was enhanced by Hans Namuth's photographs of him working: the black-and-white pictures, often blurred as Pollock danced around, stepped on, or knelt beside large canvases laid flat on the floor, a cigarette dangling from his mouth as he spattered or smeared paint with sticks, gave vivid meaning to the term "action painting" that the critic Harold Rosenberg had devised to refer to Abstract Expressionism. Early in 1956, just months before his premature death in an automobile accident, *Time* magazine gave Pollock his lasting nickname, "Jack the Dripper," in a reference to his trademark technique of applying paint.[87]

Robert Hughes observed that Andy Warhol was "the first American artist to whose career publicity was truly intrinsic."[88] Warhol not only actively courted fame, but made celebrity itself a theme of his art.[89] Neal Gabler contended that "What Warhol realized and what he promoted in both his work and his life... was that the most important art movement of the twentieth century... was celebrity. Eventually, no matter who the artist was and no matter what school he belonged to, the entertainment society made his fame his achievement and not his achievement his fame."[90] As early as 1964, *Newsweek* titled a profile of Warhol "Saint Andrew," and in 1970, *Vogue* declared that "Andy Warhol is the most famous artist in America. For millions, Warhol is the artist personified."[91] Warhol not only produced vast numbers of art works at a studio he named "The Factory," but he also managed a famous rock band, the Velvet Underground, he directed movies that some critics considered important innovations, and he published *Interview*, a magazine in which celebrities were interviewed, often by other celebrities. Warhol survived being shot by a disturbed member of his sizeable entourage, but he later died after a routine operation. After Warhol's death in 1987, the critic Arthur Danto surveyed his career, and predicted that "When the final multivolume *Popular History of Art* is published, ours will be the Age of Warhol – an unlikely giant, but a giant nonetheless."[92]

Damien Hirst may be the most famous artist working today. He freely admits that this was always his plan: "I wanted to be a famous artist." Fame allows him to achieve his real goal: "As an artist, you have a desire to communicate an idea to a hell of a lot of people on a massive scale."[93] From an early stage of his career, Hirst combined dramatic art works, including some that presented dead animals preserved in formaldehyde in large vitrines, with a public persona borrowed from British punk rockers, that has been described as an "art yobbo" image: "Hirst glared, grimaced and grinned at the camera and cultivated a puckish image by not shaving, wearing long or very short hair and a weird assortment of clothes along with oversize boots."[94] The success of his campaign was such that the critic Jerry Saltz has observed that he is "the one true pop-star artist." Interestingly, however, Hirst's success is due in part to his art's studious conceptual synthesis of many important strands of contemporary art: "His art is an original mélange, a mutant sprung from virtually every movement that preceded it."[95] Through his entrepreneurship, his flamboyant art, and his colorful personal image, Hirst has become not only the leader but also the symbol of the young British artists, or yBas, who made London a center of the art world in the 1990s: "He's their prophet and deliverer, their Elvis and ayatollah." And he achieved this through a flair for arousing controversy that even Warhol would have admired: "To his supporters, Hirst is an inspiration and lightning rod; to his critics, he's a black sheep and bad egg."[96]

Thirteen Ways of Looking at Modern Art

> The aim of the historian... is to portray time... He transposes, reduces, composes, and colors a facsimile, like a painter, who in his search for the identity of the subject, must discover a patterned set of properties that will elicit recognition all while conveying a new perception of the subject.
>
> George Kubler[97]

The necessary preliminaries are now complete. The remainder of this book will be devoted to an analytical history of art in the twentieth century. The next four chapters will give a quantitative overview of the most important figures in that history, and their achievements. The balance of the book will deal with a series of selected topics, chosen to represent key innovations in the work and behavior of artists in the twentieth century. The goal of this study as a whole is to examine systematically many old problems, and some new ones, from novel points of view, and in the process to discover patterns that will give both experts and nonspecialists a new perception of twentieth-century art, and an understanding of why it is fundamentally different from the art of all earlier times.

2

The Greatest Artists of the Twentieth Century

Introduction

The masters, truth to tell, are judged as much by their influence as by their works.

Emile Zola, 1884[1]

Important artists are innovators: they are important because they change the way their successors work. The more widespread, and the more profound, the changes due to the work of any artist, the greater is the importance of that artist.

Recognizing the source of artistic importance points to a method of measuring it. Surveys of art history are narratives of the contributions of individual artists. These narratives describe and explain the changes that have occurred over time in artists' practices. It follows that the importance of an artist can be measured by the attention to his work in these narratives. The most important artists, whose contributions fundamentally change the course of their discipline, cannot be omitted from any such narrative, and their innovations must be analyzed at length; less important artists can either be included or excluded, depending on the length of the specific narrative treatment and the tastes of the author, and if they are included their contributions can be treated more summarily. The judgments of different authors can of course differ. Surveying a large number of narratives can reduce the impact of idiosyncratic opinions, and serves to reveal the general consensus of expert opinion as to the relative importance of the artists considered.

Today, well into the first decade of a new century, it is possible to survey a large collection of narratives of the art of the past century, and

TABLE 2.1. *Greatest Artists of the Twentieth Century*

Artist	Date of Birth	Date of Death	Country of Birth
Brancusi, Constantin	1876	1957	Romania
Braque, Georges	1882	1963	France
Duchamp, Marcel	1887	1968	France
Johns, Jasper	1930	–	US
Kandinsky, Wassily	1866	1944	Russia
de Kooning, Willem	1904	1997	Netherlands
Malevich, Kazimir	1878	1935	Russia
Matisse, Henri	1869	1954	France
Mondrian, Piet	1872	1944	Netherlands
Oldenburg, Claes	1929	–	Sweden
Picasso, Pablo	1881	1973	Spain
Pollock, Jackson	1912	1956	US
Rauschenberg, Robert	1925	2008	US
Rothko, Mark	1903	1970	Russia
Warhol, Andy	1928	1987	US

Source: This and subsequent tables in this chapter are based on the data set constructed for this study. See the text and appendix for the method used and sources.

to see which artists emerge most prominently from these accounts. One result of this survey is a ranking of the greatest artists of the twentieth century.

The Ranking

> Lists seem trivial, but in fact they are crucial symptomatic indices of underlying struggles over taste, evaluation and the construction of a canon... [T]here is a complex genealogy of influence and indebtedness which is left for critics and historians to unearth.
>
> Peter Wollen, 2002[2]

The artists selected for this study are those whose major contributions were made entirely in the twentieth century and who were found to be the most important artists at particular times and places by a series of earlier surveys of art history textbooks. Specifically, fifteen different artists were found to have an average of at least two illustrations per textbook in a series of nine previous studies of artistic importance.[3] These artists are listed in Table 2.1.

For the present study a new data set was created by recording all illustrations of the work of these fifteen artists in thirty-three textbooks of art history.[4] These were all the available books, published in English,

TABLE 2.2. *Ranking of Artists by Total Illustrations*

Artist	N	Mean Illustrations Per Book
1. Picasso	395	12.0
2. Matisse	183	5.5
3. Duchamp	122	3.7
4. Mondrian	114	3.5
5. Braque	101	3.1
6. Pollock	96	2.9
7. Malevich	93	2.8
8. Warhol	85	2.6
9. Kandinsky	84	2.5
10. Johns	75	2.3
11. Brancusi	71	2.2
12. Rauschenberg	62	1.9
13. Oldenburg	58	1.8
14t. de Kooning	52	1.6
14t. Rothko	52	1.6

that surveyed the history of art in the twentieth century, and that were published in 1990 or later.

Table 2.2 ranks the fifteen artists by using the total number of illustrations of each artist's work that appeared in the thirty-three textbooks. A number of important facts emerge from this ranking.

Perhaps the most striking feature of Table 2.2 is the dominant position of Picasso. Remarkably, the textbooks surveyed contain an average of twelve illustrations of his work, more than twice as many as the average for his rival and friend, Matisse. Table 2.2 clearly demonstrates that it would be difficult to overstate the importance of Picasso for twentieth-century art.

More generally, Table 2.2 also points to the privileged position given to artistic developments in France. The top five artists are all Europeans, and all spent some if not all of their careers in Paris. Pollock ranks sixth, making him the most important American artist of the century. He is joined in the top ten by Warhol and Johns. Thus New York is given a prominent role, second to that of Paris.

Table 2.2 provides the basis for an overview of the specific roles of the most important artists of the twentieth century. The data set constructed for this study can be used to provide a more precise focus for that overview, by pointing to when each of the artists made his major

TABLE 2.3. *Best Five-Year Period in Each*
Artist's Career, by Total Illustrations

Artist	Years	Ages
Brancusi	1924–28	48–52
Braque	1907–11	25–29
Duchamp	1910–14	23–27
Johns	1955–59	25–29
Kandinsky	1910–14	44–48
de Kooning	1949–53	45–49
Malevich	1913–17	35–39
Matisse	1905–09	36–40
Mondrian	1912–16	40–44
Oldenburg	1960–64	31–35
Picasso	1906–10	25–29
Pollock	1947–51	35–39
Rauschenberg	1957–61	32–36
Rothko	1956–60	53–57
Warhol	1962–66	34–38

contribution. Thus Table 2.3 shows the five-year period in each artist's career that accounts for the most textbook illustrations. Arranging these periods in chronological order provides a precise outline for a consideration of the sequence in which the greatest artistic innovators of the twentieth century made their most important discoveries.

Henri Matisse

Painting isn't a question of sensibility; it's a matter of seizing the power, taking over from nature, not expecting her to supply you with information and good advice. That's why I like Matisse. Matisse is always able to make an intellectual choice about colors.
                    Pablo Picasso[5]

Fauvism was the first important art movement of the twentieth century. Matisse was its prime inventor and its leader. Table 2.3 shows that his greatest period began in 1905, when he and several friends, including André Derain and Maurice Vlaminck, first presented their new Fauve paintings to the public. As Matisse later summarized the movement, Fauvism built on the bright symbolist color of Gauguin and van Gogh: "Here are the ideas of that time: Construction by colored surfaces. Search for intensity of color, subject matter being unimportant. Reaction against the diffusion of local tone in light. Light is not suppressed, but is expressed by a harmony of intensely colored surfaces."[6]

The movement's name came from a facetious remark by the critic Louis Vauxcelles, who called the group "les fauves" – the wild beasts – for their reckless use of color.[7] The young painters were fully aware of the violence they had done to tradition. Derain worked with Matisse during the summer of 1905, and later recalled that explosive time: "Colors became sticks of dynamite. They were primed to discharge light."[8] Although the work was iconoclastic, it was not undisciplined. Matisse planned his paintings meticulously. For example in the spring of 1905 he exhibited a large figure painting that became a manifesto for the new style. His preparations for the work began with watercolor sketches of the bay of St. Tropez in the summer of 1904. Back in Paris, he devoted the fall and winter to making preparatory oil paintings, adding posed studies of nude figures, and producing a full-scale charcoal drawing of the whole composition. After his wife and daughter transferred this drawing to a large canvas using a traditional academic technique called pouncing, Matisse colored within the traced contours to produce the painting. The completed work was finally given a literary title of impeccable pedigree, *Luxe, calme, et volupté*, from one of the poems in Charles Baudelaire's *Les Fleurs du mal*.[9]

The conceptual nature of Fauvism was quickly recognized in Paris's advanced art world. In a review of the Salon des Indépendants in 1905, the painter and critic Maurice Denis, who had himself been a leader of the conceptual Nabi movement in the 1890s, declared that "*Luxe, calme, et volupté* is the diagram of a theory."[10] Later that year, the novelist and critic André Gide stressed the rationality of Matisse's work in a review of the Salon d'Automne:

The canvases which he paints today seem to be the demonstrations of theorems. I stayed quite a while in this gallery. I listened to the visitors and when I heard them exclaim in front of a Matisse: "This is madness!" I felt like retorting: "No, Sir, quite the contrary. It is the result of theories." Everything can be deduced, explained ... Yes, this painting is reasonable, or rather it is itself reasoning.[11]

Nor was this recognition exclusive to critics. The young painter Raoul Dufy explained that he became a convert to Fauvism instantly upon seeing *Luxe, calme, et volupté*, as its conceptual basis allowed him to understand the movement's ideas simply by viewing that painting: "I understood all the new principles of painting, and impressionist realism lost its charm for me as I contemplated this miracle of the imagination introduced into design and color. I immediately understood the new pic-torial mechanics."[12] Fauvism was in fact derived from thought rather than observation. Derain later reflected that "We painted with theories, ideas."[13]

In 1908, Matisse published an extended explanation of his artistic goals, "Notes of a Painter," which became one of the most influential statements ever made by a modern artist. He stressed that his art was not primarily concerned with observation, but rather with feelings: "What I am after, above all, is expression...I am unable to distinguish between the feeling I have about life and my way of translating it." He contrasted his goal with that of the Impressionists, who had sought to capture tran-sitory perceptions: "I prefer, by insisting upon its essential character, to risk losing charm in order to obtain greater stability." For Matisse, the purpose of art transcended superficial appearances: "one can search for a truer, more essential character...By removing oneself from the literal *representation* of movement one attains greater beauty and grandeur." Capturing the true character of an object or person required careful study before beginning the final work: "For me, all is in the conception. It is thus necessary to have a clear vision of the whole right from the beginning."[14]

In a remarkable series of interviews given throughout his career, Matisse expanded on the themes of his early statement. For example in 1925 he told a critic "the secret of my art. It consists of a meditation on nature, on the expression of a dream which is always inspired by real-ity."[15] He explained in 1929 that there were two stages in the creation of his art, as his initial emotions had to be transformed into ideas in order to make them communicable: "The painter releases his emotion by painting; but not without his conception having passed through a certain analytic state."[16] Even more simply, in 1949 he declared that "for me, it is the sensation first, then the idea."[17]

Matisse's art influenced painters throughout the twentieth century. Thus for example in 1911, Wassily Kandinsky invited Matisse to con-tribute an essay to *The Blaue Reiter Almanac*, which became the most important literary document of German expressionism.[18] Decades later, the Abstract Expressionist Mark Rothko spent hours studying Matisse's *The Red Studio* of 1911 at the Museum of Modern Art, and after Matisse's death in 1954 Rothko paid tribute to that work in his *Homage to Matisse*. Rothko explained that "When you looked at that painting, you became that color, you became totally saturated with it."[19]

Matisse's central contributions stemmed from his early realization "that one could work with expressive colors that are not necessarily descriptive colors."[20] The critic John Berger observed that "Matisse's achievement rests on his use – or in the context of contemporary Western art one could say his invention – of pure color ... He repeatedly declared that color 'must serve expression.' What he wanted to express was 'the nearly religious feeling' he had towards sensuous life – towards the blessings of sunlight, flowers, women, fruit, sleep."[21] Similarly, an art historian remarked that Matisse "saw that if they were no longer subordinated to their mimetic function, the illusionistic devices of painting (the capacity of marks and colors on a flat surface to create a whole fictional world of space and form, light and shade) were free to be a source of the deepest visual and intellectual enjoyment."[22]

Pablo Picasso and Georges Braque

Picasso is a special case who dominates this century from a great height.
Daniel-Henry Kahnweiler[23]

I have always said that Braque is my other half.
Pablo Picasso[24]

Cubism thoroughly transformed modern art. John Golding reflected that "Cubism was perhaps the most important and certainly the most complete and radical artistic revolution since the Renaissance. New forms of society, changing patronage, varying geographic conditions, all these things have gone to produce over the past five hundred years a succession of different schools, different styles, different pictorial idioms. But none of these has so altered the principles, so shaken the foundations of Western painting as did Cubism."[25] George Heard Hamilton explained that Cubism broke with the past because it "embodied for the first time in Western art the principle that a work of art, in conception as well as in appearance, in essence as well as in substance, need not be restricted to the phenomenal appearance of the object for which it stands."[26] John Berger made this same point by noting that with Cubism "the idea of art holding up a mirror to nature became a nostalgic one." Berger stressed that Cubism replaced perception with conception: "The metaphorical model of Cubism is the *diagram*: the diagram being a visible, symbolic representation of invisible processes, forces, structures."[27] Cubism was also the first movement of the modern era to find its subject matter predominantly in urban settings, often the everyday objects found in Parisian cafés, as Picasso remarked that "I want to tell something by means of the most common object."[28] The man-made, constructed subjects of Cubism paralleled the constructed artificiality of the system of symbols it used to portray them.

Cubism was primarily the result of a collaboration that stemmed from a visit Georges Braque made to Picasso's Montmartre studio late in 1907. On that occasion Braque was shocked by his first sight of Picasso's *Les Demoiselles d'Avignon*, but he subsequently came to realize that "We were both headed in the same general direction," for both he and Picasso were pursuing the constructive, spatial implications of Cézanne's late work.[29] The collaboration developed gradually, but the two worked together closely from 1909 on – in Braque's words, "like two mountaineers roped together" – until Braque joined the French army in 1914.[30] In recalling that five-year period, Picasso also stressed the extraordinary degree of cooperation: "Almost every evening, either I went to Braque's studio or Braque came to mine. Each of us *had* to see what the other had done during the day. We criticized each other's work. A canvas wasn't finished unless both of us felt it was."[31] David Sylvester compared the relationship of Picasso and Braque in these formative years of Cubism to the later relationship of the jazz musicians Dizzy Gillespie and Charlie Parker in the heyday of bebop: "It was a relationship in which two young artists who were at once men of genius and great virtuosi and who had totally contrasting temperaments were joined in the creation of a revolutionary style, inspiring each other, guiding each other through a journey in the dark, goading each other with their intense rivalry, loving each other, often disliking and distrusting each other."[32]

Picasso and Braque wanted to represent the tangible nature of objects without the use of linear perspective, which they regarded as mechanical and arbitrary. They replaced the restrictive single viewpoint of Renaissance perspective – which Braque ridiculed, saying "It is as if someone spent his life drawing profiles and believed that man was one-eyed" – with an approach that allowed them to represent their full knowledge of objects, effectively walking around their subject and presenting views of it from many different vantage points. They did this without the vivid colors used by the Impressionists, because they wanted to create solid and stable forms that represented underlying structures, rather than the momentary and changing reflections of light that dissolved the material world into flimsy and shimmering optical effects.[33] They did not replace traditional perspective and color with any single system, but over time devised a number of instruments to substitute for them.

The most striking early development was based on a logical extension of a technique developed by Cézanne. Late in his career Cézanne often used several vantage points within a single painting. Although this produced occasional anomalies, most conspicuously in the form of inconsistencies in the shapes of table tops that supported still life compositions, Cézanne did this to give solidity to the apples, baskets, and bowls that he studied and painted with infinite care.[34] Picasso and Braque reasoned that if Cézanne could break the contours of objects by viewing them from two or three different positions, they could do the same using two or three dozen viewpoints. This gave rise to the faceting the Cubists used to portray each of a number of different elements of an object from a different point of view, with each of the associated planes lighted from a different direction, and to the consequent creation of spaces that could not exist in actuality.[35]

In this early phase, in their pursuit of the reality of objects the Cubists restricted their colors to a limited range of shades of gray and brown, in order to avoid both the shimmering Impressionist coloring that dissolved substance and the arbitrary brilliance of Fauve colors.[36] Their search for a realistic way to reintroduce a wider range of colors led Picasso to create the first collage in 1912, by attaching a piece of cloth to the canvas, and later the same year prompted Braque to make the first papier collé. The materials introduced into these new genres were often actual fragments of the real objects they were used to symbolize – cigarette wrappers, newspapers, playing cards – and in other cases were commercial imitations of real objects – for example, the piece of cloth printed to imitate chair caning that Picasso used to represent a chair. When the artists began to translate the effects of collage and papier collé into paint, the result was a new flattened construction of overlapping, superimposed planes that appeared to exist within a much shallower space than the earlier fragmented facets of objects. The new phase after 1912, in which compositions were constructed from larger, flattened elements, came to be known as Synthetic Cubism, in contrast to the earlier Analytic phase, in which objects were broken into smaller fragments, each of which was shaded to create an illusion of three dimensionality.[37]

In 1921, Roger Fry described Picasso as "the painter who has had more influence on modern art than any other single man." Yet Fry also explained why he felt unable to place Picasso's achievement in perspective:

When we attempt the impossible feat of estimating the value of a contemporary artist, we generally take as a measure the case of some similar artist in the past familiar to us, the full trajectory of whose career time has enabled us to trace. But where in the past are we to find the likeness to Pablo Picasso? ... For here is an artist who has given rise to more schools of art, who has determined the direction of more artists, than any other one can think of. An artist, too, who has changed the superficial appearance of pictures more radically than any other in the whole history of the world.[38]

The survey of art history textbooks clearly confirms what virtually all art scholars recognize, that the greatest period of Picasso's career was the time of his invention and development of Cubism during his late twenties and early thirties. Much of this period was spent in his remarkable collaboration with Braque, which ended when Braque went to fight in World War I. Picasso later told his friend and dealer, Daniel-Henry Kahnweiler, "On August 2, 1914, I took Braque and Derain to the Gare d'Avignon. I never saw them again." The statement wasn't literally true, for although Braque was severely wounded in the war, Picasso did see him again, many times, between 1917 and Braque's death in 1963. But as Kahnweiler explained, "by this he meant that it was never the same."[39]

Marcel Duchamp

Duchamp was the great *saboteur*, the relentless enemy of painterly painting (read Picasso and Matisse), the asp in the basket of fruit.
Robert Motherwell[40]

Marcel Duchamp's avowed goal was to correct what he considered a basic error of art in the modern era. He argued that prior to the mid-nineteenth century "paint was always a means to an end, whether the end was religious, social, decorative, or romantic. Now it's become an end in itself."[41] Modern art had forsaken the mind in favor of the eye: "Since Courbet, it's been believed that painting is addressed to the retina. That was everyone's error. The retinal shudder!"[42] From the beginning of his career, Duchamp wanted to change this orientation: "I was interested in ideas – not merely in visual products. I wanted to put painting once again at the service of the mind."[43]

As a young painter in Paris, Duchamp's point of departure was Cubism. He later explained that the basis of his early work had been "a desire to break up forms – to 'decompose' them much along the lines the Cubists had done. But I wanted to go further – much further – in fact in quite another direction altogether." Under the influence of the early chronophotography of Etienne-Jules Marey and Eadweard Muybridge, Duchamp painted his first major work, *Nude Descending a Staircase, No. 2*, in 1912: "My aim was a static representation of movement – a static composition of indications of various positions taken by a form in

movement – with no attempt to give cinema effects through painting."[44] *Nude Descending* immediately caused a scandal. When Duchamp
submitted it to the 1912 Salon des Indépendants, it was perceived as
a parody of Cubism, and rejected.[45] The rejection by his fellow painters
confirmed Duchamp's scorn for orthodox art: "It helped liberate me completely from the past."[46] Duchamp realized that he was dissatisfied not
only with the current state of painting, but with painting itself: "The
whole trend of painting was something I didn't care to continue. After
ten years of painting I was bored with it." In pursuit of a more highly
conceptual art, "from 1912 on I decided to stop being a painter in the
professional sense."[47]

In 1913, Duchamp posed the question, "Can one make works which
are not works of 'art'?" Later that year he provided a novel answer, in the
form of "a work of art without an artist to make it."[48] By fastening a bicycle wheel to a stool, Duchamp had made the first of what he would later
name "readymades" – manufactured objects that he purchased, titled,
signed, and often inscribed with a short phrase or sentence. Duchamp
stressed that the choice of readymades was "never dictated by aesthetic
delectation," but rather was based on "a reaction of visual indifference
with at the same time a total absence of good or bad taste."[49] By presenting everyday objects such as a urinal, a bottle rack, or a snow shovel as
works of art, Duchamp dramatically raised the question of what constituted art. Decades later, he explained that the readymade demonstrated
that there could be no general definition of the essential nature of art:
"the readymade can be seen as a sort of irony, because it says here it
is, a thing that I call art, I didn't even make it myself. As we know art
etymologically speaking means to 'make,' 'hand make,' and there instead
of making, I take it readymade. So it was a form of denying the possibility
of defining art."[50]

Duchamp's work pushed conceptual art to new extremes. Indeed,
Joseph Masheck observed that Duchamp functioned differently than
artists had in the past: "In a sense he was a mute critic and aesthetician
whose works were plastic rather than verbal: although he is commonly
thought of as a conceptual plastic artist, much of his work is really reflection concretized."[51] Duchamp became a central influence on the Dada
movement that began during World War I. In 1934, André Breton, the
founder and leading spirit of Surrealism, declared that Duchamp had
been "at the very forefront of all the 'modern' movements which have
succeeded each other during the last twenty-five years."[52] With the wholesale departure of Robert Rauschenberg, Jasper Johns, and many others

from the traditional methods and materials of art from the mid-1950s on, Duchamp came to be considered by many as "the most influential artist of the second half of the twentieth century."[53] In a eulogy Johns wrote that "Marcel Duchamp, one of this century's pioneer artists, moved his work through the retinal boundaries which had been established with Impressionism into a field where language, thought and vision act upon one another. There it changed form through a complex interplay of new mental and physical materials, heralding many of the technical, mental and visual details to be found in more recent art."[54] Duchamp's contribution was placed in a broader context by the Abstract Expressionist Robert Motherwell. A painter whose career extended into the era when Rauschenberg, Warhol, and other younger artists were breaking down traditional artistic barriers, Motherwell saw Duchamp as the source of one of the two basic forces that had created a fault line in the art of the twentieth century, as artists struggled over the issue of whether art would follow fixed conventions, and respect established genres, or whether it would break existing rules, and create new art forms. Thus in 1971 Motherwell reflected that "Picasso, as a painter, wanted boundaries. Duchamp, as an anti-painter, did not. From the standpoint of each, the other was involved in a *game*. Taking one side or the other is the history of art since 1914."[55]

Wassily Kandinsky, Piet Mondrian, and Kazimir Malevich

It might be fair to say that Malevich's abstraction sprang, Athena-like, ready formed from the brow of its creator; this distinguishes Malevich's approach very sharply from that of both Mondrian and Kandinsky, who had sensed and inched their way into abstraction over a period of many years.

John Golding[56]

At the age of 30, Wassily Kandinsky gave up a career teaching law in Russia and moved to Munich to become a painter. He took with him a strong belief in the expressive power of color and design, which derived in part from the traditional folk art he had seen while doing ethnographic research in Russian peasant villages. Kandinsky's art developed slowly in Munich, because his interest in color rather than drawing did not conform to the prevailing academic orthodoxy. But he was excited by a trip to Paris in 1906, where he saw Matisse's exaggerated use of color in his early Fauve paintings. Kandinsky began to consider giving even greater emphasis to color over form: "Much encouraged, I asked myself... whether one might not simply reduce or 'distort' objects, but do away with them altogether."[57]

This initiated Kandinsky's progression toward abstraction. Yet by his own account this occurred "slowly, as a result of endless experiments, doubts, hopes, and discoveries."[58] He feared that a totally abstract art would degenerate into mere decoration, devoid of emotional or spiritual impact. He believed that non-representational art would remain meaningful only if it grew out of representation: if the artist began with objects, then veiled them by blurring or simplifying their forms, the viewer would sense their presence, and feel their impact, even if only subconsciously. Making abstract art therefore involved hiding things, for "concealment wields an enormous power in art." Even greater possibilities were raised by mixing implicit and explicit forms, "the combination of the hidden and the revealed."[59]

Kandinsky's development of abstraction therefore involved a cautious advance, as objects gradually disappeared, and it was not until 1913 that he began to make paintings that contained no recognizable references to the phenomenal world. In that year, he acknowledged that it had taken "a very long time before I arrived at the correct answer to the question: What is to replace the object? I sometimes look back at the past and despair at how long this solution took me."[60] Yet he understood that this slow progression was required by the need for gradual learning: "it is impossible to conjure up maturity at any particular time. And nothing is more damaging and more sinful than to seek one's forms by force... Thus, I was obliged to wait patiently for the hour that would lead my hand to create abstract form."[61]

The images Kandinsky created in these early abstract works were novel both for their use of autonomous color and for their creation of a new pictorial space. Brightly colored shapes float and overlap in a state of flux, without perspective or shading to create depth, in a space that suggests an indeterminate state of dreams.[62] Kandinsky explained to one collector that viewers had to learn to see these pictures "as a graphic representation of a *mood*."[63]

Piet Mondrian spent the first two decades of his career in his native Holland, but the turning point for his art occurred when he moved to Paris at the age of 40. There the impact of Cubism on his art was so decisive that his friend and biographer Michel Seuphor later declared that "We may say that it was in Paris, in 1912... that the life of the great painter began."[64] Under the influence of Cubism, Mondrian's earlier symbolist treatment of landscape evolved into progressively more simplified and fragmented forms, with increasing emphasis on horizontal and vertical lines. His subsequent development was driven by a desire to find the reality underlying the superficial appearance of objects: "The interior of things shows through the surface . . . It is this inner image that should be represented."[65]

Mondrian's belief in Theosophy led him to seek an ideal art, that would be universal and would help to create a new society by portraying a spiritual equilibrium, but it also gave him a firm conviction that progress toward this ideal could only occur gradually, "the slow and sure path of evolution."[66] The remaining decades of his career, and life, became a protracted quest for "universal beauty." In 1914, Mondrian stated his credo for a fellow artist: "I believe that it is possible by means of horizontal and vertical lines, constructed *consciously* but not *calculatingly*, guided by a higher intuition and brought to harmony and rhythm . . . to arrive at a work of art as strong as it is true . . . And *chance* must be as far removed as *calculation*."[67] Carl Holty, a younger artist who knew Mondrian late in his life, testified that he worked visually and experimentally: "There was no program, no symbols, no 'geometry' or system of measure; only intuition determined the total rhythm of the relationships, by trial and error. The given space of the canvas, the given tension of its proportion, its size, were likewise experimentally determined and varied. Intuitive experience for Mondrian could only be direct, immediate, sensual."[68]

By 1913, Mondrian had begun to make paintings that made no recognizable visual reference to real objects, and that were consequently considered to be totally abstract. It appears, however, that until 1919 he continued to use the visual stimulus of specific surroundings as the point of departure for his paintings, and in some cases he referred to these sources in his titles.[69] After 1919 his paintings continued to evolve through variations in their component elements, as Mondrian experimented with regular and irregular grids of black lines, and with compositions based on colored rectangles of varying sizes.

Mondrian's willingness to continue significant experimentation throughout his life produced a denouement that is rare if not unprecedented in the history of Western art. In 1943, working in New York after World War II had forced him to flee both Paris and London, he decided to eliminate the network of black lines that had been a central characteristic of his paintings virtually since his first encounter with Cubism.[70] One consequence of this was to give a new depth and dynamism to his very latest paintings of brightly colored bands and squares.[71] In particular

Broadway Boogie-Woogie, executed at the age of 71, is reproduced in more textbooks than any other painting Mondrian made in a career of more than 50 years. Remarkably, therefore, Mondrian's commitment to experimentation to the very end of his life allowed the last painting he ever completed to be considered by art historians the most important he ever made.

Kazimir Malevich was first exposed to advanced art when he moved to Moscow from his native Ukraine in 1907. In Moscow he met and worked with a group of talented young Russian artists, and he saw paintings by leading French artists both in exhibitions and in the private collections of two wealthy Russian merchants who were a major collectors of Matisse, Picasso, Braque, and other important young artists in Paris. Malevich quickly assimilated the innovations of Cubism and Futurism, and in 1915 made a radical leap into a new form of abstract art that he named Suprematism.

Malevich's mature work was based not only on careful planning but on explicit calculation. John Milner observed that by 1913 "Malevich began to make the mathematical basis of his work a primary consideration," working by constructing figures to fit predetermined geometric schemes.[72] Geometric calculations not only provided the basis for the forms of the paintings Malevich displayed at the landmark "0,10" exhibition in Petrograd in December 1915, at which he first presented his Suprematist compositions, but were also used to determine the arrangement of the paintings on the walls.[73]

Unlike Kandinsky and Mondrian, Malevich did not develop abstract forms from observation of objects in the external world, but instead derived them from ideas. Malevich believed that the time had come for revolutionary changes in art, to parallel those that were occurring in technology and society. Rather than transforming real objects, or breaking them into component parts, Suprematism would create symbols directly from abstract elements, "the formation of signs instead of the repetition of nature." These new signs would be ideas "flowing from our creative brain."[74] The squares and other geometric shapes in Malevich's Suprematist abstractions symbolize flight into the cosmos, but the space these figures float in is not the actual space we see by looking up at the sky: "Represented spaces, planes and lines exist only on the pictorial surface, but not in reality."[75]

Malevich's sudden plunge into abstraction contrasted dramatically with the gradual progressions into abstract art of Kandinsky and Mondrian. This was a clear consequence of his conceptual approach to art, compared to the experimental orientation of both Kandinsky and Male-vich. Thus John Golding observed that in the years immediately following his creation of Suprematism, both Malevich's painting and his thought evolved "at the same dizzying and heady rate," as he drew on a range of intellectual sources that were "astonishingly and bafflingly disparate."[76]

Just as Malevich devised and developed his form of abstract art more rapidly than Kandinsky and Mondrian, so too his subsequent experi-ence differed from theirs. Malevich made few paintings during the late 1910s and early 1920s, and when he returned to painting, his work was figurative. John Golding examined Malevich's situation:

Malevich is the true father of what we have come to call "minimal" and "conceptual" art. But he is also the prototype for countless subsequent abstract artists who having reached their goal – or at least a distillation of the ideas and sensations they were seeking to evoke – only find themselves in the tragic posi-tion of wondering how to go further, how to avoid the endless repetition of the climax of their achievement, a repetition that might ultimately only drain their art of much of its original impact or meaning. Mondrian knew how to renew himself by constantly kicking the visual ladder from under himself. Kandinsky's endlessly inquiring mind produced for him, throughout his career, a succession of alternative possibilities. Malevich had succumbed to the principle of destruction inherent in a Hegelian system of dialectics.[77]

Golding's description of the three artists' differing trajectories can be explained simply: it is possible for conceptual innovators fully to express their ideas and thus reach their goals, but experimental innovators gener-ally do not believe in definitive conclusions. The vague aesthetic goals of Kandinsky and Mondrian never allowed them to feel satisfied that they had reached a conclusion, but Malevich's demonstrations of his ideas appear to have left him with no further problems to solve, and therefore no need to continue making art.

Constantin Brancusi

Since the Gothic, European sculpture had become overgrown with moss, weeds – all sorts of surface excrescences which completely concealed shape. It has been Brancusi's special mission to get rid of this overgrowth, and to make us more shape-conscious. To do this he has had to concentrate on very simple direct shapes.

Henry Moore[78]

Constantin Brancusi arrived in Paris from his native Romania in 1904, and remained there for the rest of his life. Early in his career he worked briefly as an assistant to Auguste Rodin, but he soon left, explaining that "Nothing can grow in the shadow of the great trees."[79] Brancusi became a great sculptor by reacting against Rodin's style, but late in his career he wrote that "Without the discoveries of Rodin, my work would have been impossible." Rudolf Wittkower explained that Brancusi's art owed a great debt to the fragmentary partial figures pioneered by Rodin: "The discovery that the part can stand for the whole was Rodin's, and Brancusi along with scores of other sculptors accepted the premise."[80]

Brancusi's distinctive contribution was to bring abstraction to sculpture. He did this visually, for his forms always originated in nature. Unlike Rodin and most of his contemporaries, Brancusi did not have plaster models translated to marble by technicians, but instead worked directly in the stone. Furthermore, he did this without planning: "I don't work from sketches, I take the chisel and hammer and go right ahead."[81]

Brancusi's experimental approach meant that for him the completion of an individual sculpture was not a resolution or conclusion, but only one step in the development of a theme. This process was typically gradual and protracted: he made a series of versions of *The Kiss* over an elapsed span of more than 35 years, and he made more than two dozen related *Birds* over the course of 30 years.[82] His forms generally became progressively simpler and more abstract over time, for his goal was to portray "not the external form but the essence of things."[83] He stressed that his sculptures were not intellectual puzzles: "Don't look for obscure formulas or for mystery."[84] Brancusi considered simplicity not a goal but an incidental product of the search for reality, and David Sylvester observed that it characterized his work: "Brancusi's sculpture, at its most simple and refined, can be as pure as anything in Western art since Cycladic sculpture."[85] The process by which he made his sculptures became a physical metaphor for his visual quest for the underlying essences of objects. Thus John Golding contrasted Brancusi's method with that of Rodin: "Rodin had been essentially a modeller, with all that implies for the process of building things up additively, slapping and pressing clay into clay, twisting, bending, manipulating, gouging. Brancusi turned himself into the archetypal carver, slowly working inward, reducing and compressing, removing layer after layer until he had released his material's hidden inner life; even his obsessive polishing of his bronzes can be seen as an extension of the carving process."[86]

The trajectory of Brancusi's career was typical of an extreme experimental artist. David Lewis observed that Brancusi's work changed slowly and subtly over time: "It does not fall into clear phases like the work of most other artists, and as a result it is always difficult with Brancusi to say which sculptures belong to which year. Often a series of sculptures will span almost a lifetime and those at the end of the development will be distinguishable from those at the beginning in terms of only the slightest adjustments."[87] Sidney Geist noted a consequence of this gradual evolution: "just as there are no unsuccessful Brancusis or grave lapses in quality, so are there no towering peaks whose achievement sets them apart from the rest."[88] David Sylvester recognized Brancusi as an archetypal experimental artist: "He was an extreme instance of the seeker, with his indefatigable exploration of a few themes, eschewing duplication to create variations involving the subtlest of differences."[89] Brancusi himself described his technique in terms that left little doubt that it was equally a philosophy: "all these works are conceived directly in the material and made by me from beginning to end, and...the work is hard and long and goes on forever."[90]

Jackson Pollock, Willem de Kooning, and Mark Rothko

Every so often, a painter has to destroy painting. Cézanne did it. Picasso did it with cubism. Then Pollock did it. He busted our idea of a picture all to hell. Then there could be *new* paintings again.
Willem de Kooning[91]

The phrase "abstract expressionist" is now seen to mean "paintings of the school of de Kooning" who stands out from them as Giotto stood out from his contemporary realists.
Fairfield Porter, 1959[92]

Rothko's mixtures resulted in a series of glowing color structures that have no exact parallel in modern art.
Robert Motherwell[93]

Pollock, de Kooning, and Rothko were the most prominent members of the Abstract Expressionists, a group of New York painters who came to be recognized as the most important advanced artists to emerge after World War II, and who in the process shifted the center of the art world from Europe to the United States. The critic Clement Greenberg, who was the first important advocate for the Abstract Expressionists, shocked many people by declaring early in 1948 that "the immediate future of Western art...depends on what is done in this country," and that "American abstract painting...has in the last several years shown here and there a capacity for fresh content that does not seem to be matched...in France."[94] Although French observers denied the claims of Greenberg and other American critics for decades, even French critics and historians have now generally conceded that the leading French counterparts of the Abstract Expressionists, such as Pierre Soulages, Jean Fautrier, and Nicholas de Staël, were not the most important innovators of their time.[95]

The Abstract Expressionists were unified not by a style but by an interest in drawing on the subconscious to produce images, and doing so by working directly on the canvas by trial and error, without plans or preconceptions. Pollock's signature drip method of applying paint, with its inevitable splashing and puddling that could not be completely controlled by the artist, became the most famous emblem of this search for the unknown image, reinforced by his often-quoted statement, "When I am *in* my painting, I'm not aware of what I'm doing."[96] De Kooning also worked without a specific goal: "I find sometimes a terrific picture...but I couldn't set out to do that, you know. I set out even keeping that in mind that this thing will be a flop in all probability and, you know, sometimes it turns out very good."[97] Rothko stressed the absence of preconceived outcomes more dramatically: "Pictures must be miraculous...The picture must be for [the artist]...a revelation, an unexpected and unprecedented resolution."[98]

Pollock made his most innovative paintings during 1947–50, when he used brushes, sticks, and syringes to drip and spatter paint onto unstretched canvases spread on the floor of the Long Island barn that he used as a studio. In addition to the novel method of applying paint, these works were innovative in a number of ways. They were larger than most earlier abstract paintings; Pollock believed that "the easel picture [is] a dying form, and the tendency of modern feeling is towards the wall picture or mural."[99] They had no specific focal point, but were instead all-over compositions, with equal emphasis over the whole picture surface; Pollock declared that "My paintings do not have a center."[100] They used line in a new way, not to mark the edges of planes, or to define shapes or figures, but as an autonomous element in the composition. Thus the sculptor Richard Serra later explained that "Pollock has rid himself of figuration, meaning lines that enclose or contain or describe shapes."[101] These paintings were basically different from earlier works of art. Pollock embraced this fact, as he told an interviewer in 1950 that "My opinion is that new needs need new techniques."[102] Serra reflected that "Pollock made something never seen before that we now know of as a Pollock painting, an interlacing, tumbleweed creation that exists in a space unlike any other."[103]

De Kooning gradually developed a distinctive abstract style during the late 1940s, but his most celebrated series of works was made up of the large figurative *Women* that he executed during 1950–53.[104] His return to representation at a time when nearly all of his colleagues were committed to abstraction raised considerable controversy, but de Kooning ignored the criticism, and reflected that either option was arbitrary: "It's really absurd to make an image, like a human image, with paint today, when you think about it... But then all of a sudden it was even more absurd not to do it."[105] Unlike Pollock and many of the other Abstract Expressionists, who wanted to separate themselves from European approaches to create a distinctively American art, de Kooning had been formally trained in art in his native Holland, and felt no need to revolt against European traditions. For him, the female figure remained an important subject: "Flesh was the reason why oil painting was invented... [F]or the Renaissance artist, flesh was the stuff people were made of."[106]

Rothko first arrived at his trademark image of stacked rectangles in 1949, and during the next two decades he made it the basis for hundreds of paintings, constantly experimenting by changing the size of the canvas, the sizes of the rectangles, and the colors of the forms. Rothko defended his repetition, declaring that "If a thing is worth doing once, it is worth doing over and over again – exploring it, probing it, demanding by this repetition that the public look at it."[107] By diluting his paint and applying it in thin washes, layer over layer, he achieved luminous color effects, and viewers of his paintings often have the impression of looking into deep films of color suspended in space.[108] Although Rothko became known as a colorist, he consistently maintained that color was merely an instrument toward his true goal of evoking moods, and dealing with tragic themes.[109] Thus in 1943, in a joint statement Rothko and his fellow Abstract Expressionist Adolph Gottlieb declared that "We assert that the subject is crucial and only that subject-matter is valid which is tragic and timeless."[110] In the 1950s, Rothko continued to insist on the spiritual content of his abstract paintings, as he told the critic Selden Rodman: "I'm interested only in expressing basic human emotions – tragedy, ecstasy, doom, and so on... The people who weep before my pictures are having the same religious experience I had when I painted them. And if you, as you say, are moved only by their color relationships, then you miss the point!"[111] Although art scholars have puzzled over Rothko's claims of treating specific ideas and themes, his unusual color effects appear to transcend merely decorative interpretations, and a typical conclusion is that of Alan Bowness: "Rothko's paintings are about the working of color in space, but they are, at a fundamental level, icons for contemplation and meditation."[112]

The Abstract Expressionists invented an aggressively experimental art, in which the finished painting often visibly recorded the process of its own creation. Both artists and critics could celebrate these new forms of abstract art as an "assertion of freedom" by the artist, whose devices – "the mark, the stroke, the brush, the drip" – were "all signs of the artist's active presence."[113] In part, the influence of the Abstract Expressionists was on younger experimental artists who felt liberated by this demonstration of how art could be made. For example Richard Serra observed that in the drip paintings "Pollock allowed the form to emerge out of the materials and out of the process. For me, as a student, this idea of allowing the form to emerge out of the process was incredibly important."[114] Similarly, the painter Susan Rothenberg acknowledged that "de Kooning was always important to me because of his whole struggle to produce a painting, then becoming unsettled by it, doing something else to it, until finally it was OK by him."[115] Yet the Abstract Expressionists' influence was more general than this: they had a profound effect even on many later conceptual artists who had little interest in their ideas or methods, for they succeeded once and for all in ridding the American art world of its sense of inferiority. For generations, American painting had been a provincial and largely derivative art, and a sojourn in Paris had been a standard part of the education of an aspiring American painter. The Abstract Expressionists decisively broke with this pattern, and attitude. In 1944, Pollock told an interviewer that he felt no need to go to Europe, because "I don't see why the problems of modern painting can't be solved as well here as elsewhere."[116] Because of what he and his contemporaries accomplished over the course of the next two decades, for the remainder of the twentieth century no American artist would have to worry about that issue.

Jasper Johns and Robert Rauschenberg

The painting of a target by Jasper Johns was an atomic bomb in my training. I knew that I had seen something truly profound.
                    Ed Ruscha[117]

Rauschenberg invented more than any artist since Picasso.
                    Jasper Johns[118]

Johns and Rauschenberg became partners in designing department store window displays in New York in 1954, and lived together during most of the next seven years. This became the key formative period for the art of both, in which they made the innovations that would inspire much of the advanced art of the 1960s and beyond.

Arriving in the art world at a time when Abstract Expressionism was the dominant paradigm, Johns and Rauschenberg reacted against what they considered the exaggerated emotional and philosophical claims of the older painters for their art. Rauschenberg later recalled that "The kind of talk you heard then in the art world was so hard to take. It was all about suffering and self-expression and the State of Things. I just wasn't interested in that, and I certainly didn't have any interest in trying to improve the world through painting."[119] Similarly, Johns explained that "I'm neither a teacher nor an author of manifestos. I don't think along the same lines as the Abstract Expressionists, who took those sorts of things all too seriously."[120] Instead of self-expression, the two young artists wanted to find new ways to use art to reflect everyday life. Rauschenberg famously declared that "Painting relates to both art and life. Neither can be made. (I try to act in that gap between the two.)"[121] Johns echoed the same idea: "I'm interested in things which suggest the world rather than suggest the personality. I'm interested in things which suggest things which are, rather than in judgments."[122]

The brash and iconoclastic Rauschenberg made a number of symbolic attacks on Abstract Expressionism. In 1953, he literally erased an Abstract Expressionist work. After obtaining a drawing from Willem de Kooning for the purpose, Rauschenberg carefully rubbed out the image, then framed the smudged sheet and hand-lettered a label, "Erased de Kooning Drawing, Robert Rauschenberg."[123] In 1957, Rauschenberg mocked the supposed spontaneity and uniqueness of the Abstract Expressionists' work by making two collage paintings, *Factum I* and *Factum II*, that appeared identical, even to the drips and splashes around several large brush strokes. Most damaging, however, was Rauschenberg's innovation of a new form of art. In 1954 he began to attach real things to his canvases, in order to make his paintings independent objects rather than illusionistic representations of them: "I don't want a picture to look like something it isn't. I want it to look like something it is. And I think a picture is more like the real world when it's made out of the real world."[124] Rauschenberg named these three-dimensional works "combines," and they became so influential for successive generations of younger artists, many of whom were eager to break away from the traditional two-dimensional picture plane and the sanctity of traditional art materials, that the critic Arthur Danto observed in 1997 that "the artistic mainstream today is very largely Rauschenbergian."[125]

In January 1958 the dealer Leo Castelli presented an exhibition of paintings Jasper Johns had produced during the previous three years. The show electrified the art world: one of the paintings, *Target with Four Faces*, was reproduced on the cover of a leading art magazine, and Alfred Barr, the director of collections of the Museum of Modern Art, bought *Target with Four Faces* and two other paintings for the museum, and persuaded the architect Philip Johnson to buy a fourth painting, *Flag*, as a future gift to the museum. The show included the early paintings that have become Johns's most celebrated works. Although they were painted with visible brushstrokes that were derived from Abstract Expressionism, the motifs were presented directly, and neutrally, without any illusion of depth: as Arthur Danto observed, each painting was "at once a representation and the object of representation," a flag that was simply a flag, or a target that was simply a target.[126] Johns later explained that he chose these subjects because "They seemed to me preformed, conventional, depersonalized, factual, exterior elements."[127] Danto remarked that these paintings invalidated the aesthetic of Abstract Expressionism, not only by returning to figuration, but by doing it in such a literal way: "*Flag* reconnected art with reality. It showed how it is possible for something to be at once an artwork and a real thing."[128] Nor was it lost on younger painters that Johns' preformed and exterior images, like the real objects in Rauschenberg's combines, had a very different origin than the spontaneous images of the Abstract Expressionism. Thus Ed Ruscha recognized that "the work of Johns and Rauschenberg marked a departure in the sense that their work was premeditated, and Abstract Expressionism was not." He recalled that this had had a liberating effect on him, at a time when his art school teachers had insisted on "things that were gestural rather than cerebral." With the example of Johns, "I began to move towards things that had more of a premeditation." This allowed Ruscha to produce the paintings that made him one of the leading American painters of the 1960s: "All of my art has been premeditated; having a notion of the end and not the means to the end."[129]

Johns's targets and flags had a remarkably large and varied impact on younger artists. As a senior in college, Frank Stella saw Johns's 1958 exhibition, and was struck by "the idea of stripes... the idea of repetition."[130] This soon led to Stella's Black paintings, in which parallel stripes of black paint filled large canvases. These were exhibited in 1960, at Castelli's gallery, and subsequently became Stella's most important works. Their simplicity and symmetry in turn prompted Carl Andre and Donald Judd to make the simple, symmetrical sculptures that initiated Minimalism, one of the major art movements of the 1960s.[131] Johns's paintings of targets and flags thus led to the abstraction of Minimalism, but they also led to the figuration of Pop art, for their direct images helped inspire Andy Warhol and Roy Lichtenstein to paint straightforward images of photographs and comic strips.[132] Looking back at Johns's early work four decades later, Danto reflected that "it signaled the end of an era," by undermining Abstract Expressionism, while at the same time it "opened up the present in which we all exist artistically."[133]

Rauschenberg's use of found objects, and Johns's deadpan portrayal of two-dimensional motifs, powerfully revived Duchamp's earlier efforts to eliminate the traditional barriers between art and everyday life. And like Duchamp, their highly conceptual approaches to art raised the possibility of irony that had been altogether absent from the spiritual quests of the Abstract Expressionists. The work of Johns and Rauschenberg opened the door to a series of movements that have made art that has differed radically in form and appearance, but have consistently been characterized by the use of common images and objects and by the real or ostensible rejection of the vision of the artist as a privileged maker of hallowed objects. Thus for example the critic John Coplans declared that "It is impossible ... to discuss the origins and development of Pop Art – and especially the use of banal imagery so central to the style – without first remarking the influence of Jasper Johns and Robert Rauschenberg."[134]

Andy Warhol and Claes Oldenburg

Andy Warhol's influence on the art world cannot be overstated.
William Burroughs[135]

I think Oldenburg's work is profound ... There are few artists as good as Oldenburg.
Donald Judd[136]

Warhol and Oldenburg were two of the leading Pop artists, a movement that sprang into prominence in 1962. The subject matter of Pop art varied among artists, as did their specific methods, but a shared characteristic was the mechanical, impersonal appearance of their works. Their images were predetermined, for they were usually replications of existing advertisements, comic strips, news photographs, or other commercial images. Pop artists aggressively attacked the distinction between advanced art and commercial art, and they did this by making original works that pretended to be copies of the commercial originals.

Warhol's most important works were those that introduced Pop art to the American public, and the New York art world, in 1962. Early in the year he began to make paintings with stencils, and in June his first solo show, in Los Angeles, exhibited 32 paintings of Campbell's soup cans he had made using this process. In July, Warhol began to make paintings using silkscreen printing, which allowed him to replicate photographic images taken from magazines or newspapers, and to work much more quickly.[137] Marilyn Monroe's suicide in August prompted Warhol immediately to make a series of portraits from a publicity photograph of the actress, and these were displayed, along with paintings of Campbell's soup cans and of Coca-Cola bottles, at Warhol's first solo New York show in November.[138]

John Coplans noted that Warhol's paintings of 1962 introduced two important formal innovations: "First, the actual as against the simulated use of an anonymous and mechanical technique, and second, the use of serial forms."[139] Both were highly conceptual devices, as was his practice of painting from photographs. In 1964, the aging doyen of twentieth-century conceptual art, Marcel Duchamp, endorsed Warhol's use of seriality: "If you take a Campbell soup can and repeat it fifty times, you are not interested in the retinal image. What interests you is the concept that wants to put fifty Campbell soup cans on a canvas."[140] Warhol himself left no doubt that his interest was not in creating spontaneous or unique images, as he famously explained in a 1963 interview that "The reason I'm painting this way is that I want to be a machine."[141] Indeed, he freely admitted that he did not enjoy the process of painting – "Paintings are too hard" – and that he would be pleased not to be involved at all: "I think somebody should be able to do all my paintings for me."[142] Not surprisingly, he professed surprise that artists were held in particular esteem: "Why do people think artists are special? It's just another job."[143]

Warhol's innovations had an immediate impact on younger artists. The painter Chuck Close recalled seeing an exhibition of Warhol's work in 1964, the year Close graduated from art school: "I felt wonderful, momentary outrage, yet I was totally won over by seeing something like that in an art gallery and seeing the limits and definitions of what art could be, having to be elastic enough to incorporate it." Close, who subsequently developed his own distinctive method of painting from photographs, reflected that "We don't think of Warhol as a figurative painter essentially but that's a role that he offered, and the fact that he was working from photographs was important."[144] Mechanical reproduction, photography, and seriality have all played a central role in painting since the early 1960s, and Warhol's influence has been present in virtually all cases in which they appear.

Oldenburg's early career was marked by work in a variety of forms, including painting and wire constructions covered with cardboard and papier-mâché. Under the influence of Allan Kaprow's early happenings, Oldenburg began to stage his own happenings in New York in the early 1960s. He made plaster reliefs based on common objects to serve as props: "I take the materials from the surroundings in the Lower East Side and transform them and give them back."[145] Oldenburg's interest in transforming common objects into art led him to make his first soft sculptures in 1962, oversized replicas of cakes, hamburgers, and ice cream cones that he made from canvas and stuffed with foam rubber.

In a manifesto written in 1961, Oldenburg declared that "I am for an art...that does something other than sit on its ass in a museum." He also declared his support for an art "that embroils itself with the everyday crap," "that is comic, if necessary," and "that takes its form from the lines of life itself." His art would be made from the common objects and experiences of everyday life, including "things lost or thrown away." He opposed the glorification of the artist: "I am for an artist who vanishes, turning up in a white cap painting signs or hallways."[146]

Oldenburg's art extended sculpture, with novel images and materials. He furthermore did this with a gentle sense of irony and humor, making small things large and often monumental, and hard things soft. He acknowledged his ironic motivation in a 1965 interview, in explaining why he had made the soft sculptures: "I think it's an intention to prove that sculpture is not limited...Take a very general notion of sculpture, and if a thing is one thing why shouldn't it be its opposite?"[147] In recognition of the wide range of Oldenburg's activities, the critic Harold Rosenberg called him "the most inventive American artist of the post-Abstract Expressionist generation." Rosenberg found the unity of Oldenburg's art in his approach to all his creations: "Oldenburg has the offside mind and deadpan of the comedian-visionary."[148] Oldenburg himself pointed to a different source for this unity: "Everything I do is completely original – I made it up when I was a little kid."[149]

The conceptual content of Oldenburg's sculpture stemmed not only from the irony of enlarging and softening the objects he selected, but also from the selection of those objects, and the particular images of them he portrayed. Oldenburg explained that he not only worked with common, everyday, man-made objects, but that he worked with typical examples of their forms: "I suppose when you invent something like an ice cream cone or a machine, it goes through several states until it begins to look the way people want it to look... And after this has settled for a while you get a traditional form, and I would really prefer to work with a traditional typical form." Doing this meant that Oldenburg often had to create an ideal mental image of the object: "I work a great deal from the picture of the object that I assume people are carrying around in their minds."[150] The sculptor Donald Judd emphasized the information contained in Oldenburg's works: "The preferences of a person or millions are unavoidably incorporated in the things made."[151]

Young Geniuses and Old Masters

At the age of ten, twenty, a hundred, very young, a little older, and very old, an artist is always an artist.

Isn't he better at some times, some moments, than at others? Never impeccable, since he is a living, human being?

Paul Gauguin, 1903[152]

The data set constructed for this chapter can be used to examine the creative life cycles of the artists considered by this study. Table 2.3 shows that the nine artists categorized as conceptual innovators all had their best five-year periods during their twenties and thirties, whereas five of the six experimental artists had their best five-year periods during their forties and fifties. Even more narrowly, Table 2.4 presents the ages of the fifteen artists in the single year from which their work received the most illustrations. The ages of the nine conceptual artists in their single best years range from 25 for Johns to 37 for Malevich, all below the comparable ages for the six experimental artists, which range from 38 for Pollock to 71 for Mondrian. The median age of 33 for the conceptual artists in their best individual years is fully sixteen years below the median age of 49 for the experimental artists.

Table 2.5 presents the percentage distributions of all of each artist's illustrations over their whole careers. The differences between the conceptual and experimental artists are again clear. For eight of the nine conceptual artists – all except Matisse – more than half of their total

TABLE 2.4. *Best Single Year in Each Artist's Career, by Total Illustrations*

Artist	Year	Age
Conceptual		
Johns	1955	25
Picasso	1907	26
Braque	1911	29
Duchamp	1917	30
Oldenburg	1962	33
Rauschenberg	1959	34
Warhol	1962	34
Matisse	1905	36
Malevich	1915	37
Experimental		
Pollock	1950	38
De Kooning	1950	46
Kandinsky	1913	47
Brancusi	1925, 1928*	49, 52
Rothko	1957	54
Mondrian	1943	71

* Two years tied for most illustrations.

TABLE 2.5. *Percentage Distributions of Illustrations over Artists' Careers*

Age	20–9	30–9	40–9	50–9	60–9	70–9	80–9	90–9	Total
Conceptual									
Braque	58	28	6	3	5	0	0	–	100
Duchamp	39	48	2	4	2	5	0	–	100
Johns	60	27	7	5	1	0	–	–	100
Malevich	1	68	21	10	–	–	–	–	100
Matisse	1	44	26	7	6	4	12	–	100
Oldenburg	0	67	26	5	2	0	–	–	100
Picasso	35	25	17	14	4	2	2	1	100
Rauschenberg	10	84	3	0	3	0	0	–	100
Warhol	0	88	5	7	–	–	–	–	100
Experimental									
Brancusi	0	31	32	23	14	0	0	–	100
Kandinsky	0	1	70	20	4	5	–	–	100
De Kooning	0	2	73	13	6	6	0	0	100
Mondrian	0	11	47	20	5	17	–	–	100
Pollock	8	76	16	–	–	–	–	–	100
Rothko	0	6	17	62	15	–	–	–	100

TABLE 2.6. *Single Most Important Work by Each Artist, by Total Illustrations*

Artist, Title	Year	Age	Location
Conceptual			
Braque, *Houses at L'Estaque***	1908	26	Berne
Braque, *The Portuguese***	1911	29	Basel
Duchamp, *Fountain*	1917	30	unknown
Johns, *Three Flags*	1958	28	New York
Malevich, *Suprematist Composition:*	1918	40	New York
White on White			
Matisse, *Joy of Life*	1906	37	Merion
Oldenburg, *The Store*	1961	32	multiple
Picasso, *Les Demoiselles d'Avignon*	1907	26	New York
Rauschenberg, *Monogram*	1959	34	Stockholm
Warhol, *Marilyn Monroe Diptych*	1962	34	London
Experimental			
Brancusi, *Bird in Space*	1928	52	New York
Kandinsky, *Der Blaue Reiter*	1912	46	multiple
De Kooning, *Excavation*	1950	46	Chicago
Mondrian, *Broadway Boogie-Woogie*	1943	71	New York
Pollock, *Autumn Rhythm*	1950	38	New York
Rothko, *Red, White and Brown*	1957	54	Basel

* Two paintings tied for most illustrations.

illustrations represent work they did before the age of 40; for five of the nine, more than 80 percent of their illustrations are of work done before that age. In contrast, for five of the six experimental artists – all except Pollock – less than one-third of their total illustrations are of work they did before 40, and for four of them this share is less than 20 percent.

More narrowly still, Table 2.6 lists the single work by each artist that was most frequently illustrated. The ages of the conceptual artists when they made these works range from 26 for both Braque and Picasso to 40 for Malevich, while the ages of the experimentalists range from 38 to Pollock for 71 for Mondrian. The median age of the conceptual artists, of 31, is fully eighteen years lower than the median age of 49 of the experimentalists. Whereas eight of the ten conceptual works in the table were executed by their makers before the age of 35, and none were made after 45, all of the experimental works were made after the age of 35, and five of the six were made after 45.

Conceptual innovators tend to make their greatest contributions early in their careers, when they are least constrained by fixed habits of thought, and not yet accustomed to following the existing conventions of their disciplines. In contrast, experimental innovators generally improve with age, with the deepening of their understanding of their craft and their increasing knowledge of the subjects they are trying to represent. The greatest artists of the twentieth century clearly follow these contrasting life cycles. The conceptual painters Braque, Johns, and Picasso made their greatest contributions in their twenties, while their conceptual peers Duchamp, Malevich, Matisse, Oldenburg, Rauschenberg, and Warhol made their major contributions in their thirties. Of the experimentalists, Pollock made his greatest contribution in his late thirties, while Brancusi, Kandinsky, de Kooning, and Mondrian made theirs in their forties, and Rothko did his greatest work in his fifties. The art of the twentieth century was thus created by both young geniuses and old masters.

Conclusion

The modern artist is committed to the idea of endless invention and growth.
Meyer Schapiro, 1950[153]

The twentieth century was a time of fundamental change in advanced art, as artists embraced radically new methods and materials. This chapter used scholarly narratives of modern art to identify the most important innovators of the past century. Picasso dominates these narratives, but other artists also made key contributions in Europe early in the century, and in New York later, as the center of advanced art changed continents.

The greatest artistic innovators of the century made their discoveries in very different ways. Some, including Picasso, Matisse, and Duchamp, made sudden breakthroughs based on the formulation of new ideas. Others, including Mondrian, Kandinsky, and Pollock, made more gradual progress dictated by visual criteria. As in earlier centuries, the tension between conceptual and experimental innovation played a major role in the transformation of fine art.

The process of change continued to dominate fine art in the final decades of the twentieth century, and in fact accelerated over time. The enormous demand for innovation was a key element in making conceptual approaches to art the dominant feature of the art world in the late twentieth century. The extremely rapid pace of change created by a succession of conceptual movements in fact may account for the absence from this study of any artist who came to prominence after the early 1960s. As will be seen later in this study, there is no doubt that Robert Smithson, Bruce Nauman, Cindy Sherman, Jeff Koons, Damien Hirst, and other artists who worked in the late twentieth century have made important contributions that have changed the practices of their peers. Yet the rapidity of change in this era has limited the extent of their influence relative to that of their predecessors. A central reason for this is the nature of the conceptual changes that have occurred in art over the course of the twentieth century, for many of them have served to create new genres that have become independent specialties for many artists. The resulting fragmentation of art in the new era of pluralism restricts the proportion of the art world's territory that any single innovation can reach. Until some future innovator reverses this process by creating an art form that restores greater unity to the visual arts, the great painters of the early and mid-twentieth century may be the last in a line of giants each of whom, since the Renaissance, has for a time dominated the entire world of advanced art.

Appendix to Chapter 2
Books Surveyed for This Chapter

Adams, Laurie. 1994. *A History of Western Art.* New York: Harry N. Abrams.
Arnason, H. H. 2004. *History of Modern Art*, 5th ed. Upper Saddle River, NJ: Prentice Hall.
Bell, Cory. 2001. *Modern Art.* New York: Watson-Guptill.
Blistène, Bernard. 2001. *A History of 20th-Century Art.* Paris: Flammarion.
Bocola, Sandro. 1999. *The Art of Modernism.* Munich: Prestel.
Britt, David, ed. 1999. *Modern Art.* New York: Thames and Hudson.
Cumming, Robert. 2005. *Art.* New York: DK Publishing.
Dawtrey, Liz; Jackson, Toby; Masterson, Mary; Meecham, Pam; and Wood, Paul. 1996. *Investigating Modern Art.* New Haven: Yale University Press.
Dempsey, Amy. 2002. *Art in the Modern Era.* New York: Harry N. Abrams.
*Fer, Briony; Batchelor, David; and Wood, Paul. 1993. *Realism, Rationalism, Surrealism.* New Haven: Yale University Press.
Fleming, William. 1995. *Arts and Ideas*, 9th ed. Fort Worth: Harcourt Brace.
Foster, Hal; Krauss, Rosalind; Bois, Yve-Alain; and Buchloh, Benjamin. 2004. *Art Since 1900.* New York: Thames and Hudson.
Freeman, Julian. 1998. *Art.* New York: Watson-Guptill.
Gebhardt, Volker. 1998. *The History of Art.* New York: Barron's.
Gilbert, Rita. 1998. *Living With Art*, 5th ed. Boston: McGraw Hill.
*Harrison, Charles; Frascina, Francis; and Perry, Gill. 1993. *Primitivism, Cubism, Abstraction.* New Haven: Yale University Press.
Honour, Hugh; and Fleming, John. 2002. *The Visual Arts.* New York: Harry N. Abrams.
Hughes, Robert. 1991. *The Shock of the New.* New York: Alfred A. Knopf.

Hunter, Sam; Jacobus, John; and Wheeler, Daniel. 2004. *Modern Art*, 3rd ed. New York: Vendome Press.

Janson, H. W.; and Janson, Anthony. 2001. *History of Art*, 6th ed. New York: Harry N. Abrams.

Kemp, Martin. 2000. *The Oxford History of Western Art*. Oxford: Oxford University Press.

Lucie-Smith, Edward. 1997. *Visual Arts in the Twentieth Century*. New York: Harry N. Abrams.

Lucie-Smith, Edward. 1999. *Lives of the Great 20th-Century Artists*. London: Thames and Hudson.

Parmesani, Loredana. 2000. *Art of the Twentieth Century*. Milan: Skira.

Richter, Klaus. 2001. *Art*. Munich: Prestel-Verlag.

Sprocatti, Sandro. 1992. *A Guide to Art*. New York: Harry N. Abrams.

Stangos, Nikos, ed. 1994. *Concepts of Modern Art*, 3rd ed. London: Thames and Hudson.

Stokstad, Marilyn. 1995. *Art History*. New York: Harry N. Abrams.

Strickland, Carol; and Boswell, John. 1992. *The Annotated Mona Lisa*. Kansas City: Andrews and McMeel.

Tamplin, Ronald, ed. 1991. *The Arts*. Oxford: Oxford University Press.

Varnedoe, Kirk. 1990. *A Fine Disregard: What Makes Modern Art Modern*. New York: Harry N. Abrams.

Walther, Ingo, ed. 2005. *Art of the 20th Century*, 2 vols. Cologne: Taschen.

Wilkins, David; Schultz, Bernard; and Linduff, Katheryn. 1997. *Art Past, Art Present*, third ed. New York: Harry N. Abrams.

*Wood, Paul; Frascina, Francis; Harris, Jonathan; and Harrison, Charles. 1993. *Modernism in Dispute*. New Haven: Yale University Press.

Yenawine, Philip. 1991. *How to Look at Modern Art*. New York: Harry N. Abrams.

*These three books are a series, and are treated as a single book for this survey.

3

The Most Important Works of Art
of the Twentieth Century

Introduction

Quality in art is not just a matter of private experience. There is a *consensus* of taste.

Clement Greenberg[1]

Important works of art embody important innovations. The most important works of art are those that announce very important innovations.

There is considerable interest in identifying the most important artists, and their most important works, not only among those who study art professionally, but also among a wider public. The distinguished art historian Meyer Schapiro recognized that this is due in large part to the market value of works of art: "The great interest in painting and sculpture (versus poetry) arises precisely from its unique character as art that produces expensive, rare, and speculative commodities."[2] Schapiro's insight suggests one means of identifying the most important artists, through analysis of prices at public sales.[3] This strategy is less useful in identifying the most important individual works of art, however, for these rarely, if ever, come to market.

An alternative is to survey the judgments of art experts. One way to do this is by analyzing textbooks. The illustrations an author chooses implicitly tell us which works of art he considers most valuable in providing a narrative of the successive innovations that make up the history of art. Surveying a large number of textbooks effectively allows us to poll art historians as to which works are generally considered the most essential to this narrative. This study will identify and rank the individual works that authors of recent textbooks consider the most important ones

TABLE 3.1. *Most Important Works of Art of the Twentieth Century, in Chronological Order*

Artist, Title	Date	Location
Pablo Picasso, *Les Demoiselles d'Avignon*	1907	New York
Marcel Duchamp, *Nude Descending a Staircase, No. 2*	1912	Philadelphia
Umberto Boccioni, *Unique Forms of Continuity in Space*	1913	New York
Marcel Duchamp, *Fountain*	1917	–
Vladimir Tatlin, *Monument to the Third International*	1919	–
Pablo Picasso, *Guernica*	1937	Madrid
Richard Hamilton, *Just what is it that makes today's homes so different, so appealing?*	1956	Tübingen
Robert Smithson, *Spiral Jetty*	1970	Great Salt Lake

Source: See text.

of the twentieth century. We will then consider why each of these works is significant, and what common elements they share. The results are surprising in a number of respects; understanding why this is the case will contribute to a richer understanding of the art of the past century.

The Ranking

> In the last analysis, the artist may shout from the rooftops that he is a genius; he will have to wait for the verdict of the spectator in order that his declarations take a social value and that, finally, posterity includes him in the primers of Art History.
>
> Marcel Duchamp[4]

The data collection for the present study can begin from the results of a series of earlier surveys of textbooks. Each of these earlier studies ranked the most important artists and works of art made at specific times and places throughout the twentieth century. In all, eight individual works of art were found to have been illustrated in at least half of all the books surveyed in one or more of these earlier studies.[5] These eight works are listed in chronological order in Table 3.1.

The specific textbooks used in each of the earlier studies varied because some books did not cover the relevant times and places considered by some of those studies. To obtain a consistent ranking of the eight works listed in Table 3.1, this study consequently required a new survey, in which none of the textbooks analyzed excluded any of the eight works due to the book's specified coverage. A total of thirty-three books were found that were published since 1990 and covered all relevant genres

TABLE 3.2. *Ranking of Works*

Artist, Title	N	% of Total Books
1. Picasso, *Les Demoiselles d'Avignon*	28	85
2. Tatlin, *Monument to the Third International*	25	76
3. Smithson, *Spiral Jetty*	23	70
4. Hamilton, *Just what is it that makes today's homes so different, so appealing?*	22	67
5t. Boccioni, *Unique Forms of Continuity in Space*	21	64
5t. Picasso, *Guernica*	21	64
7. Duchamp, *Fountain*	18	55
8. Duchamp, *Nude Descending a Staircase, No. 2*	16	48

Source: This and subsequent tables are based on the data set created for this study. See the text for a description.

of art during the entire period from the earliest to the latest dates in Table 3.1.[6]

Table 3.2 presents the results of this new survey. Picasso's *Les Demoiselles d'Avignon* ranks first, illustrated in 85 percent of the textbooks surveyed. Understanding why it is the most essential work of art of the twentieth century, and why the other seven works in the table are also central to narratives of art history, requires us to consider each individually. The following sections of this chapter take up each work in turn, in the order of their production.

Les Demoiselles d'Avignon, 1907

Picasso studies an object like a surgeon dissecting a corpse.
Guillaume Apollinaire, 1913[7]

Les Demoiselles d'Avignon is clearly the most important painting of the twentieth century. With its execution, the greatest artist of the century initiated the century's most important artistic movement. Art scholars debate whether the *Demoiselles* should be considered a Cubist painting, but there is no question that it differed profoundly from all of the art that preceded it, and that it began the development of Cubism. Nor is there any debate over the painting's importance, as for example George Heard Hamilton observed that "it has been recognized as a watershed between the old pictorial world and the new," and John Russell described it as "the white whale of modern art: the legendary giant with which we have to come to terms sooner or later."[8]

The *Demoiselles* was intended to be a masterpiece. Stung by the success his rival, Henri Matisse, had gained by exhibiting his large Fauve manifesto *Le Bonheur de vivre* in the spring of 1906, later that year Picasso began to fill one sketchbook after another with preparatory drawings for his own large masterpiece.[9] William Rubin concluded that in all Picasso made between 400 and 500 studies for the *Demoiselles* – "a quantity of preparatory work unique not only in Picasso's career, but without parallel, for a single picture, in the entire history of art."[10] More than 60 square feet in size, the painting was by far the largest Picasso had ever attempted.[11]

The *Demoiselles* announced Cubism's rejection of linear perspective, which had dominated Western art since the Renaissance, and anticipated the new representation of space and construction of form that would characterize the Cubist revolution. The painting's radical formal innovations combined with its thorough disregard for conventional standards of beauty to jolt the advanced art world: not only did Matisse denounce the painting as an attempt to discredit modern art, but even Georges Braque, who would later join forces with Picasso in developing Cubism, was initially so shocked by the painting that he compared Picasso to the fairground fire-eaters who drank kerosene to spit flames.[12]

The *Demoiselles* presented a radical synthesis of a variety of earlier artistic styles that had never previously been considered to be related. The poses of the five nude women, their simplified forms, and their composition in space were derived in part from Cézanne's late paintings of bathers. The stylized and distorted features of the figures drew on Gauguin's late work, and on a number of forms of art that Picasso considered "primitive," including Greek sculpture, pre-Roman Iberian sculpture, and African carvings from the Ivory Coast. Picasso's willingness to combine elements from such highly disparate sources produced a startling visual result that dramatically announced a new era, in which artists were free to break with stylistic continuity, and to adapt to their own purposes anything that they found useful from the vast history of art.

The earliest published reference to the *Demoiselles* was by a young poet and friend of Picasso's, André Salmon. He recognized its conceptual nature, comparing the painting's figures to numbers on a blackboard, and concluding that "This is the first appearance of the painting-equation."[13] As Cubism became the most influential development in the visual arts of the twentieth century, the *Demoiselles* stood out more and more clearly as the century's greatest masterpiece. Table 3.1 confirms its privileged position among the works of art of the past century.

Nude Descending a Staircase, No. 2, 1912

The movement of form in time inevitably ushered us into geometry and mathematics.

Marcel Duchamp[14]

In 1912, Marcel Duchamp executed a painting that was almost immediately interpreted as an attack on Cubism, which was the reigning style of advanced art. Although the painting used the plastic forms and monochrome colors of Cubism, Duchamp had goals that differed considerably from those of Picasso and Braque, for as he later explained, he "wanted to create a static image of movement."[15] In doing this, he drew on a number of influences, including the chronophotography of the French scientist Etienne-Jules Marey and the photographic sequences of Eadweard Muybridge.[16] Rather than views of a stable subject from different positions, as in Cubism, *Nude Descending* presents sequential views of a moving subject from a fixed vantage point. In addition, the painting built on Cubism's divorce of the painted image from the appearance of the object represented, by beginning to translate a human form into mechanical elements. Duchamp also took the unconventional step of inscribing the picture's title in block letters below the image.

Much of the importance of *Nude Descending* stems from two episodes, both of which involved group exhibitions. The first occurred in Paris in 1912, when Duchamp submitted his new painting to the Salon des Indépendants. It was rejected, in spite of the fact that Duchamp's brothers, Jacques Villon and Raymond Duchamp-Villon, were members of the jury. The two were delegated to ask Duchamp if he would change the painting's title, but he refused, and immediately retrieved the work.[17]

Nude Descending was exhibited in Paris later in the year, but the second important event in its history was a result of its inclusion in the Armory Show in New York in 1913. This was the now-legendary exhibition that introduced advanced European modern art to the American public. Although there was widespread outrage at the work of Matisse and others, the single painting that became the focus of the greatest ridicule in the popular press was *Nude Descending*. One widely quoted critical remark described it as "an explosion in a shingle factory," and as Calvin Tomkins later explained, "To a great many visitors, the painting seemed to sum up everything that was arbitrary, irrational, and incomprehensible in the new art from Europe."[18] By the close of the show, the young Marcel Duchamp was famous in the United States, a country he had never visited.

Although it was the second of these incidents that brought public attention to Duchamp, the first was perhaps more important in making *Nude Descending* a key work in Duchamp's career. Stung by the rejection of his painting by his fellow artists, including even his brothers, Duchamp appears to have resolved to go his own way, and to carry further the radical ideas that *Nude Descending* represented.[19] As he proceeded to make increasingly extreme conceptual works, in retrospect *Nude Descending* appeared to have been an announcement of Duchamp's future agenda, which would fundamentally change the course of modern art. The importance of this was such that Arthur Danto has remarked that "the *Nude* explosively proclaimed a new era in art."[20]

Unique Forms of Continuity in Space, 1913

> The higher art raises itself, the more distant it becomes from Nature.
> Umberto Boccioni, 1911[21]

Unique Forms of Continuity in Space was also made by a young artist who wanted to adapt Cubist forms to create a representation of motion. In 1909, the Italian painter Umberto Boccioni and several of his friends joined Futurism, which had been founded as a literary movement by the poet F. T. Marinetti. One of Marinetti's main concerns was the role of speed in modern life, so the Futurist painters took as a goal the visual representation of the sensation of movement.

Early in 1912, Boccioni visited Paris, where he saw the new Cubist techniques of Picasso and Braque, which he quickly incorporated into his paintings. Boccioni also suddenly developed an interest in sculpture. John Golding has argued that while in Paris "Boccioni, summing up the scene around him with an eye that was quick and competitive, saw that there was as yet no such thing as a school of Cubist sculpture, and he sensed, very shrewdly, how he could best and most quickly make his mark."[22] In March of 1912, Boccioni wrote to a friend that "I am obsessed these days by sculpture. I think I can perceive a complete revival of this mummified art."[23]

Marinetti had introduced a novel conceptual practice in which polemical written manifestos accompanied, or even preceded, actual works of art. Following this model, in the spring of 1912, before he had begun making sculptures, Boccioni published a manifesto proposing a Futurist sculpture. To create the illusion of movement, he argued that the new approach must take account of the merging of an object with its surroundings. The problem Boccioni then confronted was how to do this in practice.

A year later, Boccioni presented 11 sculptures in an exhibition at a Paris gallery. *Unique Forms* was quickly recognized as the most important of the group, for its three-dimensional representation of power and speed. The surfaces of an advancing human figure are broken into parts, but rather than the straight lines of Cubism they are made of smooth curved planes, that appear to flow in the winds created by the figure's forward movement. The poet Guillaume Apollinaire, who was the most respected critic in Paris' advanced art world, praised *Unique Forms* as a "joyful celebration of energy."[24]

Boccioni's career as a sculptor lasted just this one year: Golding concluded that after making *Unique Forms*, "Boccioni seems to have realized that he had achieved the definitive masterpiece for which he longed."[25] He was killed in 1916, while serving in the Italian army. World War I effectively ended the Futurist movement, which became influential more for its ideas than for its successful works of art. Yet John Golding declared that "Futurism did, however, produce one major masterpiece," as *Unique Forms* came to symbolize the achievement of the movement as a whole.[26]

Fountain, 1917

The readymade can be seen as a sort of irony, because it says here it is, a thing that I call art, I didn't even make it myself.
Marcel Duchamp, 1959[27]

In New York in 1917, Marcel Duchamp provoked one of the most far-reaching controversies in modern art. He purchased a porcelain urinal, painted on its rim the name R. Mutt, then submitted it under that fictitious artist's name, with the title *Fountain*, to the first exhibition of the Society of Independent Artists, of which Duchamp was a founding member. In spite of the fact that the society's explicit policy was to exhibit any work submitted to it, the directors refused to exhibit *Fountain*. These actions triggered a critical debate over the meaning of art that continues today.

Fountain was not the first manufactured object Duchamp had made into art. He initially did this in 1913, by attaching a bicycle wheel to a stool. He then coined the term "readymade" in 1915 to refer to this and other manufactured objects that he signed and titled. *Fountain* became the most celebrated of Duchamp's readymades, however, because of the debate that attended its rejection by the Independents.

In *The Blind Man*, a magazine published by Duchamp and a few friends at the time of the Independents exhibition, an editorial defended *Fountain* against the charge that it was not a work of art: "Whether Mr. Mutt with his own hands made the fountain or not has no importance. He CHOSE it. He took an ordinary article of life, placed it so that its useful significance disappeared under the new title and point of view – created a new thought for that object."[28] This was the most extreme assertion that had ever been made of the primacy of the concept in art, for it proposed that the artist's craftsmanship could be eliminated altogether, and that a work of art could be made simply by the decision of the artist, because what mattered was the idea the work represented. *Fountain* also occasioned a debate over whether Duchamp was serious. In the same issue of *The Blind Man*, an article signed by a friend of Duchamp's noted that "there are those who anxiously ask, 'Is he serious or is he joking?' Perhaps he is both! Is it not possible?"[29]

After *Fountain* was removed from the premises of the Independents, Duchamp took it to Alfred Stieglitz's art gallery, where Stieglitz photographed it in front of a painting by Marsden Hartley. The original *Fountain* was later lost, but it lives on in written accounts of the Mutt case and in Stieglitz's famous photograph. These representations of the work are adequate, for as Octavio Paz observed of the readymades, "their interest is not plastic but critical or philosophical."[30]

The issues raised in the Mutt case were so radical that for nearly four decades after 1917 the readymades had little impact on modern art. Like a time bomb, however, Duchamp's new genre exploded into the consciousness of the advanced art world in the mid-1950s, when Rauschenberg, Johns, and other artists began to incorporate real objects into their work. Since then Duchamp has often been considered the single greatest influence on the advanced art of the second half of the twentieth century, as a succession of key contemporary artists have made works that continue to explore and expand the boundaries of art. *Fountain* has become the leading symbol of this legacy of Duchamp.[31]

Monument to the Third International, 1919

My monument is a symbol of the epoch. Unifying in it artistic and utilitarian forms, I created a kind of synthesis of art with life.

Vladimir Tatlin[32]

Vladimir Tatlin began his career as a painter, but on a trip to Paris in 1913 he was inspired by the new sculptures of Boccioni and Picasso, and he returned to Moscow as a sculptor. Tatlin had always believed that artists should rely not only on vision but on knowledge, and as a sculptor he devised novel forms by organizing miscellaneous found objects into three-dimensional constructions using formal geometric planning.

After the 1917 Revolution, Tatlin became a leader of the movement to use art in the service of the new social order. In 1919 the Soviet government commissioned him to design a monument to the Third International, which Lenin had recently founded to promote global revolution. Tatlin's goal in doing this was to create a revolutionary new art form to celebrate the new revolutionary society.

Tatlin's *Monument to the Third International* was actually designed as a building that would house the Third International. It was to be a tower 1,300 feet high that would span the Neva river in Petrograd. The design was worked out by the end of 1919, and a model of it, about 20 feet tall, was exhibited the next year.[33] The design embodied many layers of symbolism. The tower appeared to lean forward, befitting a progressive new form of government. The spiral shapes that dominated the design symbolized rising aspirations and triumph, while the use of two intertwined spirals symbolized dialectical argument and its resolution. Earlier, static governments were housed in static, immobile buildings, but the new government should have an active, mobile architecture. The lowest of the building's three levels, where the International's congress would meet, was to rotate fully on its axis once a year; the second level, which would contain the International's executive bodies, was to rotate once a month; and the highest level, which was reserved for newspaper and other information services to provide propaganda to the international proletariat, was to rotate once a day. The progressively smaller areas of the higher floors reflected the increasing concentration of power in smaller and more authoritative bodies.[34] The monument was intended to have an immediate effect on anyone who entered it, for it was to be "a place of the most intense movement; least of all should one stand still or sit down in it, you must be mechanically taken up, down, carried away against your will."[35] New technology would help to create new art forms that would help to achieve new social objectives.

Tatlin claimed the design for the *Monument* could be carried out, but he was not an engineer, and it is unlikely that this dynamic new architecture could actually have been built. This was never attempted, but in the Soviet Union the model of the *Monument,* and photographs of the model after the original was lost, became popular symbols of the idea that advanced art could serve the purposes of the new Soviet society. Today the tower's image survives as the visual embodiment of the ambitious goals of early Communism. The fact that it was never built is perhaps appropriate in view of the stark contrast between the hopeful symbolism of the image and the disastrous consequences of those goals.

Guernica, 1937

In the panel on which I am working which I shall call *Guernica* . . . I clearly express my abhorrence of the military caste which has sunk Spain in an ocean of pain and death.

Pablo Picasso, 1937[36]

On April 26, 1937, the Basque town of Guernica was destroyed by German bombers acting for General Franco. On May 1, the day after the first photographs of the devastated town were published, Picasso began working on a mural that was more than 25 feet long and 11 feet tall, by far the largest work he had ever made. He was working under extreme time pressure, for he had been commissioned to paint a mural for the Spanish pavilion at the Paris World's Fair, which was scheduled to open in early May. In the event the fair's opening was delayed, and the Spanish pavilion opened even later, but Picasso nonetheless created *Guernica* in just 10 weeks from the first sketches to the final canvas.

There is a remarkable body of documentation concerning the planning and execution of *Guernica*. More than fifty preparatory drawings for the painting have survived, most dated with the day they were made, and the painting was photographed at least ten times during the course of its execution by Picasso's companion Dora Maar, who was a professional photographer. This evidence has provided the basis for detailed scholarly analyses of the changing forms of the painting's figures both before and during the execution of the final work. Interestingly, however, the two scholars who have done the most intensive studies of *Guernica* have both stressed the unity of Picasso's initial overall conception of the painting. Picasso's first six sketches for the painting were done on May 1. Herschel Chipp remarked that these revealed that

By the end of the first day of work, Picasso had performed a most remarkable feat: in a few hours he had formulated the basic conception of *Guernica* . . . The heroic bull towering over the scene of chaos, the agonized horse writhing on the ground, and screaming toward the sky, and the female observer surveying the carnage – all were to remain an integral part of the final painting, five or six intervening weeks of continual change notwithstanding.[37]

Rudolf Arnheim made a similar observation, of a central concept that persisted from beginning to end:

While the work was going on, there were changes of emphasis and proportion, and there were many experiments in trying to define the content by working out its shape. A germinal idea, precise in its general tenor but unsettled in its aspects, acquired its final character by being tested against a variety of possible visual realizations.[38]

Before the modern era, the importance of art depended in large part on its subject matter: the greatest paintings had to treat religious themes, or show classical heroes in triumph. This changed with the advent of modern art, as the Impressionists and their successors painted nature, or scenes of everyday life. Cubism then retreated into even more restricted subject matter, with images made up almost exclusively of studio props. *Guernica* was a dramatic departure, for it demonstrated that the most advanced forms of modern art, that had previously been used only for private expression, could be used to make a large-scale public work that dealt forcefully with the most important issues facing modern society.[39] *Guernica* did not make an innovation in form, but rather put Cubist forms to a novel use. Ernst Gombrich remarked that "It is not the least moving aspect of the search for an expressive symbol to communicate his grief and anger that in the end Picasso reverted to his earlier invention."[40] In this *Guernica* became an inspiration for later modern artists who wanted their work to make social and political statements.

Just What Is It That Makes Today's Homes So Different, So Appealing?, 1956

Contemporary art reacts slowly to the contemporary stylistic scene. How many major works of art have appeared in the twentieth century in which an automobile figures at all?
Richard Hamilton, 1962[41]

In London in the early 1950s, Richard Hamilton was a member of the Independent Group made up of young artists and critics who wanted to create an art that reflected recent developments in popular culture and technology. In 1956 the group organized an exhibition, titled "This is Tomorrow," at the Whitechapel Art Gallery, and Hamilton agreed to make a poster for the show.

Hamilton went about his task systematically. He began with a list of fifteen categories of interest: Man, Woman, Humanity, History, Food,

Newspapers, Cinema, TV, Telephone, Comics, Words, Tape recording, Cars, Domestic appliances, and Space. Hamilton, his wife, and another artist then searched through piles of magazines, many of which had been brought back from the United States by a fellow Independent Group member, cutting out illustrations that could represent the categories on Hamilton's list. Hamilton then selected one image for each category, and combined them into a small collage, which showed a male bodybuilder and a female pin-up in a fictitious living room furnished with a wide range of consumer goods and advertising logos. The work's title was itself a caption from a discarded photograph.

Just what is it? is a complex work, made up of many separate images, a number of which have multiple meanings. For example the ceiling is actually a photograph of the Earth made from outer space, a lampshade is made of the Ford insignia, and a carpet is a detail of a photograph of hundreds of people on a beach. In a prominent position, the word "Pop" appears in large letters on a Tootsie roll pop held by the bodybuilder. Commercial products abound: a canned ham is displayed on a coffee table, a framed comic book hangs on the wall, a tape recorder sits on the floor, and a theatre marquee seen through a window advertises *The Jazz Singer.*

Hamilton and his friend Eduardo Paolozzi were pioneers of British Pop art, which preceded its American relative. In general, British Pop was subtler and more complex visually than American Pop, but the broad appeal of the leading Americans lay in large part in the brashness, simplicity, and large size of their works.[42] In spite of the fact that Warhol, Lichtenstein, Oldenburg, and other American Pop artists would overshadow Hamilton and his British colleagues, *Just what is it?,* made years before Warhol had begun to reproduce magazine photographs or Lichtenstein had begun to mimic comic strips, has justifiably been described as "an icon of early Pop," for its prophetic presentation of the commercial images that would transform advanced art in New York in the early 1960s.[43]

Spiral Jetty, 1970

I think the major issue now in art is what are the boundaries. For too long artists have taken the canvas and stretchers as given, the limits.
Robert Smithson, 1969[44]

The 1970s began an era of pluralism in art that has continued to the present, marked not only by the proliferation of styles but also by the creation of a number of new artistic genres. In one of these new genres, Robert Smithson created a rare synthetic masterpiece that has become the most frequently illustrated work in the entire history of American art.

Smithson was a leader of the Earth art movement, in which a number of young artists decided not only to place their art in the landscape, away from galleries and other traditional settings for art, but to use the landscape itself to make their art. Smithson was the first to use the term "earthwork" to refer to the objects he and his colleagues created in remote areas.[45] In Smithson's mature projects, Earth art became a complex conceptual activity that consisted not only of the construction of large-scale monuments from earth and stone, but also involved written texts, "nonsites" (indoor earthworks), films, and extensive documentation, in the form of photographs and maps.

Spiral Jetty is located in an isolated area of Utah's Great Salt Lake. After Smithson had planned its form, and staked out its boundaries, the 1,500-foot-long jetty was created over a period of three weeks by a five-man crew using a tractor and two dump trucks to move more than 6,500 tons of mud, salt crystals, and rocks. The construction of the jetty was filmed by a professional photographer according to a detailed plan Smithson had prepared. Two years later Smithson published an essay on the jetty, that in the span of just ten pages ranges from the origins of Smithson's interest in salt lakes to the structure of the film Smithson made about it, passing through references to more than a dozen academic disciplines, and comparisons of the jetty's shape to a dozen other objects, both natural and artificial.[46]

In *Spiral Jetty*, Smithson managed to incorporate a remarkable number of issues that were central to the advanced art of the 1960s. The most general unifying feature of the art of the period was its conceptual orientation, and Smithson made his work the focal point of an enormously varied body of ideas. The shapes of all his works were simple, drawing on Minimalist sculpture, the leading movement of the mid-1960s. Yet in *Spiral Jetty* Smithson made his own adaptation of Minimalism, with a larger scale and an elegant curved shape. The remote location of the *Jetty* drew on the anti-commercial, anti-gallery sentiment that was shared by many young artists at the time. The base materials used to make the *Jetty*, and the difficulty of viewing it, served further to defy the traditional methods and presentation of fine art. Smithson's complex written text reflected a vital tradition of conceptual art, in using language to accompany objects, that dated back to Futurism. His consideration of how natural forces would change the *Jetty* over time, not only due to erosion but also from the deposit of salt crystals, was a product of his long-standing fascination with entropy. The extensive use of photography and film to present *Jetty* to a broader public reflected a trend of the 1960s to use mechanical reproduction as part of, or in lieu of, works of art. Smithson's sophisticated conceptual approach to art appealed not only to other artists, but also to art scholars: thus Kirk Varnedoe described Smithson as "the kind of artist who, if he didn't exist, would have to be invented by graduate students."[47]

Smithson was killed in 1973, at the age of 35, when the small plane from which he was photographing the staked-out plans for a new work in Amarillo, Texas, crashed into a hillside. His premature death, in the process of making his art, added poignancy to accounts of the brief life of the brilliant young artist who created monumental works in remote places. But Smithson had already succeeded in creating new forms of art by breaking old boundaries, physical as well as intellectual, and he had guaranteed continuing attention to these innovations by creating the most indispensable masterpiece in American art.

Creative Careers

This century's most practiced creators of legendary works have, of course, been Picasso and Duchamp.

David Sylvester, 1995[48]

As the preceding discussions have shown, all eight of the works of art considered in this chapter were made by conceptual innovators, whose innovations embody new ideas that the artists formulated before executing their works. Earlier research has found that the most important conceptual innovations, which make radical departures from established conventions, tend to occur early in artists' careers, before they have become constrained by fixed habits. Table 3.3 largely supports this generalization. Thus the median age of the artists when they executed these eight works was 31.5 years. Seven of the eight works were made by artists aged 35 or younger, and the most important of the eight was made by Picasso when he was 26. One of these works was made by an older artist, as Picasso produced *Guernica* at 56, but he had made his greatest innovation fully 30 years earlier.

An interesting feature of conceptual creativity is that important conceptual innovations can be made by relatively unimportant artists. Thus in a number of cases fine art has produced one-hit wonders – artists who

TABLE 3.3. *Artists' Ages at Time of Execution of Most Important Works*

Artist, Title	Age
1. Picasso, *Demoiselles*	26
2. Tatlin, *Monument*	35
3. Smithson, *Spiral Jetty*	32
4. Hamilton, *Just what is it?*	34
5t. Boccioni, *Unique Forms*	31
5t. Picasso, *Guernica*	56
7. Duchamp, *Fountain*	30
8. Duchamp, *Nude Descending*	25

formulated a single important idea, and embodied it in an individual work that consequently dominates their careers.[49] Table 3.4 shows that three of the eight works considered here clearly dominate the careers of their makers, as the *Monument to the Third International, Just what is it?*, and *Spiral Jetty* all account for at least 60 percent of the total illustrations of these three artists' work in the thirty-three textbooks surveyed. Yet although this phenomenon is possible, it is of course not necessary. It is striking that four of the eight works considered here were made by two artists who rank among the very greatest figures in modern art: Picasso is by far the greatest artist of the past century, and Duchamp ranks third, after only Picasso and Matisse, among the greatest artists of the twentieth century.[50] Both Picasso and Duchamp are archetypal cases of the versatile conceptual artists who have become a prominent feature of twentieth-century art.[51]

TABLE 3.4. *Illustrations of Most Important Works as Percentage of Artists' Total Illustrations in Books Surveyed*

Artist, Title	N	Artist's Total Illustrations	%
1. Picasso, *Demoiselles*	28	395	7
2. Tatlin, *Monument*	25	42	60
3. Smithson, *Spiral Jetty*	23	34	68
4. Hamilton, *Just what is it?*	22	34	65
5t. Boccioni, *Unique Forms*	21	55	38
5t. Picasso, *Guernica*	21	395	5
7. Duchamp, *Fountain*	18	122	15
8. Duchamp, *Nude Descending*	16	122	13

Conceptual Creativity

To paint, then, in the twentieth century requires no elaborate skill in drawing, no stock of conventional knowledge, but sensibility, feeling, and a strong impulse to creation. The painter has ceased to be a craftsman or a learned man; he is a creator in the pure sense of the philosophers.

Meyer Schapiro, 1957[52]

The eight works considered here all represent important conceptual innovations in the art of the twentieth century. Some of the century's most important artistic movements are not represented among these landmark works: in some cases this is because experimental artists produced large bodies of work from which no individual landmarks emerged, while in other cases conceptual artists embodied an innovation in several major works that competed with each other, so that none emerged as a dominant statement. Some of the works examined here do symbolize entire movements, as Boccioni's *Unique Forms* stands for Futurism, Hamilton's *Just what is it?* represents Pop art, Smithson's *Spiral Jetty* stands for Earth art, and most notably, Picasso's *Demoiselles* represents Cubism.

Most of the works considered here made important formal innovations in art, but it is not surprising that a number of them also made powerful statements about social and political developments. In the latter works, Picasso, Boccioni, Tatlin, Hamilton, and Smithson were all involved in commenting on the societies they lived in, whether in praise (Boccioni and Tatlin), protest (Picasso and Smithson), or a combination of the two (Hamilton). To some extent, these works reflect the changing attitudes of artists over time, from an enthusiastic embrace of modern technology (Boccioni) and political revolution (Tatlin), to a more ironic celebration (Hamilton), and to pessimism (Smithson). Kirk Varnedoe recognized Tatlin's tower and Smithson's jetty as ideological bookends for the century: "The millennial, utopian optimism about the order of the spiral [in Tatlin's *Monument*] perhaps finds its opposite number in Smithson's *Spiral Jetty*... a monument of dystopian, millennial pessimism."[53] As a political statement, *Guernica* stands alone as the most forceful artistic expression of outrage of the century. Robert Hughes remarked that *Guernica* was the last great history painting, in a line that included masterpieces by Goya and Delacroix: "It was also the last modern painting of major importance that took its subject from politics with the intention of changing the way large numbers of people thought and felt about power." Hughes further reflected that with the subsequent rise of mass media, *Guernica* marked the end of a particular belief in the political role of fine art: "the idea that an artist, by making painting or sculpture, could insert images into the stream of public speech and thus change political discourse has gone, probably for good, along with the nineteenth-century ideal of the artist as public man."[54]

Conceptual innovation is in no way a new or recent development; it can in fact be traced back at least as far as one of the most important early developments in the history of Western art, the introduction of linear perspective, which made Masaccio's *Tribute Money* one of the most frequently reproduced paintings ever executed.[55] What was new in the twentieth century, however, was the extremity of conceptual innovation, as the importance of the artist's idea has been increased relative to the significance of the artist's execution of the work. Thus among the works considered here, Duchamp's *Fountain* involved no work of the artist's hand other than a signature, Tatlin's *Monument* survives only in photographs of a model that was built by Tatlin and several assistants, and *Spiral Jetty* was produced by construction workers following Smithson's design and direction. The first two of these today exist only in photographs, whereas the third was invisible for nearly 30 years under the water of Great Salt Lake, and is still seen almost exclusively in photographs, for even after a potential viewer travels to Golden Spike National Historic Site, access to *Spiral Jetty* requires a 16-mile trip on a gravel road that has many large lava rocks embedded in it.[56]

Even in cases in which an artist's new ideas are complemented by virtuosity in execution, the great value placed on rapid conceptual innovation differentiated the twentieth century from earlier periods with respect to artistic practice. The evidence of this chapter underscores the distinctive nature of conceptual innovation in the twentieth century, for only in the twentieth century would a ranking of the eight most important individual works of art include not only the traditional genres of painting and sculpture but no less than three other genres – readymade, collage, and earthwork – that did not even exist when the century began. In 2001, Arthur Danto observed that "We are living in a conceptual art world."[57] The evidence of this chapter suggests that we have in fact been living in a conceptual art world for more than a century.

4

The Greatest Artistic Breakthroughs
of the Twentieth Century

Breakthroughs

[The artist] has to make an enormous effort to lift himself above his contemporaries. This results in what we often call the "breakthrough," that
every artist on the path to success has to make.

Sir Alan Bowness[1]

The true subject of art history is the narrative and analysis of the succession of innovations that have changed the practices of artists over
the course of time. This is a source of considerable confusion not only
among the public at large, but even among many art scholars, for there
is a persistent belief that art history is the story of the lives of great
artists. However widespread, this belief is mistaken. Artists' contributions to their discipline do not consist of their entire body of work, but
rather only that part of it that embodies inventions that are subsequently
deemed useful by other artists. The chief curator of painting and sculpture
at New York's Museum of Modern Art, perhaps the world's preeminent
museum of twentieth-century art, recently expressed this succinctly in
explaining the mission of his institution: "MOMA is a museum interested
in telling the story of successive innovations rather than a museum interested in the longevity of individual careers."[2] Scholarly surveys follow this
same model, as for example in the statement that opens the preface to
their recent textbook, *Art Since 1900*, Hal Foster, Rosalind Krauss, Yve-
Alain Bois, and Benjamin Buchloh declare not that their work is arranged
around the careers of artists, but rather that "This book is organized as
a succession of important *events*, each keyed to an appropriate date, and
can thus be read as a chronological account of twentieth-century art."[3]

Although a vast body of scholarship has concentrated on the specific discoveries made by great artists, art historians consistently treat each of these discoveries in isolation, and there has been remarkably little systematic comparative treatment of these events. This chapter will begin to remedy this neglect, by using the scholarly narratives of scores of art historians as the basis for empirical analysis of the most important breakthroughs made by the greatest artists of the past century in the course of following their paths to success. Performing this analysis can increase our understanding of artistic creativity, at the same time that it deepens our insight into the nature of the greatest artistic innovations of the twentieth century.

Data

> There is, it seems, a graph of creativity which can be plotted through an artist's career.
>
> Sir Alan Bowness[4]

The data used here were drawn from all available textbooks of art history, published in English since 1990, that survey the art of the twentieth century.[5] From these thirty-three books, listings were made of all the illustrations of works by nineteen artists: fifteen of these artists were identified by an earlier study as the most important artists of the twentieth century, while the remaining four were identified by a second study as having executed individual works that ranked among the most important of the twentieth century.[6] The full sample of these nineteen artists is shown in Table 4.1.

The data set constructed in this way can be used to create a profile for each artist, showing how many illustrations of his work the textbooks contain from each year of his career. Because the illustrations were chosen by the books' authors to show readers the most important developments in advanced art, the individual years, or periods of years, from which the most illustrations of an artist's work are reproduced can be presumed to identify the most important portions of each artist's career.[7]

These profiles furthermore reveal not only at what stage of his career an artist made his greatest contribution, but also how suddenly and how quickly he made them. Comparisons across artists of the numbers of illustrations of their work from specified periods of time can furthermore allow us to judge which artists' breakthroughs were most important, in the collective judgment of art historians.

TABLE 4.1. *Artists Included in This Chapter*

Artist	Date of Birth	Date of Death	Country of Birth
Boccioni, Umberto	1882	1916	Italy
Brancusi, Constantin	1876	1957	Romania
Braque, Georges	1882	1963	France
Duchamp, Marcel	1887	1968	France
Hamilton, Richard	1922	–	England
Johns, Jasper	1930	–	US
Kandinsky, Wassily	1866	1944	Russia
de Kooning, Willem	1904	1997	Netherlands
Malevich, Kazimir	1878	1935	Russia
Matisse, Henri	1869	1954	France
Mondrian, Piet	1872	1944	Netherlands
Oldenburg, Claes	1929	–	Sweden
Picasso, Pablo	1881	1973	Spain
Pollock, Jackson	1912	1956	US
Rauschenberg, Robert	1925	2008	US
Rothko, Mark	1903	1970	Russia
Smithson, Robert	1938	1973	US
Tatlin, Vladimir	1885	1953	Russia
Warhol, Andy	1928	1987	US

Source: For the construction of this and subsequent tables in this chapter, see text.

Durations

Many artists do their best work in a relatively short period.
Sir Alan Bowness[8]

Table 4.2 ranks the best individual years of all the artists in the sample for this study. This ranking is not restricted to each artist's best year, so some artists appear more than once, while other sample members do not appear at all.

Perhaps the most striking feature of Table 4.2 is the dominant position of Picasso. Not only does he rank in first place for his work of 1907, with nearly a third more illustrations than the second-place entry, but in all he has no less than four individual years that rank among the greatest fifteen of the century. Even more remarkably, three of these years rank among the top five overall.

It is no surprise that Picasso's work of 1907 ranks as the greatest one-year achievement of the twentieth century, for it was in that year that he painted *Les Demoiselles d'Avignon*, which ranks as the century's

TABLE 4.2. *Best Years in Careers of Greatest*
Twentieth-Century Artists

Artist	Age	No. of Illustrations	Year
1. Picasso	26	61	1907
2. Warhol	34	46	1962
3. Picasso	31	42	1912
4. Matisse	36	37	1905
5. Picasso	56	36	1937
6. Pollock	38	34	1950
7. Malevich	37	31	1915
8. Boccioni	31	28	1913
9t. Duchamp	30	25	1917
9t. Tatlin	34	25	1919
11t. Duchamp	25	24	1912
11t. Smithson	32	24	1970
13. Braque	29	23	1911
14t. Hamilton	34	22	1956
14t. Picasso	29	22	1910

most important individual work of art.[9] The privileged place of that painting, and of Picasso's work of that year, are a consequence of the fact that this announced the beginning of the Cubist revolution, which would become by far the most influential development of the century in the visual arts. Experimental artists develop their contributions gradually, and late works in their mature signature styles are typically the most important examples of experimental artists' innovations, but conceptual artists often arrive at their contributions precipitously, and therefore it is generally the earliest works in a new style that are the most important. Cubism was a quintessentially conceptual innovation, a symbolic language that Picasso created in order to represent his knowledge of objects rather than to describe their appearance. Although Picasso, later joined by his friend Braque, would go on to develop Cubism in a number of important respects, the movement's greatest innovation occurred at its outset. Picasso clearly understood this, for he spent months making an unprecedented number of preparatory sketches and studies, then executed the *Demoiselles* on a canvas far larger than any he had previously attempted. Thus although Picasso did not make mature Cubist paintings in 1907, his work of that year unambiguously declared the radical new approaches to the representation of space and the construction of form that would stand as Cubism's most important legacy to modern art. There is consequently no surprise that his work of 1907 leads Table 4.2, for it was in that year that the century's greatest artist announced the century's greatest artistic innovation. It is difficult to overstate its impact. John Golding, a historian of the movement, opened his study of it by placing it in this perspective:

Cubism was perhaps the most important and certainly the most complete and radical artistic revolution since the Renaissance. New forms of society, changing patronage, varying geographic conditions, all these things have gone to produce over the past five hundred years a succession of different schools, different styles, different pictorial idioms. But none of these has so altered the principles, so shaken the foundations of Western painting as did Cubism.[10]

The importance of Cubism is again underscored by the third-place ranking of Picasso in Table 4.2 for 1912. This was a key year in the development of Cubism, for it was during 1912 that the progressive flattening by both Picasso and Braque of the faceted objects in their paintings marked the passage from early, or analytical, Cubism to late, synthetic Cubism. In part this progression was a consequence of a dramatic innovation by Picasso, announced in his famous *Still Life with Chair Caning* of 1912, in which he pasted a small piece of oil cloth to the canvas. This small painting thus became the first collage. This marked a radical departure from artistic tradition, for by attaching a real object to his canvas Picasso violated the two-dimensional surface of the picture plane that Western painters had respected for five centuries. This apparently innocuous act was the seminal event for the unprecedented proliferation of artistic genres that would occur over the course of the twentieth century.[11]

Picasso's third entry in Table 4.2, which ranks fifth overall, is for 1937. Although this came more than two decades after the initial period during which Picasso and Braque had developed Cubism, Picasso's innovation of 1937 was nonetheless a significant development of the application of Cubism. During a ten-week period in the spring and early summer of 1937, Picasso painted *Guernica*, a mural that was nearly five times as large as the *Demoiselles d'Avignon*. Picasso made the enormous painting to express his outrage at the destruction of the Basque town of Guernica, and the slaughter of its entire population, by German bombers acting for General Franco. The painting was an artistic landmark because of its subject matter, for it demonstrated that Cubism, which had previously been restricted to private subjects, could be used to make a powerful public statement. For this *Guernica* became an inspiration to advanced artists who wanted to use their art for political and social ends.

A striking feature of Table 4.2 is the position of Warhol, who ranks second for his work of 1962. This was the year in which Warhol made his most celebrated works, which became the most famous images of the Pop movement. Early in the year he painted thirty-two portraits of Campbell's soup cans – one for each flavor the company made – which were exhibited in July in Los Angeles, in Warhol's first one-man show. He made these paintings with stencils. In August, Warhol began to make paintings by silkscreening, a technique he would use for the rest of his life, and he quickly made a series of portraits of actors and singers based on magazine photographs.[12] Marilyn Monroe committed suicide in August, and Warhol decided to paint a series of portraits of her. In November, Warhol had his first New York show. It included both *Marilyn Diptych* and *Green Coca-Cola Bottles*, which became his two most important individual paintings.[13]

Warhol's position in Table 4.2 is a consequence of the enormous influence of his work on generations of conceptual artists from the 1960s on, and of his precipitous arrival at his key innovations. Early in 1962, Warhol was still engaged primarily in his successful career as a commercial artist (when the paintings of Campbell's soup cans were first exhibited in Los Angeles, they were priced at $100 each, which was one-tenth as much as Warhol was then getting for a commercial drawing). The immediate impact of the Campbell's soup can paintings on the art world, which was triggered by an article in *Time* magazine even before his Los Angeles show opened, within months made Warhol into the leader of the dominant new art movement of its time.[14] Critics immediately recognized the conceptual nature of his art, as for example in an assessment of Pop art the editor of *Artnews* observed that "Today, the sole requirement of a work of art is intent; what the artist says, goes."[15] And it was the conceptual nature of the art that allowed Warhol's sudden transformation from a commercial artist to an advanced artist, for as his biographer noted, "From the first Campbell's soup can onwards Warhol was at his purest as a conceptual artist."[16] During the single year of 1962, Warhol arrived at his key formal innovations, the production of serial forms and the use of a mechanical technique to make paintings of photographic images.[17] And because what mattered was not the appearance of the works but the idea that motivated them, there was no need for Warhol or his assistant Gerard Malanga to spend years, or even months, perfecting their use of silkscreens (indeed, Malanga later recalled that he and Warhol often made mistakes, but Warhol never rejected anything, saying "It's part of the art"), and it was the very earliest paintings that embodied these innovations that became Warhol's canonical works.[18]

Matisse ranks fourth in Table 4.2, for his work of 1905. Although Matisse made a number of contributions in the course of a long career, the most important was his first innovation, the development of Fauvism. The movement was a conceptual one, in which Matisse and several younger painters, inspired by the strong colors and flattened forms of van Gogh and Gauguin, went beyond those earlier symbolists in the expressive use of pure, bright colors and simplified shapes. Matisse was recognized as the leader of the Fauve movement, which began abruptly in 1905, and ended abruptly in 1907. Fauvism became important for its influence on a series of expressionist painters, beginning with the German Die Brücke and Blue Rider movements. Although Matisse made Fauve paintings for three years, the conceptual nature of the contribution meant that the most important were those that announced the innovation, and these were the paintings of 1905 that were exhibited at the Salon d'Automne of that year.

Although there are six experimental artists in the sample for this study, only one appears in Table 4.2. This imbalance is a consequence of the absence of sudden breakthroughs by experimental artists, whose work typically evolves gradually. Yet Jackson Pollock nonetheless ranks sixth for his work of 1950. Pollock's most celebrated innovation was the drip method he developed, in which he poured and spattered paint onto the canvas, breaking the connection between the touch of the artist's brush and his paintings. Pollock used the drip method in novel ways, to make "all-over" compositions that lacked any central focal point of interest. He achieved this by creating lines that for the first time in western art did not indicate the edges of planes, and consequently did not bound shapes or figures, but rather served as an autonomous visual element.[19] These innovations are generally considered to have been used most effectively in the large paintings Pollock made during the four-year period from 1947 to 1950.[20] It is not the paintings from the earliest of these four years that most often appear in textbooks, however, but those from the last year of the period, in 1950. Because Pollock's contribution was not an idea, it is not its first appearance that is most important. Instead, because the contribution was aesthetic, it is the latest and most sophisticated embodiments of the new techniques that are most important. A common misconception about Pollock's drip style is that it represented a lack of control. Pollock vehemently denied this, famously responding to a *Time* magazine article that described his style as chaos with a telegram that declared "NO CHAOS DAMN IT."[21] As William Rubin later pointed out, Pollock's method involved a number of choices that had to be made jointly, and that doing this successfully required considerable skill, that developed over time: "It may very well be that the physical mastery needed to control a larger 'figure' in this technique partly explains why the more bodily inflected patterns of the wall-size pictures came only after three years of working with it."[22]

Malevich ranks seventh in Table 4.2. He was one of the three great pioneers of abstraction, as he, Kandinsky, and Mondrian all developed their own distinctive forms of non-representational art during the mid-1910s. Yet the arrival of the conceptual Malevich was more sudden than those of the experimental Kandinsky and Mondrian, as John Golding recognized: "It might be fair to say that Malevich's abstraction sprang, Athena-like, ready formed from the brow of its creator; this distinguishes Malevich's approach very sharply from that of Mondrian and Kandinsky, who had sensed and inched their way into abstraction over a period of many years. It is this that makes Malevich's art so exhilarating."[23] The gradual progress of Kandinsky and Mondrian, rather than any lack of importance of their achievements, accounts for their absence from Table 4.2, for Mondrian's work overall received substantially more total illustrations in the textbooks than Malevich's, and Kandinsky's only slightly fewer than that of Malevich.[24] In contrast, the suddenness of Malevich's arrival at abstraction accounts for his high position in Table 4.2, for his entry is for 1915, the year he executed his first abstract paintings, and presented them, with attendant fanfare that included publication of the *Suprematist Manifesto*, at a Moscow exhibition titled "The Last Exhibition of Futurist Painting." The abruptness of Malevich's departure into abstraction was not accidental, for he wrote that "in art it is not always a case of evolution, but sometimes also of revolution."[25] The conceptual nature of Malevich's work is reflected in his meticulous use of geometric calculation not only in the preparation for these paintings, but also in their arrangement at the exhibition, as well as in the assertion in his written text that the abstract forms in those paintings symbolized the triumph of modern technology over space and time.[26]

Duchamp is the only artist other than Picasso who has more than one entry in Table 4.2. Duchamp was a radical and protean conceptual innovator, who made a series of largely unrelated innovations that all served to challenge basic conventions of advanced art. Duchamp's highly conceptual approach allowed his innovations to be embodied in individual landmark works, and his two entries in Table 4.2 represent the years in

TABLE 4.3. *Best Three-Year Periods in Careers of Greatest Twentieth-Century Artists*

Artist	Ages	N	Years
1. Picasso	24–6	80	1905–07
2. Picasso	31–3	74	1912–14
3t. Matisse	36–8	67	1905–07
3t. Warhol	34–6	67	1962–64
5t. Malevich	35–7	49	1913–15
5t. Pollock	36–8	49	1948–50
7. Boccioni	29–31	44	1911–13
8t. Duchamp	25–7	43	1912–14
8t. Picasso	27–9	43	1908–10
10. Duchamp	30–2	40	1917–19
11t. Braque	27–9	38	1909–11
11t. Picasso	54–6	38	1935–37
13. Picasso	40–2	37	1921–23
14. Kandinsky	45–7	36	1911–13
15. Matisse	40–2	31	1909–11

which he made his two most celebrated works, which both rank among the most frequently reproduced works of the century: thus in 1912 he painted *Nude Descending a Staircase, No. 2*, and in 1917 he signed a porcelain urinal to create the readymade *Fountain*.[27] Both of these works created immediate controversy, not only among the general public but also among advanced artists – *Nude Descending* for what was taken to be its attack on Cubism, and *Fountain* for its implicit assertion that art could be made merely by a decision of the artist. Although for a time *Nude Descending* was considered the more important of these works, their relative positions in Table 4.2 may reflect the fact that the influence of *Fountain* has grown in recent decades, so that many in today's art world consider it to have been the most influential individual work for the advanced art of the second half of the twentieth century.[28]

To consider the possibility that breakthroughs can occur within short periods longer than one year, Table 4.3 ranks the best three-year periods, again by total illustrations, for the same artists listed in Table 4.1. The results are broadly similar to those of Table 4.2, but some significant changes appear. Three artists who were ranked in Table 4.2 disappear from Table 4.3. Each of the three – Tatlin, Smithson, and Hamilton – made a single important conceptual innovation, which in each case was embodied in a single important work, but none of the three made any significant developments beyond this contribution.[29]

Picasso holds the top two positions in Table 4.3, as well as three others in the ranking; remarkably, he accounts for five of the century's fifteen most important three-year periods in the careers of individual artists. What is interesting, however, in comparing his performance in Tables 4.2 and 4.3 is that the period in Picasso's fifties when he produced *Guernica* becomes less important when the longer span of three years is considered, whereas all three of Picasso's highest ranked entries in Table 4.3 are from the years from 1905 to 1914, when the young artist was first developing Cubism. This underscores the density of innovation during this first decade of Cubism, whereas in contrast *Guernica* appears as an isolated achievement of Picasso's later years, which he did not subsequently develop in any significant way. Exceptionally, Picasso was able to make a major innovation at the age of 56 – fully nineteen years beyond the age of any other conceptual artist listed in Table 4.2 – but even he could not recapture the remarkable ability to make one discovery after another that he had enjoyed during his twenties and early thirties.

Kandinsky joins Pollock as a second experimental entrant in Table 4.3. The years represented, 1911–13, are the ones in which Kandinsky's cautious and gradual approach finally produced abstract forms. In an essay of 1913 he looked back on the evolution of his work, and stressed not only the difficulty of his progress, but also his expectation that it had not yet reached an end:

Only after many years of patient toil and strenuous thought, numerous painstaking attempts, and my constantly developing ability to conceive of pictorial forms in purely abstract terms, engrossing myself more and more in these measureless depths, did I arrive at the pictorial forms I use today, on which I am working today and which, as I hope and desire, will themselves develop much further.

Although he expressed frustration with the slow pace of his development – "I sometimes look back at the past and despair at how long this solution took me" – he understood that it was not his nature to solve problems conceptually: "My only consolation is that I have never been able to persuade myself to use a form that arose within me by way of logic . . . I could not devise such forms, and it disgusts me when I see them."[30]

Finally, to consider even more gradual breakthroughs, Table 4.4 ranks the same artists' best five-year periods. The rankings do not change dramatically, but several interesting differences appear. Braque, who had ranked thirteenth and eleventh, respectively, in Tables 4.2 and 4.3, moves

TABLE 4.4. *Best Five-Year Periods in Careers of Greatest Twentieth-Century Artists*

Artist	Ages	N	Years
1. Picasso	25–9	116	1906–10
2. Matisse	36–40	86	1905–09
3. Picasso	30–4	84	1911–15
4. Warhol	34–8	69	1962–66
5. Braque	26–30	63	1908–12
6. Malevich	34–8	61	1912–16
7. Pollock	35–9	58	1947–51
8. Boccioni	27–31	52	1909–13
9. Kandinsky	44–8	51	1910–14
10. Duchamp	24–8	46	1911–15
11t. Duchamp	30–4	45	1917–21
11t. Johns	25–9	45	1955–59
13. Picasso	39–43	44	1920–24
14. Picasso	52–6	43	1933–37
15. Mondrian	39–43	38	1911–15

up to fifth place in Table 4.4, for the years 1908–12. These were the years when Braque and Picasso worked together "like two mountaineers roped together," in Braque's famous description, to develop Cubism. Picasso was the more gifted of the two, and he was bolder and more daring in his art. In spite of Braque's more cautious approach, however, in 1908 and 1911 he produced individual paintings that appear in more textbooks than any single work of Picasso's from the period apart from the *Demoiselles d'Avignon*. Reviewing an exhibition of the art of Picasso and Braque from these years, John Golding reflected that "it told the story of how one of the most protean of all artists was prepared temporarily to accept the support and the stimulus offered to him by a fellow artist so much less talented than himself, and of how that artist accepted the challenge involved and in the process transformed himself into a major painter."[31] Virtually all successful modern artists have initially developed their art in the company of other talented young artists. David Sylvester compared these collaborations to jazz musicians' jam sessions, "the paradigm of a situation in which artists are simultaneously supporting and competing with each other."[32] The early collaboration of Picasso and Braque was the most important of these episodes for the art of the twentieth century, just as that of Monet with Bazille, Renoir, and the other Impressionists had been for the modern art of the nineteenth century. That three of the top five entries in Table 4.4 represent a single ten-year period in the development of Cubism further emphasizes the preeminent place of that movement in twentieth-century art. All three of these occurred during 1906–15. The collaboration of Picasso and Braque ended when Braque went to serve in the French army. Picasso later told his dealer and friend, Daniel Kahnweiler, "On August 2, 1914, I took Braque and [André] Derain to the Gare d'Avignon. I never saw them again."[33] Although Braque was severely wounded in the war, Picasso did see him again, many times, between 1917 and Braque's death in 1963. But the relationship between the two artists had changed, and the exhilaration of creating Cubism was over. Picasso went on to other achievements, but none was nearly as exciting, or as important, as what he and Braque had accomplished in their youth.

Another interesting feature of Table 4.4 involves two great experimental artists, as Kandinsky moves up into the ninth rank, and Mondrian makes an appearance for the first time in this chapter's rankings, in the lowest position. Both artists benefit from consideration of a longer period, as both are ranked in Table 4.4 for the period in the early 1910s when they and Malevich pioneered abstraction. That Mondrian worked even more cautiously, and progressed even more slowly than Kandinsky, is witnessed by the fact that Mondrian ranks well below Kandinsky in Table 4.4 in spite of the fact that he has substantially more total illustrations than the Russian artist in the textbooks overall, for that larger number is spread more evenly over a period of five decades.[34] For Mondrian, progress in art could only occur slowly. In 1937, he wrote that "One can rightly speak of an *evolution in plastic art*. It is of the greatest importance to note this fact, for it reveals the true way of art; the only path along which we can advance." The term "evolution" was not a casual choice, for Mondrian cautioned, "It is a mistake to try to go too fast."[35]

Table 4.4 provides clear evidence of the difference in the creative life cycles of conceptual and experimental innovators. Twelve of the entries in the table are for conceptual artists, whereas three are for experimental innovators. The median age of the conceptual artists when they began the periods listed in the table was 30, whereas the corresponding median age of the experimental artists was 39. Great conceptual innovators, like Picasso, Warhol, and Duchamp, mature rapidly and peak early in their lives, whereas great experimental artists, like Mondrian, Kandinsky, and Pollock, develop slowly and make their greatest contributions at older ages.

Conclusion

> Of all the revisions of pictorial language proposed in the 20th century, cubism has been the most radical.
>
> Sir Alan Bowness[36]

Artistic innovation in the twentieth century was dominated to a remarkable degree by one man. By the measure of textbook illustrations, Picasso alone accounts for three of the five most creative individual years of the century, five of the fifteen most creative three-year periods, and two of the three most creative five-year periods. Today, after the close of the twentieth century, we can see not only how Picasso's specific artistic innovations dominated the agenda of advanced artists throughout the first half of the century, but also how the manifestation of his versatile conceptual creativity became the prototype for some of the most important conceptual innovators throughout the entire century.[37] David Sylvester recognized the historical departure represented by Picasso, when he reflected that "Picasso is a kind of artist who couldn't have existed before this century, since his art is a celebration of this century's introduction of a totally promiscuous eclecticism into the practice of art."[38]

Cubism was equally clearly the preeminent artistic movement of the twentieth century. Working together during the period from 1908 until Braque left to serve in the French army in 1914, Picasso and Braque created a revolution that not only transformed painting, but also had a profound impact on sculpture, architecture, cinema, and virtually every other form of visual art, and beyond this to poetry and literature, as faceting and fragmentation were applied to words as well as to images. The work of Picasso and Braque in these years accounts for three of the five most important five-year periods of individual artistic creativity of the century. These two young conceptual innovators created a new synthesis of earlier artistic elements that overturned the synthesis of an equally young conceptual innovator, Masaccio, who had worked in Florence nearly five centuries before, as Cubist space and form abruptly and decisively replaced Renaissance perspective as the dominant paradigm in advanced art. Sylvester again recognized both the significance of this episode and its nature, as he observed that

The story of the rise of Cubism is one of the most wonderful chapters in the history of art. There is something deeply moving about the way this pair of artists in their late twenties found themselves subverting six centuries of European painting while seeing themselves – quite rightly – as the successors to a line that stretched from Poussin to Chardin to Corot to Cézanne.[39]

This chapter also provides an important result for our understanding of American art, by revealing that Andy Warhol's work of 1962 constituted the greatest breakthrough of a single year ever made by an American artist. Warhol's silkscreened paintings based on photographs of Marilyn Monroe, Coca-Cola bottles, and other icons of American popular culture not only became the most celebrated images of Pop art, but also raised issues of "time, sequence, duration, repetition, and seriality" that have influenced younger artists from the 1960s through the present.[40]

The empirical analysis of this chapter highlights the difference in the creative processes of conceptual and experimental innovators, for it points out that conceptual artists not only innovate earlier in their careers than their experimental counterparts, but also that they innovate more rapidly. Evidence presented in Chapter 2 showed that three of the ten greatest artistic innovators of the twentieth century were experimental artists, as were five of the greatest fifteen.[41] When we examine short periods of innovative breakthroughs, however, using the same data set as Chapter 2, the experimental artists are much less prominent. Thus experimental artists account for only one of the fifteen most important individual years of creativity of the century, for only two of the fifteen most important three-year periods, and for only three of the fifteen most important five-year periods. The difference in the results of the two studies is a consequence of the fact that many conceptual artists arrive at their greatest contributions suddenly, while many experimental artists arrive at their greatest achievements much more gradually: the shorter the periods within artists' careers we study, the greater the advantage of conceptual over experimental innovators.

One further important difference between the two types of innovator also appears in the data analyzed here. Because experimental innovators are rarely satisfied that they have achieved their goals, they are often tied to a single problem for an entire career. In contrast, conceptual innovators often believe that they have conclusively achieved specific goals, and can consequently move on to other problems, and to make different contributions. This diversity of conceptual innovators is reflected in the fact that the three artists who make more than a single appearance in any of the tables in this chapter were all conceptual artists. All three – Picasso, Matisse, and Duchamp – are among the protean conceptual innovators who made multiple contributions to modern art.

5

The Greatest Women Artists
of the Twentieth Century

Introduction

Recent decades have witnessed an intense interest in the role of women in the art of the past. Scores of museum exhibitions have been devoted to the work of women artists, and scores of monographs have examined the contributions of women to our artistic heritage.

As is common in the humanities, however, the scholarly attention devoted to the role of women artists has been qualitative rather than quantitative. As a result, we now have a large amount of scholarship that analyzes the contributions of individual women artists, or of particular groups of women artists, but we do not have studies that provide systematic evaluation of the relative importance of different women artists. This chapter will begin to remedy this deficiency.

Specifically, this chapter will investigate the question of which women made the greatest contributions to art during the past century. Women played a far greater role in the art of the twentieth century than in any earlier time. So for example the third edition of Nancy Heller's *Women Artists*, published in 1997, a textbook written "to provide a richly illustrated overview of some of the most interesting professional women painters and sculptors in the Western world, from the Renaissance to the present," devotes fully 144 pages to the twentieth century, substantially more than the total of only 97 pages devoted to all earlier centuries. This concentration is a product of the fact that the twentieth century witnessed, in Heller's words, "a profusion of women artists."[1]

Following the practice used in a series of earlier studies, this chapter will measure the relative importance of the members of a sample of artists by the number of illustrations of their work contained in art history textbooks. As discussed above, this measure draws on the judgments of large numbers of art scholars as to which artists, and works of art, are most central to the narrative of the history of art.[2] Interestingly, a number of scholars have specifically cited textbooks of art history as evidence of the neglect of women artists in earlier times. For example Thomas McEvilley observed that the 1970 edition of H. W. Janson's *History of Art* contained no mention of any woman artist, and Nancy Heller noted that the 1986 edition of Janson's book contained only 19 illustrations of works by women.[3] One indication of the recent increase in the attention paid to women artists is that the 2007 edition of Janson's book contains 40 illustrations of works by women. The present study will use not only the latest edition of Janson's text, but also more than two dozen other recent textbooks, to produce the first systematic survey of the judgments of art scholars on the relative importance of the greatest women artists of the twentieth century.

The Ranking

This study began by identifying all the women artists who worked in the twentieth century who had a total of four or more illustrations of their art included in five leading textbooks of art history published from 2000 to 2005.[4] There were twenty-five such artists. A data set was then created by recording all illustrations of the work of these twenty-five artists in twenty-nine textbooks of art history published in English from 1995 on.[5] All of these books examined the art of at least the entire twentieth century, so that all twenty-five artists were eligible to appear in every book, regardless of where and when they worked.

A ranking of the ten artists (actually eleven, because of a tie) whose work was most often illustrated in the twenty-nine texts is presented in Table 5.1. Overall, the ranking is dominated by Americans. In addition to the four artists who were born in the United States, three others – Bourgeois, Hesse, and Nevelson – spent their careers in the United States. The youngest woman in the table, Cindy Sherman, is also the highest ranked.

Careers

This chapter will examine the nature and timing of the major contributions of the five highest-ranked women in Table 5.1. The data set constructed for this study can help to identify those contributions, by

TABLE 5.1. *Greatest Women Artists of the Twentieth Century*

Artist	Date of Birth	Date of Death	Country of Birth	N
1. Cindy Sherman	1954	–	USA	38
2. Georgia O'Keeffe	1887	1986	USA	30
3t. Louise Bourgeois	1911	–	France	27
3t. Eva Hesse	1936	1970	Germany	27
5. Frida Kahlo	1907	1954	Mexico	25
6t. Barbara Kruger	1945	–	USA	23
6t. Jenny Holzer	1950	–	USA	23
8t. Louise Nevelson	1899	1988	Russia	22
8t. Bridget Riley	1931	–	England	22
8t. Natalia Goncharova	1811	1962	Russia	22
8t. Käthe Kollwitz	1867	1945	Germany	22

Source: This and Tables 5.2–5.3 are based on the data set constructed for this study. See the text for the method of construction, and the appendix to this chapter for a list of the sources used.

pointing to when they occurred – the periods in these artists' careers that are most heavily represented by textbook illustrations.

Table 5.2 shows the five-year period in the career of each of the top five women from Table 5.1 from which the textbooks include the largest number of illustrations. There is substantial variation in the ages at which these periods occurred. Thus whereas Sherman's best five-year period ended when she was 28, and those of both Kahlo and Hesse ended when they were 34, O'Keeffe did not complete her best period until the age of 43, and Bourgeois, remarkably, did not complete hers until the age of 84. Why the timing of these artists' most important periods differed so radically is one topic of interest for this study.

The following sections of this chapter will consider each of the artists listed in Table 5.2, in chronological order of their prime periods as identified in that table.

TABLE 5.2. *Best Five-Year Period in Each Artist's Career, by Total Illustrations in Textbooks*

Artist	N	Years	Ages
1. Sherman	17	1978–82	24–28
2. O'Keeffe	13	1926–30	39–43
3t. Bourgeois	9	1991–95	80–84
3t. Hesse	24	1966–70	30–34
5. Kahlo	14	1937–41	30–34

Georgia O'Keeffe

I think that what I have done is something rather unique in my time and that I am one of the few who gives our country any voice of its own – I claim no credit – it is only that I have seen with my own eye and that I couldn't help seeing with my own eye.

Georgia O'Keeffe, 1945[6]

Georgia O'Keeffe was an experimental artist, whose paintings were based on vision. When the director of the Cleveland Art Museum asked her to write a description of one of her paintings, she protested that "It is easier for me to paint it than write about it and I would so much rather people would look at it than read about it. I see no reason for painting anything that can be put into any other form as well." But the brief account she then provided ended by stressing the central importance for her art of her perception of color: "Color is one of the great things in the world that makes life worth living to me and as I have come to think of painting it is my effort to create an equivalent with paint color for the world – life as I see it."[7]

The visual basis of O'Keeffe's art was clear to those who knew her work. For example in 1927 the critic Lewis Mumford observed that O'Keeffe's art originated in images rather than ideas: "hers is a direct expression upon the plane of painting, and not an illustration by means of painting of ideas that have been verbally formulated."[8] A decade later the painter Marsden Hartley agreed, writing of O'Keeffe that "She is satisfied that appearance tells everything and that the eye is a better vehicle of truth for picture purposes than the mind can ever be."[9] O'Keeffe painted to capture the beauty and color she saw around her. Her sensitivity to the colors and shapes of her surroundings is manifest in the vivid description of her home in New Mexico that she sent to a friend, the painter Arthur Dove, in 1942:

I wish you could see what I see out the window – the earth pink and yellow cliffs to the north – the full pale moon about to go down in an early morning lavender sky behind a very long beautiful tree covered mesa to the west – pink and purple hills in front and the scrubby fine dull green cedars – and a feeling of much space – It is a very beautiful world.[10]

The strength of O'Keeffe's feeling for the beauty of the world led her to defend her artistic goal in an era when beauty in art had fallen out of fashion, as in 1960 she remarked that "I'm one of the few artists, maybe the only one today, who is willing to talk about my work as pretty. I don't mind it being pretty."[11] Similarly, when it had become fashionable for artists to declare that their work expressed their emotions, O'Keeffe persisted in maintaining that her art was visual: "I never think about expressing anything. I'm not so wonderful that my thoughts should be expressed that way."[12]

O'Keeffe did not plan her paintings. A *New Yorker* profile in 1929 reported that "She does no under-painting on her canvases; she rarely even blocks out her design in advance."[13] O'Keeffe believed that achievements were made in a body of work rather than in individual paintings: "Success doesn't come with painting one picture. It results from taking a certain definite line of action and staying with it."[14] Throughout her career, she tended to work in series, with multiple variations on a particular theme. Sometimes these would comprise four or five paintings done within a few weeks, but sometimes they were much more extended. For example between 1946 and 1960 she made more than twenty paintings of the patio door of her adobe house in Abiquiu. She told Katharine Kuh that she had bought the house because of that door: "I'm always trying to paint that door – I never quite get it. It's a curse – the way I feel I must continually go on with that door." She couldn't explain why the door interested her: "I wish I knew. It fascinates me." When Kuh asked why she painted in series, O'Keeffe replied that "I have a single-track mind. I work on an idea for a long time. It's like getting acquainted with a person, and I don't get acquainted easily."[15] Even O'Keeffe's abstract paintings were based on the observation of nature, for they grew out of progressive simplification of the shapes of real objects over the course of a series of works: "Sometimes I start in very realistic fashion, and as I go from one painting to another of the same thing, it becomes simplified till it can be nothing but abstract."[16] The process of simplification was gradual, based on visual inspection: "Details are confusing. It is only by selection, by elimination, by emphasis, that we get at the real meaning of things."[17]

O'Keeffe believed that artists had to develop slowly. In 1928, at the peak of her accomplishment, she told an interviewer that "The notion that you can make an artist overnight, that there is nothing but genius, and a dash of temperament in artistic success is a fallacy. Great artists don't just happen, any more than writers, or singers, or other creators. They have to be trained, and in the hard school of experience."[18] In 1960, looking back on forty years of O'Keeffe's art, the curator Daniel Catton Rich observed that her style had evolved gradually: "Her work shows a complete organic growth. There have been no sudden reversals, no abrupt shifts in style."[19] Like many other experimental artists O'Keeffe did not believe in the reality of achieving success, but instead valued the process of seeking greater clarity of vision: "Whether you succeed or not is irrelevant, there is no such thing. Making your unknown known is the important thing – and keeping the unknown always beyond you. Catching, crystallizing your simpler clearer vision of life – only to see it turn stale compared to what you vaguely feel ahead – that you must always keep working to grasp."[20] When the Museum of Modern Art honored her with a retrospective exhibition in 1946, O'Keeffe told the responsible curator that she was flattered, but then immediately returned to her dissatisfaction with her achievement: "I can not honestly say to myself that I could not have been better."[21]

The period the textbooks identify as that of O'Keeffe's most important work was marked both by her paintings of New York and by a continuation of the series of large paintings of individual flowers that she had begun in 1924.[22] O'Keeffe had moved to New York in 1918, but it was only in 1926 that she began to paint the city, with simplified and often elongated geometric shapes of the skyscrapers dramatically illuminated, and sometimes partially obliterated, by reflected sunlight or neon signs. The familiar magnification of the flower paintings was also influenced by the pace of life in the city, as O'Keeffe later recalled that "I said to myself – I'll paint what I see – what the flower is to me but I'll paint it big and they will be surprised into taking time to look at it – I will make even busy New Yorkers take time to see the flowers."[23]

Frida Kahlo

The only thing I know is that I paint because I need to, and I paint always whatever passes through my head, without any other consideration.
Frida Kahlo[24]

Frida Kahlo's art was dominated by images of herself to an extent that may be unique among important painters. More than one third of all her paintings, and all of her most celebrated paintings, were self-portraits. Thus twenty-four of the twenty-five illustrations of her work in the textbooks surveyed for this study were self-portraits, including her most famous single painting, *The Two Fridas* (1939), which accounts for seven of the illustrations. Kahlo used her own image as a vehicle to explore not only her own life, but also a wide range of issues involving religion, politics, and society. On the occasion of a recent exhibition of her work, Tanya Barron stressed the great variety and range of Kahlo's artistic sources:

Frida Kahlo built up a complex symbolic language, a repertoire of signs and emblems . . . which she gave a particularly personal and often highly idiosyncratic character. Her visual language is eclectic, encompassing European fine art traditions from Bosch and Brueghel to avant-garde movements such as Surrealism, Mexican colonial-era art, the Mexican avant-garde of her contemporaries (including her husband Diego Rivera), popular and folkloric Mexican art and culture, as well as belief systems as different as Catholicism, Eastern spirituality, Aztec culture and religion, ancient Egyptian belief, European philosophy, psychoanalysis and Communism. She often combines varied references together in a single image, speaking on multiple levels and creating an especially private and cryptic language.[25]

Much of the critical analysis of Kahlo's work involves its relationship with Surrealism. When the poet and founder of Surrealism, André Breton, visited Mexico in 1938 and saw Kahlo's art, he declared that she in fact belonged to that movement: "her work has blossomed forth, in her latest paintings, into pure surreality, despite the fact that it had been conceived without any prior knowledge whatsoever of the ideas motivating the activities of my friends and myself."[26] Although Kahlo welcomed the attention, and placed *The Two Fridas* in a major Surrealist exhibition in Mexico City in 1940, she never fully accepted her categorization as a Surrealist, and in later years vehemently denied the affiliation altogether. But she did recognize that her work shared some common ground with that of the Europeans:

I adore surprise and the unexpected. I like to go beyond realism. For this reason, I would like to see lions come out of that bookshelf and not books. My painting naturally reflects these predilections and also my state of mind. And it is doubtless true that in many ways my painting is related to that of the Surrealists. But I never had the intention of creating a work that could be considered to fit in that classification.[27]

In spite of the fact that Kahlo had developed her art independently, her biographer Hayden Herrera argued that Surrealism affected her work in what became her prime period:

Frida was surely one for whom contact with Surrealism served to reinforce both a personal and a cultural inclination toward fantasy. Though she was a Surrealist discovery rather than a Surrealist, there is a definite change in her work after her direct contact with Surrealism in 1938 . . . After 1938 her paintings become more complex, more penetrating, more disturbingly intense.[28]

After her participation in the International Exhibition of Surrealism in 1940, Kahlo gained increasing recognition, and her paintings rose in value. At the same time, some of the intensity of her earlier work was lost. Herrera observed that the paintings she produced after 1940 were "generally larger-scale than those she had done in the 1930s, and they appear to have been aimed at a broader audience, to be less like private talismans or votive images."[29] Her growing reputation also led to more commissions from patrons: "Frida's portraits of others are almost always less vibrant and original than her subject paintings and self-portraits – perhaps because, in painting a specific individual, she did not feel free to project all her complex fantasy and feeling – her 'own reality' – onto the image."[30]

Kahlo's distinctive contribution lay in the difference between her symbolism and that of the European Surrealists. Unlike Surrealism, which attempted to create visual metaphors for the experience of dreams and the unconscious, Kahlo's art was a personal and direct expression of her thoughts and emotions. As Herrera observed, Kahlo's symbolism was "almost always autobiographical and relatively simple." In 1952 Kahlo herself declared that "I do not know whether my paintings are Surrealist or not, but I do know that they are the frankest expression of myself."[31] The next year she made a key distinction in distancing herself from the Surrealists' goals: "They thought I was a Surrealist, but I wasn't. I never painted dreams. I painted my own reality."[32]

Breton stressed the expressive power of Kahlo's art by describing it as "a ribbon around a bomb."[33] By effectively making Surrealism an autobiographical project, Kahlo later became a model for many younger women artists who wanted to use their art to express their own feelings about their lives and their societies. So for example a Kahlo self-portrait that showed her growing from the earth like a plant was a direct inspiration for the celebrated earth/body sculptures the performance artist Ana Mendieta made during the 1970s.[34] An art historian recently noted that Tracey Emin's trademark works are also related to Kahlo's art:

Her quilted, embroidered, and appliquéd blankets with their angry, desperate confessional declarations look back to the tradition of women's craft activities, and to the example of Frida Kahlo's autobiographical, populist symbolism and style. Such works affectingly, but also knowingly, restage Kahlo's manner and her suffering persona in the contemporary idiom of street and fashion-magazine graphics or political murals.[35]

Peter Wollen observed that the themes of Kahlo's art had a powerful appeal for women artists in the 1970s:

Her art was intimate, private and personal; it was about her identity as a woman and a Mexican; it was about the body – very specifically the female body and, even more specifically, her own; it was about babies or the lack of them, clothes and their signification, the contradictory projection of both strength and weakness. It was in violent contrast to the pretentious asceticism of much late modernism, to its vatic emptiness, to the tedious aspiration of being high art, to its ultra-refined painterliness.

Even more generally, Wollen noted that Kahlo's art addressed a number of concerns that were central to the advanced art of the 1970s and beyond: "Whether we look at Kahlo from the vantage-point of women's art, Third World art or surrealism; whether we are interested in the appropriation of vernacular forms or the crossover between outsider and fine art, we will find Kahlo's paintings staring us right in the face."[36]

Eva Hesse

First feel sure of idea, then the execution will be easier.
Eva Hesse, notebook entry, 1965[37]

Trained initially as a painter, Eva Hesse began to make sculptures in 1964, just six years before her death at the age of 34. Yet as a young artist in New York, she was in contact with some of the leading advanced artists of the late 1960s, including Robert Smithson, Sol LeWitt, Donald Judd, and Robert Ryman. Hesse's exposure to these artists profoundly affected her art, and between 1966 and 1970 she created new sculptural forms that were based on Minimalism, the dominant movement of the time, but that made distinctive departures from it.

Minimalist sculpture typically used unyielding materials, including aluminum, steel, and wood, to make rigid, austere, geometric forms. In contrast, Hesse used unconventional and often pliable materials, such as wire, latex, and rubber tubing, to make related forms that were often irregular and imprecise in appearance. These included elements drawn from the work of a number of artists who had influenced her. So for example the tangled ropes in some of her works were often considered three-dimensional references to Jackson Pollock's dripped webs of paint. The frequent repetition of elements within her sculptures was inspired by LeWitt : "Series, serial, serial art, is another way of repeating absurdity."

The tubing that projects out from the empty frames that Hesse mounted on walls may have been extensions of the hooks that break the surface of some of Jasper Johns's paintings. And the humor that Hesse considered to be basic to her work may have originated in the work of Claes Oldenburg.[38]

Hesse was determined to make an important contribution to art. This ambition was reflected in her desire to make radical departures, as for example in 1960, at the age of 24, she wrote in her diary that "I will paint *against* every rule I or others have invisibly placed."[39] Although she did not know where to start to do this at the time, her determination led to quick results once she solved that problem. Hesse first began experimenting with sculpture in December of 1964, using discarded materials in the abandoned factory where she and her husband, who was also a sculptor, were working during a year in Germany. Barely more than a year later, in January of 1966, she made *Hang-Up*, the large wall-mounted sculpture that has become her most celebrated individual work, and that accounts for five of the illustrations of her work in the texts used for this study.[40] Shortly before her death, Hesse told an interviewer that *Hang-Up* was "I think the most important statement I made." Describing it as "really an idea piece," Hesse remarked that "It's the most ridiculous structure I have ever made and that is why it is really good."[41]

Hesse's unconventional materials and irregular forms brought humor and absurdity to Minimalism, which had previously been humorless and ascetic. Rosalind Krauss summarized Hesse's contribution as "countering the formalist dialogue of the 1960s with the message of expressionism."[42] Kim Levin stressed that Hesse's art adapted the formal tools of Minimalism to her own ends, producing "a new kind of Expressionism, abstract and Minimalist in form."[43] That Hesse could make a substantial contribution to advanced art in such a brief career was a result of the conceptual nature of her art. Lucy Lippard described Hesse as "a pivotal figure and a synthesizer," and like many other young conceptual innovators, Hesse combined previously unrelated elements to create a synthesis that yielded a novel and unexpected result.[44]

Cindy Sherman

These are pictures of emotions personified, entirely of themselves with their own presence – not of me.
Cindy Sherman, about *Untitled Film Stills*, 1980[45]

Cindy Sherman gave up painting for photography in art school: "I was initially in school for painting and suddenly realized I couldn't do it any more, it was ridiculous, there was nothing more to say . . . [T]hen I realized I could just use a camera and put my time into an idea instead."[46] In 1977, the year after she graduated, she began to make the series of sixty-nine photographs, *Untitled Film Stills*, that is generally considered her most important work, and accounts for more than a third of her illustrations in the texts used for this study. Each photograph in the series portrayed Sherman as a character in what appeared to be 1940s, 1950s, and 1960s B-movies. Rosalind Krauss explained that the point of the *Film Stills* was "the simulacral nature of what they contain, the condition of being a copy *without* an original."[47] Sherman intended her photographs to be unconvincing imitations of publicity film stills from the era: "My 'stills' were about the fakeness of role-playing as well as contempt for the domineering 'male' audience who would mistakenly read the images as sexy."[48]

Throughout her career, Sherman has used herself as a model. Her photographs are not self-portraits, however, because the costumes and settings clearly signal that in each case she is playing a role. Precisely what the role is remains unclear: "I didn't want to title the photographs because it would spoil the ambiguity."[49] This ambiguity allows many interpretations, and Sherman's work has become the basis for an imposing body of analysis by a large number of scholars and critics, who use her photographs to consider how women have been represented, and more generally how identity is constructed, through the media. As early as 1990, Arthur Danto remarked that "Sherman's brilliant appropriation, in the late 1970s, of the format of the 'still,' with its implied narrative in which she was the nameless starlet, became the focus of so much neostructuralist, radical feminist, Frankfurt School Marxist and semiological hermeneutics that one is convinced there must be whole programs of study in institutions of higher learning in which one can major, or even earn a doctorate, in Sherman Studies."[50]

Although Sherman does not reject the academic analysis of her work, she denies that it captures her intentions: "I've only been interested in making the work and leaving the analysis to the critics. I could really agree with many different theories in terms of their formal concepts but none of it really had any basis in my motivation for making the work." She pays little attention to criticism of any kind: "It's the way I feel about the art world and the critical world; after being around for a while, I don't take anything that seriously in this field. So I'm making fun of it all, myself included." She wants her art to reach a wide audience: "I just want to be accessible. I don't like the elitism of a lot of the art that looks like it's so difficult, where you must get the theory behind it before you can understand it."[51] It was this concern with accessibility that led her to mimic movie ads: "I wanted to imitate something out of the culture, and also make fun of the culture while I was doing it."[52]

Sherman entered the art world at a time when it was in a highly conceptual phase, and Peter Schjeldahl noted that she and some of her peers added to its visual vocabulary: "it was precisely in the art historical muddle of the early '70s that Sherman and her keenest contemporaries found their orientation, not by rejecting conceptualism but by bringing a particular grist to its mill: images."[53] Sherman and others made photography more central to contemporary art at the same time that they changed the practices of the genre. Lisa Phillips explained that, "Cindy Sherman, along with other contemporaries, such as Richard Prince, Barbara Kruger, and Sherrie Levine, have diverted the official course of the history of photography by rejecting its most revered conventions: the sacredness of the photographic paper, of the camera, the perfect exposure, and the immaculate print."[54] Sherman emphasizes that she considers herself an artist who uses photography rather than a photographer.[55] She is not concerned, for example, with whether she takes a photograph or has someone take it for her.[56]

After the black and white *Stills* of 1977–80, Sherman began to use color, initially to make pictures of herself in more elaborate costumes and settings, and later to make pictures of dolls, often grotesquely mangled, and often featuring sexual themes. Yet her early work is disproportionately represented in the textbooks, and the *Untitled Film Stills* are likely to remain her most important contribution. Sherman's most important innovation lies in her nostalgic use of the formulaic methods used for movie stills in the 1950s. Her later creation of shocking images is likely to prove less distinctive than her early images of apparently familiar scenes. In Sherman's words, the *Stills* "should trigger your memory so that you feel you have seen it before. Some people have told me they remember the movies that one of my images derives from, but in fact I had no film in mind at all."[57] This parallels Jeff Koons's statement about his celebrated *Banality* statues, "where I did not work with direct ready-made objects but created objects with a sense of ready-made inherent in them."[58] Sherman explained that she stopped making the *Stills* when she ran out of clichés.[59] And it was in large part because of the use of clichés that her early work had such a great impact on an art world that valued novel uses of irony.

In a review of an exhibition in 1989, Schjeldahl remarked on the beauty and range of Sherman's pictures, and predicted that "she may very well emerge in eventual retrospect as the single most important American artist of the '80s."[60] Sherman has had enormous success. In 1987, at the age of 33, she had a full-scale exhibition at New York's Whitney Museum, and in 1997 the Museum of Modern Art in New York presented an exhibition, sponsored by the pop singer Madonna, in honor of the museum's acquisition of a complete set of the *Untitled Film Stills*. Sherman's work has also helped to raise the position of photography in the art world. Thus in 1987 the curator of her Whitney exhibition claimed that "She has accomplished what photographers have been pursuing for a century – true parity with the other two arts."[61] And in 1995, a dealer's guide to the art market commented that "Cindy Sherman has performed some sort of modern-day alchemy. She has convinced the art market that her photographs should be priced like paintings."[62]

Louise Bourgeois

I am a long-distance runner. It takes me years and years and years to produce what I do.

Louise Bourgeois[63]

Louise Bourgeois was a contemporary of the Abstract Expressionists – she was born a year before Jackson Pollock – and like them she spent her career working experimentally to create a visual art that would explore the unconscious. Her statements about her art parallel the attitudes of her contemporaries. In 1954 she described art as a quest into the unknown: "The finished work is often a stranger to, and sometimes very much at odds with what the artist felt or wished to express when he began." Fifteen years later, she stressed that an entire career was properly devoted to a single elusive goal: "for a lifetime I have wanted to say the same thing. Inner consistency is the test of the artist. Repeated disappointment is what keeps him jumping." Two decades later, her work still hadn't reached a conclusion: "That's why I keep going. The resolution never appears: it's like a mirage." She did not make art for pleasure, but out of necessity: "I do sculpture because I *need*, not because I have fun. I have no fun at all – everything I do is a battlefield, a fight to the finish." Artistic style emerged from abnegation and adversity: "My style, the way I work comes from all the temptations I have resisted, all the fun I didn't have, all the regrets." In 1993 the 82-year-old artist explained to an interviewer that the prestige of having her work exhibited in the United States pavilion at the Venice Biennale was not important to her: "Personally, no exhibition is important. The progression in the work is important. The self-knowledge that I get and that all artists get – I'm not special – the self-knowledge is its own reward." She believed firmly in the value of experience: "You know, artists improve... Otherwise, what's the use of working?"[64]

Like the Abstract Expressionists, Bourgeois was deeply influenced early in her career by Surrealism. But her art diverged significantly from the main concerns of Abstract Expressionism. The dominant genre of that movement was painting, but Bourgeois early gave up painting for sculpture. William Rubin commented that "The organic, biomorphic language of the abstract side of Surrealist art *wants* to be three-dimensional, wants materials of more organic allusiveness than paint. Louise Bourgeois understood this, and picked up where certain veins of Surrealist art had left off."[65] From the beginning of her career, Bourgeois' exploration of the unconscious was more intensely personal and autobiographical than those of the Abstract Expressionists. Thus in 1994 she stated that "All my work in the past fifty years, all my subjects have found their inspiration in my childhood." She told a critic that one of her better-known sculptures, *The Destruction of the Father*, was made "to exorcise the fear. And after it was shown – there it is – I felt like a different person. Now, I don't want to use the term *thérapeutique*, but an exorcism *is* a therapeutic venture. So the reason for making the piece was catharsis."[66]

The art world's recognition of the importance of Bourgeois' work came gradually and late in her career. In 1971, when asked whether she had received as much recognition of her work as she would like, Bourgeois answered "No. But recognition will come in time, and this is enough for me."[67] Ten years later, when Bourgeois was 70, the critic Kay Larson chose Bourgeois as her nominee for a feature in *Artnews* on "Artists the Critics are Watching." Larson explained that "Perhaps Louise Bourgeois is an idiosyncratic choice for an article on 'emerging' artists. Yet she was the first to come to mind when considering artists of high caliber whose work came to my attention during the past season."[68] In 1982, when Bourgeois was given an exhibition at a major museum, the critic Robert Hughes commented that "Louise Bourgeois is certainly the least-known artist ever to get a retrospective at New York's Museum of Modern Art."

He went on to explain that two recent developments had increased interest in Bourgeois' art:

One was the collapse of the idea that art had only one way, the abstract track, forward into history. This made Bourgeois' idiosyncratic kind of late surrealism well worth examining. The second, which made it look more interesting still, was feminism. The field to which Bourgeois' work constantly returns is female experience, located in the body, sensed from within.[69]

Bourgeois' success in creating new visual forms has affected many younger artists. For example the British sculptor Rachel Whiteread recently named Bruce Nauman and Bourgeois as the two greatest influences on her work, explaining "They're the yin and yang of me, the conceptual and the emotional sides."[70]

Although Louise Bourgeois was born more than forty years before Cindy Sherman, Table 5.2 shows that her most illustrated period occurred more than a decade later than that of Sherman. As a late bloomer, Bourgeois is extraordinary even among great experimental artists, for the most illustrated period in her career did not begin until she reached the age of 80. In 1988, she continued to maintain that art should not be made primarily from the art of the past, as in the practice of the reigning conceptual artists, but should grow out of perception and experience:

Art is not about art. Art is about life, and that sums it up. This remark is made to the whole academy of artists who have attempted to derive the art of the late 1980s, to try to relate it to the study of the history of art, which has nothing to do with art. It has to do with appropriation.[71]

For Bourgeois, the greatest art came with age, for with time "you become better in every way, morally, intellectually ... You become better, which is really the Chinese philosophy – the wisdom of the elders."[72]

Old Masters and Young Geniuses

Conceptual innovators generally make their major contributions earlier in their careers than do experimental innovators. Table 5.2 shows that this is true for the artists considered here. The three conceptual artists – Sherman, Hesse, and Kahlo – began their best periods at 24, 30, and 30, respectively, whereas the experimental O'Keeffe began hers at 39, and Bourgeois at 80.

Conceptual innovators also generally make their major contributions more suddenly than their experimental counterparts. Table 5.3 shows

TABLE 5.3. *Best Single Year in Each Artist's Career, by Total Illustrations in Textbooks*

Artist	N	Year	Age	% of Total Illustrations
1. Sherman	8	1978	24	21
2. O'Keeffe	4	1926	39	13
3t. Bourgeois	3	1968, 1993 (tie)	57, 82	11
3t. Hesse	8	1966	30	30
5. Kahlo	8	1939	32	32

that this is also true for the artists considered here. Thus 21 percent of Sherman's total illustrations are of work done in her single best year, as are 30 percent of Hesse's and 32 percent of Kahlo's, whereas only 13 percent of O'Keeffe's total illustrations, and 11 percent of Bourgeois's, are accounted for by their best individual years.

The composition of retrospective exhibitions provides an independent source of evidence on the timing of artists' most important contributions. In general, the museum curators who organize these exhibitions include larger numbers of works from the periods of artists' careers that they consider the most important.[73] For comparison to the evidence of textbook illustrations, Table 5.4 uses the most recent major retrospective for each of the five artists to identify both the best single year and the best five-year period in their careers.

The retrospectives and the textbook illustrations yield nearly identical results for four of the artists. Thus for O'Keeffe the best single year identified by the two sources is the same; there is a difference of just one year between the two sources for Hesse and Kahlo; and there is a difference of just two years for Sherman. Similarly, the best five-year periods identified by the two sources are exactly the same for O'Keeffe and Kahlo, and they differ by just one year for both Sherman and Hesse. For these four artists it is therefore clear that the textbooks and the retrospectives agree on when in their careers they produced their most important work.

For Bourgeois, the two sources do not yield identical results, but they do agree on the basic pattern of her career. In both sources, there are ties for her best single year: in both cases, one of the two years was age 57, while the other two years were considerably later, at 82 and 91. The textbooks identify her best five-year period as her early eighties, and the retrospective as her late fifties. All of this evidence is consistent with

TABLE 5.4. *Best Single Year and Best Five-Year period in Each Artist's Career, by Total Works in Retrospective Exhibitions*

Artist	Best Year	Age	Best 5-Year Period	Age
1. Sherman	1980	26	1977–81	23–27
2. O'Keeffe	1926	39	1926–30	39–43
3t. Bourgeois	1968, 2002 (tie)	57, 91	1967–71	56–60
3t. Hesse	1965	29	1965–69	29–33
5. Kahlo	1938	31	1937–41	30–34

Note: For Bourgeois, the tabulation excluded works on paper, and included only works exhibited at all locations.

Sources: Amanda Cruz, Elizabeth Smith, and Amelia Jones, *Cindy Sherman: A Retrospective* (Chicago: Museum of Contemporary Art, 1997).
Lloyd Goodrich and Doris Bry, *Georgia O'Keeffe* (New York: Whitney Museum of American Art, 1970).
Frances Morris, ed., *Louise Bourgeois* (London: Tate Publishing, 2007).
Helen Cooper, *Eva Hesse: A Retrospective* (New Haven: Yale University Press, 1992).
Emma Dexter and Tanya Barson, *Frida Kahlo* (London: Tate Publishing, 2005).

the conclusion that Bourgeois had no single period that clearly stands out as her greatest, and equally indicates that all of her most important periods were at advanced ages, beginning in her late fifties and running, remarkably, through her early nineties.

Conclusion

Artistic importance depends on influence: the most important artists are those who have the greatest impact on the future course of their discipline. As many art historians have stressed, in the past discrimination made it extremely difficult for women artists to become genuinely important. Since the 1970s this has changed, however. Not only have recent women artists had greater opportunities to become influential, but some women who worked in earlier times have been rediscovered, and have had new opportunities to influence new generations of artists.

A survey of twenty-nine textbooks found that art historians generally consider Cindy Sherman to be the most important woman artist of the past century. Sherman entered the art world in the late 1970s, and has had an impact not only on women's art, but also on the importance of photography, and its use in advanced art. Two of the other artists ranked in the top five by the art historians – Bourgeois and Hesse – both made their major contributions after the mid-1960s, and a third, Kahlo, has probably had a greater impact on art since her rediscovery in the 1970s and 1980s than she did in her own time.

This study furthermore demonstrates that the creativity of important women artists is not the exclusive domain of either the young or the old. Sherman, Hesse, and Kahlo are all conceptual artists, and all made major contributions early in their careers, whereas O'Keeffe and Bourgeois are experimental artists, and were at their best only after decades of experience. Bourgeois' case is extraordinary, for she persevered in developing her sculpture in spite of decades of neglect and indifference from the art world, and she has made her greatest work beyond the age of 80, an achievement that has been matched by few in the history of art.

Appendix to Chapter 5

Books Surveyed for This Chapter

The five books used to select the artists for the chapter are indicated by asterisks.

Adams, Laurie. 2007. *Art Across Time*, 3rd ed. New York: McGraw Hill.

*Arnason, H. H. 2004. *History of Modern Art*, 5th ed. Upper Saddle River, NJ: Prentice Hall.

Barnes, Rachel, et al. 1996. *The 20th Century Art Book*. London: Phaidon.

Bell, Cory. 2001. *Modern Art*. New York: Watson-Guptill Publications.

Blistène, Bernard. 2001. *A History of 20th-Century Art*. Paris: Flammarion.

Bocola, Sandro. 1999. *The Art of Modernism*. Munich: Prestel.

Britt, David, ed. 1999. *Modern Art*. New York: Thames and Hudson.

Buchholz, Elke Linda. 2003. *Women Artists*. Munich: Prestel.

Chadwick, Whitney 2002. *Women, Art, and Society*, 3rd ed. London: Thames and Hudson.

Cottington, David. 2005. *Modern Art*. Oxford: Oxford University Press.

Cumming, Robert. 2005. *Art*. New York: DK Publishing.

Davies, Penelope, et al. 2007. *Janson's History of Art*, 7th ed. Upper Saddle River, NJ: Pearson Prentice Hall.

Dawtrey, Liz, et al., eds. 1996. *Investigating Modern Art*. New Haven: Yale University Press.

*Dempsey, Amy. 2002. *Art in the Modern Era*. New York: Harry N. Abrams.

Foster, Hal; Rosalind Krauss; Yve-Alain Bois; and Benjamin Buchloh. 2004. *Art Since 1900*. New York: Thames and Hudson.

Freeman, Julian. 1998. *Art*. New York: Watson-Guptill Publications.

Gilbert, Rita. 1998. *Living With Art*, 5th ed. Boston: McGraw Hill.

Grosenick, Uta, ed. 2005. *Women Artists in the 20th and 21st Century*. Cologne: Taschen.

Heller, Nancy. 1997. *Women Artists*, 3rd ed. New York: Abbeville Press.

Honour, Hugh, and John Fleming. 2002. *The Visual Arts*, 6th ed. New York: Harry N. Abrams.
*Hunter, Sam; John Jacobus; and Daniel Wheeler. 2004. *Modern Art*, 3rd ed. New York: Vendome Press.
Johnson, Paul. 2003. *Art*. New York: Harper Collins.
*Kemp, Martin, ed. 2000. *The Oxford History of Western Art*. Oxford: Oxford University Press.
Lucie-Smith, Edward. 1997. *Visual Arts in the Twentieth Century*. New York: Harry N. Abrams.
Parmesani, Loredana. 2000. *Art of the Twentieth Century*. Milan: Skira.
Richter, Klaus. 2001. *Art*. Munich: Prestel.
*Stokstad, Marilyn. 1995. *Art History*. New York: Harry N. Abrams.
Walther, Ingo, ed. 2005. *Art of the 20th Century*. Cologne: Taschen.
Wilkins, David; Bernard Schultz; and Katheryn Linduff. 1997. *Art Past, Art Present*, 3rd ed. New York: Harry N. Abrams.

6

Creating New Genres

Conceptual Artists at Work and Play in the Twentieth Century

Introduction

What is sculpture? What is painting? Everyone's still clinging to outdated ideas, obsolete definitions, as if the artist's role was not precisely to offer new ones.

Pablo Picasso[1]

The twentieth century was a time of extremely rapid and sustained artistic innovation. One striking feature of this is the increase in the number of kinds of art that occurred during the century. Even casual observers of the art world are aware that some of the most popular forms among contemporary artists, including video and installation, are of recent vintage. Yet although all narratives of the art of the past century discuss many new art forms, none has systematically surveyed these innovations. Doing so shows that dozens of new genres of art were invented during the twentieth century, and reveals some surprisingly strong general characteristics that unite what have usually been considered as widely disparate artistic forms, lacking any overall coherence or commonality. Overall, this survey clarifies our understanding of how and why the art of the twentieth century stands apart from earlier art.

Format

This chapter will present a chronological narrative of forty-nine artistic genres that were invented during the twentieth century. These vary considerably in importance: some are widely used today, while others are rare or extinct. Of the forty-nine genres, twenty-two are contained as

entries in the *Oxford English Dictionary*. Each of these, when first mentioned, will be footnoted to its *OED* entry; unless noted otherwise, these
references will be to the second edition, as reprinted in 1991. Another
twenty-seven genres are included in this chapter: all of these are discussed
in a leading textbook of art history. When first mentioned, each of these
nine genres will be footnoted to the relevant discussion in the fifth edition
of H. H. Arnason's *History of Modern Art*. *To facilitate locating all the
genres discussed within this chapter, each of the twenty-two that appear
in the OED will be marked by a single asterisk the first time it appears in
the text, while each of the other twenty-seven genres will be marked by
two asterisks.*

A note is in order here on the precise nature of the terms selected for
discussion. "Genre" can be used to refer to the style of works of art, but
this is not the concern here: this chapter is *not* about the invention of
Fauvism, Cubism, and the many other schools or styles of art invented
in the last century. Rather, this chapter is concerned with new *categories*
of art. Each of these constitutes a new art form. In each case, the words
included in the chapter can be applied not only to a type of art in general,
but can designate a single work – for example a collage, or a joiner, to
anticipate the first and last genres chronologically.

The Beginning

Early in 1912, Pablo Picasso made a small oval painting that included a
piece of oil cloth, printed to imitate chair caning, glued to the canvas. As
John Golding later explained, "This was the first *collage*,* that is to say the
first painting in which extraneous objects or materials are applied to the
picture surface."[2] The invention of collage "struck the most violent blow
yet at traditional painting," because it violated a fundamental tradition
that had been honored since the Renaissance, that nothing other than
paint should be placed on the two-dimensional surface of the support,
and because it did this in a particularly irreverent way, by using "bits of
rubbish."[3]

Art historians have long considered collage a far-reaching innovation:
so for example Golding commented that "The aesthetic implications of
collage as a whole were vast, and its invention was to lead to a whole
series of developments in twentieth-century art."[4] In the discipline of
art history, however, it has not generally been appreciated just how vast
the implications of the innovation of collage have been, for these go
far beyond aesthetic considerations. When he made *Still Life with Chair*

Caning, Picasso set in motion a remarkable series of events that would make the art of the twentieth century fundamentally different from that of all earlier centuries. During the next six decades, the invention of dozens of new artistic genres would radically transform the functions as well as the appearance of art.

That collage initiated this process is fitting for a number of reasons. The inventor himself was an archetype. Not only was Picasso the most important artist of the twentieth century, but when he made *Still Life with Chair Caning* at the age of 31, he became the first in the line of dozens of young innovators who would transform twentieth-century art by creating new genres. And like virtually all of those later innovators, Picasso was a conceptual artist, whose contributions were the embodiments of new ideas. Collage was an archetypal conceptual innovation, for it dramatically and decisively broke the rules of an existing art form. And it was also an archetype in that, like many of the later conceptual innovations in twentieth-century art, it was synthetic, and involved combining previously disparate elements into a single work.

The 1910s

The impact of Picasso's example in creating a new genre was almost immediate. Since 1909, Picasso had worked closely with Georges Braque in developing Cubism. The two spent August of 1912 working together in Sorgues, a small town in the South of France. Picasso left to return to Paris at the beginning of September. In Picasso's absence, within the next few weeks, Braque created the first papier collé,* *Fruit Dish and Glass*, by attaching three pieces of wallpaper, printed to resemble wood-grain, to a charcoal still life.[5] Braque later recalled, "After having made the [first] papier collé I felt a great shock, and it was an even greater shock for Picasso when I showed it to him."[6] Papier collé was obviously related to the innovation of collage, but it produced an effect that Picasso had not recognized. In the earlier stages of Cubism, Picasso and Braque had largely abandoned color as a result of their concern with using shading to give solidity to the flat planes of the fragments into which they broke the objects they represented. Papier collé presented a way to reintroduce color into their art, for it showed how they could symbolize objects through the use of flat colored planes. This ushered in a new synthetic phase in the two artists' development of Cubism. Thus George Heard Hamilton pointed to the rapid development from Braque's innovation: "The skill and authority with which both artists manipulated their discoveries can be seen in *papier collés* executed only a few months later, where an 'analytical' fragmentation of objects was succeeded by their 'synthetic' construction from forms not originally derived from them."[7]

A trip to Paris in 1913 prompted the young Russian artist Vladimir Tatlin to give up painting in favor of sculpture. His key experience in Paris was a visit to Picasso's studio, where Tatlin saw some small three-dimensional works that Picasso had made, in a Cubist idiom, from pieces of paper, sheet metal, and wire. Upon his return to Moscow later in 1913, Tatlin began to make sculptures with the same kinds of scrap materials Picasso had used, but which Tatlin systematically organized into forms through the use of geometric planning. Searching for a name for his new works, Tatlin tried several, including painterly relief – signifying the works' intermediate position between painting and sculpture – before settling on the name counter-relief.**[8] Tatlin chose this name to emphasize his objection to traditional sculptural relief, and it has become associated with his innovation.[9] Tatlin's emphasis on the use of common materials that were not associated with the tradition of fine art struck a responsive chord with a number of young Russian artists who wanted to create forms for a new mass audience, and over the course of the next few years the concept of construction* came to be associated with Tatlin's work.[10] The precise date when this began is unclear, but by 1920 the term construction was used by Russian artists to refer both to a process for making art works and to the final result of that process.[11] By that time, Tatlin had been recognized as the founder of Constructivism, with followers who included Naum Gabo and Alexander Rodchenko. In keeping with Tatlin's initial concerns, Constructivism used mathematical planning and modern technology to explore the artistic qualities of common materials.

Late in his life, Marcel Duchamp recalled:

In 1913 I had the happy idea to fasten a bicycle wheel to a kitchen stool and watch it turn . . .

In New York in 1915 I bought at a hardware store a snow shovel on which I wrote "In Advance of the Broken Arm."

It was around that time that the word "readymade"* came to mind to designate this form of manifestation.[12]

The real fame of the readymade dates from 1917, when the American Society of Independent Artists declined to exhibit a porcelain urinal that Duchamp had purchased, signed with the fictitious name R. Mutt, and titled *Fountain*. The ensuing controversy produced a heated debate over the boundaries of art that became a central issue in generating the art of the second half of the twentieth century. It is primarily because of this that many art critics consider Duchamp the greatest influence on the art of that era.[13]

The highly conceptual nature of Duchamp's work has proved irresistible to many conceptual art scholars, and there has been a vast outpouring of analysis of his art, and his life. An issue that has been relatively neglected, however, in this great body of work is that of the origins of the readymade. Duchamp himself did not discuss the inspiration for this innovation, beyond describing it as a "happy idea" he had in 1913, in the passage quoted above. Few scholars appear to have considered whether Duchamp's idea might have been related to Picasso's innovation of collage just one year earlier. In 1971, the critic Clement Greenberg did make this connection, writing of Duchamp that:

He would seem to have attributed the impact of Cubism – and particularly of Picasso's first collage-constructions – to what he saw as its startling difficulty; and it's as though the bicycle wheel mounted upside-down on a stool and the store-bought bottle rack he produced in 1913 were designed to go Picasso one better in this direction.[14]

In this regard, it is interesting to note that although *Fountain* was effectively unaltered from the object Duchamp purchased, the same was not true of the first readymade, in which Duchamp fastened together, or collaged, two disparate objects. Although there is no evidence that Duchamp saw Picasso's collage, an obvious feature of conceptual art is that it is often not necessary to see an innovation in order to understand its significance, and this is clearly true for collage.[15] It appears likely that Duchamp's enormous influence on the art of the late twentieth century was made possible by Picasso's key early innovation.

A number of artists associated with the Dada movement began to create new genres during World War I. In several cases, these artists and their innovations subsequently became important in Surrealism. An example of this is the biomorph,* that Jean Arp first created in 1915 or 1916.[16] Arp was one of the founders of the first Dada group, in Zurich, and he later became an influential Surrealist. The shapes of the biomorphs came from Arp's interest in automatism, and appear to be related to plants or primitive animal forms. William Rubin observed that Arp's biomorphism gained currency as "the nearest thing to a common form-language for the painter-poets of the Surrealist generations."[17]

During this same time Arp was devising a new type of relief, intermediate between painting and sculpture, that he called constructed paintings.**[18] These were Arp's response to Cubist collages. He would make drawings, usually using organic forms like the biomorphs, then give them to a carpenter who would cut the shapes from thin layers of wood. Arp painted each of the pieces, then glued a number of them together, often superimposing them to create reliefs of varying depths. Although these reliefs were always abstract, they suggested plants or primitive animal forms, and Arp used the term "earthly forms" to describe them.[19]

Arp's interest in automatism soon produced another new genre. In 1916 and 1917 he began to make collages in which torn pieces of paper were fixed to a support in the positions they supposedly fell into when dropped from above.[20] Although Arp's greatest concern with these collages was in the use of accident in creating works of art, just as the Dada poet Tristan Tzara made poems from words cut out of newspapers and drawn from a hat or scattered on a table, it was a different aspect of the creation of these works – the tearing of the pieces of paper – that resulted in their designation as the first examples of a new genre, papier déchiré.*[21]

In the winter of 1918–19 the German artist Kurt Schwitters began to make collages from scraps of waste paper and other discarded material. When these were first exhibited in 1919 Schwitters chose the word merz** to describe them.[22] The term originated from one of the first such collages, *Merzbild*, which was titled from a scrap of paper that had been cut from an advertisement for a bank – the Kommerz-und Privatbank – in which the syllable "merz" could be read. Schwitters declared that "*Merzbilder* are abstract works of art. The word Merz denotes essentially the combination of all conceivable materials for artistic purposes." Over time, Schwitters came to apply the term to nearly all his works, as he considered merz a principle of working, using individual units of diverse materials in a constructive way: "Merz stands for freedom from all fetters, for the sake of artistic creation."[23]

Photomontage* was invented by Dada artists in Berlin by 1919 in an attempt to create a new art form, based on photography, that would replace easel painting.[24] Although it failed to achieve this goal, it quickly spread from its initial use, of creating biting political and social commentary and satire, to the commercial advertising profession. William Rubin argued that photomontage was a misnomer for photo-collage, because the images were not montaged in a darkroom but were instead made by pasting superimposed photographs onto a support, but photomontage nonetheless came to be the accepted term for the works of a number of Berlin Dadaists, especially John Heartfield, George Grosz, Raoul

Hausmann, and Hannah Höch.[25] Hausmann explained that the name had an ideological motivation: "We called this process photomontage because it embodied our refusal to play the part of the artist. We regarded ourselves as engineers, and our work as construction: we *assembled* (in French: *monter*) our work, like a fitter." He observed that the technique "introduced the simultaneous juxtaposition of different points of view and angles of perspective, as in a kind of motionless moving picture."[26]

In the Vitebsk art school in 1919, the Russian artist El Lissitzky, who was a Suprematist disciple of his fellow faculty member Kazimir Malevich, developed his own form of abstract painting. He called it Proun,** the title he subsequently gave to all his abstract paintings.[27] The exact source of the term Proun is uncertain, but it appears to have been an acronym referring both to new art and to the name of the Vitebsk art school. Lissitzky's paintings were strongly architectural, and he explained that "A Proun is a station for changing trains from architecture to painting."[28] He later expanded Proun to include sculpture, and a room-sized work he created for a Berlin art exhibition in 1923.[29]

The 1920s

In Paris late in 1921, the American Dada painter and photographer Man Ray began to make photographs without a camera. Under the influence of Duchamp, Man Ray had become interested in making works of art without traditional means. After using an airbrush to make paintings without touching the canvas, Man Ray began to make photographs by placing objects on photographic paper and exposing it to light. This was not a new process, for it had been used in the nineteenth century. But instead of making static images, as in the earlier instances, Man Ray moved the light source and shifted the objects, creating new visual effects suggesting depth and movement. To honor his invention of this new practice, Man Ray named his new works rayograms.*[30]

In early 1922, apparently unaware of Man Ray's invention, in Berlin the Hungarian artist Laszlo Moholy-Nagy independently made works using virtually the same process, which he called photograms.*[31] Moholy-Nagy was a Constructivist, and was interested in mechanical interactions of light and motion. The images he produced differed considerably in appearance from those of Man Ray, but they were basically similar in consisting of photographs made without a camera.

The German artist Max Ernst discovered frottage* in 1925.[32] As a Surrealist, Ernst was always alert to new ways of drawing on the

subconscious, and he later recorded an experience he had on August
10, 1925:

Finding myself one rainy evening in a seaside inn, I was struck by the obsession
that showed to my excited gaze the floor-boards upon which a thousand scrub-
bings had deepened the groove. I decided then to investigate the symbolism of
this obsession and, in order to aid my meditative and hallucinatory faculties, I
made from the boards a series of drawings by placing on them, at random, sheets
of paper which I undertook to rub with black lead.[33]

The success of this new means of producing images prompted Ernst
to extend it, and to make rubbings of a wide range of objects. He concluded that frottage was "the real equivalent of that which is already
known by the term *automatic writing*." Like Rimbaud's desire to allow
his subconscious to write poetry, Ernst believed his subconscious could
now create images: "by widening in this way the active part of the mind's
hallucinatory faculties I came to assist *as spectator* at the birth of all my
works, from the tenth of August, 1925, memorable day of the discovery
of *frottage*."[34]

Exquisite corpse** was invented in 1925 by the Surrealist poet André
Breton.[35] It originated in a word game motivated by the Surrealists' love of
accidental and irrational effects. Each of a group of friends would write
a word or phrase on a piece of paper, then fold the paper so the next
participant could not see the previous entries. The first result obtained in
this way gave the game its name: "The exquisite/corpse/shall drink/ the
young/wine."[36] The game was readily extended to drawing, and provided
a means for creating composite irrational images: Breton remarked that
"With the *Exquisite Corpse* we had at our disposal – at last – an infallible
means of sending the mind's critical mechanism away on vacation and
fully releasing its metaphorical potentialities."[37]

1930s

In 1922, while working as a professor at the Weimar Bauhaus, Laszlo
Moholy-Nagy conceived the idea of a light-and-motion machine. After
eight years of calculation and design, Moholy-Nagy produced a kinetic,
motor-driven construction that he named a light-space modulator.**[38]
These machines were made with metal and glass, and when they were
set in motion their rotation produced silhouette displays on objects that
surrounded them. The light-space modulator combined both Constructivist concerns with working mechanisms and Suprematist interests in

the machine as spectacle, while its conception and creation typified the artist-engineer ideal of the Bauhaus.[39]

In 1930 the young American sculptor Alexander Calder visited the Paris studio of Piet Mondrian. Calder later recalled that the sight of Mondrian's colored rectangles gave him a shock. He suggested to Mondrian that "perhaps it would be fun to make these rectangles oscillate," and although the painter immediately rejected the suggestion, Calder seized on this goal, of combining abstraction and movement.[40] Calder began to make wire sculptures with revolving elements; some were driven by small electric motors, others with hand cranks. In 1932, a friend brought Marcel Duchamp to see these sculptures. Duchamp liked them, and arranged for Calder to exhibit them at a Paris gallery. Calder later wrote: "I asked him what sort of a name I could give these things and he at once produced 'Mobile'* . . . Duchamp also suggested that on my invitation card [for the exhibition] I make a drawing of the motor-driven object and print: CALDER: SES MOBILES."[41] The term mobile was later extended to the wire sculptures that Calder began to make later in 1932 that did not have motors, but that were instead moved by air currents.

Many of Calder's fellow artists attended his exhibition of mobiles. Calder recalled that in reacting to the mobiles, one of them had retrospectively named another genre: "Jean Arp said to me, 'Well, what were those things you did last year – stabiles?'* Whereupon, I seized the term and applied it first to all the things previously shown at Percier's [gallery] and later to the large steel objects I am involved in now."[42]

In Paris in 1933, the photographer Brassaï began to publish pictures of such discarded objects as crumpled bus or Metro tickets, or lumps of toothpaste or shaving cream. Brassaï's close-up photographs transformed these chance shapes into evocative images. The Surrealist painter Salvador Dali declared that these forms were subconsciously made art, and named them involuntary sculptures.**[43]

Surrealism had a particular concern with objects that were not intended to be artistic. As early as 1923, Breton had called for "the concrete realization . . . of objects perceived only in dreams."[44] An exhibition in Paris in 1936 dedicated to the Surrealist object included a number of types of objects, including "natural objects, interpreted natural objects, perturbed objects, found objects,* mathematical objects, Readymades, etc."[45] In an essay written for the exhibition, Breton described "the surrealist aim of bringing about *a total revolution of the object* through various measures, including: . . . showing it in whatever state external forces such as earthquake, fire or water may have left it; retaining it just because of the doubt surrounding its original function; or because of the ambiguity resulting from its totally or partially irrational conditioning by the elements, entailing its dignification through chance discovery (the 'found object')."[46] Found objects could be natural objects, such as stones or plants, or such manufactured objects as a shoe, a toy, or a loaf of bread.[47]

1940s

In 1946 the Argentine artist Lucio Fontana began to call his works of all kinds – paintings, sculptures, and architecture – spatial concepts.**[48] Fontana wanted to eliminate the barriers among the genres of art, to emphasize that what mattered in any format was the primacy of mental conception, before the manual realization occurred. All of Fontana's art was intended to represent a new idea of space.

In 1949 two young French artists proposed a new form of collage that came from the streets of Paris. In that year Raymond Hains and Jacques de la Mahé Villeglé first dismounted a long section of torn posters from their original locations on walls and fences and transferred them to canvas.[49] In tribute to the process of removal, they named their new work décollage.**[50]

The same year marked the first appearance of the environment.*[51] Early in 1949, in a Milan gallery Lucio Fontana exhibited *Ambiente nero*, or *Black Environment*, in which an abstract shape covered with phosphorescent varnish hung from the ceiling, lit only by black light. The work consisted of the entire space of the gallery, which surrounded the viewer.[52] This was part of Fontana's Spatialist program aimed at transcending painting and sculpture by developing color and form into surrounding space. During the 1960s, the term environment was extended to a wide variety of works of art that the spectator had to walk into.[53]

1950s

Assemblage* is perhaps the single exception to the rule that the new genres of the twentieth century were all invented by conceptual artists.[54] In 1953, the experimental painter Jean Dubuffet began to make lithographs from collages of torn fragments of a variety of colored and printed papers.[55] In the belief that the term "collage" should be reserved for works made during the 1910s and 1920s, Dubuffet gave his works the new name of assemblages d'empreintes (imprint assemblages).[56] In 1955 Dubuffet extended this technique to oil paintings: he would begin by making a large number of paintings, then cut them into pieces, and create new works by fitting these pieces together and gluing them onto clean canvases. He called the resulting works tableaux d'assemblages (painting assemblages).[57] True to his experimental nature, Dubuffet made his assemblages to achieve a visual effect, for he found that combinations of small pieces of paper or canvas covered with many different colors achieved a "lively scintillation" that he could not obtain through other means. Equally experimental was his attitude that the works he produced in this way were "not so much undertaken with the idea of realization as in the spirit of preliminary research, with a view to future realizations."[58]

Assemblage came to be used to describe a wide range of works of art, but its typical application was not to the collages of pieces of paper or canvas that Dubuffet had made. Instead, in the catalogue for a major exhibition titled *The Art of Assemblage*, presented at the Museum of Modern Art in New York in 1962, William Seitz explained that the works included nearly all shared two characteristics: "1. They are primarily *assembled* rather than painted, drawn, modeled, or carved. 2. Entirely, or in part, their constituent elements are preformed natural or manufactured materials, objects or fragments not intended as art materials."[59] Interestingly, therefore, the three-dimensional works made of manufactured objects that are now commonly called assemblages are far in spirit and appearance from the two-dimensional works of paper and canvas to which Dubuffet first gave the name.[60]

In 1954 the young artist Robert Rauschenberg began using the term combine-painting, or simply combine,** to refer to paintings to which he attached real objects.[61] Initially the combines were intended to be mounted on walls, but over time some came to be free standing. Two combines – *Bed* (1955) and *Monogram* (1959) – are among the five works made by American artists in the 1950s that are most frequently reproduced in textbooks of art history.[62] The term combine has never been extended to works by artists other than Rauschenberg, and is in fact generally restricted to works he made during 1954–64.[63] But the combines are widely considered the most important works ever made by Rauschenberg, who is in turn considered one of the most influential artists of his generation.[64] One indication of their importance is that New York's Metropolitan Museum, which rarely presents exhibitions of the work of living artists, recently hosted a show titled *Robert Rauschenberg Combines*, which included 170 of the works.[65] Arthur Danto contended that the combine *Bed* (1955) was a pivotal work between the past and the future of advanced art, "pointing in one direction back to the metaphysics of paint, which defined Abstract Expressionism . . . and, in the other, to the uninflected display of commonplace objects, which in various ways was to define Pop."[66]

Early in his career the Swiss artist Jean Tinguely became fascinated with making kinetic sculptures that would incorporate chance into the process of making art. In 1955, Tinguely made a drawing machine that, in the words of his friend Pontus Hulten, "demonstrated that a work of art is not something finished or final, but something that makes its own life . . . [T]he work of art itself has creative powers."[67] Tinguely later made a series of machines that produced drawings, as well as others that made paintings, that he called meta-matics.**[68] The meta-matics could produce thousands of works of art without ever making two identical images.

The Italian conceptual artist Piero Manzoni began to make works he called achromes** in 1957.[69] The first achromes were made with kaolin – white clay – on canvas, but later Manzoni extended the name to white works made from other materials, including plaster or cotton balls. Whatever the medium, the achromes were "monochrome works with neutral surfaces that were emphatically devoid of any imagery."[70] The achromes were motivated by Manzoni's concern with the infinite. Their white surface was not a symbol, "just a white surface that is simply a white surface and nothing else"; although the achrome could not actually be infinite, it was "repeatable to infinity."[71]

In 1958 in Paris, Christo Javacheff began to encase objects. He began by wrapping an empty paint can in canvas, tying it with twine, and coating it with varnish.[72] Over time he went on to wrap larger objects, usually with cloth, and his wrapped** projects became some of the most prominent large-scale art works of the 1960s and beyond.[73] These included wrapping one million square feet of the Australian coastline in 1969, eleven small islands in Miami's Biscayne Bay in 1983, the Pont Neuf in Paris in 1985, and the Reichstag in Berlin in 1995. Christo's wrappings have been considered to grow out of the tradition of Tatlin and the Russian Constructivists of using "real materials in real space," and Christo has explained that his work relates to "territory limits."[74]

In 1958, Lucio Fontana began to make *tagli*** (slashes, or cuts).[75] These were monochrome paintings on canvas that Fontana slashed one or more times with a razor blade. Following Fontana's practice since 1946, all were titled *Spatial Concepts*, then the tagli were given subtitles – *Expectation* for those with a single cut, and *Expectations* for those with two or more. The cuts were a logical extension of an earlier set of paintings in which Fontana had made holes in the canvases. The laceration was a precise and calculated gesture that took only a moment, and was irreversible. For Fontana, cutting into the featureless monochrome canvas was analogous to cutting into all of cosmic space.[76]

One of the cultural trademarks of the early 1960s was baptized in 1958, when Allan Kaprow coined the term "happening"* to refer to a new form of performance.[77] As a young artist in the 1950s, Kaprow was preoccupied with the Duchampian question, What is art? He began to fill gallery spaces with trash and other real objects, in keeping with one current view that art was anything, but he soon tired of this permissiveness: "'anything' was too easy. If anything was art, nothing was art."[78] His new answer was to invent the happening, "a collage of rather abstract events for moveable audiences." The first happening, titled *Eighteen Happenings in Six Parts*, was presented in October, 1959, at the Reuben Gallery in New York. For Kaprow,

The Happening seemed to me a new art form that couldn't be confused with paintings, poetry, architecture, music, dance, or plays. As residues of a European past, these old forms of art had lost their artness for me by overexposure and empty worship. Happenings were fresh.[79]

Over time, Kaprow became disturbed when his new happenings began to settle into conventions, and became "just another version of vanguard theater." He decided to avoid this by doing events only once, and by encouraging spontaneity in their execution.[80] Happenings subsequently had no structured beginning, middle, or end; they were fluid and open ended. They had no plot, and were improvised. Chance played a key role in happenings, and they could not be reproduced.[81] However, the author or authors of any particular happening did present a program and a sequence of events for viewing, and the actions could often be interpreted as symbolic.[82]

Happenings came to be emblematic of popular culture in the early 1960s, and were promoted by the mass media as evidence of the emergence of new and more accessible forms of art; it was in this spirit that the Supremes released a song titled "The Happening" in 1966. Happenings could easily be emulated, and they spread rapidly around the world, in the process influencing the work of artists as diverse as Robert Rauschenberg, Joseph Beuys, and Yves Klein. The highly conceptual nature of the genre was particularly attractive to artists who, like Kaprow, were also cultural critics, and Kaprow was proud of the large body of writing that quickly grew up around happenings.[83]

In 1959, Wolf Vostell and Nam June Paik began to include televisions in their environmental works; this marked the first use of the twentieth-century's new mass medium in advanced art. Yet Amy Dempsey argues that "the symbolic birth of Video* Art occurred later in 1965 when Paik purchased Sony's new Portapak hand-held video camera."[84] Paik predicted that "as collage techniques replaced oil paint, the cathode ray tube will replace the canvas."[85] Video has become an important medium in advanced art, through the work of Paik, Ana Mendieta, Bruce Nauman, Bill Viola, Tony Oursler, and others. Many young artists today work primarily or exclusively in video, including such prominent figures as Pipilotti Rist, Steve McQueen, who won England's Turner Prize in 1999, and Matthew Barney.

In 1959, Gustav Metzger published "Auto-Destructive Art," a manifesto on the relationship between creation and destruction in art. In his scheme auto-destructives* were to be public monuments, created by collaborations between artists and scientists, that would symbolize the decay and disaster that resulted from the political and technological developments of the Cold War.[86] Metzger did not actually build these monuments, but in 1960 the sculptor Jean Tinguely made what would become the most celebrated artistic auto-destructive, *Homage to New York*, "a kinetic assemblage of junk and found objects meant to destroy itself in a performance that took place in MOMA's [Museum of Modern Art's] sculpture garden."[87] Tinguely stopped making auto-destructives in 1964, and the genre did not spread among visual artists. Metzger's influence might have been greater in another of the arts, however. Thus the English musician Pete Townshend, who had learned Metzger's theory as a student at Ealing Art College, made his show-ending auto-destructive act of smashing his guitar the trademark of his rock band, The Who. Townshend began the practice in 1964, and it quickly became famous; the band's singer, Roger Daltrey, later recalled that "After two years, people were just coming to see us smash up all our gear. The music meant nothing."[88]

The 1960s

The French conceptual artist Yves Klein dreamed of flying effortlessly into the void, and in 1960 he devised a new means of creating images that represented weightless human bodies in space. Under his direction, nude models would apply his trademark blue paint to their bodies, then press themselves against large sheets of paper tacked to the wall or spread on the floor. These paintings were first made at Klein's Paris apartment, in front of a small number of his friends. One of those present, the critic Pierre Restany, gave the works the name Klein subsequently adopted, of anthropometries.**[89] The use of "living brushes" was consistent with Klein's conceptual belief that the artist should conceive works of art but not personally produce them: "True 'painters and poets' don't paint and don't write poems."[90]

Also in 1960, Klein began to make cosmogonies** – paintings created by natural forces.[91] These were produced by painting leaves, grass, and plants and imprinting them on canvases, or by coloring sheets of paper or canvases with pigment, then exposing them to rain or wind.[92] Klein recalled one trip from Paris to Nice: "I placed a canvas, freshly coated with paint, upon the roof of my white Citroen. As I zoomed down Route Nationale 7 at the speed of 100 kilometers an hour, the heat, the cold, the light, the wind, and the rain all combined to age my canvas prematurely."[93] Like the anthropometries, the cosmogonies were conceived but not directly produced by the artist.

In 1958, Klein's obsession with space had led him to present an exhibition at Iris Clert's Paris gallery titled *Le Vide* (*The Void*) that consisted of empty space. The French artist Arman, a friend of Klein's, proposed that Klein's show should logically be followed by *Le Plein* (*The Full*), but it took two years to convince Clert, so Arman's show appeared in 1960, when he filled the gallery with trash.[94] This initiated Arman's production of poubelles** (trash cans), usually smaller, table-top works, consisting of discarded objects encased in plexiglass boxes.[95] Some of these were symbolic portraits of friends, for which the artist coaxed people to give up their favorite possessions to be permanently preserved. Arman's use of trash to make works of art symbolized the transience of men's lives, while the personalized collections further reflected the tastes and interests of individuals.

Arman also began making accumulations** in 1960.[96] Each of these comprised a large collection of a single type of manufactured object – such as headlights, alarm clocks, padlocks, ladies' shoes, or bottle caps – in a wooden box. Initially the objects were used domestic goods, while over time Arman began to choose new industrial goods. The size of the accumulations varied, depending on the artist's judgment of what constituted a "critical mass." Arman contended that he did not discover accumulation, but that it discovered him, for he saw spontaneous, man-made accumulations at flea markets, junk yards, and hardware stores. Accumulations were intended to display the power contained in masses of similar objects.[97]

Klein and Arman were both members of a group of young French artists that Pierre Restany named the Nouveaux Réalistes (New Realists). In 1960 another member of the group, César, exhibited sculptures he called compressions,** made by crushing automobile bodies into brightly colored blocks of steel.[98] Compressions might be made with whole auto bodies, or with collections of a single body part, such as bumpers. Crushing auto bodies allowed César to avoid the gestural methods of the Abstract Expressionists and the Tachistes, for the compressions were the product of a mechanical gesture of only one moment.[99]

In 1961 the French artist Niki de Saint Phalle began to make shot-reliefs** by shooting a rifle at bags of liquid paint suspended above reliefs made with plaster and other objects on wood.[100] When hit by bullets, the bags dripped paint down onto the plaster – in the words of Pierre Restany, "in a colorful fashion worthy of Pollock's best."[101] For de Saint Phalle, the act was symbolic: "I was shooting at my own violence and the violence of the times. By shooting at my own violence I no longer had to carry it inside of me like a burden."[102] She considered painting a communal activity, so she invited others to shoot; among those who participated in making shot-reliefs were Jean Tinguely, Yves Klein, Jasper Johns, and Robert Rauschenberg.[103]

In Rome in 1961, Piero Manzoni first signed human beings and declared them to be works of art, or living sculptures.**[104] An accompanying certificate of authenticity specified whether the individual was a work of art in whole, or only in the (body) part signed, and whether the person was always a work of art or only during certain activities. Among those in the highest category of works of art, in whole until death, were the artist Marcel Broodthaers and the linguist Umberto Eco.[105] Manzoni's action effectively extended Duchamp's readymades from manufactured objects to human beings. In 1969 the London-based artists Gilbert and George pronounced themselves living sculptures. Their art was initially made up of performances they called actions, the first of which, *The Singing Sculpture,* consisted of singing a music hall song, "Underneath the Arches," for eight hours on each of two consecutive days. Subsequently they have worked in a wide variety of forms, consistently aimed at making art more widely accessible and at breaking down artistic and societal taboos. Their art is always based on their own experiences, and they consider themselves to be living sculptures at all times. Gilbert and George have influenced Damien Hirst and other young British artists in their example of artists as performers, and in their enthusiasm for making art from everyday urban life.[106]

The Pop artist Claes Oldenburg made the first soft sculpture* in 1962.[107] These were originally made as props for happenings Oldenburg produced, but Oldenburg soon began to make large stuffed cloth articles of food, including hamburgers, ice cream cones, and slices of cake, which he presented at an exhibition at a New York gallery in 1962. Soft sculpture was quickly perceived as a radical challenge to traditional conceptions of sculpture, for instead of being rigid and resistant, Oldenburg's stuffed works were malleable and pliable.[108] The humor of Oldenburg's soft sculptures, and their surprising consistency, helped to make them one of the most distinctive contributions to early Pop art.

In 1962, Gerhard Richter made his first photopainting.**[109] He later recalled that "I had had enough of bloody painting, and painting from a photograph seemed to me the most moronic and inartistic thing that anyone could do." Working from photographs reduced the number of necessary decisions: "Not having to invent anything any more, forgetting everything you meant by painting – color, composition, space – and all the things you previously knew and thought."[110] Richter's photo paintings characteristically included the blurring and graininess of old photographs or amateur snapshots.

One of the most esoteric new genres was the creation of an English conceptual artist named John Latham. Latham developed a philosophy that held in part that instrumental reason and its tool, language, played a central role in the creation of social oppression and war. Beginning in 1964 his attack on language, and its institutionalization in books, was embodied in towers of books, or skoobs* (books spelled backwards), that he burned.[111] Book burning did not become popular among artists, and Latham appears to have been the sole artistic creator of skoobs.

It is not known exactly when the term installation* began to be used for art works, but sometime in the mid-1960s it emerged as a general name for environmental works, including assemblages and happenings.[112] Today many artists produce large, often room-sized works they call installations. These are extremely varied in intent and appearance, and share only the two characteristics that they usually involve a number of disparate objects, and they surround the viewer. Prominent artists whose current output consists primarily or entirely of installations include Christian Boltanski, Maurizio Cattelan, Tracey Emin, Roni Horn, Yayoi Kusama, and Bill Viola. Kristine Stiles observed that "By 1970, installation had become so prevalent and multifaceted that the French artist Daniel Buren would observe: 'Hasn't the term *installation* come to replace [the term] *exhibition?*' "[113]

Another label that first began to be used for works by visual artists during the mid-1960s is performance.*[114] This grew out of a tradition that included the work of Futurist and Dada artists early in the twentieth century, as well as collaborative works created by the composer John Cage, the choreographer Merce Cunningham, Robert Rauschenberg, and others at Black Mountain College in North Carolina in the early 1950s.[115] It is uncertain when the term performance began to be used for these multi-disciplinary activities, but the published notebooks of Carolee Schneeman, who became an important performance artist, contain discussions using the name performance art written in 1962–63.[116] Several of the most influential artists of the late 1960s and the 1970s became known for their live or videotaped performance works, including notably Joseph Beuys, Bruce Nauman, and Gilbert and George.

Two new genres originated in the art of Robert Smithson. The broader of the two, earthwork,** was first named by Smithson in a 1969 article, and came to be widely used to refer to the large landscape works he and such other artists as Walter De Maria and Michael Heizer constructed in remote areas.[117] The name appears to have been taken from the title of a science fiction novel, Brian Aldiss's *Earthworks*, that Smithson bought in the course of a documented excursion he had made in 1967.[118] The narrower and more specific term, non-site,** was devised by Smithson in 1968 to refer to the works he made for display in art galleries.[119] In Smithson's usage, the site works were the large-scale projects he created in, and from, the landscape, which could only be viewed in their original locations, while the non-sites were made up of documentation and natural material taken from those sites, to be displayed indoors.[120]

In 1968, the Minimalist artist Sol LeWitt began to make wall drawings.**[121] LeWitt explained that he "wanted to do a work of art that was as two-dimensional as possible," and that it consequently seemed "more natural to work directly on walls than to make a construction ... and then put the construction on the wall." In LeWitt's scheme, "the artist conceives and plans the wall drawing," which is then "realized by draftsmen."[122] Wall drawings can be moved from place to place, by recreating the work in a new location, but each is supposed to exist in only one place at a time, so when a new version is made, the old one is supposed to be painted over.

The 1970s

In 1973, while using the newly invented Polaroid SX-70 camera, Lucas Samaras discovered that while the photograph developed, its surface remained soft, and that he could manipulate the image by pressing and pushing the emulsion.[123] This allowed him to combine his earlier interests in transformation and photographic self-portraits.[124] The result was the photo-transformation,** in which Samaras's face and body appear distorted and mutilated.[125] Samaras has explained these images as the product of the fears that haunted him from his childhood in wartime Macedonia.[126]

The 1980s

In 1982, David Hockney began to use a Polaroid camera to make series of photographs of selected subjects, taken from different angles. He then assembled these series into composite images he called joiners.**[127] Hockney's purpose was to pursue Cubist discoveries about pictorial space, dispensing with the one-point perspective established in the Renaissance in favor of images that more accurately mimicked actual human perception, with "many points of focus and many moments."[128]

Young Geniuses

For forty-four of the new genres discussed above, it is possible to identify a particular innovator (or innovators, in the case of Hains and Villeglé) and a date of first appearance with reasonable confidence. For these genres, Table 6.1 shows the ages of these artists at the time of the innovations.

Pablo Picasso initiated this stream of innovations when he was 31 years old, and perhaps appropriately this is the overall median age of the forty-five artists listed in Table 6.1 when they created their new genres. Thirty-six of the forty-five innovators, or 80 percent were below the age of 35; apart from the experimental Dubuffet, only Lucio Fontana was above the age of 50 when he made an innovation. Table 6.1 thus clearly confirms that new genres are generally created by young conceptual innovators.

TABLE 6.1. *Ages of Artists at Time of Inventing New Genres*

Date	Genre	Artist	Age
1912	collage	Picasso	31
1912	papier collé	Braque	30
1913	counter-relief	Tatlin	28
1915	readymade	Duchamp	28
1916	biomorph	Arp	30
1916	papier dechiré	Arp	30
1916	constructed paintings	Arp	30
1919	merz	Schwitters	32
1919	Proun	Lissitzky	29
1921	rayogram	Man Ray	31
1922	photogram	Moholy-Nagy	27
1925	frottage	Ernst	34
1925	exquisite corpse	Breton	29
1930	light-space modulator	Moholy-Nagy	35
1932	mobile	Calder	34
1932	stabile	Calder	34
1933	involuntary sculptures	Brassaï	34
1946	spatial concepts	Fontana	47
1949	décollage	Hains	23
		Villeglé	23
1949	environment	Fontana	50
1953	assemblage	Dubuffet	52
1954	combine	Rauschenberg	29
1955	meta-matic	Tinguely	30
1957	achrome	Manzoni	24
1958	wrapping	Christo	23
1958	happening	Kaprow	31
1958	tagli	Fontana	59
1959	auto-destructive	Metzger	33
1960	cosmogonies	Klein	32
1960	poubelles	Arman	32
1960	accumulations	Arman	32
1960	compressions	César	32
1960	anthropometry	Klein	32
1961	living sculpture	Manzoni	28
1961	shot-reliefs	Saint Phalle	31
1962	photo paintings	Richter	30
1962	soft sculpture	Oldenburg	33
1964	skoob	Latham	43
1965	video	Paik	33
1968	non-site	Smithson	30
1968	wall drawing	LeWitt	40
1969	earthwork	Smithson	31
1973	photo-transformations	Samaras	37
1982	joiners	Hockney	45

Source: See text.

Conclusion

The twentieth century witnessed an unprecedented proliferation of artistic genres. In 1910, visual art consisted primarily of painting, and to a lesser extent sculpture. Today, less than one hundred years later, many visual artists spend most or all of their time making installations, videos, collages, performances, and a host of other types of work that did not exist in 1910. This has had profound implications for artists and their roles. Apart from the enormous changes in the appearance of art, the proliferation of genres has fragmented the art world. Early in the twentieth century, a great artist could influence nearly all advanced visual artists, but in contrast, a century later it is virtually impossible for any one artist to influence artists making such different types of art as painting, photographs, videos, and installation.

Surprisingly, very few of the new genres were the result of new technology. Video was of course a twentieth-century invention, but nearly all the other genres described above use technologies available in 1900.

The dramatic increase in new artistic genres was a product of both new practices and new attitudes. Not only did many artists want to do new things, but they often wanted to underscore the novelty of these new things, by giving them new names. The self-consciousness with which many artists devised new practices, as well as the attitude that celebrated the novelty of those practices, was a feature of the conceptual approach to art that accounted for nearly all the new genres discussed above. To a greater extent than had ever before been true, the art of the twentieth century was dominated by a rapid succession of conceptual movements, from Fauvism and Cubism onward. All of these conceptual movements were dominated by young artists. It is young practitioners who generally break rules most decisively and conspicuously in all intellectual disciplines. This is true not only because young practitioners, who are new to a field, may have less respect for its traditions, but also because their elders have become so accustomed to the rules of an activity that they are often hardly aware of the rules' existence, and impact. Seeing these rules with a fresh eye, brash young members of a discipline may consciously decide to depart from them. Creating a new genre is one obvious way of violating the existing rules.

The enumeration of new genres presented in this chapter raises some puzzles that have not been analyzed, or even recognized, by art scholars. A striking puzzle involves chronology. The roll call of young conceptual innovators carried out above ends abruptly with the 1960s: only Lucas

Samaras named a new genre in the 1970s, and only the middle-aged David Hockney created one in the 1980s. Thus the 1960s, which witnessed the creation of more than a dozen new genres, was followed by three decades that together produced only two. It would appear that artists working in the 1970s, 1980s, and 1990s were no longer concerned with creating new genre trademarks for their movements or their own work. It should be emphasized that the small number of new genres christened after 1970 does not mean that the creation of new art forms that violated the boundaries of existing genres had ceased. Important young conceptual artists in fact continued to create new forms. It is easy to imagine the 23-year-old Cindy Sherman, beginning to make the *Untitled Film Stills* in 1977, declaring that she had invented the un-self-portrait; or the 26-year-old Jeff Koons, putting a Hoover vacuum in an acrylic box in 1981 and naming it a consumer case; or the 26-year-old Damien Hirst, suspending a tiger shark in a vitrine in 1991 and calling it an animal house. That neither these artists nor their admirers gave genre names to these novel art forms may have been a product of the general recognition that it was no longer necessary. In 1996, for example, Hirst declared that whatever he did, "it's all art to me," and explained that "I wanted to be stopped, and no one has stopped me. I just wanted to find out where the boundaries were. So far, I've found out there aren't any."[129] Thus perhaps by 1970 the creation of new genres had become so thoroughly taken for granted in the art world that there was no longer a need to call attention to it: photographs of the artist in disguise are automatically associated with Sherman, just as consumer goods and dead animals in vitrines are automatically associated with Koons and Hirst, respectively, even without the self-conscious device of a genre name. Novelty is so pervasive that it is almost assumed that important conceptual artists will produce a new trademark product.

Early in the twentieth century, the explosion of new genres was triggered by the young genius who became the most dominant artist of the century. When Picasso invented collage in 1912, he not only made a specific contribution that soon led to extensions by Braque, Tatlin, Duchamp, and other young conceptual artists, but he also provided a new model of artistic behavior that became an inspiration for many other young artists throughout the century, of the daring and iconoclastic young innovator. As early as 1912, the older, experimental artist Wassily Kandinsky could already foresee what he considered the unfortunate consequences of the younger artist's versatile brilliance, as he described Picasso as a fearless mountain climber: "often driven wildly onward, Picasso throws himself from one external means to another. If a chasm lies between them, Picasso makes a wild leap, and there he is, standing on the other side, much to the horror of his incredibly numerous followers."[130] From Duchamp and Arp through Manzoni, Smithson, and beyond, many young conceptual artists learned the lesson that was a key part of Picasso's legacy, that horrifying the art world could be a direct route to importance.

7

And Now for Something Completely Different

The Versatility of Conceptual Innovators

Introduction

In recent decades, it has become fashionable for scholars of art history to disdain systematic comparison or generalization. Much recent scholarship in the discipline considers one artist, or even one work, at a time. Art historians' unwillingness, or inability, to carry out systematic comparative analyses has often led to a failure to recognize and understand important patterns of artistic behavior. This chapter examines a striking example of such a failure, in which a form of creative behavior that has become enormously important in the art of the twentieth century has been neglected because every instance of it has been treated as idiosyncratic.

The following section of this chapter documents an observation that art historians have made about what they consider a puzzling practice of modern painters. Specifically, in three separate instances, a scholar commented on the behavior of a single painter, then attempted to explain the behavior by considering only that one artist. Although the observation was precisely the same in all three cases, the scholars were different in each case, the artist in question was also different, and none of the scholars showed any awareness of any other instance of this observation. My contention is that the failure to recognize the commonality of the artistic behavior at issue precluded satisfactory explanation of it. The practice noted by the scholars is in fact not unique to any artist, but rather is characteristic of a class of artists. The general explanation for the three painters' behavior is both simpler and more powerful than explanations that appeal to individual idiosyncrasy. Understanding this explanation furthermore allows us to recognize the same phenomenon in other arts.

The One-Man Group Exhibition: Three Episodes

In 1985, the eminent art historian Meyer Schapiro began an essay titled "The Unity of Picasso's Art" with the following observation:

Picasso's art presents itself to us today as an example of a lifework that one cannot describe in terms of any single set of characteristics. If the works of Pablo Picasso were not identified directly with his name, if they were shown together in a big exhibition, it would be rather difficult to say that they were the work of one man.[1]

In 1996 the art historian David Campbell opened a paper titled "Plotting Polke" with the following observation:

One of the most intriguing aspects of Sigmar Polke's work is the way it defies attempts to read it as a unified project. So marked is the sense of aesthetic and thematic disjuncture in the work that visiting a Polke exhibition is often like wandering around a group show.[2]

And in an article written in 2002, the philosopher and critic Arthur Danto observed that:

visitors to the magnificent Museum of Modern Art retrospective of [Gerhard] Richter's work since 1962 . . . are certain to be baffled by the fact that he seems to vacillate between realism and abstraction, or even between various styles of abstraction, often at the same time. These vacillations seemed to me so extreme when I first saw a retrospective of Richter's work in Chicago in 1987, that it looked like I was seeing some kind of group show.[3]

It is striking that three different observers, writing about three different artists, all used exactly the same metaphor, of a one-man exhibition that appeared to be a group show. In all three cases, furthermore, the phenomenon of an artist producing unrelated works was not merely a puzzling practice involving appearances, but raised deeper problems for the observers. For Schapiro, it raised a question about commitment:

There exists in [Picasso's] practice a radical change with respect to the very concept of working, of production. Working involves, at least within our tradition, the commitment to a necessary way of working. If you can work in any other way you please, then no one way has a necessity; there is an element of caprice or arbitrariness of choice.[4]

Campbell made a similar observation:

As a result of this aesthetic mobility, doubts arise about his artistic integrity . . . This reaction, no doubt anticipated by Polke, has the unfortunate consequence of questioning the control, conviction, and seriousness of his artistic programme.[5]

And Danto also made a similar comment:

For most artists in America, it is important that they be stylistically identifiable, as if their style is their brand. To change styles too often inevitably would have been read as a lack of conviction.[6]

In the essays quoted, Schapiro, Campbell, and Danto all proceeded to discuss the problem of why an artist would work in multiple styles, and all offered explanations. It is not my concern here to evaluate those explanations, except to note that each concentrated on the work and practice of the single artist under consideration, without systematic comparison or examination of the work of any other artist. I believe that these explanations cannot allow us to understand the basic source of the variety of styles used by each of the three artists, nor can they allow us to resolve satisfactorily the question of these artists' integrity. For I believe that there is a general explanation for these three cases, that also applies to the work and practices of many other artists.

Conceptual Innovators

The practice of an artist working in multiple styles is characteristic of a number of conceptual innovators. This is a class of artists whose work is intended to communicate their emotions or ideas. Conceptual painters often plan their works carefully, to carry out specific goals. In a general description of conceptual innovators, in 2001 I wrote the following:

Because their goals are precise, conceptual artists are often satisfied that they have produced one or more works that achieve a specific purpose. Unlike experimental artists, whose inability to achieve their goals often ties them to a single problem for a whole career, the conceptual artist's ability to be satisfied that a problem has been solved can free him to pursue new goals. The careers of some important conceptual artists have consequently been marked by a series of innovations, each very different from the others.[7]

Picasso, Polke, and Richter are all examples of important conceptual innovators who have made more than a single innovation.

Table 7.1 presents the distribution over the three artists' careers of all the illustrations of their work contained in a large number of survey textbooks of art history. This shows that Picasso and Polke both fit the pattern most common to conceptual innovators, of producing their most important contributions early in their careers. For Picasso this was the invention of Cubism in 1907, at the age of 26. Art historians

TABLE 7.1. *Percentage Distributions of Textbook Illustrations over Artists' Careers*

Age	20–9	30–9	40–9	50–9	60–9	70–9	80–9	90–9	Total
Artist									
Picasso	35	25	17	14	4	2	2	1	100
Polke	67	7	19	7	0	–	–	–	100
Richter	0	40	7	47	6	0	–	–	100

Source: Picasso: See Table 2.5.
Polke and Richter: Cory Bell, *Modern Art* (New York: Watson-Guptill, 2000); Jonathan Fineberg, *Art Since 1940*, 2nd ed. (New York: Harry N. Abrams, 2000); David Hopkins, *After Modern Art, 1945-2000* (Oxford: Oxford University Press, 2000); Martin Kemp, ed., *The Oxford History of Western Art* (Oxford: Oxford University Press, 2000); Bernard Blistene, *A History of 20th-Century Art* (Paris: Flammarion, 2001); Edward Lucie-Smith, *Movements in Art Since 1945*, new ed. (London: Thames and Hudson, 2001); Klaus Richter, *Art* (Munich: Prestel, 2001); Michael Archer, *Art Since 1960*, new ed. (London: Thames and Hudson, 2002); Amy Dempsey, *Art in the Modern Era* (New York: Harry N. Abrams, 2002); Hugh Honour and John Fleming, *The Visual Arts: A History*, 6th ed. (New York: Harry N. Abrams, 2002); H.H. Arnason, *A History of Modern Art*, 5th ed. (Upper Saddle River, NJ: Prentice Hall, 2004); Sam Hunter, John Jacobus, and Daniel Wheeler, *Modern Art*, 3rd ed. (New York: Vendome Press, 2004); Pascale Le Thorel-Daviot, *Nouveau Dictionnaire des Artistes Contemporains* (Paris: Larousse, 2004); Gill Perry and Paul Wood, eds., *Themes in Contemporary Art* (New Haven: Yale University Press, 2004); Hal Foster, Rosalind Krauss, Yve-Alain Bois, and Benjamin Buchloh, *Art Since 1900* (New York: Thames and Hudson, 2004); Ingo Walther, ed., *Art of the 20th Century*, 2 vols. (Cologne: Taschen, 2005).

have analyzed in detail the sources of Cubism, as Picasso synthesized elements taken from African art, early Iberian sculpture, and the paintings of Cézanne and Gauguin.[8] Yet the synthesis was a revolutionary one, for it challenged the traditional purpose of painting. As John Berger observed, with Cubism

The concept of painting as it had existed since the Renaissance was overthrown. The idea of holding up a mirror to nature became a nostalgic one... Painting became a schematic art. The painter's task was no longer to represent or imitate what existed... The metaphorical model of Cubism is the *diagram*: the diagram being a visible, symbolic representation of invisible processes, forces, structures.[9]

Thus the young Picasso pioneered a conceptual form of art in which the artist would no longer present visual descriptions of objects, but would instead symbolize his knowledge of them.

Polke's most important contribution was the invention of German Pop art in 1963, when he was 22 years old. Polke's early Pop works were influenced by illustrations of paintings by Warhol and Lichtenstein that he first saw in 1962. He followed Warhol in taking images from magazine photographs, and like Lichtenstein he constructed these images by mimicking the benday dots that form photographs in newspapers and magazines. But Polke adapted both of these devices to his own purposes, as he avoided the glamorous individuals and sensational events chosen by Warhol in favor of more pedestrian subjects, and he gave greater emphasis than Lichtenstein to the benday dots, thus making the photographic images of his paintings compete with the patterns created by the irregularly colored dots. The result was recognizable as Pop art, but in a form distinctively different from those of the American artists.[10] Yet German Pop art shared its conceptual basis with its older American relative, as it used mechanical reproduction, or its appearance, to recreate images drawn from popular culture.

Richter's career pattern is quite different. The absence of any illustrations of his work prior to the age of 30 is understandable as a consequence of his delayed exposure to advanced art. Richter was born and raised in East Germany, and his early studies in art were done there. His first opportunity to study advanced art did not occur until he moved to West Germany in 1961. When he enrolled in the Düsseldorf Kunstakademie in that year he was 29, nine years older than his classmate Polke. He joined Polke in creating German Pop art in 1963, while both were still students.

The early innovations of conceptual innovators are generally formal ones, made by synthesizing earlier artists' work. This was true of Picasso's early innovations in Cubism, and of Polke's and Richter's early Pop art. In most cases, conceptual artists' creativity declines considerably after these early contributions, generally because they become accustomed to working in the style or with the technique they invented in their youth. In some cases, however, these artists may be jarred out of this process of repetition. Such was the case with both Picasso and Richter.

In 1937, at the age of 56, Picasso painted *Guernica* in response to the destruction of the Basque town of Guernica by German bombers during the Spanish Civil War. This painting became one of the most important works not only of Picasso's career, but of twentieth-century art. In 1988, at the age of 56, Richter executed fifteen paintings based on photographs of the dead bodies of three members of the urban guerilla Baader-Meinhof group, who had died in a German prison in 1977. These paintings became the most controversial, and celebrated, works of Richter's career. What is clear is that these unusual creative revivals, relatively late in these two conceptual artists' careers, were the product of enormously strong stimuli. Thus while he was working on *Guernica*, Picasso declared his outrage against the Spanish fascists: "My whole life as an artist has been nothing more than a continuous struggle against reaction and the death of art. How could anybody think for a moment that I could be in agreement with reaction and death?"[11] Similarly, at a press conference in 1988, Richter spoke of his need to make his Baader-Meinhof paintings: "The deaths of the terrorists, and the related events both before and after, stand for a horror that distressed me and has haunted me as unfinished business ever since, despite all my efforts to suppress it."[12] The declining creativity of conceptual artists with age is not a physiological phenomenon, but is rather the product of habit, as an artist's ways of thinking become ingrained over time. In some cases, including those of Picasso and Richter, the artist's reaction to an external event is so powerful that it destroys some of the artist's habits, and results in a novel artistic contribution.

Picasso famously declared that "I paint objects as I think them, not as I see them."[13] Richter equally expressed his belief in the conceptual nature of art, writing to a friend that "Pictures are the idea in visual or pictorial form." Richter often paints from photographs, and he has explained that this eliminates the need to make decisions in the process of executing his works: "When I paint from a photograph, conscious thinking is eliminated." The image was predetermined and preconceived: "by painting from photographs, I was relieved of the need to choose or construct a subject."[14]

In 1984, Richter explained his stylistic versatility to an interviewer, recalling that earlier in his career he had deliberately "created some space for myself, protected myself, as it were, against being tied down, in order to maintain the freedom to do what I like – to try anything I like, and not to become an artist-painter who is tied down to a single trick." He recognized that there were benefits associated with working in a single style: "you can be very successful with a trick like that, because it makes you easier to recognize." But he observed that his strategy of deliberately varying his styles could also lead to success: "it works this way too. It has now become my identifying characteristic that my work is all over the place."[15] The critic Peter Schjeldahl agreed, as he observed of Richter that "His range of styles – from Pop to Minimalist to Photo-Realist and several varieties of abstract – has seemed perversely promiscuous, as if he were heaping obloquy on the very idea of style."[16]

Integrity and Style

In questioning the seriousness or integrity of these conceptual artists, Schapiro, Campbell, and Danto followed a number of earlier observers.

As early as 1919, Piet Mondrian wrote from Paris to his fellow painter Theo van Doesburg in Holland with a report on the art world: "I also went to the Picasso exhibition. Old and new work, not much changed, but I thought his latest work less serious, less convincing. I hear he is doing other work, not to make money, but *because he wants to be versatile*!! That's right: his work can't be convincing then, can it?"[17] In 1921, the German artist Oskar Schlemmer wrote to a friend of his reaction to a book that surveyed Picasso's career: "I was amazed at the versatility of the man. An actor, the comic genius among artists? For everything is there: he could easily assume the role of any artist of the past or of any modern painter."[18] Interestingly, however, in 1921 the painter and critic Amédée Ozenfant had specifically explained Picasso's practice. Writing in a Paris journal, Ozenfant remarked on the clarity of Picasso's intent, and the precision with which he expressed himself: "When he paints a picture, he knows what he wants to say and what kind of picture will in fact say it: his forms and colors are judiciously chosen to achieve the desired end, and he uses them like the words of a vocabulary." Continuing the parallel between plastic forms and language, Ozenfant responded to critics who believed that Picasso's execution of representational works meant that he had repudiated Cubism: "Can such people not understand that Cubism and figurative painting are two different languages, and that a painter is free to choose either of them as he may judge it better suited to what he has to say?"[19]

Ozenfant anticipated the concerns of Schapiro, Campbell, and Danto, and his response to them was thus to explain the attitude of the conceptual artist who is free to change forms and styles as he changes problems. Implicitly, these three observers were all judging the conceptual artists in question by the standard of experimental artists. A colleague of Campbell's, writing in the same symposium, did this explicitly, comparing Polke's practice with that of the experimental Abstract Expressionists:

[Polke] signals no single-minded commitment to a worthy programme (such as the pursuit of pure painterliness associated with American Abstract Expressionism, the paradigmatic intentionality of post-war avant-gardes). Critics who are primed to look for evidence of such integrity of purpose, of prolonged "struggle" with an heroic problematic, find none in Polke, and may assume therefore that he is opportunistic and undiscriminating.[20]

The conceptual Picasso's ability to choose styles to fit his changing ideas could not have differed more from that of an experimental painter like Cézanne, who undertook a lifelong quest to create a style that would allow him to achieve a single goal, and the same is true of the conceptual Polke and Richter in comparison with the experimental Abstract Expressionists. These conceptual artists' periodic alternation of styles, like their rapid development of new styles over the course of their careers, reflected the basis of their art in ideas that could be formulated and expressed quickly, whereas the experimental artists' steadfast commitment to a single style, that could evolve only gradually over time, was a product of the visual nature of their art, and the impossibility of fully achieving their elusive goals. It is critical to recognize that rapid changes of approach and style, which would signal insincerity on the part of an experimental artist, can be signs of vitality for conceptual innovators.

Picasso as Prototype

> This will be Picasso's main contribution to art. To have been able to start from a new source, and to keep this freshness with regard to whatever new expressions mark the different epochs of his career . . . Picasso in each one of his facets, has made clear his intention to keep free from preceding achievements.
>
> Marcel Duchamp, 1943[21]

A succession of observers have commented on Picasso's frequent and sudden changes of style. As early as 1912, in his celebrated book, *On the Spiritual in Art*, the artist Wassily Kandinsky remarked on Picasso's abrupt and radical changes, and noted that these shocked even Picasso's admirers:

> Led on always by the need for self-expression, often driven wildly onward, Picasso throws himself from one external means to another. If a chasm lies between them, Picasso makes a wild leap, and there he is, standing on the other side, much to the horror of his incredibly numerous followers. They had just thought they had caught up with him; now they must begin the painful descent and start the climb again.[22]

In the same year, Roger Fry observed that "It is dangerous and difficult to speak of Picasso, for he is changing with kaleidoscopic rapidity . . . He is the most gifted, the most incredibly facile of artists."[23] In 1920, when Picasso was still not yet 40 years old, the English critic Clive Bell remarked that "His career has been a series of discoveries, each of which he has rapidly developed. A highly original and extremely happy conception enters his head . . . Forthwith he sets himself to analyze it . . . Before long he has established what looks like an infallible method for producing an effect of which, a few months earlier, no one had so much as dreamed."[24] In 1925 the Spanish artist Josep Llorens Artigas observed that Picasso painted "with neither law nor system, and he adopts for each work original attitudes and solutions, thus creating that stylistic inconsistency which is the dominant note in his painting, we might say, 'his own style.'"[25] In 1928 the German poet and critic Carl Einstein recognized that Picasso was a "pluralistic spirit," who could not be constrained by any single method, but who worked in a "polyphony of styles." Einstein described Picasso as "a man who has blown apart, as none other has, the limitations, the obsessional narrowness, of the practices of art."[26] Decades later the English novelist and critic John Berger observed that Picasso's work was made up of "sudden inexplicable transformations," and declared that "In the life work of no other artist is each group of works so independent of those which have just gone before, or so irrelevant to those which are to follow."[27] Picasso's biographer Pierre Cabanne made the same point by contrasting Picasso and Cézanne: "There was not one Picasso, but ten, twenty, always different, unpredictably changing, and in this he was the opposite of a Cézanne, whose work... followed that logical, reasonable course to fruition."[28] Meyer Schapiro remarked on a consequence of Picasso's changes: "There is no example in all history of another painter who has been able to create such a diversity of works and to give them the power of successful art."[29]

Art scholars have been struck, however, not only by the fact that Picasso frequently changed styles, but that he often alternated between two styles, using two very different manners to make different works at the same time. Thus Schapiro remarked that in 1921, "In the morning he made Cubist paintings; in the afternoon he made Neoclassical paintings." In a recognition similar to that of Ozenfant, Schapiro then observed: "So that for him the two styles were both available and belonged to two different aspects of his personality."[30] Jack Flam later echoed Schapiro, noting that "As early as 1915 Picasso had begun making meticulously rendered realistic drawings, and by the early 1920s he was alternating between a full-blown neoclassical style and more planar and abstract Synthetic Cubist imagery."[31]

What was startling about Picasso's practice was not simply that he made significant changes in style: Schapiro pointed out, for example, that in the 1880s an English writer had remarked that major works Raphael had made a decade apart could have been by different artists.[32] What was novel in Picasso's approach was the frequency of his changes, and his ability to shift back and forth between styles. Flam reflected on the latter:

Picasso was able effectively and convincingly to employ conflicting styles at will, and he used these with great energy – another instance of his uncommon sensitivity to the arbitrariness of different languages. In fact, he was probably the first Western artist to insist willfully and persistently on the relative arbitrariness of the means of pictorial representation.[33]

Picasso thus appears to mark a turning point, for the first time using stylistic change as a deliberate strategy, a systematic practice that he used to achieve multiple goals. The English critic David Sylvester recognized this when he explained in 1996 why Picasso himself had been the key problem facing critics in the twentieth century: "Picasso is a kind of artist who couldn't have existed before this century, since his art is a celebration of this century's introduction of a totally promiscuous eclecticism into the practice of art."[34] In a century marked by a heightened demand for innovation in art, Picasso's demonstration of how an individual artist could innovate frequently and radically became an inspiration for some of the most imaginative conceptual artists who came after him.

In a rare extended interview he gave to a friend in 1923, Picasso expressed his belief that the artist was free to choose styles as he wished, because styles were no more than forms of communication. Thus he declared that "We all know that Art is not truth. Art is a lie that makes us realize truth... The artist must know the manner whereby to convince others of the truthfulness of his lies." He explained that he chose styles that suited the problem at hand: "If the subjects I have wanted to express have suggested different ways of expression I have never hesitated to adopt them... Whenever I had something to say, I have said it in the manner in which I have felt it ought to be said. Different motives inevitably require different methods of expression." One key consequence of this he stressed was that changes in an artist's style should not be interpreted as growth or improvement, but should be recognized merely as a succession: "Variation does not mean evolution. If an artist varies his mode of expression this only means that he has changed his manner of thinking, and in changing, it might be for the better or it might be for the worse." He insisted that his own history was a case in point: "The several manners I have used in my art must not be considered as an evolution, or as steps toward an unknown ideal of painting. All I have ever made was made for the present."[35]

Late in his life, Cézanne wrote to his friend and dealer Ambroise Vollard of his frustration:

I am working doggedly, for I see the promised land before me. Shall I be like the Hebrew leader or shall I be able to enter? ...
    I have made some progress. Why so late and with such difficulty? Is art really a priesthood that demands the pure in heart who must belong to it entirely?[36]

Picasso understood the importance of Cézanne's art not only for his own innovations, but for the advanced art of the early twentieth century in general: thus in 1943 he told a friend that Cézanne "was my one and only master...He was like a father to us all."[37] Yet unlike Cézanne, for Picasso art was not a lifelong quest along a single path toward an unknown goal of the true style, but rather the expression of a series of ideas, often unrelated, using whatever means were appropriate. Declaring that "when I paint my object is to show what I have found and not what I am looking for," Picasso became a model for many later conceptual finders.[38] In changing styles at will, he also became a prototype of a new form of conceptual artist, for whom style would not be a matter of integrity, but merely a convenient vehicle for expression.

Followers

The analysis presented above improves our understanding of the methods and art of Picasso, Polke, and Richter. Yet the significance of the analysis extends far beyond these three important artists – to other painters, and to practitioners of other arts.

Considering first other visual artists, versatility has been a characteristic of a number of the most important conceptual innovators of the twentieth century. A prime early example is Marcel Duchamp. In his 1913 book, *The Cubist Painters*, the poet and critic Guillaume Apollinaire began his treatment of Duchamp's work with a comment that parallels those of Schapiro, Campbell, and Danto, as he observed that "Marcel Duchamp has not yet painted enough pictures and his work is too varied for us to assess his true talent from the available evidence."[39] Nearly a century later, the conceptual artist William Anastasi recalled that when he first saw a collection of Duchamp's art, "What struck me about it was not only that Duchamp's work was different from everybody else's, but that every Duchamp was so completely different from every other Duchamp."[40] Francis Naumann observed that Duchamp's "working method involved a constant search for alternatives – alternatives not only to accepted artistic practice, but also to his own earlier work."[41] John Coplans remarked that "Duchamp is the preeminent example of the didactic revolutionary among artists. Duchamp made each of his works, step by step, a special lesson. Never repeating himself, he made of inconsistency an unbreakable law."[42] William Rubin declared of the period 1911–15, when Duchamp was in his mid-20s, that "No four years in the work of any other modern painter . . . witness so many radical departures in method and idea." Rubin understood that Duchamp could change his art so quickly and decisively because of his conceptual approach: "Duchamp advances speculatively, not by painting but *through cerebration*; the finished work represents the plastic re-creation of a reality which has grown to maturity in the mind."[43]

Duchamp's variations occurred within a very different volume of output from that of Picasso, for unlike Picasso, who made many works within each of his adopted styles, Duchamp made very few works of art. Early in his career, the rejection of his *Nude Descending a Staircase, No. 2* by the 1912 Salon des Indépendants, because the judges considered it an attack on Cubism, led Duchamp to the conclusion that that movement had grown dogmatic and rigid in just a few years, and prompted him to vow never to become set in his own taste. Because he reasoned that taste was a product of habit, he determined to avoid repetition. It was in view of this that he once remarked that "I've had thirty-three ideas; I've made thirty-three paintings."[44] Duchamp was among the most protean of conceptual innovators, and his career was marked by the production of a series of works that had little in common other than their conceptual origins and their purpose of undermining basic conventions of Western art.

Late in his life, Duchamp recalled that his many early abrupt changes stemmed from an attitude that he had shared with Francis Picabia, another conceptual painter who was his closest friend when the two were beginning their careers: "Fundamentally, I had a mania for change, like Picabia. One does something for six months, a year, and one goes on to something else. That's what Picabia did all his life."[45] Picabia recognized his conceptual orientation early in his career, when his grandfather, an amateur photographer, warned him to give up painting, arguing that color photography would make painting obsolete. The young artist rejected that advice, thinking that "You can photograph a landscape, but not the forms that I have in my head."[46] William Camfield, a biographer of Picabia, observed that "his art functioned with a responsiveness approaching that of speech. It was called up to express his thoughts, emotions and reveries."[47] In a tribute to Picabia, Duchamp described his career as "a kaleidoscopic series of art experiences... hardly related to one another in their external appearances." Duchamp considered his old friend a liberator: "In his fifty years of painting Picabia has consistently avoided adhering to any formula or wearing a badge. He could be called the greatest exponent of freedom in art."[48]

Picabia made frequent changes in style a deliberate policy, declaring that "If you want to have clean ideas, change them as often as you change your shirts."[49] Camfield noted that over a career of fifty years his paintings "ranged over styles related to Impressionism, Neo-Impressionism, Fauvism, Cubism, abstract art, figurative art, Dada and Surrealism."[50] Picabia was the only child of an affluent family, and the combination of his opulent lifestyle and artistic versatility caused critics to question his sincerity and commitment: "Early in his career, Picabia was labeled a millionaire joker."[51] Picabia understood that this perception was the cost of what he considered the proper approach to art, and advised other artists that "There is only one way to save your life; sacrifice your reputation."[52]

Like many other conceptual artists, Picabia's styles usually grew directly out of the work of earlier artists. Thus Camfield observed that "So frequently... was Picabia's work an apparent response or reaction to the art of others that this phenomenon looms as a basic element in his creative process."[53] Roberto Ohrt stressed the enormous range of these sources: "The spectrum of quotes that Picabia uses in his art points to a lexical archive containing visual art throughout the ages and from all regions."[54] Camfield concluded that both Picabia's use of earlier art and his need for change "amounted to much more than the inconstancy of a playboy artist: it was a profound element of his character."[55] And, also like many other conceptual artists, Picabia was skeptical of the idea that an artist might improve with age. Thus late in his life he told a young artist that "Experience is absolutely useless."[56]

Man Ray was a close friend of both Duchamp and Picabia. He collaborated with Duchamp on a series of artistic works, including a celebrated photograph, *Elevage de poussière*, a close-up picture Man Ray made of dust that had settled on Duchamp's *Large Glass*, that the two artists both signed.[57] Man Ray began his career as a painter, but became widely known as a photographer. As a Dada and later Surrealist, he invented a method for making photographs without a camera, that he named Rayographs, and he made a number of Surrealist objects. An admirer observed that "Critics were confused by an artist who so easily turned from one medium to another."[58] On one occasion, when Man Ray was asked why he had painted his Paris street in an academic style that contrasted sharply with his Surrealist paintings, he replied that "I did this simply because I was not supposed to – that some of my contemporaries feel the urge also to do such a work but do not dare – and I enjoyed contradicting myself."[59] Duchamp saluted the conceptual nature of Man Ray's photography, writing that "it was his achievement to treat the camera as he treated the paint brush, a mere instrument at the service of the mind."[60]

The painter Richard Hamilton, who was one of the key figures in developing English Pop art, in 1956 systematically constructed a collage, titled *Just what is it that makes today's homes so different, so appealing?*, that became a Pop icon and one of the most important works of art of the twentieth century.[61] Yet Hamilton made no other works in the same style, and throughout his career his art has been marked by extreme diversity. Harold Rosenberg observed that "Hamilton's career is one of continual transition."[62] As Richard Morphet wrote in the catalogue to a 1970 retrospective of Hamilton's work, "Before as well as after 1956, Hamilton had painted each work in the style best suited to it, however sharp an idiomatic shift this might entail."[63]

Early in his career, Hamilton made a series of drawings to illustrate Joyce's *Ulysses*. To reflect Joyce's verbal stylistic changes, each of Hamilton's illustrations was done in a different style, as he tried to create visual equivalents for Joyce's verbal devices.[64] Hamilton later reflected that studying *Ulysses* had taught him a lesson that he applied to his art: "Joyce's readiness to ape the manner of other writers and genres . . . freed me from inhibitions about the uniquely personal mark that every painter is supposed to strive for."[65]

The English art historian Edward Lucie-Smith recognized the conceptual source of Hamilton's variations in style, observing that his "productions tend to differ radically from one another because each is the embodiment of an idea and the idea itself has been allowed to dominate the material form."[66] David Sylvester remarked that Hamilton's development as an artist was marked by unpredictability, and explained that this was a product of the fact that his works were generally exercises, in which the subjects were dictated by Hamilton's continuing interest in understanding new styles: "he first gets interested in some form or other of visual communication and . . . he then finds the sorts of subject-matter which suit that language or technique or method."[67]

Hamilton was a devoted follower of Duchamp; he spent several years translating and publishing Duchamp's notes for *The Large Glass*, and in 1966 he produced a replica of that work, which Duchamp co-signed.[68]

In 1977, Hamilton wrote that he admired Duchamp above other artists: "I've found his work more interesting, more exciting, more durable, than any other." He respected Duchamp for "the variety in his work. He covered so much ground... Once he'd done something, he was likely to turn his attention to another thing." Hamilton tried to do the same with his own art: "In this century, at all events, there are no techniques more valid than others."[69]

Jasper Johns described Robert Rauschenberg as the artist who "invented the most since Picasso."[70] Early in his career Rauschenberg made a series of radical innovations, all the embodiments of new ideas, and all motivated by his stated goal of working in the gap between art and life. Among these early works was a drawing by Willem de Kooning that Rauschenberg carefully erased. Rauschenberg explained that "the whole idea just came from my wanting to know whether a drawing could be made out of erasing"; the critic Harold Rosenberg described it as a turning point in contemporary art:

Art-historically, the erasing would be seen as a symbolic act of liberation from the pervasive force of Abstract Expressionism... "Erased de Kooning" became the cornerstone of a new academy, devoted to replacing the arbitrary self of the artist with predefined processes and objectives – that is to say, Minimalism and Conceptualism.[71]

Rauschenberg's most celebrated innovation was his creation of a new artistic genre in 1954, at the age of 29. During that year he began to attach more and more real objects to his paintings – "I think a picture is more like the real world when it's made out of the real word" – until the works became three-dimensional and often free-standing, prompting Rauschenberg to give them a new name, of "combine."[72] Two of the early combines, *Bed* (1955) and *Monogram* (1959), are among the half-dozen American art works of the 1950s and early 1960s that are most often reproduced in textbooks of art history.[73]

The diversity of Rauschenberg's work has troubled many critics. Thus Calvin Tomkins conceded that "There would always be critics for whom Rauschenberg was too protean, too experimental, or too outrageous to be taken seriously as an artist," and Robert Mattison remarked that "The majority of commentators have viewed Rauschenberg's art as a random accumulation of unrelated objects and images, and the artist himself has encouraged such interpretations."[74] Throughout his career, Rauschenberg has demonstrated his desire to create new works unrelated to his earlier ones. In 1964, Rauschenberg received his first major honor when he was awarded first prize for painting at the Venice Biennale. The next day, he telephoned from Venice to a friend in New York, to ask him to go to Rauschenberg's studio and destroy all his old silk screens. According to Calvin Tomkins, "There were about a hundred and fifty screens all told, representing a sizable financial investment as well as a rich bank of images. Destroying them was a form of insurance against the pressure to repeat himself."[75] Recently Rauschenberg explained that he tries to clear his mind before he begins to work: "Everything I can remember, and everything I know, I have probably already done, or somebody else has." He regards the accumulation of knowledge as his enemy: "Knowing more only encourages your limitations."[76]

Controversy still surrounds much of Rauschenberg's work, but there is little disagreement on two propositions. One is that his influence on recent art has been enormous: so for example Arthur Danto wrote in 1997 that "the artistic mainstream today is very largely Rauschenbergian."[77] The other is that, like many conceptual innovators, Rauschenberg's significant contributions were made early in his career. As the English critic Richard Cork regretfully concluded in 1981, "No *enfant* was more *terrible* than Rauschenberg in his heyday, but the trouble is that even the most precocious child has to grow up. Now well into his fifties, he has long since outlived the effervescence which once gave his work such an infectious sense of involvement with urban life."[78]

Andy Warhol's friend and biographer, David Bourdon, wrote that "Warhol strove to be a jack-of-all-arts. It wasn't enough for him to be recognized merely as an artist, filmmaker, and show-business entrepreneur. He fantasized about having a hit movie playing at Radio City Music Hall, a Broadway show at the Winter Garden, a television special, a book on the bestseller list, a Top-40 record, and the cover of *Life*. He truly believed he could keep several careers going simultaneously, winning acclaim in all of them."[79] Although he didn't accomplish all those goals, Warhol did make significant contributions in areas far from painting, most notably with movies. In a history of film, Robert Sklar wrote in 1993 that "The most significant alternative filmmaker of the 1960s may turn out to be the famed Pop artist Andy Warhol."[80] In 1966, the director and critic Jonas Mekas reviewed Warhol's *The Chelsea Girls* in *The Village Voice* as "a very important film." He declared that "This is the first time I see in cinema an interesting solution of narrative techniques that enable cinema to present life in the complexity and richness achieved by modern literature."[81] The critic Geoff Andrew observed that Warhol's style in film raised questions about the nature of the medium, and remarked that

"It is perhaps appropriate therefore that its relationship to mainstream cinema is also primarily conceptual."[82]

David Hockney, the most important English painter of his generation, is a versatile conceptual artist who was brilliant early in his career.[83] In 1962, his final year as a student at London's Royal College of Art, for his entry in the school's student exhibition Hockney executed a series of four paintings, each in a different style, that he titled collectively *Demonstrations of Versatility*. Hockney later explained that "I deliberately set out to prove I could do four entirely different sorts of picture, like Picasso." He emphasized the point by giving each painting an individual title that identified its style.[84] A few years later, Hockney remarked that he often deliberately painted different parts of a single picture in different styles.[85] Marco Livingstone, a friend and biographer of Hockney, explained that his deliberate use of contrasting styles was his way of "seeking refuge from the Abstract Expressionist ... notion of painting as existential autobiography." Hockney wanted to make it clear that he was not a visual seeker, but a conceptual finder: "Just as an image was selected rather than simply discovered in a haphazard manner, so a particular style could be quoted rather than adopted unthinkingly. In so doing, the artist declared the preeminence of choice and control in the making of his picture."[86]

In 1968 the young Argentine conceptual artist Nicolas Garcia Uriburu decided to serve both his interest in nature and his desire to make his art more widely accessible by making water the support for his work. On June 19, during the Venice Biennale, Uriburu used 30 kilograms of the chemical fluorescein to turn the Grand Canal bright green for the day. This was the first of Uriburu's "colorations," with later examples including the East River in New York, the Seine in Paris, and the River Plate in Buenos Aires.[87] Uriburu later made works in a number of other genres to dramatize the pollution of the environment. He made a series of green paintings of the map of South America – often reversed from its familiar orientation to place the southern tip at the top instead of the bottom of the continent – to protest the destruction of the continent's natural resources by North America. He bottled and labeled polluted water from the River Plate and other sources; one such series, made in 1981 with water from the Rhine, was jointly signed by Uriburu and Joseph Beuys.[88] In Tokyo, Uriburu made sculptures by wiring together cylindrical piles of the wooden chopsticks discarded by the restaurants he frequented, and attaching labels: "Eating each day you destroy a forest."[89] Uriburu has also painted the plants that are indigenous to South America. The critic Pierre Restany observed that Uriburu's work is unified not by a common style or form, but by a commitment to ecological awareness and Latin American identity.[90]

Bruce Nauman is among the most influential artists working today: as early as 1990, Peter Schjeldahl described him as "a maverick who at one time or another has affected the course of just about every visual medium except painting, earning a prestige among serious younger artists like that of no one else since Jasper Johns."[91] Early in his career, Nauman was influenced by a retrospective exhibition of the work of Man Ray: "To me Man Ray seemed to avoid the idea that every piece had to take on a historical meaning. What I liked was that there appeared to be no consistency to his thinking, no one style."[92] Throughout his career, Nauman has done conceptual work in a wide range of genres. Schjeldahl remarked that "Artists in the late 1960s were optimistic about the aesthetic potential of technologies and systems, and Nauman played with most of them – video, film, photography, light, sound, language, mathematics, holography, and more – to memorable effect. His work was Duchampian in its wit and insolence, in its teeming paradoxes, puns, and other forms of mental short-circuitry."[93] One of Nauman's most celebrated early works, a photograph of himself spouting water from his mouth titled *Self-Portrait as a Fountain*, was a tribute to Duchamp's famous readymade, *Fountain*. Nauman explained the diversity of his work by saying "I've never been able to stick to one thing."[94] He also explained that the variety of his output has always made his work a struggle: "I realized I would never have a single process; I would always have to reinvent it over and over again . . . On the other hand, that's what is interesting about making art, and why it's worth doing: it's never going to be the same, there is no method."[95] The difficulty of his art was a consequence of its purpose: "I think the hardest thing to do is to present an idea in the most straightforward way."[96] In a review of a Nauman retrospective in 1994, Michael Kimmelman observed that "His signature style is the lack of one . . . Even more than with Gerhard Richter or Sigmar Polke, you begin to understand Mr. Nauman only once you see the eclecticism."[97] Schjeldahl agreed: "There is no Nauman style."[98]

Damien Hirst's art is enormously varied, in subject as well as genre. His works include dead animals – whole or sectioned – suspended in tanks filled with formaldehyde, giant ash trays filled with cigarette butts, a ping pong ball suspended on a column of air, paintings of colored circles, and photo realist paintings of images ranging from pills in a medicine cabinet to the aftermath of a suicide bombing in Baghdad. Louisa Buck described

Hirst's philosophy, and traced its source: "At the heart of Hirst's success – or, according to some, his fatal flaw – is his impudent updating of Marcel Duchamp's conviction that anything can be art if the artist says so. According to Hirst, the only artistic parameters that exist are those that you draw up for yourself. Whether he is making a video for the Brit-pop band Blur, producing artwork for a Dave Stewart album, decorating a fashionable restaurant, or slicing up a pig to make a sculpture, it is all art. 'I just wanted to find out where the boundaries were,' he says. 'I've found out that there aren't any. I wanted to be stopped, and no one will stop me.'"[99] Hirst's art draws on a wide range of earlier styles and artists. As Jerry Saltz observed, "Hirst's work has always been derivative; that's one of its strengths. His art is an original melange, a mutant sprung from virtually every movement that preceded it."[100] Interestingly, Hirst echoed Schapiro, Campbell, and Danto in commenting on the diversity of his own production: "I curate my own work as if I were a group of artists."[101] He also explained that he deliberately avoids consistency: "I'm aware that a lot of the things I make at the moment are kind of the same idea. I worry about that. I mean, I don't want to make 'Damien Hirsts.'"[102]

Beyond Painting

Versatility has spread beyond visual art, and has also become a characteristic of many important twentieth-century conceptual innovators in arts other than painting. A few examples can illustrate this. Ezra Pound was one of the most influential poets of the early twentieth century. He was famously precocious, as his early achievements included the invention of a new poetic doctrine, Imagism, at the age of 27. The critic Hugh Kenner remarked on the conceptual nature of the innovation: "The imagist... is not concerned with getting down the general look of the thing... The imagist's fulcrum... is the process of cognition itself."[103] The literary historian Donald Stauffer remarked on the extraordinary diversity of Pound's work:

Taken as a whole, Pound's early poetry – published in five separate volumes between 1909 and 1915 [when Pound was 24–30 years old] – is an astonishing display of variety and versatility... [H]e wrote poems in a wide range of styles and modes: Catullan satire, Imagesque poems, Browningesque dramatic monologues, impressions, manifestoes, and translations from the Anglo-Saxon and Chinese.[104]

Pound's friend James Joyce was a conceptual innovator in fiction. One obituarist described Joyce as "the great research scientist of letters, handling words with the same freedom and originality that Einstein handles mathematical symbols," and observed that "even the strongest of his characters seems dwarfed by the great apparatus of learning that he brings to bear on them."[105] In *Ulysses*, widely considered the most influential novel of the twentieth century, Joyce deliberately adopted different styles in different chapters. The critic Edna O'Brien remarked that the styles were "so variable that the eighteen episodes could really be described as eighteen novels between the one cover."[106] The surprising juxtapositions of styles in *Ulysses* led the French critic Pierre Courthion to compare the book to the protean work of Picasso.[107] Terry Eagleton observed that "*Ulysses* is an enormous repertoire of 'packaged' styles and discourses, no one of which is absolute." Considering Joyce's oeuvre as whole, Eagleton posed the question "What... is James Joyce's style?," and reflected that "The question is almost impossible to answer, as it is not in the case of Jane Austen or William Faulkner." Eagleton recognized that Joyce's prose did not have the consistency of these two experimental writers: "His writing is motley, hybrid, mongrelized, a thing of shreds and patches. Words are shot through with other words, one style is bounced off another, one language folded within a second."[108]

Five decades after *Ulysses*, Thomas Pynchon, another conceptual innovator, published a novel that is frequently compared to Joyce's masterpiece.[109] One scholar remarked that "the prose style of *Gravity's Rainbow* is not a single style but an impressive compendium of many styles which contribute considerable power to the paradox within the novel," while another observed that the book's narrative styles range "from Kabbalistic revelation, to formulaic romance, to folk-myth, to cinematic parody, to comic book classic, to technological manual, to sewer fantasy, to rocket graffiti."[110] In a review of *Gravity's Rainbow*, Richard Poirier declared that "At thirty-six, Pynchon has established himself as a novelist of major historical importance."[111]

When a friend told John Cage that he planned to lecture on Cage's musical style, the composer replied, "You have a problem – there are so many."[112] Cage is known for the diversity of his many innovations, including the prepared piano, compositional techniques that incorporate chance, and his work $4'33''$, in which a pianist sat for that length of time without touching the keyboard.[113] Cage was prompted to write $4'33''$ when his friend Robert Rauschenberg exhibited his early white paintings, a series of panels with no images, that changed in appearance as shadows or reflections moved across them. The composer and critic Kyle Gann called August 29, 1952, the date of the work's first performance, a landmark in American music history, explaining that 4'33" "requested a new attitude toward listening, and toward the concept of music itself."[114] Just as Rauschenberg's paintings were intended to demonstrate that there was no such thing as an empty canvas, Cage's composition proved that sounds are always present.[115] Cage was a conceptual innovator, who consistently worked to expand the boundaries of music, and who was committed to persistent radical change: "If my work is accepted, I must move on to the point where it isn't." His answer to a question about his philosophy was a self-reflexive pun that could serve as a conceptual credo: "Get out of whatever cage you find yourself in."[116] Cage devoted much of his career to a variety of approaches to a goal that was not aural but conceptual, of "giving up control" over music, "so that sounds can be sounds."[117] John Rockwell concluded that

Cage's music has undergone shifts of style and emphasis, as with almost all composers. In his case, though, the shifts have been radical ones, complete transformations of method, performing forces and sheer sound. What has remained constant is his questing spirit of adventure, his determination to seem fresh and even outrageous, and his meditative epistemology.[118]

In 1968, the film critic Manny Farber began an essay about Jean-Luc Godard by stressing the diversity of the director's movies:

Each Godard film is of itself widely varied in persona as well as quality. Printed on the blackboard of one of his Formicalike later films, hardly to be noticed, is a list of African animals: giraffe, lion, hippo. At the end of this director's career, there will probably be a hundred films, each one a bizarrely different species, with its own excruciatingly singular skeleton, tendons, plumage . . . Unlike Cézanne, who used a three-eighths-inch square stroke and nervously exacting line around every apple he painted, the form and manner of execution changes totally with each film.

Farber recognized that the diversity of Godard's films was a product of the director's conceptual approach:

Braining it out before the project starts, most of the invention, the basic intellectual puzzle, is pretty well set in his mind before the omnipresent [cinematographer Raoul] Coutard gets the camera in position . . . Each of his pictures presents a puzzle of parts, a unique combination of elements to prove a preconceived theory.[119]

Three decades later, the critic Peter Wollen observed that Godard had made an additional fifty films since Farber had written his essay, and declared that "just as Farber predicted, each film seems to be *sui generis*, quite unlike any of his previous work, the same only in being so unpredictably, inconsistently different." In Godard's constant quotation from old Hollywood films and his equally consistent disregard for all of the conventions of those films, Wollen recognized a key characteristic of the conceptual artist, who borrows the techniques of his predecessors but often transforms them for uses that would appall those earlier practitioners: "Godard's films showed a contradictory reverence for the art of the past and delinquent refusal to obey any of its rules."[120] Godard himself consistently maintained that film was simply one possible means for expressing his ideas: "I think of myself as an essayist... only instead of writing, I film them. Were the cinema to disappear, I would simply accept the inevitable and turn to television; were television to disappear, I would revert to pencil and paper. For there is a clear continuity between all forms of expression. It's all one."[121] Gerald Mast summarized the common thread in Godard's work: "Godard films are consistent in their inconsistency, their eclecticism, their mixing of many different kinds of ideas and cinematic principles."[122]

Mast noted that Godard's New Wave colleague François Truffaut "also delighted in mixing cinematic styles."[123] Pauline Kael declared that "What's exciting about movies like [Truffaut's] *Shoot the Piano Player* and [Godard's] *Breathless* (and also [Truffaut's] superb *Jules and Jim*, though it's very different from the other two)... is that they, quite literally, move with the times. They are full of unresolved, inexplicable, disharmonious elements."[124] Karel Reisz and Gavin Millar contended that the apparent incoherence of Truffaut's movies was an imitation of real life: "The swift changes of mood and pace that characterize his films are an attempt to match his form more nearly to the way life usually develops."[125] Truffaut's own account of his work was a bit different, however, comparing it not to life but to other forms of popular art: "For me the cinema is a show, and I compare a film to an act in the circus, or in a music hall." He conceded that *Shoot the Piano Player* "seems to contain four or five films," but explained "that's what I wanted. Above all I was looking for an explosion of the genre (the detective film) by mixing genres (comedy, drama, melodrama, the psychological film, the thriller, the love film, etc.). I know that the public detests nothing more than changes in tone, but I've always had a passion for changing tone."[126]

Conclusion

How can you say one style is better than another? You ought to be able to be an Abstract-Expressionist next week, or a Pop artist, or a realist, without feeling you've given up something.

Andy Warhol, 1963[127]

Conceptual innovators pose specific problems, and solve them. Their recognition that they have reached a goal can free them to pursue another one: that project is finished, their curiosity about it is satisfied, and they can go on to something else, perhaps completely different. This behavior is logical and reasonable to the conceptual artist, but appears problematic from the vantage point of his experimental counterpart. Experimental innovators' problems are generally broader, their goals less distinct. They are rarely satisfied that they have reached their goals, and many in fact come to doubt that their goals can be reached at all: the more they progress, the more distant their goal appears. Their persistent dissatisfaction with their efforts, and their skepticism about the possibility of conclusive resolution of artistic goals, lead them to question the commitment and sincerity of any artist who changes styles, and goals, with any frequency.

Interestingly, recognition of the versatility of a number of important conceptual innovators in art during the past century adds a dimension to our appreciation of the significance of Picasso. Some of the greatest artists of the past influenced other artists not only through their innovations in style, but by providing new models of how artists create their work. So for example the greatness of Raphael and Titian is due not solely to their innovations in composition, form, and color, but also to the fact that Raphael inspired generations of conceptual painters with his meticulous planning of his canvases, and that Titian equally inspired generations of experimental painters with his unplanned direct approach to painting, and the repeated revisions by which he brought his works to completion.[128] In light of the present investigation, it appears similarly that Picasso's greatness lies not only in his innovations in form and subject, but also in his creation of a new model of artistic behavior, that of the versatile conceptual artist who makes frequent and precipitous changes in the style and form of his work. In 1943, when a visitor to Picasso's studio remarked that a statue Picasso had made from a child's scooter was not really a sculpture, the artist exclaimed: "What is sculpture? What is painting? Everyone's still clinging to outdated ideas, obsolete definitions, as if the artist's role was not precisely to offer new ones."[129] It was this realization, that artists could innovate freely and often by formulating new ideas and definitions, that made Picasso the prototype of the versatile conceptual innovator.

The parallel observations of Meyer Schapiro on Picasso, David Campbell on Polke, and Arthur Danto on Richter clearly demonstrate the dangers that attend the neglect of a comparative approach in the analysis of art – a neglect that is not only widespread, but is actually celebrated by many contemporary humanists. These art scholars' surprise at the practices of these painters is a consequence of their failure to recognize that the practices are common among a class of artists, those I call conceptual. And the scholars' questions about the artists' integrity of purpose are equally a consequence of their failure to understand the systematic differences that exist in the practices and attitudes of conceptual and experimental artists. More specifically, art historians' failure to recognize the common basis of the behavior of versatile conceptual innovators has resulted in an incomplete understanding of the practices of some of the most influential innovators of the past century, including Picasso, Duchamp, Picabia, Beuys, Rauschenberg, Klein, Hockney, Nauman, Koons, and Hirst. We should also expect more names to be added to this list in future, because of the heavy emphasis on conceptual innovation in the contemporary art world: as Gerhard Richter observed in 1977, "changeable artists are a growing phenomenon. Picasso, for instance, or Duchamp and Picabia – and the number is certainly increasing all the time."[130]

8

You Cannot Be Serious

The Conceptual Innovator as Trickster

The Accusation

The artist does not say today, "Come and see faultless work," but "Come and see sincere work."

Edouard Manet, 1867[1]

When Edouard Manet exhibited *Le Déjeuner sur l'herbe* at the Salon des Refusés in 1863, the critic Louis Etienne described the painting as an "unbecoming rebus," and denounced it as "a young man's practical joke, a shameful open sore not worth exhibiting this way."[2] Two years later, when Manet's *Olympia* was shown at the Salon, the critic Félix Jahyer wrote that the painting was indecent, and declared that "I cannot take this painter's intentions seriously." The critic Ernest Fillonneau claimed this reaction was a common one, for "an epidemic of crazy laughter prevails . . . in front of the canvases by Manet." Another critic, Jules Clarétie, described Manet's two paintings at the Salon as "challenges hurled at the public, mockeries or parodies, how can one tell?"[3] In his review of the Salon, the critic Théophile Gautier concluded his condemnation of Manet's paintings by remarking that "Here there is nothing, we are sorry to say, but the desire to attract attention at any price."[4]

The most decisive rejection of these charges against Manet was made in a series of articles published in 1866–67 by the young critic and writer Emile Zola. Zola began by declaring that those who laughed at Manet were fools: "There isn't the least thing laughable in all this. There is only a sincere artist following his own bent." Zola made a bold prediction: "I am so sure that Manet will be one of the masters of tomorrow that I should believe I had made a good bargain, had I the money, in buying all his canvases today. In fifty years they will sell for fifteen or twenty times more." Zola, who would later gain fame as a literary realist, specifically defended Manet's integrity and sincerity as a visual realist: "He has then courageously set himself in front of a subject, he has seen this subject in broad areas of color, by strong contrasts, and he has painted each thing as he has seen it. Who dares here to speak of paltry calculation, who dares to accuse a conscientious artist of mocking art and himself?" Zola underscored the point: "Manet paints in an unaffected and completely serious manner."[5]

Zola's contention that Manet was not deliberately provoking attacks on his work was clearly correct, for Manet disliked criticism, and reacted badly to it. In 1865, the poet Charles Baudelaire, a friend of Manet's, wrote to another friend of Manet's distress at the controversy over *Olympia*: "He strikes me as depressed and overwhelmed by the shock." Another close friend of Manet's, Antonin Proust, noted in 1865 that the criticism of the artist's work had demoralized him: "However disposed he may have been to work had he received encouragement, his fervor collapsed before the cruelty and injustice of those who did not understand him."[6] Looking back on this period later in his life, Manet admitted the damage the critics had done: "The attacks directed against me broke me in the mainspring of life. No one knows what it is to be consistently insulted. It disheartens you and undoes you."[7]

A number of visitors to Pablo Picasso's Montmartre studio early in 1907 were shocked by the large new painting that would later be titled *Les Demoiselles d'Avignon*. Among those visitors was Georges Braque, whose reaction to the painting was to compare Picasso to the fairground fire-eaters who swallowed tow and drank kerosene in order to spit flames.[8] Yet Braque soon realized that Picasso's new work was not a stunt, and little more than a year later he joined Picasso in the development of Cubism. Picasso had little interest in publicizing his new work, and in fact did not exhibit the *Demoiselles* for nearly a decade.

Manet and Picasso were both young conceptual artists who produced radical innovations that shocked many in the art world. Their willingness to violate cherished conventions early in their careers made it tempting for detractors to dismiss them as immature tricksters who were playing practical jokes merely to gain attention. These charges appear to have been unfounded with respect to both Manet and Picasso. Yet in the modern era, as the recognition that important art must be conspicuously innovative has become widespread, the potential for artists to gain attention by presenting radical innovations that can be seen as tricks has become real.

The danger in doing this is that once an action comes to be generally considered as a trick or hoax, the perpetrator can be discredited, and any benefit from the earlier publicity can be lost. To be of lasting value to the artist, any action that gains attention by being condemned as a trick or joke therefore has to have the potential for the artist to maintain that it is in fact a serious contribution. Direct denials are usually unpersuasive in the face of such attacks, however, so subtler defenses are necessary if the artist is to weather these critical firestorms. With the proper response from the artist, the effect of the attacks can be reversed, and transformed into a positive force in establishing the importance of the art. Specifically, if the artist can avoid becoming defensive in the face of the criticism, the anger and hostility of the critics can be interpreted as proof that the artist's innovation has successfully controverted some central tenet of previous artistic practice. Then the more vehement the denunciations, the greater the evidence they provide of the significance of the new contribution.

The twentieth century has witnessed a series of artists whose behavior conforms with this insight. A series of young conceptual artists have offered radically innovative works that have been seen by many in the art world as tricks or hoaxes. Confronted by these charges, the artists have either remained silent, or have offered only enigmatic or elliptical statements in defense of their work. In this way, these artists have gained publicity not only initially, as a result of the criticism that has greeted their work, but also subsequently, as a result of the debate that has ensued over whether their work is to be dismissed as a hoax or valued as a novel contribution to art. For these artists, ambiguity has become a positive and powerful force in establishing the value of their art, and advancing their careers. If the artist achieves just the right balance, admirers and detractors can debate indefinitely whether his work is a joke or a serious contribution, a crude parody or a sophisticated new idea. Such debates confer substantial benefits on the artist.

The Prototype

> I suppose every young generation needs a prototype. In this case, I play that role. I'm delighted to.
> Marcel Duchamp[9]

Marcel Duchamp was modern art's original model of the contrary, enigmatic maverick as conceptual innovator. Duchamp posed radical conceptual challenges to conventional art, and increased the effectiveness of these attacks by skillfully evading the question of whether his actions were taken in earnest.

In conversations with the critic Pierre Cabanne recorded late in the artist's life, Duchamp recalled lessons he had learned as a young painter in Paris. One concerned the value of silence. Cubism had been the exciting new development of the time, and although minor artists attempted to explain it to the public, the true leader of the movement didn't: "Picasso never explained anything. It took a few years to see that not talking was better than talking too much."[10] Another lesson, that he should remain aloof from other artists, came from a painful personal experience. Not only was Duchamp's own contribution to Cubism, *Nude Descending a Staircase, No. 2*, rejected by the Salon des Indépendants in 1912, but it was Duchamp's two older brothers, the painter Jacques Villon and the sculptor Raymond Duchamp-Villon, who were delegated to deliver the news of the rejection to Duchamp. Stung both by the rejection and by his brothers' lack of loyalty, Duchamp reflected that the incident had liberated him: "I said, 'All right, since it's like that, there's no question of joining a group – I'm going to count on no one but myself alone.'"[11] He admitted, however, that a young colleague had taught him yet another lesson. Francis Picabia, who subsequently became Duchamp's closest friend, demonstrated how an artist could exert a contrary influence, from outside the groups that dominated the advanced art world of the day. Duchamp explained that Picabia was "a negator. With him it was always, 'Yes, but...' and 'No, but...' Whatever you said, he contradicted. It was his game."[12]

These early lessons all contributed to the persona that Duchamp appears to have deliberately created, in which irony and ambiguity became powerful weapons in an attack on received practices and positions. In one exchange with Cabanne, Duchamp explained that he avoided all fixed attitudes:

Cabanne: One has the impression that every time you commit yourself to a position, you attenuate it by irony or sarcasm.
Duchamp: I always do. Because I don't believe in positions.
Cabanne: But what do you believe in?
Duchamp: Nothing, of course! The word "belief" is another error. It's like the word "judgment," they're both horrible ideas.[13]

This detached and lofty persona became the foundation for Duchamp's one-man crusade to reverse the direction of modern art. He observed that in the modern era artists had been freed from the demands of patrons, but he regretted that artists had used their new-found freedom to produce an art that lacked intellectual content, and was devoted merely to pleasing the eye:

That famous liberation of the artist at the time of Courbet changed the status of the artist from the employee of a patron or collector to a free individual. By "free," I mean the artist was able to paint what he wanted... This liberation in the nineteenth century took the form of impressionism, which in a way was the beginning of a cult devoted to the material on the canvas – the actual pigment. Instead of interpreting through the pigment, the impressionists gradually fell in love with the pigment, the paint itself. Their intentions were completely retinal and divorced from the classical use of paint as a means to an end. The last hundred years have been retinal... Today abstract expressionism seems to have reached the apex of this retinal approach. It's still going strong but I doubt whether this is the art of the future. One hundred years of the retinal approach is enough. Earlier, paint was always a means to an end, whether the end was religious, political, social, decorative or romantic. Now it's become an end in itself.[14]

Duchamp's goal was to restore art to what he considered its proper conceptual purpose: "I wanted to get away from the physical aspect of painting... I was interested in ideas – not merely in visual products. I wanted to put painting once more at the service of the mind."[15]

Duchamp's most radical assault on retinal art was his invention of the readymade, manufactured objects that he selected and designated as works of art. Characteristically, he avoided discussing the precise signifi-cance of his new genre: "I've never been able to arrive at a definition or explanation that fully satisfies me. There's still magic in the idea, so I'd rather keep it that way than try to be exoteric about it."[16] Yet in a talk at New York's Museum of Modern Art, Duchamp stressed that aesthetic considerations played no role in his selection of objects: "A point which I want very much to establish is that the choice of these 'readymades' was never dictated by aesthetic delectation. This choice was based on a reaction of visual indifference with at the same time a total absence of good or bad taste."[17]

Duchamp made the first readymade in 1913, by attaching a bicycle wheel to a stool, and he coined the term "readymade" two years later. But the fame of the readymade dates from 1917, and the first exhibi-tion of the newly established American Society of Independent Artists. The society had been established the year before, to promote advanced American art by holding annual exhibitions with a policy of "no jury, no prizes." Duchamp was a member of the board of directors, and his anti-authoritarian attitude was reflected in the society's stated policy of inclusiveness, as any artist who joined the society was entitled to show two works. A week before the first exhibition opened, Duchamp purchased a porcelain urinal, signed it with the fictitious name R. Mutt, titled it *Fountain*, and submitted it, along with R. Mutt's membership fee, to the society. *Fountain* outraged many of the society's organizers, and the board of directors voted to reject it. Duchamp immediately resigned from the board in protest.[18]

Duchamp later admitted to Cabanne that submitting *Fountain* to the Independents had been "rather provocative":

Cabanne: Well, since you were looking for scandal, you were satisfied?
Duchamp: It was, indeed, a success. In that sense.
Cabanne: You really would have been disappointed had the *Fountain* been welcomed . . .
Duchamp: Almost. As it was, I was enchanted.[19]

The society's refusal to exhibit *Fountain*, technically in violation of its own policy not to judge submissions, allowed Duchamp both to highlight the hypocrisy of established artists and to publicize in stark form the nature of his conceptual challenge to the artistic conventions of the day. In *The Blind Man*, a small magazine published by Duchamp and a few friends in the wake of the incident, an article signed by Louise Norton lamented that "Like Mr. Mutt, many of us had quite an exorbitant notion of the independence of the Independents. It was a sad surprise to learn of a Board of Censors sitting upon the ambiguous question, What is ART?" That question was so radical that it had little immediate impact, but its challenge reemerged in the late 1950s, when a number of young artists set out to break down the traditional barriers surrounding art, and it then became perhaps the single most potent force generating the art of the remainder of the twentieth century. And many of the central figures in the production of that art were furthermore influenced by an aspect of Duchamp's behavior that was also identified by Louise Norton, who declared that: "there are those who anxiously ask, 'Is he serious or is he joking?' Perhaps he is both! Is it not possible?"[20]

With the *Fountain* incident, Duchamp thus not only provided future conceptual artists with an agenda, of challenging the boundaries of art, but also gave them a powerful stance from which to pursue it. This stance used irony and detachment effectively to insulate the innovator from criticism, for whenever provocative conceptual acts produced the inevitable reaction of outrage from critics and other artists, the innovator could express his amusement, and the criticism could be interpreted as proof of the value of the innovation. Thus Norton explained, "there is among us today a spirit of 'blague' arising out of the artist's bitter vision of an over-institutionalized world of stagnant statistics and antique axioms . . . [O]ur artists are sometimes sad, and if there is a shade of bitter mockery in some of them, it is only there because they know that the joyful spirit of their work is to this age a hidden treasure."[21] As the critic Harold Rosenberg later observed, "In the case of Duchamp . . . the antagonism he arouses is an essential element of his role, and even, if one wishes, of his greatness and profundity."[22] Yet Thomas Hess recognized that Duchamp's stance afforded him an extraordinary protection: "Marcel Duchamp over the years brilliantly has consolidated a position that is practically invulnerable to serious criticism."[23]

Duchamp's preeminence as the great artistic trickster of the twentieth century is widely recognized. One recent statement is that of Roger Shattuck: "Marcel Duchamp appointed himself the court jester of twentieth-century art. We have had many eccentrics, fanatics, and experimenters, but only one astute wag who understood that he could mix enigma and spoof in approximately equal proportions and be tolerated as a contraband artist."[24] Arthur Danto flatly declared that "Duchamp's gestures of 1913–17 were jokes."[25] Danto pointed to a major consequence of the conceptual orientation of Duchamp, and named his primary heirs: "Since Duchamp, it has been possible to be a visual artist without being a painter, a sculptor, a draftsman, or even a photographer, or without displaying much by way of skill in the incidental employment of these crafts, as long as one has the right sort of transfigurative intelligence. His two greatest followers have been Andy Warhol and Joseph Beuys." Danto also stressed the extreme conceptual nature of these three artists' innovations: "it is only necessary to recall the large retrospective exhibitions of Duchamp and Warhol at the Museum of Modern Art, or of Beuys at the Guggenheim, to appreciate that we are dealing with a form of artistic creativity of an altogether different genre than that of Matisse or Motherwell or Pollock or de Kooning. These were aggregates of puzzling objects, often aesthetically repellent but always conceptually exalting. They were shows one had to think one's way through, one object at a time."[26] Harold Rosenberg isolated another central legacy of Duchamp's career: "Duchamp placed innovative art under permanent suspicion of being a hoax." Rosenberg furthermore pointed out a distinctive characteristic of Duchamp's art that would also become part of the model he created for later conceptual artists: "Picasso is undoubtedly at least equal to Duchamp as an art-world presence, but when one thinks of Picasso there is a strong inflection toward the objectively interrelated mass of his creations, whereas in regard to Duchamp the works are reflected in the changing silhouette of their creator. Every Duchamp piece is a piece of Duchamp, and derives its meaning from the spectator's total impression of the artist."[27]

The Followers

I'm not more intelligent than I appear.

Andy Warhol[28]

Joseph Beuys was among the most controversial of Duchamp's heirs. Throughout his career, an active debate continued between his admirers and his detractors: "Beuys is credited with brilliance, insightfulness, and lyricism, as well as fraudulence, hokum, and preposterous simplicity. Which is the real Beuys?"[29] Beuys created a complex persona, based in large part on a myth he created about an experience he claimed to have had as a fighter pilot in World War II. In his account, after his Luftwaffe plane had been shot down in the Crimea, Tartar tribesmen saved his life, salving his injuries with animal fat, and wrapping him in felt to warm him. Fat and felt subsequently became key elements in his art, and throughout his life he always wore a felt Stetson hat, supposedly necessitated by injuries to his head suffered in the plane crash. The hat was just one of Beuys' props. Irving Sandler described the ensemble:

To be effective Beuys had to attract the attention of the media. To this end he fashioned a memorable – a trademark – persona that featured a felt hat (atop his sallow, hollow-cheeked face), an apple green fisherman's vest, jeans, heavy shoes, fur-lined overcoat, and knapsack.[30]

A Danish critic remarked of Beuys that "If you go by appearances, he is a fantastic figure, half-way between a clown and gangster."[31]

Beuys wanted to expand the concept of art: in his philosophy, anything can be seen as art, and everyone is an artist. He referred to all his varied activities – sculpture, performance, teaching, and ecological and political activism – as "social sculpture," and he declared that "My objects are to be seen as stimulants for the transformation of the idea of sculpture, or of art in general."[32] His work was both highly conceptual and very personal: confronted by a Beuys retrospective exhibition, Rosalind Krauss remarked that "One is almost helpless without the explanations supplied by the artist."[33] As a biographer explained, "Beuys was an enigma; he did everything differently. But everything he did was unmistakably the man himself: the sculpture *Joseph Beuys.*"[34]

The variety of Beuys' activities defies any attempt to summarize the nature of his work, and the complexity of his discourse makes any description of his motivations problematic. In 1965 he created one of his most celebrated works, *How to Explain Pictures to a Dead Hare*, in a Dusseldorf gallery. After pouring honey over his head and covering his face with gold leaf, Beuys walked around the gallery and talked about the paintings to a dead hare he held in his arms, letting it touch the pictures with its paw. After finishing the tour, Beuys sat and thoroughly explained the pictures to the hare. In 1974, Beuys enacted *I Like America and America Likes Me* by having himself locked in a New York art gallery for three days with a live coyote. Beuys wrapped himself in felt, and had only a shepherd's crook to defend himself. The two lived peacefully together in their cage.[35]

Beuys became a role model for many young European artists, because of his concern for the democratization of art, his use of art for political and social protest, and his close personal identification of art with the constructed image of the artist. His career presented a basic ambiguity: "Beuys is self-consciously paradoxical – unashamedly double. He presents himself as a shaman and showman – mystic and spectacle – simultaneously. His integrity consists in his openness about his seemingly unresolvable 'duplicity'."[36] He became a cult figure: "No other artist (with the possible exception of Andy Warhol, who certainly generated a totally different kind of myth) managed – and probably never intended – to puzzle and scandalize his primarily bourgeois art audience to the extent that he would become a figure of worship."[37] Beuys appears to have been ambivalent toward Duchamp: in 1964 he participated in a television program titled *The Silence of Marcel Duchamp is Overrated*; he resented a remark made by Duchamp that denigrated the Performance art of the 1960s as unoriginal; and he insisted that his celebrated sculpture *Fat Chair* had nothing to do with Duchamp's readymades.[38] Yet it is difficult to believe that Beuys's careful construction of his own artistic myth, and his skillful use of ambiguity in doing so, was not based on a thorough understanding of Duchamp's earlier practice. Thus for example Johannes Cladders argued that Duchamp and Beuys were the two twentieth-century artists who had been most mythologized, and observed that "I think Beuys felt himself to be in competition with his fellow 'myth.'"[39]

Calvin Tomkins judged that "It may be that Andy Warhol was Duchamp's truest heir – the one artist who pushed the implications of

Duchamp's ideas to conclusions that not even Duchamp had foreseen. Publicity, repetition, and all-out commercialism, the elements on which Warhol's art was based, can each be seen as the flip side of Duchampian indifference."[40] Harold Rosenberg declared that "The innovation of Andy Warhol consists not in his paintings but in his version of the comedy of the artist as a public figure," and conceded that "his performance goes beyond that of Marcel Duchamp."[41] For Kirk Varnedoe, "Warhol is to the emperor's new clothes what Chanel is to the little black dress. He may not have invented the concept, but he has become its spokesperson."[42] Kelly Cresap, who titled his book about Warhol *Pop Trickster Fool*, observed that "In recent years scholars have alternately characterized Warhol as a sixties intellectual; as someone who had the saving grace of being 'never in the least intellectual'; and as 'the great idiot savant of our time'. . . Warhol's ability to generate concern about his intelligence easily qualifies as one of the most inspired and effortlessly self-regenerating publicity stunts of his career – a nearly irresistible tactic for attracting an audience and holding it in his spell."[43] Matthew Collings' analysis of Warhol recalls Louise Norton's question concerning whether Duchamp couldn't be simultaneously serious and joking: "An important thing about Warhol . . . was his way of being original and at the same time staging originality. With him, it was a massive staging, with all pretense of not staging absolutely stripped away."[44]

In interviews, Warhol blithely offered radical challenges to traditional conceptions of art. For example in 1963 he told an interviewer that differences among artistic approaches were overrated: "How can you say one style is better than another? You ought to be able to be an Abstract-Expressionist next week, or a Pop artist, or a realist, without feeling you've given up something." And he maintained that the same was true of differences among artists: "I think it would be great if more people took up silk screens so that no one would know whether my picture was mine or somebody else's."[45] Nor was he concerned with the issue of what constituted his work: "I think somebody should be able to do all my paintings for me." Cresap detailed Warhol's challenges to the reigning art of the preceding generation:

Warhol played the role of vacuous fraud to the hilt, performing a series of ruses or "dupes" upon the ground rules of the previous artistic dispensation. If late-modernist art was promoted as a strenuous, "heroic" undertaking, Warhol proclaimed how easy and fun painting was. In contrast to the image of the isolated genius creating art ex nihilo, he pinched ideas from friends, lifted images wholesale from preexisting photos and logos, and enlisted labor-saving assistants. Where

Jackson Pollock forcefully confronted his canvases in a style known as "action" painting, Warhol abandoned painterly gestures in favor of overhead projection, stencil-work, silkscreen transfer, and gridlike repetition. His statement "I want to be a machine" mercilessly deflates the Romantic pretensions of Pollock's statement, "I am nature."[46]

Warhol generally declined to discuss his background. As he told one interviewer, "I'd prefer to remain a mystery, I never like to give my background and, anyway, I make it all up different every time I'm asked. It's not just that it's part of my image not to tell everything, it's just that I forget what I said the day before and I have to make it up all over again." In fact, he claimed, there wasn't much to know about him: "If you want to know all about Andy Warhol, just look at the surface: of my paintings and films and me, and there I am. There's nothing behind it."[47] The curator Henry Geldzahler commented on Warhol's success in creating his own image:

There is a quality to Andy Warhol's public persona that inspires endless discussion, quite unlike that of any other artist. Such discussions inevitably center on the question of his intentions and the artist's control over the meanings in his work which are often subtle and contradictory. He has cultivated to perfection a naïve blankness, a bottomless well of innocence when forced to declare himself on an issue . . . The truth is that those of us who have been among his close friends for the past twenty years or more have exactly the same questions about Warhol's intent and control as does the informed public.[48]

A series of artists have followed Duchamp, Beuys, and Warhol, in skillfully creating ambiguous personas that reinforce the impact of their provocative, and often shocking, conceptual innovations. Yves Klein (1928–62) was a contemporary of Warhol's. A friend of Klein's, the sculptor Jean Tinguely, called him "the greatest provocateur I have ever known."[49] The poet and critic John Ashbery observed that "In his art and in his life, Klein was a perfect example of a poker face, or, as the French say, a *pince-sans-rire*. Needless to say, he was dismissed by conservative critics as a practical joker."[50] One of those critics, *The New York Times'* John Canaday, observed of a retrospective of Klein's work in 1967, five years after the artist's death, that "The prodigious exaltation of nonsense is the really troubling thing about this exhibition." Canaday described Klein as "one of the truly great vaudevillians," and concluded that the artist "presented as liberations of the spirit a series of tricks that are more accurately interpretable as symptoms of art's mortal illness."[51]

Klein had a lifelong fascination with representations of space, and the infinite. In pursuit of transcending physical limitations, in 1958 he announced that "My paintings are now invisible and I would like to show them in a clear and positive manner, in my next Parisian exhibition at Iris Clert's."[52] Shortly thereafter Klein presented an exhibition, titled *The Void*, at Clert's gallery. Two days before the opening, Klein covered the gallery's windows with his patented International Klein Blue paint. Working in seclusion, Klein emptied the gallery of all its furniture and painted its walls white. He then "projected mental images onto the transparent space, creating immaterial paintings... in mid-air by prolonged concentration." On the evening of April 28, for the exhibition's opening the front door was flanked by two Republican Guards in full dress uniform, which usually signified a formal state event. The otherwise empty gallery was packed with invited guests – whose invitations had been mailed with International Klein Blue stamps – and a crowd of several thousand people outside were unable to enter. Police and fire trucks were eventually called to disperse the crowd. In a speech delivered at 1:00 AM at the famous café La Coupole, Klein told those assembled that they had been present at a historic moment in the history of universal art: "In my modest person... four millennia of civilization have found their exhaustive conclusion."[53] Critical reactions to the exhibition varied widely, from one review that compared the gallery to a "freshly limewashed cowshed" to another that characterized the gallery as "a void to fill with dreams."[54] Klein considered the show a great success, and during the next four years he presented several other public displays of the void.

Nor did Klein stop with exhibitions, for in 1959 he began to sell the void. He created receipts for what he called *Zones of Immaterial Pictorial Sensibility*, and offered them at prices ranging from 20–160 grams of gold. Purchasers were offered the option of keeping the receipts or, to realize the "authentic immaterial value" of the work, of purchasing and then burning them. In the latter case, Klein would throw half the gold he had received into an ocean or river. At least three of these ritual transfers took place in 1962 in Paris, on the banks of the Seine. A purchaser who participated in one of these ritual transfers of immateriality, which were performed formally and solemnly, later wrote that he had had "no other experience in art equal to the depth of feeling of [the sale ceremony]. It evoked in me a shock of self-recognition and an explosion of awareness of time and space."[55]

Throughout his career, Klein devised a number of ways to create paintings that were not the direct product of the artist's hand. These included making nude models into "living brushes," by having them cover themselves with blue paint and then press themselves against canvases tacked to the wall or laid on the floor; driving his car on a highway with a canvas covered with wet paint tied to the roof; and scorching patterns into canvases with blow torches. All of these techniques stemmed from his belief in the immaterial and conceptual nature of art: "True 'painters and poets' don't paint and don't write poems."[56]

After Klein's premature death, critics debated the meaning of his art. A French admirer, Pierre Restany, declared that "His career was marked by conquest stages that are practically myths incarnated in deeds."[57] Harold Rosenberg described Klein as "a highly inventive showman." Rosenberg concluded that "Klein's talent lay neither in his works nor in the originality of his ideas but in his way of staging them and himself."[58] Interestingly, in spite of his dismissal of Klein's art, Rosenberg accurately identified a key element of his impact on the art of the 1960s, for Klein's flamboyant staging of his exhibitions and the execution of his works became one of his legacies for artists who would be increasingly interested in the relationship between performance and art objects. Thus Thomas McEvilley observed of Klein that "his career as a whole can be described best as a sustained seven-year-long performance."[59] As a result, Klein's ambiguity remains at the center of his legacy. In terms that echo Louise Norton's question, the art historian Paul Wood recently concluded that "One suspects that part of the problem that Klein presents for historians of the avant-garde is that he was capable of being both funny and serious, mystical and materialist, and often both at the same time."[60]

During the early 1960s, the Italian conceptual artist Piero Manzoni (1933–63) made a series of works that explored issues similar to those of Klein, including the void and the physical relationship of the artist to his work. In 1998, Julia Peyton-Jones observed that "commentators have positioned Manzoni as an artist who continues to shock, 35 years after his death ... Manzoni's audacity has placed him among the *enfants terribles* even of our own time."[61]

In 1961, Manzoni created *Magic Base*: "as long as any person or any object stayed on this base he, or it, was a work of art." Later the same year, Manzoni made the *Base of the World*, a large iron pedestal turned upside down in a Danish park that made the whole world a work of art.[62] Also in 1961, Manzoni began making human beings into works of art by signing them. These "living sculptures" were given receipts by Manzoni specifying whether the whole person or only the body part signed by him was a work of art, and whether they were art at all times or only during certain activities.

Manzoni's most provocative work was the production of a series of ninety small cans, each numbered and signed by the artist, titled *Merda d'artista*, with labels in four languages reading "Contents: 30 gr. net; freshly preserved; produced and tinned in May 1961." Manzoni sold these cans at prices equal to the current market value of 30 grams of gold.[63] Richard Cork later wrote of Manzoni's attitude in producing these works:

An instinctive showman, Manzoni played the part of artistic insurgent with relish. He even posed for a photograph, canned shit in hand, next to a lavatory bowl. A puckish grin animates his plump face, and his eyes gleam in brazen defiance of all those who dismissed him as a charlatan.[64]

The *Merda d'artista* have raised a series of questions that have fueled debate ever since Manzoni's premature death. From one vantage point, they are demonstrations that carry to an extreme the Duchampian proposition that anything so designated by the artist can be a work of art – not only clean and aesthetically attractive manufactured objects, but even the most taboo waste product of the human body. The commercial language of the label presents the can's contents as a consumer item, but it cannot be consumed. Indeed, there is a persistent debate about what the cans actually contain. Manzoni made the cans by himself, in a secluded place, and a recent survey of owners of the cans found considerable disagreement over whether they really contain the material described on their labels. Because Manzoni sealed the cans, it is generally accepted that opening one destroys it as a work of art, so the debate over what is inside them cannot be settled.[65]

In 2004, Jeremy Lewison, the director of acquisitions for the Tate Modern in London, explained his museum's purchase of a *Merda d'artista* by saying that "From our point of view, this is already a classic work of art." Interestingly, Lewison also remarked that "we wanted to complement our Manzoni collection and continue to build it up, just as we have recently been building up our Duchamp collection."[66] In 2003 no. 77 of *Merda d'artista* was sold at a London auction for $27,000. Manzoni had implicitly compared himself to an alchemist in his original pricing of these works, but their subsequent appreciation to values much greater than that of gold reflected the inspiration they provided to the younger Italian Arte Povera artists in the late 1960s for their aggressive use of unconventional materials in making art. Manzoni had written in 1957 that the common problem of misunderstanding that faced contemporary art was a consequence of the artist's need to be "the herald of . . . new human conditions; he discovers new totems and taboos latent in his time but not yet recognized, combining them in a new civilization."[67] Whether *Merda d'artista* was seriously intended to be an element of a new civilization, and whether it has become such an element, continue to be debated today.

In 1969, Gilbert Proesch (1943–) and George Pasmore (1942–), who work professionally as Gilbert & George, declared themselves to be living sculptures. In their first notable work, they painted their faces and hands bronze and sang "Underneath the Arches," a music hall song, for eight hours at a stretch for two consecutive days. Since then, they have made works in a variety of media, many involving photographs of themselves, both clothed and naked, and many using profane titles and written texts to make jarring and obscene statements about sex, religion, race, and other subjects that arise in the course of their daily lives in London. They were awarded the third annual Turner Prize in 1986, and the description of their work on that occasion began by observing that "Gilbert and George have constantly attempted to address themes and subjects from human experience in such a way that their work would be accessible to untutored audiences."[68]

In 2000, Louisa Buck noted that although Gilbert and George, together with only David Hockney and Damien Hirst, are probably Britain's best-known living artists, mixed feelings persist about them, because of a basic ambiguity concerning their work and lives: "Is their fused artistic persona an ongoing continuation of their 1960s decision to become 'Living Sculpture,' or an attention-seeking joke at the world's expense?"[69] Although the two often appear in public, and have given extensive interviews, they never appear out of character, which includes their trademark matching tweed suits and their formal and paradoxical statements about themselves and their art. Thus the critic Matthew Collings wrote that:

Ever since they started, people would ask if they really were like the way they behaved publicly. Their funny, stiff, upright manner and stiff suits. Didn't they drop the act in private, or when they were among friends? But they never do drop the act, and they really are sincere artists, although it's hard to know why that's good. I mean they really are good but it's hard to explain how being sincere and totally made-up at the same time can work, and why that should result in excellence.[70]

Buck pointed to the same issue by comparing the British artists to an earlier figure in the lineage of conceptual tricksters: "In a career spanning some thirty years, the living logo that is G & G has followed in the footsteps of Andy Warhol in achieving the three-way formula for contemporary artistic success: ubiquity, inscrutability and – above all – controversy."[71] David Sylvester's analysis of Gilbert and George referred back to an earlier artistic ancestor. Reflecting that the mystery surrounding their partnership makes their art problematic, he observed that "Not the least problematic element is the question whether G&G's 'real' work is the corpus of their artefacts or is the living sculpture," then remarked that "It was surely Marcel Duchamp who first invented that problem of where the real work lay... Gilbert and George, like Duchamp, never forget the importance of keeping us guessing." But Sylvester was at pains not to trivialize the art of Gilbert and George, or of their forerunner, as he immediately proceeded to discuss "the risk that I have been making G&G and Duchamp himself sound like smart alecs rather than seriously subversive artists who take serious chances."[72]

In a typical statement, in 1986 Gilbert and George elaborated on their motto, "Art for All," declaring that "We want Our Art to speak across the barriers of knowledge directly to People about their Life and not about their knowledge of art." They have consistently denounced modern art: "The twentieth century has been cursed with an art that cannot be understood."[73] Because of this, they stress that their own art avoids traditional artistry in favor of ideas: "You don't see the brush strokes, the handwritten message that every artist is so proud of. We always said that we wanted to make pictures that shoot from the brain like a laser."[74] Their views on art history are proudly xenophobic, as they scorn "Monet or Manet or these lock-jaw names. Disgusting. Art from wine-growing countries." They want their art to break with tradition: "We would like very much to make an art that has nothing to do with the art world, just with the public."[75] And they consistently profess their sincerity: "I'll tell you where there's irony in our work: nowhere, nowhere, nowhere. Every time we see that word in an article about us we go to the dictionary and I still don't understand the bloody meaning of the word. And we hate it."[76]

Louisa Buck observed that "From the beginning of their joint career, Gilbert and George have deliberately embraced extremes of tastelessness. But they've always made a point of combining outrage with ambiguity. Often, the more crudely shocking the content, the more complex the reading."[77] Their iconoclastic stance, with its emphasis on embracing the daily life of the city, has made Gilbert and George a role model for many of the successful young British artists who have become prominent in the past decade. Thus Julian Stallabrass explained that "Gilbert and George were important examples in their manipulation and provocation of the media, their ambivalent attitude to political correctness (highly conservative in their image and their statements but not above complaining of gay-bashing when they were attacked for those views), in their overt populism and in the performative aspect of their art."[78] The most successful of all of these younger artists, Damien Hirst, cited Gilbert and George as proof of the bias of the contemporary art world: "I can't help thinking if Gilbert and George were American, they'd be much more significant."[79]

In 1988 the critic Peter Schjeldahl wrote: "Jeff Koons makes me sick. He may be the definitive artist of this moment, and that makes me sickest."[80] In 2004, Arthur Danto observed that "It is widely acknowledged that Jeff Koons is among the most important artists of the last decades of the twentieth century." Yet, Danto continued, if there were a poll of critics and other art experts, "we would encounter a fair amount of resistance to the idea that Koons is anything more than a clever opportunist who has pulled the wool over the rest of the Art World's eyes." Danto understood what this meant: "That by itself would be evidence of his importance."[81]

The phases of Koons' career are well known in the art world, from the Hoover vacuums in plexiglass cases of the early 1980s, through the floating basketballs in tanks of the mid-1980s, the manufactured porcelain statues of the late 1980s, the explicit photographs of Koons having sex with La Cicciolina, the Italian star of adult films who was then his wife, in the early 1990s, to the large composite paintings of recent years. Koons greatly admires Andy Warhol, and his attitudes and practices follow Warhol in a number of respects. Among these is his use of artisans and assistants to execute his works. In 1999, for example, Koons produced a series of seven paintings, each 3 by 4.3 meters in size, for an exhibition at the Guggenheim Museum in Berlin. He began each by using a computer to create a composite image from photographs he had taken from magazines and books. The resulting computer image was then made into a slide, which was projected onto a canvas, on which it was traced. In rushing to meet the deadline for the Berlin show, Koons had a total of forty-seven artists painting, in shifts, twenty-four hours a day, seven days a week.[82] The statues which are among Koons' most famous works (including the nearly 6-foot long ceramic portrayal of Michael Jackson and his pet chimpanzee, Bubbles, which sold at auction in 2001 for $5.6 million) are made by craftsmen in France, Germany, and Italy.[83]

Koons has complemented his works with statements that are striking in their simplicity and apparent ingenuousness. He openly admits his interest in publicity: "I want to have an impact in people's lives. I want to communicate to as wide a mass as possible." Subtlety was not an element in achieving this: "My art has always used sex as a direct communication line to the viewer."[84] He embraces commercial success: "the seriousness with which a work of art is taken is interrelated to the value it has. The market is the greatest critic."[85] He does not feign modesty: "I'm making some of the greatest art being made now . . . In [the 20th century] there was Picasso and Duchamp. Now I'm taking us out of the twentieth century." He does not claim artistic sophistication: "My work has no aesthetic values . . . I believe that taste is really unimportant." And he stresses that his work has no hidden meanings: "A viewer might at first see irony in my work, but I see none at all. Irony causes too much critical contemplation." His commitment to his art is complete: "My art and my life are totally one."[86] Irving Sandler compared Koons's behavior to that of a predecessor: "Koons spun a web of words around his vacuum cleaner – and all of his subsequent – works, explicating them in an utterly serious and seemingly candid manner in frequent public appearances. Like Warhol he can be considered as much a performance artist as a producer of art objects."[87]

Critics have long puzzled over Koons's work, and his persona. In 1988, Schjeldahl asked: "So who is the joke on? Is Koons playing the fool for his audience or making fools of them? It's useless to ask, because his irony isn't a vector but a spiral, showing a special smirk to every available point of view."[88] In 2004, Danto traced Koons's artistic genealogy: "The conceptual development of art from Duchamp through Warhol to Koons is like the punctuated evolution of science from Galileo through Newton to Einstein." Danto recognized that Koons owed the basis of his artistic existence to these forebears: "Koons has found a way of making high art out of low art – but in a way that would not have been a possibility until the conceptual revolutions of Duchamp and Warhol."[89] Koons embraced a similar genealogy in the course of explaining why he was not troubled by the negative judgments of his work by the critic Hilton Kramer: "I always know everything's OK when Hilton attacks me because in the same breath he always attacks my heroes. He says Jeff Koons had to occur since Jasper Johns painted his American flag. And the flag couldn't have occurred without Duchamp. And after Johns it was Andy . . . That sounds wonderful to me – Duchamp, Johns, Andy Warhol. Such good company!"[90] Like Duchamp and Warhol before him Koons has influenced younger artists not only by producing new forms of art, but by creating a living model for an artist's behavior. So for example not only do Damien Hirst's famous steel and glass cases, that contain a variety of household objects and dead animals, owe a direct debt to Koons's many sealed cases, but Hirst has explained that he admires Koons for deliberately constructing "Jeff Koons, the Artist."[91] It is also apparent that Hirst has taken to heart another of Koons' aphorisms: "The trick is to be outrageous but not offensive."[92]

An art historian wrote in 2005 that "Perhaps more than any other contemporary artist, Tracey Emin has come to stand in Warhol's footsteps, occupying the space of artist-celebrity that he carved out for himself, but also developing it in significant respects."[93] A frequent observation about the young British artists, of whom Emin is a prominent member, is that their art deals with contemporary life.[94] In Emin's case, the life in question is her own:

Emin's exclusive subject matter is her personal life, and that life, as read off from the art, has included underage sex, rape, abortion, bouts of serious depression and long periods of drunkenness... Most famously, Emin made a tent, *Everyone I Have Ever Slept With (1963–1995)*, the inside of which is covered with numerous sewn dedications to lovers, her twin brother and grandmother, a teddy bear and her aborted foetus.[95]

Her presentation of her life is obviously subjective: "in her published statements, as in her works of art, there is a continual slippage between memories of an event and poetic imagining. Her eccentricities and the awkwardness of her expression assure her viewers that the art is authentic and sincere."[96] Emin denies any ironic intent: "Everything that I do is totally sincere."[97]

Early in her career Emin was known for boorishness, and for her liberal use of profanity at drunken public appearances, but Matthew Collings observed in 2001 that her image had subsequently become more nuanced:

Recently public feeling toward Emin has changed slightly from loving to loathe her, to loving to love her. She is still a by-word for artistic charlatanism, and TV and radio personalities will never miss a chance to curry favor by sneering at her. But somehow she's become a by-word for public outbreaks of sentimentalism as well – the nation seems to be able to cope with the contradiction... [Y]ou can hardly get past two or three short paragraphs [of newspaper articles about her] before the writer will be blubbing like crazy, out of a sense of identification with Emin's pain, and the pain of international women; and referring to her as "Tracey" or "Trace," or the favorite – "our Trace."[98]

A historian observed that "like Warhol, Emin appears to use ambiguity as a strategy." He noted that although "her work gives a first impression of a self-absorption, clamor for attention, and a desire to shock that are naïve and even childish," in fact her art makes informed and sophisticated references to both earlier art and popular culture. In a number of works, Emin also alludes to her own celebrity, and to the popular image of herself as a drunken and sexually liberated wild child. This scholar pointed out that this creates a basic ambiguity: "Emin's work both is and is not what it appears at first sight to be. It *is* all those things 'we' see on first impression, but it is *also* the reputation that inescapably accompanies each exhibition of it, brought by its audiences, as well as the mechanisms – above all, of 'celebrity' – by which that reputation is produced and sustained."[99]

When Damien Hirst won the Turner Prize in 1995, an English critic denounced him as a trickster: "If Damien Hirst is anything, he is the ringmaster of his own career – on to his next trick, his next sensation, before the audience starts to think. There are the freak shows of the animals, the jolly paintings, his beaming self."[100] On the same occasion, another critic hailed Hirst as an artist for the ages: "Hirst's work acknowledges a buried sense of loss and longing for completeness that some psychoanalysts believe is universal."[101] Virginia Button summed up the debate, observing that "There seemed to be no middle ground as far as critical response to Hirst's work was concerned: was he a contemporary genius or arch hoaxer intent on conning the public?"[102]

Hirst is the most flamboyant of the young British artists who became a powerful force in contemporary art during the 1990s. In 1988, when he was still a student at Goldsmiths' College, Hirst curated *Freeze*, the first of what became a series of group exhibitions of the work of many of his fellow students held in an empty warehouse in London's Docklands, that has become legendary as the public debut of many of the leading members of the group. In 1991, on a commission from the collector and dealer Charles Saatchi, Hirst made perhaps his most famous work, a 14-foot tiger shark suspended in a formaldehyde solution that he titled *The Physical Impossibility of Death in the Mind of Someone Living*.

Hirst is widely recognized as the leader of what many consider the most vibrant art movement of the past two decades. As the American critic Jerry Saltz observed in 2000, "Ask anyone on the London scene, 'Did Damien set this in motion? Is he one of the reasons for the new Tate?' and you'll see how much influence he's had. He's their prophet and deliverer, their Elvis and ayatollah."[103] Hirst's critical reputation in England is such that a *Financial Times* columnist could recently compare him to the greatest artist of the past century, seriously posing the question "Will Damien Hirst, the one-time *enfant terrible* of 'Brit art,' be seen in the same light as Picasso by 2050?"[104] Hirst's success in the market is hardly less impressive. A work of his surpassed $2 million at auction in 2004, and in 2005 a front-page story in the *New York Times* reported that *The Physical Impossibility* had been sold privately to an American collector for $8 million.[105] Hirst announced in the spring of 2006 that his next project, to be displayed at a new London gallery in 2007, would consist of a human skull cast in platinum, completely encased in diamonds. He would collaborate with a London jeweller on the project, which would use 8,500 diamonds, and cost an estimated £8–10 million to produce. *The Observer* reported that the work, to be titled *For the Love of God*, would be the most expensive work of art ever created, and that the asking price would be £50 million. Hirst described the work as a celebration of life and a defiance of death: "I've always adhered to the principle that the simplest ideas are the best, and this will be the ultimate two fingers up to death."[106]

Hirst is a celebrity. In 2000, Louisa Buck observed that "Such is Damien Hirst's current status that it wouldn't really affect his reputation if he gave up making art altogether."[107] Julian Stallabrass remarked that "Hirst is as much or more known for his lifestyle as for his art, and he takes care to ensure that the two are thoroughly entangled." Observing that Hirst's work is "spectacular and attention-seeking," Stallabrass argued that:

This courting of publicity was cloaked with an all-knowing irony... A facile postmodernism, the basis for a ubiquitous irony, was the foundation of this new art, one which took no principle terribly seriously. The new art would be quite as dreadful as the philistines said it was... but this time deliberately so: it would use the philistines' energy and power in the mass media against them.[108]

Hirst has readily conceded that he welcomes public attention: "As an artist, you have a desire to communicate an idea to a hell of a lot of people on a massive scale." Yet he denies that he has created a new persona to gain fame: "I'm not prepared to do that." Interestingly, however, Hirst declared that he admired Jeff Koons for doing just this, explaining that "he actually made a concerted effort to do it as part of his art." Hirst admired Koons's sacrifice: "he gave up his life to become his own idea of himself." But Hirst condemned the hypocrisy of other artists who denied they had become actors in order to gain success: "What I hate is a hell of a lot of artists who I know, who are alive, have done that and won't admit it." Hirst did not believe this applied to him, and in fact he maintained that he did not feel famous: "I just think everyone's famous, but not me."[109]

Arthur Danto noted that Hirst has been called the "hooligan genius" of British art, but defended his art on conceptual grounds:

Putting a huge fish in a large tank of formaldehyde sounds easy enough... But imagining doing it requires a degree of artistic intuition of a very rare order, since one would have to anticipate what it would look like and what effect it would have on the viewer. The work in fact has the power, sobriety, and majesty of a cathedral.[110]

Louisa Buck stressed the two sides of Hirst: "being a dab-hand at spectacle and having an engaging way with the popular has also concealed Hirst's ability to be a serious – and in many ways, traditional – artist who knows art history well enough to employ a keen formalism and sense of scale, and who still believes that art should grapple with the hefty issues of what it is to be human, to live and to face death."[111] Matthew Collings commented on Hirst's shrewd cultivation of his public image:

In interviews, he acts like a mad genius-artist. The media assume this is the only way a modern genius-artist can possibly behave. They take it for granted it's a mark of his genius that he actually does behave like that. So you've got to admit he's got a good sense of the media and he understands how that mind set works, although you might still question if that's really such an amazing achievement for an artist. He never actually says anything genuinely compromising or revealing, but we're all supposed to be amazed at his shocking candor anyway.[112]

As early as 1995, David Sylvester identified Hirst's ancestry: "Duchamp... has been the veritable patron saint of the most conspicuous art made since the mid-1960s (Damien Hirst is an obvious example)."[113] Louisa Buck pointed to another of his ancestors: "Hirst doesn't make great claims for his art: like a true child of Warhol he professes to be happy with any response."[114]

Consequences

I've played my part as artistic clown.
Marcel Duchamp, 1957[115]

Duchamp was a kind of French Buster Keaton.
Harold Rosenberg[116]

During the course of the past century, a series of important artistic innovators have been accused of being tricksters: their major works have shocked many viewers, have often been considered tasteless or vulgar, and have been judged by many to be jokes. In many cases, these artists' silence or deadpan denials that their works are jokes has led to extended and often heated debate over whether the works are intended as serious contributions. Art scholars and critics who have studied these artists have frequently concluded that their behavior is entirely deliberate. In this view, the artists have employed a strategy in which an initial radical contribution that has provoked widespread criticism, and often outrage, is followed either by the artist's refusal to defend the work, or by statements in its defense that are obviously ironic. The result of this strategy has been to create a basic ambiguity, and the degree of its success can be measured by the number of admirers and detractors who subsequently become engaged in the debate over the significance of the work in question. In every such case, a key element of this debate has concerned the motives and sincerity of the artist.

The strategy of the artist as trickster is a twentieth-century innovation. A number of artists in earlier centuries were accused of perpetrating hoaxes, but these accusations generally failed to generate sustained interest or discussion, typically because they were clearly false. As a young artist, Marcel Duchamp learned a series of lessons that led him to devise this strategy, and his behavior made him a prototype for a number of later artists.

The provocative nature of the trickster model, and the importance of Duchamp, Beuys, Warhol, and the other artists treated in this chapter, has generated considerable attention from art scholars, and there now exist many detailed analyses of the behavior of each of these artists. As is frequently the case in the humanities, however, there has been a failure to generalize about this behavior. Thus, although studies of artists like Klein or Manzoni virtually always mention Duchamp as a predecessor, these references are usually cursory, and the bulk of the analysis devoted to the artist in question inevitably considers that artist's behavior in isolation. A consequence of this is that although we have dozens of monographic studies of the individual artists treated here, we do not have a single study of the general model of the behavior of the artist as trickster. Because the many instances of this behavior have not been linked to all the others, there has been a failure to appreciate how important this model has been overall to the art of the twentieth century. This chapter has obviously not considered all the cases of this behavior, but the nine instances examined here are all major modern artists, and clearly demonstrate how central the model has been to the art of the past century.

A number of common features of this behavior have often been overlooked. One, noted above, is that this behavior is a new phenomenon in the twentieth century. Another is that the behavior has been restricted to conceptual innovators. Radical conceptual innovators are iconoclasts, and they are usually young when they make their most important contributions. Duchamp and his followers have taken advantage of their youth, often feigning naivete and ignorance of tradition to heighten the public image of them as brash, arrogant, and impudent. And the large conceptual component of their innovations has made ambiguity a particularly powerful tool. Thus just as the Futurists discovered that written manifestos, containing complex intellectual rationales for their conceptual art works, could be valuable tools in increasing the audience for those works, so the trickster conceptual innovators of the past century recognized that ambiguity, and the debate that it produced over the meaning and sincerity of their works, could be attractive accompaniments to their works for many critics and collectors.

The model of the artist as trickster has effectively made the work of art inseparable from the personality of the artist. Prior to Duchamp, many art scholars studied the ideas and attitudes of artists in order to illuminate the meaning of their art, but many others considered this unnecessary, on the grounds that the significance of the work of art was embodied in the work itself. From Duchamp on, the work of the trickster artists effectively eliminated the latter option. With Duchamp, Beuys, Warhol, and their trickster peers, we can never look at their work without thinking not only of their ideas – what is the artistic significance of a manufactured object purchased at a hardware store, or a silkscreen of a photograph taken from a magazine – but also of their attitudes – was *Fountain* or *Fat Chair* really intended to be taken seriously? In this sense, the model of the trickster has produced a type of conceptual art that is more personal than most other forms of art.

Late in his life, Marcel Duchamp gave a lecture titled "The Creative Act." He reflected that "art history has consistently decided upon the virtues of a work of art through considerations completely divorced from the rationalized explanations of the artist." Ultimately, he concluded that the reason for this was that "the creative act is not performed by the artist alone; the spectator brings the work in contact with the external world by deciphering and interpreting its inner qualifications and thus adds his contribution to the creative act."[117] In the final chapter of a recent monograph on Duchamp, three art scholars observe that with this formulation "Duchamp strikes at the heart of the modernist idea of the self-sufficiency of the work of art, its immutable and independent quality, in his ideas about the spectator, who, for him, is the other pole of the creation of art." With undisguised admiration, the three close the chapter by reflecting that Duchamp's emphasis on the importance of the spectator is a form of "abnegation" or "self-effacement as an artist."[118] What the three fail to notice, however, is that the behavior described in this chapter can be seen as a clever way for the artist to reverse the circumstance identified in Duchamp's lecture, that "the artist... plays no role at all in the judgment of his own work."[119] For when the viewer stands before the work of the trickster artist, perhaps to a greater extent than for any earlier art the viewer's critical reaction is dominated by the effort to analyze the artist's intentions. Ever the master of irony, Duchamp appears to have devised a way of manipulating the spectator's judgment that is neither abnegating nor self-effacing, for even decades after his death Duchamp is present whenever a viewer confronts his art, wondering whether he was serious or joking, and having to consider that perhaps he was both.

9

Painting by Proxy

The Conceptual Artist as Manufacturer

Introduction

It sometimes seems to me that the labor of the artist is of a very old-fashioned kind; the artist himself a survival, a craftsman or artisan of a disappearing species, working in his own room, following his own home-made empirical methods, living in untidy intimacy with his tools... Perhaps conditions are changing, and instead of this spectacle of an eccentric individual using whatever comes his way, there will instead be a picture-making laboratory, with its specialist officially clad in white, rubber-gloved, keeping to a precise schedule, armed with strictly appropriate apparatus and instruments, each with its appointed place and exact function... So far, chance has not been eliminated from practice, or mystery from method, or inspiration from regular hours; but I do not vouch for the future.

Paul Valéry, 1936[1]

In 1955, in the A.W. Mellon Lectures in the Fine Arts at the National Gallery of Art, Washington, the French philosopher Étienne Gilson, a member of the Académie Française, presented his analysis of the art of painting. These lectures were published in both English and French in 1958.[2] Early in this discussion, Gilson reflected on the essence of painting:

The nature of painting is such that the artist who conceives the work is also the one who executes it. This proposition is not necessarily true of the sculptor, but it is assuredly true of the painter. Except for tasks of secondary importance that can easily be left to his assistants, it is the painter himself who confers the material and physical existence upon the work he conceives.[3]

The touch of the painter created the work of art: "It is the hand of the painter that embodies in actually existing physical objects the conceptions

184

of his mind." Unlike poets, playwrights, novelists, and composers, who are white-collar workers, painters necessarily work with their hands: "when all is said and done, painters (and sculptors) are related to manual laborers by a deep-rooted affinity that nothing can eliminate." Gilson underscored this point: "As often as not, a painter has to don working clothes in the same way as a mechanic or any other artisan. He does not resent dirtying his hands with paint."[4] Nor could the artist choose whether or not to execute his own paintings: "a painter is the sole and total cause of his work."[5]

In considering the issue of authenticity, Gilson described what he called an extreme case in which an artist, presented with an imitation of his work done by another artist, might add his own touches to the painting and then sign it:

Is such a painting authentic? No, since most of it has not been done by the painter himself. Yes, since, after being done in his own manner, this work of art has been completed by the painter himself and finally acknowledged by him as his own work.[6]

The case for authenticity thus involves the physical touch of the artist. Gilson was of course aware that a number of Old Masters had routinely made paintings in collaboration with others, but he noted that in every case these collaborations involved "a master and assistants working together under his direction and responsibility."[7] In two examples he discussed, both Rubens and Delacroix used assistants to paint parts of the works that the masters completed.[8]

Gilson stressed that his account of art rested in large part on the views of artists: "painters will perhaps notice how careful I have been to listen to what they themselves had to say concerning the nature of their own work."[9] He gave no indication that his analysis of the nature of painting would meet with any disagreement from artists. Yet even as he wrote, his statement of the nature of painting had been contradicted by the practice of at least one significant painter of the early twentieth century. Interestingly, it had also been rejected in theory by the private statements of the greatest painter of the twentieth century. And more importantly, within just a few years after Gilson wrote, major artists would create important paintings that clearly controverted Gilson's definitions, and their practices would change the mainstream of advanced art. Today some of the greatest artists do not touch their paintings, and some do not even supervise those who do touch these works. Recent innovations in art have radically changed the nature of painting, so that many painters have joined their literary and musical peers as white-collar workers. And recent research on artistic creativity has given us an understanding of the common elements that underlie this new practice.

Old Masters

Before examining the experience of the twentieth century, it is useful to return briefly to an earlier time. Recent investigations of the practices of two great seventeenth-century painters provide some valuable clues to the source of the novel practices of more recent artists.

Peter Paul Rubens and Rembrandt van Rijn were both recognized by contemporaries as among the most talented painters who worked in the seventeenth-century Netherlands. Both Rubens in Antwerp and Rembrandt in Amsterdam maintained sizable workshops where they were surrounded by numerous pupils and assistants.[10] Yet the two painters ran their workshops very differently.

Rubens collaborated with his assistants in the execution of large numbers of paintings. Zirka Filipczak described his practice:

Rubens provided the crucial invention for each piece but delegated much of the actual execution to others. To this end, he provided his pupils, assistants, and collaborators with models for the general composition of a picture in the form of preparatory drawings and, especially, *disegni coloriti* or oil sketches. He often also furnished models for individual parts of the work, such as head studies, many of which he kept on file in his studio. With works largely executed by his assistants, Rubens generally retouched the final product in order to restore the spark of life where it had been dulled by uninspired execution.[11]

There was considerable variation in the amount of work the master did personally, and the cost of his paintings varied accordingly. So for example, in 1618, Rubens wrote to a patron that paintings not entirely by his hand "are rated at a much lower price."[12]

Recent scholarship has revealed that Rembrandt's practice was very different. Svetlana Alpers concluded that "So far as we know he almost never collaborated on paintings with assistants."[13] Unlike the joint products made by Rubens and his assistants, in Rembrandt's studio the works were all made separately, so that Rembrandt was "a master surrounded by student-assistants each eventually producing paintings on their own for sale."[14] Josua Bruyn stressed this difference: "being an assistant in Rembrandt's studio meant taking one's own share in the studio's output rather than – as was the case with, for instance, Rubens – assisting the master in the execution of large paintings."[15]

Alpers explained that Rubens's method of making paintings allowed a division of labor:

He developed a painting factory: assistants specialized in certain skills – landscapes, animals, and so on – and the master devised a mode of invention employing a clever combination of oil sketches and drawings. These permitted his inventions to be executed by others, sometimes with final touches to hands or faces by the master himself.[16]

Rembrandt worked very differently, making paintings without preparatory sketches and drawings. Ernst van de Wetering concluded that "Rembrandt . . . rarely prepared his paintings with the aid of drawings."[17] Alpers agreed that "Rembrandt's habit was not to work out his inventions in advance through drawings, but rather to invent paintings in the course of their execution."[18] Because Rembrandt's method of working did not separate invention and execution, his workshop could not operate like that of Rubens, for without drawings or other plans to guide them, his assistants could not actually work on his paintings: "Rather than executing his inventions . . . Rembrandt's students had to make paintings like his."[19]

Art historians have long recognized that some Old Masters worked collaboratively, like Rubens, and that others, like Rembrandt, did not. Thus, for example, Alpers observed that "While Raphael and Rubens could work with a team, Leonardo and most notably Michelangelo, could not."[20] Alpers suggested that these differences could have been due to personality – Rembrandt "was not a man who got on easily with others" – but it is more likely that a general explanation lies in what Alpers calls the artist's "pictorial personality."[21] Raphael, like Rubens, was a conceptual artist who made meticulous plans for his paintings that could then be carried out by others, much as some architects make detailed blueprints that others can follow in building their projects.[22] In contrast, Leonardo and Michelangelo, like Rembrandt, were experimental artists who were not comfortable planning their works, and who had to execute their own paintings because they did not believe in separating invention and execution.[23] Important conceptual painters who were capable of planning their works in advance could hire assistants to execute paintings, based on their blueprints – preparatory drawings and oil sketches – whereas experimental painters generally would be incapable of collaborating with others, because of their inability to anticipate the final appearance of their paintings.

Interestingly, we know that the different methods by which painters produced their works were familiar to seventeenth-century Dutch painters. In his book, *Introduction to the Higher Education of the Art of Painting*, published in 1678, the painter Samuel van Hoogstraten, a former student of Rembrandt, described a contest that was supposed to have occurred in Holland around 1630, in which three painters were given the task of painting a landscape within a specified time limit before an audience of art connoisseurs.[24] The first painter immediately began to paint finished forms, by routine. The second painter began by covering his canvas with a variety of colors, "here light there dark more or less like a variegated agate or marbled paper," then created houses, ships, and other forms that were suggested by these random markings: "In short, his eye, as though looking for forms that lay hidden in a chaos of paint, steered his hand in true wise so that one saw a complete painting before one realized what he intended." The third painter initially appeared to be doing nothing – "it seemed at first even that he was deliberately wasting time, or knew not how he should begin" – but in fact he was creating a mental image of the finished work: "he was first forming in his imagination the whole conception of his work; he was first making the painting in his mind before he put his brush into the paint." In the end, the third painter was judged the winner, for he had "in his well-chosen naturalness and in the art something extraordinary," which was considered superior to the first painter's works "that flow easily from the hand," or the second painter's works made "by searching and finding in random images."[25]

The first artist in the account, who produced conventional and repetitive works, was not a potential innovator. The second artist was an experimental painter, who found his subject as he worked, whereas the third artist was a conceptual painter, who preconceived images before executing them. Although the work of the conceptual painter was deemed the best because the academic tradition accorded its greatest honors to art that originated in ideas, Hoogstraten's anecdote demonstrates that seventeenth-century artists were aware of both the experimental and the conceptual approaches to painting.

Understanding the differences in the practices of conceptual and experimental Old Masters provides a useful background for our consideration of the twentieth century, when some conceptual artists would delegate even more of the work involved in executing their paintings. And for this purpose the practice of Rubens yields one more interesting insight. The specific case is not strictly relevant to this inquiry, because it involves the production of prints rather than paintings, but it is suggestive.

When Rubens completed a painting he sometimes had a printmaker produce copies of the work; this was common among a number of masters of the time, for the circulation of numerous and relatively inexpensive prints allowed their work to become known much more widely throughout Europe. Following the normal practice, Rubens would generally provide a drawing of his painting that the printmaker would translate into his medium. Late in his life, however, Rubens departed from this practice:

In a few exceptional cases in the late 1630s, Rubens provided inventions without preparing any model. Crippled by gout, he sometimes found it difficult to work on the small scale that was necessary in preparatory drawings for frontispieces. This physical limitation led him to experiment with a novel procedure. He dictated his ideas to Erasmus Quellinus who then recorded them in a drawing. The frontispieces engraved after this type of drawing bore the following credits: "Erasmus Quellinius delineavit, Pet. Paul. Rubenius invenit, Corn. Galleus junior sculpsit." Even though he had not lifted a pencil in the manual execution of a work, Rubens was thus recognized as the inventor of a visual image – a revolutionary idea in the 17th century.[26]

Rubens' practice in these cases can logically be seen as a preview of the behavior of many conceptual painters of the second half of the twentieth century.

Young Geniuses

In the *Dada Almanac*, published in Berlin in 1920, an article jointly authored by the artist Jean Arp, the poet Tristan Tzara, and a writer named Walter Serner proposed that paintings could be executed by proxy: "the good painter was recognized, for instance, by the fact that he ordered his works from a carpenter, giving his specifications on the phone."[27] This idea evidently resonated with Laszlo Moholy-Nagy, a young Hungarian painter who was then working in Berlin. Under the influence of Constructivism and Suprematism, Moholy-Nagy was searching for new ways of making art that would replace easel painting, in which engineer-artists would provide designs for works of art that could be mass produced. In 1922, Moholy-Nagy designed three colored compositions on graph paper and had them manufactured from industrial enamel. A biographer of the artist noted that "The result was not an industrial product, not even a model, but a perfectly composed and artistically constructed work of art: a Suprematist composition appearing not on canvas but on a slightly curved metal plate."[28] Moholy-Nagy ordered the three works in person, but when they were completed, he declared "I might even have done it over the telephone!," and in later years they were given the name "telephone pictures."[29]

Moholy-Nagy was a protean conceptual artist. He became an influential teacher at the Bauhaus, and he made contributions in areas as diverse as photography, industrial design, documentary films, and the design of stage sets for opera and theatre. He did not pursue the concept of the telephone pictures, and it does not appear that they influenced the course of advanced art. Yet Moholy-Nagy's execution of the Dada idea has led some art scholars to consider him "a visionary in regard to Minimal Art and the modern concept of anonymous authorship."[30]

The idea of painting by proxy recurred in later years. An interesting instance appears in Françoise Gilot's account of her life with Picasso. Gilot, who was herself a painter, wrote of an incident in 1948 when Picasso was working on a large painting, *La Cuisine*. After he had completed the basic forms, he told Gilot: "I see two possible directions for this canvas. I want another one just like it, to start from. You make a second version up to this point and I'll work on it from there. I want it tomorrow." Because of the little time available, Gilot called Picasso's nephew, Javier Vilato, who was also a painter, and asked him to help her. Working together, the two completed the task, and Picasso subsequently made two different versions of the painting. Gilot recalled that she did similar jobs for Picasso on several occasions to save him time when he wanted to develop a composition in two different ways: "That gave him a chance to get to the main point quickly and work over it longer." She noted that "For Pablo my collaboration was a practical demonstration of the truth of one of his favorite aphorisms: 'If I telegraph one of my canvases to New York,' he said, 'any house-painter should be able to do it properly. A painting is a sign – just like the sign that indicates a one-way street.'"[31]

The 1960s witnessed a series of departures from Gilson's characterization of the nature of painting, the first of which occurred at the very beginning of the decade. Early in 1960, in Paris Yves Klein began to create paintings with what he called "living brushes." Nude models would cover themselves with Klein's patented International Klein Blue paint, then press themselves against large sheets of paper tacked to the wall or laid on the floor. In one production in March 1960, one hundred invited guests filled a Paris art gallery and listened to a small orchestra as they watched three nude models create the paintings that the critic Pierre Restany had named "anthropometries." Klein, dressed formally in a tuxedo and white tie, stood nearby giving the models instructions and directions as they worked. This performance was documented by hired photographers, as were a number of subsequent sessions. On some later occasions, Klein added white gloves to his formal attire, to underscore his physical separation from the execution of the paintings. As he explained,

In this way I stayed clean. I no longer dirtied myself with color, not even the tips of my fingers. The work finished itself there in front of me, under my direction, in absolute collaboration with the model. And I could salute its birth into the tangible world in a dignified manner, dressed in a tuxedo.[32]

The process satisfied Klein's conception of the artistic process, because he believed that the artist should conceive works of art but not personally produce physical objects. Using living brushes allowed him to retain control of the production of the paintings without any direct physical contact: "Detached and distant, the work of art must complete itself before my eyes and under my command."[33]

Unlike Moholy-Nagy's telephone paintings, Klein's anthropometries became influential for advanced art. Klein was the most important French painter of his generation, and the anthropometries became his most important works.[34] Many younger artists were impressed both by Klein's detachment from the execution of his paintings and by the flair of the performances at which he produced them.

Klein eliminated the artist's touch from the creation of paintings, but retained personal control over the assistants who executed them. In 1962, Robert Rauschenberg dispensed with the latter as well. In 1951, as a student at Black Mountain College, Rauschenberg had made the *White Paintings*, a series of canvases to which he applied white paint evenly with a roller. Although these were ostensibly empty canvases, shadows and reflections served to create images, demonstrating to Rauschenberg's satisfaction that there was in fact no such thing as an empty canvas. The impact of the *White Paintings* was considerable, for when the composer John Cage saw them he responded by writing his famous 4'33", which demonstrated that there was in fact no such thing as silence.[35]

The original *White Paintings* disappeared; Rauschenberg often painted over his works, and these seven unmarked canvases must have been particularly inviting targets. In 1962, Pontus Hulten, the director of Stockholm's Moderna Museet, contacted Rauschenberg to request the *White Paintings* for an exhibition. Rauschenberg told Hulten the paintings had been lost, but sent him the measurements of the panels together with samples of the white pigment and canvas, and Hulten had them recreated.[36] This may have marked the first time that an important artist had authorized the execution of his paintings without supervising the execution, or even seeing the result. It is presumed that Hulten destroyed the paintings after exhibiting them, because when Rauschenberg's dealer, Leo Castelli, wanted to exhibit the works in 1968, Rauschenberg had his current assistant, the painter Brice Marden, prepare a new set.[37]

Andy Warhol may have done more than any other artist of his generation to subvert traditional practices and attitudes associated with painting. Both his paintings and his statements about them systematically undermined the generalizations Gilson had made in 1958. Early in 1962, Warhol began to use stencils, and with them he made the thirty-two paintings of Campbell's soup cans that were exhibited at his first solo show, at Los Angeles' Ferus Gallery in June.[38] In July, Warhol discovered that he could work much more quickly by silkscreening his paintings. During the next three months he made 100 pictures, including the portraits of Marilyn Monroe and the images of Coca-Cola bottles that became the basis for his first solo show in New York, at the Stable Gallery in November.[39]

Warhol's paintings exploded on the art world, and almost overnight he came to be seen as the leader of the controversial new Pop movement. The demand for his paintings soared, and in 1963 he hired Gerard Malanga as an assistant to make them. Later in the year, Warhol moved his studio into a warehouse and factory building that became the first of four of his studios to be called the Factory. During this time Warhol began making statements embracing the use of mechanical processes and stressing his personal detachment from the execution of his art. For example in a 1963 interview published in a leading art magazine, he declared "I think somebody should be able to do all my paintings for me," and explained his use of screening by stating "The reason I'm painting this way is that I want to be a machine."[40] In another interview the same year, when he was asked what his profession was, Warhol responded "Factory owner."[41] In his practice, the mechanical process of silkscreening, the use of magazine photographs as the images of his paintings, and the serial repetition of these images not only from one work to another, but often within a single work, all served to emphasize the absence of the human element in general in the execution of the works and the absence of Warhol's touch in particular.

There is uncertainty about the actual division of labor between Warhol and his assistants. In a 1965 interview he declared that "Gerard does all my paintings," and in 1966, when asked about his role in making the paintings, he replied "I just selected the subjects." Years later, however, he insisted that "I really do all the paintings," disowning an earlier statement to the contrary by explaining "We were just being funny."[42] Concerning the early years, Malanga recalled that "When the screens were very large, we worked together; otherwise I was left to my devices."[43] Malanga further explained that the need for the artist's personal quality control was ruled out by Warhol's philosophy:

Each painting took about four minutes, and we worked as mechanically as we could, trying to get each image right, but we never got it right... Andy embraced his mistakes. We never rejected anything. Andy would say, "It's part of the art."[44]

The mechanical production of Warhol's paintings led to concerns about forgery. Warhol publicly dismissed these in a 1981 interview, confidently stating that "If there are any fakes around I can tell."[45] According to Malanga, however, the problem was more serious: "Unlike Rauschenberg, Andy never destroyed his screens after they were used, and for this reason he has always been worried about the possibility of a forgery. If somebody faked his art, he could never hope to identify it."[46]

Sol LeWitt was a leading member of the Conceptual art movement of the late 1960s. In a manifesto published in 1967, LeWitt stated a basic tenet:

In conceptual art the idea or concept is the most important aspect of the work. When an artist uses a conceptual form of art, it means that all of the planning and decisions are made beforehand and the execution is a perfunctory affair. The idea becomes a machine that makes the art.

LeWitt spelled out one immediate consequence: "This kind of art... is usually free from the dependence on the skill of the artist as craftsman."[47] Two years later, LeWitt again stressed the primacy of planning: "Once the idea of the piece is established in the artist's mind and the final form is decided, the process is carried out blindly."[48]

In 1968, LeWitt made the first example of what would become his trademark form of art, works drawn or painted directly onto walls. In a 1971 statement defining the genre, he described the possibility of a complete separation between the originator of the work and the person who executed it:

The artist conceives and plans the wall drawing. It is realized by draftsmen (the artist can act as his own draftsman); the plan (written, spoken, or drawn) is interpreted by the draftsman.

LeWitt specified that the artist and draftsman would "become collaborators in making the art." He went on to treat the issue of the validity of the finished work:

> The wall drawing is the artist's art, as long as the plan is not violated. If it is, then the draftsman becomes the artist and the drawing would be his work of art, but art that is a parody of the original concept.
>
> The draftsman may make errors in following the plan. All wall drawings contain errors, they are part of the work.[49]

LeWitt went on to produce hundreds of wall drawings. Yet he never specified who would determine whether the plan for a particular wall drawing was violated, or according to what criteria. In practice, this determination obviously could not always be done by the artist, for even during his lifetime LeWitt often did not see the final works. It is possible for purchasers of the drawings to have them executed by LeWitt's designated assistants, but this was not required by any of the artist's statements, and LeWitt encouraged the owners of simple wall drawings to execute them themselves.[50]

When the touch of the artist is no longer necessary for the creation of a painting, the question arises of what determines authenticity. Warhol never fully confronted this question. One result is that there are frequent disputes over whether specific works can properly be sold as his, and the decisions of official experts on the authenticity of particular works by Warhol often appear arbitrary. LeWitt did deal with this problem, however. Purchasers of wall drawings receive certificates of authenticity, signed by the artist; these are often accompanied by diagrams of the works.[51] The economic value of the wall drawings is considerably increased by the fact that they can be moved from place to place, simply by painting them in a new location. Each drawing is supposed to exist in only one location at a time, so when a new version is executed the old one is supposed to be painted over.

Since the 1960s it has become commonplace for successful painters to employ assistants who perform most or all of the labor involved in executing their finished works. There are too many cases of this to catalogue in full. Several important contemporary artists can serve as examples.

In 1988, Peter Schjeldahl remarked that Jeff Koons "may be the definitive artist of this moment," and in 2004, Arthur Danto confirmed that "It is widely acknowledged that Jeff Koons is among the most important artists of the last decades of the twentieth century."[52] The value of Koons's art is considerable; his works have sold at auction for more than $1 million on more than twenty occasions. In an interview in 2000 with the English critic David Sylvester, Koons gave a detailed account of the preparation of seven large paintings, each more than 135 square feet in size, for an exhibition at the Guggenheim Museum in Berlin. Koons began by taking images from magazines and books, and arranging them into composites with a computer: "After I have an image on a computer file that I like, we make a digital slide. And then the slide is projected and we draw out the image on the canvas." The painting was then done by hired assistants. Because the work was done under time pressure, Koons brought in more assistants than usual:

We were up to forty-seven at the end. There were a lot of people mixing color. And we had two different shifts, so the studio was going twenty-four hours a day, seven days a week, always with half the staff there working to complete the paintings.

Koons emphasized his complete control of the execution:

I mean, physically, I could execute these paintings, and they would look identical to the paintings that are there now. But I wouldn't have been able to finish one painting in this time frame. So the thing is to be able to bring in a staff. And I've worked with my main staff now for about five years, so they already know what I want. And they know my vocabulary and they understand that there's no room for interpretation.

Referring to the practices of Raphael and Rubens, Sylvester asked why, unlike those masters, Koons chose not to do any of the paintings himself. Koons responded not only by saying that his time was required for super-vision, but also by reflecting that participating in the work of painting would actually interfere with his growth as an artist:

When you have forty-seven people doing something, I have to be watching all the process. Also, my vocabulary isn't just the execution of it; it's also a continued conception of where I want my work to go in another area. So it has to do more with the reality of being able to be in a position where I can continue to grow as much as possible as an artist, instead of being tied down in the execution of the work.[53]

Damien Hirst is widely recognized as the leader of the young British artists, who rose to prominence in the 1990s and in the process made London the center of the contemporary art world. Commenting in 2000 on Hirst's role in London's art, an American critic remarked that "He's their prophet and deliverer, their Elvis and ayatollah," whereas in 2005 a *Financial Times* columnist asked rhetorically, "Will Damien Hirst, the one-time *enfant terrible* of 'Brit art', be seen in the same light as Picasso by 2050?"[54] Unlike Koons, Hirst does not make preparatory drawings directly on a computer, but has his drawings transferred to a computer by an assistant: "I'll do a drawing and then I'll have it done by somebody who's got a computer. It's like a fabrication drawing, basically, so it can be made from that drawing."[55] When asked why he didn't execute his own works, Hirst answered in conceptual terms:

You've got an idea, or you've got a vision, and you've got to see that vision through. It's like thinking, "I'm an artist; I've got to paint my own paintings." And the logical extension of that is "Yeh, but who's making my paints?"[56]

Although Hirst did not mention Marcel Duchamp, the last sentence appears to refer to a comment made by Duchamp in 1961, in defending his readymades against the charge that because they were manufactured they could not be works of art: "Since the tubes of paint used by the artist are manufactured and readymade products we must conclude that all the paintings in the world are 'readymades aided' and also works of assemblage."[57]

Hirst also defended his practice of using assistants to make his famous spot paintings, on the grounds that the assistants did better work than he did:

I only ever made five spot paintings. Personally. I can paint spots. But when I started painting the spots I knew exactly where it was going, I knew exactly what was going to happen, and I couldn't be fucking arsed doing it. And I employed people. And my spots I painted are shite. They're shit. I did them on the wrong background, there's the pin-holes [from the compass] in the middle of the spots which at the time I said I wanted, because I wanted a kind of truth to it. Under close scrutiny, you can see the process by which they were made. They're shit compared to ... The best person who ever painted spots for me was Rachel [Howard]. She's brilliant. Absolutely fucking brilliant. The best spot painting you can have by me is one painted by Rachel.[58]

When Gordon Burn observed that it seemed to be part of Hirst's aesthetic to have someone else between him and the art, with the spot paintings as an example, Hirst replied: "The dots are boring [to make]. And I love other people."[59] In discussing the exclusion of emotion by the grid structure of the spot paintings, Hirst made a comment that echoed Warhol: "I want them to look like they've been made by a person trying to paint like a machine."[60]

Conclusion

In 1958, Étienne Gilson stated what he considered a basic and immutable fact about painting:

In painting, it is impossible to distinguish between art itself and execution, as if art were wholly in the mind and execution wholly in the hand. Art here is *in* execution, and if it is true to say that the intellect of the painter is engaged in all the motions of the hand, it is equally true to say that a painter could entertain no thought about his art if his hand were not there to give to the word "art" a concrete meaning.[61]

Within just two years, however, advanced artists had begun a series of innovations that separated the conception and execution of paintings in precisely the way that Gilson had declared impossible. Yves Klein's use of living brushes allowed him to supervise the execution of his anthropometries without dirtying himself with paint. Robert Rauschenberg could provide instructions for re-creating his *White Paintings* on another continent. Andy Warhol's use of silkscreens removed the human touch from painting altogether. On a number of occasions Warhol declared he played no part in the execution of his works. Sol LeWitt's philosophy of conceptual art separated execution from conception in principle, and his practice with his wall drawings put this into effect. And many of the most important artists active today, including Jeff Koons and Damien Hirst, rarely if ever touch the paintings that are produced by dozens of hired assistants and are sold as works by these masters.

Gilson made two basic mistakes. One was to state rules of art, and to declare that these were immutable. In doing this he failed to recognize the force of the conceptual impulse in twentieth-century art. The story of art in the past century is in large part one of young iconoclastic innovators systematically breaking every significant rule, tradition, or convention that they could identify. Thus Klein was 32 when he first used living brushes, Rauschenberg was 37 when he authorized Hulten to recreate the *White Paintings*, Warhol was 34 when he began to silkscreen his paintings, and LeWitt was 39 when he declared the freedom of the artist from the need to execute his own paintings. Earlier in the twentieth century, conceptual artists had broken the traditional association of painters with trademark styles by beginning to change their styles at will, and had created new genres of art that intentionally broke the rules of the time-honored forms of painting and sculpture.[62] Gilson might have anticipated that conceptual artists would find a way to break the rules of painting he published in 1958. When Klein, Warhol, and others promptly did this, they were effectively demonstrating that artists, not scholars or critics, determine the nature of art.

Yet Gilson did not err only in failing to foresee the conceptual innovations of the 1960s, for his account of the history of painting missed a basic distinction in artistic practice that had existed since the Renaissance. Gilson declared that "it cannot be doubted that the art of the painter resides in his hands, in his fingers, and probably still more in his wrists, at the same time that it resides in his intellect."[63] Yet Vasari knew that the relative importance of the hand and the intellect varied enormously in the art of even the greatest painters.[64] A number of art historians have documented, and puzzled over, the fact that some Old Masters were better able than others to delegate the work of painting to assistants, thus allowing these masters, including Raphael and Rubens, to produce many more square feet of finished paintings than such others as Leonardo, Michelangelo, and Rembrandt. The basic difference appears to lie in the ability of conceptual innovators, from Raphael on, to produce a high degree of separation between invention and execution, whereas for Leonardo and his fellow experimental innovators invention and execution were inseparable. Gilson is thus just one of many art scholars who have failed to perceive the distinction between conceptual and experimental innovators, and consequently have failed to understand its implications. For the studio practices of such conceptual artists as Klein, Rauschenberg, Warhol, LeWitt, Koons, and Hirst can be seen as logical extensions of the earlier practices of their conceptual predecessors Raphael and Rubens. This process has produced some unexpected results. So for example the touch of the artist's hand, once regarded as the tangible demonstration of genius, is now seen by one of today's leading artists as an unnecessary and time-consuming feature of painting that actually interferes with his growth as an artist.

In 1958, Étienne Gilson claimed that "The art of the painter is an art of the whole man."[65] This is no longer true. Contrary to more than five centuries of tradition, during the second half of the twentieth century many painters ceased to be manual laborers who dirty their own hands with paint, and have instead become manufacturers, who hire employees to make paintings according to their plans. As Damien Hirst recently put it, "The painter has stopped being this hairy guy with paint all over him. He became a guy in a suit, or a lab coat probably."[66] Making the touch of the artist irrelevant to the authenticity of the painting is one significant element in the conceptual revolutions that made the art of the twentieth century so different from the art of all earlier centuries.

Co-Authoring Advanced Art

Introduction

Consistent co-authorship of painting or other works of advanced visual art did not occur prior to the late twentieth century. In recent decades, however, this practice has been followed by a handful of teams of important artists. Yet the history of visual artists working together suggests that co-authorship is likely to become more widespread in the future, and for this reason the practice is of greater interest than would be warranted by the limited number of artists who have already adopted it. A brief survey of this history can help us to understand its recent emergence.

Before Modern Art

Joint production of paintings was an accepted practice in the Renaissance, as eminent masters presided over studios that might comprise dozens of students and assistants. So for example Vasari reported that when Raphael became successful he employed a large number of assistants and "was never seen at court without some fifty painters."[1] John Pope-Hennessy noted that in this phase of his career "Raphael over a large part of his work became an ideator instead of an executant," as he made detailed preparatory drawings or cartoons for works that would then be painted by assistants.[2] Raphael's practice of having his plans executed by others was a consequence of his conceptual approach to art, for he clearly considered the essence of his works to lie in their conception. Art scholars have generally agreed, as for example E. H. Gombrich described Raphael's images as "ideas come to life."[3] Like other conceptual masters of his time, Raphael consequently did not hesitate to present joint products of his studio as his own work. Yet although several artists might work on a single painting, it was very rare for the finished product to bear the signature of more than one artist, for in virtually all cases there was a clear distinction between the roles of the master and his assistants.

Occasional instances can be found prior to the modern era in which two independent masters jointly produced a painting. One example is the case of Peter Paul Rubens (1577–1640) and Jan Brueghel the Elder (1568–1625), the two most important painters in Antwerp in the early seventeenth century. The two were good friends, and they executed about two dozen paintings together between 1598 and Brueghel's death in 1625. Although only one of these paintings was actually signed by both artists, Anne Woollett observed that their joint works "are distinguished by the evident separateness of their hands in a composition," and that "their established specialties and styles of painting serve as the visual equivalent of a signature."[4]

In general, Brueghel appears to have initiated the joint paintings, carrying out the drawing of the overall composition and much of the painting, including landscape and other natural motifs, which were his specialty. Rubens then painted the figures, which were his particular strength. That the paintings contain few significant pentimenti (changes made during the process of execution) suggests that the compositions were planned carefully in advance. Scholars assume that the two painters worked on these paintings sequentially, and that in fact each probably worked in his own studio, with the canvases being moved back and forth. That both Brueghel and Rubens were conceptual artists, who were accustomed to painting from preliminary drawings, obviously facilitated the process, for neither typically found it necessary to alter work the other artist had already done on a particular painting.[5]

Although the older Brueghel was more established when the two artists began working together, Rubens soon gained greater prominence, and ultimately became a much more famous painter. So for example a survey of eighteen recent textbooks of art history found a total of sixty-five illustrations of paintings by Rubens, compared to six for Brueghel. The textbooks also show that the joint paintings were not among Rubens's most important contributions, for only two of his illustrations are of co-authored paintings.[6]

The Twentieth Century

Co-authorship of paintings and other works of visual art became much more common in the twentieth century, as a number of groups of conceptual artists produced significant numbers of joint productions, that two or more artists would sign. So for example many co-authored works were made by Dada artists in the late 1910s and early 1920s, by Russian Suprematists and Constructivists during the 1920s, by Surrealists from the 1920s on, and by members of the Cobra group from the late 1940s on. Co-authored works consequently exist by many prominent artists, including the Dada artists Jean Arp, George Grosz, and Raul Hausmann, the Russians Kazimir Malevich and Georgii and Vladimir Stenberg, the Surrealists Joan Miró, Yves Tanguy, Salvador Dali, and Roberto Matta, and the Cobra painters Asger Jorn, Pierre Alechinsky, and Karel Appel.[7] In fact, the Surrealists produced hundreds of drawings, each of which was co-authored by three or four artists: these were the products of a game the group often played, that they named Exquisite Corpse.[8]

Yet although there were many co-authored works made by artists in these groups during the first half of the twentieth century, these works did not make co-authorship an important phenomenon in the visual arts. The co-authored works were rarely significant efforts: although they were often produced by important artists, in no instance did they rank among those artists' most important contributions. The co-authored works were typically minor pieces, made quickly, and often, as in the case of the Surrealists' Exquisite Corpse drawings, primarily for the artists' amusement. Very few artists in the first half of the twentieth century consistently co-authored works with one other artist and devoted significant effort to this joint activity. In a few exceptions to this last generalization, including the case of Jean Arp and his wife, Sophie Taeuber-Arp, both artists had made substantial bodies of work before they began working together, and one of the partners had a considerably greater reputation based on the earlier work, so the joint work was typically overshadowed by the more prominent artist's productions.

Throughout most of the century, an effective barrier to the serious and sustained production of co-authored art remained in place. Specifically, co-authorship was prevented by the traditional conception of the artist as an autonomous agent. Curiously, this conception persisted in spite of the fact that both patrons and critics have long recognized that Western art has always been in many respects a communal activity: the workshops of the Old Masters, where many paintings were jointly made by several artists, and the many stylistic groups in which modern artists worked closely together – Impressionism, Fauvism, and Cubism, to name a few – immediately provide evidence of this recognition. Yet critics and collectors nonetheless appear to have insisted that individual works be identified with the name of a single artist.

In the second half of the twentieth century, significant cases of co-authorship have become more common in advanced art. In a number of cases, this is a consequence of instances in which a husband and wife who were already both working as artists decided to sign all their works jointly. Examples of this include Edward Kienholz and Nancy Reddin, Claes Old-enburg and Coosje van Bruggen, and Christo and Jeanne-Claude Javach-eff. Although some of the work these artists have made has achieved prominence, in general these teams' joint work has been overshadowed by the reputations established earlier by the more eminent of the two part-ners. So for example an art scholar remarked that "Although [Kienholz] has included his wife's name as co-creator, he has not yet allowed her to have great impact on his style." The same scholar judged that "Although the Oldenburgs' collaboration is acknowledged, . . . the style belongs to the husband," and that in yet another case, "the ideas are Christo's; the financial organization Jeanne-Claude's."[9]

A new practice emerged in the late twentieth century, however, in which teams of two artists working together from the beginning of their careers, making all of their art jointly, have become significant contribu-tors to advanced art. In most cases these artists have had family relation-ships: they include husbands and wives (Bernd and Hilla Becher), brothers (Mike and Doug Starn, Jake and Dinos Chapman), and partners in long-term relationships (Gilbert and George, Tim Noble and Sue Webster). A survey of twenty textbooks of art history published since 1990 serves to measure the relative importance of the most prominent of these recent artistic teams. Most notable is the success of Gilbert and George, as Table 10.1 shows that they have an average of almost one illustration per book. Gilbert and George appear to be genuine innovators in creating a suc-cessful model of artistic co-authorship, and their case is consequently of considerable interest.

Gilbert and George

Gilbert Proesch (1943–) and George Pasmore (1942–) met in 1967, when they were students in the sculpture department of St. Martin's School of Art in London. Both were dissatisfied with the formalist orientation of the

TABLE 10.1. *Total Illustrations of Work of*
Five Artistic Teams in Twenty Textbooks

Artist	N
1. Gilbert and George	18
2. Bernd and Hilla Becher	10
3t. Jake and Dinos Chapman	4
3t. Mike and Doug Starn	4
5. Komar and Melamid	3

Sources: See text and appendix.

program: "They taught you to think solely about form: Extraordinary! The entire course was about the work's form, color, shape, weight. The teachers didn't think about content, meaning didn't come into it."[10] They decided that together they would create a new type of art, in which they themselves would become the art. The critic David Sylvester later found the key to their art in its beginning: "everything they've done depends from that marvelous wheeze they had as students that a couple of artists could be living sculptures."[11] Gilbert agreed: "we decided we were the object and the subject. And I think that was the biggest invention we ever did . . . We made a decision, like another artist who tells himself the most important thing is the form. And for us the most important thing was us as objects speaking to the world."[12] An element of the decision was that the two would be a single artist: "Two people make one artist. We think that we are an artist." When asked if each could make art individually, Gilbert responded "I think it would be totally impossible."[13]

As part of their position that they are a single artist, Gilbert and George deny that their work is the product of any functional division of labor: "All those partnerships you think of, it's one person doing one thing and another doing another, bringing their different talents to bear on something. We don't think we're doing that. We never see it that we are doing a picture together in that way."[14] Early in their career, Gilbert and George made large charcoal drawings based on photographs, but they abandoned these, in part because some viewers would attempt to separate their contributions. To make this impossible, their subsequent work has been based on photography: "We invented a technical form to make one art that doesn't distinguish between us. You don't see the brush strokes, the handwritten message that every artist is so proud of."[15] This served their original decision to become one artist, for "it was a way of getting away from self."[16]

Gilbert and George have explained why they consider their practice of making art together to be advantageous: "We can never have self-doubt. Because the normal artist is always asking himself questions, he is sitting in front of the canvas saying, 'Should I put another green cow in the corner, should I change the color of the sky?,' and no answer comes back. Whereas with two people you've always got an answer. Self-doubt is vanishing. As long as the other always says yes – and we always say yes to each other. I think we share an enormous sense of purpose. I think that's our greatest strength."[17] When they are asked how they resolve disagreements about their work, they deny that they have any: "we never argue."[18]

When Gilbert and George left St. Martin's, they set out to become successful artists: "We were desperate to draw attention to ourselves." In 1969, dressed in matching tweed suits, with bronze paint on their faces and hands, they sang an old music hall song, "Underneath the Arches," continuously for eight hours in Charing Cross, one of the busiest spots in London. Titled *Singing Sculpture*, the work became famous, and during the next five years they presented it in clubs, art schools, and museums throughout Europe, Australia, Asia, and the United States.[19] Gilbert and George consider *Singing Sculpture* to have been their first work, and it remains their most important: photographs of it appear in eight of the 20 textbooks surveyed by this study, whereas none of their other works appears in more than two books.

Gilbert and George have consistently maintained that art should be conceptual. In a 1982 interview they declared that "Art is completely abstract, intellectual," in 1987 they stated that "Art is pure thought," and in 1993 they explained that "Art is about having new ideas."[20] What matters to them is not the process of making art, but the result: "The work is totally unimportant except for the end result. It is only the message that is important."[21] In pursuit of powerful images, over time their works have become larger and more colorful, recently filling large walls with grids of panels made with digital technology. Their images nearly always feature themselves, often dressed in their trademark tweed suits, but occasionally in the nude, and they frequently include enlarged photographs of bodily fluids and waste products, with provocative texts referring to religion, homosexuality, male prostitution, AIDS, and other topics of obvious social significance. They contend that their goal is to influence people: "We are not here to reflect or illustrate life. We want to form it, change it."[22] Curiously, however, although the images and language in their works are often shocking, their messages are generally unclear: as

David Sylvester noted, "there is something deeply equivocal about what is expected of us." Sylvester placed this within a conceptual tradition: "Gilbert and George, like Duchamp, never forget the importance of keeping us guessing."[23]

The Next Generation

Gilbert and George appear to be appreciated more in England than elsewhere: Louisa Buck recently observed that they, along with Damien Hirst and David Hockney, are Britain's best-known living artists, and in 2002 Hirst complained that "I can't help thinking if Gilbert and George were American, they'd be much more significant."[24] The impact of the pair in England may account for the greater prominence in London of artistic teams of the next generation. So for example the younger team of sculptors Tim Noble (1966–) and Sue Webster (1967–) announced their first exhibition by making flyers on which they superimposed photographs of their own faces on a picture of Gilbert and George.[25]

Louisa Buck listed several ways in which Jake (1966–) and Dinos (1962–) Chapman are indebted to their older colleagues: "Like contemporary art's other famous double act, Gilbert and George (for whom they once worked as assistants), the Chapmans have benefitted from the PR advantages of presenting a twinned front. They have also embraced scandal and outrage by creating images that many people find offensive ... while declaring that they are only dealing with what is already floating in the cultural ether. More significantly, however, the Chapmans have followed the example of Gilbert and George by presenting often outrageously transgressive subject matter in a way that appears mechanical and pristine – thus further distancing themselves from the work."[26]

The Chapman brothers' art is highly conceptual: "They play with visual and verbal correspondences, create hilariously vulgar and impenetrably obscure associations, layer images onto existing historical imagery and cyclically reconfigure motifs that reappear in different guises. They employ word games, visual puns, illogical anachronism and time leaps, biological shifts and moral conundrums, unexpected variations in scale and sudden alterations between media to create both amusing and unsettling ambiguities."[27] One of their characteristically conceptual practices is to base their art on earlier artists' work. Early in their careers they became fascinated with Francisco Goya's series of etchings, *The Disasters of War*, and they proceeded to make a number of works based on it. These include *Insult to Injury*, of 2003. After purchasing an edition of Goya's

Disasters series for £25,000, they defaced or (in their word) "rectified" Goya's black-and-white images by drawing colored cartoon faces over those of some of the original figures, and occasionally adding helmets decorated with swastikas. They presented these "improved" works in an exhibition titled *The Rape of Creativity*.[28] When some critics expressed outrage at what they called an act of vandalism, the Chapmans made two arguments in their defense. One was economic: noting that each of the 80 etchings in their series sold for £13,500, they asked how an act that raised the value of a work of art could be considered vandalism. The other argument was canonical, as the brothers pointed to the famous precedent of the young Robert Rauschenberg erasing a drawing by Willem de Kooning to create a new work of art in 1953.[29]

The comparison between the Chapmans' *Insult to Injury* and Rauschenberg's *Erased de Kooning Drawing* is of course inexact, because rather than eliminating Goya's work, the Chapmans added to it, and thus effectively made themselves co-authors of Goya's. The Chapmans have made other works that refer to artistic co-authorship, including a set of etchings, titled *Exquisite Corpse*, that mimic the composite drawings made in the course of the game of that name by the Surrealists, in which each of several panels on a folded sheet of paper was drawn by a different artist who could not see the forms made by preceding participants. The frequency with which the Chapmans appropriate other artists' images and practices implies that one of the themes underlying their work is in fact artistic collaboration. Consistent with this, they have spoken of the history of art as a continuity, and have claimed that "We're trying to diffuse the creative importance of the artist in the process of making art."[30]

Artistic Teams

The twentieth century has seen a number of significant instances of two young conceptual artists working closely together. Several of these episodes have attained almost mythic status. From 1909 until the outbreak of World War I, Picasso and Braque joined forces in developing Cubism. Picasso recalled how closely they worked together: "At that time our work was a kind of laboratory research from which vanity was excluded."[31] Braque similarly stressed that they cooperated to solve problems: "In the early days of Cubism, Pablo Picasso and I were engaged in what we felt was a search for the anonymous personality. We were inclined to efface our own personalities in order to find originality. Thus it often happened that amateurs mistook Picasso's painting for mine and mine for Picasso's. This was a matter of indifference to us because we were primarily interested in our work and in the new problem it presented."[32]

Jasper Johns and Robert Rauschenberg worked closely together during the late 1950s, when both were making what proved to be their most important innovations. Rauschenberg recalled that "Jasper and I literally traded ideas."[33] Johns stated that "I suppose I learned more about painting from Bob than I learned from any other artist or teacher, and working as closely as we did and more or less in isolation, we developed a strong sense of kinship. When that ended, each of us seemed to develop – where there had been none before – some sense of self-interest."[34] At a time when the two artists were receiving little encouragement from the art world at large, Rauschenberg explained that the support they got from each other gave them "permission to do what we wanted."[35] Today Johns and Rauschenberg object to comparisons between their early working relationship and that of Picasso and Braque, pointing out that unlike the two young Cubists, they never shared an artistic style. During that early time, however, they nonetheless drew comfort from the parallel they perceived between their situation and that of the Cubists. Thus Johns recently told a journalist, "I remember once, I was reading Gertrude Stein's *Autobiography of Alice B. Toklas* to him, reading it out loud, and Bob turned and said, 'One day they'll be writing about us like that.'"[36]

Like these other pairs of young artists before them, Gilbert and George faced considerable opposition to their work early in their careers. One example occurred shortly after they left St. Martin's, and had begun to present themselves as living sculptures. Hoping to get support from their former teachers, they went back to see several, including Anthony Caro, the most eminent sculptor at St. Martin's. "We went to a pub near his studio and sat and had half a bitter and a cheese roll, and explained where we wanted to take our art. He listened very carefully, quite politely. Then he said, 'I hope very much that you don't succeed, but I rather think you might.'"[37] Like the young Picasso and Braque, and the young Johns and Rauschenberg, the young Gilbert and George joined together to solve problems, with a primary emphasis on artistic concepts, rather than the personality of the artist. And like those earlier teams, Gilbert and George made their early innovations in the face of considerable adversity. Unlike their earlier counterparts, however, Gilbert and George not only worked *as if* their art was a joint product, but actually formally co-authored their work. And unlike the earlier teams, Gilbert and George did not part company after an initial period of discovery: in 2007, their retrospective exhibition at London's Tate Modern Museum surveyed work that they had done over the course of 38 years, from 1969 through 2006. In their complete and consistent co-authorship of their work, and the degree of their success, Gilbert and George effectively became pioneers of a new practice in advanced art. They have succeeded in convincing the art world that a pair of individuals can jointly make a significant contribution. The introduction to the booklet distributed at their recent retrospective exhibition in London includes a sentence that simultaneously points to the English art world's view of their importance and the complete acceptance of the pair as a unit, noting that "it is fitting that *Gilbert & George: Major Exhibition* is the largest retrospective of any artist to be held at Tate Modern."[38]

As the survey of art history textbooks demonstrates, Gilbert and George are the most successful team working today, but they are not unique among contemporary artists in their consistent production of co-authored art. Key aspects of their practice also appear to be common to other contemporary artistic teams. So for example, the photographers Bernd and Hilla Becher have explained that in their practice "there is no division of labor in the sense that one person is always responsible for one aspect or phase of the work. Both of us do everything: at times we each do a certain task and then we swap... Outsiders cannot tell who has taken a particular photo and we also often forget ourselves. It simply is not important."[39] And Jake and Dinos Chapman have declared that they always work together in order to suppress their individual preoccupations: "We work together as a means to avoid coalescing into a single boring artist preoccupied with all things personal and internal."[40]

The Future of Co-Authorship in Art

Co-authorship has become not only common but typical in many academic disciplines. Although it is not common in visual art, in recent decades it has become a consistent practice for a handful of important pairs of artists, and it is now widely accepted by art critics as well as collectors. For example Gilbert and George were awarded the English Turner Prize in 1986, and Jake and Dinos Chapman were short-listed for that prize in 2003, as Jane and Louise Wilson had been in 1999. And a number of artistic teams, including Gilbert and George, Bernd and Hilla Becher, Tim Noble and Sue Webster, Peter Fischli and David Weiss, and Jake and Dinos Chapman, have all had individual works sell for $100,000 or more at auction.

Throughout the past century, a number of pairs or small groups of young conceptual artists have worked closely together, often to solve specific technical problems, and to give each other encouragement while breaking accepted rules of art. During most of the century, these artists did not actually co-author their works, perhaps in part because they feared this would not be accepted by others in the art world. This is no longer true, for co-authored art is now exhibited in the most important museums of modern art, and generates substantial prices at auction. In view of this, it is likely that in future increasing numbers of young artists will not only make their work jointly, but will present it explicitly as their joint product. It is also likely that, as in the past, these teams will generally be made up of conceptual artists, for ideas appear to be more readily exchanged and negotiated than visions.

Appendix to Chapter 10

Books Surveyed for This Chapter

The textbooks used to construct Table 10.1 are listed here. The artists included in Table 10.1 are all co-authors whose work was illustrated in at least two of the three books asterisked below.

Adams, Laurie. 2007. *Art Across Time*, 3rd ed. Boston: McGraw Hill.

*Archer, Michael. 2002. *Art Since 1960*, new ed. London: Thames and Hudson.

*Arnason, H. H. 2003. *History of Modern Art*, 5th ed. Upper Saddle River, NJ: Prentice Hall, 2004.

Blistène, Bernard. 2001. *A History of 20th-Century Art*. Paris: Flammarion.

Britt, David, ed. 1999. *Modern Art*. New York: Thames and Hudson.

Cumming, Robert. 2005. *Art*. New York: DK Publishing.

Dempsey, Amy. 2002. *Art in the Modern Era*. New York: Harry N. Abrams.

Foster, Hal, et al. 2004. *Art Since 1900*. New York: Thames and Hudson.

Gilbert, Rita. 1998. *Living with Art*, 3rd ed. Boston: McGraw Hill.

Honour, Hugh, and John Fleming. 2002. *The Visual Arts*, 6th ed. New York: Harry N. Abrams.

Hopkins, David. 2000. *After Modern Art*. Oxford: Oxford University Press.

*Hunter, Sam; John Jacobus; and Daniel Wheeler. 2004. *Modern Art*, 3rd ed. New York: Vendome Press.

Lucie-Smith, Edward. 2001. *Movements in Art Since 1945*. London: Thames and Hudson.

Lucie-Smith, Edward. 1997. *Visual Arts in the Twentieth Century*. New York: Harry N. Abrams.

Parmesani, Loredana. 2000. *Art of the Twentieth Century*, Milan: Skira.

Perry, Gill, and Paul Wood, eds. 2004. *Themes in Contemporary Art*. New Haven: Yale University Press.

Sandler, Irving. 1996. *Art of the Postmodern Era*. New York: Harper Collins.
Stangos, Nikos, ed. 1994. *Concepts of Modern Art*, 3rd ed. London: Thames and Hudson.
Stokstad, Marilyn. 1995. *Art History*. New York: Harry N. Abrams.
Walther, Ingo, ed. 2005. *Art of the Twentieth Century*. Cologne: Taschen.

I I

Language in Visual Art

Introduction

A distinctive feature of visual art in the twentieth century is its use of language. Words had appeared in paintings and sculptures since classical times, but their use was generally restricted to a few specific functions. From an early date, inscriptions served religious purposes, identifying the protagonists in a biblical scene or referring to a relevant biblical text. Artists' signatures identified the person responsible for a work, and dates were often included to specify when a work was completed. And artists sometimes included the title of a painting within the work's image.[1] In the early twentieth century, however, some artists began using language in their works for very different reasons. Over time this practice spread, as words and even sentences became more conspicuous in a number of artists' work. Eventually, in some cases language became more important than images, and for some artists words replaced images altogether.

The introduction of language into art for new purposes is a symptom of the increasingly conceptual nature of visual art during the twentieth century. The increasing acceptance of the use of language equally became an independent factor fueling the conceptual orientation of art, for the possibility of using language appealed to many young artists with conceptual goals: the example of important visual artists whose work featured language helped make visual art an attractive activity for many conceptually oriented artists, and provided them with points of departure for new conceptual innovations.

TABLE 11.1. *Total Illustrations of Works Including Letters or Words,*
by Artist

Artist	Illustrations	Year of Birth	Year of Death
1. Marcel Duchamp	21	1887	1968
2. Pablo Picasso	17	1881	1973
3. Georges Braque	15	1882	1963
4. Richard Hamilton	12	1922	–
5t. Max Ernst	11	1891	1976
5t. Joseph Kosuth	11	1945	–
7. Andy Warhol	10	1928	1987
8t. Raoul Hausmann	9	1886	1971
8t. Roy Lichtenstein	9	1923	1997
8t. René Magritte	9	1893	1967
8t. Francis Picabia	9	1879	1953
8t. Ed Ruscha	9	1937	–
13t. Marcel Broodthaers	8	1924	1976
13t. Stuart Davis	8	1894	1964
13t. Jenny Holzer	8	1952	–
13t. Jasper Johns	8	1930	–
13t. Barbara Kruger	8	1945	–
13t. Kazimir Malevich	8	1878	1935
13t. Bruce Nauman	8	1949	–
13t. Kurt Schwitters	8	1887	1948

Source: See text and appendix.

Word Counts

Determination of which twentieth-century artists made the most important use of language was done by surveying thirteen textbooks, all of which covered the art of the entire century, and all of which were published in 2000 or later. The ranking of Table 11.1 was made by counting all illustrations in these books of works that included letters or other inscriptions, excluding artists' signatures. The artists listed are the twenty who had the most such works illustrated in the books surveyed.

The inscriptions included in the works counted for Table 11.1 vary enormously, from a few stenciled letters or a word fragment torn from a newspaper, through a cartoon caption or the label of a commercial product, to full sentences or even paragraphs of printed text. Understanding why artists used words in these many varied forms is central to this analysis of the role of language in twentieth-century art. But in spite of the diversity, the listing of artists in Table 11.1 provides a good basis for identifying the most influential uses of language in visual art in the past century. The following sections of this chapter will consider how and why each of these artists used language, ordered chronologically by the most important appearances of language in their art.

Language in Art

In the fall of 1911, Georges Braque used stencils to paint letters and numerals on two paintings. On one, *Le Portugais*, the letters included the word "BAL."[2] This marked the introduction of lettering into Cubist painting. The act cannot have been a casual one: Braque had been working closely with Pablo Picasso in developing the new form of art, and the two were so sensitive to the appearance of their works that for a time they had put their signatures on the backs of their paintings, in order not to interfere with the compositions.[3] Picasso quickly seized on Braque's new practice. Before the year was out he had inscribed "MA JOLIE" at the bottom of his painting *Woman with a Guitar*, and the next year he prominently placed the letters "JOU" on the first collage, *Still Life with Chair Caning*. Letters began to appear in almost all of the two artists' paintings. When Braque made the first papier collé in 1912, *Fruit Dish and Glass*, he included the letters "BAR." And when Picasso responded with his first papier collé, *Guitar, Sheet Music and Glass*, one of the pieces of paper pasted to it was torn from a newspaper, including the letters "JOU."[4]

Braque's use of a stencil had set in motion a process that would have an enormous impact on both the form and content of advanced art in the twentieth century. Braque would later say that he had done this "as part of a desire to come as close as possible to a certain kind of reality." The stenciled letters called attention to the two-dimensional surface of the painting, and thus created a contrast, effectively pushing other elements of the painting back into space, and pointing to the solidity of the shaded facets of the objects depicted: as Braque put it, "they were forms which could not be distorted because, being quite flat, the letters existed outside space and their presence in the painting, by contrast, enabled one to distinguish between objects situated in space and those outside it."[5] John Golding observed that the stenciled letters and numbers also served to emphasize the nature of Cubist paintings as *objects*. Picasso and Braque often spoke of "le tableau objet," and Golding argues that this represented a new concept of paintings "as constructed objects having their own independent existence, as small, self-contained worlds, not reflecting the outside world but recreating it in a completely new form." The artificial letters and numerals emphasized the novelty of the form of the paintings because – just like the pieces of cloth or paper, or fragments of glass or tin that the Cubists would later attach to their canvases – they were foreign to the traditional practice of painting, and therefore made the viewer aware of the material existence of the work as an object. Braque's first use of a stencil thus became a conceptual prelude to both collage and papier collé.[6]

Braque's use of letters also affected the content of his paintings. The word "BAL" in *Le Portugais* referred to a popular dance, and this reference to low culture was not an isolated event. Picasso's inscription, "MA JOLIE," was not only a coded reference to a new love who would soon replace his current companion, but also the refrain of a song that was popular at the moment.[7] And when Picasso began to attach pieces of newspaper to his paintings, he consistently cut them from the sensationalistic *Le Journal*, an inexpensive paper aimed at a wide audience, rather than more sophisticated newspapers intended for more prosperous readers.[8] By bringing popular images and artifacts squarely into their new art, Kirk Varnedoe observed that Braque's lettering and Picasso's enthusiastic response "initiated a sequence of events that was decisive for the whole future process of modern art's engagement with the materials of popular culture." The departure could not have failed to amaze the advanced art world, because of the stark contrast between the austerity and cerebrality of the images the Cubists had developed by 1911 and the banality of the references to popular culture they introduced thereafter. Varnedoe drily commented that "having perfected an exquisite, chamber-music harmony, Picasso and Braque seem to have decided that the perfect next step was to add a kazoo counterpoint."[9]

At a general level, the introduction of letters into their works by Braque and Picasso underscored the radically conceptual nature of their innovation in creating Cubism. Letters that did not function as illusionistic elements of images were obviously a conceptual device, and the challenge they posed to viewers to decipher their meanings within these paintings added another level of difficulty for viewers already faced with the problem of interpreting the fragmented motifs of these works. Conceptual artists had made images that carried symbolic meanings throughout the history of western art, but the signs they used for these were generally familiar and easily understood by their intended audiences. What was novel in the practice of Picasso and Braque, so much so as to inaugurate a new era of conceptual art, was the use of signs that were not generally familiar to any audience, and that consequently had to be studied and learned, like a new or unfamiliar language. As early as 1915, Daniel-Henry Kahnweiler, who was the dealer for Picasso and Braque during their collaboration, wrote explicitly of Cubism as a new language, noting that its images could not be immediately understood "when the spectator is unfamiliar with the new language."[10] Picasso echoed this metaphor in 1923, when he told Marius de Zayas that "The fact that for a long time cubism has not been understood and that even today there are people who cannot see anything in it, means nothing. I do not read English, an English book is a blank book to me. This does not mean that the English language does not exist, and why should I blame anybody else but myself if I cannot understand what I know nothing about?"[11] Fragments of words, or incomplete sentences, were obvious puzzles, and they reinforced the basic message that the entire works in which they appeared were puzzles. But letters and words were a particular kind of puzzle, for they are associated with reading, and their inclusion thus carried the implication that Cubism itself was a symbolic language, that the observer had to decipher or translate. The letters in Cubist paintings have therefore been seen as indicators of a transition in conceptual art, in which spectators would no longer simply be viewers, but would instead become readers.

Art historians have attempted to find political or social commentary in the specific newspaper clippings Picasso chose to include in his papiers collés. Yet the ambiguous fragments of words and phrases he used do not appear to offer decisive support for these specific interpretations, nor does the fact that he offered virtually no independent statements on these subjects. Varnedoe concluded that "An attempt to decrypt from these works specific messages about the epoch would seem simplistic, in a context where elusive complexity is the defining order; and it would go against the grain of the way the words, and the structure of the works as a whole, consistently work to subvert single-minded clarity. The world of words the Cubists made in these *papiers collés* is not merely an edited shorthand for the one that surrounded them." Varnedoe observed that one consequence of this lack of a specific message was that the Cubists' new device could be adapted to many varied purposes: "Cubist works with words, like Cubism in general, appeared to many contemporaries to provide a language without an ideology, in a time when there were numerous ideologies in search of a language. If the inner circle who made this language never said what it meant, others nonetheless quickly saw what they could do with it."[12]

In Moscow, Kazimir Malevich had already been following the lead of the Cubists from a distance, and in 1914 he made a series of paintings that transformed the Cubists' use of language for his own purposes. In contrast to the subdued palette of Picasso and Braque, the bright colors of Malevich's paintings suggest his excitement with the new methods of Cubism, as does the intricacy of his use of collage, with many more small painted and pasted elements placed against or upon each other, and with more abrupt transitions than in the more sedate compositions of the Cubists. So for example Rainer Crone and David Moos described Malevich's *Lady at the Poster Column* of 1914, a large painting with a wide variety of collage elements, as a "sensorial bombardment of pictorial and 'verbal' information that confronts the viewer in a similar fashion to a passerby absorbing advertisements and announcements."[13] Although the specific words and phrases resist unambiguous interpretation, both the active compositions of Malevich's paintings and the use of fragments from both Russian and French newspapers appear to express Malevich's enthusiasm about the cosmopolitanism and dynamism of life in the modern city, and his approval of the sophistication of life in Moscow in particular.[14]

In view of the fact that Marcel Duchamp's avowed primary goal was to reverse what he considered the unfortunate tendency of modern painting to create visual products and instead "to put painting once again at the service of the mind," it is not surprising that he quickly embraced the Cubists' introduction of language into art.[15] And because Duchamp's "mania for change" made him avoid repetition, it is not surprising that he used language in a series of very different ways in his art.[16] In 1912, *Nude Descending a Staircase, No.* 2 shocked both the public and Duchamp's fellow artists in part because of its title, which Duchamp inscribed in block capitals at the bottom of the canvas. Duchamp later recalled that much of the negative reaction to the painting at the time stemmed from the attitude that "a nude should be respected. It should not descend a staircase because that is ridiculous."[17] Indeed, when the artist's two brothers famously came to break the news to him that the painting had not been accepted by the 1912 Salon des Indépendants because of its perceived challenge to Cubism, their mission was in fact not to tell him of a rejection, but to urge him to alter the painting in order to make it acceptable: according to Duchamp's account of the meeting, they asked "'Couldn't you at least change the title?' They thought it was too much a literary title, in a bad sense – in a caricatural way . . . Even their little revolutionary temple couldn't understand that a nude could be *descending* the stairs. Anyway, the general idea was to have some changes, something to make it possible to show it, because they didn't want to reject it completely." Duchamp declined, and retrieved the painting.[18] He claimed he did not explain his intransigence to his brothers at the time, but when he referred to the episode in an interview years later, he indicated that he considered that title and its appearance on the image a significant conceptual innovation. Thus he noted that the furor over *Nude Descending* was "Probably because of the shock value due to its title, which by the way already predicted the use of words as a means of adding color or, shall we say, as a means of adding to the number of colors in a work."[19]

Later in 1912, Duchamp painted *The Passage from the Virgin to the Bride*, and again wrote the name of the painting at the bottom. Like *Nude Descending, The Passage* was concerned with the representation of time. In the later painting, however, Duchamp might have used typography to communicate a sly message. Thus Duchamp wrote *LE PASSAGE* in capitals, and *de la vierge à la mariée* in lower case. Thierry de Duve suggested that this may stress that the passage in question in fact occurs at a single moment in time.[20]

In 1913, Duchamp created the first of his readymades, which would become one of the most controversial artistic innovations of the century. In a brief speech he made about that innovation in 1961, Duchamp commented on the role of language: "One important characteristic was the short sentence which I occasionally inscribed on the 'readymade.' That sentence instead of describing the object like a title was meant to carry the mind of the spectator towards other regions more verbal."[21] Perhaps the most celebrated example of this occurred in 1919, when Duchamp bought a postcard of the *Mona Lisa*, pencilled on the image a mustache and goatee, and wrote at the bottom "L.H.O.O.Q." Read aloud in French, the letters produce a short sentence that is generally translated as "She's got a hot ass."[22] The juvenile word puzzle reinforced the offensive defacement of the portrait's image to produce what Varnedoe described as "a cynical, knowing irreverence, and . . . sniping use of crudely barbed wit against established shibboleths." Varnedoe characterized Duchamp's presentation of the postcard as a readymade as "arguably the first modern work to incorporate graffiti into its strategies."[23]

Stuart Davis developed a distinctive early style that combined the flat colored planes of synthetic Cubism with characteristically American symbols and images. During the 1920s, in paintings that mimicked collage, Davis paid homage to Lucky Strike and other popular American cigarette brands, copying their colorful packaging and bold lettering in compositions that sometimes also included newspapers and comic strips, with legible headlines and titles. Davis's jazz age celebrations of popular and commercial images have often been considered an anticipation of American Pop art of the 1960s.[24] In 1921, Davis recorded his belief that he was bringing to painting an artistic appreciation for a distinctively American modernity that had previously been expressed only in poetry: "I feel that my tobacco pictures are an original note without parallel so far as I can see... In poetry we have Lindsay, Masters, Sandburg and Williams, all in some way direct descendants of Whitman our one big artist. I too feel the thing Whitman felt and I too will express it in pictures – America – the wonderful place we live in."[25]

Four of the artists listed in Table 11.1 – Max Ernst, Raoul Hausmann, Francis Picabia, and Kurt Schwitters – were members of the Dada movement, which originated in 1916 as a protest against World War I. Both Dada and its successor, Surrealism, were dedicated to making art from the irrational and the unconscious. Both also began as literary projects before they expanded into visual art. For this reason, William Rubin observed that "The preoccupation with the use of words *in* images, and vice versa, was natural for the poet-painters of Dada and Surrealism." He also noted that language played a greater role in Dada's art than in that of their predecessors: "The Dadaists went far beyond the Cubists in composing pictures with letters and words connected syntactically."[26]

Dada was not a style but an attitude, and the four artists of Table 11.1 illustrate its diversity. All made art that differed greatly in appearance, and their use of language was equally diverse. Ernst devised a novel way of making collages, in which random combinations of photographs, newspaper clippings, and illustrations from advertising catalogues would suggest new and unexpected forms to him. He would then develop these, by drawing or painting, and often by adding words: "thus I obtained a faithful fixed image of my hallucination and transformed into revealing dramas my most secret desires – from what had been before only some banal pages of advertising."[27] Ernst merged mechanical and biomorphic shapes to create "enigmatic forms and fantastic beasts," and while his works are obviously symbolic, they do not yield obvious messages or clear interpretations.[28] The titles of his paintings added to their enigmatic quality, so Ernst often inscribed them below the images, as he did, for example, in his first major Surrealist painting in 1921, writing "CELEBES" below the image of a mechanical monster that bore some resemblance to an elephant. Much of Ernst's audience would not have been expected to recognize the painting's title, *The Elephant of Celebes*, or its subject as references to an obscene German schoolboy rhyme.[29]

Hausmann was one of a group of Berlin Dada artists who pioneered the use of photomontage. Together with Hannah Höch and John Heartfield, he used photographic images from newspapers and magazines, combined with words and sentences cut from newspapers, to produce biting political satire and angry social commentary. Berlin Dada was the most explicitly political of the Dada groups, and relied most heavily on photographs and texts drawn from the mass media for its art, in order to "attack the bourgeoisie with distortions of its own communications imagery."[30]

Picabia was a close friend of Duchamp, and shared the latter's taste for a number of artistic devices, including symbolic mechanical forms and the use of verbal puzzles. Picabia inscribed the title "UDNIE" on one of his most important paintings, and "EDTAONISL" on another; numerous attempts to decipher the meanings of those words have been no more definitive than suggested interpretations of the paintings' abstract forms. When a journalist asked him to explain the titles, Picabia compared his work to musical harmonies, and asked: "why not accept a sign that does not evoke accepted conventions?"[31]

Schwitters created a distinctively personal form of Dada that originated in the structure and materials of Cubist collage. Yet instead of placing a few pieces of newspaper into a painted composition, Schwitters made compositions by fitting together large numbers of small items drawn from his preferred materials – discarded tram tickets, receipts, and other small pieces of waste paper and cloth – so that the collage elements became the primary features of the works, and retained their original identity to a greater extent than in Cubist paintings or the collages of Berlin Dada.[32] As a result, the words printed on many of the elements in Schwitters' collages do not pose puzzles, or ask for symbolic interpretation, but instead contribute to the compositions as if they were abstract forms.

Language played a central role in the single most famous painting ever produced by René Magritte, a leading Surrealist. In 1929, Magritte painted *The Treachery of Images*, in which the meticulously painted image of a briar pipe was placed above the inscription "Ceci n'est pas une pipe" (this is not a pipe). The painting was one of scores of works that Magritte called "word-pictures," that he began making in 1927 and continued to produce throughout the remaining 40 years of his life. The format of the painting recalls traditional grammar-school object lessons, in which a photograph or careful drawing of a common object is presented above a caption with its name, and the parallel is reinforced by the schoolroom penmanship that Magritte mimicked for the inscription.[33]

The imitation of the familiar and trustworthy object lesson makes the unexpected and anomalous denial of the inscription all the more jarring, and this is precisely what has made the painting so successful. For instead of instructing viewers in vocabulary, Magritte was demonstrating a proposition from an essay titled "Words and Images" that he wrote in 1929: "Everything tends to suggest that there is little connection between an object and what represents it."[34] This statement was a product of Magritte's interest in the writings of the philosopher Ludwig Wittgenstein, who stressed the arbitrary nature of the relationship between words and the objects they name. Implications of *The Treachery of Images* include the facts that an image of a pipe is not an actual pipe, and that there is no natural relationship between the word and the object. The painting's controversion of the way in which we are accustomed to using language makes it an example of Magritte's contention that "my paintings are a kind of defiance of 'common sense.'"[35] *The Treachery of Images* was the single most famous instance of what Suzi Gablik described as the mission of Magritte's life: "to overthrow our sense of the familiar, to sabotage our habits, to put the real world on trial."[36]

In 1956 the English artist Richard Hamilton made a small collage, *Just what is it that makes today's homes so different, so appealing?*, that embraced popular culture by including product labels and other commercial imagery carefully cut from magazine advertisements, comic books, and newspapers. The work was a caricatural but nonetheless enthusiastic British view of contemporary American consumer culture, and its words, including the logo for Ford automobiles, the title of Al Jolson's movie *The Jazz Singer*, and the label of a Tootsie pop, were a key element in establishing Hamilton's belief that mass entertainment and modern technology could make a positive contribution to fine art.[37]

Jasper Johns's early paintings famously portrayed familiar objects – "things the mind already knows."[38] In some cases, words appeared on objects he painted or sculpted, including cans of Savarin Coffee and Ballantine Ale. In other cases Johns stenciled letters or numbers on his paintings, as part of his search "for subject matter that was recognizable." Like the flags and targets he had painted, letters and numbers became common objects in an uncommon setting: "everyone had an everyday relationship to numbers and letters, but never before had they seen them in the context of a painting. I wanted to make people see something new."[39] In other paintings, Johns achieved a different kind of surprise by stenciling the names of colors on his paintings, often – but not always – in a color different from the color named. He explained that "I liked it that the meaning of the words either denied or coincided in the colored paintings . . . Those paintings to me were an accomplishment in ambiguity that previous paintings had not matched."⁴⁰

It is not surprising that the two leading painters of the Pop art movement appear in Table 11.1. The most famous images of both Andy Warhol and Roy Lichtenstein included language, in Warhol's case the labels of the Campbell's soup cans that introduced Pop to a wide audience in 1962, and in Lichtenstein's the phrases that appear in bubbles to communicate the thoughts or exclamations of comic strip characters, or the onomatopoetic words that provide the sound effects for the explosions or collisions in those same enlarged comic strip frames. The language of these paintings is obviously a key element, for the carefully designed labels of popular products in a supermarket or the bold and simple language of comic strip characters are essential to their identity, and this is a basic concern of Pop art. Thus the critic Lawrence Alloway observed that "The communication system of the twentieth century is, in a special sense, Pop Art's subject."⁴¹ The selection of familiar images by Warhol, Lichtenstein and their colleagues allowed "American Pop art of the 1960s [to] become, more swiftly and perhaps more widely than any other kind of modern art, genuinely popular."⁴²

Toward Language as Art

In the work of all the artists surveyed to this point, language appeared as an adjunct to images: in most cases words played a clearly subordinate role, while in a few cases words were central, and might even be considered as important as the images. During the 1960s, however, visual artists began to feature language more prominently: for some artists words became more important than images, and for others words replaced images altogether, as words effectively became the images. Four artists who appear in Table 11.1 – Marcel Broodthaers, Joseph Kosuth, Ed Ruscha, and Bruce Nauman – represent this new tendency as it appeared in the 1960s, whereas two others – Barbara Kruger and Jenny Holzer – illustrate its development beyond that decade.

Broodthaers was a starving Surrealist poet who publicly declared in 1964 that he had decided to make visual art in order "to sell something and succeed in life." Inspired by the success of Pop art, "The idea of inventing something insincere finally crossed my mind, and I set to work straightaway."⁴³ His first sculpture consisted of a package of the remaining copies of a book of his poetry, half-embedded in plaster. The books remained visible, but they could not be opened unless they were removed from the plaster. Broodthaers intended the work to pose a frustrating choice for the viewer: "Here you cannot read the book without destroying its sculptural aspect." Yet he observed that viewers did not recognize this problem at all: he was the only one who saw the irony in the fact that his poems had had no significant audience, but that an object made entirely of those poems succeeded in attracting a sizeable audience after the poems were made inaccessible.[44] Broodthaers devoted much of his effort to a critique of the institutions of the art world, with a series of works that involved what he considered the contradictory relationship between artistic and commercial values. The most ambitious of these was a simulated museum, an installation that included a wide variety of objects and displays, as well as all the kinds of equipment necessary to transport and display art in a museum. Words played a prominent role in this notional modern art museum, for in addition to signs specifying hours of admission and other practical information for visitors, every exhibit had a card reading "This is not a work of art." The latter stemmed directly from Broodthaers's fascination with Magritte's caption, "This is not a pipe." Broodthaers's target was what he considered the arbitrary ability of museums to confer value on objects by declaring them to be art and displaying them: since his museum was fictitious, his signs testified to the fact that he lacked this ability.[45]

While still a student at New York's School of Visual Arts, Kosuth made *One and Three Chairs*, which would become his single most celebrated work.[46] It consists of a wooden folding chair, a photograph of that chair, and an enlarged photograph of the dictionary definition of the word "chair." A different chair would be used in each location where the work was exhibited, and a new photograph would be taken of that chair. Kosuth liked this procedure because "it meant you could have an art work which was that *idea* of an art work, and its formal components weren't important."[47] In a subsequent series titled *Art as Idea as Idea*, Kosuth eliminated two of the three elements, and these works consisted exclusively of photostats of dictionary definitions of selected words.

Early in his career, Kosuth decided that being an artist meant questioning the nature of art. He reasoned that this couldn't be done using painting or other traditional means, because to use these implicitly accepted the nature of art. His solution lay in the use of language: "It seemed to be the only possibility with the potential for being a neutral non-material." Making works entirely out of language avoided "the mystified experience of aesthetic contemplation . . . Texts are human marks, language is daily, banal; no magical worlds to enter, no theatrical suspension." Using only language allowed him to focus on the essential: "Works of art are analytic propositions."[48] Kosuth has consistently maintained the extreme conceptual position that "art's viability is not connected to the presentation of visual ... experience," and his admirers agree. For example the philosopher Jean-François Lyotard observed that "Kosuth's work is a meditation on writing."[49]

Language has played an important role in Ruscha's paintings throughout his career. He initially became known for his images of such California icons as Standard gas stations, the Hollywood sign, and the 20th Century Fox logo, all of which prominently featured words. From the mid-1960s he increasingly painted single words, often portraying them as three-dimensional objects. He explained his interest in words as a result of the influence of the printed media: "I guess I'm a child of communications ... I felt newspapers, magazines, books – words – to be more meaningful than what some damn oil painter was doing." The words he selected came from popular culture: "The content was important ... I responded to contemporary life, city life; the words I picked were pulled off the street, for their street power." Once the words were chosen, the painting had been conceived: "I don't know what motivates me, but each of the works is premeditated. I don't stand in front of a blank canvas waiting for inspiration." What matters to him is the effect of the language on him: "It might be the power of the word or words that I'm glorifying." His paintings are made from his ideas, but they are not designed to send messages: "Whether or not the work communicates anything to anyone is not important to me. The work is my indulgence. I don't set out to get something across." In general, Ruscha distrusts art as communication: "That's where the trouble begins, when artists try to communicate."[50] But the words in his paintings take on visual interest as objects from the clever and often elegant designs Ruscha devises for them: as Peter Schjeldahl put it, "Ruscha makes loaded words and phrases sit for their portraits."[51]

Nauman gave up painting while he was in art school because "I couldn't get enough of what I was interested in into paintings. For example, language."[52] He has made language into three-dimensional forms, and presented it in photographs and neon signs. Whatever the medium, Nauman's concern is with the properties of words. His use of words was influenced by Wittgenstein's discussion of language games. As Arthur Danto observed, Nauman often works by taking words apart: "Thus he finds the word EAT in DEATH. Or he finds that EROS spelled backward is SORE. He discovers shapes within the shapes of words or expressions, and presents them to us as if they mean something beyond the fact that one shape occurs within another. One genre of his work consists in neon signs, in which, for example, we are to join him in seeking the connection between VIOLINS and VIOLENCE and SILENCE... Is there a connection? Other, that is, than at the level of sound?"[53] It is unlikely that Nauman would be troubled by Danto's skepticism. In a 1987 interview, Nauman was asked whether he really meant the statement presented by one of his celebrated early neons, which read *The True Artist Helps the World by Revealing Mystic Truths*. His response was non-committal: "It's one of those things you say to figure out what you think about it yourself." He explained that his work wasn't intended to answer questions: "it's more that I figure out what those questions are."[54]

Kruger and Holzer both became prominent during the 1980s. Both exemplify a novel phenomenon of the time, of artists using the technologies of advertising and the mass media to attempt to reach a public much larger than the usual audience for advanced art. Kruger and Holzer did this in order to provoke and influence public discourse. Both are examples of the artist as activist, and the use of art as a political instrument.

Kruger began her career as an extremely successful graphic designer, as she became the chief designer of *Mademoiselle* magazine at the age of 22. Her experience in advertising taught her the importance of creating a sense of immediacy and urgency, and when she became an artist she created a distinctive format that used language and photography as a vehicle for social criticism. Her work aimed to make people aware of how they are unconsciously indoctrinated by the many forms of propaganda that surround and bombard them in their daily lives. Danto commented on the intent of one of her most celebrated messages: "'I shop therefore I am' was meant to bring to consciousness what, when one thought it through, was not simply a fairly innocent distraction but a kind of willing collaboration in a social system. The shopper is an agent of her own oppression. The work is a piece of consciousness-raising."[55] More generally, Linda Weintraub concluded that "Kruger subverts established ideological and economic values by inserting an outsider's perspective into the information stream. She asserts the female point of view." Kruger's goal has been to transform passive observers into active thinkers: "her work fortifies the public against the perils of mind control."[56]

Holzer gave up abstract painting while she was an art student, and began to make art from language: "I wanted to write so that I could be very direct. I could say exactly what I wanted on any subject, and I could address specific topics. This is impossible to do with abstract painting. That's how I came to use language. I had the desire to be explicit and I felt the need to study dearly held beliefs."[57] Her texts have appeared in a wide range of forms often devoted to advertising, including posters, t-shirts, magazines, billboards, television, and her signature medium, LED (light-emitting diode) signs.[58] She initially used electronic signs simply to reach a large audience, but she found that "A great feature of the signs is their capacity to move, which I love because it's so much like the spoken word: you can emphasize things; you can roll and pause, which is the kinetic equivalent to inflection in the voice."[59] Her most celebrated works, a series of several hundred aphorisms called *Truisms* that she made early in her career, were intended as political activism, but not as advocacy of any specific position – indeed, the claims of individual truisms often contradict each other. Holzer has explained that the goal was "to show that truths as experienced by individuals are valid. I wanted to give each assertion equal weight in hopes that the whole series would instill some sense of tolerance in the onlooker."[60] She is concerned with the visual presentation of her art, but each work begins with a text: "Language has been the core because the writing holds most of the subject matter."[61]

Conclusion

Prior to the modern era, when words appeared in paintings for purposes other than to identify the artist, they usually served conceptual ends – to identify the figures in a religious painting, to make clear the allegorical content of an image, or to specify the identity and position of a person shown by a portrait. Words rarely appeared in works by experimental painters, who were generally concerned with images rather than messages. This pattern continued in modern art, even as words began to be used for a variety of new purposes. Remarkably, all twenty artists in Table 11.1 – those twentieth-century artists who have the most works using language illustrated in art history textbooks – are conceptual artists.

Braque and Picasso introduced letters and words into their paintings for formal reasons, and this motive was a consideration for many of the artists who followed them in the practice. But the Cubists also used language to refer to popular culture, and this intention ran through many later artists' use of language, including Malevich, Davis, Hamilton, Warhol, Lichtenstein, and Ruscha. Duchamp quickly followed the Cubists in using language, but since his constant concern was to increase the conceptual orientation of visual art, he consistently used letters and words to make puns and to pose verbal puzzles. His friend Picabia appears to have done the same, and his admirer Johns later followed suit. A succession of artists used language to engage with philosophy and semiotics: prominent figures considered here were Magritte, Broodthaers, Kosuth, and Nauman. And a number of artists used language for political or social commentary. The Berlin Dada artists, of whom Hausmann was a leading member, pioneered this practice, and they were followed in it by many others later in the century, including Kruger and Holzer.

Language has played a prominent role in the visual art of the past century, and this is one more way in which the twentieth century differs significantly from all earlier periods. The use of words in paintings and other genres spread very rapidly after Braque's initial stencilings of 1911, and the uses to which visual artists put words quickly proliferated. The twentieth century was a time of extended conceptual innovation, and language is a powerful and versatile conceptual tool. Once Braque and Picasso had pioneered its use in painting, many other conceptual visual artists recognized the value of words, and even texts, for their own purposes. The diversity of the specific uses of language surveyed above is symptomatic of the increasing diversity over time in the conceptual uses of visual art. Throughout the century, the increasing role of language was an obvious product of the fact that much of visual art was progressively less something to be looked at, and increasingly something to be read. One end-point of this tendency occurred at an exhibition in 1972, as the critic Brian O'Doherty observed of Joseph Kosuth's installation at Leo Castelli's New York gallery that "It is not a looking room; it is a reading room."[62]

Appendix to Chapter 11

Books Surveyed for This Chapter

Adams, Laurie. 2007. *Art Across Time*, 3rd ed. New York: McGraw Hill.

Arnason, H.H. 2004. *History of Modern Art*, 5th ed. Upper Saddle River, NJ: Prentice Hall.

Bell, Cory. 2001. *Modern Art*. New York: Watson-Guptill Publications.

Blistène, Bernard. 2001. *A History of 20th-Century Art*. Paris: Flammarion.

Cumming, Robert. 2005. *Art*. New York: DK Publishing.

Davies, Penelope, et al. 2007. *Janson's History of Art*, 7th ed. Upper Saddle River, NJ: Pearson Prentice Hall.

Dempsey, Amy. 2002. *Art in the Modern Era*. New York: Harry N. Abrams.

Foster, Hal, et al. 2004. *Art Since 1900*. New York: Thames & Hudson.

Honour, Hugh, and John Fleming. 2002. *The Visual Arts*, 6th ed. New York: Harry N. Abrams.

Hunter, Sam; John Jacobus; and Daniel Wheeler. 2004. *Modern Art*, 3rd ed. New York: Vendome Press.

Kemp, Martin, ed. 2000. *The Oxford History of Western Art*. Oxford: Oxford University Press.

Parmesani, Loredana. 2000. *Art of the Twentieth Century*. Milan: Skira.

Richter, Klaus. 2001. *Art*. Munich: Prestel.

12

Portraits of the Artist

Personal Visual Art in the Twentieth Century

Introduction

I am making a study of the soul, as I can observe myself closely and use myself as an anatomical testing ground for this soul study.
Edvard Munch, 1908[1]

In an essay written for a 1999 exhibition of Rembrandt's self-portraits, the scholar Ernst van de Wetering, professor of art history at the University of Amsterdam and chairman of the Rembrandt Research Project, noted that Rembrandt "had painted himself before the mirror on at least forty occasions, had etched himself thirty-one times, and had made a handful of drawn self-portraits." On the basis of this enumeration, van de Wetering made a dramatic declaration: "This segment of his oeuvre is unique in art history, not only in its scale and the length of time it spans, but also in its regularity."[2]

Van de Wetering's striking claim is not even close to being accurate. The scholar Iris Müller-Westermann observed that Edvard Munch "recorded himself in more than seventy painted works and about twenty graphic self-portraits, as well as in more than one hundred watercolors, drawings, and studies; sometimes year by year, at times monthly or even daily."[3] Munch thus executed considerably more oil portraits of himself than Rembrandt, and Munch's total of more than 190 images of himself in all media was more than double Rembrandt's total of approximately 90.[4] Rembrandt first painted himself at age 20, and continued to do so until near the end of his life at age 63, but this span of 43 years also falls far short of the 62 years that separated Munch's first self-portrait at age 19 from his last at age 81.[5]

That such an erudite scholar would make such a clear misstatement may be symptomatic of a failure of art historians to recognize a phenomenon that began in the late nineteenth century and became more common in the twentieth. This involves not simply self-portraiture, but a broader artistic practice. Specifically, the twentieth century is the first in which a large number of visual artists made most or all of their art about themselves and their own lives. Before the modern era, many painters made occasional self-portraits, but the bulk of their work treated subjects that did not involve them personally. For example Rembrandt's paintings of himself probably made up considerably less than 20 percent of his total output of paintings, and were greatly outnumbered by the biblical scenes and commissioned portraits that were the products expected by most purchasers of oil paintings in the seventeenth century.[6] It was only in the modern era, with the increased autonomy that was a consequence of the development of a competitive market for advanced art, that painters could not only make self-portraits a larger share of their total output, but that those who wished to do so could make most or even all of their works about their own lives – images of people and things they themselves knew and cared about.

Poets

> I write very personal poems but I hope that they will become the central theme to someone else's private life.
> Anne Sexton[7]

Although scholars have not drawn attention to the growing importance of personal visual art, the same is decidedly not true for poetry. The present consideration of the practice of visual artists can consequently benefit from the conclusions of some analyses of personal poetry.

In 1984 the literary critic Alan Williamson observed that "what is most exciting and original about the poetry of the last twenty-five years is its individualism: its willingness to set values of universality at risk, in favor of the authenticity of specific autobiography." For Williamson, the distinctive feature of "the personal poetry that emerged in the late 1950s ... [was] its tendency to make candor an aesthetic value and to suggest that complete self-definition is a sufficient and possible goal for lyric poetry."[8] This was not a new claim. In 1973, Robert Phillips declared that "we are living in a great Age of Autobiography," in which the most distinguished contributions were those of poets whose work was called "confessional." This poetry was generally highly subjective, privileged the personal over the universal, was written in the language of ordinary speech, often took alienation as a theme, and recognized no subject matter as off limits. Assuming objectivity to be impossible, the confessional poets were explicitly subjective: "Whatever the cost in public exposure or private anguish, their subjects are most often themselves, and always the things they most intimately know." The common characteristic of confessional poetry was the centrality of the poet's self: "It uses the self as a poetic symbol around which is woven a personal mythology."[9]

Confessional poetry was a reaction against the doctrine of persona, which was the reigning orthodoxy of advanced poetry for much of the first half of the twentieth century. *Persona* – originally the Latin word for the mask an actor wore onstage – was the term used by Ezra Pound, T.S. Eliot, and others to stress the distinction between the poet and the speaker of a poem: the "I" of a poem was not the poet, but a mask created by him.[10] This separation generally implied not only detachment but also objectivity on the part of the poet. Thus Eliot explained that "Poetry is not a turning loose of emotion, but an escape from emotion; it is not the expression of personality, but an escape from personality."[11]

During the 1950s, Allen Ginsberg and Robert Lowell were prominent younger poets who reacted against the impersonality and absence of passion in contemporary poetry, and who "created art out of the confusion of their lives."[12] As their influence spread, some critics identified a change in regime. In 1972, for example, Lionel Trilling declared that "Within the last two decades English and American poets have programmatically scuttled the sacred doctrine of the *persona*, the belief that the poet does not, must not present himself to us and figure in our consciousness as a person, as a man speaking to men, but must have an exclusively aesthetic existence."[13]

In heralding this revolution, the poet and critic Donald Davie proclaimed that "A poem in which the 'I' stands immediately and unequivocally for the author" was "essentially and necessarily superior to a poem in which the 'I' stands not for the author but for a *persona* of the author's."[14] Davie cited Robert Lowell's prize-winning *Life Studies*, a pioneering work of the new poetry, as an example in which the speaker was unequivocally the poet himself.[15] In fact, however, Lowell explained that the autobiographical poems in *Life Studies* were "not always factually true. There's a good deal of tinkering with fact." Yet although Lowell conceded that he had "invented facts and changed things," he stressed that his goal was nonetheless to create the appearance of truth: "you want the reader to say, This is true . . . [T]he reader was to believe he was getting the *real* Robert Lowell."[16] The poet John Berryman resolved the contradiction between Davie's criterion of the poet as speaker and Lowell's practice of mixing fiction with fact by observing that *Life Studies* was clearly based on Lowell's personal experience rather than on invention and symbol, but that "the 'I' of a poem can never be identical with the actual author," even if only because of the incompleteness of art: "The necessity for the artist of selection opens inevitably an abyss between his person and his persona."[17]

Robert Elliott observed of *Life Studies* that for many readers "a substantial part of the fascination, the strength, the poignancy of these poems resides in their claim to the truth."[18] Yet not all confessional poetry shared Lowell's goal of the appearance of truth. For example Lowell himself observed that the poetry of his former student Sylvia Plath was "personal, confessional, felt, but the manner of feeling is controlled hallucination, the autobiography of a fever." Lowell remarked that in her final poems, "Plath becomes herself, becomes something imaginary, newly, wildly, and subtly created – hardly a person at all, or a woman, certainly not another 'poetess,' but one of those super-real, hypnotic, great classical heroines."[19]

Several issues raised in these analyses of confessional poetry can be useful in considering personal visual art. One key question involves how objectively or subjectively the poet – or artist – treats his own experience. Another involves explicitness: if the author employs symbols, are their meanings accessible or are they esoteric? And another important issue concerns sincerity – whether the work is intended to convince the reader that the speaker is the real author, as opposed to an obviously exaggerated or distorted persona.

Vincent van Gogh (1853–1890)

Painters . . . dead and buried speak to the next generation or to several succeeding generations through their work.
Vincent van Gogh, 1888[20]

The prototype of the visual artist who made his art entirely out of his own life was Vincent van Gogh. This was recognized by Meyer Schapiro, who observed that "van Gogh converted all [his] aspiration and anguish into his art, which thus became the first example of a truly personal art, art as a deeply lived means of spiritual deliverance or transformation of the self."[21] George Heard Hamilton stressed the integration of van Gogh's words and images in creating this art: "His autobiography in the form of some 755 letters to his devoted brother Theo and a few friends is one of the most relentless documentations of the search for self in literary history. In his paintings and drawings, van Gogh also illustrated that life, literally and figuratively. Each of his pictures was a stage in his search, each 'a cry of anguish,' as he said, so that to understand his art it is not enough to judge it in purely artistic terms."[22] Schapiro further recognized that van Gogh's enterprise was a distinctive product of the new role of art in the secular modern era, and that van Gogh provided a model for the pursuit of that role: "he responded, as others did in his time, to the new function of art in the West, as an alternative to older moral-religious means. But failing in this heroic effort to save himself, as his suicide shows, he nevertheless sealed this function by his great example and the authenticity of his work; he showed that art could reach that intimacy and intensity of the striving, loving, anguished self."[23]

Van Gogh was an archetypal example of a conceptual artist whose work was intended to express his own emotions. From an early stage of his career as a painter, he resolved to ignore his critics and "to paint what I feel and feel what I paint."[24] Embracing precedents he saw in Poussin, "in whose pictures all reality is at the same time symbolic," and in the work of the writer Guy de Maupassant, who asserted "the artist's liberty to exaggerate, to create in his novel a world more beautiful, more simple, more consoling than ours," van Gogh created a personal symbolic language that pervaded his entire oeuvre.[25] So for example one of the last paintings he made before leaving his parents' home in Holland in 1885 was *Open Bible* – a still life in which a large bible, open at Isaiah, lay open next to a small, battered paperback copy of Emile Zola's *La Joie de Vivre*. H.R. Graetz explained that the contrast between the books represented a temporal and generational shift: "The little novel lying in front of the weighty Bible symbolizes the opposition between the modern way of life and the strong religious tradition with the condemnation in Isaiah of joy in living – of *joie de vivre*." The image also expressed van Gogh's anguish from his relationship with his disapproving father: "His break away from these strong ties of his earlier life – father and church – did not take place without pain; it is reflected in the contrast between the powerful Bible with its reinforced edges and the tiny, frayed

Joie de Vivre with its visible marks of injury."[26] Schapiro observed that because of his persistence in painting symbolically his own life, van Gogh "is able to transpose to the canvas with a singular power the forms and qualities of things; but they are things that have touched him deeply," so that a painting that portrayed nothing but a pair of worn boots – a motif he executed no less than eight times – became "a piece from a self-portrait."[27] When van Gogh painted portraits, they were not of patrons, but of people he cared deeply about, for his goal was not to generate income but instead to make a psychological statement – "to paint portraits which would appear after a century to the people living then as apparitions. By which I mean . . . using our knowledge of and our modern taste for color as a means of arriving at the expression and the intensification of the character."[28]

Van Gogh realized that viewers of his paintings would not understand all the personal meanings they held for him.[29] Because of the remarkable explanation of his life, and work, recorded in the letters that Theo carefully saved, it is possible to recognize, as Schapiro did, that "Every stage of his art has a profound personal meaning, it engages him completely, and could only have been produced in the place where he had lived and worked."[30] But even before the letters were published, van Gogh's art was widely appreciated, because of the obvious power of the conceptual plastic devices he created. Thus Hamilton concluded that van Gogh's art was "totally self-expressive. When it achieves . . . a more than personal power and beauty, it is expressive to such a degree that it became almost immediately . . . one of the principal sources for the broader currents of European Expressionism."[31]

Edvard Munch (1863–1944)

My art is a self-confession. Through it, I seek to clarify my relationship with the world.

Edvard Munch, 1932[32]

One of the earliest expressionist artists to be influenced by van Gogh was the Norwegian Edvard Munch. Munch saw a memorial exhibition of ten paintings by van Gogh in Paris in 1891, and the sharp, exaggerated diagonal that van Gogh used to express sadness soon became one of Munch's favorite compositional devices.[33] The example of van Gogh's life remained vivid to Munch throughout his own life. More than four decades after his first exposure to van Gogh's art, Munch reflected that

"During his short life, van Gogh did not allow his flame to go out. Fire and embers were his brushes during the few years of his life...I have thought, and wished...to follow in his footsteps. Not to let my flame burn out, and with burning brush, to paint to the very end."[34]

Early in his career, Munch's conception of art was deeply affected by Hans Jaeger, a charismatic philosopher who was the leader of a group of Norwegian bohemians. One of Jaeger's tenets was that the individual could become free only through self-examination.[35] Munch's self-portraits were his response. Thus Arne Eggum observed that "To Munch, the self-portrait was a mirror to reflect fundamental problems regarding our own existence. The great majority of them have a very personal stamp, and most of them were never exhibited by Munch himself."[36] But all of Munch's paintings pursued the goal he took from Jaeger, as did the notebooks he called his "soul's diary": "When I write these notes, it is not to describe my own life...Just as Leonardo da Vinci studied the recesses of the body and dissected human cadavers, I try from self-scrutiny to dissect what is universal in the soul."[37] Munch believed that his own experience could be of value to others. Thus he reflected that his focus on himself "could...be called egotism. However, I have always thought and felt that my art might be able to help others to clarify their own search for truth."[38]

Because of his desire for universality, Munch struggled to develop a vocabulary of signs and symbols that would communicate the intensity of his feelings to viewers of his paintings. The most famous instance of this stemmed from a memory he described in his diary in January of 1892:

I was walking along the road with two friends. The sun set. I felt a tinge of melancholy. Suddenly the sky became a bloody red.
    I stopped, leaned against the railing, dead tired, and I looked at the flaming clouds that hung like blood and a sword over the blue-black fjord and the city.
    My friends walked on. I stood there, trembling with fright. And I felt a loud, unending scream piercing nature.[39]

Munch wanted to paint the experience of this episode, but a friend recalled that he was frustrated by the fear that others wouldn't see it as he had: "He was in despair because the miserable means available to painting were not sufficient."[40] Yet he was determined to try nonetheless, and during the next two years he made a series of preparatory sketches and paintings. As he worked, the scene became increasingly simplified with flat, stylized areas of color, and progressive suppression of descriptive detail. In the celebrated final version of *The Scream*, which Munch completed in the fall of 1893, the central figure turns to face the viewer: "Its completely flat body loses all effects of human anatomy and twists like a worm to conform to and extend the fjord landscape."[41] The distorted figure, and the horror of its features as it presses its hands against the sides of its head, have been widely seen as an early psychological expression of the anxiety of modern man.

Munch's conception of art was highly personal: he wrote in his diary that "Art is one's heart-blood."[42] Throughout his life, he kept with him a newspaper clipping of a review of an exhibition of his work in Paris in 1897, that read in part:

> The man and his work are indeed inextricably bound together; one serves to clarify and illuminate the other. His work lays bare thoughts that are felt, experienced . . . Munch, by means of his skill as a painter, opens his soul to us, revealing its most secret corners.[43]

Frida Kahlo (1907–1954)

Where is the "I"?

Frida Kahlo, 1938[44]

Frida Kahlo began painting at the age of 19, as a result of an accident that almost killed her. A collision between a tram and the bus she was riding on severely damaged her spine and legs, and forced her to remain in bed, immobile for months. Out of boredom, she began painting portraits of her family and friends to amuse herself. She also hung a mirror beside her bed, and painted herself. When her injuries made it impossible for her to pursue the medical studies she had planned, she made painting her career.

The accident left Kahlo permanently wounded: she had more than thirty surgical operations during the remaining 28 years of her life, including the eventual amputation of one leg, and she lived in constant pain. The accident also influenced the character of her art. Her biographer Hayden Herrera observed that "it was the accident and its aftermath that led her eventually, as a mature painter, to chart her state of mind – to set down her discoveries – in terms of things done to her body . . . [I]n her paintings Frida was intent on making painful feelings known."[45] Kahlo herself explained that from the time of the accident, she used art to express her own reality: "my obsession was to begin again, painting things just as I saw them with my own eyes and nothing more . . . Thus, as the accident changed my path, many things prevented me from fulfilling the desires which everyone considers normal, and to me nothing seemed more normal than to paint what had not been fulfilled."[46]

Kahlo deliberately created a persona with her art. Gannit Ankori noted that "she was an expert at hiding behind masks and facades of her own construction. It is no coincidence that she was nicknamed by [her husband Diego] Rivera and by her closest friends *la gran ocultadora* – 'the great concealer.'"[47] Kahlo was fascinated by her own appearance, and she surrounded herself with mirrors.[48] In her 28 years as an artist, "Kahlo produced over one hundred images that explore aspects of her complex identity in relation to her body, to her genealogy, to her childhood, to social structures, to national, religious and cultural contexts, and to nature."[49]

Kahlo's approach to art was quintessentially conceptual. Ankori described her as "a highly sophisticated and erudite artist who constructed each painting with utmost care, and with deliberate artistic and expressive considerations."[50] Herrera noted that her subjects invariably "came from a world close at hand – friends, animals, still lifes, most of all from herself. Her true subjects were embodied states of mind, her own joys and sorrows."[51] In many of her paintings Kahlo mimicked the narrative style of Mexican folk art – "the drawing is naively painstaking, the color choices are odd, the perspective is awkward, space is reduced to a rudimentary stage, and action is condensed to highlights. Adherence to appearances is less important than... dramatization."[52]

Kahlo's construction of her persona was not limited to her art. In spite of a 21-year age difference, she married – and divorced and remarried – the flamboyant and egomaniacal Diego Rivera, who was widely recognized as the greatest Mexican painter of his time. Their tempestuous relationship, and his numerous affairs, made their marriage the subject of constant gossip. From early in her career, Kahlo dressed exclusively in the colorful long dresses, jewelry, and often also the headdresses of Mexico's Tehuana region. André Breton described her as "adorned like a fairy-tale princess," and when she and Rivera visited San Francisco, the photographer Edward Weston remarked that "Dressed in native costume even to huaraches, she causes much excitement on the streets... People stop in their tracks to look in wonder."[53] Kahlo's dramatic beauty attracted many admirers, and she was rumored to have had affairs with several famous artists and other prominent figures of both sexes.[54]

Kahlo developed a complex symbolic visual vocabulary, based on colors, objects, and forms, that ran through her entire oeuvre.[55] Yet she wanted her work to affect even viewers who had not studied her life: Herrera concluded that "Although Frida's paintings served a private function, they were meant . . . to be accessible in their meaning."[56] The graphic images of her many self-portraits do make clear what one critic wrote in a eulogy for Kahlo: "It is impossible to separate the life and work of this singular person. Her paintings are her biography."[57]

Francis Bacon (1909–1992)

My whole life goes into my work.
Francis Bacon[58]

Francis Bacon developed slowly as an artist: "I seem to have been a late starter in everything. I think I was kind of delayed, and I think there are those people who are delayed."[59] His goals were visual: "I'm probably much more concerned with the aesthetic qualities of a work than, perhaps, Munch was."[60] His art was not intended to make a statement: "I'm not really trying to *say* anything, I'm trying to *do* something."[61] Indeed, for Bacon the test of a successful image was that it not be susceptible to any logical verbal explanation: "After all, if you could explain it, why would you go to the trouble of painting it?"[62]

Bacon stressed the importance to his art of what he called *accident*: "I don't in fact know very often what the paint will do, and it does many things which are very much better than I could make it do."[63] He found that distortions occurred in his images as he worked: "I terribly don't want to make freaks, though everyone seems to think that that's how the pictures turn out."[64] A biographer argued that Bacon's experimental inability to anticipate or control the final appearance of his paintings was one source of his reluctance to paint commissioned portraits. Thus Michael Peppiatt described an episode when Bacon painted a commissioned portrait of a friend, the photographer Cecil Beaton. When Beaton described the finished work as the portrait of a "monster cripple," Bacon agreed to make a second attempt. Although Bacon felt the second portrait was a success, when Beaton again found it shocking, Bacon destroyed it in embarrassment.[65] A friend and biographer, John Russell, contended that the distortions in Bacon's portraits were actually a result of his attempt to represent individuals as he perceived them, as each portrait offered "a superimposition of states, in which certain characteristics of the person concerned appear with exceptional intensity, while others are obliterated."[66]

As Bacon matured, the subjects of his work changed: "When I was young I needed extreme subject matter for my paintings. Then as I grew older I began to find my subject matter in my own life."[67] During the 1960s his primary subject matter was his friends: "It's through my life and knowing other people that a subject has really grown."[68] For example one posthumous exhibition of Bacon's portraits presented fifty paintings of nine people, including fourteen of the painter Lucian Freud.[69] Knowing his subjects was key to Bacon's practice: "I couldn't do people I don't know very well. I wouldn't want to. It wouldn't interest me to try and do them unless I had seen a lot of them, watched their contours, watched the way they behaved."[70] The importance of familiarity was magnified by Bacon's recognition that semblance was not solely a visual phenomenon: "Every form you make has an implication, so that, when you are painting somebody, you know that you are, of course, trying to get near not only to their appearance but also to the way they have affected you." He wanted his portraits to have what he called "the living quality;" the problem "was to find a technique by which you can give over all the pulsations of a person."[71] The distortions of Bacon's portraits might be understood as a product of both this elusive goal and his conception of relationships: "I've always thought of friendship as where two people tear each other apart and perhaps in that way learn something from one another."[72] Bacon wanted the result of his efforts to transcend the appearance of individuals: "In catching the 'likeness' of his friends, Bacon also caught their dominant characteristics, which in turn, he hoped, would give the portraits greater universality as images of human beings not bound to specific circumstances."[73]

The focus of Bacon's attention narrowed even further in the early 1970s. In the fall of 1971, the day before a major retrospective exhibition of Bacon's work at Paris' Grand Palais was to be opened in a formal ceremony, Bacon's companion for much of the previous decade, George Dyer, was found dead of an overdose of drugs and alcohol in their Paris hotel room. For several years thereafter, Bacon's paintings consisted almost exclusively of images of Dyer and himself. Bacon brought his mourning for Dyer to an end in a large triptych of 1973, which effectively reenacted his death. Yet self-portraits remained a dominant element in Bacon's art for the rest of his life. He claimed that he hated his own appearance, but "it's all I've got left to paint now."[74] In spite of the deaths of nearly all of the friends who had been the subjects of his art, and his own failing health, Bacon continued to paint until his death at the age of 82. That the force of his art is not generally considered to have diminished would not have surprised him, for he believed that "Painting is an old man's business."[75]

Louise Bourgeois (1911–)

All the work of an artist is the realization of a self-portrait. But very often it is unconscious. Very often, you do not realize that you reveal yourself that much.

Louise Bourgeois, 1995[76]

In 1982, at the age of 71, Louise Bourgeois was given her first major exhibition, a retrospective at New York's Museum of Modern Art. In an autobiographical slide show prepared for that exhibition, for the first time Bourgeois publicly told a story from her childhood that she described as the motivation for everything she had ever done as an artist. Beginning with the title "Child Abuse," Bourgeois revealed that a young English woman who had been hired as a teacher for Bourgeois and her sister had in fact been the live-in mistress of Bourgeois's father for a decade, with the knowledge of Bourgeois's mother. Bourgeois declared that she had felt betrayed both by her parents and by the teacher, and that her work as an artist had been motivated by her anger: "Everyday you have to abandon your past or accept it and then if you cannot accept it you become a sculptor."[77]

Bourgeois had always been reticent about her past, and her explosive revelation prompted a reevaluation of her work. She had previously conceded that her work had always been sexually suggestive: "Sometimes I am totally concerned with female shapes – clusters of breasts like clouds – but often I merge the imagery – phallic breasts, male and female, active and passive."[78] Yet Bourgeois worked visually, and although her sculptures clearly included elements that derived from human anatomy, the final forms of her work resisted precise interpretation. Thus she explained that "my sculptures are improvisational (i.e. free – the final result has only a distant relation to the initial drawings with which they start), but with an obsessive intention and theme."[79] Her motivation had consistently come from her early life: "My childhood has never lost its magic, it has never lost its mystery, and it has never lost its drama."[80] Yet her motives were not conscious: "After a work is finished, then you say, Ah my God! *This* is what I meant."[81] And even then, the meanings of her work remained obscure to viewers: "I work very hard and I never – never! – get people to understand what I mean."[82] Ultimately, the work was independent: "a work of art has to stand by itself, so . . . it is totally unnecessary to ask me what I want you to see in a piece, because you are supposed to see it by yourself."[83] In view of her complete commitment to a visual experimental approach, it is perhaps not surprising that Bourgeois' favorite artist is Francis Bacon: "I like the way he talks and I like his kind of subjects, and I like his rendering. It's simply true."[84]

During the 1990s, Bourgeois made a series of installations called *Cells*, large wire cages that contained a variety of objects. In *Cell (Choisy)*, the objects included a model of one of her childhood homes, carved in pink marble. She explained that "To have really gone through an exorcism, in order to liberate myself from the past, I have to reconstruct it, ponder about it, make a statue out of it and get rid of it through making sculpture." The work's resemblance to a prison was not incidental: "I have been a prisoner of my memories and my aim is to get rid of them."[85] Bourgeois believes that her love of her work has allowed her to repair the damage of her early life: "When I see [my sculptures] I say: Louise, you turned a trauma into a very human, a very happy person." Over time, she has gained artistic sophistication: "All the time, and more and more, I become more skillful, clearer, so there is an increasing pleasure."[86] She considers tenacity a virtue: "I am a long-distance runner and I am also a lonely runner and that's the way I want it."[87]

Joseph Beuys (1921–1986)

> I did already a sculpture when I was born, on the first day. So every point of my life was considered under the point of view of sculpture. That is the whole biographical thing I did personally.
>
> Joseph Beuys[88]

Joseph Beuys believed that creative lives were the product of a small number of "key experiences."[89] On the occasion of a retrospective exhibition of Beuys's work at the Guggenheim Museum in 1979, the curator Caroline Tisdall wrote that for Beuys, "One event was absolutely determining. In 1943 the [Luftwaffe bomber] that Beuys was flying was hit by Russian flak and crashed in a snowstorm in the Crimea. He was found unconscious among the wreckage by Tartars." She then quoted Beuys:

> Had it not been for the Tartars I would not be alive today . . . [I]t was they who discovered me in the snow after the crash, when the German search parties had given up. I was still unconscious then and only came round completely after twelve days or so, and by then I was back in a German field hospital . . . [The Tartars] covered my body in fat to help it regenerate warmth, and wrapped it in felt as an insulator to keep the warmth in.

Tisdall then commented, "It is certainly true that without this encounter with the Tartars ... Beuys would never have turned to fat and felt as the material for sculpture."[90]

In 1980, the art historian Benjamin Buchloh described Beuys's account of this episode as a "spectacular biographic fable." Buchloh went on to consider inconsistencies in Beuys's account. Among these were the photographs that purported to show Beuys with his wrecked plane. Buchloh asked, "Who would, or could, pose for photographs after the plane crash, when severely injured? And who took the photographs? The Tartars with their fat-and-felt camera?" In sum, Buchloh contended that "Beuys' 'myth of origin'... is an intricate mixture of facts and memory material rearranged according to the dynamics of the neurotic lie: that myth-creating impulse that cannot accept, for various reasons, the facticity of the individual's autobiographic history as such."[91] In 2001, Gene Ray noted that subsequent research had provided evidence that Beuys did crash in the Crimea, though in 1944 rather than 1943, and that the day after the crash he was delivered to a German field hospital. Beuys could thus possibly have been tended to by nomadic tribesman for one day, rather than the twelve he claimed. Ray argued that it was possible "that Beuys did not so much lie about his experiences under the Nazis before and during the war, as inadequately address the full truth about them."[92]

Although much remains uncertain about the facts of this episode, it is striking how often Beuys's story is simply reported as a factual account.[93] Careful observers, however, recognize that "Beuys constructed a persona," and that the only real dispute concerns whether this enterprise was "honest creativity or hocus-pocus." Most of Beuys's artistic output, including the numerous objects made from fat and felt, can only be understood through reference to his myth of origin: "The material remains of Beuys' work are the detritus of an operation that begins ... at the point at which he sacrificed his true identity for an assumed persona. He raided his previous life for symbolism redeemable to this objective, and in his subsequent life everything similarly ceded priority to its symbolic projection."[94]

One of Beuys's central ideas was what he called "social sculpture," his desire to expand the concept of art to include the entire process of living. In keeping with this goal, he did not restrict his own activities to producing art objects: among other projects, he became an early ecological activist, and ran for the European Parliament as a founding member of the Green Party, and he and the writer Heinrich Böll founded a Free International University for Creativity and Interdisciplinary Research, based on a radical approach to education in which there would be no entrance tests, no exams, no limits on enrollment, and no age limits for students.[95]

Donald Kuspit observed that Beuys's art was entirely personal: "The art of most artists does not seem to demand that we think of their lives... But Beuys' art arises directly from his life, and directly raises the question of art's role in life, and life's role in art."[96] Merilyn Smith noted a consequence of the inseparability of Beuys' life and art: "it is inconceivable that any single work by Beuys would be so self-sufficient as to survive without attribution... [E]ach of his statements is but a sentence in the large biography."[97]

Bruce Nauman (1941–)

I was using my body as a piece of material.
Bruce Nauman, 1970[98]

In 1964, during Bruce Nauman's first semester as a graduate student in art, "one day he had a revelation – that it didn't make sense for students to sit in a circle all drawing a model in the middle." On the spot, he decided he would use his own body as the subject of his art.[99] During the next few years, Nauman did this in a variety of ways, in a diverse range of genres, to produce a series of works that made him one of the most influential American artists of the late twentieth century.[100] These included neon sculptures (e.g., *Neon Templates of the Left Half of My Body Taken at Ten-Inch Intervals*, 1966), videos (e.g., *Thighing*, 1967), fiberglass, wax, or plastic sculptures cast from parts of his body (e.g., *From Hand to Mouth*, 1967) or from objects he used (e.g., *A Cast of the Space Under My Chair*, 1968), photographs (e.g. *Self-Portrait as Fountain*, 1967), and films (e.g., *Walking in an Exaggerated Manner Around the Perimeter of a Square*, 1968).[101]

Nauman's art is highly conceptual, and the concepts that interest him involve the relationship of the artist to the making of art – "investigation of the function of an artist."[102] As a result, his use of his body in his art is not aimed at exploring his own personality, or at presenting his own biography. He uses himself rather as a model – one example of an artist. The uses are consequently quite impersonal, because he does not want to focus attention on his specific characteristics, but instead to achieve universality. So for example in 1970 he explained that "I use the figure as an object... [T]he problems involving figures are about the figure as an object, or at least the figure as a person and the things that happen to a person in various situations – to most people rather than just to me or one particular person."[103] Similarly, in 1987 he observed that "if you examine yourself you make certain propositions that help with the work, certain conclusions. Other people are interested because these are common experiences."[104]

In 1993, Neal Benezra contrasted the practices of Nauman and Joseph Beuys. Benezra noted that "Beuys placed himself at the very epicenter of his work – making his persona indispensable to its presentation and meaning. In contrast,... Nauman has established quite another model. Whereas Beuys was a quintessentially 'public' figure, Nauman sees himself in a different role: 'When I give a public presentation of something I did in the studio, I go through an incredible amount of self-exposure which can also function, paradoxically, as a defense. I will tell you about myself by giving a show, but I will only tell you so much.' While he has often employed his own body as 'raw material,' he has also taken great care to mask his presence psychologically."[105]

Cindy Sherman (1954–)

[P]eople seem to think that I must be revealing something of a personal or autobiographical nature, and they are constantly looking for it in the work.
Cindy Sherman, 1995[106]

During 1977–80, Cindy Sherman made a series of sixty-nine black-and-white photographs, collectively called the *Untitled Film Stills*. She appeared in each photograph, always alone. In each photograph she wore different clothing, and in each she was shown in a different setting. These photographs are considered her most important work. Sherman has explained that the motifs grew out of her past: "As a child, I played dress-up, and it was fun because it was artificial. It still is artificial to do any of that, so in the mid-seventies when I was starting to do black and white work, it seemed interesting to be collecting these costumes that were relics of an earlier age." The *Stills* mimicked the artificiality of old movies: "It was just about me dealing with these role models from film."[107]

Art scholars have engaged in complex theoretical analyses of Sherman's photographs. For example one recently described her as "a postmodern feminist, skillfully manipulating media imagery to reveal the phallogo-centric basis of a male-dominated society."[108] Sherman has no objection to the extensive critical attention to her work, but she denies that it accurately represents her intentions: "I could agree with many different theories in terms of their formal concepts but none of it really had any basis in my motivation for making the work."[109] Contrary to the complexity and subtlety of the critical analyses, Sherman considers her work to be direct and simple: "I'm doing one of the most stupid things in the world which I can't even explain, dressing up like a child and posing in front of a camera trying to make beautiful pictures. And people seem to fall for it." Her real anxiety about her work concerns what might be an obvious inference from it: "I have this enormous fear of being misinterpreted, of people thinking the photos are about me, that I'm really vain and narcissistic." In fact, her goal was universality: "I'm trying to make people recognize something of themselves rather than me."[110] Her intended message involved attitudes: "The role-playing was intended to make people become aware of how stupid roles are, a lot of roles, but since it's not all that serious, perhaps that's more the moral to it, not to take anything too seriously."[111]

Although the meanings of Sherman's work have been hotly debated, there is widespread agreement that her use of her own image is not a result of either introspection or narcissism. For example Arthur Danto remarked that "the stills do not compose a sequential exploration of her own features, nor do they stand as a monument to feminine vanity."[112] Verena Lueken stressed that the *Film Stills* were not self-portraits: "She is her own model and, as is the case with all models, this does not make her the subject of her art."[113] Peter Schjeldahl agreed that Sherman cast herself in a role: "Sherman the performer is wholly obedient to Sherman the director. In herself, she has an extraordinary actress – selfless and undemanding, game for unflattering angles."[114] And Danto offered personal testimony that the *Stills* were in fact not about Sherman's own identity: "I cannot imagine anyone who could recognize Sherman from the stills. Though I had studied and indeed written about them, so little does she resemble her images that I was surprised to see what she looked like when we met."[115]

Tracey Emin (1963–)

What you see is what I am.

Tracey Emin[116]

Tracey Emin's art is highly diverse in form, but not in subject: "Emin's exclusive subject matter is her personal life, and that life, as read off from the art, has included underage sex, rape, abortion, bouts of serious depression and long periods of drunkenness. These are represented in words and pictures, in small, edgy monochrome prints and in large assemblages of sewn material carrying inarticulate messages of love and hate."[117] The work embodies a basic ambiguity, for "it is understood to promulgate a populist version of the hackneyed Romantic myth of the artist as creative primitive, while nonetheless, in the more sophisticated context of the art world, cunningly exploiting the incongruity of its own naiveté for conceptual effect. It thus manages to achieve the marketing coup of being simultaneously popular and elitist."[118]

Public debate over Emin's art reached a peak in 1999, when she was shortlisted for the Turner Prize, and her exhibition at the Tate Gallery included *My Bed*, an installation in which a rumpled and urine-stained bed was surrounded by detritus that included blood-stained underwear, discarded food packages, empty vodka bottles, and used condoms. Some critics dismissed the work as a bad joke, as the editor of *Art Review* sneered that "Any list with Emin cannot be taken seriously," and the British Secretary of State for Culture commented that the work of some young British artists "was giving the country a bad name abroad." Yet in spite of the elitist attacks and dismissals, the accessibility of Emin's art made her display the sensation of the exhibition, and a *Financial Times* critic observed that she had become the "people's choice."[119] Deborah Cherry noted, however, that a more serious issue emerged from the debate: "The question that most preoccupied London critics was whether Tracey was telling the truth. If art is no more and no less than the artist's life, then authenticity becomes a key benchmark for a critical practice that judges the artist rather than the work. Whereas those who supported her argued for the unmediated translation of life into art, less enthusiastic reviewers questioned her genuineness."[120]

The form and content of Emin's art originated in a decision she made after graduating from the Royal College of Art, where she had been intensely unhappy. She destroyed all her previous work, gave up painting, and reacted against the goal of becoming a "picture-maker" by making herself the subject of her art: "I realized I was much better than anything I ever made . . . I was my work."[121] She adopted as the themes of her work all the ways her background made her an outsider in the posh world of English art: "The fact that I'm not Anglo Saxon, I'm half Cypriot. The fact that my dad came here in 1948. The fact that my father never went to school. The fact that I'm the first woman in my family to have an education . . . The fact that I left school at thirteen . . . The fact that I haven't got a rounded British accent. The fact that I'm not middle class. The fact that I had to work really hard to get through things."[122] The style of her work reinforced this content, as for example in her monoprints "it is the act of rapid drawing, combined with quickly executed texts, that makes these works analogous to the unrehearsed, firsthand accounts of someone reporting a catastrophic or shocking event."[123] Yet Julian Stallabrass has noted that there is an ambiguity in Emin's statements and in her art, for "there is a continual slippage between memories of an event and poetic imagining."[124]

Emin has consistently maintained that her art is both genuine and sincere. In an interview with the rock musician David Bowie, she denied that she ever uses irony: "Everything that I do is totally sincere."[125] She told another interviewer that "I work with what I know. It is always based on some real event, something that happened."[126] Her art is direct: "Art has always been, a lot of the time, a mysterious coded language. And I'm just not a coded person." Her goal is always to make a statement to a wide audience: "I want society to hear what I'm saying. I'm not only talking to galleries, museums and collectors. For me, being an artist . . . [is] some kind of communication, a message."[127]

For Emin's admirers, the perception of sincerity is the basis for much of her appeal. Jennifer Doyle noted that "Emin's work seems to offer itself up as an 'unedited' incorporation of the remains of a messy sex life, as a fantasy of a (nearly) unmediated encounter with the artist herself." Admirers can therefore identify with the art: "Reviews almost invariably describe weeping young women who identify with Emin's narratives of abuse, humiliation, rebellion. These spectators are so moved because they feel the work is not so much about 'Trace' as it is about them."[128] These spectators validate Emin's claim that although her own experience serves as her point of departure, "it goes beyond that. I start with myself and end up with the universe."[129]

Emin's considerable recent success, which has brought her both fame and fortune, poses an interesting potential problem for her personal art. Stallabrass observed that "Emin's celebrity is a problem for her work because it might compromise her authentic primitive self – thus her continued mining of her childhood, adolescence and home-town happenings, the ineluctable past time of innocence and its first loss, and thus her neglect of later events."[130] Emin freely acknowledges her change in status, as in 2000 she told a tabloid reporter "I'm not an outsider at all. I go to all the parties."[131] She also acknowledges that her audience might consequently lose sympathy with her: "oh well she made all this work about how hard life was, now what's she going to do, make work about jumping into rich people's swimming pools with bottles of champagne?"[132] She maintains, however, that the true basis of her art has not changed, because her inner life has not been affected by the outward changes in her status: "On the outside it might look like my life is very comfortable, but inside my life is still in turmoil over things. I still go to bed crying, I still pray to God for a better life, I still curl up in a small fetal shape and cower from the world and those feelings never change."[133]

Conclusion

> I purposely bought a mirror good enough to enable me to work from my image in default of a model, because if I can manage to paint the coloring of my own head, which is not to be done without some difficulty, I shall likewise be able to paint the heads of other good souls, men and women.
>
> Vincent van Gogh, 1888[134]

In the late nineteenth century, Vincent van Gogh initiated a new form of artistic behavior, by making his work entirely out of the experiences of his own life. He was soon followed by Edvard Munch, and their examples reverberated throughout the art of the twentieth century. For example Francis Bacon considered van Gogh "one of my great heroes," and Tracey Emin left her first course of art education "in love with Edvard Munch."[135]

In considering the practices of van Gogh, Munch, and seven of the most important artists who followed them in making their art from their own lives, this study found several significant tendencies. In most of these cases, the artist's biography was key: the subject of the art was the artist's own life, and knowledge of the biography was consequently valuable for an understanding of the art. This was not universally true, however. Although both Bruce Nauman and Cindy Sherman used images of themselves in their most important works, the art was not genuinely personal, for they effectively served only as models or actors, whose true identity was not relevant to the art's message.

All but two of the artists considered here were conceptual innovators. In a majority of the cases, their message was expressed through a personal symbolism that ran through much or all of their work. Thus van Gogh, Munch, Kahlo, Beuys, and Emin all relied heavily on personal symbols that became themes of their art over time. Although a complete under-standing of these symbols requires extensive study, and is therefore not available to most viewers, for most of these artists the basic ideas of their work are clear even to casual observers. The obvious exception to this is Beuys, whose work is nearly meaningless to anyone unfamiliar with his personal history, and the myths he created around it.

Any artist who frequently makes self-portraits, or uses only subjects that are of personal significance, risks being accused of narcissism, or self-absorption. The probability of this accusation may increase if the artist exaggerates or distorts the appearance of his or her subjects in the interest of personal expression. So it is not surprising that at some point this charge has been leveled against each of the artists considered here. Yet in spite of the fact that all these artists have prominently featured themselves and their immediate interests in their work, and have obviously departed considerably from objective portrayals, all have attracted admirers who consider the significance of the work to transcend its ostensible subject matter.

Personal poetry has primarily been the domain of conceptual artists, including prominently John Berryman, Allen Ginsberg, Sylvia Plath, Theodore Roethke, and Anne Sexton. The same is true of visual art, as van Gogh, Munch, Kahlo, Beuys, Nauman, Sherman, and Emin all used their work to express ideas and emotions. In neither art was this conceptual predominance a complete monopoly, however. Thus just as Robert Lowell used confessional poetry experimentally, to describe his own life and his relationships with his family and close friends, so Bacon used personal painting to explore his vision of himself and his closest friends, and Bourgeois has used personal sculpture to delve into her perceptions of her past and her relationships with family members.

Vincent van Gogh was a self-taught painter: early in his career, he wrote to his brother Theo that "I have had no 'guidance or teaching' from others to speak of, but taught myself; no wonder my technique, considered superficially, differs from that of others."[136] For him art was not merely a career, but a means of expressing his deepest beliefs. Thus, in 1884, he wrote to a fellow painter of his conviction that "art is something which, although produced by human hands, is not created by these hands alone, but something which wells up from a deeper source in our souls."[137] Van Gogh was never taught the traditional academic hierarchy of artistic subjects, and he had no interest in learning it, for to him there were no uninteresting or unimportant people or places. He saw valuable motifs wherever he was. He believed that his task was to develop a language that would communicate the strength of his feelings for the world around him, including his own image: "it is difficult to know yourself – but it isn't easy to paint yourself either," he wrote to his brother, less than a year before his death.[138] For him it seemed natural to paint the people he cared most about, the things he saw every day, and the places where he chose to live. Although he didn't think of this practice as novel, others soon recognized that it was an innovation that would help them to pursue, or achieve, their own artistic goals. Personal art thus became a key element of van Gogh's legacy, and a distinctive feature of the artistic freedom of the twentieth century.

13

The Rise and (Partial) Fall of Abstract Painting in the Twentieth Century

Introduction

The abstract painter denounces representation of the outer world as a mechanical process of the eye and the hand in which the artist's feelings and imagination have little part. Or in a Platonic manner he opposes to the representation of objects, as a rendering of the surface aspect of nature, the practice of abstract design as a discovery of the "essence" or underlying mathematical order of things.

Meyer Schapiro, 1937[1]

Abstraction is perhaps the single most distinctive development in twentieth-century painting. It is also among the most misunderstood, not only by the general public, but also by many in the art world. In part this is a consequence of its variety, for artists have made nonrepresentational art from many different motives, using many different techniques. This chapter will trace the changing role of abstraction in painting over time, considering the goals of some of its most important practitioners, and examining their methods. Before presenting a chronological treatment, however, it is valuable to begin with a cautionary lesson.

Deceptive Appearances

[W]ith Mondrian, arriving at the idea was of exceptional importance. The conception came before the painting; it was the primary act of creation.

Harold Rosenberg, 1971[2]

When Piet Mondrian died in 1944, the critic Clement Greenberg declared that his painting "takes its place beside the greatest art." Greenberg went on to defend what he considered the mechanical nature of Mondrian's art: "Perhaps Mondrian will be reproached for the anonymity with which he strove for the ruled precision of the geometer and the machine in executing his paintings: their conceptions can be communicated by a set of specifications and dimensions, sight unseen, and realized by a draftsman. But so could the conception of the Parthenon."[3]

In 1995 the scholars Angelica Rudenstine, Yve-Alain Bois, Joop Joosten, Hans Janssen, and John Elderfield called attention to a "a problem of perception" involving Mondrian's art: "Mondrian's early partisans praised his work as a blueprint for modern architecture or typography, as 'formal experimentation' destined to be 'applied' in various fields; and his neo-plastic work has often been characterized (admiringly) as that of a geometric designer." They emphasized that their research had led them to a very different conclusion about Mondrian's working process: "As becomes especially clear from this selection of unfinished works, Mondrian's abstract work was far from geometric or mathematical in its origin or expression; rather, it was the product of a highly intuitive mind and hand, gradually working toward carefully modulated but far from measurable composition solutions."[4]

Accounts by friends of Mondrian testify to the absence of calculation or preconception in his art. An artist who knew him in Paris in the 1920s recalled watching him work: "If the black line was too thick, he'd take a piece of white paper, or a paper of about the same color as the color planes next to that line, and then he pasted it onto the canvas, and then held it at a distance to see 'is the line the way I want it or not.'"[5] When the artist Charmion von Wiegand first met Mondrian in New York late in his life, she recorded that "He explained that he did not work with instruments nor through analysis, but by means of intuition and the eye. He tests each picture over a long period by eye: it is a physical adjustment of proportion through training, intuition, and testing."[6]

Von Wiegand became a close friend of Mondrian's, and studied his art. Interestingly, she reported that although he famously restricted his palette to primary colors, their precise composition was never constant: "his hues changed in every picture. His red was never the same red, nor his blue the same blue. It had to be in perfect equilibrium with the whole painting and the proportions of each plane. He was very aware of how color interaction can change a hue and make a red look bluer or a blue look redder." She was shocked when she first saw what would prove to be his last completed painting, *Broadway Boogie Woogie*, with its many small colored squares that violated Mondrian's published generalizations about his art. She recalled that "I exclaimed: 'But Mondrian, it's against the theory!' I remember him standing back from the painting, squinting his eyes, and saying, 'But it works. You must remember, Charmion, that the paintings come first and the theory comes from the paintings.'"[7] The painter Carl Holty, who also knew Mondrian in New York, wrote of his constant revision of his works in progress: "Watching the pictures change into others as he worked, I asked him whether he wasn't losing good pictures in numbers because of his exigence. He said, 'I don't want pictures. I just want to find things out.'"[8]

On the basis of an intensive technical study of Mondrian's late paintings, Ron Spronk concluded that "He scraped away paint and often stripped parts of the paint surface and ground layer to the bare canvas. These reworkings left their marks on the paintings. Many of them are visible to the naked eye or can be seen with a microscope; others are hidden by (sometimes multiple) layers of thick paint and need to be revealed by other means."[9] One example among many is afforded by *Composition with Red, Yellow, and Blue*, which Mondrian dated as completed in 1942. The painting was photographed in 1934, and again in 1936, and it was recently X-rayed by the San Francisco Museum of Modern Art. Spronk reported in part that "Close comparison of the images from April-May 1934, 1936, the present state, and the X-radiograph shows changes to the composition both before and after the first state was completed in 1935. Between the 1934 photograph and the completion of the first state, the left vertical black line was shifted to the left, the yellow color field was enlarged downward and the top horizontal brought down accordingly, and the lower horizontal line was moved up. The black bar at upper left was widened and moved up, while the lower black bar was widened and moved down. In the final, 1942 state Mondrian added the blue field, the black and red bars at lower left, and the central horizontal black line. The upper black bar was changed to a red bar, moved upward, and widened. The lower black bar of the first state was brought down still further."[10]

Technical examination of his paintings and eyewitness accounts by Mondrian's friends thus support the artist's own claims that his art was made empirically and visually rather than theoretically and mathematically. Both Clement Greenberg and Harold Rosenberg were deceived by the appearance of his completed paintings into drawing the false conclusion that Mondrian worked mechanically, by preconception.[11] Mondrian was not a conceptual artist, who privileged ideas, and for whom conception preceded execution, but rather an experimental innovator, who allowed theory to emerge from his paintings, who worked by trial and error, and whose primary goal was to learn from the process of making his paintings. The cautionary lesson is clear. If even highly respected critics can make such basic errors, it must always be kept in mind that simply looking at a painter's finished works is not sufficient to understand how and why they were made: the appearance of paintings alone cannot be assumed to reveal the methods and goals of the artist.

The Pioneers

We, the abstractionists of today, will be regarded in time as the "pioneers" of abstract art, who had the good fortune, through clairvoyance, to live perhaps centuries ahead of our time.
Wassily Kandinsky, 1922[12]

Abstract painting was first developed in the years immediately before and after the outbreak of World War I. The three great pioneers – Kandinsky, Mondrian, and Malevich – independently arrived at very different forms of abstraction, through different means, from very different motives. Yet all three made their discoveries with the confident belief that abstract art would play an active role in creating a better world in the future, whether by directly affecting social behavior or by complementing the impact of political institutions.

In an essay titled "Reminiscences," written at the height of his career in 1913, Kandinsky described the development of his art. He recalled a key event that occurred in 1896, when he was 30, which contributed to his decision to become a full-time artist. At an exhibition of the art of the French Impressionists in Moscow, for the first time he came upon a painting that was not obviously realistic: "That it was a haystack, the catalogue informed me. I didn't recognize it. I found this nonrecognition painful, and thought that the painter had no right to paint so indistinctly." In spite of his discomfort, Kandinsky discovered that the painting had seized his imagination: "I noticed with surprise and confusion that the picture not only gripped me, but impressed itself ineradicably upon my memory, always hovering quite unexpectedly before my eyes, down to the last detail.... What was ... quite clear to me was the unsuspected power of the palette, previously concealed from me, which exceeded all my dreams. Painting took on a fairy-tale power and splendor. And, albeit unconsciously, objects were discredited as an essential element within the picture."[13] Kandinsky's account revealed that he was intensely affected by a visual event, as his first sight of a Monet not only demonstrated the power of color, but also planted the seed that would eventually grow into the realization that effective art need not be representational.

Another pivotal event occurred several years later, after Kandinsky had moved to Munich to study painting:

I was enchanted on one occasion by an unexpected spectacle that confronted me in my studio. It was the hour when dusk draws in. I returned home with my painting box having finished a study, still dreamy and absorbed in the work I had completed, and suddenly saw an indescribably beautiful picture, pervaded by an inner glow. At first, I stopped short and then quickly approached this mysterious picture, on which I could discern only forms and colors and whose content was incomprehensible. At once, I discovered the key to the puzzle: it was a picture I had painted, standing on its side against the wall.

The next day, Kandinsky was unable to recapture his enchantment with the picture: "even on its side, I constantly recognized objects, and the fine bloom of dusk was missing." He drew a simple but momentous conclusion: "Now I could see clearly that objects harmed my pictures."[14]

The empirical and visual source of Kandinsky's belief in the validity of abstract art points to his experimental nature as an artist. The same is true of the extended process by which he gradually developed his form of abstract art. Thus he reflected in 1913 that "Only after many years of patient toil and strenuous thought, numerous painstaking attempts, and my constantly developing ability to conceive of pictorial forms in purely abstract forms, engrossing myself more and more in these measureless depths, did I arrive at the pictorial forms I use today, on which I am working today and which, as I hope and desire, will themselves develop much further." He recognized that this laborious and slow process was necessary, for he had to proceed intuitively, letting forms appear as he worked: "My only consolation is that I have never been able to persuade myself to use a form that arose within me by way of logic, rather than feeling. I could not devise such forms, and it disgusts me when I see them. Every form I ever used arrived 'of its own accord,' presenting itself fully fledged before my eyes, so that I had only to copy it, or else constituting itself actually in the course of work, often to my surprise."[15] What Kandinsky came to understand was that he could only create his art gradually, and that abstraction could only come at the end of a "long path, which I *had* to follow."[16]

Kandinsky considered painting as a "struggle with the canvas," in the course of which he "derived spiritual experiences from the sensations of colors on the palette."[17] While he worked, an inner voice was constantly sensitive to the appearance of the developing image: "The artist 'hears' how something or other tells him: 'Hold it! Where? The line is too long. It has to be shortened, but only *a little bit!' 'Just a little bit, I tell you.'* Or: 'Do you want the red to stand out more? Good! Then add some green. Now they will "clash" a little, take off a little. But only *a little*, I tell you.'" Response to the work in progress was essential: "One must have the perception to 'listen' when the voice sounds. Otherwise, no art."[18] The importance of vision led Kandinsky to reject systems: "My advice, then, is to mistrust logic in art."[19]

Kandinsky evolved gradually from a painter of landscapes into a painter of images abstracted from landscapes. Unlike most experimental artists, he routinely made preparatory drawings, watercolors, and even oil sketches for his early abstract paintings. Unlike conceptual artists, however, for whom a painting is often an enlarged replica of a final preparatory image, Kandinsky's paintings are generally the last, most abstract, stage of a progression, in which the image became progressively more divorced from reality as each sketch moved farther from the recognizable forms of the first drawing. Thus when Kandinsky spoke of hiding or concealing objects in the approach to abstraction, he was not referring to a process that occurred in the course of application of successive layers of paint to single canvas, but rather one that was carried out in a series of separate works. One consequence of this is that ambiguous objects in his early abstract paintings can often be identified by consulting the related preparatory works. Vivian Barnett made this point in discussing a key series of early abstractions:

Kandinsky's *Improvisations* . . . retain unmistakable references to his favorite, recurrent motifs. They contain multiple and abstract images of horses, riders, boats, rowers, waves, cannons, graveyards, citadels and reclining lovers . . . In formulating the *Improvisations* between 1911 and 1913, the artist made preparatory watercolor sketches. By studying a group of related watercolors with the final oil version, it becomes clear that Kandinsky moved away from the object, obscuring the specific motif so only allusions to its representational origins are retained. Sometimes he executed a detailed watercolor on which he based a canvas . . . In the large oil paintings the forms have been obscured to an even greater degree than in the preparatory study. The images have been abstracted from nature to such an extent that they cannot easily be identified or "read."[20]

Scholars have remarked on the causes and consequences of Kandinsky's experimental approach. Alan Bowness observed that during his approach to abstraction "Kandinsky was a man struggling in the dark. He was aware of this – it is part of his historic importance that he admitted that neither the creation nor the appreciation of a work of art is an exclusively conscious process."²¹ Kandinsky's friend and biographer Will Grohmann stressed that he achieved abstraction not decisively, from theory, but tentatively, from experience:

> It is only with the greatest caution that Kandinsky made the transition to abstract forms. Had he been guided by theory alone, he could easily, after he wrote *On the Spiritual in Art* (i.e., from 1910 onward), have completely eliminated naturalistic elements from his painting. In actual fact it took him four years to reach that point, and he was still painting landscapes as late as 1913. Kandinsky did not want to paint decorative works, states of mind, or music. He consciously aimed at the pictorial, and for this reason he had to try to retain the forms he had intuitively experienced, but at the same time he filled them with the content of his lived experience.²²

Analyzing Kandinsky's work of this transitional period, David Sylvester compared his practice to that of another great experimental painter: "The incompleteness of these paintings – the way that passages are left unresolved – is something like the incompleteness of an unfinished Cézanne still life."²³

Mondrian's development of abstract art also originated in a process of simplification of real scenes: as he wrote in 1914, "I am seeking to approach truth as closely as possible, and to abstract everything from it until I reach the foundations (always visible foundations!) of things."²⁴ He carried out this process gradually and tentatively. A Dutch friend recalled being with Mondrian in Domburg in 1914: "On a walk beside the ocean, late in the evening, under a radiant, starry sky, he took a tiny sketchbook out of his pocket and made a scribbled drawing of a starry night. For days he worked over that suggestive little scribble. Every day he took a tiny step further away from reality and came a tiny step nearer to the spiritual evocation of it."²⁵ The critic Michel Seuphor, a friend of Mondrian's, recalled his extreme attention to detail, finding progress in changes so small that others might fail to notice: "Even so, it's another step,' he once said to a friend who was studying a new picture of his, 'or don't you think so? Don't you find that it represents even a little step forward?'"²⁶ For Mondrian, this process of incremental change made all his work part of a single continuous progression: "I began as a naturalistic painter. Very quickly I felt the urgent need for a more concise form of expression and an economy of means. I never stopped progressing toward abstraction. One period flows logically from the one before."²⁷ The cumulative effect of Mondrian's many marginal changes was very great. David Sylvester observed that "A Mondrian retrospective is not just a procession of great pictures, but a progression which in itself is an aesthetic experience: the trajectory of a man's art becomes as much a thing of beauty as the art."[28]

Mondrian not only made changes from one painting to the next, but also within the execution of individual works. Joop Joosten and Angelica Rudenstine stressed that "Mondrian's compositional method was anything but systematic or mathematical... Nothing was predetermined. Reworking, rethinking, and refining characterized his resolution of every problem."[29] His revisions often occurred over extended periods. For example when Mondrian traveled to New York in 1940, he took with him seventeen paintings that he had started in Paris and London during the preceding five years. He exhibited these "transatlantic paintings" in New York in 1942, and he inscribed on them dates indicating the intervals during which he had revised them: thus *Composition with Red, Yellow, and Blue*, which was discussed above, was dated 1935–42.[30] Technical analysis of these transatlantic paintings led Ron Spronk to conclude that "Mondrian routinely reworked his compositions in his New York years, and these revisions were often elaborate and invasive."[31] Even the size of his paintings was provisional, as throughout his career, Mondrian's uncertainty about his finished works led him "to create most of his paintings on supports whose final size was determined during the working process."[32] Charmion von Wiegand recalled that "Mondrian was never *finished* with a painting, which further proves that he had no predetermined compositional ideas. He would change a picture over and over again." When she asked him why he didn't make a series of paintings instead of repeatedly revising *Victory Boogie-Woogie*, the large work that remained unfinished at his death, Mondrian replied, "It is not important to make many pictures but that I have one picture right."[33]

Although the appearance of their paintings differed enormously, the experimental artists Kandinsky and Mondrian both arrived at non-representational images by a gradual and visual process of abstraction from nature. The conceptual Malevich did not. In 1916, he declared that "The artist can be a creator only when the forms in his picture have nothing in common with nature."[34] Nor must progress necessarily be gradual: "in art it is not always a case of evolution, but sometimes also of revolution."[35] He firmly believed that art should follow rules: "in constructing painterly forms it is essential to have a system for their construction, a law for the constructional inter-relationships of forms."[36] These rules should be derived from theory: "The system, hard, cold and unsmiling, is brought into motion by philosophical thought."[37]

John Milner observed that by 1913, when he began the key period in his development of abstract art, Malevich and his colleagues Lyubov Popova and Vladimir Tatlin "were all three *constructing* figures on the basis of geometry." Rather than simpifying natural objects, they were using mathematical relationships to create generalized forms: "Individuality, likeness and character were all of secondary importance." Milner concluded that "In preferring generalized form to specific detail, and the approach of constructing with geometry, these painters relinquished the whole realist tradition."[38] Larissa Zhadova explained that Suprematism, which Malevich designated as the successor to Cubism and Futurism, was intended to symbolize the cosmos, but not to resemble it: "His pictures can be described as images of the world's cosmic space. But they are not copied from nature; this is not the space one sees by looking at the blue sky above one's head. They are hypothetical images, conceptual images, plastic formulation images, 'factorizations' carried out by the artist's imagination."[39]

Malevich considered Suprematism a radical new departure, that would effectively negate all previous representational painting.[40] The apocalyptic tone of the manifesto Malevich wrote for the 1915 exhibition that announced the arrival of the new art underscored the drama of the breakthrough, as he announced that "I have transformed myself into the *zero of form*, and dragged myself out of the *rubbish-filled pool of Academic art.*" Denouncing the imitation of nature as the cowardly act of artists lacking in creativity, he declared that "*to gain the new artistic culture*, art approaches creation as an end in itself and domination over the forms of nature." The emblem of the new movement was to be his painting, *Black Square*: "The square is a living, royal infant. It is the first step of pure creation in art." Art would be changed forever: "Our world of art has become new, non-objective, pure." He closed with an appeal to all: "We, Suprematists, throw open the way to you. Hurry! – For tomorrow you will not recognize us."[41] John Golding contended that Malevich's art justified his rhetoric: "To be confronted by Malevich's radical new abstract work is like travelling in uncharted territory."[42]

Kandinsky's early experiences in Russia, which included ethnographic research on folk art and a commitment to the Russian Orthodox Church, gave him an awareness of the moral aspects of art, and an abiding belief in its healing and redemptive properties.[43] Mondrian believed in Theosophy, and from it he became convinced that all life is directed toward evolution, and that the purpose of art is to give expression to that evolution.[44] Kandinsky and Mondrian thus both believed that the beauty of abstract art could accomplish utopian social goals, but they were vague in explaining how and when this might occur. Malevich had more immediate goals, as in 1918 he took Russia's political revolution as a model for art: "The social revolution which smashed the chains of capitalist slavery, has not yet smashed the old tables of aesthetic values." He was confident, however, that art had a key role to play in the new society, as the next year he asserted that "The aesthetic, the pictorial, takes part in the construction of the whole world."[45]

The three pioneers of abstract painting were all important figures in early twentieth-century art: Kandinsky was a leader of German Expressionism, Mondrian was initially the leader of the Dutch De Stijl movement, and Malevich was the founder of Russian Suprematism. Yet Paris remained the center of advanced art, and the dominant figures there had the broadest influence overall. The Cubists Picasso and Braque approached abstraction before World War I, but their decision to stop short of it, together with Matisse's steadfast dedication to representation, prevented abstraction from taking the central place in advanced painting early in the century.

Abstract Expressionism

The consciousness of the personal and spontaneous in the painting and sculpture stimulates the artist to invent devices of handling, processing, surfacing, which confer to the utmost degree the aspect of the freely made. Hence the great importance of the mark, the stroke, the brush, the drip, the quality of the substance of the paint itself, and the surface of the canvas as a texture and field of operation – all signs of the artist's active presence. The work of art is an ordered world of its own kind in which we are aware, at every point, of its becoming.

Meyer Schapiro, "Recent Abstract Painting," 1957[46]

It was only after World War II, with the emergence of Abstract Expressionism in New York and Tachisme in Paris, that abstraction became the dominant form of advanced art. The leading Abstract Expressionists, including Jackson Pollock, Willem de Kooning, Mark Rothko, Arshile Gorky, Barnett Newman, Franz Kline, and Robert Motherwell, became more influential than their counterparts in Paris, the most prominent of whom were Pierre Soulages, Jean Fautrier, Hans Hartung, and Nicolas de Staël.[47] Although the two groups had little contact during their formative years, and had little direct influence on each other artistically, they shared a number of basic characteristics, including their belief in the need to create new forms of art and their conviction that this should be done experimentally, by trial and error, rather than conceptually, by the application of theory. Although these artists came to maturity little more than three decades after the pioneers of abstraction, two world wars and a great economic depression had occurred in this relatively brief span, so it is not surprising that they did not share either the optimistic utopianism of the pioneers, or their belief in the power of art to improve society. Instead, the artists who led the new movements in both New York and Paris were individualistic, and their goals were more personal and introspective than those of their predecessors. So for example in 1948 Barnett Newman declared that American painters, "free from the weight of European culture" and its "outmoded images," were creating a new art for a new age: "Instead of making *cathedrals* out of Christ, man, or 'life,' we are making them out of ourselves, out of our own feelings."[48]

The Abstract Expressionists were deeply influenced by Surrealism, which was the most important European development in advanced art between the wars. Most generally, the Abstract Expressionists took from the Surrealists the idea of drawing on the subconscious to produce new, personal images. For example in 1943, Mark Rothko and Adoph Gottlieb wrote a statement of their beliefs, which included the propositions that "To us art is an adventure into an unknown world," that "This world of the imagination is ... violently opposed to common sense," and that "It is our function as artists to make the spectator see the world our way – not his way."[49] Jackson Pollock explained in 1950 that modern artists wanted to express the aims of contemporary society: "we have a mechanical means of representing objects in nature such as the camera," and consequently, "The modern artist, it seems to me, is inventing and expressing an inner world."[50]

A number of the Abstract Expressionists, including Pollock, borrowed the device of automatism from the Surrealists, in order to accomplish their goal of painting from the unconscious. Yet the Americans used this technique differently from the Europeans. André Masson, Joan Miró, and other Surrealists often began their paintings with random markings, then finished them by developing the figures and symbols they found to be suggested by these markings. In contrast, the Americans did not use automatism to create figurative works, but instead used the initial markings as the basis for coherent but still abstract compositions. Pollock and other Abstract Expressionists thus adapted automatism to their own purposes, in order to create a new and more spontaneous way of producing abstract images. Pollock explained in 1948 that "When I am *in* my painting, I'm not aware of what I'm doing. It is only after a sort of 'get acquainted' period that I see what I have been about."[51] Pollock's celebrated drip method of applying paint, with the inevitable spattering and puddling that could not be completely controlled by the artist, was one means of escaping from preconceived ideas and forms.

Whether or not they used the technique of automatism, the Abstract Expressionists almost unanimously subscribed to the belief that the artist should work without preconception. Indeed, perhaps the most basic shared characteristic of the group was their goal of allowing unexpected forms to emerge during the process of painting. Pollock declared that, while working, "I have no fears about making changes, destroying the image, etc., because the painting has a life of its own. I try to let it come through."[52] Rothko explained that "I think of my pictures as dramas; the shapes in the pictures are the performers. Neither the action nor the actors can be anticipated, or described in advance." The painter's initial ideas were only a point of departure: "Ideas and plans that existed in the mind at the start were simply the doorway through which one left the world in which they occur... The picture must be for [the artist], as for anyone experiencing it later, a revelation."[53] De Kooning reflected that "I find sometimes a terrific picture... but I couldn't set out to do that, you know."[54] The importance of the working process to their art in fact led one of the group's leading supporters, the critic Harold Rosenberg, to suggest in 1952 that they should properly be called "action painters," on the grounds that their paintings were records of the act of their own making. Rosenberg argued that "At a certain moment the canvas began to appear to one American painter after another as an arena in which to act – rather than as a space in which to reproduce, re-design, analyze or 'express' an object, actual or imagined. What was to go on the canvas was not a picture but an event."[55] To increase the visual impact of their gestures, many of the Abstract Expressionists worked on wall-sized canvases that allowed the viewer to become engulfed by their images.

For most of the Abstract Expressionists, repeated revision of their works in progress was a routine consequence of their uncertain goals. The painter and critic Elaine de Kooning described how intensively her husband worked on his paintings in the early 1950s: "He worked on these one at a time – just all day, every day. Even the small ones. Even if it took a year... [O]n any given canvas, I saw hundreds of images go by. I mean, paintings that were masterpieces. I would come in at night and find they had been painted away."[56] Because they wanted to discover new forms and images, some of the artists spent much of their time looking at their works in progress. An assistant who worked for Rothko during the 1950s recalled that he "would sit and look for long periods, sometimes for hours, sometimes for days, considering the next color, considering expanding an area." A biographer concluded that "since the late 1940s Rothko, building up his canvases with thin glazes of quickly applied paint, had spent more time considering his evolving works than he had in the physical act of producing them."[57]

Their uncertainty about their goals equally led to difficulties in deciding when a painting was finished. During the last decade of his life, Pollock painted on lengths of canvas unrolled and laid flat on the floor, and he often began without determining either the size or orientation of the finished work. His widow, the painter Lee Krasner, recalled how this complicated the process of completing a picture: "Sometimes he'd ask, 'Should I cut it here? Should this be the bottom?' He'd have long sessions of cutting and editing... Those were difficult sessions. His signing the canvases was even worse. I'd think everything was settled – tops, bottoms, margins – and then he'd have last-minute thoughts and doubts. He hated signing. There's something so final about a signature."[58] Barnett Newman stressed the continuity in his own enterprise by declaring that "I think the idea of a 'finished' picture is a fiction. I think a man spends his whole lifetime painting one picture or working on one sculpture."[59]

The Abstract Expressionists worked for long periods to create their mature styles, and the eventual results were so novel and radical that even the artists themselves were uncertain about their achievement. For example Robert Motherwell wrote of helping a friend, William Baziotes, hang the paintings for Baziotes's first gallery exhibition in 1944. When they finished, Motherwell recalled that Baziotes was seized by anxiety: "Suddenly, he looked at me and said, 'You're the one I trust; if you tell me the show is no good, I'll take it right down and cancel it.' At that moment, I had no idea whether it was good or not – it seemed so far out; but I reassured him that it was – there was nothing else I *could* do." Motherwell's doubt went beyond the immediate issue of the quality of Baziotes's paintings: "You see, at the opposite side of the coin of the abstract expressionists' ambition and of our not giving a damn, was also not knowing whether our pictures were even pictures, let alone whether they were any good."[60] Similarly, Lee Krasner remembered that during the early 1950s, even after he had been recognized as a leader of the Abstract Expressionists, Jackson Pollock had shared the same doubt, as one day "in front of a very good painting... he asked me, 'Is this a painting?' Not is this a good painting or a bad one, but *a painting*! The degree of doubt was unbelievable at times."[61]

The Tachistes were as diverse stylistically as the Abstract Expressionists, and each of them also developed signature abstract forms based on distinctive gestures. Their commitment to an experimental method was strikingly similar to that of the Americans. So for example Pierre Soulages explained that he painted by instinct: "Often I decide to do something, to intervene in a certain way and I don't know why, and I don't seek to know why." He discovered forms as he worked: "It's a kind of dialogue between what I think is being born on the canvas, and what I feel, and step by step, I advance and it transforms itself and develops, becomes clearer and more intense in a way that interests me or not. Sometimes it surprises me; those aren't the worst times, when I lose my way and another appears, unexpectedly." The decision that a painting was finished was made on visual grounds, over a period of time: "When I see that I can't add much without changing everything, I stop and consider that the picture is finished for the moment ... Then I turn the picture to the wall and I don't look at it for several days, several weeks, sometimes several months. And then when I look at it again, if it still seems to accomplish something, if it seems alive, then it can leave the studio."[62]

The generation of artists who came to maturity after World War II represented the high point of abstraction in the twentieth century: this was the one generation in which virtually all of the most important painters made their greatest contributions in an abstract idiom.[63] The pioneers of abstraction had confidently believed that abstraction would be the art of the future, but for them this had been a matter of faith. During the early 1950s the Abstract Expressionists and their supporters could legitimately feel that abstraction had become the dominant form of advanced art. Remarkably, within a decade after the end of World War II, Pollock, de Kooning, Rothko, and a few dozen other artists had simultaneously shifted the center of the art world from Europe to the United States, and made Abstract Expressionism the dominant style of advanced American painting.[64] They firmly believed that they were creating the art of the future. For example in the early 1950s, Mark Rothko told a friend, the sculptor David Hare, that he and his colleagues were "producing an art that would last for a thousand years."[65] Similarly, Adolph Gottlieb told an interviewer that "We're going to have perhaps a thousand years of nonrepresentational painting now."[66] And unlike the diverse attitudes of the pioneers, the abstraction that emerged at mid-century was based on a shared set of attitudes and practices. David Sylvester summarized these, observing that "Most of the artists whose styles were formed in the 1940s subscribed to the idea that making art meant feeling one's way through unknown territory... Art was the lonely journey of existentialist man... This common ethical ideal led to a generally shared attribute of style: the way in which the work was made was more or less visible in the end-product."[67]

After Abstract Expressionism

Especially in the last fifty years, a lot of abstract art has demonstrated that our intelligence innovates not by making things up out of whole cloth or by discovering new things about nature, but by operating with and upon the repertoire of the already known; by adapting, recycling, isolating, recontextualizing, repositioning, and recombining inherited, available conventions in order to propose new entities as the bearers of new thought.

Kirk Varnedoe, 2003[68]

Although a number of important Abstract Expressionists worked through the 1960s, the demise of Abstract Expressionism as the central form of advanced art began when Jackson Pollock died in an automobile accident in 1956, progressed further when Jasper Johns had his first gallery exhibition in New York in 1958, and was effectively completed when Andy Warhol and Pop art exploded on the art world in 1962. Nearly all of the forms of abstract painting that have been developed since Pollock's death have been reactions to Abstract Expressionism.

A basic division appears among the abstract painters who came to maturity during the late 1950s and the 1960s. One group followed the Abstract Expressionists, trying to extend their art while accepting their basic attitudes and methods. Another group rebelled against Abstract Expressionism, and created a variety of new forms of abstraction that nearly always consisted of a direct and negative comment on the older art. This basic division followed a clear pattern, for the followers of the Abstract Expressionists were experimental artists, whereas those who repudiated Abstract Expressionism were conceptual.

The following discussion will briefly examine the motives and methods of some of the key figures in each of the two camps. It should immediately be emphasized that during the past five decades, styles of abstraction have proliferated. The reasons for this will be seen here, but one consequence is that no treatment on the scale of this one can possibly be complete in coverage, as there are too many important artists, who have created too many different approaches to abstraction, to examine all of them even briefly. What this discussion will do is to consider how, and why, some of the most important painters from the late 1950s on have gone about making abstract art.

Most of the key experimental abstract painters of recent times first emerged during the late 1950s, as direct followers of the Abstract Expressionists – often students and friends of the older artists. These were primarily younger artists who were inspired by the beauty of the Abstract Expressionists' art, and excited by their conviction and commitment to existentialist ideals. For example Helen Frankenthaler recalled that when she first saw Pollock's paintings in 1951, shortly after she had graduated from college and moved to New York to become an artist, "It was as if I suddenly went to a foreign country but didn't know the language, but had read enough and had a passionate interest, and was eager to live there. I wanted to live in this land; I *had* to live there, and master the language."[69] Frankenthaler followed Pollock in applying paint without touching the canvas. She achieved novel results, however, by pouring thinned pigment onto canvas that had not been primed: the diluted paint soaked into the fabric of the canvas, and produced a visual effect closer to watercolor than to traditional oil painting. Kenneth Noland and Morris Louis emulated Frankenthaler's new technique, and produced new forms of abstraction that featured pure colors stained into canvases that were often as large as Pollock's late works. The paint was absorbed into the canvas, and the pigment consequently did not create the surface texture that was visible in Pollock's paintings. Because there was nothing to distract from the effect of the areas of color, this art was often called "color-field" abstraction.[70]

A number of younger experimental painters followed the Abstract Expressionists in developing their own distinctive abstract forms, that became recognizable as their signature marks or gestures. Joan Mitchell and Sam Francis were prominent among these. The beauty of their work was based on the interaction of their imaginative use of color and their free, often calligraphic brushstrokes.[71]

The first-generation Abstract Expressionists were all born before 1920. Most of their second-generation followers, including Frankenthaler, Noland, Mitchell, and Francis, were born between 1920 and 1930. Relatively few important experimental abstract painters emerged from later birth cohorts. One who did is Brice Marden, who was born in 1938. Marden is an avowedly visual artist who works without preconception: "If you're not working with preconceived forms and thinking, then you can concentrate on expression." He hopes to make discoveries while working: "There are times when a work has pulled ahead of me and goes on to become something new to me, something that I have never seen before; that is finishing in an exhilarating way."[72] Marden admires Cézanne's "intense, long, slow process of working, looking, assimilating."[73] Marden has also acknowledged his debt to Pollock. In 1989, he explained that Pollock's approach had affected his attitude toward his own art: "The great thing about Pollock ... was his conviction that each work is part of a continuing quest. To be an artist is not about making individual works. To be an artist is to do your work and let your work express the evolution of a vision."[74]

Marden's comments about Cézanne and Pollock focus on central elements of the experimental approach to art in general. The long, slow process of development and the conviction that the artist is engaged in a quest for a personal vision together point to a shared characteristic of all the experimental abstract painters discussed here, from Kandinsky and Mondrian through the two generations of Abstract Expressionists – namely the goal of creation by the individual of a unique signature style. At some point in their careers, each of these artists became committed to abstraction, and for nearly all of them this subsequently became a lifelong commitment to that form. Even in those cases, including Pollock and de Kooning, in which the artist returned to varieties of figuration, this occurred gradually, and within an aesthetic of color, brushstrokes, and forms that demonstrated clear continuities with their earlier non-representational work.

The conceptual approaches to abstraction that have been developed since Pollock's death are generally very different. Not only are they extremely diverse in style and purpose, as will be described below in a number of specific cases, but almost without exception they do not have the characteristic of commitment. Since the demise of Abstract Expressionism, conceptual painters have developed the novel practice of part-time abstraction – of alternating between making representational paintings and abstract paintings. And beyond this absence of commitment to abstraction, most of these artists have lacked a commitment even to a single style of abstraction. One of the most important painters of the era, Andy Warhol, clearly demonstrates both of these practices. Thus although Warhol's most celebrated paintings, including those of Marilyn Monroe and Campbell's soup cans, were based on photographs, he made non-representational paintings at a number of points in his career, and he made these abstract paintings in a number of completely different ways, in completely different styles. Not surprisingly, Warhol explained that this should not be a source of concern: "an artist ought to be able to change his style without feeling bad."[75] Many of his fellow conceptual artists shared this opinion, and this is a distinctive feature of conceptual abstraction since the late 1950s.

The aesthetic of Abstract Expressionism and Tachisme was a powerful presence in the advanced art world of the 1950s, and ambitious young conceptual artists quickly rebelled against it on both sides of the Atlantic. Robert Rauschenberg is a prominent early example of an artist who was deeply influenced by the Abstract Expressionists, but who reacted against their art in a number of ways. Rauschenberg conceded that he owed a great debt to the Abstract Expressionists, but he stressed that "I was never interested in their pessimism or editorializing. You have to have time to feel sorry for yourself if you're going to be a good Abstract Expressionist, and I think I always considered that a waste."[76] His artistic rejections of Abstract Expressionism were not subtle. For example in 1953 the 28-year-old Rauschenberg carefully erased a drawing by de Kooning that the older artist had given him, somewhat reluctantly, for this purpose. Rauschenberg framed the work, and titled it *Erased de Kooning Drawing*. He considered it "a legitimate work of art, created by the technique of erasing."[77] Harold Rosenberg described this as a turning point: "Art-historically, the erasing could be seen as symbolic act of liberation from the pervasive force of Abstract Expressionism... 'Erased de Kooning' became the cornerstone of a new academy, devoted to replacing the arbitrary self of the artist with predefined processes and objectives."[78]

Many of the conceptual reactions to Abstract Expressionism not only appear to comment on that style, but to do so ironically. In 1957, Rauschenberg produced *Factum I* and *Factum II*, two paintings with collage elements, done in an Abstract Expressionist style, that appear identical, even to the drips of paint that run down from the smeared brushstrokes. The two paintings have been widely interpreted as a par-ody of the Abstract Expressionists' insistence on spontaneity and unique-ness.[79] Their somewhat obscure titles may underscore this challenge, for an obsolete definition of "factum" is from mathematics: "the product of two or more factors." The two paintings are in any case early examples of preconceived, conceptual abstract paintings that are designed to appear unplanned and experimental.[80]

As a young artist in Paris during the 1950s, Yves Klein explored the use of pure color to represent the infinite in nature, an interest that he had developed looking at the sea and sky during his childhood on the Mediterranean coast of southern France. He wanted to make abstract paintings, but he strongly rejected the attitudes of the Tachistes, and their emphasis on the use of gesture as personal expression: "I detest artists who empty themselves in their paintings, as is often the case today . . . In place of thinking of beauty, goodness, truth, they render, ejaculate, spit out all their horrible, impoverished and infectious complexity in their paintings as if to relieve themselves."[81] In 1955, Klein began to make monochrome paintings, each a single uniform color, most often the intense ultramarine pigment he patented as International Klein Blue, or IKB. Initially he gave each of these paintings its own distinctive surface texture, but within a few years he stopped doing this, and began applying the paint to uniform flat surfaces with a roller, to eliminate any gestural traces of the artist's hand. Klein explained that "My personal psychology does not impregnate the painting when I paint with a roller, only the color value itself radiates in pure and inherent quality."[82]

In 1960, Klein began to make what a friend, the critic Pierre Restany, named his anthropometries, in which nude models pressed themselves against canvases tacked to the wall, or rolled on canvases laid on the ground, after covering themselves with blue paint. From then until his premature death in 1962, at the age of 34, Klein devised a series of other novel ways to produce abstract paintings. For example he painted with fire, by using a blow torch to scorch the surface of a specially prepared canvas; with wind, by coating a canvas with wet paint, strapping it to the roof of his car, and driving from Paris to Nice; and with rain, by putting a freshly painted canvas outside to be marked by a spring shower. (He also attempted to record the impact of lightning on a canvas, but noted that "Needless to say, the last-mentioned ended in a catastrophe.") In a 1961 manifesto, Klein discussed these methods, and specifically responded to critics who claimed that the anthropometries were a form of action painting: "I would like now to make it clear that this endeavor is opposed to 'action painting' in that I am actually completely detached from the physical work during its creation."[83] Throughout his brief career Klein made abstract paintings without using the traditional method of applying paint with a brush. In effect, much of his oeuvre can be thought of as answering a question: how many ways could a conceptual artist think of to make paintings that resembled gestural abstractions, but in which the forms were created by means other than the artist's personal gestures in applying paint to a canvas?

Jasper Johns's famous early work reacted against the attitudes of the Abstract Expressionists, in its preconceived depiction of everyday objects.

As he later recalled, "There was this idea associated with Abstract Expressionist painting that the work was a primal expression of feelings, and I knew that was not what I wanted my work to be like."[84] Johns's most celebrated works remain his early, representational paintings of flags, targets, numerals, and maps, but at several points in his career he has made non-representational paintings. Many of these have consisted of groups of parallel cross-hatched line segments, fitted together like flagstones on a patio. Kirk Varnedoe has observed that these paintings parody Pollock. Like Pollock's large, all-over compositions, Johns's abstractions have no central point of interest. Yet in each case, Johns's composition presents "a systematization of the idea of gestural abstraction. Its complexity can be reduced to modular form." Johns thus transforms Pollock's improvised experimental art into a planned conceptual form: "It is a calculated program, quite the opposite of Pollock's sense of automatic release. You do not need a roadmap to recognize that there is an order to this picture; you understand that it is fragmented, not continuous, and that it is plotted."[85]

The entire Pop art movement was in large part a reaction against Abstract Expressionism, and many of its members mocked the older artists not only with words but with works of art. Warhol's famous statement of 1963, that "The reason I'm painting this way is that I want to be a machine," was an obvious affront to artists whose goal was self-expression, but he did not limit his challenges to interviews.[86] The most insulting of Warhol's parodies of Abstract Expressionism was the series of *Oxidation* paintings he produced during 1978. Large canvases – up to 25 feet long – were spread on the floor of his studio and coated with copper paint. Warhol, his assistants, and occasionally visitors to his studio then urinated on the canvases, producing abstract images where the acid in the urine oxidized the metallic base, turning it from copper into shades of green and brown.[87] Their large size, their flowing liquid forms, and their execution on canvas laid flat on the floor all made these works immediately recognizable as references to Pollock's drip paintings, which had emerged as the most famous emblems of Abstract Expressionism.[88]

The Warhol paintings that are generally considered his most important abstractions are the series of 102 works, titled *Shadows*, that he made during 1978–79. Large paintings, each 6 feet by 4 feet, were produced by silkscreening a single enlarged photograph that an assistant took of the shadows cast by cardboard cutouts.[89] In each painting, a black form that resembles the bold brushstrokes of the Abstract Expressionist Franz Kline is placed on a colored monochrome background. Although the use of a number of different ground colors makes the appearance of the paintings differ, the same shape recurs in every work, making the series an ironic comment on Abstract Expressionist uniqueness and spontaneity.

Warhol subsequently produced other abstract works. In 1983, he made a large silkscreened painting from an enlarged photograph of lengths of yarn of various colors tangled in interlocking loops against a white background. The resemblance to Pollock's drip paintings is obvious.[90] In 1984, Warhol made the *Rorschach* series. After pouring black paint onto a large canvas laid on the floor, he folded the canvas to duplicate the image. Warhol improvised his own abstract compositions, in the mistaken belief that psychiatric patients created their own ink blots for Rorschach tests. He later explained that he would have preferred to enlarge the standard images: "I wish I'd known there was a set."[91] The symmetry of the black forms has been considered to be an ironic comment on the paintings of the Abstract Expressionist Robert Motherwell, which often consisted of abstract black forms on a white ground, while Warhol's method of pouring paint onto unprimed canvas parodied the stain paintings of Helen Frankenthaler and Morris Louis.[92]

In addition to his famous early paintings based on comic strips, during the 1960s Roy Lichtenstein made a series of works based on paintings by great modern artists. Having quoted paintings by Cézanne, Picasso, and Mondrian by reproducing specific paintings by each artist using his trademark benday dots, he found himself "inevitably led to the idea of a de Kooning." Instead of reproducing the image of a painting, however, as he had done for the earlier artists, Lichtenstein found that he "was very interested in characterizing or caricaturing a brushstroke." During 1965–66, he made a series of large *Brushstroke* paintings, each of which presented stylized characterizations of one or more magnified brushstrokes: thick black outlines, the spaces enclosed by them filled with solid colors, set against backgrounds of Lichtenstein's imitations of benday dots. Lichtenstein made these forms by brushing black paint onto transparent plastic sheets, allowing the paint to shrink and dry, then projecting the result onto a canvas, and tracing the enlarged contours. Although the brushstrokes were not actually copied from de Kooning, Lichtenstein conceded that they "obviously refer to Abstract Expressionism."[93]

Lichtenstein's *Brushstrokes*, which he intended to look as brushstrokes would appear in a comic strip, are clearly parodies. David Sylvester observed that "we see his meticulous imitations of slashing brushmarks as a joke about the Abstract Expressionist cult of heroic spontaneity . . . [T]he basic irony is simply the notion of representing the appearance of *any* spontaneous daub with obvious deliberation and care."[94] Kirk Varnedoe agreed: "He takes the lavish, heated, inimitable, signature brush stroke of painters like de Kooning... and shows that it can be codified – freeze-dried, if you will – as if in comics, undermining as insincere the rhetoric and scale of these painters. Everything that is supposed to be ethereal, ineffable, ambiguous, or soulful about abstract expressionism is rendered as die-cut, stamped form, reduced literally to comic formulae in these hard-won brush strokes by Lichtenstein."[95]

Frank Stella rejected representational painting when he was in junior high school: "I wasn't very good at making things come out representationally, and I didn't want to put the kind of effort that it seemed to take into it." During his high school and college years, he painted in a style derived from Abstract Expressionism. In his senior year of college, however, he saw Jasper Johns's first exhibition in New York, and he was strongly affected by the patterns of the targets and flags, "the idea of stripes... the idea of repetition. I began to think a lot about repetition." He soon began to react against "the romance of Abstract Expressionism... which was the idea of the artist as a terrifically sensitive ever-changing, ever-ambitious person... I began to feel very strongly about finding a way [of working] that wasn't so wrapped up in the hullabaloo,... that wasn't constantly a record of your sensitivity."[96]

Stella promptly devised a new approach, based on his rejection of the idea of the painting as a record of process: "I didn't want to record a path. I wanted to get the paint out of the can and onto the canvas." He also rejected the goal of recording the artist's subconscious feelings: "I always get into arguments with people who want to retain the old values in painting... [T]hey always end up asserting that there is something there besides the paint on the canvas. My painting is based on the fact that only what can be seen there *is* there." He disliked the visual complexity of gestural abstraction: "One could stand in front of any Abstract-Expressionist work for a long time, and walk back and forth, and inspect the depths of the pigment and the inflection and all the painterly brushwork for hours. But I wouldn't particularly want to do that and also I wouldn't ask anyone to do that in front of my paintings. To go further, I would like to prohibit them from doing that in front of my painting." Toward this end, he wanted his paintings to present simple and straightforward images: "All I want anyone to get out of my paintings, and all I ever get out of them, is the fact that you can see the whole idea without any confusion... What you see is what you see." And he rejected the older artists' uncertainty: "We believe that we can find the end, and that a paint-ing can be finished. The Abstract Expressionists always felt the painting's being finished was very problematical."[97] Stella left no doubt that he val-ued ideas over technique: "I do think that a good pictorial idea is worth more than a lot of manual dexterity."[98]

Stella's objections to gestural abstraction led him to make a series of abstract works called the Black paintings, which he completed at the age of 24. These paintings, which remain his most important works, effectively made the repetitive patterns of Johns's targets and flags non-representational, as he used housepainters' brushes to fill large canvases with parallel stripes of black paint, each approximately $2\frac{1}{2}$ inches wide, in a variety of simple geometric patterns.[99] Harold Rosenberg belittled Stella's paintings as "the most professorial paintings in the history of art," arguing that they represented the result of formalist art criticism rather than artistic self-discovery: "He wished to negate not only the content of Abstract Expressionism but its gesture, too."[100] Stella followed the Black paintings with a series of paintings that used aluminum paint to create geometric patterns. These effectively enacted his wish to prohibit viewers from standing in front of his works for an extended period, for as he conceded, the aluminum paint was "repellent" to look at: "these would be very hard paintings to penetrate...It would appear slightly reflective and slightly hard and metallic."[101] Stella's "slap in the face" to Abstract Expressionism had a considerable impact, for his avoidance of the gestural brushstrokes and tactile surfaces of Abstract Expressionism in favor of simple geometric patterns produced with anonymous techniques and industrial materials gave a powerful stimulus to the young artists who went on to create Minimalism, by making simple geometric sculptures out of industrial, manufactured materials.[102]

Gerhard Richter is widely considered one of the most influential painters of recent decades. His reputation rests largely on an innova-tion of the early 1960s, in which he responded to Pop art's revival of figuration by devising a new, distinctive style of representational painting based on photographs. But he is also known for the great stylistic vari-ety of his work, and it is consequently not surprising that he has made abstract paintings. What is striking is how many distinctly different styles of abstraction he has devised, each based on a different method. His out-put is so large and varied that no simple summary of his approaches is possible, but many of his paintings fall into groups, to which he gives collective titles.

In 1966, Richter began making large paintings he called Color Charts, which consisted of grids of rectangular blocks of color that were copies of sample cards from paint manufacturers. The earliest Color Charts had small numbers of colors, but over time Richter increased these by mixing colors to make new shades; by 1974 he made a painting with 4096 different colors.[103] The paintings were made systematically, as Richter and his assistants applied the paint as smoothly as possible, and distributed the blocks of color randomly on the support. The Color Charts thus blended accident and preconception, as Richter observed that "I found it interesting to tie chance to a wholly rigid order."[104]

In the early 1970s, Richter made the Gray Paintings, monochrome works with a variety of surface textures, some with visible brushstrokes, others with smooth surfaces. In the late 1970s he began several series of Abstract Pictures, which he continued over the following decades. Some of these, often called the "soft abstractions," were made by taking photographs of small sections of earlier paintings, then enlarging them by projecting them onto new canvases. With scale enlargements of 100:1, the new works become both non-representational and blurred. Another series of abstract paintings was made by drawing rigid squeegees vertically or horizontally over the surfaces of large canvases that had been covered with a variety of colors, often chosen at random. Richter would repeat this process many times, each time applying more paint, then scraping the surface – in one documented case, a painting went through thirty-three discrete stages – with the effect that the final paintings generally bear visible traces of many colors in many layers.[105]

A theme that runs through Richter's statements in interviews and published writings is that his art is motivated by ideas. In considering Richter's alternation between forms, Varnedoe remarked that he was "programmatic in his gambits between abstraction and representation," and in pondering Richter's methods in making non-representational paintings, Varnedoe further observed that "He comes to his abstraction from a climate of dead cynicism and irony."[106]

Conclusion

The standard history of abstraction, and the one that the satirists and ironists of the 1980s would write, smugly and in self-congratulation, is a history of faith and its loss, a history of illusions replaced by knowing, of dreams dispelled by reality.

Kirk Varnedoe, 2003[107]

Early in the twentieth century, three great artists pioneered a radical new form of painting. All three came from places that lay outside the central traditions of western modern art – Kandinsky and Malevich from Russia, Mondrian from Holland – but each was heavily influenced by mainstream artistic movements of their time – Kandinsky by Fauvism, Mondrian by Cubism, and Malevich by both of those movements, as well as by Futurism. They proceeded in very different ways, the experimental Kandinsky and Mondrian gradually and visually, the conceptual Malevich precipitously and theoretically, in arriving at their discoveries. Their specific goals for their art also differed greatly, but they shared a basic optimism, and a belief that the new forms of art they were pioneering would not only be the advanced art of the future, but would directly and powerfully contribute to improving human society.

Abstraction became the dominant form of advanced painting during the decade following the end of World War II. The rise of abstraction coincided with the rise of New York as the center of the advanced art world, as a group of ambitious young experimental artists worked for decades in what proved to be a successful attempt to transform themselves from art world outsiders into the new leaders of modern art. Only thirty years, but also two world wars and a worldwide depression, separated their arrival at their mature art from the pioneers' original discoveries, so it is hardly surprising that the Abstract Expressionists were less optimistic than their predecessors, and few if any of them genuinely believed that their art would have a real impact on society at large. They were committed, however, to using art as a vehicle for learning about themselves: as they experimented with new ways to use paint to create novel images, they hoped that the forms they discovered on their canvases would reveal new insights into the sources of their own feelings and motivations.

The dominance of abstraction as the leading form of advanced painting was cut short abruptly during the late 1950s and early 1960s by the innovations of a succession of young conceptual artists; the hegemony of Abstract Expressionism did not last a millennium, as some of its leading members had expected, but barely a decade. The rise of conceptual approaches in advanced art, from the late 1950s on, greatly reduced the importance of abstract painting. In part this was a consequence of the return to figuration in painting, while in part it was also a product of a general deemphasis of painting in favor of new genres of art, many of which were devised as rejections of Abstract Expressionist painting.

Yet although abstract painting declined in importance, it did not disappear altogether from advanced art after 1960. It persisted, but in a new role that many analysts have found puzzling. For example in an essay of 2002 the critic Arthur Danto, a thoughtful observer of the contemporary art world, looked back to what he called "the art wars of the mid-twentieth century," and reflected that "it says something about human passion that the distinction between figuration and abstraction was so vehement that, in my memory, people would have been glad to hang or shoot one another, or burn their stylistic opponents at the stake, as if it were a religious controversy and salvation were at risk. It perhaps says something deep about the spirit of our present times that the decisions whether to paint abstractly or realistically can be as lightly made as whether to paint a landscape or still life – or a figure study – was for a traditional artist."[108] Although Danto did not attempt to explain the difference between these two eras, the answer in fact appears to lie in the analysis outlined in the two preceding sections of this chapter. At mid-century, disputes over the relative merits of figuration and abstraction were spearheaded by experimental artists, who were deeply committed to just one or the other as a superior path to artistic truth. Thus an Abstract Expressionist who returned to figuration – as both Pollock and de Kooning did, temporarily, during the 1950s – might be denounced by his colleagues or the critics who championed abstraction as reactionary traitors to the cause.[109] In contrast, by 2002 a host of conceptual artists alternated between these forms frequently and at will, since they considered them no more than different languages, each with its own advantages in expressing certain ideas. No critic would have thought to call them traitors, for there were no commitments or causes at stake.

Abstract painting thus underwent a series of remarkable transformations within little more than five decades. When it first appeared on the eve of World War I, its creators had no doubt that it would not only dominate the future of art, but that it would play a central role in creating a better world. Three decades later, it did become the central form of advanced painting in the hands, and gestures, of the Abstract Expressionists. The cataclysmic events that separated Pollock and his colleagues from the pioneers of abstraction produced a radical diminution in the later artists' expectations for the role of art in society at large, but they were nonetheless committed to a quest for the personal image, and to abstraction as a vehicle for exploration and personal discovery. Within a decade after Pollock's death, however, abstract painting was largely taken over by conceptual artists, the most prominent of whom saw it as no more than a part-time style, and many of whom used it primarily to mock the seriousness of earlier abstract painters. Today abstraction is seen by most artists as a particular strategy, and considered by most of those who employ it as merely one available means among many of making their personal artistic statements.

14

The Globalization of Advanced Art in the Twentieth Century

Art and Globalization

The whole work, called art, knows no borders or nations, only humanity.

Wassily Kandinsky and Franz Marc, 1911[1]

During the twentieth century, the center of the advanced art world shifted from Paris to New York. Yet Paris and New York were not the only places where important innovations were produced. A number of other major cities also served, more briefly, as centers of creative activity.

Throughout the modern era, important artists have originated in diverse places: no one nativity has had a monopoly. During the twentieth century, however, there was a marked increase in the diversity of the geographic origins of innovative artists.

Both the proliferation of artistic centers and the growing number of nationalities represented by important modern artists are important aspects of the globalization of advanced art in the twentieth century. Both are also consequences of the increased diffusion of artistic innovations. Over time, new artistic techniques and styles have spread both more rapidly and more widely than previously. This increased diffusion has in turn been a consequence of the increasingly conceptual nature of advanced art during the past century.

This chapter will provide an overview of how and when the central locations of advanced art changed during the twentieth century. This will be done by surveying some of the key movements. For each, the sources and implications of its principal innovations will be considered.

Before examining this chronology, however, it is necessary to understand the role of location: how does place matter to the creation of advanced art?

The Importance of Place

> No artist is known – at least not where the evidence is clear enough – to have arrived at important art without having effectively assimilated the best new art of the moment, or moments, just before his own.
>
> Clement Greenberg, 1971[2]

Globalization involves not only the movement of goods, but also the movement of people and ideas. For advanced art, a central element of globalization has been the spread of important innovations – the geographic diffusion of new techniques and styles. In considering the role of location, there are two basic questions. First, how does location affect the ability of artists to make new discoveries? And second, what affects the spread of these discoveries?

Art scholars typically contend that no general understanding of the conditions surrounding artistic innovation is possible: they argue that these innovations are too diverse and too idiosyncratic to be reduced to systematic patterns. Yet this is wrong: it is no more true of art than of any other intellectual activity. There are general conditions under which artistic innovations occur, and identifying these conditions leads to a recognition of how location matters for the production of advanced art.

Location matters to artists primarily early in their careers, because of the need for contact with other artists. Important contacts are of two types. Significant new contributions to advanced art – changes in existing practices – can only be made by artists who understand the advanced techniques or styles they are trying to add to, or replace. Apprenticeship with an important artist of an earlier generation is the best route to this understanding. These apprenticeships can occur within formal art schools or in informal relationships, but in either case they normally occur in artistic centers.

After they have learned the state of existing artistic practice from one or more older artists, young artists need to develop their art with other like-minded and talented artists of their own generation. The crucial role of collaboration in the development of all the important movements in the history of modern art has long been a commonplace of art history. The Abstract Expressionist Barnett Newman in fact argued that the first of these great movements set the pattern for later ambitious young artists, for "it was not until the impressionists that a group of artists set themselves a communal task: the exploration of a technical problem together."[3] Location matters for these collaborations because it is only in artistic centers that groups of talented young artists can be formed and sustained. Whether small or large, it is in these groups that young artists can develop, or begin to develop, the innovations that will become their contributions.

A key to understanding the accelerating pace of globalization of advanced art in the twentieth century lies in recognizing that both of these necessary forms of contact between artists can differ, depending on the nature of the art in question. The goals of experimental artists are imprecise, and not readily formulated or expressed, so older artists typically influence younger ones by demonstrating how they work. Instruction occurs gradually, face to face. In contrast, conceptual teachers can often simply tell their students why and how they work, and young artists can consequently learn conceptual approaches more quickly. For these same reasons, collaborations among young artists may proceed at very different rates. Experimental artists, who work by trial and error to develop new physical processes of making art – for example, devising new ways of applying paint to canvas to achieve a desired visual effect – develop their art more slowly than conceptual artists, who can exchange ideas and produce innovations more quickly.

As conceptual approaches become more extreme, these relationships can be altered even more. Most notably, direct contact between teacher and student might not only be reduced, but eliminated altogether, as craft and technique give way to ideas. A talented young conceptual artist might learn a new technique simply by visiting the studio of an older conceptual innovator. Direct contact between older and younger artists might not even be necessary: the younger artist might learn merely by seeing an innovative conceptual work, or even by hearing, or reading, a description of it. In these latter instances, the importance of location for apprenticeships can disappear, for conceptual artists can learn from artists they have never met, and this learning can occur anywhere.

The basic difference in the ways that experimental and conceptual innovations can be produced implies that conceptual innovations can not only be created more quickly, but can also be transmitted more quickly, than experimental contributions. This recognition provides a basis for understanding the accelerating pace of artistic globalization in the twentieth century.

The Age of Manifestos[4]

It is from Italy that we launch through the world this violently upsetting
incendiary manifesto of ours.

F.T. Marinetti, 1909[5]

In two leaflets published in 1910, five young Italian painters – Umberto
Boccioni, Carlo Carrà, Luigi Russolo, Giacomo Balla, and Gino Severini –
issued an artistic call to arms. Declaring that they would "Destroy the
cult of the past, the obsession with the ancients, pedantry and academic
formalism," and "Sweep the whole field of art clean of all themes and
subjects which have been used in the past," they promised a new form
of painting that would capture the speed of contemporary life: "The
gesture which we would reproduce on canvas shall no longer be a fixed
moment in universal dynamism. It shall simply be the *dynamic sensation*
itself."[6] George Heard Hamilton later observed that "These were brave
words with which to attack academic idealism and naturalism, but the
pictorial and sculptural correlatives for them had still to be found."[7]

These two leaflets, the first two manifestos of Futurist painting, were
the first instances of a novel conceptual device that would have a profound impact on the globalization of visual art for the next six decades.
Futurism was the first important movement in visual art that began as
a literary movement. It was founded by the Italian poet F.T. Marinetti,
who made the manifesto, written with what he called "*precise* accusation, *well-defined* insult," into the characteristic literary form of the
movement. Marjorie Perloff observed that "as what we now call a conceptual artist, Marinetti was incomparable . . . The novelty of Italian Futurist
pronouncement, sufficiently aestheticized, can, in the eyes of the mass
audience, all but take the place of the promised art work."[8]

As vivid descriptions of new – or intended – forms of conceptual art, the
manifestos became powerful tools for the rapid diffusion of Futurist innovations. Thus John Golding noted that Kazimir Malevich and other Russian artists "first learned of Futurism through its pamphlets or manifestos.
These were invariably blueprints for art that was about to be produced,
rather than justifications or explanations of literature, painting and sculpture already in existence, and this explains why the influence of Italian
Futurism was to be incalculable and yet entirely disproportionate to that
of its artistic and intellectual achievements: it provided artists all over the
world with instant aesthetic do-it-yourself kits."[9] As Golding implied, the
Futurist manifestos' ideas were often more compelling to their audience

than their associated works of art. For example the German Expressionist painter Franz Marc wrote to his friend Wassily Kandinsky in reference to the Futurists in 1912 that "I cannot free myself from the strange contradiction that I find their ideas, at least for the main part, brilliant, but am in no doubt whatsoever as to the mediocrity of their works."[10]

The key to the success of the Futurist manifestos stemmed from their ability to give verbal expression to visual art, and this was a direct consequence of the movement's highly conceptual motivations and methods. Perloff stressed that "it is not enough to say of ... Futurist manifestos that theory preceded practice ... For the real point is that the theory ... *is* the practice ... To talk about art becomes equivalent to making it."[11] And to read about art became equivalent to seeing it. Once this was true, artistic innovations could diffuse much more rapidly than previously, for mailing and reading pamphlets could be done much more quickly and inexpensively than transporting paintings and presenting them in formal exhibitions.

The Futurist manifesto proved a more influential innovation than Futurist painting. Malevich was among the earliest painters outside Italy to recognize the value of published statements to fledgling conceptual art movements. Thus, in 1915, when he launched his own new movement in an exhibition in Petrograd, it was accompanied by a manifesto titled *From Cubism and Futurism to Suprematism*. Although he praised Futurism in his manifesto, Malevich was at pains to emphasize that he had now gone beyond it: "We have abandoned Futurism: and we, the most daring, *have spat on the altar of its art*" – in itself, as Golding noted, a very Futurist thing to say.[12] For decades thereafter, manifestos became a distinctive feature of nearly all self-respecting conceptual art movements, and the manifestos often contain echoes of Marinetti or his intellectual heirs. For example Perloff remarked that "From [Marinetti's] *Down with the Tango and Parsifal* (1914) to Tristan Tzara's first Dada manifesto, the *Manifesto of Monsieur Antipyrine* (1916), is a shorter step than the Dadaists would have liked us to think," and in turn Tzara's manifesto influenced Dada's artistic successor: "its coterie address, its complex network of concrete but ambivalent images, and its elaborate word play and structuring look ahead to André Breton's first Surrealist manifesto of 1924." Of a later era, Perloff observed of the 1967 essay in which Robert Smithson first published the word "earthworks," that was to become the emblem of his artistic movement, "'The Monuments of Passaic' is reminiscent of Russian Futurist manifestos, especially Malevich's *From Cubism and Futurism to Suprematism*."[13]

Paris

There is a theory I have heard you profess, that to paint it is absolutely necessary to live in Paris, so as to keep up with ideas.

Paul Gauguin to Camille Pissarro, 1881[14]

Early in the modern era, Paris was the exclusive source of advanced art. Thus in 1913 the poet Guillaume Apollinaire, who was perhaps the most sophisticated critic of his time, could look back on the history of modern painting and conclude that "in the nineteenth century Paris was the capital of art." The credit went primarily to French citizens: "The greatest names in modern painting, from Courbet to Cézanne and from Delacroix to Matisse, are French." Yet Paris' artistic greatness was not exclusively a national achievement: "Englishmen like Constable and Turner, a German like Marées, a Dutchman like van Gogh, and a Spaniard like Picasso have all played major roles in this movement, which is a manifestation not so much of the French genius as of universal culture."[15]

No artist of the late nineteenth century who did not go to Paris to study the most advanced art of the moment could become an important figure in the development of modern art. The artistic education and maturation of Vincent van Gogh illustrate this necessity. As an aspiring artist in Holland in 1884, van Gogh had never seen Impressionist paintings, the most important recent advanced artistic innovation. Nor could he understand Impressionism from the written descriptions he received from his brother Theo, who was an art dealer in Paris: "from what you told me about 'impressionism,' I have indeed concluded that it is different from what I thought, but it's not quite clear to me what it really is."[16] Van Gogh joined his brother in Paris in 1886, and his art was transformed, as the instruction of Camille Pissarro changed not only his use of color but his entire conception of the possible uses of art. Thus Meyer Schapiro remarked that "In Paris he discovered the senses, the world of light and color which he had lacked, and which he now welcomed as a release from past repressions and a narrow, no longer vital, religion and village world."[17] Van Gogh was fully aware of the importance of this education for his art, as early in his stay in Paris he wrote to a fellow painter who had remained in Antwerp that "There is but one Paris... What is to be gained is progress and what the deuce that is, it is to be found here." He cautioned that living in Paris was costly, and that art dealers there neglected young artists in favor of established masters, "But for adventurers as myself, I think they lose nothing in risking more."[18] In Paris, van Gogh also met Paul Gauguin, Emile Bernard, and a number of other young artists who were developing a new Symbolist art. Having accepted the brilliance of Impressionist color, these artists were beginning to use these colors for expressive purposes, and this adaptation became the basis for van Gogh's distinctive contribution to modern art. He left Paris in 1888 for Arles, where he soon arrived at what Schapiro called "his first new art...transfigured by what he had learned in Paris, or could now learn by himself thanks to his Paris experience."[19] Mark Roskill observed that for both van Gogh and Gauguin "impressionism provided a basic vocabulary...which they in turn built upon and manipulated for special purposes."[20] Van Gogh realized that his teacher Pissarro would be dismayed by his departure from Impressionist goals and practices, as he wrote to Theo from Arles that "I should not be surprised if the impressionists soon find fault with my way of working...Because instead of trying to reproduce exactly what I have before my eyes, I use color more arbitrarily, in order to express myself forcibly."[21]

Van Gogh's experience is remarkable for the astounding rate at which he assimilated the advanced art of the moment, and then used it as the basis for his own contribution. This speed is an obvious consequence not only of his great talent, but also of his highly conceptual approach to art. But his experience is typical in its structure, for ambitious young artists of his time needed to gain a Paris education in advanced art before going on to their personal achievements. Thus at the other end of the artistic spectrum, 14 years before van Gogh's arrival in Paris, Paul Cézanne left his home in Aix to live in Pontoise, a village near Paris, where, in Roger Fry's words, he "became in effect apprentice to Pissarro."[22] Just as he would later do for van Gogh, Pissarro initiated Cézanne into the motives and means of Impressionism, and Cézanne's palette and his conception of art were transformed. Fry explained that Pissarro's instruction "turned him away from the inner vision and showed him the marvelous territory of external vision, a country which invited his adventurous spirit to set out on the discovery of new experiences."[23] Because of Cézanne's visual and experimental approach, this discovery required not merely a few months or years, as for van Gogh, but instead decades, and Cézanne did not achieve his greatest innovations until more than 30 years after he first travelled to Pontoise. But throughout his life he remained acutely aware of the crucial role of the education he had received from "the humble and colossal Pissarro," as in an exhibition catalogue in Aix in 1902 he had himself listed as "Pupil of Pissarro," and in 1906, a month before his death, he wrote to his son "long live...Pissarro, and all those who have an impulse towards color."[24] The persistent gratitude of van Gogh and Cézanne to Pissarro did not arise from personal idiosyncrasies, but rather from their understanding that their education in the advanced art of the moment had been necessary for their own artistic achievements. And the basis of that education was not created by one person, but by many artists working in one place, as Pissarro reflected when economic necessity forced him to give up his Paris studio: "I shall much regret no longer having one foot in Paris. This was very useful for me, since it enabled me to keep up with everything that concerns painting."[25]

Paris retained its position as the center of the advanced art world into the twentieth century. The first two important movements of the new century – Fauvism and Cubism – both originated there. Both were conceptual in nature, both were created by small groups of young artists, and both spread rapidly. Cubism proved to be the more influential of the two, and its career created a new model of artistic globalization.

Cubism

This creative tendency is now spreading throughout the universe.
Guillaume Apollinaire, 1913[26]

Cubism originated in a partnership between the young Spaniard Pablo Picasso and the young Frenchman Georges Braque. Picasso later stressed "how closely we worked together. At that time our work was a kind of laboratory research from which every pretension or individual vanity was excluded."[27] Braque similarly recalled that "Picasso and I were engaged in what we felt was a search for the anonymous personality. We were inclined to efface our own personalities in order to find originality."[28]

Several themes frequently recur in art scholars' discussions of Cubism. One is the great speed at which Cubism spread. A second is how widely it diffused. And a third is that many of the artists who adopted Cubism put it to uses very different from those for which it was initially developed. For example all three of these themes appear in a brief introductory statement by Douglas Cooper to his book, *The Cubist Epoch*:

Cubism originated in Paris between 1906 and 1908 and was the creation of Picasso and Braque...Within four years, however, the pictorial methods and technical innovations of those two young painters had been seized on by other artists – in France, Germany, Holland, Italy, Czechoslovakia, Russia, America and, to a much lesser degree, in England – who either imitated them or tried to transform them by imaginative efforts into new types of artistic expression. A knowledge of Cubist methods and possibilities spread rapidly, and by this means Cubism played some part in the technical and stylistic adventures which constitute virtually all the avant-garde developments in western art between 1909 and 1914.[29]

These same themes also recur in discussions of one specific innovation of the Cubists, collage. For example Marjorie Perloff wrote that "The rapid dissemination of [collage] . . . is in itself remarkable . . . [T]he first collages, Picasso's *Still Life with Chair Caning* and Braque's *Fruit Dish*, were both made in 1912 . . . Within a few years, collage and its cognates – montage, construction, assemblage – were playing a central role in the verbal as well as the visual arts."[30]

Cubism is a highly conceptual artistic language, based on the thoughts of artists rather than their perceptions. Thus John Golding remarked that "The Cubism of Picasso and Braque was to be essentially conceptual. Even in the initial stages of the movement, when the painters still relied to a large extent on visual models, their paintings are not so much records of the sensory appearance of their subjects, as expressions in pictorial terms of their idea or knowledge of them."[31] The shock that many contemporary artists and critics experienced upon first exposure to the radical appearance of Cubist paintings has often obscured the fact that the most distinctive stylistic devices of the new art – the faceting of objects, and the juxtaposition of images viewed from different vantage points – could quickly be understood and adopted by artists who wanted to work in a Cubist idiom. This understanding did not require contact with Picasso or Braque, but could be acquired simply by seeing Cubist paintings, and the rapid spread of Cubism was the product in large part of the display of paintings by Picasso, Braque, and their Paris followers at exhibitions throughout Europe and the United States in the years between 1910 and the outbreak of World War I.[32]

The device of collage was even simpler, and even more readily adapted to alternative purposes, than the style of Cubism in general. Collage was so highly conceptual that it could be adopted by artists who had not even seen examples of its use, but who had merely heard descriptions of it. A remarkable demonstration of this is contained in a recollection by the Italian painter Gino Severini of his first acquaintance with collage (which he refers to by the name of its close relative, papier collé, the device in which Braque began to paste pieces of paper to his canvases, shortly after Picasso had created collage by pasting a piece of oil cloth to one of his paintings). Severini, who had been living in Paris at the time, provided a description of a sequence of conversations that served to carry the new technique from Paris to Italy, and to translate it from Cubism to Futurism:

As regards the so-called *papiers collés* I can tell you with precision that they were born in 1912 in the zone of Montmartre. As I remember it, Apollinaire suggested the idea to me after having spoken of it to Picasso, who immediately painted a small still-life onto which he applied a small piece of waxed paper (the type that was used for the tablecloths in the bistros of Paris). I tried to glue some *paillettes* [spangles] and multicolored sequins onto forms of ballerinas in movement. I next saw a collage of Braque, perhaps the first, made of what seemed to be wood and large sheets of white paper on which he had sketched to a large extent with black crayon. During my trip to Italy in August of 1912 I naturally spoke about the technique to Boccioni and he, in turn, to Carrà. During 1913 the first futurist experiments in this field saw the light of day.[33]

Severini's narrative provides vivid evidence of the highly communicable nature of collage. Thus by his account his own first use of the technique resulted not from contact with Picasso, or even the sight of one of Picasso's works, but rather from a conversation with a friend of Picasso's, Guillaume Apollinaire, who was not a painter, but a poet. Severini could in turn pass on verbal instructions that allowed Boccioni to make his own use of collage, and to continue the process of diffusion by word of mouth.

Severini's experience also demonstrates the extreme versatility of collage. In 1912, as he described, he attached sequins to a painting of dancers – *Dynamic Hieroglyphic of the Bal Tabarin*, which became his most celebrated painting.[34] Thus unlike Picasso and Braque, who consistently used fragments of newspaper, wallpaper, and other scraps of waste materials in their collages to evoke the dark and tranquil atmosphere of cafes, Severini used sparkling sequins to recreate the excitement of "the fairy ambiance of light and color" that he experienced in the night clubs of Paris.[35] And although collage was devised by Picasso and Braque for the purposes of Cubism, which was an art of still life and subdued colors, Severini could immediately adapt it to Futurism, which instead stressed speed, motion, and bright colors.

Futurism

We may declare, without boasting, that the first Exhibition of Italian Futurist Painting... is the most important exhibition of Italian painting which has hitherto been offered to the judgment of Europe.

For we are young and our art is violently revolutionary.

Umberto Boccioni, Carlo Carrà,
Luigi Russolo, Giacomo Balla,
Gino Severini, 1912[36]

Speed – the dynamism, excitement, and novelty of modern city life and technology – was the hallmark of Futurism. It was the theme of

Marinetti's founding manifesto in 1909, and it later became the theme of Futurist painting and sculpture. Futurist painting rejected the aims of Cubism, but borrowed its formal devices. Unlike the Cubists, who painted still lifes by analyzing arrangements of studio props, the Futurists wanted to make art from the streets of the city, and to paint riots, carnivals, and speeding trams. Yet in creating images that would capture the interaction of objects in motion, Futurist painters found the multiple viewpoints and intersecting planes of Cubism to be valuable tools.

Apart from Severini, who moved to Paris in 1906, the Futurist painters lived in Italy. Their knowledge of the innovations of Cubism was acquired primarily on short visits to Paris. An example of how quickly these young conceptual artists could assimilate the art of the moment is afforded by a brief visit Boccioni made to Severini in Paris early in 1912, on his way back to Milan from an exhibition in Berlin. Neither of the two painters had ever made sculptures, but Severini recalled that during this visit Boccioni "expressed a particular interest in sculpture. All day every day he would discuss the subject. To sate his appetite for exploring the problems of sculpture, I took him to visit Archipenko, Agero, Brancusi, and Duchamp-Villon, who were the most daring avant-garde sculptors of the moment." Severini and Boccioni were close friends, having met a dozen years earlier when both were teenaged art students in Rome, and Severini afforded Boccioni the full benefit of his knowledge of Paris: "I took him along, like a brother, everywhere I usually went myself . . . He lived like a real Parisian in Paris, not like a visitor."[37]

After a few frenetic days of visiting artists' studios by day and bars and clubs by night, Boccioni returned to Milan. Severini was stung when, only two weeks later, Boccioni published in Milan his *Technical Manifesto of Futurist Sculpture*: "During our discussions and visits to various sculptors in Paris, Boccioni had not once mentioned this manifesto, so it surprised and saddened me to have to acknowledge that these speed 'records,' these feverish searches for novelty for the sake of novelty itself, and a lack of sincerity on his part, would inevitably cause deep wounds in our relationship."[38] In typical Futurist fashion, Boccioni's manifesto stridently rejected the sculpture of the time – "All the sculpture . . . to be seen in all European cities presents such a pathetic spectacle of barbarism, ineptitude and tedious imitation that my Futurist eyes turn away from it with the deepest loathing" – so Severini also felt deeply embarrassed before his colleagues in Paris: "it seemed to all my friends who had recently received him that I had been his accomplice, and I must confess that I found this very distasteful."[39]

The sculptors whose work Boccioni had seen in Paris were concerned with extending Cubism to three dimensions, and Boccioni wanted to go beyond their experiments to create the appearance of motion. Over the course of the next year, he completed eleven sculptures. Several of these were dramatically fragmented striding figures that appeared to be blown by powerful winds created by their own rapid progress. Boccioni arranged for these sculptures to be exhibited at a Paris gallery in June of 1913, barely a year after he had first taken up the art.

Apollinaire reviewed Boccioni's new work favorably, crediting him with introducing movement into sculpture: "Varied materials, sculptural simultaneity, violent movement – these are the innovations contributed by Boccioni's sculpture."[40] Boccioni was elated, writing to a friend that "Apollinaire is completely won over to Futurism." He described a dinner that he had had with Apollinaire and Marinetti: "We talked from seven until three in the morning. We came out drunk and exhausted. After these discussions, which are true conquests by magnetism, I end up sad and discouraged. I think about what I would have done by now if I had grown up with Paris or Berlin as my environment."[41]

This episode affords a number of insights into the progress of globalization in the highly charged European art world immediately before World War I. A few days of inspecting the most advanced sculpture of the time in Paris were sufficient to serve as the point of departure for Boccioni's own conceptual efforts to make new innovations in sculpture. He then accomplished this successfully – so successfully that one of these sculptures became one of the most important works of art of the twentieth century – in a period of barely more than one year, in spite of the fact that he had never sculpted before.[42] Yet beyond the remarkable speed of Boccioni's internalization of the state of the art, and the no less remarkable speed of his own contribution, the episode also gives an interesting glimpse into the psychology of a young conceptual artist, who was willing to embarrass his closest friend in order to gain publicity for his own art, in pursuit of what Severini ruefully called "speed records" – "feverish searches for novelty." And finally, the highly pressured atmosphere of the art world is suggested by Boccioni's ambivalent reaction to his critical success in Paris. Although the artist was only 31 years old, he could not simply enjoy Apollinaire's praise and his own knowledge of his accomplishment, but instead immediately reflected sadly that he could have made greater contributions even earlier if he had grown up in a center of the art world.

Expressionism

> There is an artistic tension all over Europe. Everywhere new artists are greeting each other; a look, a handshake is enough for them to understand each other!
>
> Franz Marc, 1912[43]

The earliest of the groups that came to be identified with German Expressionism originated in Dresden in 1904, when four art students formed the Brücke, or Bridge. These young painters rejected the formal art of the academies, and wanted to create a more passionate art of self-expression, portraying the excitement and anxiety of modern urban life by devising new means that would replace description of contemporary subjects with psychological statements.

The artists of the Brücke were young revolutionaries, anxious to deny any influence of earlier artists in order to stress their own originality. Yet art scholars have found strong visual evidence of influence of a kind that underscores the rapid transmission of conceptual innovations. Thus late in 1905 a Dresden art gallery exhibited fifty paintings by Vincent van Gogh, and early the next year a Dresden art association presented twenty paintings by Edvard Munch.[44] A biographer of Ernst Kirchner, the leading member of the Brücke, identified a series of specific influences of van Gogh and Munch on Kirchner's paintings of 1906–08, including his use of symbolism, his composition, the thick impasto of the paint surface, the large size and unusual length of brush strokes, and the expressive and often arbitrary use of color.[45] A historian of German Expressionism observed that in spite of the denials of the young painters, "it would seem that Munch and van Gogh influenced the Brücke artists in their formative years," and that when the Galerie Arnold exhibited van Gogh's work in 1905, "The violence of van Gogh's expression must have made an enormous impression on the young Dresden painters... The ecstatic expression of a personal symbolism, leading to a subjective unity of form and content, made van Gogh of the greatest importance to the expressionists."[46] The speed with which the innovations of van Gogh and Munch could be assimilated by the young conceptual painters simply upon seeing examples of their art was a direct result of the conceptual clarity of those innovations. Thus Robert Jensen has argued that van Gogh's art could become influential so rapidly throughout Europe precisely because of its highly conceptual nature: "much of van Gogh's stylistic contributions to modern art can be summarized by a few characteristics that could easily be taken up by other artists."[47] For young painters impatient to make a new art that allowed them to express strong emotions, the innovations of van Gogh and Munch came as a powerful and immediate revelation of new means of expression.

Over time, the innovative bold use of color by Matisse and the Fauves also became a major influence on the Brücke and other German expressionist painters. Matisse was in fact invited, but declined, to contribute an essay to the *Blaue Reiter Almanac*, which was published in 1912 by a group of artists who collectively called themselves the Blue Rider. The *Almanac* was a rare case in which an important experimental artist – Wassily Kandinsky – made common cause with a group of conceptual painters, most notably his younger co-editor Franz Marc, to produce a group manifesto. In keeping with the unusual intellectual basis of this alliance, the *Almanac* was an unusual manifesto. Rather than a highly focused and precise description of a new style or artistic project, the *Almanac* was eclectic in the extreme. For example none of its fifteen essays was coauthored, and less than half were written by members of the Blue Rider group. Four of the essays were about music rather than visual art, and the *Almanac* also included a poem, and a script for a stage performance written by Kandinsky. But perhaps the most remarkable dimension of the *Almanac's* eclecticism lay in its many illustrations, which totaled more than 140 images. George Heard Hamilton summarized them as follows:

Reproductions of paintings and drawings by members of the group, principally the two editors, by Macke, Campendonk, Kubin, and Klee, and by the North German Expressionists were outnumbered three to one by illustrations of primitive, folk, and children's art. In addition to objects from Africa and the South Seas, examples of medieval German sculpture and woodcuts ("primitive" in the stylistic sense), Egyptian paper puppets, Japanese woodcuts and drawings, and Russian popular prints and sculpture, there were no less than seventeen examples of Bavarian *hinterglas* painting (devotional images painted on the reverse of panes of glass) and other votive paintings... Nine drawings by children constitute one of the first instances of the publication of such work for artistic reasons. There were also seven reproductions of paintings by Henri Rousseau... Of the Post-Impressionists there were only five reproductions after Cézanne, Gauguin, and van Gogh.

Hamilton's comment on this surprising collection of images was that "emphasis fell on the psychological immediacy of unsophisticated expression, supposedly to be found in the direct statements of persons artistically untrained or belonging to less complex societies."[48] Although neither

Kandinsky nor Marc was directly influenced by most of the forms of primitive art illustrated in the *Almanac*, the selection did reflect the appreciation for Russian folk art that Kandinsky had developed while doing ethnographic research in northern Russia during his university studies. More generally, the images may have been part of Kandinsky's justification for his challenge to conventional western art. When the *Almanac* was published, Kandinsky was in the process of abandoning representation, an iconoclastic act that he rationalized at the time as the product of his need to follow his own intuition: "The most important thing in the question of form is whether or not the form has grown out of inner necessity."[49] Decades later, in a memorial for Marc, Kandinsky explained that the artistic forms included in the *Almanac* demonstrated that what was important in art was not adherence to rules or conventional styles, but the expression of genuine feeling born of spiritual motivation: "My idea then was to point out by means of examples that the difference between 'official' and 'ethnographic' art had no reason to exist; that the pernicious habit of not seeing the organic inner root of art beneath outwardly different forms could, in general, result in total loss of reciprocal action between art and the life of mankind."[50] The many forms of primitive art illustrated in the *Almanac*, like the inclusion of music and poetry in the book, were thus a plea by the editors for tolerance and freedom in art. A new era of art lay ahead – Marc wrote in the *Almanac* that "we are standing today at the turning point of two long epochs" – but a genuinely spiritual art could emerge only with liberation from the restrictions of the past, as Kandinsky concluded that "*The future* can be received only through freedom."[51]

The *Blaue Reiter Almanac* was a product of the age of manifestos, but unlike those of the Futurists or Suprematists, it did not advocate a specific style or program, and it cannot have communicated equally specific ideas to its readers. Yet in spite of its diffuse message, its inclusive approach to art, not only over time but also across space, must have impressed many in its audience as a powerful appeal for the globalization of advanced art. As Kandinksy and Marc wrote of their planned volume in 1911, "It should be almost superfluous to emphasize specifically that in our case the principle of internationalism is the only one possible."[52]

Moscow

The center of political life has moved to Russia . . . A similar center must be formed for art and creativity.

Kazimir Malevich, 1919[53]

Malevich left Russia only once, in 1927, when his greatest innovations were well in the past, and he never visited Paris. Yet early in his career, he worked in Moscow with a number of talented young artists, including the painters Mikhail Larionov, Natalia Goncharova, and Vladimir Tatlin, and his early development came at a time when two wealthy Russian merchants, Sergei Shchukin and Ivan Morozov, were building great collections of modern French art in Moscow.[54]

Shchukin and Morozov made their collections available for young artists to study, and their impact on Russian art was considerable. Malevich was an extremely fast learner: John Golding commented that his "intellect, though untutored, was voracious and quick."[55] Within barely a decade, Malevich systematically worked his way through nearly every significant development of modern art, in chronological order. His paintings not only bear strong evidence of the influences he absorbed, but in many cases this influence can be traced to specific paintings he saw in Moscow. Thus for example two of Malevich's self-portraits, of 1907 and 1909, used colors and compositional devices favored by Gauguin, whose paintings filled a wall in Shchukin's mansion; Malevich's *Bather* of 1911 in subject and form resembled the recent work of Matisse, who carried out major commissions for Shchukin, and twenty-one of whose paintings hung in Shchukin's "Matisse room"; and by 1912 Malevich's paintings demonstrated an acquaintance with Cubist paintings owned by Shchukin and Morozov.[56] In 1912–13, the particular form of Cubism developed by Fernand Léger in Paris became an important influence on Malevich's art. In this case, Malevich knew the geometric, tubular forms of Léger's recent work not only from paintings, but also from photographs carried from Paris to Moscow by a young Russian painter, Alexandra Exter, who divided her time between the cities, and who studied with Léger during her visits to Paris.[57] Malevich's *Woman at a Tram Stop* of 1913 clearly demonstrated an acquaintance with Picasso's recent synthetic Cubism, and his 1914 *Woman at a Poster Column* used Cubist collage forms and techniques.[58]

Malevich made his own artistic breakthrough in 1915, when he created his distinctive form of abstraction. Yet his paintings from the preceding decade clearly reveal the direct influence of the most recent innovations of the most important painters in Paris, in spite of the fact that he had never worked with, or even met, any of these artists. Even Malevich's radical leap of 1915, in which he launched the Suprematist movement with an exhibition that included his painting *Black Square*, demonstrated his full understanding of the process of conceptual innovation as it had developed in Western Europe. Thus not only did the flat geometric shapes of his abstractions reflect his analysis of the synthetic Cubist paintings and collages of Picasso and Braque, but the exhibition was accompanied by a Suprematist manifesto, which stated an ambitious intellectual rationale for the art, reflecting lessons Malevich had learned from the Futurists about the value of published theoretical declarations for new conceptual art movements.[59]

Malevich was the first major innovator of the modern era to make an important contribution to the mainstream of advanced art, based on a firm understanding of the most significant recent developments in that art, without having travelled to the center of the art world, or having contact with the artists whose work provided the basis for his own discoveries. He was clearly aided in this by the stimulation and companionship of a number of other talented young artists who were going through a similar development. But that he was able to become a major innovator without ever leaving Moscow was due to his strong conceptual orientation, which allowed him to assimilate the conceptual innovations that dominated advanced art in the late nineteenth and early twentieth centuries without learning them at their source. And in this he became a prototype for other young conceptual innovators later in the century, whose ability to understand the conceptual innovations of others at a distance, and to use them as the basis for their own discoveries, would speed the globalization of advanced art.

Unlike Malevich, Vladimir Tatlin did visit Paris, where he spent one month in the spring of 1913. This brief visit not only changed the form of Tatlin's art, but also led to a fundamental change in his artistic philosophy.

John Milner wrote that Tatlin "travelled west as a mature painter. He returned the constructor of reliefs."[60] Tatlin was 28 at the time of his visit to Paris. He had been a boyhood friend of Mikhail Larionov, and since 1910 he had lived in Moscow studying art and working with Larionov and a group of his peers. Like Malevich and the other young Russian painters in this group, Tatlin had been influenced by the French paintings that had been brought to Moscow. The geometric forms of Cubism had a particularly large impact on Tatlin's painting, because of his conceptual orientation. Thus Milner observed that "The distinction between observing the visual world and constructing visual objects had become a recurrent dichotomy in Tatlin's painting and drawing by 1912 . . . As

Tatlin grew less concerned with observation and the recording of visual impressions, his art became an investigation, in visual terms, of the process of creativity."[61]

Marjorie Perloff described Tatlin's visit to Picasso's Montparnasse studio in Paris in 1913 as "legendary."[62] In fact, he probably visited the studio several times, perhaps with the Lithuanian sculptor Jacques Lipchitz, who lived in Paris, as translator.[63] Upon his return to Moscow, Tatlin ceased making paintings, and began making sculptures, out of found materials, that appear to be based on small works that Picasso had made during the preceding year. George Heard Hamilton observed that one of these sculptures, Tatlin's *Relief*, of 1914, "composed of a worn board, a broken piece of glass, a bit of old iron, and a tin can with part of its label still attached, was, if the date is correct, one of the first 'works of art' in Western culture to have been assembled of untreated junk."[64]

Tatlin's conversion changed his career definitively, as he soon gained prominence as a sculptor. The ideas he had taken from Picasso's studio proved to be the key to the form of his sculptures, as he made what he called counter-reliefs in a Cubist idiom, and he followed Picasso's practice in making them from materials that had originally been intended for non-art purposes. These humble materials in turn came to be the basis for his new philosophy of art, which occasioned a break with Malevich. The Suprematist Malevich stood for the idea that painting could make a contribution to the new Soviet society by remaining apart from daily life, whereas Tatlin rejected painting as decadent and bourgeois, and advocated making art an immediate part of workers' daily lives. In his new art of Constructivism, works would be made from common materials, using industrial manufacturing techniques, and would consist of three-dimensional objects that would not hang flat on walls, but would instead project outward into real space.

Tatlin's trip to Paris, and particularly the visits he made to Picasso's studio, could change the course of his career so precipitously because of the highly conceptual nature of the Cubist works he saw, and his own extremely conceptual approach to art. Scholars have consistently emphasized not only the speed with which Tatlin assimilated the Cubist innovations he saw in Paris, but also how quickly he adapted them to his own purposes, to make a closely related but clearly distinct contribution of his own. Thus whereas Picasso remained committed to representation, and used found objects to make visual puns that suggested recognizable forms, Tatlin constructed his works abstractly, so that scraps of wood, metal, or glass no longer suggested familiar objects.[65] But Tatlin did not simply make novel sculptures, for his conceptual inclination led him to create a philosophy and an entire artistic movement, Constructivism, based on the insights he had gained in a few visits to Picasso's studio.

Dada

Dada was not an artistic movement in the accepted sense; it was a storm that broke over the world of art as the war did over nations.

Hans Richter[66]

Like Futurism, Dada was a highly conceptual movement that originated in literature before spreading into visual art. Unlike Futurism and nearly all other previous movements, however, Dada did not begin with a positive program, but as a protest. One of the most important Dada painters, Jean Arp, explained that "Revolted by the butchery of the 1914 World War, we in Zurich devoted ourselves to the arts. While the guns rumbled in the distance, we sang, painted, made collages and wrote poems with all our might. We were seeking an art based on fundamentals, to cure the madness of the age."[67] Dada had no coherent philosophy. The painter Hans Richter described its goals as "riot, destruction, defiance, confusion . . . In art, anti-art."[68] Many Dadaists considered it their purpose to attack all conventional values and practices: thus Arp stated that "The Dadaist thought up tricks to rob the bourgeois of his sleep."[69] The poet Hugo Ball observed that "Art is for us an occasion for social criticism."[70] Although the Dadaists would have liked to have an impact on society at large, their true target was advanced art. Thus the historian Dietmar Elger remarked that "While the Dadaists could not abolish war, the political power structures, or the class system in society, they could make their point by smashing the formal structure of pictures and poems."[71]

Because Dada was not tied to specific products or practices, there is considerable imprecision in tracing its origins. Thus in his history of Dada written in 1965, Richter remarked that "Where and how Dada began is already almost as hard to determine as Homer's birthplace." He explained that the uncertainty arose from the fact that "around the year 1915 or 1916, certain similar phenomena saw the light of day (or night) in different parts of the globe, and . . . the general label of 'Dada' can be applied to all of them." He continued, however, by remarking that "it was only in *one* of these that the magic fusion of personalities and ideas took place which is essential to the formation of a movement."[72] This was Zurich, where in February of 1916 Hugo Ball founded the Cabaret

Voltaire, which he described in a public announcement as "a group of young artists and writers... whose aim is to create a center for artistic entertainment."[73] Ball was soon joined by the poet Tristan Tzara and a host of other enthusiastic young artists, so that within a month of the first performance at the Cabaret Voltaire, Ball recorded in his journal that "Everyone has been seized by an indefinable intoxication. The little cabaret is about to come apart at the seams and is getting to be a playground for crazy emotions."[74] Considerable debate would later arise over how and when the movement gained its name, but a widely accepted version is that Ball and the poet Richard Huelsenbeck found the word "dada" by chance in a French-German dictionary. Huelsenbeck later explained that "Dada means hobby-horse in French. We were impressed by its brevity and suggestivity, and in a short time dada became the label for all the artistic activities we were engaging in at the Cabaret Voltaire."[75] The Cabaret Voltaire became associated with the outrageous and the absurd, as young artists created new forms, including the "simultaneous poem," which Ball described as "a contrapuntal recitative in which three or more voices speak, sing, whistle, etc., at the same time in such a way that the elegiac, humorous, or bizarre content of the piece is brought out by these combinations." From the beginning, however, the absurdity of Dada had a somber undertone, as Ball reflected that "What we are celebrating is both buffoonery and a requiem mass."[76]

Dada was created by young artists. Among the early members of the group in Zurich in 1916, Ball was 30, as was Tzara, Arp was 29, Huelsenbeck was 24, the Romanian painter Marcel Janco was 21, and Richter was 28. Richter reflected that this was not an accident: "we were all in our twenties and ready to defy all the fathers in the world in a way that would rejoice the heart of Freud's Oedipus."[77] Their defiant and iconoclastic attitude quickly produced a flow of conceptual innovations in literature and visual art, as Richter explained that "our freedom from preconceived ideas about processes and techniques frequently led us beyond the frontiers of individual artistic categories... As the boundaries between the arts became indistinct, painters turned to poetry and poets to painting. The destruction of the boundaries was reflected everywhere. The safety-valve was off."[78]

The rapid geographic spread of Dada has often been remarked by art scholars. So for example William Rubin observed that Dada "arose in a number of cities in Europe, and in New York, in part spontaneously and in part through the interchange of ideas."[79] Specific Dada techniques equally spread rapidly. For example the Berlin Dada artist Hannah Höch reflected that "When, in 1919, the Dadaists grasped the possibility of forming new shapes and new works through photography and made their aggressive photomontages, it happened, strangely enough and simultaneously, in a number of quite diverse countries, in France, Germany, Russia, and Switzerland."[80] Throughout Dada's history, the movement of ideas was facilitated by the many small magazines that the group's members produced. Table 14.1 presents a partial listing of Dada magazines. Some of these were published monthly, over several years, while others lasted only one or two issues. But the large numbers of both titles and editors clearly reflect the movement's enthusiasm for the genre, as the twenty-five magazines listed in Table 14.1 had almost as many different editors. Contributors to the magazines numbered in the hundreds: few Dada artists failed to contribute texts or images to Dada magazines, and many contributed both. In Zurich, Dada magazines began to appear within a few months after the opening of the Cabaret Voltaire, and Tzara soon emerged as the primary editor. Richter recalled that "Tzara was the ideal promoter of Dada, and his position as a modern poet enabled him to make contact with modern poets and writers in other countries . . . It was . . . through these contacts that Dada later became something more than a solitary Alpine flower, became in fact an international movement."[81]

Dada was also spread by the frequent travels of its rootless young practitioners. The movement was initially created by refugees from World War I, as Elger noted that it was no coincidence that the young artists who founded Dada in Zurich did not include a single native-born Swiss.[82] As they continued on their travels, they carried with them ideas and examples that could quickly influence young artists elsewhere. Thus Richter observed that "when Richard Huelsenbeck arrived in Berlin from Zurich at the beginning of 1917, he found the right setting and the right colleagues to set off the Dada bomb which had been perfected and tested in Zurich."[83] Dada had already effectively been created in America in 1915, when Francis Picabia and Marcel Duchamp, who had worked together as young artists in Paris, were reunited in New York, and were joined by the young American artist Man Ray as the central figures in what became an influential branch of the movement.[84]

Although Dada artists often attempted to avoid stylistic consistency, themes did appear in the art of the major Dada centers. In Zurich, accident played an important role in many of the literary improvisations of the Cabaret Voltaire, and chance also became a concern for a number of visual artists.[85] For example Arp incorporated accident into his paintings and collages by allowing fragments of paper to fall freely onto a surface;

TABLE 14.1. *Dada Magazines*

Title	Editors	Place	Dates
Cabaret Voltaire	H. Ball	Zurich	1916
Dada	T. Tzara	Zurich	1917–18
Anthologie Dada	T. Tzara	Zurich	1919
Bulletin Dada	F. Picabia	Paris	1920
Dadaphone	T. Tzara	Paris	1920
Dada Intirol	T. Tzara	Tarrenz, Austria	1921
Der Zeltweg	O. Flake, W. Serner, T. Tzara	Zurich	1919
The Blindman	M. Duchamp, Man Ray	New York	1917
Rongwrong	M. Duchamp, Man Ray	New York	1919
New York Dada	M. Duchamp, Man Ray	New York	1921
Club Dada	R. Huelsenbeck, F. Jung, R. Hausmann	Berlin	1918
Der Dada	R. Hausmann, J. Heartfield, G. Grosz	Berlin	1919–20
Jedermann Sein Eigner Fussball	W. Herzfelde	Berlin	1919
Der Blutige Ernst	J. Hoexter, C. Einstein, G. Grosz	Berlin	1919–20
Die Pleite	C. Einstein	Berlin	1919–20
Die Freie Strasse	J. Heartfield, J. Booder	Berlin	1916–18
Der Ventilator	J. Baargeld, M. Ernst	Cologne	1919
Bulletin D	J. Baargeld, M. Ernst	Cologne	1919
Die Schammade	J. Baargeld, M. Ernst	Cologne	1920
Merz	K. Schwitters, El Lissitzky	Hanover	1923–32
391	F. Picabia	Barcelona, New York, Zurich, Paris	1917–20
Pilhao-Thibaou	F. Picabia	Paris	1921–24
Cannibale	F. Picabia	Paris	1920
La Pomme de Pins	F. Picabia	St. Raphael	1922
Littérature	L. Aragon, A. Breton, P. Soupault	Paris	1919–24

Sources: Dawn Ades, *Dada and Surrealism Reviewed* (London: Arts Council of Great Britain, 1978); Hans Richter, *Dada* (London: Thames and Hudson, 1965).

although he adjusted their positions before fixing them in place, he contended that chance had influenced the final patterns. This innovation later influenced the Surrealist practice of beginning paintings with random markings. In New York, the interests of Duchamp and Picabia focused Dada on creating works that posed intellectual puzzles, often using enigmatic mechanical abstract forms. In Berlin, which suffered much more intensely than the neutral Zurich or New York, German artists responded to Richard Huelsenbeck's call "to make literature with a gun in hand," using their new technique of photomontage to make violent and bitter political statements.[86] In spite of these marked differences in the interests of artists in different places, however, many artists in all these cities consistently identified themselves as members of the international Dada movement, in recognition of the fact that they were united by a common attitude of protest that they expressed in highly conceptual approaches to art.

In an incisive analysis of the achievements of Dada, Werner Haftmann observed that Dada's formal innovations and techniques can be traced almost exclusively to three major movements that immediately preceded it. Thus Dada's improvisatory cabaret technique, its use of manifestos as a literary genre, the typography of its publications, and its development of photomontage all derived from Futurist practices and concepts; Dada's use of collage was inspired by Cubism; and Dada's free use of color and spontaneous use of artistic materials derived from Expressionism. Haftmann argued that Dada's originality lay in synthesis: "Dada took up all these separate ideas, assembled them and established them as a unified expression of experiences and emotions that were wholly of the present." These connections produced Dada's most basic contribution: "Dada led to a new *image of the artist.*"[87] George Heard Hamilton concluded that Dada, "as much as any artists since and more than most, proved that the artist's decision alone determines what art is, and what is art. They inserted deep in the aesthetic of modern times the inescapable conviction that even if the material existence of the work of art claims our attention first, the work itself originates only in the confrontation of matter with mind."[88] The conclusions of Haftmann and Hamilton underscore the fact that Dada was a quintessentially conceptual movement, that innovated in classic conceptual fashion by creating unexpected syntheses of elements drawn from earlier art.

The highly conceptual nature of Dada eventually resulted in a number of fundamental ironies. Dada was intended to be anarchic, spontaneous, and ephemeral, without regard for history: Marcel Janco declared that "No Dadaist will write his memoirs!"[89] In fact, the literary orientation of the movement's members and the verbal character of many of its activities led to an outpouring of published memoirs and histories of the movement by former participants that is matched by few, if any, other artistic movements.[90] Dada was intended not as art, but as anti-art. For example John Heartfield declared that Berlin Dada "was not, and did not want to be art or an art movement . . . it was a political renunciation of art," Georges Hugnet concluded that "Dada was against art," and Georges Ribemont-Dessaignes described Dada as "a permanent revolt of the individual against art."[91] Yet as Richter recognized, the goal of making anti-art was impossible: "A work of art, even when intended as anti-art, asserts itself irresistibly as a work of art. In fact, Tzara's phrase 'the destruction of art by artistic means' means simply 'the destruction of art in order to build a new art.' This is precisely what happened."[92] Objects produced by Dada artists rose inexorably in value, and hundreds of Dada works were exhibited at New York's orthodox Museum of Modern Art as early as 1936, when it presented an encyclopedic survey, *Fantastic Art, Dada, Surrealism*.[93] And finally, several basic ironies were caused by the effect stressed by the present study, that Dada could diffuse rapidly, often almost spontaneously, because of its highly conceptual nature. Thus for example a bitter dispute raged for decades over who founded the Dada movement.[94] Another, equally bitter, focused more narrowly on who first used the word "Dada" to refer to the movement.[95] And yet another was an extended argument over whether Raoul Hausmann and Hannah Höch or George Grosz and John Heartfield should be credited with the invention of photomontage.[96] The irony of these debates is considerable, for Dada was intended to abolish bourgeois values and traditional conceptions of artistic invention: in Jean Arp's account of the movement's youthful idealism, he recalled that "We wanted an anonymous and collective art."[97] But as in many other instances, youthful revolutionaries became aging reactionaries, and this manifested itself in a concern for property rights, the most bourgeois of values, as Elger observed that "In the battle of priorities – and not just in the disputes concerning the origins of the word Dada – most Dadaists suddenly became deadly serious."[98] The difficulty of establishing where and when the highly conceptual practices of Dada originated meant that, once begun, battles over intellectual property rights would be nearly impossible to resolve.

Surrealism

Surrealism is not a new means of expression . . . It is a means of total liberation of the mind.
    We are determined to make a Revolution.
                    Louis Aragon, André Breton, et al.,
                        *Declaration of the Bureau de
                        Recherches Surréalistes*, 1925[99]

Although Dada outlived World War I, with the end of the war its true raison d'etre had disappeared, and the movement's energy quickly dissipated. Surrealism soon emerged as Dada's successor: in Hans Richter's succinct formulation, "Surrealism devoured and digested Dada."[100] In a number of ways, Surrealism resembled its predecessor. For example Surrealism was also initiated as a literary project, and only later added visual art to its program. Unlike Dada, however, Surrealism was created primarily by a single poet, who remained firmly in charge of the movement throughout its career, formally recruiting new members to its cause, and excommunicating those who failed to conform to its requirements. Also unlike Dada, for most of its history Surrealism was located entirely in a single place.

André Breton, who was often called the pope of Surrealism, did not present Surrealism as simply a new artistic movement, but instead as a way of freeing artistic imagination from reason and convention. Thus in his initial *Manifesto of Surrealism* in 1924, he defined Surrealism as "Psychic automatism in its pure state, by which one proposes to express – verbally, by means of the written word, or in any other manner – the actual functioning of thought. Dictated by thought, in the absence of any control exercised by reason, exempt from any aesthetic or moral concern."[101] Breton did not restrict Surrealism to future actions, so he felt free retroactively to appropriate the work of earlier artists, as he did in his manifesto, describing such authors as Hugo, Poe, Rimbaud, and Jarry as Surrealists, as well as such painters as Seurat, Matisse, Picasso, Duchamp, and de Chirico.[102]

Breton created Surrealism in Paris, and the first visual artists who formally affiliated themselves with the movement were former Dada painters who returned to the city in the years following the end of World War I. Over time, Breton added a number of younger artists, including practitioners of such other arts as sculpture and photography. Although all Surrealism's artists were recruited in Paris until World War II forced Breton to flee to New York, the visual movement of Surrealism was not dominated by French nationals. Of the most important Surrealist artists, only André Masson and Yves Tanguy were French, whereas Max Ernst and Jean Arp were German, Salvador Dali and Joan Miró were Spanish, René Magritte and Paul Delvaux were Belgian, Giorgio de Chirico was Italian, Alberto Giacometti was Swiss, Roberto Matta was Chilean, and Man Ray was American. Although Paris remained the center of the advanced art world during the 1920s and 1930s by attracting talented artists from all over Europe, the heterogeneous origins of the artists who comprised its most important movement during these decades already pointed to France's decline as a producer of great modern artists.

Surrealism was exceptional among twentieth-century visual art movements in including both experimental and conceptual branches. George Heard Hamilton remarked that "There are such painters as Masson and Miró who have investigated the spontaneous reaction of the hand to the medium, and there are those who have found for their hallucinations visual metaphors of great clarity and precision, among them Tanguy, Dali, Magritte, Delvaux, and Brauner."[103] The first group, who stressed spontaneity, worked visually and experimentally, whereas the second, who privileged precision, carefully planned their conceptual works. As Hamilton's summary suggests, conceptual Surrealists predominated numerically over their experimental counterparts, though over time the experimentalists would prove at least as influential, if not more so.

William Rubin observed that "During the thirties Surrealist art sustained its position as the leading vanguard movement largely through default. Its pioneer years in the previous decade had witnessed a phenomenal variety of stylistic and iconographic inventions; but like many other modern movements, Surrealism could not sustain momentum for more than five or six years."[104] The lack of new art movements as challengers to Surrealism must have been in large part a consequence of the great economic depression of the 1930s, while the decline of Surrealist creativity reflected the exhaustion of the early creativity of its many conceptual members. When Breton moved to New York in 1941, he officially took Surrealism with him, and several New York galleries exhibited the work of Surrealist artists in exile, including Ernst, Masson, Matta, and Tanguy. Yet the movement's importance as a creator of new art lay in the past, as World War II produced a vacuum in the world of advanced art. The remaining significance of Surrealist artists would be in influencing a new generation of artists who would come to prominence after the war.

Abstract Expressionism

Q: Would you like to go abroad?

A: No. I don't see why the problems of modern painting can't be solved as well here as elsewhere.

Interview with Jackson Pollock, 1944[105]

In 1946, the American critic Clement Greenberg respectfully declared that "The School of Paris remains still the creative fountainhead of modern art, and its every move is decisive for advanced artists everywhere else – who are advanced precisely because they show the capacity to absorb and extend the preoccupations of that nerve-center."[106] Just two years later, however, new evidence from both sides of the Atlantic had caused Greenberg to change his mind, and in 1948 he proclaimed the fall of Paris and the rise of New York:

If artists as great as Picasso, Braque, and Léger have declined so grievously, it can only be because the general social premises that used to guarantee their functioning have disappeared in Europe. And when one sees, on the other hand, how much the level of American art has risen in the last five years, with the emergence of new talents so full of energy and content as Arshile Gorky, Jackson Pollock, David Smith ... then the conclusion forces itself, much to our own surprise, that the main premises of Western art have at last migrated to the United States, along with the center of gravity of industrial production and political power.[107]

Not surprisingly, the emerging American artists were aware of this shift in the art world's center before it was recognized even by sympathetic critics. Thus in 1945 the painter Barnett Newman had observed that whereas Paris' status in the art world had been severely damaged by the war, New York's stature had actually been increased by the war's effects:

With the large immigration of refugee painters who have acted as a stimulus, New York artists have begun to feel themselves the leaders and bearers of the artistic tradition of Europe instead of, as heretofore, only its reflection. The longstanding inhibiting position that made New York a mirror of Paris disappeared in 1940, and suddenly the artists of New York had to stand on their own feet.[108]

During the 1930s and 1940s, New York was the scene of the development of the most important experimental art movement of the century, as a large group of painters gradually created a novel form of abstract art. They were aware that their progress was slow and painstaking. For example, in 1945 Mark Rothko wrote to Barnett Newman that the recent development of his work had been exhilarating even though it had caused him many headaches: "Unfortunately one can't think these things out with finality, but must endure a series of stumblings toward a clearer issue."[109] They were also aware that few outside their circle of fellow artists took any interest in their efforts. Adolph Gottlieb later recalled that "We were like the people who are nothing but chess players or tennis bums and who refuse to do anything useful. And we felt that we were willing to go all our lives and do this despised kind of painting without any hope of success."[110] Yet in retrospect the Abstract Expressionists recognized that the absence of attention to their work in the early years had allowed them the necessary time to develop their art without external pressure. Thus, in 1969, when the famous 66-year-old Mark Rothko was awarded an honorary degree by Yale University – from which Rothko had dropped out 46 years earlier, in anger at the school's anti-Semitism and anti-intellectualism – he spoke briefly and nostalgically of the golden age he had found in the art world of his youth, that no longer existed because of the very success of his own cohort:

When I was a younger man, art was a lonely thing: no galleries, no collectors, no critics, no money. Yet it was a golden age, for then we had nothing to lose and a vision to gain. Today it is not quite the same. It is a time of tons of verbiage, activity, a consumption . . . I do know that many who are driven to this life are desperately searching for those pockets of silence where they can root and grow. We must all hope that they find them.[111]

The freedom afforded them by the art world's indifference to their early efforts was a common theme among the Abstract Expressionists. For example Adolph Gottlieb recalled that "Nothing could have been worse than the situation in which we were, so we tried desperate things," and Robert Motherwell reflected that "No one thought we could ever produce truly great modern painting, only Europeans could. So we had nothing to lose by risking all."[112] But it wasn't merely critics, dealers, and collectors who lacked confidence in the young American artists, for they themselves were dogged by the persistent uncertainty of experimental innovators. For example the experimental Abstract Expressionists failed to produce the manifestos that earlier conceptual movements had used to attract attention to their art, and Motherwell later explained that "the very nature of a manifesto is to affirm forcefully and unambiguously, and not to express the existential doubt and the anxiety that we all felt."[113]

Many of the leading Abstract Expressionists served informal apprenticeships in New York with a few key figures. Rothko, Gottlieb, Newman, and a number of their peers attended weekly sketching sessions throughout the 1930s and early 1940s at the New York apartment of the older American painter Milton Avery. Avery was an experimental painter who had been deeply influenced by Matisse early in his career, and had spent decades developing his own mature style based on the expressive use of subtle color harmonies. Although Avery never fully abandoned representation, the simplified shapes and blurred outlines of the objects in his images could be seen by his younger protégés as a step toward the creation of textured and flattened fields of color that were not constrained by figuration. The importance of the younger painters' direct contact with Avery was eloquently expressed in a eulogy in which Rothko paid tribute to his friend and teacher: "This conviction of greatness, the feeling that one was in the presence of great events, was immediate on encountering his work. It was true for many of us who were younger, questioning, and looking for an anchor... The instruction, the example, the nearness in the flesh of this marvelous man – all this was a significant fact – one which I shall never forget."[114] Several others among the Abstract Expressionists were influenced by a painter closer to their own age, but who brought to New York a charismatic personality and an impressive Paris reputation as the youngest of André Breton's recruits to Surrealism. Motherwell described Roberto Matta as "the most energetic, enthusiastic, poetic, charming, brilliant young artist that I've ever met," and recalled that during a trip the artists made together to Mexico, "In the three months of that summer of 1941, Matta gave me a ten-year education in surrealism."[115] The Abstract Expressionists often spoke of their desire to create images from the subconscious, yet their interest in Surrealism was not in the work of the artists who produced precise dream images, but rather in that of those who used paint spontaneously. Thus they admired the paintings of Miró and Masson, and they learned about those painters' techniques from Matta, who had developed his personal experimental form of Surrealism using fluid color and shallow spaces in an abstract tradition that had been initiated by Kandinsky.[116] In addition to Motherwell, Matta's technique had a direct impact on Pollock, William Baziotes, and Arshile Gorky. Motherwell gave credit to Matta for introducing the Abstract Expressionists to the use of automatism, which he identified as the key to the development of their art: "my conviction is that, more than any other single thing, the introduction and acceptance of the theory of automatism brought about a different look into our painting... It was the germ, historically, of what later came to be called abstract expressionism."[117]

In spite of the great differences in their mature styles, during the 1940s and early 1950s the Abstract Expressionists shared a strong common identity as members of a collective enterprise. In regular meetings at a series of galleries, cafeterias, and bars, including the now-legendary Cedar Street Tavern, the artists argued and discussed their work, and in the process both encouraged and challenged one another. In 1954, Baziotes described this: "Contact with other artists has always been of great importance to me. When the artists I know best used to meet ten or twelve years ago, the talk was mostly of ideas in painting. There was an unconscious collaboration between artists. Whether you agreed or disagreed was of no consequence. It was exciting and you were compelled to paint over

your head. You had to stay on a high level or drown."[118] Similarly, a
biographer of Rothko observed that "all of these artists knew each other,
viewed each other's work and formed a social network... During the
late forties, in the absence of sales and critical recognition, this loose field
of social relations, with artists attending each other's shows, engaging
in conversations, spending Saturday afternoons at a gallery like Parsons'
or Saturday evenings in an apartment like Ferber's – all these provided
a stimulating, supportive context for innovation as well as relief from
'crushing' isolation."[119]

The Abstract Expressionists were not concerned primarily with ideas
or the philosophy of painting, but rather with the process of painting
and the discovery of new images. For them, innovations emerged from
physical activity: thus Robert Motherwell could declare that "I think the
deepest discoveries in art have to do with the artist's materials, the liquids,
grounds, instruments, brushes, sticks, palette knives, pen points, whatever."[120] The experimental art that emerged triumphant in New York
in the early 1950s was widely copied by artists elsewhere. In 1955, for
example, William Seitz observed that "it is impossible to convey fully the
degree to which Abstract Expressionism has become a universal style,"
so that "the uniting features of the style can now be found in England,
France, Germany, Italy, Spain, and even Japan."[121] Abstract Expressionism did not travel well, however. Only in Paris did an important group
of painters emerge who shared the attitudes and values of the American
Abstract Expressionists, and their art was developed independently of
that of New York, with considerably less impact on the advanced art
world than that of the Americans.[122] The only group of followers of the
Abstract Expressionists who came to be considered important contributors to advanced art were the younger artists who worked in New York
during the 1950s and 1960s, who were labeled the second-generation
Abstract Expressionists, and their importance was also considerably less
than that of their first-generation predecessors.[123] The experimental character of Abstract Expressionism appears to account for the inability of
artists outside New York to make important contributions by emulat-
ing the school's methods and images, for Abstract Expressionism was
based on subtle and complex uses of materials, that could not be system-
atized or even precisely described. So for example in 1948, when four
of the leading Abstract Expressionists established a school – that proved
unsuccessful and short lived – they offered no formal courses because, as
Robert Motherwell explained, "The way to learn to paint... is to hang
around artists."[124] Aspiring artists who were unable to hang around the

pioneering Abstract Expressionists proved unable to use their discoveries as the basis for any significant new contributions to advanced art. And even those young experimental artists who were able to spend time with their first-generation predecessors in New York quickly found their own innovative efforts overshadowed by the bolder and more radical innovations of a new generation of young conceptual artists.

Pop Art

Pop is Instant Art.

Robert Indiana, 1963[125]

Pop Art burst on the New York art world in 1962. A *New York Times* review of one group exhibition in that year opened with the statement "It's mad, mad, wonderfully mad," and an article in *Art International*, titled "'Pop' Culture, Metaphysical Disgust, and the New Vulgarians," declared that "The truth is, the art galleries are being invaded by the pin-headed and contemptible style of gum chewers, bobby soxers, and worse, delinquents."[126]

The contrast between Pop Art and Abstract Expressionism could hardly have been greater. The Abstract Expressionists had complex and uncertain goals, and pursued them cautiously by developing highly personal gestures; the Pop artists had simple goals, which they accomplished summarily with straightforward execution. The Abstract Expressionists rejected all preconception, for they wanted to discover images, and their own identity, in the process of painting; the leading Pop artists reproduced existing images – often familiar, commercial products – using impersonal, and often actually mechanical, techniques. The Abstract Expressionists considered art to be an existentialist quest, with the goal of asserting the freedom of the individual; Pop was an art about mass production, that often used techniques of mass production in its own execution. Andy Warhol explained that "I'm for mechanical art. When I took up silk screening, it was to more fully exploit the preconceived image through the commercial techniques of multiple reproduction," while Roy Lichtenstein stated that "I want my painting to look as if it had been programmed. I want to hide the record of my hand."[127]

Unlike Abstract Expressionism, which depended critically on the subtleties of the application of paint and the creation of personal forms by the individual artist, Pop was so completely preconceived that a number of Pop artists, including Warhol, did not have to execute their own paintings. In view of the fact that these artists could fully communicate their intentions to assistants, it is not surprising that their work could readily be understood by others. Thus the Pop painter Robert Indiana described Pop as "straight-to-the-point, severely blunt, with as little 'artistic' transformation and delectation as possible," and he observed that "Its comprehension can be as immediate as a Crucifixion."[128] A younger artist, Larry Bell, remarked in 1963 on the rapid diffusion of Pop: "It is quite unique to these past few years that a generation of artists should have its influence on a second generation before it has even resolved its own philosophy. Modern means of communication and Pop Art are a romance that must have been made in heaven."[129] To understand and emulate Pop art, other artists not only didn't have to have direct contact with the innovative Pop artists, they didn't even have to see their original works: Pop's images were taken directly from magazines and other modern means of communication, and as Bell recognized, they were readily transmitted by those same means.

In 1963, Roy Lichtenstein predicted that Pop would spread to Europe: "Everybody has called Pop Art 'American' painting, but it's actually industrial painting... Europe will be the same way soon, so it won't be American; it will be universal."[130] Although Lichtenstein didn't know it at the time, his prediction had already come true. In 1962, Gerhard Richter and Sigmar Polke were students at the Düsseldorf Academy of Art. The most influential teacher at the academy, Joseph Beuys, was proselytizing for his new conception of Social Sculpture, and he denounced painting as a reactionary activity. Richter and Polke reacted in the typically perverse fashion of young conceptual innovators: "Polke and Richter thought long and hard about whether they were 'allowed to paint,' decided they were not, and for that reason took it up with a vengeance."[131] The troublesome question remained, however, of how to paint without embracing past traditions. The key discovery occurred in 1962, when a fellow student, Konrad Lueg, showed Polke and Richter an art magazine that contained illustrations of Pop paintings by Lichtenstein and Warhol. Richter almost immediately began to base his paintings on photographs: "I had had enough of bloody painting, and painting from a photograph seemed to me the most moronic and inartistic thing that anyone could do... I simply copied the photographs in paint and aimed for the greatest possible likeness to photography."[132]

Working together, the young German painters created a new art they variously called Capitalist Realism, German Pop, or Pop Art. Richter noted that "We have worked out our ideas largely by talking them through . . . And so the exchange with other artists – and especially the collaboration with Lueg and Polke – matters a lot to me: it is part of the input that I need."[133] In the spring of 1963, Richter, Polke, Lueg, and a fourth young painter presented an exhibition of their work in Düsseldorf. In a press release, Richter declared this the "first exhibition of 'German Pop Art.'" He explained that Pop had inaugurated an aesthetic revolution: "Pop Art has rendered conventional painting . . . entirely obsolete, and has rapidly achieved international currency and recognition." Curiously, he went on to argue that "Pop Art is not an American invention, and we do not regard it as an import – though the concepts and terms were mostly coined in America and caught on more rapidly there than in Germany. This art is pursuing its own organic and autonomous growth in this country."[134]

Richter has not denied the importance of American Pop art for his early development.[135] Although he did not explain his claim that Pop was not an import to Germany, it is likely that what he had in mind was that he and Polke did not simply follow the styles of Warhol or Lichtenstein, but that they adapted the innovations of the Americans to their own purposes. Thus although the Photo Paintings Richter began to produce in 1962 are generally recognized as his first significant contribution, they do not in any way resemble the paintings of any American Pop artist, and Richter went on in later years to make paintings, based on photographs, in a variety of other styles. Polke's early Pop paintings not only did not resemble American Pop, but also had little in common with those of Richter. Polke seized particularly on Lichtenstein's mimicry of the benday dots that create newspaper photographs, but his paintings were very different in appearance from those of Lichtenstein.[136] Thus Richter's claim that Pop art had had "its own organic and autonomous growth" in Germany may have been a reference to the flexibility of the ideas and techniques of Pop, for artists anywhere could readily understand the practices of Warhol and Lichtenstein, and could equally readily transform them according to their own tastes. Richter and Polke would go on to become two of the most important painters of the late twentieth century, and their success would rest largely on the practice of painting from photographs, with techniques that often imitated photographic elements, but both would use motifs and methods that made their paintings distinctively their own.

In an amusing anecdote, Arthur Danto reported a later instance of the diffusion of Pop, similar to that of its adoption by Richter and Polke, that underscores even more forcefully the unimportance of the actual appearance of the original art for its ability to influence artists in distant places:

The dissident artists, Vitaly Komar and Alexander Melamid told me that they discovered Pop Art from seeing it in half-tone illustrations in various art magazines that had clandestine circulation in the Soviet Union, and appropriated its strategies for their own subversive purposes in a movement they called "Zotz Art." One result of *Glasnost* was the ceremonial exchange of art exhibitions, which is one of the ways in which nations symbolically express friendship for one another; and the Zotz artists could scarcely contain their excitement when a show of American Pop Art in Moscow was announced. What they were unprepared for, Alex Melamid remembers, was how *beautiful* Pop Art was![137]

An early debate about Pop art, never resolved, concerned whether Pop was intended to celebrate or to mock contemporary commercial culture.[138] Another perennial dispute has questioned whether Pop's use of photography was sincere or ironic. The ambiguities that have fuelled these debates appear to have made a sizeable contribution to the influence of Pop art. Thus since the invention of Pop, commercial motifs could become subjects for artists with a wide range of ideologies. The Pop practice of painting from existing photographs equally created a vast new store of images for advanced artists: as David Sylvester observed, "all of Warhol's mature work is as if inspired by a revelation that a modern painter could and should exploit the photograph as Renaissance painters exploited classical antiquities."[139] It was because Pop opened up these new conceptual opportunities that its influence not only spread rapidly, but has continued to resonate in the advanced art world for decades.

Conceptual Art

In conceptual art the idea or concept is the most important aspect of the work.

Sol LeWitt, 1967[140]

During the late 1960s a number of artists in New York began to identify their work as Conceptual Art. In a number of respects, Conceptual Art paralleled the earlier Dada movement. Like Dada, Conceptual Art was a protest. Thus in 1968, Sol LeWitt, a key member of the movement, observed that "American life is rapidly breaking down. We have riots, wars, etc. The middle class morality is breaking down... There is no reason that the artist should feel he is part of something that is so decadent and so completely without any purpose."[141] Another important

Conceptual artist, Joseph Kosuth, later explained that Conceptual art was "the art of the Vietnam war era."[142] Like Dada, Conceptual artists attacked the values of advanced art. The critic Lucy Lippard explained that "it was usually the form rather than the content of Conceptual art that carried a political message ... Anti-establishment fervor in the 1960s focused on the de-mythologization and de-commodification of art, on the need for an independent (or 'alternative') art that could not be bought and sold by the greedy sector that owned everything that was exploiting the world and promoting the Vietnam war."[143] And like Dada, Conceptual art spread rapidly across space. The critic Peter Wollen observed that "To grasp the spread of conceptualism as a broad global movement, it is essential to understand both that it was multi-polar in its origins and that it was the creation of a very small, but very vocal and productive, phalanx of artists, strategically situated in New York and committed to a typically avant-garde strategy, complete with manifestos, journals and theoretical statements."[144]

Although its rhetoric often exceeded its practices, Conceptual art went beyond Dada in defining new artistic forms that would be more strictly conceptual than any earlier art. In a famous early manifesto in 1967, LeWitt declared that in Conceptual Art execution would be strictly subordinated to conception: "When an artist uses a conceptual form of art, it means that all of the planning and decisions are made beforehand and the execution is a perfunctory affair. The idea becomes a machine that makes the art." Two years later, LeWitt explained that execution was in fact not a necessary element of art: "Ideas can be works of art ... All ideas need not be made physical."[145] Kosuth made parallel statements, in 1967 declaring that "All I make are models. The actual works of art are ideas," and in 1969 observing that "art's viability is not connected to the presentation of visual (or other) kinds of experience."[146] On the basis of theoretical statements in this vein, in 1968 Lucy Lippard and John Chandler, two critics who were supporters of Conceptual Art, made a bold prediction: "a number of artists are losing interest in the physical evolution of the work of art. The studio is again becoming a study. Such a trend appears to be provoking a profound dematerialization of art, especially of art as object, and if it continues to prevail, it may result in the object's becoming wholly obsolete."[147]

Inspired by the concept of dematerialization, in 1968 the dealer Seth Siegelaub created an exhibition titled *The Xerox Book*, that had no physical manifestation other than a Xeroxed book. Each of seven Conceptual artists – Kosuth, LeWitt, Carl Andre, Robert Barry, Douglas Huebler,

Robert Morris, and Lawrence Weiner – was asked to submit twenty-five pages of material on standard sheets of paper, with whatever texts or images they pleased, and their submissions were Xeroxed.[148] Siegelaub chose Xeroxing instead of higher quality reproduction because it was "really just for the exchange of information... Xerox just cuts down on the visual aspect of looking at the information." He believed that he had successfully dematerialized the art gallery: "I've just, in a sense, eliminated the idea of space. My gallery is the world now."[149]

The rapid geographic diffusion of Conceptual Art was highlighted by a 1970 exhibition at New York's Museum of Modern Art, titled *Information*. Intended as "'an international report' of the activity of younger artists," over 100 artists from more than a dozen countries were invited to submit their work. The show's curator, Kynaston McShine, observed that the artists shared a concern with "the general social, political, and economic crises that are almost universal phenomena of 1970. If you are an artist in Brazil, you know of at least one friend who is being tortured; if you are one in Argentina, you probably have had a neighbor who has been in jail for having long hair, or for not being 'dressed' properly; and if you are living in the United States, you may fear that you will be shot at, either in the universities, in your bed, or more formally in Indochina."[150] The seven artists from the *Xerox Book* were all included in *Information*, and they were joined by such other prominent artists as the Germans Bernd and Hilla Becher and Joseph Beuys, the French Daniel Buren, the English Gilbert and George, the Dutch Jan Dibbets, the Italian Michelangelo Pistoletto, the Japanese On Kawara, and a host of other Americans including John Baldessari, Bruce Nauman, Yoko Ono, Ed Ruscha, and Robert Smithson. Many of the submissions consisted exclusively of written texts, while many combined texts and photographs.

In the catalogue for *Information*, McShine observed that with modern technologies of communication and transportation, "it is now possible for artists to be truly international; exchange with their peers is now comparatively simple... It is no longer imperative for an artist to be in Paris or New York."[151] In an interview the previous year, Seth Siegelaub had given an enthusiastic and detailed analysis of the connection between the new Conceptual Art and globalization:

I like the idea of things, information, people, ideas moving back and forth. And now that has much to do with a quality of the art, too. It can travel very easily, and it can be seen on a primary level, not just photographs of something but the something itself. The idea of primary information as opposed to secondary or tertiary information. Or hearsay. It's happening very, very quickly. And it makes communications even quicker. Just send a letter in the mail and you know what it's about. You don't have to wait for a painting to arrive, like someone in Paris wouldn't see a Pollock until the late fifties or early sixties, whenever the show took one over. Those days are over. And the idea that people can make art wherever they live, that they don't have to necessarily come to New York and be part of the scene, I like that too.[152]

Conceptual Art proved no more successful than Dada in destroying the commercial values of advanced art. As early as 1973, Lucy Lippard acknowledged her disappointment that "Hopes that 'conceptual art' would be able to avoid the general commercialization, the destructively 'progressive' approach of modernism were for the most part unfounded." The formerly anti-materialist Conceptual artists had been co-opted: "the major conceptualists are selling work for substantial sums here and in Europe; they are represented by (and still more unexpected – showing in) the world's most prestigious galleries." Lippard was forced to concede that "art and artist in a capitalist society remain luxuries."[153] Yet although ideas had not replaced objects, texts had not replaced images, and Xeroxed copies had not replaced paintings, the Conceptual Art movement did demonstrate how rapidly highly conceptual artistic practices could spread. The catalogue of the Museum of Modern Art's 1970 *Information* show provides powerful evidence of this. Thus just a few years after New York artists had begun to provide formal definitions of Conceptual Art, the movement had made converts, or at least attracted adherents, in more than a dozen different countries, and artists throughout Western Europe and South America could use written texts, diagrams, and newspaper photographs to create works that can hardly be distinguished in style or substance from the products of the movement's pioneers in New York.

London

The center of the fucking art world's in England. You know that, don't you?

Damien Hirst, 2000[154]

In the late 1990s, a number of English critics began to claim that London had displaced New York as the center of the advanced art world, as a result of the achievements of the young British artists, or yBas. The yBas first burst onto the art scene in 1988, in *Freeze*, a group exhibition of 16 young artists held in the vacated Port of London Authority Building in London's Docklands. The show was curated by Damien Hirst, who was then an art student at London's Goldsmiths College, and the exhibitors were Hirst's fellow students or recent graduates of Goldsmiths.[155] *Freeze* was soon followed by a series of similar group exhibitions, which were held in empty warehouses, and the artists involved, with others of their generation, gained a common identity as a new movement. The label for the group was cemented by a series of five group shows presented by the collector and dealer Charles Saatchi, beginning in 1992, titled *Young British Artists*.

In 1995 Richard Cork, the art critic for *The Times*, wrote that "New art in this country enjoys an outstandingly high reputation today. Curators, critics and collectors in many different countries are excited about the vitality of British artists." With some surprise, Cork observed that the yBas "have proved that Britain is capable of producing a remarkably self-assured and inventive generation busily redefining accepted ideas about what art can be," and he speculated that "they may well go on to win for modern British art an even higher reputation than the one it already enjoys."[156] In 1997, London's Royal Academy of Arts hosted *Sensation*, an exhibition of the work of forty-four young British artists, drawn entirely from the collection of Charles Saatchi. In surveying the accomplishments of these artists, Norman Rosenthal, the Royal Academy's Exhibitions Secretary, observed that "the latest new generation of British artists is having considerably more impact than its predecessors." He cautiously raised the possibility that the yBas had already elevated London to art world preeminence:

Can London become the unchallenged center for the practice and presentation of contemporary art? In the past, Paris, New York and even Düsseldorf have been able aggressively to claim this role, by virtue of the density of activity in each city over considerable periods of time, with many artists, as well as collectors and galleries, contributing to the debate with originality and daring. If London could now claim such a position, that would be a first, and surely grounds for celebration.[157]

And in 1998, in an early example of the definite assertion of English success, the critic Matthew Collings flatly declared: "Always remember, New Yorkers, young British art now dominates the world, even your world."[158]

The art of the yBas is extremely diverse, and does not share any common style. The critic Richard Shone generalized about the yBas:

> none was motivated by didactic, socio-political issues; all took for granted the lessons of conceptual and minimal art; none was...a legibly figurative artist; and many introduced autobiographical and personal elements into their work. Materials used were invariably demotic, drawn from their immediate environment...Most difficult of all to characterize is perhaps a shared directness and confidence in their imagery, whether dealing in grand, universal themes or in more particular observations from contemporary life.[159]

Michael Craig-Martin, an artist and teacher at Goldsmiths College who is often considered the godfather of contemporary British art because he was the key tutor for the *Freeze* exhibitors, stressed the clarity of their work in explaining its broad appeal: "In my view it never occurred to artists of this generation to make art that people wouldn't get and wouldn't like. They thought that if people didn't get it, then they must have done something wrong. Now that is not what artists of my generation behaved like. There is now a transparency to it all."[160] The art of many of the yBas was eclectic, moving freely from style to style, and often from one medium or genre to another. One source of this eclecticism was a decision by Goldsmiths College in the 1970s to abolish divisions between departments, so students would feel free to work in any medium they chose.[161]

The yBas were young and confident. Surveying their work in 1999, Arthur Danto saw "the brashness of art students the world around. There is an exuberance, a confidence, a swagger unfortunately not to be found in the demoralized American art world of today."[162] Damien Hirst epitomized this attitude, as in 1999 he looked back on the yBas' early achievements: "I mean, all us lot, we fucking caned the fucking art world. Absolutely totally phenomenal. We caned the fucking art world as *kids*."[163] It was their brashness that allowed the highly conceptual yBas to revolutionize British art, and to circumvent existing art world constraints by presenting their work directly to the public.

The art of the yBas had what Julian Stallabrass called "an accessible veneer," with many references to mass culture that the general public would understand.[164] Beneath this veneer, however, the yBas made liberal use of art history. Nearly all the yBas were trained in art schools that stressed a highly conceptual approach to artistic practice, so they were thoroughly familiar with earlier art even though they often feigned ignorance of it. So for example Damien Hirst, who has cultivated a public image based on the oafish and boorish behavior of punk rock musicians, with an appropriately irreverent disrespect for artistic traditions, acknowledged that one of his most celebrated early works was influenced by several leading American conceptual artists: "in my fly-killer piece [*A Thousand Years*, 1990], the lights were like Dan Flavin and the box was like Sol LeWitt. I put all that in knowingly." He explained that he and his peers deliberately did not base their art on a single predecessor, but on many: "at a certain point everyone at Goldsmiths believed that rather than avoiding taking directly, we could take from everybody . . . It was just getting all these influences and piling them together into our own thing."[165] Like many other conceptual artists, the yBas consistently based their innovations on syntheses of earlier art. Thus Chris Townsend and Mandy Merck observed that "For a movement so relentlessly appraised in terms of novelty, . . . the yBas seemed to depend upon strategies of the 're.' Think reprise; think reply; think repeat; think reinterpretation."[166] And as is also common among conceptual artists, the yBas often based their innovations on the art of their immediate predecessors. For example Tracey Emin and Sarah Lucas both borrowed from the American conceptual artist Bruce Nauman in specific works, and Rachel Whiteread's trademark practice of casting negative spaces, that runs through her entire oeuvre, has been seen as a reaction to a single work Nauman made in 1968, *A Cast of the Space Under My Chair*.[167] In recognition of the yBas' debt to American artists of the generations preceding theirs, after Matthew Collings informed New York of the end of its reign over the world of advanced art, he added: "we bow the knee to you and salute you, for your past achievements. We got all the ideas for our present achievements from you."[168]

One of the most distinctive features of the yBas is their celebrity: few contemporary art movements have been of such great interest to so large a public. As one English journalist remarked, "Fame is part of their story."[169] This is not merely incidental, but is part of a conscious strategy. Damien Hirst, the most prominent yBa, explained that he deliberately set out to change the public's perception of artists: "I grew up in box office . . . When I decided I wanted to be an artist, art became box office. I went in there and thought, 'I want to entertain, with art.' Not: 'I want to rot in a garret and chop my ear off.'" Hirst's attitude toward publicity is simple: "I think all publicity helps everything."[170] But the celebrity of the yBas is not limited to Hirst. Michael Craig-Martin remarked on a change in emphasis: "British contemporary art has shifted its focus from an interest in the object itself to an interest in the artist as genius."[171]

Julian Stallabrass has argued that there is a paradox at the center of much of contemporary art: "while the means by which that art is pursued are steadily less expressive of the artist's personality, more reliant on conventional ideas than feelings, more the assemblage of ready-made elements than the creation of organic compositions, the personality of the artist, far from shrinking, has greatly expanded, sometimes overshadowing the work."[172] In fact, however, this is not at all paradoxical. In most cases, the fame of the yBas has been a direct product of shocking works of art, including Hirst's dead, often sectioned, animals, suspended in formaldehyde; Tracey Emin's soiled bed, littered with blood-stained underwear and used condoms; Jake and Dinos Chapman's mocking images of mutilated corpses, taboo sexual fantasies, and Nazi symbolism; and Chris Ofili's painting of the Virgin Mary surrounded by lumps of dried elephant dung and pornographic photographs. The shocking content of these works raised the same question about the intentions of these artists that had echoed throughout the world of advanced art ever since Marcel Duchamp submitted a porcelain urinal to the first exhibition of the American Society of Independent Artists in 1917: is he serious or is he joking? For the yBas, as for Duchamp, Beuys, Warhol, and a series of later conceptual artistic tricksters, that question of intent necessarily led to a consideration of the personality of the artist.[173] As attentive students of art history, Hirst, Emin, and a number of their peers learned this lesson from their illustrious predecessors, just as they learned that the publicity value of the debate engendered by that question would grow over time if they could avoid resolving the issue. Hirst, Emin, the Chapmans, and Ofili are conspicuous among those yBas who have carefully constructed public personas that allow the debates over their sincerity to be rekindled with each new exhibition, in the process raising their profiles ever higher among the British public.

In 2001, the American critic Jerry Saltz wrote of the yBas as a group in a way that is reminiscent of descriptions of the Abstract Expressionists, an earlier group of important artists who did not share a common style: "the British have something we lack, and that is community, by which I mean a small group of people who spend a fair amount of time together, stay up late, and probably drink and argue about art with one another . . . [T]here's a sense of camaraderie that's absent here." In Saltz's account, the East End of London appears to have become as central to contemporary art as Greenwich Village was in the 1950s: "The Chapmans run a tiny gallery out of Jake's house, next door to Chris Ofili's, a block from Gilbert & George's. Tracey Emin lives nearby; so do Peter Doig,

Marc Quinn, Gary Hume, Wolfgang Tillmans, Tim Noble and Sue Webster, and Rachel Whiteread. Locals boast 'the highest concentration of working artists in Europe'."[174] There is little doubt that London has been a more important artistic center than New York for the cohort of artists born during the 1960s: Hirst, Whiteread, Emin, Lucas, the Chapmans, Ofili, and their peers have had considerably greater success than most of their American contemporaries.[175] Yet it may be premature to conclude that London has definitively replaced New York as the major generative center for advanced art. As Norman Rosenthal recognized, during the 1960s and early 1970s Düsseldorf's Academy of Art produced a remarkable series of painters, including Gerhard Richter, Sigmar Polke, Blinky Palermo, Jörg Immendorff, Anselm Kiefer, and Markus Lüpertz. Yet Düsseldorf could not sustain this level, and is no longer considered a major artistic center. As a major international center for finance and culture, London has obvious advantages over Düsseldorf that bode well for its continued success in advanced art, but it will require at least another creative generation to demonstrate that London will become the next New York rather than the next Düsseldorf.

Globalization, Nativity, and Identity

> Basquiat was intent on being a mainstream artist. He didn't want to be a black artist.
>
> Arden Scott[176]

In recent decades, there has been a considerable amount of discussion in the art world about the globalization of advanced art. These discussions have often failed to distinguish among three separate phenomena.

One of these is a consequence of recent increases in the prosperity of a number of places that were traditionally not connected to mainstream western art. In these countries, including conspicuously China and India, increasing wealth has led to the rise of thriving markets for local contemporary art. In a number of instances, young artists in these countries have created new forms of conceptual art, based in part on borrowing from western styles.

A prime example of this is the painter Wang Guangyi, who is a leading member of China's New Art Movement, that began in the late 1980s.[177] In 1988, at the age of 31, Wang established himself as a rebel artist with a daring series of eight large paintings of Chairman Mao, that mimicked the billboard portraits that had been widely displayed during

Mao's reign, but had disappeared after his death. In 1990, Wang began a new series of large paintings that became his trademark works. These combined Chinese socialist propaganda with Pop art. The most famous of these juxtaposed an image of revolutionary soldiers with the Coca-Cola logo. Each painting in the series combined the main title *Great Criticism* – an ironic reference to Mao's constant criticism of bourgeois values – with a subtitle that was the name of a famous western brand– such as Canon, Swatch, and M&Ms. In a special tribute, one of the paintings was subtitled *Andy Warhol*. Wang's work became the basis for a new genre in Chinese art, Political Pop.

Wang Guangyi wanted to become famous in order to improve China's image: "From the start, I was determined to produce art that was contemporary, Chinese, and that would be accorded international respect." He believed that Chinese artists had to demonstrate their familiarity with western art to dispel the image of China as culturally backward: "We wanted to engage the West on equal terms. To do this we had to understand western art theories."[178] He and other contemporary Chinese artists did this, borrowing both the techniques and the ironic attitudes of American Pop art. Wang's work gained international recognition as a new and innovative form of Chinese art, and it has sold for high prices in both western and Chinese markets. Yet it has had little impact on western artists.[179] This has been a general pattern. Young conceptual artists who have remained in their countries of origin have borrowed styles and techniques from advanced western art, and many have gained fame and fortune in their home countries. Yet to date few developments created by those working outside western centers have had a significant impact on the mainstream of advanced western art.

Two other facets of globalization have affected the form and content of recent western art, however. One of these is a continuation and extension of a process that has been important throughout the modern era, the migration to western artistic centers of young artists from an increasingly wide range of countries. Prominent recent examples include the Cuban-born Felix Gonzalez-Torres (1957–96), who spent his career in New York, and the Chinese artist Cai Guo Quiang (1957–), who left his native country for Japan, and later New York. Other important contemporary artists, including the Italian Maurizio Cattelan (1960–) and the Japanese Takashi Murakami (1963–), have maintained studios both in their native countries and New York.

To date there has been no systematic study of the changing composition by nativity of leading contemporary artists, but there are some

TABLE 14.2. *Number of Different Countries of Birth of Artists Mentioned in* Art Since 1960, *by Birth Cohort*

Decade of Artist's Birth	Number of Countries
1890–99	6
1900–09	5
1910–19	8
1920–29	18
1930–39	27
1940–49	22
1950–59	26
1960–69	23

Sources: Michael Archer, *Art Since 1960*, second ed. (London: Thames and Hudson, 2002).

indications that this aspect of globalization has progressed in recent times. So for example Table 14.2 is based on an analysis of a textbook published in 2002 titled *Art Since 1960*, written by an English art historian named Michael Archer. The present analysis was done by identifying the country of birth of every artist mentioned in the text. Table 14.2 presents the number of different countries of origin of these artists, distributed according to the artists' birth cohorts. The evidence shows a substantial increase in the number of countries represented over time. So for example the artists considered in the book who were aged 41–50 in 1960, the book's starting point, had been born in a total of just eight different countries, whereas those aged 31–40 came from eighteen different countries, and those aged 21–30 were from twenty-seven different countries. Disaggregated analysis of the evidence reveals that a number of Asian and African countries, including China, India, Korea, Morocco, and Tunisia, were represented for the first time in Archer's book by artists born in the 1930s, who were in their twenties and thirties during the 1960s, when conceptual approaches became dominant in advanced western art.

A third aspect of globalization that has become increasingly important in recent times is related to the last one mentioned, but is conceptually distinct from it. This is the adoption of visual elements from the art of places that have not been part of the western mainstream, by artists who are working in western centers. This practice has of course been present throughout the modern era, as Gauguin, Picasso, and others drew elements of their styles from art forms they considered "primitive."[180] The novel aspect of this practice in recent times, however, is that these borrowings have increasingly been done by artists who assert that they are reclaiming their own national or ethnic heritage. Thus whereas some of the artists who have engaged in this practice are themselves migrants to the West, others were born in the West, but are drawing on the art of their parents' countries of origin, or on their ethnic backgrounds more generally.

Consider several examples of immigrants who drew on the art of their countries of origin. Ana Mendieta (1948–85) arrived in the United States as a Cuban refugee at the age of 12. After attending art school, while working as an artist in New York she pursued her long-time interest in Afro-Cuban iconography, and her art was directly influenced by her study of the rituals of Santería. She explained that "In my work I am in a sense reliving my heritage. My sources are memories, images, experiences, and beliefs that have left their mark in me."[181]

Anish Kapoor (1954–) was born in India, but attended art school in London, and settled permanently in England. On a trip to India in 1979, he saw the curved forms that Hindu art used to represent the feminine deity, and these had a major impact on the development of his style. He has become one of the most important sculptors working today, and was awarded the Turner Prize in 1991.[182]

Takashi Murakami (1962–) combined a childhood love of Japanese animation art with the Pop commercial aesthetic of Jeff Koons that he discovered in New York. As the self-proclaimed Japanese Andy Warhol, Murakami created a conceptual fusion of style and content that he calls "superflat," in a joint reference to the traditional flat appearance of Japanese visual art and to the Japanese tendency to flatten or disregard the boundaries between artistic genres.[183]

It is no more difficult to find significant examples of western-born artists who imported artistic elements they considered their inheritance. Jean-Michel Basquiat (1960–88) was born in New York, but his art reflected both his father's Haitian nativity and his mother's Puerto Rican origins. Thus many of his paintings included words in the Caribbean Spanish his mother spoke to him, and a number of his paintings portrayed the suffering of Africans in the transatlantic slave trade.[184] Basquiat explained that these works were personal: "I've never been to Africa . . . But I have a cultural memory. I don't need to look for it; it exists. It's over there, in Africa. That doesn't mean that I have to go live there. Our cultural memory follows us everywhere."[185]

Yinka Shonibare (1962–) was born in London to Nigerian parents. He attended art school in London, and settled there. In art school, he was doing a series of works about Soviet perestroika, when a tutor remarked that "it's not really you though, is it?" Thinking "Okay, you want ethnic, I'll give you ethnic," Shonibare went to Brixton Market, where he bought *ankara*, African-print cloth, and he has featured this cloth in nearly all his subsequent work. He has explained that although this cloth is African, it was originally made in Indonesia, and was later produced industrially in Manchester. Shonibare thus actually uses *ankara* "to challenge the idea of authenticity in arts . . . so the fabrics are for me a metaphor for something which is multicultural and essentially hybrid like my own identity."[186]

Chris Ofili (1968–) was born in Manchester, to parents who were natives of Nigeria. At the age of 24, as a student at London's Royal College of Art, Ofili visited Zimbabwe on a traveling scholarship. There he saw ancient cave paintings made with brightly colored dots. And it was in Zimbabwe that he had the idea of adding an African material – dried elephant dung – to his paintings, to lend an African element to his western surfaces. Both brightly colored dots and dried elephant dung subsequently became key characteristics of Ofili's paintings, which won him the Turner Prize in 1998.[187]

Globalization in a Conceptual Era

> The art of the world has come out of the capitals of the world, because it is only in the capitals of the world, at certain favored periods, that the best minds among the older men and the ready minds of the younger enthusiasts have mingled and taken fire from one another.
>
> Ezra Pound, 1913[188]

Overall, much of the twentieth century was a time of rapid globalization for advanced art. Artists who originated in a larger number of countries than in earlier periods made important contributions, and they did so in a larger number of places than their predecessors had earlier in the modern era. Many important innovations also diffused much more rapidly, and widely, than in earlier times.

The dominance of conceptual forms of art during most of the twentieth century was largely responsible not only for the increased speed with which innovations were made, but also for the greater speed with which they diffused geographically. Collage was an early example of a major innovation that was so highly conceptual, and so versatile in its uses, that artists could adapt it to their own purposes simply after hearing descriptions of it, without even seeing actual examples. The innovations of such movements as Dada and Pop put greater emphasis on ideas relative to execution than virtually any earlier artistic movements, and this allowed many of their new practices to spread almost spontaneously. Throughout much of the century, the great importance of written manifestos was symptomatic of the centrality of conceptual innovation, and these manifestos contributed to the rapid spread of the conceptual practices of the movements that produced them.

The dominance of artistic centers was reduced by the progress of globalization. During the twentieth century it became possible, for the first time in the modern era, for artists to make important contributions to the artistic mainstream without working in the art world's central place. For most of the first century of modern art, Paris was the single source of important innovations in advanced art. Today, in an era of highly conceptual art, it appears unlikely that any one place could again hold this position so completely for so long. Yet predictions like those that some art scholars and critics made in the late 1960s, that place would no longer matter for artistic innovation, appear to have been wrong. As in the past, it remains true today that artists who have already created novel styles or methods can work nearly anywhere they please, but also as in the past, it is unlikely that any contemporary artist can develop, or at the very least begin to develop, significant innovations anywhere other than in one of the central locations of the art world. The mainstream of western art still runs through central places. There may no longer be one single central place: as discussed above, both New York and London have been places where artists could make important innovations in recent times. And it is possible that the number of these artistic centers may increase in the future, particularly if advanced art remains highly conceptual. Yet it is unlikely that this number will increase greatly. With the highly conceptual emphasis of recent art, direct contact with the leading innovators of the preceding generation has become less important for aspiring artists than in the past, but contact with talented peers is still essential, and the places where this is possible will remain limited.

15

Artists and the Market

From Leonardo and Titian to Warhol and Hirst

Introduction

There's a real sense that when you start quantifying artistic output in dollars
and cents, those things are tangents to what we really should be talking
about.

Michael Rooks, curator, Museum of Contemporary Art, Chicago[1]

In an era in which many previously forbidden subjects, including race, sex,
religion, and drugs, have become favored themes for public discussion,
the nexus between money and art remains perhaps the last taboo topic
for many art scholars and critics. The extent of this prudish distaste
may account for the relative neglect of a striking recent innovation by a
number of important conceptual artists, who have decisively broken with
a tradition that has ruled the art world since the Renaissance. A brief
history of the relationship between artists and the market can serve to
place this innovation in perspective.

The Renaissance Ideal

A mind intent on gain will rarely obtain the reward of fame with posterity.

Leon Battista Alberti, 1435[2]

During the Middle Ages, artists were considered craftsmen. Painters'
guilds were first founded in Italy late in the thirteenth century, and from
there this practice spread throughout Europe. Sculptors and architects
were also organized in guilds, along with masons and bricklayers. As

the social and economic status of artists improved, objections to guild supervision appeared. In 1434, for example, Filippo Brunelleschi refused to pay his dues to the guild of building workers, and the guild's officials had him thrown in prison. He was freed eleven days later, after the intervention of church authorities, and he returned to his work on the great dome of Florence's cathedral. In spite of the decline of the authority of guilds over artists, the widespread perception of artists as craftsmen who earned money by manual labor persisted. So for example Michelangelo's biographer Condivi reported that the master's family regarded his choice to become an artist as shameful.[3]

As artists increasingly asserted their freedom, a new model of the artist emerged. A key element of this was economic. As craftsmen, medieval artists had been paid like other manual laborers, at fixed rates per day. During the fifteenth century artists began to challenge this practice. For example the archbishop of Florence noted in the mid-fifteenth century that "Painters claim, more or less reasonably, to be paid for their art not only according to the amount of work involved, but rather according to the degree of their application and experience." Margot and Rudolf Wittkower recently recognized the turning point marked by the spread of this claim during the course of the following century: "The time had come when great artists could ask and would receive star fees and were capable of amassing wealth undreamed of by fourteenth and fifteenth century masters."[4]

With artists' new economic status came a desire to improve their image with new forms of behavior. In the early fifteenth century, the painter Cennino Cennini advised his peers that their conduct should reflect their newly elevated status: "Your life should always be regulated as if you were studying theology, philosophy or other sciences." Cennini observed that the dignity of their position equally had implications for their motivations: "There are some who follow the arts from poverty and necessity . . . but those who pursue them from love of the art and noble-mindedness are to be commended above all others." The Wittkowers noted that the idea that artists should work not for economic gain but for love of their profession became a well-established convention.[5] For example in his treatise *On Painting*, written in 1435, Leon Battista Alberti told aspiring artists that painting "brings pleasure while you practice it, and praise, riches and endless fame when you have cultivated it well." He encouraged them to pursue fame, but warned them against coveting riches: "You who strive to excel in painting, should cultivate above all the fame and reputation which you see the ancients attained, and in so doing it will be a good thing to remember that avarice has always been the enemy of renown and virtue."[6] Similarly, about 1510, Leonardo da Vinci advised painters to concentrate on the quality of their work rather than on the money that work would earn them, for "The glory of the excellence of mortals is much greater than that of their riches."[7] And in 1548 the Venetian painter Paolo Pini declared that "A painter should, above all, abhor all the vices such as cupidity, that vile and despicable part of human nature..."[8] Thus during the fifteenth and sixteenth centuries, artists were elevated from manual to intellectual workers. Artists should consequently emulate the dignity of scholars so art would be perceived as a calling rather than a trade. The Wittkowers noted that the new image of the artist was also based on the topos "that the morality of the man and the quality of his work are inseparable"; thus "the lofty art of a Raphael could only result from a high-minded soul."[9]

The principle that the price of an artist's work would be determined by the artist's skill rather than his time gave great artists enormous leverage, and many used this to their advantage. For example the Wittkowers observed that "Titian looked after his financial interests with skill, patience and tenacity...The image of the 'typical' artist unconcerned with the value of money most certainly did not fit him." His behavior was not a secret: "His contemporaries took it for granted but posterity has often forgotten that he hardly ever used his brush except on commission. Works which bear the stamp of incontestably sincere emotional experience and unrivaled technical mastery were to him so many objects of trade, barter and bribe once they were ready to leave his studio." Titian shrewdly used his art to advance his career: "Time and again we find Titian painting a portrait for no other reason than that the sitter's influence might be advantageous to him." Furthermore, "Titian's cupidity is not at all exceptional," for a number of other Renaissance masters, including Bramante, Raphael, and Michelangelo, used their genius to accumulate substantial fortunes.[10]

Although many artists would be interested in, and motivated by, the prospect of financial gain, the convention that artists should not openly and publicly appear to be concerned with money became a legacy of the Renaissance. Thus when the French government authorized the establishment of a Royal Academy of Fine Arts in Paris in 1648, members of the Academy were required to appear to be above commercial activity: the founding statutes included a rule forbidding any Academician from opening a gallery to sell his work, "nor to do anything to permit the confounding of two such different things as a mercenary profession and the status of Academician."[11] Katy Siegel and Paul Mattick observed that of course these artists lived by selling their work, "But the higher social status embodied in the work of academic art was expressed by a theoretical disdain for monetary considerations; the fine artist, like the aristocrat who was his ideal customer, worked in theory not for money but for personal and national glory."[12]

The Rise of the Market for Modern Art

Now there is in your canvases a vigor; . . . they will undoubtedly be appreciated one day. When we see that the Pissarros, the Gauguins, the Renoirs, the Guillaumins do not sell, one ought to be almost glad of not having the public's favor, seeing that those who have it now will not have it forever, and it is quite possible that times will change very shortly.

Theo van Gogh to his brother Vincent, 1889[13]

An interesting change in the attitude of some members of the art world toward prices occurred in Paris in the late nineteenth century, as a consequence of a change in art market institutions. During the final quarter of the century, the patronage system in which the government was the dominant purchaser of advanced art was progressively replaced by a competitive market for art. The effective monopoly of the Academy's official Salon as the only venue for the legitimate presentation of new art to the public was undermined by the establishment, from 1874 on, of the principle that smaller artist-organized Salons would henceforth present the most important new art.[14] The existence of an independent, competitive market for art prompted a change in critical attitudes toward prices. In 1878, for example, in a defense of the Impressionists, the critic Théodore Duret declared that "it is necessary that the public who laughs so loudly over the Impressionists should be even more astonished! – this painting sells."[15] Robert Jensen explained that Duret's claim was an instance of a new strategy: "The challengers to the French Academy used market value to demonstrate how previously disfranchised artists (and that could mean almost anyone who was not a member of the Academy) were vindicated by later prices, consequently demonstrating their right of place in the pantheon of great artists."[16] Using market prices as evidence of artistic success would outlive the fight against the Academy. For example, in her 1940 biography of Roger Fry, Virginia Woolf wrote of the pain he had suffered when the Post-Impressionist exhibition he presented in London in 1910 was widely ridiculed, but she concluded that "Time...has vindicated Roger Fry, if money is any test. Shares in Cézanne have risen immeasurably since 1910. That family who accumulated works by Matisse must today be envied even by millionaires."[17]

In the twentieth century, the group exhibitions of the artists' Salons were eventually superseded by the galleries of private dealers as the primary locus of the competitive market for new advanced art. The first important artist to rise to prominence by exhibiting in galleries rather than in group shows was Pablo Picasso. Picasso claimed that he regarded dealers to be the enemies of artists, but his actions call this claim into question. Early in his career, Picasso used his art to cultivate key figures in Paris' art world, as he made portraits of the poet and critic Guillaume Apollinaire, and the collector Gertrude Stein. Yet he devoted more extensive efforts to portraying dealers, as he carefully cultivated central figures in the art market who could sell his work and spread his reputation with major exhibitions and publications. Few artists can have painted more portraits of dealers. During the early period in which he was establishing himself as a leading artist, Picasso painted the dealers Pedro Manach (1901), Clovis Sagot (1909), Ambroise Vollard (1901, 1910, 1915), Daniel-Henry Kahnweiler (1910), Wilhelm Uhde (1910), Léonce Rosenberg (1915), André Level (1918), Paul Rosenberg (1919), and Berthe Weill (1920), and in 1918 he also painted portraits of the wife of Georges Wildenstein and of the wife and daughter of Paul Rosenberg.[18] When the young Catalan painter Joan Miró first arrived in Paris in 1919, he was given a warm welcome by Picasso. Yet Miró wrote to a friend that although he considered Picasso a great painter, he found the atmosphere of his studio depressing: "Everything is done for his dealer, for the money. A visit to Picasso is like visiting a ballerina with a number of lovers."[19]

Early in his career, Picasso privately told Kahnweiler, "I'd like to live like a poor man with a lot of money."[20] As he became the dominant painter of the twentieth century, Picasso's wealth was increased by the skill with which he "applied his remarkable talents to winning the support of those who could enhance his reputation and bring acclaim to his art – the dealers, critics, collectors, and curators who constituted his primary audience."[21] Yet Picasso was careful to keep private his considerable interest in the material rewards of art, and it did not become part of the colorful image that made him the epitome of the modern artist for a vast admiring public.

If I Can Make It There

American culture has in any case seldom fed our painters and sculptors as it has our novelists and poets.

Clement Greenberg, 1947[22]

After World War II, the center of the art world shifted to the United States, as the Abstract Expressionists emerged as the leading artists of their generation. The problems that advanced artists faced in America were very different from those that confronted aspiring European artists. The Impressionists and those artists who followed them in Paris came of age in a culture that had supported high art for centuries; the artist's problem was to establish his place within the succession of important contributors to that tradition. In contrast, the United States did not have a tradition of producing, or supporting, large numbers of advanced painters. Thus in 1954 the Abstract Expressionist painter Adolph Gottlieb recalled that "By the age of 18, I clearly understood that the artist in our society cannot expect to make a living from art; must live in the middle of a hostile environment; cannot communicate through his art with more than a few people; and if his work is significant, cannot achieve recognition until the end of his life (if he is lucky), and more likely posthumously."[23] Barnett Newman explained that when he and his colleagues were developing their art, "we had no general public . . . There were just a few galleries . . . It was not, in that sense, a true marketplace."[24]

Under the circumstances, a recurring theme of the few critics who vigorously championed the Abstract Expressionists was the difficulty the artists faced in trying to create innovative new art in spite of the lack of support from a society that did not appreciate high culture. Thus in 1947 Clement Greenberg published an assessment of "The Present Prospects of American Painting and Sculpture," in which he contended that the future of American art depended on a band of fifty artists who were struggling to create an art of genius. He concluded on a pessimistic note: "Their isolation is inconceivable, crushing, unbroken, damning. That anyone can produce art on a respectable level in this situation is highly improbable. What can fifty do against a hundred and forty million?"[25] Similarly, Harold Rosenberg lamented that "there is no audience for contemporary art and no luxury for artists. Both attention and cash go to kitsch."[26]

Over time, however, public recognition of the achievement of the Abstract Expressionists produced a growing demand for their work. In 1955 *Fortune* magazine reported that the "art market is boiling with an activity never known before," and, using the language of stock markets, described the work of the Abstract Expressionists as "speculative or 'growth' issues" that were likely to gain rapidly in value in the near future.[27] It was not long before some in the art world perceived a danger in this newfound prosperity. In a speech in 1957, Meyer Schapiro, who was widely respected as one of the most distinguished art scholars alive, gave a passionate defense of non-representational painting against the perennial charges that abstract painters lacked artistic skills, and that their work lacked real meaning. Yet Schapiro closed his speech on a cautionary note, observing that "If painting and sculpture provide the most tangible works of art and bring us close to the activity of the artist, their concreteness exposes them, more than the other arts, to dangerous corruption." This corruption came via the market: "Paintings are perhaps the most costly man-made objects in the world . . . [This] stamps the painting as an object of speculation, confusing the values of art. The fact that the work of art has such a status means that the approach to it is rarely innocent enough; one is too much concerned with the future of the work, its value as an investment, its capacity to survive in the market and to symbolize the social quality of the owner." For Schapiro, "the artist is one of the most moral and idealistic of beings," who "cannot live by his art." Although he was too polite to identify the villains, it is clear that for Schapiro dealers and collectors were responsible for perverting the activity, so that "Painting is the domain of culture in which the contradiction between the professed ideals and the actuality is most obvious and often becomes tragic."[28] For at least one great scholar, the Renaissance ideal of artistic behavior was alive and well in New York in the midst of the booming art market of the late 1950s.

Andy Warhol

I have a Fantasy about Money: I'm walking down the street and I hear somebody say – in a whisper – "There goes the richest person in the world."
Andy Warhol, 1975[29]

Andy Warhol decisively broke with the hallowed tradition of five centuries that the artist should appear to be unconcerned with money. He was fascinated with money, he loved earning it, and he never attempted to hide this.

Warhol created a revolution in modern art in 1962, when he began to use the mechanical technique of silkscreening to make multiple photographic images on canvas. His most celebrated works with the technique in that year are the serial portraits of Marilyn Monroe that he made after hearing the news of her death in August: the single painting of his that is most often reproduced in art history textbooks, the *Marilyn Diptych*, comprises five rows of ten pictures of the actress.[30] Interestingly, however, Warhol's adoption of silkscreening was prompted by a different motif. Early in 1962, he made a number of large drawings of paper money, in several denominations. His decision to repeat these images in grid compositions prompted him to try simple printing techniques. He found, however, that cutting stencils or carving rubber stamps was too difficult for the complicated, detailed images he had in mind. At the suggestion of his assistant, who was a commercial artist, Warhol took his drawings of dollar bills to a printing shop, which converted them into silkscreens. As a result, Warhol's paintings of dollar bills – including the 82-inch by 92-inch *200 One Dollar Bills*, which consists of twenty rows of ten one-dollar bills – became the first works in which he used the silkscreen technique that became his basic method of making paintings for the rest of his career.[31]

It was not an accident that Warhol was engaged in making images of money. He often asked his friends for suggestions of motifs, and in his memoir of the 1960s he recalled that "finally one lady friend of mine asked me the right question: 'Well, what do you love most?' That's how I started painting money."[32] In addition to the paintings of dollar bills, during 1962 Warhol also made paintings of sheets of trading stamps and postage stamps. His friend and biographer David Bourdon observed that these choices arose from "Warhol's persistent wish to achieve a sort of artistic alchemy, transforming ordinary paint into actual cash. Warhol loved few things better than to barter his art for objects that had more value, at least in his eyes. He earnestly yearned for the power to transmute virtually everything he touched into something of greater financial worth."[33]

Even when Warhol's early Pop paintings did not involve images of money or other financial instruments of exchange, they often made direct reference to commerce, using techniques that reinforced the images. Thus Kirk Varnedoe observed that "Warhol painted Campbell's soup cans in a way that played on the intuition that the sale of art and the sale of commodities were not very different from each other. But he gave them a snappy, cheeky, upbeat rhythm by injecting some of the bright colors and the crassness of commerce into the language of his painting."[34] In a 1966 interview, Warhol remarked that "I've heard it said that my paintings are as much a part of the fashionable world as clothes and cars," and he added that "I don't think there's anything wrong with being fashionable or successful."[35] In his memoir, he ignored the mystique of the art world by directly comparing art to fashion, explaining that "To be successful as an artist, you have to have your work shown in a good gallery for the same reason that, say, Dior never sold his originals from a counter in Woolworth's. It's a matter of marketing."[36]

In 1975, Warhol published *THE Philosophy of Andy Warhol*. As David Bourdon observed, Warhol's remarks in the book "are conspicuously devoid of any idealism concerning the making of art or its role in society and offer little evidence that he considered painting to be an honorable profession."[37] In a chapter titled "Art," for example, Warhol asked "Why do people think artists are special? It's just another job."[38] Warhol was much more enthusiastic in discussing the relationship between art and business. In an often-quoted passage, he declared that "Business art is the step that comes after Art . . . Being good in business is the most fascinating kind of art. During the hippie era people put down the idea of business – they'd say 'Money is bad,' and 'Working is bad,' but making money is art and working is art and good business is the best art."[39] And he openly declared his favorable attitude toward currency: "Cash. I just am not happy when I don't have it."[40]

Warhol's practice provides considerable evidence that these musings were not mere provocations, but reflected real beliefs on his part. He had begun making commissioned silkscreen portraits early in his career, including the well-known painting of one of his first collectors, *Ethel Scull Thirty-Six Times*, in 1963. In the early 1970s, however, he focused more intensively on this activity: "Wooing prospective clients provided him a pretext for becoming more social than ever, attending as many as three dinner parties in one evening . . . In contrast to his bohemian consorts of the past, he now concentrated his attentions on the wealthy, partying socialites who constituted the glittery jet set – the Beautiful People." Warhol's concern with his income made him "especially keen to find long-term clients whose insatiable vanity would necessitate a new portrait every year." A portrait, which consisted of a single forty-inch-square painting made from a silkscreen of a Polaroid photograph, cost $25,000, and the client could purchase addition panels for $5,000 each. Warhol enlisted "his dealers, friends, and employees in the quest for new clients, offering them a twenty percent commission." The efficiency of Warhol's enterprise made portraits his principal source of income, and clearly supported his assertion in *THE Philosophy* that "I wanted to be an Art Businessman or a Business Artist."[41] When his portraits were shown in an exhibition at the Whitney Museum in 1979, many critics expressed their distaste for Warhol's social role: Peter Schjeldahl lamented that "Warhol in the seventies emerged as something he was once prematurely accused of being: a servant to the rich," while Robert Hughes sneered that Warhol was "obsessed with serving the interests of privilege."[42]

Interestingly, there is a consistency to Warhol's statements and artistic practices that art scholars often overlook or ignore. Just a few months before his death in 1987, when he was asked by an interviewer to comment on his "transformation from being a commercial artist to a real artist," Warhol responded, "I'm still a commercial artist. I was always a commercial artist." He explained that his assertion was based on his view that a commercial artist was "someone who sells art."[43] Warhol's art from 1962 on, which exploded on the art world as the single most important body of work of the Pop movement, was based on a number of practices that originated in his earlier, highly successful career as a commercial artist. From the time of his arrival in New York in 1949, after graduating from Carnegie Institute of Technology with a major in painting and design, Warhol quickly began to get jobs making illustrations for leading fashion magazines and department stores. His specialty came to be drawings of women's shoes, and his primary source of income for a number of years was the I. Miller shoe store, which regularly published his illustrations in the fashion pages of the *New York Times*. By the mid-1950s, Warhol was so busy that he began to hire assistants to help him with his drawings. One of these assistants helped Warhol improvise simple printing techniques to allow them to reproduce his drawings for a number of uses. Thus several of the more controversial practices Warhol used in producing his paintings from 1962 on, including the use of assistants to execute the works, and the use of mechanical printing techniques, originated in his career as a commercial artist. Furthermore, the assistant who introduced Warhol to silkscreening, Nathan Gluck, was the same one who had earlier helped him devise the printing techniques he had used to save time in making his ads for women's shoes.[44] During the 1980s, Warhol painted a number of images for advertising campaigns, including vodka, mineral water, automobiles, and Campbell's soup: "Some critics thought his career had gone full circle, beginning with and returning to advertising art. But Warhol brazenly disagreed: 'I was always a commercial artist.'"[45] Warhol's claim might not have been ironic or disingenuous, for it is possible that, as he consistently maintained, he saw no real difference between his works that were published in newspapers and those that would hang in museums.

In his memoir, Warhol recalled that in the early 1960s he had asked his friend Emile de Antonio why Robert Rauschenberg and Jasper Johns didn't like him. De Antonio's response included Warhol's open acknowledgment of his career as a commercial artist: "When *they* do commercial art – windows and other jobs I find them – they do it just 'to survive.' They won't even use their real names. Whereas *you've* won *prizes*! You're *famous* for it!" Warhol was hurt, but he recognized the truth in de Antonio's explanation: "I was well known as a commercial artist. I got a real kick out of seeing my name listed under 'fashion' in a novelty book called *A Thousand New York Names and Where to Drop Them*. But if you wanted to be considered a 'serious' artist, you weren't supposed to have anything to do with commercial art. De [Antonio] was the only person I knew who could see past those old social distinctions to the art itself." Warhol decided not to care about the disapproval of Rauschenberg and Johns: "There was nothing wrong with being a commercial artist."[46] Warhol's account of this episode reinforces the view that he saw no difference between commercial and fine art, but considered this only a distinction imposed by others.

With both his actions and words, Warhol blatantly and publicly violated both key elements of the Renaissance ideal that had bounded artists' behavior for five centuries, as he not only flaunted his fascination with money and wealth, but also openly demeaned the dignity of his profession. The superficial, nakedly commercial persona he projected served to complement the garishly colored images, often derived from publicity photographs, of celebrities and consumer goods that appeared in his paintings. Indeed, Warhol not only created images for commercials, but he registered with an agency to become a celebrity model, and he personally endorsed products.[47] In these as in other aspects of his behavior, Warhol enlarged the range of attitudes that artists could present to the public, and that could be tailored to the particular forms of conceptual art they created.

After Warhol: Artists

It was in creating the creator of his works that Warhol proved genuinely creative, and penetrating to the point of subversion. The archetype of the modern artist has been the Dandy, Baudelaire's detached and intellectually tormented "hero of modern life." This figure survived in a variety of versions to the threshold of the sixties . . . Warhol buried the Dandy under an avalanche of soup cans.

Harold Rosenberg[48]

Warhol's new model of the artist as materialist was not emulated by large numbers of other artists. Some of his fellow Pop artists shared his attitudes, though generally in less extreme and flamboyant forms. During the early 1960s, for example, Claes Oldenburg periodically presented exhibitions titled "The Store" at his storefront studio on New York's Lower East Side, for which he would fill the space with manufactured objects he bought and coated sloppily with commercial enamel paint. In the first such show in 1961 prices started at $21.79 for a painted plastic oval mirror, and increased to a maximum of $899.95 for a mannequin representing a bride. This initial exhibition lost money, but the prices of Oldenburg's projects soon rose substantially during the Pop art boom that began in 1962.[49] In a 1961 manifesto, Oldenburg also expressed the view that artists should not be the objects of great interest, as he wrote that "I am for an artist who vanishes, turning up in a white cap painting signs or hallways."[50]

Unlike Pop art, which was based heavily on commercial imagery and accepted the idea that art is a commercial product, the major artistic movements of the later 1960s rejected what they considered to be the excessive materialism of western society. Many of these artists opposed the business orientation of the art world, and rebelled against its institutions by attempting to create art forms that could not be sold in galleries or exhibited in museums. Robert Smithson wanted art to be "free for all," and he and his fellow earth artists made huge works out of the landscape in remote locations.[51] George Maciunas was "against art-object as non-functional commodity – to be sold and to make livelihood for an artist," and he became a leader of the Fluxus movement, which created performance pieces that disappeared after a single presentation.[52] Douglas Huebler declared that "The world is full of objects . . . I do not wish to add any more."[53] He and a number of colleagues who called themselves Conceptual artists attempted to dematerialize their art, by presenting their ideas in forms such as xeroxed sheets or printed sentences for which "no one, not even a public greedy for novelty, would actually pay money, or much of it."[54]

No true successor to Warhol in the lineage of the artist as avowed materialist appeared until the rise of Jeff Koons in the late 1980s. Koons's art, which included such consumer goods as vacuums and basketballs in display cases, and framed advertisements and posters, owes a great debt to Pop art, which he has freely acknowledged: "I love Pop art, and I really want to play with aspects of Pop."[55] It also appears that Koons's stated philosophy about the relationship between artistic success and the market was made possible by the new model of the artist that Warhol had created.

Koons's stated goal was "for art to have as much political impact as the entertainment industry, the film, the pop music and the advertising industries." Accomplishing this required recognition of a change that had occurred in the position of the artist: "At one time, artists had only to whisper into the ear of the King or Pope to have political effect. Now, they must whisper into the ears of millions of people." This insight led to Koons's desire "to communicate with as wide an audience as possible."[56] He did this by making art that is about "aspects of entertainment."[57] Interestingly, Koons's desire to become an artist, and the form of his early art, were influenced by his interest in salesmanship. He told an interviewer that as a child he enjoyed selling things door-to-door, because he liked both earning money and having the feeling of helping people. When he first arrived in New York these early experiences caused him to work in sales, first selling memberships in the Museum of Modern Art, then selling commodities and stocks on Wall Street. He retains a high regard for salesmen: "I feel salesmen are on the front line of culture." His early sculptures with vacuums were a tribute: "One of the reasons I did my vacuum-cleaner pieces was the door-to-door salesman." Making art now gives Koons the same pleasure he got selling chocolates as a child: "One of the reasons that I want to make artworks is to meet people's needs and to give support to them."[58]

Koons has explained that his philosophy made him want his work to sell for the highest prices possible: "It's not about greed. It's about demanding to be taken seriously on a political stage. What I'm saying is that the seriousness with which a work is taken is interrelated to the value that it has." For Koons, the market is consequently the most important voice in the art world: "The market is the greatest critic."[59] He contends that this is actually universally recognized: "everyone knows that the true political power, where the negotiating really takes place, is in the market." He believes that those in the art world who claim that their own judgments are superior to those of the market are merely trying "to conserve their little bit of power ... What they're really saying is that they're not going to let the market dictate the situation." In fact, however, Koons believes that the judgment of the market necessarily transcends that of individuals: "of course the market represents the only true power because it absorbs all their ideas and a lot of other ideas besides."[60]

Thus Koons, like Théodore Duret, appeals to market success as evidence of widespread approval of innovative art – indeed, he recently observed that the high auction prices for contemporary art in recent years "demonstrate how much we love each other."[61] Yet that an artist is willing to announce this philosophy publicly is likely a consequence of Warhol's pioneering embrace of commercial success.

Damien Hirst has made a fortune as a celebrity artist in a country that he believes disapproves of successful artists: "I think in England especially, people are anti any kind of success really. You're struggling and you cut your ear off; they like that kind of artist. Whereas if you're making money . . . They'd rather you were working on a building site and painting in a garret somewhere. I'd say that's a problem." He has seen through the pretense, and recognizes that the art world has materialistic values: "I have proved it to myself that art is about life and the art world's about money. And I'm the only one who . . . knows that. Everyone lies to themselves to make it seem like it's the other way. But it isn't." For him art and money are inseparable: "I find the money aspect of the work part of its life . . . [P]eople buy it and pay money for it and it becomes a commodity and still manages to stay art, I find that really exciting." He is not troubled by the fact that the market determines the value of art: "I'm one of the few people in the world who can say, 'I know what everything is worth.' . . . Everything in the whole world is worth what anyone else is prepared to pay for it. And that's it. Simple."[62]

Hirst confidently believes in the economic efficiency of the art market: "I think people always buy good art, and I think I've always been aware of that." In view of this, he is not at all surprised that his work is in great demand: "I've sold everything I've ever made." Because he believes market valuations are meaningful, he insists on receiving high prices for his work. For example in 2000, when Charles Saatchi offered £950,000 for Hirst's sculpture *Hymn*, Hirst insisted that Saatchi pay the full asking price of £1 million. Hirst felt he owed this to other artists: "I think with a benchmark of a million pounds you owe it to everyone around you and behind you to take the money." But he also enjoyed the success: "I like saying when somebody says, 'How much did you sell it for?' 'One. A long one.'"[63]

Interestingly, Hirst initially became widely known not for his art, but for his entrepreneurship. In 1988, Hirst, who was then an art student at Goldsmiths College, curated *Freeze*, a group exhibition, in an empty Port Authority building in London's Docklands. Nearly all the exhibitors were fellow students of Hirst's at Goldsmiths. *Freeze*, and several similar group shows that soon followed, launched the careers of Matt Collishaw, Gary Hume, Sarah Lucas, Fiona Rae, and a number of other successful artists. *Freeze* is now regarded as the key event that initiated the process leading to the recognition of a new art movement, the young British artists, of which Hirst is the acknowledged leader. Although *Freeze* was a student enterprise, its success has been attributed to its professionalism, including the use of several commercial galleries' mailing lists and the publication of an elaborate catalogue.[64] Nearly all of Hirst's subsequent activities have equally reflected his flair for entrepreneurship, as he has consistently attracted publicity. This publicity is often generated by economic considerations. Thus Julian Stallabrass observed, "Try to find one of the many popularizing articles about Damien Hirst... which does not mention money."[65] Hirst's recent work, *For the Love of God*, is an obvious case in point. Photographs of the sculpture, a platinum human skull covered with diamonds, have been featured in newspapers around the world. And prominently featured in virtually every news story about the work is its price of £50 million – which has almost certainly become the most famous asking price in the history of art.[66]

The ability of Hirst's materialist image to generate free publicity is probably unrivaled by that of any other artist, except perhaps the model's inventor. A recent illustration is afforded by the reaction to the announcement that Hirst's sculpture, *The Physical Impossibility of Death in the Mind of Someone Living*, will be displayed on loan at the Metropolitan Museum of Art. This prompted not only a news story in the *New York Times*, but remarkably also an editorial.[67] The editors took direct aim at Hirst as a materialist, taunting that he "has gone from being an artist to being what you might call the manager of the hedge fund of Damien Hirst's art." They further declared that "No artist has managed the escalation of prices for his own work quite as brilliantly as Mr. Hirst." If Andy Warhol were still alive, it is likely that he would be proud of Hirst for successfully provoking such impressive free publicity, though it is also likely that Warhol would be at least a bit offended by the *Times*' judgment that Hirst has surpassed him as a career manager.

Hirst has acknowledged his respect for both Andy Warhol and Jeff Koons; interestingly, he has praised Warhol for his honesty.[68] Hirst's understanding of the relationship between art and money, and his openness in discussing it, appear to owe a considerable debt to the ideas and behavior of both Warhol and Koons.

After Warhol: Scholars and Critics

[W]ith a few illustrious exceptions, seemingly designed to recall the ideal, painters and writers are deeply self-interested, calculating, obsessed with money and ready to do anything to succeed.

Pierre Bourdieu, 1986[69]

Even in the post-Warhol era, many in the art world remain squeamish about the relationship between money and art. It is still not uncommon for critics and scholars to denounce prices as meaningless. Thus for example in 1978, Robert Hughes of *Time* declared that "the price of a work of art is an index of pure irrational desire."[70] In the same vein, Sotheby's chief auctioneer considers the market to be "magical."[71] And sounding very much like a nineteenth-century French academician, in 2005 the dean of the Yale University School of Art declared that "We don't consider success in the marketplace has anything to do with being a successful artist."[72] Art markets appear to be a source of embarrassment for these sensitive aesthetes, and their discomfort appears to increase as the level of art prices rises.

Yet in recent decades some prominent members of the art world have taken a more positive view of the relationship between prices and artistic quality. In 1989, for example, Peter Schjeldahl, who would later go on to become an art critic for the *New Yorker*, attended his first art auction. He wrote that he was driven to this by the fact that the booming art market was "a bigger story than anything that might conceivably be happening in studios, galleries, or museums." Although Schjeldahl was hardly overjoyed by the prominence of money in the art world, which he described as an "atrocious situation," he had to concede that the relative prices produced by the session he witnessed at Christie's were generally reasonable: "I must admit that the artistic judgment of current big bucks is better than the average among, say, critics." He understood that this should not be surprising: "Like the prospect of being hanged, shelling out millions may concentrate the mind wonderfully." And he also recognized that high art prices could have a favorable impact on the future supply of art: "Moreover, I foresee as a sure, short-term bet the rise of ambitious artists intimately attuned to the psychic wave-lengths of major money. Some of these artists, of whom Jeff Koons is a harbinger, will be very good, and I will like them."[73] (Peter Schjeldahl, meet Damien Hirst.)

Also in 1989, in London the art historian Sir Alan Bowness, the former director of the Tate Gallery, gave a lecture about the process by which artists become successful. He began by explaining to his audience that the art market absorbs the work of vast numbers of artists, the great majority of whom are journeymen. A small number, however, are artists of genius, whose work becomes the focus of museum collections. And he explained that it is the work of the most important artists that brings the highest prices: "It is only the museum artists whose work begins to rise to exceptional prices, and of course it is the very rarity of such artists in a supply-and-demand market that accounts for the phenomenal prices achieved today in the auction houses."[74]

Conclusion

> In the history of art, as in more materialistic matters, money talks vividly.
> Let us not be ashamed to listen.
>
> Alfred H. Barr, Jr., 1929[75]

The Italian Renaissance transformed artists from manual workers into intellectuals. Painters would no longer be paid as craftsmen, at fixed daily rates, but would instead themselves set prices that took into account their often exceptional skills. This transformation made it possible for artists to charge "star fees" for their paintings, and to accumulate wealth that might sometimes equal that of their patrons.

Yet this increase in status imposed new responsibilities. If artists were to be as affluent as aristocrats, they should also behave like them. One element of this was that they should appear to be unconcerned with such crass matters as their own incomes. A legacy of the Renaissance therefore came to be the convention that although artists might greedily pursue financial gain in private, they should never publicly appear to be interested in monetary rewards, but should be perceived to work for the glory of art, and the honor of the patrons and institutions they served.

As long as the market for fine art was dominated by patronage, the prices of works of art received little public attention, for these were negotiated privately by artists and aristocrats or church officials. Yet in Paris during the course of the nineteenth century a competitive market for fine art was created. Auction outcomes became a subject of discussion within the art world, and some critics began to comment on the validating function of prices generated in this new market setting. Artists, however, continued to behave according to the Renaissance ideal, and to avoid public expressions of their interest in turning artistic success into financial gain.

This behavior on the part of artists persisted even as the market for art expanded and attracted more widespread attention during the early twentieth century. So for example although there was great public interest in Picasso, who came to symbolize the modern artist for a large audience, this interest focused chiefly on his enormous artistic creativity and his many love affairs, with remarkably little discussion of his sizeable fortune, and even less of the shrewd business tactics that had helped him to gain it.

The rise of Andy Warhol not only radically changed the appearance of fine art, but also abruptly broke with established convention by presenting a new model of artistic behavior. Warhol made no secret of his fascination with money, and his avid pursuit of it. Because Warhol's persona was as controversial as his art, his departure from the Renaissance ideal of the artist became known not only throughout the art world but to a much wider public. Never again would it be automatically assumed that an artist would not openly acknowledge money as a primary motivation.

Since Warhol's innovation, relatively few artists have adopted his model of the artist as materialist, but those who have include Jeff Koons and Damien Hirst, both of whom are leading members of their respective cohorts. Both have been important artistic innovators, but both have gained far greater celebrity than other artists who might be considered to have made contributions of comparable importance. Warhol's model can clearly be useful for artists who want to gain both fame and fortune, and it is likely that it will continue to be the choice of some important artists in future, even if their numbers are not large.

Art historians have consistently failed to recognize that artists' behavior has been motivated directly by market considerations throughout western history. In the early modern era, for example, the Impressionists' establishment of their epoch-making independent exhibitions was a result of their frustration at their inability to advance their careers in the official Salon. Not only was their new style a challenge to the conservative standards of the Salon juries, but the experimental Impressionists found themselves at a disadvantage in creating the large and complex paintings that showed to best advantage in the vast crowded Salon galleries. Thus as Frédéric Bazille complained in 1866, "In order to be noticed at the [Salon] exhibition, one has to paint rather large pictures that demand very conscientious preparatory studies and thus occasion a good deal of expense; otherwise one has to spend ten years until people notice you, which is discouraging."[76] Bazille and his friend Monet failed in their attempt to hold an independent exhibition in 1867, but in 1874, after Bazille's death in the Franco-Prussian War, Monet succeeded in raising the necessary funds. The Impressionist exhibitions from 1874 on featured many smaller paintings by Monet, Pissarro, Degas, and others, fulfilling Bazille's original account of the plan he and Monet had formulated for a show "where we'll exhibit as many of our works as we wish," a format tailored to an experimental approach that naturally produced groups of smaller paintings rather than imposing individual works.[77]

Monet eventually achieved considerable financial success. Yet it should not be assumed that artists who failed to achieve this success were not equally motivated by the market. Vincent van Gogh is a striking example of an artist who famously failed to achieve success in the market during his lifetime, but who devoted considerable thought and effort to becoming financially successful. Inspired by the success the Impressionists had achieved as a group, van Gogh tried to create a collective identity for a group of artists he hoped would follow in their path: thus he coined the term "painters of the Petit Boulevard" to refer to himself and his younger colleagues, including Emile Bernard and Henri de Toulouse-Lautrec, to distinguish them from the established Impressionists, whom he called the "painters of the Grand Boulevard." Cornelia Hamburg noted that "van Gogh was tireless when it came to promoting the new avant-garde," as his letters to his art dealer brother contain a series of schemes to enrich these artists, from organizing exhibitions in southern France, to trying to gain access to new markets in the Netherlands and England, where he imagined there would be a lively market for his work and that of his friends.[78] Examples like these of Monet and van Gogh could be multiplied indefinitely: rich or poor, the vast majority of artists have been motivated by the pursuit not only of fame, but also of fortune.

Long before Andy Warhol, Théodore Duret established the principle that prices provide evidence of artistic success. What is disappointing, however, is how poor the quality of the art world's economic discourse remains even in the post-Warhol era. It continues to be fashionable among many critics and scholars to claim that art markets are irrational, and that prices have no value as indicators of artistic importance. These claims are both ignorant and foolish.[79] Art scholars must overcome their distaste for economics, and become more sophisticated in examining how changes in art markets have influenced artists' attitudes and behavior.

16

The State of Advanced Art

The Late Twentieth Century and Beyond

Pluralism, Postmodernism, and Perplexed Art Pundits

Painters no longer live within a tradition and so each of us must recreate
an entire language.

Pablo Picasso[1]

Well, thank God, art tends to be less what critics write than what artists
make.

Jasper Johns[2]

In 2005, Peter Schjeldahl wrote in the *New Yorker* that "The contemporary art world of the 1980s blew apart into four main fragments . . . Eventually, even the fragments disintegrated, becoming the sluggish mishmash that has prevailed in art ever since."[3] The idea that
advanced art had become fragmented in the late twentieth century was not
a new one. In 1984, for example, the art historian Corinne Robins titled
her survey of American art during 1968–1981 *The Pluralist Era*, and on
the first page observed that "the Pluralism of the seventies . . . effectively
did away with the idea of dominant styles for at least a decade."[4] Over
time, another term gained currency to describe the situation, as in 2000,
Jonathan Fineberg explained in his textbook, *Art Since 1940*, that what
had emerged in the seventies was *postmodernism*, "an inclusive aesthetic
that cultivates the variety of incoherence."[5]

Whatever name they give to the situation, there is widespread agreement among art critics and scholars that they have lost the ability to
provide any convincing overall narrative or explanation for the art of the

late twentieth century and beyond. The critic Arthur Danto, for example, remarked in 1997 that "contemporary art no longer allows itself to be represented by master narratives at all."[6] One of the most remarkable admissions to this effect was made in 2004 by Hal Foster of Princeton University. On page 679 of *Art Since 1900* – the final page of a textbook that he co-authored with Rosalind Krauss of Columbia, Yve-Alain Bois of Harvard, and Benjamin Buchloh of Columbia – Foster raised "a question we haven't confronted," and reflected as follows:

> Are there plausible ways to narrate the now myriad practices of contemporary art over the last twenty years at least? I don't point to this period of time arbitrarily: in the last several years the two primary models we've used to articulate different aspects of postwar art have become dysfunctional. I mean, on the one hand, the model of a medium-specific modernism challenged by an interdisciplinary postmodernism, and, on the other, the model of a historical avant-garde (i.e. ones critical of the old bourgeois institution of art such as Dada and Constructivism) and a neo-avant-garde that elaborates on this critique... Today the recursive strategy of the "neo" appears as attenuated as the oppositional logic of the "post" seems tired: neither suffices as a strong paradigm for artistic or cultural practice, and no other model stands in their stead; or, put differently, many local models compete, but none can hope to be paradigmatic. And we should note too that the methods discussed again here – psychoanalysis, Marxian social history, structuralism, and poststructuralism – are hardly thriving.

Foster's statement is startling, for it is no less than a declaration by a leading art scholar, made with the tacit approval of three others, that no existing analysis can account for the art of recent decades. The interest of this conundrum is heightened by the fact that – as Foster immediately proceeded to observe – contemporary art is thriving in the marketplace.[7]

What the art experts have consistently failed to recognize is that what they call pluralism or postmodernism did not arise spontaneously in the late twentieth century, but was instead a logical – indeed, systematic – extension of practices that originated at the beginning of the twentieth century, and that developed throughout the decades that followed. This chapter will present a new explanation for the nature of contemporary art, based on the proposition that it is the consistent product of a specific type of artistic creativity, operating in a particular market environment.

The Rise of a Competitive Market for Art

The market is the greatest critic.

Jeff Koons[8]

Understanding the art of the late twentieth century requires a new analysis of the art of the twentieth century as a whole. This analysis is based on the recognition that conceptual innovation has played a more prominent role in the art of the past century than it had in earlier times.

Both experimental and conceptual innovators have played important roles throughout the history of western art. For example the Old Masters Jan van Eyck, Masaccio, Giorgione, Raphael, Caravaggio, and Vermeer were great conceptual innovators, while Leonardo, Michelangelo, Titian, Hals, Velazquez, and Rembrandt were great experimental innovators.[9] The conceptual innovators Courbet, Manet, Gauguin, and van Gogh were among the greatest artists of the nineteenth century, as were the experimental innovators Degas, Cézanne, Monet, and Renoir.[10] For centuries, neither type of innovator dominated advanced art. This balance changed, however, in the twentieth century, as conceptual innovators gained an advantage over their experimental counterparts. This advantage stemmed from a change in the structure of the market for advanced art, that began with the Impressionists.

In 1874, frustrated at their lack of success in having their paintings accepted and displayed at the official Salon, the annual or biennial exhibition operated by the Academy of Fine Arts, Claude Monet, Camille Pissarro, and a group of their friends organized an independent exhibition that included paintings by twenty-nine artists. Although its full significance would not be recognized until much later, the first Impressionist exhibition began a new era, in which the reputations of advanced artists would no longer be created in the Salon, but would instead be made in independent group exhibitions. The most important of these would be the eight Impressionist exhibitions held during 1874–86, and the Salon des Indépendants, which was held annually from 1884 on. Analytically, the critical change that the Impressionists initiated in 1874 was the elimination of the official Salon's monopoly of the ability to present fine art in a setting that critics and the public would accept as legitimate. The Salon consequently would no longer determine whether an aspiring artist could have a successful career.[11]

A competitive market for advanced art did not immediately come into existence, however, because of the slow emergence of private galleries that were willing to sell the work of younger artists: it was not until the early twentieth century that the number of independent entrepreneurial galleries would grow large enough to create a genuinely competitive market.[12] The increase in these galleries reflected the growing awareness of the potential gains from investing in innovative art, as the prices of work not only by Monet and the other Impressionists but also by the Post-Impressionists Cézanne, van Gogh, and Gauguin began to increase during the 1890s. By 1910, the leading critic of the advanced art world, the poet Guillaume Apollinaire, observed that "The plethora of individual exhibitions tends to weaken the effect of the large annual salons. The public is less keen, since many painters have already shown in the galleries the most important, if not the best, examples of their work during the year."[13] Over time, private galleries would replace group exhibitions altogether as the key exhibition places for new advanced art, not only in Paris, but also in other art centers.

The first artist to rise to prominence by exhibiting in galleries rather than group shows was Pablo Picasso. Early in his career, Picasso used his art to cultivate merchants in the art market who could sell his work and spread his reputation. It is possible that no artist has painted more different dealers: during his first two decades in Paris, Picasso executed portraits of no less than nine dealers, and the wife of a tenth.[14] Picasso's portraits of Ambroise Vollard, Daniel-Henry Kahnweiler, Paul Rosenberg, and a succession of other gallery owners stand today as powerful visual evidence of the birth of a new regime in the history of art markets that in turn created a new era of artistic freedom.

The story of the Impressionists' challenge to the official Salon has long been a staple in narratives of art history, but art scholars have never fully appreciated the significance of the changes it initiated. Innovation had always been the hallmark of important art, but from the Renaissance on nearly all artists were constrained in the extent to which they could innovate by the need to satisfy powerful individual patrons or institutions. The overthrow of the Salon monopoly of the art market in Paris started a process that led to the creation of a competitive market for the innovative work of advanced artists. This removed the constraint of patronage, and gave artists a greater freedom to innovate. In this new regime, artists would no longer have to satisfy the demands or tastes of any powerful individual patron or jury, but could gain professional and economic success by finding a dealer who would give them exhibitions, and a few collectors who would consistently buy their work. These collectors might become friends or acquaintances of the artists, or they might simply buy their paintings from a private dealer. And more than one dealer might exhibit the work not only of an established artist, but even of a promising young talent. Attracting the attention of both dealers and collectors could be achieved by making conspicuous innovations, and this could be done most readily by conceptual artists. Perhaps not surprisingly, the first great artist to take real advantage of competition among dealers was the greatest of the ambitious young conceptual innovators of the new era.

The Dematerialization of Style

How can you say one style is better than another? You should be able to be an Abstract Expressionist next week, or a Pop artist, or a realist, without feeling you've given up something.

Andy Warhol[15]

In 1985, the eminent art historian Meyer Schapiro observed that "If the works of Pablo Picasso were not identified directly with his name, if they were shown together in a big exhibition, it would be rather difficult to say they were the work of one man."[16] In 1996, the art historian David Campbell observed that "visiting a [Sigmar] Polke exhibition is often like wandering around a group show."[17] And in 2002, the critic Arthur Danto observed that "when I first saw a retrospective of [Gerhard] Richter's work . . . it looked like I was seeing some kind of group show."[18] It is striking that three different authors used precisely the same metaphor to describe their bewilderment at the stylistic versatility of three different painters. Yet each made this observation in isolation, without recognizing the common element in the practices of the artists in question. Nor are these three artists the only ones who have prompted this reaction. For example the artist William Anastasi recalled that what had struck him when he first saw the Arensberg collection at the Philadelphia Museum was "that every Duchamp was so completely different from every other Duchamp."[19] And in 1949, in a tribute to his old friend Francis Picabia, Marcel Duchamp described Picabia's career as "a kaleidoscopic series of art experiences . . . hardly related to one another in their external appearances."[20]

The practice of stylistic versatility is a pattern that has been followed by a series of important artists of the past century. It is a practice that has been consciously learned by these artists, from the example of their predecessors. Bruce Nauman's art, for instance, is so varied in form that Peter Schjeldahl declared in 2002 that "There is no Nauman style."[21] Nauman has explained that early in his career he was influenced by a retrospective exhibition of the work of Man Ray, a friend and collaborator of Duchamp and Picabia: "What I liked was that there appeared to be no consistency to his thinking, no one style."[22] And Gerhard Richter observed in 1977 that "changeable artists are a growing phenomenon. Picasso, for instance, or Duchamp and Picabia – and the number is certainly increasing all the time."[23]

Throughout the twentieth century, a succession of important artists – including, for example, not only Picasso, Duchamp, Picabia, Richter, Polke, and Nauman, but also Max Ernst, Richard Hamilton, Robert Rauschenberg, Andy Warhol, David Hockney, Jeff Koons, Damien Hirst, and Tracey Emin – have changed styles frequently and at will. This practice has been a novel feature of twentieth-century art that was initiated by Picasso. Thus, in 1943 Marcel Duchamp observed that "Picasso in each one of his facets, has made clear his intention to keep free from preceding achievements," and, in 1996, the eminent English critic David Sylvester reflected that "Picasso is a kind of artist who couldn't have existed before this century, since his art is a celebration of this century's introduction of a totally promiscuous eclecticism into the practice of art."[24]

Style had traditionally been regarded as the essential signature of the artist, but Picasso considered it instead to be merely a means of expression: "Whenever I had something to say, I have said it in the manner in which I have felt it ought to be said." This attitude implied that he could change styles as the need arose: "Different motives inevitably require different methods of expression."[25] Instead of treating style as the artist's personal hallmark, and as something to be painstakingly crafted, Picasso had created a radical new conceptual approach that reduced style to a convenient means of making a specific statement. In this new formulation, the artist could introduce new styles at will, or alternate between existing styles, as a matter of convenience. This was a powerful new conception of the role of style that could readily be adopted by other conceptual artists.

It was not long before other artists followed Picasso's lead. Duchamp adopted an even more extreme position, in an attempt to eliminate style altogether. His introduction of the readymade was one manifestation of his desire to abolish taste, which he considered to be a product of repetition.[26] Avoiding repetition would consequently eliminate taste, and incidentally style, so Duchamp's goal was to make just one work for each idea: "I've had thirty-three ideas; I've made thirty-three paintings."[27] Duchamp's friend Picabia shared his belief in frequent change, declaring that "If you want to have clean ideas, change them as often as you change your shirts."[28] Dada became the first artistic movement that effectively made the elimination of style a collective goal, as the painter Hans Richter explained that the movement aimed at "riot, destruction, defiance, confusion. The role of chance, not as an extension of the scope of art, but as a principle of dissolution and anarchy."[29]

Picasso, Duchamp, Picabia, and the Dadas created a legacy that reverberated throughout advanced art in the generations that followed. Following their examples, artists could treat style not as a goal, but as a strategy, and if they wished, they could dispense with it altogether.

One key characteristic unifies all the stylistically versatile artistic innovators of the twentieth century, from Picasso and Duchamp through Hirst and Emin: all are conceptual artists. Their behavior in changing styles made their careers differ radically from those of experimental artists. For the century's great experimental innovators, from Mondrian and Kandinsky through Pollock and Rothko and beyond, art remained a lifelong quest along a single path toward the one true personal style. Their styles evolved over time, slowly and gradually. Even late in the century, the experimental painter Brice Marden explained that he was inspired by Cézanne's "intense, long, slow process of working, looking, assimilating," and the experimental sculptor Louise Bourgeois reflected that her style had been hard won: "My style, the way I work comes from all the failures, all the temptations I have resisted, all the fun I didn't have, all the regrets."[30]

The protean innovator is a radical conceptual creation of the twentieth century, and as Gerhard Richter recognized, its importance has increased over time. By the end of the twentieth century, many of the central figures in advanced art, including Rauschenberg, Richter, Koons, Hirst, and Emin, were conceptual contributors to the dematerialization of style. For example Richter could reflect in 1984 that "It has now become my identifying characteristic that my work is all over the place."[31]

The Balkanization of Advanced Art

What is sculpture? What is painting? Everyone's still clinging to outdated ideas, obsolete definitions, as if the artist's role was not precisely to offer new ones.

Pablo Picasso, 1943[32]

Art used to mean paintings and statues. Now it means practically anything human-made that is unclassifiable otherwise.

Peter Schjeldahl, 2005[33]

The pluralism of the late twentieth century was not solely the product of the dematerialization of style, for it was also caused by another powerful trend that had also been active throughout nearly the entire century, and that was also initiated by Picasso. This trend affected not only the appearance of art, but its very substance.

In 1912, Picasso glued a piece of oil cloth to a small oval painting. *Still Life with Chair Caning* became one of the most important works of art of the twentieth century, for it was the first *collage* – "the first painting in which extraneous objects or materials are applied to the picture surface." Collage violated a tradition that had been honored by artists since the Renaissance that nothing other than paint should be placed on the two-dimensional surface of the support, and John Golding observed that "The aesthetic implications of collage as a whole were vast."[34] Yet the implications of collage went far beyond the aesthetic, for when he invented a new genre, Picasso set in motion a process that would make the art of the twentieth century fundamentally different in form from that of all earlier centuries.

Collage was an archetypal conceptual innovation, for it broke the rules of an existing art form so decisively that it was immediately recognized as a new genre. And its example quickly inspired other conceptual innovators. Before 1912 was out, Picasso's fellow Cubist Georges Braque had made the first papier collé. In 1913, after a visit to Picasso's studio, the Russian artist Vladimir Tatlin made the first counter-relief. Also in 1913, Marcel Duchamp made the first readymade.

And on and on. *During the twentieth century, more than four dozen new artistic genres were invented, virtually all by conceptual innovators.*[35] These were not all of equal importance: many gained few followers, and some remained the exclusive domain of their inventors. Yet some rose to great prominence, and a key result of this proliferation of genres was that over the course of the twentieth century the world of advanced art became balkanized. This process was at work throughout the century, but during the first half of the century two world wars and a great depression appear to have restricted its progress by limiting the demand for new art. In contrast, the prosperity of the 1960s and after, which created a strong demand for innovative art, provided the basis for the widespread adoption of new genres by ambitious young artists. At the beginning of the twentieth century, important artists were either painters or sculptors. In contrast, by the century's end, painters and sculptors had been joined by sizeable numbers of artists who devoted themselves to such other genres as collage, installation, photography, and video.

And the real extent of balkanization is even greater than a listing of active genres implies, for in many cases in which recent artists have not given new names to their innovative practices, they have nevertheless radically expanded the boundaries of existing genres. It is highly unlikely, for example, that Rodin or Brancusi would recognize as sculpture many of the recent works that are given that label. Arthur Danto noticed this: "some of the most interesting artists of the middle to late sixties – Bruce Nauman, Robert Morris, Robert Irwin, Eva Hesse – began as painters, but found painting constraining. It is not as though they turned to sculpture as such, for the connotation of sculpture would have been no less constraining at the time. All that the work of these artists had in common with sculpture was a real third dimension, which somehow seems of marginal relevance, the way it is undeniable but also irrelevant that dance is three-dimensional."[36]

One important tendency of balkanization has been to limit the importance of individual artists. In art, as in other intellectual activities, importance is a function of influence, and balkanization has tended to limit the sphere of influence of artists. Until recently, a painter could influence nearly all advanced artists, so Picasso, Pollock, or Warhol could be dominant figures in the entire art world. Today it is more difficult for any one artist to reach all these groups. This trend away from dominant individual artists is heightened by the nature of conceptual artists' life cycles, for many young innovators have failed to make any later significant contributions.[37]

The State of Advanced Art

On the morning of Sunday, February 22 with the news that Andy Warhol was dead, I ran to the window expecting to hear seismic noises coming from the city outside, and to witness a transfiguration, I don't know of what... but of something. The shock of so enormous an absence would surely register, it seemed, on reality itself.
Critic Lisa Liebmann, 1987[38]

Who made the most important art of the late twentieth century? As for earlier periods, one way to answer this question is by using narratives of art history. In order to focus not on the greatest artists who were alive late in the century, but rather on who was actually making the most important art in the specific period of interest, in this case textbook illustrations were selected according to when the illustrated works were executed. Therefore, for all available textbooks published in 2000 or

TABLE 16.1. *Ranking of Artists by Total Illustrations of Works Executed in 1975 or Later*

Artist	N	Date of Birth	Date of Death	Country of Birth
Cindy Sherman	25	1954	–	United States
Gerhard Richter	23	1932	–	Germany
Jeff Koons	22	1955	–	United States
Damien Hirst	19	1965	–	England
Anselm Kiefer	18	1945	–	Germany
Jean-Michel Basquiat	15	1960	1988	United States
Rachel Whiteread	14	1963	–	England
Matthew Barney	12	1967	–	United States
Richard Serra	12	1939	–	United States
Jake and Dinos Chapman	11	1966, 1962	–	England
Jenny Holzer	11	1950	–	United States
Richard Prince	11	1949	–	United States
Julian Schnabel	11	1951	–	United States
Jeff Wall	11	1946	–	Canada

Source: See text and appendix.

later, all illustrations were tabulated that represented works of art made in 1975 or later. Based on this survey, Table 16.1 presents the ten artists (actually 15, because of ties) who had the most works illustrated in the textbooks. It should be noted that although such major figures as Jasper Johns, Robert Rauschenberg, and Andy Warhol remained active after 1975, they do not appear on the list, because illustrations of works they made prior to 1975 were not counted for this study, and works they made in 1975 and beyond were illustrated less frequently than those of the artists included in Table 16.1.

The twenty-one books surveyed included twenty-five illustrations of photographs by Cindy Sherman. An earlier chapter found that she was the most important woman artist of the twentieth century, and the present one shows that she also has the distinction of being the most important artist overall in the period from 1975 to the present.[39] In this the textbooks support the recent judgment of Peter Schjeldahl that Sherman is "the era's most original artist."[40]

The ranking of Table 16.1 strongly underscores the dominance of conceptual art in the late twentieth century and beyond. Of the fifteen artists included in the ranking, only one – Richard Serra – was an experimental innovator.[41] And consistent with the trend toward conceptual approaches, it is significant that Serra was the second-oldest of the fifteen artists listed.

Table 16.1 clearly reflects the balkanization of advanced art in the 1970s and beyond. Thus only four of the artists listed – Richter, Kiefer, Basquiat, and Schnabel – were exclusively painters. Six – Koons, Hirst, Whiteread, Serra, and the Chapmans – were primarily sculptors, but several of these, most notably Koons and Hirst, worked with materials, including the vitrines for which both are known, that were not traditionally those used by sculptors. Three of the artists – Sherman, Prince, and Wall – worked exclusively or primarily in photography, while Barney worked primarily in video, and Holzer extensively in installation. It should also be noted that Koons and Hirst are prime examples of conceptual artists who routinely work in a number of different genres.[42]

Table 16.1 points up several significant trends of the late twentieth century. One is the growing prominence of women artists, as Whiteread and Holzer join Sherman in the ranking.[43] Another is the increasing importance of co-authorship in advanced art, as Jake and Dinos Chapman appear in the ranking.[44] In spite of the progressive globalization of advanced art, a majority – eight of fifteen – of the artists were born in the United States, but the presence of Richter and Kiefer attests to the importance of Düsseldorf in training painters, and the success of London in the 1990s is reflected in the presence of four of the young British artists – Hirst, Whiteread, and the Chapmans.[45]

The evidence of Table 16.1 can help us to explain a view that became common among art critics and scholars in the latter decades of the twentieth century that advanced art was no longer producing individual artists comparable in stature to the greatest artists of earlier periods. For example the critic Calvin Tomkins declared in 1988 that "The last two decades have produced no artists on the level of Pollock and de Kooning, much less Picasso and Matisse."[46] There has of course long been a tendency to denigrate contemporary artists as inferior to the giants of the past. Beyond this perennial doubt, however, in recent decades the structure of the art world has itself created a new basis for the perception that today's artists do not match the greatness of their predecessors. I believe that this perception is due in large part to the balkanization of advanced art. Table 16.1 provides clear evidence that the leading artists of the late twentieth century were distributed among a larger number of different genres than had been true in the past.[47]

The analysis applied throughout the present study suggests a straightforward explanation for the proliferation of both styles and genres that occurred in the late twentieth century. Quite simply, both appear to have been consequences of the extended dominance of conceptual approaches to art in a time of heightened demand for artistic innovation. Thus a series of young conceptual innovators, including nearly all the artists listed in Table 16.1, devised radical new approaches to old genres, or effectively transformed old genres into new ones, and in the process divided advanced art into a larger number of nearly unrelated activities than had ever previously been the case. Advanced artists of this period had increasingly diverse interests and objectives. And this meant that the potential sphere of influence of any individual artist became more circumscribed than in the past. For most of the first seven decades of the twentieth century, important painters worked for an audience that potentially included most, if not all, advanced artists. Andy Warhol may have been a member of the last cohort of artists whose influence could have extended to a sizeable majority of advanced artists. By the 1970s, it appears this situation had changed in a basic way. Painting no longer dominated the attention of advanced artists; many were committed to other activities. Sherman could potentially influence photographers, Richter might influence painters, Koons might influence sculptors, but it was now difficult if not impossible for any one artist to influence all these groups. Because the importance of an artistic innovator depends directly on the extent of his or her influence, one consequence of this balkanization of advanced art was that to many observers, it seemed that there was no artist of a stature comparable to that of the great painters of earlier eras.

A Conceptual World

I paint objects as I think them, not as I see them.
Pablo Picasso[48]

The radical changes in art and society that were set in motion during the early years of the twentieth century gave rise to a new kind of artist, whose first obligation was to invent or discover a new self. Tradition, skill, rigorous training, formal knowledge: All the old requirements fell away or became optional.
Calvin Tomkins[49]

In 2001, Arthur Danto declared that "We are living in a conceptual art world."[50] The observation was accurate, but tardy. The conceptual art world of the late twentieth century developed clearly and directly from the earlier conceptual innovations of Picasso, Duchamp, and their many heirs. Art scholars' failure to understand this process has led to their inability to make sense of contemporary art.

Art scholars invariably approach the history of art as the analysis of styles. This left them helpless when style dematerialized in the work of many artists late in the twentieth century. *Art scholars don't understand that style was one casualty of the conceptual revolutions in twentieth-century art.* Art scholars have long stubbornly refused to recognize the fundamental role of markets and economic incentives in advanced art. They have also resisted systematic analysis of artists' differing approaches to creativity. Yet adopting these analytical tools is essential to an understanding of the nature of contemporary art. Conceptual and experimental artists had coexisted throughout the entire history of western art, but the constraints imposed by patronage had the effect of making it possible for scholars to treat their works as comparable products for the period prior to the modern era. With the rise of a competitive market for advanced art, and the recognition by those in the art world that investments in new innovative art would eventually yield high financial returns, the rewards for radical and conspicuous innovation increased, and conceptual artists could respond to these incentives more quickly and decisively than their experimental counterparts.

Duchamp versus Picasso

I really don't think much about past art, I guess. Duchamp, of course. I find his life and work a constant inspiration.

Robert Rauschenberg[51]

The greatest idea of the twentieth century was collage. I just see it all like collage.

Damien Hirst, 1994[52]

Publicly a work becomes not just intention, but the way it is used ... You can't control that kind of thing.

Jasper Johns[53]

The development of advanced art in the twentieth century has sometimes been described as a battle between the legacies of Pablo Picasso and Marcel Duchamp. An example of this formulation was given by the painter Robert Motherwell in 1971:

Picasso, in questioning himself about what art is, immediately thought, "What is not?" ... Picasso, as a painter, wanted boundaries. Duchamp, as an anti-painter, did not. From the standpoint of each, the other was involved in a *game*. Taking one side or the other is the history of art since 1914, since the First World War.[54]

From the vantage point of this formulation, Duchamp's key contribution was the readymade, for its rejection of traditional aesthetic and artistic values. For example Thomas McEvilley declared in 2005 that "the Readymade has exerted more influence on the sculpture of the last two generations than all other models and influences put together."[55] Quantitative support for this view was provided by an English survey of 500 artists, curators, critics, and dealers taken in 2004, in which Duchamp's readymade *Fountain* was voted the most influential work of modern art, primarily because of overwhelming support from the artists included among those polled.[56] A commentator on that survey observed that "there is a new generation out there saying, 'Cut the crap – Duchamp opened up modern art,'" supporting Calvin Tomkins's conclusion more than two decades earlier that "by the end of the nineteen sixties Duchamp was widely recognized as the most influential artist of the second half of the twentieth century."[57]

Duchamp served as an inspiration for many younger conceptual artists in the second half of the twentieth century who wanted to break down the barriers between art and everyday reality. A central element of this desire was a rejection of the traditional boundaries that defined the arts, and specifically an attack on painting, the most powerful of the visual arts. A prominent early statement of this agenda was made in 1959 by Robert Rauschenberg, who declared that "Painting relates to both art and life. Neither can be made. (I try to act in that gap between the two.)"[58] In 1997, Arthur Danto recalled that he had been "dazzled by the idea of the 'gap between art and life' as a possible site for artistic activity," and he contended that Rauschenberg had succeeded in defining it in his innovative works of the 1950s: "one gets the sense that the Combines touch both these domains as boundaries, with art symbolized by raw paint, and life by odds and ends of real things with antecedent identities." To Danto, Rauschenberg's combines, which combined painting with real objects, marked a turning point, by creating a bridge between the art of the past and future, "pointing in one direction back to the metaphysics of the paint, which defined Abstract Expressionism (and hence art, in Rauschenberg's vocabulary), and, in the other, to the uninflected display of commonplace objects, which in various ways was to define Pop." Danto considered the impact of Rauschenberg's use of common objects to have been so great that he declared that "the artistic mainstream today is very largely Rauschenbergian."[59]

Yet to conclude that Duchamp clearly exerted a greater influence than Picasso on the art of the late twentieth century may ignore the complexity of Picasso's legacy. And this is true not merely because Duchamp's innovation of the readymade may have been a direct response to Picasso's invention of collage.[60] More fundamentally, collage has been recognized by a series of observers as a primary basis for the twentieth-century revolt against the traditional boundaries of the arts, and to have done this precisely by bringing elements of everyday life into art. Thus as early as 1915, the Dada poet Tristan Tzara recorded the "great uproar" caused by an exhibition of collages in Zurich, for the works were "neither art nor painting."[61] Tzara considered the invention of collage "the most revolutionary moment in the evolution of painting," because the new genre incorporated "a piece of everyday reality."[62] Similarly, the Dada poet Richard Huelsenbeck wrote in 1920 of Picasso's invention of "the new medium" of collage: "He began to stick sand, hair, post-office forms and pieces of newspaper onto his pictures, to give them the value of a direct reality, removed from everything traditional." Collage brought a new value to art: "it participates in life itself."[63] This early assessment of the function of collage has equally been shared by later analysts, and has been seen as the source of many of the forms of more recent conceptual innovations. For example in 1975, the critic Harold Rosenberg declared that "Collage changed the relation between painting and the world outside painting. The combining of formal qualities with crude fact in Cubist collage contained the seeds of anti-art that have flourished in the half-century that followed."[64] Collage thus was recognized from an early date as the catalyst for the introduction of real objects into fine art, and as the beginning of the attack on painting as the dominant form of fine art.

Collage was chronologically the first of the twentieth century's scores of new artistic genres. In many respects it was also the emblematic new genre of twentieth-century conceptual art. Collage was created by sticking together material elements that had previously been considered unrelated. In this it served directly as a model for a significant number of new genres that followed it, in sticking things together: these include papier collé, papier dechiré, photomontage, merz, and décollage. Even Rauschenberg's combines were genetically related to collage. Like collage, the combines grew directly out of painting. Some combines came to be free standing, but the earliest combines were made by attaching found objects to painted canvases. And although it was later abbreviated, the name initially given to these works was "combine painting."[65] Even when new genres did not literally involve sticking things together, the metaphor of collage as a combination of unrelated elements remained in artists' minds. For example in 1966, Allan Kaprow defined his own new genre, the Happening, as "a collage of events." In 1958, when Kaprow was first creating this genre, which was intended to unite all the traditional arts, he explained that "this idea of a total art has grown from attempts to extend the possibilities of one of the forms of painting, collage, which has led us unknowingly toward rejecting painting in any form."[66] For Damien Hirst, collage provided a model not only for his works of art, but also for the curatorial activities that first brought him to prominence in London's art world. Thus he told a critic that after he had organized *Freeze* and several other warehouse shows, "People in the art world got after me and said, 'You've got to decide whether you're an artist or a curator,' and I kept saying 'Why?' If you go out and buy objects and arrange them in a sculpture, why can't you do it with art works? It's all art to me."[67] For Kaprow, Hirst, and others, collage thus became a metaphor for conceptual innovation in general, and Picasso's innovation was seen as the historical point of origin for their later efforts.

An objection might be made to this claim for Picasso's influence, on the grounds that the work of artists like Rauschenberg and Kaprow violated his own intentions. Thus whereas Duchamp avowedly wanted to change the course of art, and was pleased by the success the readymades had in undermining the importance of painting, Picasso's firm belief in the primacy of painting would certainly have led him to disapprove of the hybrid genres that were inspired by collage. It might be maintained that since this effect of collage violated his intentions, he should receive no credit for this element of his legacy.

This argument can be immediately dismissed, however, for it is based on a misunderstanding of the nature of influence. An example from Picasso's own early work provides a telling demonstration. In 1922, the eminent English critic Clive Bell published a book of essays on modern art titled *Since Cézanne*. Bell defended this title for a book that ranged widely over forms and styles of art on the grounds that "there is hardly one modern artist of importance to whom Cézanne is not father or grand-father." Among his progeny, two were preeminent: "Matisse and Picasso are the two immediate heirs to Cézanne."[68] Cézanne never met either Matisse or Picasso, and he did not see their seminal early contributions. Yet Cézanne's experimental art was based on decades of painstaking efforts to devise better means of recording his visual perceptions, and it is inconceivable that he would have embraced the conceptual devices of either Fauvism or Cubism. Clive Bell recognized the conceptual basis of the art of Matisse and Picasso, observing in *Since Cézanne* that "in the six-teen or seventeen years which have elapsed since the influence of Cézanne became paramount theory has played a part which no critic or historian can overlook." In crediting Cézanne's legacy with this development, it did not bother Bell that Cézanne had been an implacable opponent of theory in painting: so for example among Cézanne's opinions that had been quoted in a celebrated article published by the painter Emile Bernard in 1904 was the view that the artist "must avoid thinking like a writer, which so often distracts the painter from his true goal – the direct study of nature – and causes him to waste his time in intangible theories."[69] Nor did Cézanne's commitment to an experimental approach prevent either of the younger conceptual innovators, Matisse or Picasso, from declaring their debt to his art.[70] The fact of Cézanne's influence on Matisse and Picasso stands completely independent of whether he would have approved of the form that influence took. This earlier example of the protean nature of influence clearly demonstrates that an artist's influence does not depend on his goals or intentions, but rather on the value of his innovations for other artists. The use of collage, by Rauschenberg and others, to achieve artistic goals that Picasso would have rejected thus does not in any way affect our assessment of the extent of Picasso's influence.

Duchamp's emphasis on highly conceptual approaches to art, and his rejection of painting, made him appear to many younger artists as a patron saint of their activities, whereas Picasso's professed adherence to the traditional values of painting throughout most of his life led many younger artists to ignore, or reject, him as a model. Yet it appears misguided to describe the art of the late twentieth century as a victory for the legacy of Duchamp over that of Picasso, for two reasons. Perhaps the less important is that Duchamp's key contribution may have been crucially indebted to an innovation of Picasso. More generally, however, it would appear that the radical conceptual innovations of both artists, perhaps no less Picasso's collage than Duchamp's readymade, exerted an enormous influence on the advanced art of the second half of the twentieth century and beyond.

Conceptual Revolutions in Twentieth-Century Art

Another important value of the modern artist is that his art is completely free. There are no rules, no hierarchy of privileged qualities, no absolute standards, characteristics, or codified methods, and there are no privileged materials.

Meyer Schapiro, 1948[71]

Art is invention, exciting and fantastic... When someone tells me I can't do something, so far I've always found out that I can.

Damien Hirst, 1996[72]

As discussed above, art critics and scholars have been at a loss to explain the development of advanced art in the late twentieth century. Perhaps their most basic problem is that they have failed to recognize the full significance of a shift that occurred in art in the late nineteenth and early twentieth centuries. In a classic narrative of this period, George Heard Hamilton aptly described this shift:

In the half-century between 1886, the date of the last Impressionist exhibition, and the beginning of the Second World War, a change took place in the theory and practice of art that was as radical and momentous as any that had occurred in human history. It was based on the belief that works of art need not imitate or represent natural objects and events. Therefore artistic activity is not essentially concerned with representation but instead with the invention of objects variously expressive of human experience, objects whose structures as independent artistic entities cannot be evaluated in terms of their likeness, nor devalued because of their lack of likeness, to natural things.[73]

Neither Hamilton nor his fellow art scholars understood that this momentous change was not simply a transformation in the appearance of art, but at a deeper level signaled the beginning of a change in the very behavior of artists, that would progress further over time, and that later in the century would produce forms of art that defied all earlier definitions of art.

Art scholars have been unable fully to understand the nature of the shift Hamilton described because they have failed to understand its causes. Curiously, art scholars have rarely offered any analysis of why this radical change in art occurred at this specific time; indeed, they have rarely even raised this question. One exception is Arthur Danto, who in 1992 described the process of departures or subtractions from the art of the preceding centuries, that had begun in the 1880s and continued over the course of the following decades, which in sum had made it "possible for something to be art which resembled as little as one pleased the great art of the past." Yet Danto pleaded ignorance as to the timing of this shift: "Why the history of erasures began to take place in, as I see it, the late nineteenth century I have no clear idea, any more than I have a clear idea why, in the early fourteenth century, the Vasarian conquest of visual appearances should have begun."[74] Remarkably, Danto thus contended that an event that occurred within the past century was as inscrutable as one that had occurred fully five centuries earlier. What Danto failed to see was that understanding the causes of this shift was critical to understanding its consequences. For the change in the structure of the market for advanced art that occurred in the late nineteenth and early twentieth centuries not only triggered the shift that Hamilton and Danto described, but continued to play a key role in fuelling the rapid rate of innovation of advanced art throughout the twentieth century, and beyond.

Art scholars invariably comprehend the history of art as the analysis of styles. Concerning the first century of modern art, they have generally observed that the most important change was an acceleration in the development of new styles. As discussed above, they have recognized that the proliferation of styles in the late twentieth century has made their analytical approach problematic, yet they have failed to understand the causes of this, and they have consequently been unable to develop an alternative approach.

What art scholars have not understood is that the acceleration in the rate of artistic innovation in the early twentieth century not only caused styles to develop more rapidly, and to multiply, but that in the hands of conceptual artists style began to be undermined altogether. Picasso pioneered the creation of the single most influential style of the century, but he also initiated a practice, in changing styles at will, that later conceptual artists would extend into a virtual elimination of personal or individual style. Duchamp's invention of the readymade was the most provocative of his acts, but his entire career can be seen as an effort to eliminate style from art. Dada was the first group movement that explicitly set out to destroy style. The legacies of Picasso, Duchamp, and Dada became powerful forces in the second half of the twentieth century, as conceptual innovators used a wide variety of objects in new ways to produce art that did not appear to reflect the personality of the artist.

Confronted by a contemporary art world that is marked by a wide diversity of styles and genres, and by important artists, including Richter, Koons, Hirst, and Emin, whose art seems characterized only by inconsistency, art scholars have responded by declaring that advanced art has become random or incoherent. Yet this is wrong: the multiplicity of styles in contemporary art, and the apparent lack of recognizable style or genre of many important artists, do not imply that art is random. They are manifestations of important systematic patterns that dominate contemporary art. To see these patterns, however, it is crucial to recognize that they are not based on style.

Throughout the twentieth century, great experimental artists, from Mondrian and Kandinsky, through Pollock and de Kooning, to Serra and Bourgeois, have painstakingly pursued aesthetic goals through the gradual development of a personal style. Yet from Picasso and Duchamp, through Rauschenberg and Warhol, to Koons and Hirst, conceptual innovators have discovered that new and more radical forms of art can be developed much more quickly by reducing style to a short-run strategy rather than a long-run goal. This discovery has led them to make rapid changes of style, and to create works that violate the boundaries of traditional artistic genres. Conceptual innovators have also engaged in a series of other behaviors that are novel within the context of art history. Thus they have intentionally provoked observers to debate the question of whether their work is serious or a joke; they have had their work executed entirely by others, thus stressing that their contribution is the concept; they have consistently co-authored their work; they have extended the use of language in art, and in some instances made visual art almost entirely out of language; and they have created personal art, making their work entirely out of their own lives. These are all significant features of conceptual twentieth-century art: all are patterns, involving systematic artistic behavior, but these patterns have generally been overlooked by art scholars because they do not involve style.

Art historians thus failed to recognize that the shift described by George Heard Hamilton was not merely a change in the appearance of art, but was one symptom of a more basic change that would continue into the future – a change in the behavior of artists, as conceptual artists became more extreme in their pursuit of innovation than ever before in the history of art. Nor could art historians understand why this latter change occurred. Art scholars have consistently ignored the economic basis of artistic behavior, but artists' responses to the new market structure hold the key to the new era of conceptual artistic revolution. The new and more radical approaches adopted by conceptual artists in the twentieth century were a direct result of the rise of a competitive market for art. As discussed earlier, this new market structure was the outcome of a process that began when the Impressionists' group exhibitions effectively overthrew the Salon monopoly of the ability legitimately to present fine art to the public, and that progressed as the value of the work of the Impressionists and Post-Impressionists rose in value over time, thus demonstrating the investment value of innovative art. Picasso was the prototype of the conceptual innovator who maximized the economic value of his inventiveness in the new market setting, and Duchamp quickly followed him by making logical extensions of many of his innovations. Much of the history of the art of the twentieth century is comprised of the novel products and practices devised by scores of conceptual artists who followed in the footsteps of those early masters of the new era of artistic freedom, and this era of conceptual revolutions continues to characterize the art of our world today.

Appendix to Chapter 16
Books Surveyed for This Chapter

Adams, Louise Schneider. 2007. *Art Across Time*, 3rd ed. Boston: McGraw Hill.

Archer, Michael. 2002. *Art Since 1960*, 2nd ed. London: Thames and Hudson.

Arnason, H.H. 2004. *History of Modern Art*, 5th ed. Upper Saddle River, NJ: Pearson Prentice Hall.

Bell, Cory. 2001. *Modern Art*. New York: Watson-Guptill.

Bell, Julian. 2007. *Mirror of the World*. New York: Thames and Hudson.

Buchholz, Elke Linda, et al. 2007. *Art*. New York: Abrams.

Collings, Matthew. 2004. *This is Modern Art*. London: Weidenfeld and Nicolson.

Cottington, David. 2005. *Modern Art*. Oxford: Oxford University Press.

Cumming, Robert. 2005. *Art*. London: DK Publishing.

Davies, Penelope, et al. 2007. *Janson's History of Art*, 7th ed. Upper Saddle River, NJ: Pearson Prentice Hall.

Dempsey, Amy. 2002. *Art in the Modern Era*. New York: Harry N. Abrams.

Fineberg, Jonathan. 2000. *Art Since 1940*, 2nd ed. New York: Harry N. Abrams.

Foster, Hal; Rosalind Krauss; Yve-Alain Bois; and Benjamin Buchloh. 2004. *Art since 1900*. New York: Thames and Hudson.

Honour, Hugh and John Fleming. 2002. *The Visual Arts*, 6th ed. New York: Harry N. Abrams.

Hopkins, David. 2000. *After Modern Art*. Oxford: Oxford University Press.

Hunter, Sam; John Jacobus; and Daniel Wheeler. 2004. *Modern Art*, 3rd ed. New York: Vendome Press.

Kemp, Martin, ed. 2000. *The Oxford History of Western Art*. Oxford: Oxford University Press.

Lucie-Smith, Edward. 2001. *Movements in Art Since 1945*, new ed. London: Thames and Hudson.

Parmesani, Loredana. 2001. *Art of the Twentieth Century*. Milan: Skira.

Richter, Klaus. 2001. *Art*. Munich: Prestel.

Taylor, Brandon. 2005. *Contemporary Art*. Upper Saddle River, NJ: Pearson Prentice Hall.

Notes

Introduction

1 Apollonio, *Futurist Manifestos*, p. 30.
2 Greenberg, *The Collected Essays and Criticism*, Vol. 4, p. 300.
3 Lippard, *Changing*, pp. 27–31.
4 Sylvester, *About Modern Art*, p. 30; Galenson, "And Now for Something Completely Different," pp. 17–27, and Chap. 7, this text.

Chapter 1

1 Bourgeois, *Destruction of the Father, Reconstruction of the Father*, p. 166.
2 Rosenberg, *The Tradition of the New*, p. 37.
3 Baudelaire, *Art in Paris, 1845–1862*, p. 126.
4 Baudelaire, *The Painter of Modern Life and Other Essays*, pp. 3–4, 13.
5 Danto, *Embodied Meanings*, p. 85.
6 Cézanne, *Letters*, p. 313.
7 Malevich, *Essays on Art, 1915–1933*, Vol. 1, p. 89.
8 Johns, *Writings, Sketchbook Notes, Interviews*, p. 19.
9 Rosenberg, *Discovering the Present*, pp. 111–18.
10 Bowness, *The Conditions of Success*, pp. 7, 11, 16.
11 Rosenberg, *Discovering the Present*, p. 118.
12 Sickert, *The Complete Writings on Art*, p. 253.
13 Ashbery, *Reported Sightings*, p. 392.
14 Malevich, *Essays on Art, 1915–1933*, Vol. 1, p. 170.
15 Steinberg, *Other Criteria*, p. 7.
16 Planck, *Scientific Autobiography and Other Papers*, pp. 33–34.
17 Barr, *Picasso*, p. 273; Penrose, *Picasso*, p. 159.
18 Gilot and Lake, *Life With Picasso*, pp. 268–70.
19 Gablik, *Conversations Before the End of Time*, pp. 459–61, 464.
20 Malevich, *Essays on Art, 1915–1933*, Vol. 1, p. 95.
21 Kandinsky and Marc, *The "Blaue Reiter" Almanac*, pp. 170–72.

22 Rosenberg, *Art on the Edge*, p. 162.
23 Rosenberg, *The De-Definition of Art*, p. 56.
24 Barr, *Picasso*, p. 270.
25 Varnedoe, *Pictures of Nothing*, p. 41; Baudelaire, *Art in Paris*, p. 127.
26 Bowness, *Modern European Art*, p. 73.
27 For more extensive discussion of these types, see Galenson, *Old Masters and Young Geniuses*, Chaps. 1–2.
28 Bockris, *Warhol*, p. 320.
29 Breslin, *Mark Rothko*, p. 427.
30 De Duve, *Kant after Duchamp*, p. 216.
31 Ashton, *The Writings of Robert Motherwell*, p. 239.
32 Terenzio, *The Collected Writings of Robert Motherwell*, p. 137.
33 Breslin, *Mark Rothko*, p. 433.
34 Tomkins, *Off the Wall*, p. 185.
35 Fry, *Last Lectures*, pp. 14–15.
36 Fry, *Last Lectures*, pp. 3, 15.
37 Woolf, *Roger Fry*, pp. 286–87.
38 Bowness, *The Conditions of Success*, p. 51.
39 Kandinsky, *Complete Writings on Art*, pp. 769–70.
40 Kandinsky, *Complete Writings on Art*, p. 787.
41 Kandinsky, *Complete Writings on Art*, p. 786.
42 Kandinsky, *Complete Writings on Art*, p. 828.
43 E.g., see Galenson, *Artistic Capital*.
44 Cézanne, *Letters*, p. 281.
45 Sickert, *The Complete Writings on Art*, p. 254.
46 Richter, *The Daily Practice of Painting*, p. 93.
47 For elaboration of the argument presented in this and the following paragraph, see Galenson and Jensen, "Careers and Canvases."
48 Bourdieu, *The Field of Cultural Production*, pp. 242–43.
49 Gauguin, *The Writings of a Savage*, p. 225.
50 Galenson and Jensen, *Careers and Canvases*, p. 148
51 Van Gogh, *The Complete Letters Vincent van Gogh*, Vol. 2 p. 515.
52 E.g., see Pissarro, *Letters to His Son Lucien*, pp. 162–63, 174.
53 Galenson and Jensen, *Careers and Canvases*, pp. 156–58; Galenson, *Anticipating Artistic Success*, pp. 11–12.
54 Fitzgerald, *Making Modernism*, Chapter 1.
55 Apollinaire, *Apollinaire on Art*, p. 75.
56 Fitzgerald, *Making Modernism*, p. 5.
57 Fitzgerald, *Making Modernism*, pp. 10, 29–30.
58 Coen, *Umberto Boccioni*, p. xlii.
59 Fitzgerald, *Making Modernism*, pp. 33–44.
60 Bowness, *The Conditions of Success*, p. 39.
61 Richardson, *A Life of Picasso*, pp. 297–98; Fitzgerald, *Making Modernism*, Chap. 1.
62 Albert Elsen clearly described this shift from patronage to artistic freedom in sculpture: "Until Rodin, great sculptors throughout history provided images by which their sponsors obtained a sense of identity . . . The sculptor's culture

came from the city, court, or cult that commissioned the work...What has been broken in [the twentieth] century is that part of the tradition in which great sculptors played a role...Rodin came to epitomize, at modern sculpture's beginning, the clash between sculpture made from private values, and expectations based on public norms;" *Origins of Modern Sculpture* (New York: George Braziller, 1974), pp. 27–29.

63 Danto, *After the End of Art*, pp. 75, 137.
64 Eggum, *Munch and Photography*, p. 6.
65 Flam, *Matisse on Art*, p. 54.
66 Brassaï, *Conversations with Picasso*, p. 55.
67 Richardson, *A Life of Picasso*, Vol. 2, p. 108.
68 Flam, *Matisse*, pp. 183, 197, 269, 315.
69 Hamilton, *Painting and Sculpture in Europe, 1880–1940*, p. 237.
70 Rubin, *"Primitivism" in 20th Century Art*, p. 10.
71 Hirst and Burn, *On the Way to Work*, p. 169.
72 Lynes, *Good Old Modern*.
73 Heilbrun and Gray, *The Economics of Art and Culture*, p. 191.
74 Schubert, *The Curator's Egg*, pp. 70–79; Meyer, *The Art Museum*, pp. 106–17.
75 Schubert, *The Curator's Egg*, chap. 6.
76 Button, *The Turner Prize*.
77 Berger, *The Success and Failure of Picasso*, p. 3.
78 Wittkower and Wittkower, *Born Under Saturn*, p. 40.
79 Wittkower and Wittkower, *Born Under Saturn*, p. 278.
80 Van de Wetering, *Rembrandt*, pp. 265–66.
81 Walker, *Art and Celebrity*, p. 197.
82 Cottington, *Modern Art*, p. 74.
83 Walker, *Art and Celebrity*, p. 197.
84 Brassaï, *Conversations with Picasso*, p. 50.
85 Cottington, *Modern Art*, p. 90.
86 Karmel, *Jackson Pollock*, p. 63.
87 Friedman, *Jackson Pollock*, p. 213.
88 Pratt, *The Critical Response to Andy Warhol*, p. 149.
89 Cottington, *Modern Art*, p. 91.
90 Gabler, *Life the Movie*, p. 135.
91 Pratt, *The Critical Response to Andy Warhol*, pp. 8, 60.
92 Pratt, *The Critical Response to Andy Warhol*, p. 207.
93 Hirst and Burn, *On the Way to Work*, pp. 86, 72.
94 Walker, *Art and Celebrity*, p. 244.
95 Saltz, *Seeing Out Loud*, pp. 218–19.
96 Saltz, *Seeing Out Loud*, p. 220.
97 Kubler, *The Shape of Time*, p. 12.

Chapter 2

1 Courthion and Cailler, *Portrait of Manet*, p. 160.
2 Wollen, *Paris Hollywood*, pp. 217, 222.

3   Five of these studies are included in Galenson, *Artistic Capital*; see table
    1.3, p. 7; table 2.1, p. 25; table 3.2, p. 48; table 4.3, p. 68; and table 7.5,
    p. 111. The other studies are Galenson, "One-Hit Wonders," table 7, p. 107;
    Galenson, "Toward Abstraction," table 2, p. 100; Galenson, "Who Are the
    Greatest Living Artists?"; and Galenson and Weinberg, "Age and the Quality
    of Work," table 4, p. 774.
4   On the use of illustrations as a measure of importance, see, e.g., Galenson,
    Artistic Capital, pp. 5–6.
5   Gilot and Lake, *Life with Picasso*, p. 272.
6   Flam, *Matisse on Art*, p. 84.
7   Barr, *Matisse*, p. 56.
8   Spurling, *The Unknown Matisse*, p. 323.
9   Spurling, *The Unknown Matisse*, pp. 293–94.
10 Barr, *Matisse*, p. 61.
11 Barr, *Matisse*, p. 63.
12 Barr, *Matisse*, p. 61.
13 Giry, *Fauvism*, p. 250.
14 Flam, *Matisse on Art*, pp. 37–40.
15 Flam, *Matisse on Art*, p. 80.
16 Flam, *Matisse on Art*, p. 85.
17 Flam, *Matisse on Art*, p. 185.
18 Flam, *Matisse on Art*, p. 2.
19 Breslin, *Mark Rothko*, p. 283.
20 Flam, *Matisse on Art*, p. 177.
21 Berger, *Selected Essays*, p. 35.
22 Cottington, *Modern Art*, p. 46.
23 Kahnweiler, *My Galleries and Painters*, p. 152.
24 Zurcher, *Georges Braque*, p. 85.
25 Golding, *Cubism*, rev. ed., p. 15.
26 Hamilton, *Painting and Sculpture in Europe*, p. 235.
27 Berger, *Selected Essays*, pp. 72, 84.
28 Gilot and Lake, *Life with Picasso*, p. 74.
29 Richardson, *A Life of Picasso*, 2:83.
30 Cooper, *The Cubist Epoch*, p. 42.
31 Gilot and Lake, *Life with Picasso*, p. 76.
32 Sylvester, *About Modern Art*, p. 445.
33 Richardson, *A Life of Picasso*, 2:103–05; Golding, *Cubism*, rev. ed., pp. 65,
    185.
34 Loran, *Cézanne's Composition*, p. 76; Golding, *Cubism*, rev. ed., pp. 69–70;
    Schapiro, *Modern Art*, p. 27.
35 Hamilton, *Painting and Sculpture in Europe*, p. 238.
36 Hamilton, *Painting and Sculpture in Europe*, p. 246.
37 Golding, *Cubism*, rev. ed., pp. 114–17.
38 Fry, *A Roger Fry Reader*, p. 343.
39 Kahnweiler, *My Galleries and Painters*, p. 46.
40 Cabanne, *Dialogues with Marcel Duchamp*, p. 12.
41 Kuh, *The Artist's Voice*, pp. 89–90.

42 Cabanne, *Dialogues with Marcel Duchamp*, p. 125.
43 Sanouillet and Peterson, *The Writings of Marcel Duchamp*, p. 125.
44 Cabanne, *Dialogues with Marcel Duchamp*, pp. 30, 34; Sanouillet and Peterson, *The Writings of Marcel Duchamp*, p. 124.
45 Tomkins, *Duchamp*, pp. 81–83.
46 Cabanne, *Dialogues with Marcel Duchamp*, p. 31.
47 Tomkins, *The Bride and the Bachelors*, pp. 24–25.
48 Kuenzli and Naumann, *Marcel Duchamp*, p. 33.
49 Sanouillet and Peterson, *The Writings of Marcel Duchamp*, p. 141.
50 Ades, Cox, and Hopkins, *Marcel Duchamp*, p. 151.
51 Masheck, *Marcel Duchamp in Perspective*, p. 4.
52 Breton, *Surrealism and Painting*, p. 86.
53 Tomkins, *Off the Wall*, p. 125.
54 Cabanne, *Dialogues with Marcel Duchamp*, p. 109.
55 Cabanne, *Dialogues with Marcel Duchamp*, p. 12.
56 Golding, *Paths to the Absolute*, p. 67.
57 Kandinsky, *Complete Writings on Art*, p. 806.
58 Kandinsky, *Complete Writings on Art*, p. 806.
59 Kandinsky, *Complete Writings on Art*, pp. 170–71.
60 Kandinsky, *Complete Writings on Art*, p. 370.
61 Kandinsky, *Complete Writings on Art*, p. 396.
62 Hamilton, *Painting and Sculpture in Europe*, pp. 212–13.
63 Kandinsky, *Complete Writings on Art*, p. 403.
64 Seuphor, *Piet Mondrian*, p. 96.
65 Seuphor, *Piet Mondrian*, p. 117.
66 Seuphor, *Piet Mondrian*, p. 117.
67 Blotkamp, *Mondrian*, p. 81.
68 Cooper and Spronk, *Mondrian*, p. 18.
69 Blotkamp, *Mondrian*, pp. 66–127.
70 Blotkamp, *Mondrian*, p. 240.
71 Schapiro, *Modern Art*, pp. 256–57.
72 Milner, *Kazimir Malevich and the Art of Geometry*, pp. 60–63.
73 Milner, *Kazimir Malevich and the Art of Geometry*, pp. 124–25.
74 Malevich, *Essays on Art*, 1:92, 94.
75 Zhadova, *Malevich*, p. 53; Crone and Moos, *Kazimir Malevich*, p. 158.
76 Golding, *Paths to the Absolute*, p. 74.
77 Golding, *Paths to the Absolute*, p. 78.
78 Moore, *Henry Moore*, p. 145.
79 Geist, *Brancusi*, p. 2.
80 Wittkower, *Sculpture*, pp. 253–55.
81 Geist, *Brancusi/The Kiss*, p. 99.
82 Geist, *Constantin Brancusi*, p. 21.
83 Hamilton, *Painting and Sculpture in Europe*, p. 462.
84 Geist, *Brancusi*, p. 151.
85 Sylvester, *About Modern Art*, p. 429.
86 Golding, *Visions of the Modern*, p. 190.
87 Lewis, *Constantin Brancusi*, p. 19.

88	Geist, *Constantin Brancusi*, p. 23.
89	Sylvester, *About Modern Art*, p. 431.
90	Geist, *Brancusi/The Kiss*, p. 99.
91	Blesh, *Modern Art USA*, pp. 253–54.
92	Porter, *Art In Its Own Terms*, p. 36.
93	Terenzio, *The Collected Writings of Robert Motherwell*, p. 198.
94	Greenberg, *The Collected Essays and Criticism*, 2:193.
95	Galenson, *Artistic Capital*, chap. 4.
96	Friedman, *Jackson Pollock*, p. 100.
97	Sylvester, *Interviews with American Artists*, p. 57.
98	Breslin, *Mark Rothko*, p. 240.
99	Karmel, *Jackson Pollock*, p. 17.
100	Karmel, *Jackson Pollock*, p. 78.
101	Kimmelman, *Portraits*, p. 52.
102	Karmel, *Jackson Pollock*, p. 20.
103	Kimmelman, *Portraits*, p. 54.
104	Carmean and Rathbone, *American Art at Mid-Century*, p. 157.
105	Sylvester, *Interviews with American Artists*, p. 48.
106	Hess, *Willem de Kooning*, p. 142.
107	Breslin, *Mark Rothko*, p. 526.
108	Breslin, *Mark Rothko*, pp. 316–17.
109	De Kooning, *The Spirit of Abstract Expressionism*, p. 170.
110	Harrison and Wood, *Art in Theory*, p. 569.
111	Rodman, *Conversations with Artists*, pp. 93–94.
112	Bowness, *Modern European Art*, p. 147.
113	Newman, *Selected Writings and Interviews*, p. 251; Schapiro, *Modern Art*, p. 218.
114	Kimmelman, *Portraits*, p. 54.
115	Kimmelman, *Portraits*, p. 115.
116	Karmel, *Jackson Pollock*, p. 15.
117	Ruscha, *Leave Any Information at the Signal*, p. 11.
118	Tomkins, "Everything in Sight," p. 75.
119	Tomkins, *The Bride and the Bachelors*, p. 210.
120	Johns, *Writings, Sketchbook Notes, Interviews*, p. 136.
121	Harrison and Wood, *Art in Theory*, p. 736.
122	Johns, *Writings, Sketchbook Notes, Interviews*, p. 113.
123	Tomkins, *Off the Wall*, pp. 96–97.
124	Tomkins, *Off the Wall*, p. 87.
125	Danto, *The Madonna of the Future*, p. 273.
126	Danto, *The Madonna of the Future*, p. 236.
127	Johns, *Writings, Sketchbook Notes, Interviews*, p. 113.
128	Danto, *The Madonna of the Future*, p. 236.
129	Ruscha, *Leave Any Information at the Signal*, pp. 117–18.
130	Rubin, *Frank Stella*, p. 12.
131	Galenson, *Artistic Capital*, pp. 54, 129; Battcock, *Minimal Art*, pp. 119, 262, 309.
132	Madoff, *Pop Art*, pp. 96, 189–90, 208, 294, 309.
133	Danto, *The Madonna of the Future*, p. 236.

134 Coplans, *Provocations*, p. 94.
135 McShine, *Warhol*, p. 427.
136 Madoff, *Pop Art*, p. 225.
137 Garrels, *The Work of Andy Warhol*, pp. 86–88.
138 Bockris, *Warhol*, pp. 151–55.
139 Coplans, *Andy Warhol*, p. 49.
140 Tomkins, *Marcel Duchamp*, p. 415.
141 Goldsmith, *I'll Be Your Mirror*, p. 18.
142 Bockris, *Warhol*, p. 163; Goldsmith, *I'll Be Your Mirror*, p. 17.
143 Warhol, *THE Philosophy of Andy Warhol*, p. 178.
144 Storr, *Chuck Close*, pp. 87–89.
145 Prather, *Claes Oldenburg*, p. 2.
146 Madoff, *Pop Art*, pp. 213–15.
147 Sylvester, *Interviews with American Artists*, p. 214.
148 Rosenberg, *The De-definition of Art*, pp. 118–20.
149 Prather, *Claes Oldenburg*, p. 1.
150 Sylvester, *Interviews with American Artists*, pp. 206–07.
151 Madoff, *Pop Art*, p. 225.
152 Gauguin, *The Writings of a Savage*, p. 267.
153 Schapiro, *Worldview in Painting*, p. 142.

Chapter 3

1 Greenberg, *The Collected Essays and Criticism*, 4:118.
2 Schapiro, *Worldview in Painting*, p. 204.
3 E.g., see Galenson, "Who Are the Greatest Living Artists?"
4 Sanouillet and Peterson, *The Writings of Marcel Duchamp*, p. 138.
5 Galenson, *Artistic Capital*, table 1.3, p. 7; table 2.2, p. 26; table 8.3, p. 129; Galenson, "One-Hit Wonders," tables 8, 12, pp. 108–110; Galenson, "The Greatest Artists of the Twentieth Century."
6 These books are listed in the appendix to Chap. 2, this text.
7 Apollinaire, *The Cubist Painters*, p. 13.
8 Hamilton, *Painting and Sculpture in Europe*, p. 235; Russell, *The Meanings of Modern Art*, p. 97.
9 Richardson, *A Life of Picasso*, 1:411–14.
10 Rubin, Seckel, and Cousins, *Les Demoiselles d'Avignon*, pp. 14, 119.
11 Rubin, *Pablo Picasso*.
12 Richardson, *A Life of Picasso*, 2:45, 83.
13 Gersh-Nesic, *The Early Criticism of André Salmon*, p. 40.
14 Cabanne, *Dialogues with Marcel Duchamp*, p. 31.
15 Cabanne, *Dialogues with Marcel Duchamp*, p. 30.
16 Cabanne, *Dialogues with Marcel Duchamp*, p. 34; Sanouillet and Peterson, *The Writings of Marcel Duchamp*, p. 124.
17 Tomkins, *Duchamp*, pp. 81–83.
18 Tomkins, *Duchamp*, pp. 116–17.
19 Tomkins, *The Bride and the Bachelors*, p. 22.
20 Danto, *The Madonna of the Future*, p. 179.
21 Coen, *Umberto Boccioni*, p. 234.

22 Golding, Boccioni's *"Unique Forms of Continuity in Space,"* p. 14.

23 Golding, Boccioni's *"Unique Forms of Continuity in Space,"* p. 14.

24 Apollinaire, *Apollinaire on Art*, p. 321.

25 Golding, Boccioni's *"Unique Forms of Continuity in Space,"* p. 28.

26 Golding, Boccioni's *"Unique Forms of Continuity in Space,"* p. 3.

27 Ades, Cox, and Hopkins, *Marcel Duchamp*, p. 151.

28 Tomkins, *Duchamp*, p. 185.

29 Masheck, *Marcel Duchamp in Perspective*, p. 71.

30 Masheck, *Marcel Duchamp in Perspective*, p. 84.

31 Recent evidence of this was provided by an English survey of 500 artists, curators, critics, and dealers, commissioned by the sponsor of the Turner Prize. *Fountain* was voted the most influential work of modern art, ahead of *Les Demoiselles d'Avignon*, which placed second. The surprising success of *Fountain* in the poll was attributed to overwhelming support from the artists who responded; Higgins, "Work of art that inspired a movement . . . a urinal."

32 Lodder, *Russian Constructivism*, p. 65.

33 Lodder, *Russian Constructivism*, p. 60.

34 Milner, *Vladimir Tatlin and the Russian Avant-Garde*, chap. 8.

35 Lodder, *Russian Constructivism*, p. 56.

36 Barr, *Picasso*, p. 202.

37 Chipp, *Picasso's Guernica*, p. 78.

38 Arnheim, *The Genesis of a Painting*, pp. 134–35.

39 Hamilton, *Painting and Sculpture in Europe*, pp. 458–59.

40 Gombrich, *Preference for the Primitive*, p. 237.

41 Hamilton, *Collected Words*, p. 35.

42 Madoff, *Pop Art*, p. xvii.

43 Livingstone, *Pop Art*, p. 36.

44 Flam, *Robert Smithson*, p. 175.

45 Flam, *Robert Smithson*, p. 68.

46 Flam, *Robert Smithson*, p. 143–53.

47 Varnedoe, *Pictures of Nothing*, p. 168.

48 Sylvester, *About Modern Art*, p. 353.

49 Galenson, "One-Hit Wonders," pp. 101–17.

50 See Chap. 2, above.

51 See Chap. 7, below.

52 Schapiro, *Worldview in Painting*, p. 193.

53 Varnedoe, *Pictures of Nothing*, pp. 266–67.

54 Hughes, *The Shock of the New*, pp. 110–111.

55 Jensen, "Anticipating Artistic Behavior," p. 144.

56 Galenson, *Artistic Capital*, pp. 126, 253.

57 Danto, *Unnatural Wonders*, p. 99.

Chapter 4

1 Bowness, *The Conditions of Success*, p. 50.

2 Solomon, "Frank Stella's Expressionist Phase," p. 47.

3 Foster, Krauss, Bois, and Buchloh, *Art Since 1900*, p. 12. The italics are mine.
4 Bowness, *The Conditions of Success*, p. 51.
5 These books are listed in the appendix to Chap. 2.
6 See Chaps. 2 and 3.
7 For discussion and examples, see Galenson, *Artistic Capital*, chaps. 1–2.
8 Bowness, *The Conditions of Success*, p. 51.
9 See Table 3.2.
10 Golding, *Cubism*, rev. ed., p. 15.
11 See Chap. 6, below.
12 Garrels, *The Work of Andy Warhol*, p. 87.
13 Galenson, *Artistic Capital*, p. 50.
14 Bockris, *Warhol*, pp. 145–48.
15 Madoff, *Pop Art*, p. 101.
16 Bockris, *Warhol*, p. 145.
17 Madoff, *Pop Art*, p. 296.
18 Bockris, *Warhol*, p. 170.
19 Karmel, *Jackson Pollock*, pp. 97–103, 118–75.
20 E.g., see Karmel, *Jackson Pollock*, pp. 126, 266; Varnedoe, *Jackson Pollock*, pp. 48–62.
21 Friedman, *Jackson Pollock*, p. 160.
22 Karmel, *Jackson Pollock*, p. 170.
23 Golding, *Paths to the Absolute*, p. 67.
24 See Table 2.2, above.
25 Malevich, *Essays on Art*, 1:94.
26 Golding, *Paths to the Absolute*, p. 62–67.
27 See Table 3.2, above.
28 Higgins, "Work of art that inspired a movement . . . a urinal."
29 For discussions, see Chap. 3, above.
30 Kandinsky, *Complete Writings on Art*, p. 370.
31 Golding, *Visions of the Modern*, p. 67.
32 Galenson, *Old Masters and Young Geniuses*, pp. 18–19; Sylvester, *About Modern Art*, p. 445; Bowness, *The Conditions of Success*, pp. 51–54.
33 Kahnweiler, *My Galleries and Painters*, p. 46.
34 See Table 2.2, above.
35 Henkels, *Mondrian*, pp. 16–17.
36 Bowness, *Modern European Art*, p. 105.
37 See Chap. 7, below.
38 Sylvester, *About Modern Art*, p. 30.
39 Sylvester, *About Modern Art*, p. 447.
40 Madoff, *Pop Art*, p. 299.
41 See Chap. 2, above.

Chapter 5

1 Heller, *Women Artists*, p. 111.
2 For discussion, see Galenson, *Artistic Capital*, pp. 4–6.

3 Rosen and Brawer, *Making Their Mark*, p. 187; Heller, *Women Artists*, p. 8.
4 See the appendix to this chapter for a list of these books.
5 See the appendix to this chapter.
6 Slatkin, *The Voices of Women Artists*, p. 231.
7 Slatkin, *The Voices of Women Artists*, p. 226.
8 Lynes, *O'Keeffe, Stieglitz and the Critics*, p. 264.
9 Hartley, *On Art*, p. 106.
10 Messinger, *Georgia O'Keeffe*, p. 141.
11 Kuh, *The Artist's Voice*, p. 194.
12 Drohojowska-Philp, *Full Bloom*, p. 450.
13 Lynes, *O'Keeffe, Stieglitz and the Critics*, p. 303.
14 Lynes, *O'Keeffe, Stieglitz and the Critics*, p. 288.
15 Kuh, *The Artist's Voice*, pp. 190–91.
16 Goodrich and Bry, *Georgia O'Keeffe*, p. 19.
17 Lynes, *O'Keeffe, Stieglitz and the Critics*, p. 180.
18 Lynes, *O'Keeffe, Stieglitz and the Critics*, p. 288
19 Drohojowska-Philp, *Full Bloom*, p. 478.
20 Drohojowska-Philp, *Full Bloom*, p. 240.
21 Drohojowska-Philp, *Full Bloom*, p. 413.
22 Messinger, *Georgia O'Keeffe*, pp. 79–88; Goodrich and Bry, *Georgia O'Keeffe*, p. 17.
23 Wagner, *Three Artists (Three Women)*, p. 70.
24 Herrera, *Frida*, p. 254.
25 Dexter and Barson, *Frida Kahlo*, p. 55.
26 Breton, *Surrealism and Painting*, p. 144.
27 Herrera, *Frida*, p. 255.
28 Herrera, *Frida*, pp. 256–57.
29 Herrera, *Frida*, p. 316.
30 Herrera, *Frida*, p. 322.
31 Herrera, *Frida*, pp. 258, 263.
32 Herrera, *Frida*, p. 266.
33 Breton, *Surrealism and Painting*, p. 144.
34 Chadwick, *Mirror Images*, pp. 164–67. In 1979 a friend held a costume party for which guests were to dress up as their favorite artist, and Mendieta attended as Frida Kahlo; Viso, *Ana Mendieta*, p. 71.
35 Cottington, *Modern Art*, p. 89.
36 Wollen, *Paris Manhattan*, pp. 240, 246.
37 Lippard, *Eva Hesse*, p. 32.
38 Lippard, *Eva Hesse*, pp. 172, 96, 197.
39 Lippard, *Eva Hesse*, p. 14.
40 Lippard, *Eva Hesse*, p. 56.
41 Nemser, *Art Talk*, p. 180.
42 Nixon, *Eva Hesse*, p. 28.
43 Levin, *Beyond Modernism*, p. 62.
44 Lippard, *Eva Hesse*, p. 196.
45 Stiles and Selz, *Theories and Documents of Contemporary Art*, p. 791.

46 Kimmelman, *Portraits*, p. 146.
47 Krauss, *Cindy Sherman*, p. 17.
48 Slatkin, *The Voices of Women Artists*, p. 312.
49 Sherman, *The Complete "Untitled Film Stills,"* p. 7.
50 Meyer, *Brushes with History*, p. 445.
51 Slatkin, *The Voices of Women Artists*, pp. 313–16.
52 Nairne, *State of the Art*, p. 132.
53 Schjeldahl and Phillips, *Cindy Sherman*, p. 7.
54 Schjeldahl and Phillips, *Cindy Sherman*, p. 13.
55 Kimmelman, *Portraits*, p. 148.
56 Sherman, *The Complete "Untitled Film Stills,"* pp. 14–15.
57 Schjeldahl and Phillips, *Cindy Sherman*, p. 14.
58 Danto, *Unnatural Wonders*, p. 293.
59 Sherman, *Untitled Film Stills*, p. 14.
60 Schjeldahl, *The "7 Days" Art Columns*, p. 114.
61 Schjeldahl and Phillips, *Cindy Sherman*, p. 13.
62 Polsky, *Art Market Guide*, p. 129.
63 Bourgeois, *Destruction of the Father, Reconstruction of the Father*, p. 261.
64 Bourgeois, *Destruction of the Father, Reconstruction of the Father*, pp. 66, 91, 162, 169, 218, 262, 318.
65 Wye, *Louise Bourgeois*, p. 11.
66 Bourgeois, *Destruction of the Father, Reconstruction of the Father*, pp. 277, 158.
67 Bourgeois, *Destruction of the Father, Reconstruction of the Father*, p. 97.
68 Wye, *Louise Bourgeois*, p. 33.
69 Hughes, *Nothing If Not Critical*, p. 285.
70 Wullschlager, "Rachel Whiteread."
71 Bourgeois, *Destruction of the Father, Reconstruction of the Father*, p. 166.
72 Bourgeois, *Destruction of the Father, Reconstruction of the Father*, p. 319.
73 Galenson, *Painting Outside the Lines*, pp. 26–29, 181–90.

Chapter 6

 1 Brassaï, *Conversations with Picasso*, p. 69.
 2 Golding, *Cubism*, rev. ed., p. 103; *OED*, 3:469.
 3 Golding, *Cubism*, rev. ed., p. 103.
 4 Golding, *Cubism*, rev. ed., p. 105.
 5 *OED*, 11:166.
 6 Richardson, *A Life of Picasso*, 2:249.
 7 Hamilton, *Painting and Sculpture in Europe*, p. 247.
 8 Arnason, *History of Modern Art*, pp. 208–09; also see Hunter, Jacobus, and Wheeler, *Modern Art*, p. 159.
 9 Andrews, *Art Into Life*, p. 21.
10 *OED*, 3:794.
11 Dabrowski, "The Russian Contribution to Modernism," chaps. 2–3.
12 Sanouillet and Peterson, *The Writings of Marcel Duchamp*, p. 141; *OED*, 13:270.

13 E.g., Tomkins, *Off the Wall*, p. 125.

14 Masheck, *Marcel Duchamp in Perspective*, p. 126; also see p. 11.

15 For discussion, see Galenson, *Old Masters and Young Geniuses*, pp. 86–93, and Chap. 14, this text.

16 *OED*, 2:209.

17 Rubin, *Dada, Surrealism, and Their Heritage*, p. 40–41.

18 Arnason, *History of Modern Art*, p. 245.

19 Hancock and Poley, *Arp*, pp. 62–67.

20 That the papers were not actually placed in this way is confirmed by Rubin, *Dada, Surrealism, and Their Heritage*, p. 41.

21 *OED*, 11:166; Arnason, *History of Modern Art*, p. 292.

22 Arnason, *History of Modern Art*, pp. 256–57.

23 Elderfield, *Kurt Schwitters*, pp. 12, 27, 50, 94.

24 *OED*, 11:725.

25 Rubin, *Dada, Surrealism, and Their Heritage*, p. 42; Evans and Gohl, *Photomontage*, pp. 10–16.

26 Richter, *Dada*, p. 118.

27 Arnason, *History of Modern Art*, p. 205; Hamilton, *Painting and Sculpture in Europe*, p. 317.

28 Hamilton, *Painting and Sculpture in Europe*, p. 317.

29 Arnason, *History of Modern Art*, p. 205; Hamilton, *Painting and Sculpture in Europe*, pp. 317–18.

30 Baldwin, *Man Ray*, p. 96; *OED*, 13:243.

31 *OED*, 11:721; Baldwin, *Man Ray*, pp. 98–99.

32 *OED*, 6:223.

33 Ernst, *Beyond Painting*, p. 7.

34 Ernst, *Beyond Painting*, pp. 8–9.

35 Arnason, *History of Modern Art*, p. 288.

36 Breton, *Surrealism and Painting*, p. 288–89.

37 Breton, *Surrealism and Painting*, p. 290.

38 Arnason, *History of Modern Art*, p. 344.

39 Passuth, *Moholy-Nagy*, pp. 53–55.

40 Calder, *Calder*, p. 113.

41 Calder, *Calder*, p. 127; *OED*, 9:929.

42 Calder, *Calder*, p. 130; *OED*, 16:429.

43 Arnason, *History of Modern Art*, p. 326; Tucker, *Brassaï*, p. 76.

44 Rubin, *Dada, Surrealism, and Their Heritage*, p. 143.

45 Rubin, *Dada, Surrealism, and Their Heritage*, p. 211; *OED Additions Series*, 2:97.

46 Breton, *Surrealism and Painting*, p. 280. Duchamp later explained that the readymades were not related to found objects: "My Ready-Mades have nothing to do with the *objet trouvé* because the so-called 'found object' is completely directed by personal taste. Personal taste decides that this is a beautiful object and is unique. That most of my Ready-Mades were mass produced and could be duplicated is another important difference"; Kuh, *The Artist's Voice*, pp. 90–92.

47 Rubin, *Dada, Surrealism, and Their Heritage*, p. 144.

48 Arnason, *History of Modern Art*, p. 465; Crispolti and Meessen, *Lucio Fontana*, p. 136.

49 Taylor, *Collage*, p. 148.

50 Arnason, *History of Modern Art*, p. 515; Hunter, Jacobus, and Wheeler, *Modern Art*, p. 331.

51 *OED*, 5:315.

52 Crispolti and Meessen, *Lucio Fontana*, pp. 142–43; Perry and Wood, *Themes in Contemporary Art*, p. 199.

53 Kaprow, *Assemblage, Environments and Happenings*, p. 159.

54 *OED*, 1:705.

55 Galenson, *Artistic Capital*, pp. 73–77; Selz, *The Work of Jean Dubuffet*, pp. 84–85.

56 Seitz, *The Art of Assemblage*, p. 150; Selz, *The Work of Jean Dubuffet*, p. 84.

57 Selz, *The Work of Jean Dubuffet*, pp. 116–23.

58 Selz, *The Work of Jean Dubuffet*, pp. 121, 105.

59 Seitz, *The Art of Assemblage*, p. 6.

60 Dempsey, *Art in the Modern Era*, pp. 215–16.

61 Arnason, *History of Modern Art*, p. 484; Hunter, Jacobus, and Wheeler, *Modern Art*, pp. 300–01; Dempsey, *Art in the Modern Era*, p. 205.

62 Galenson, *Artistic Capital*, p. 50.

63 Dempsey, *Art in the Modern Era*, p. 206.

64 E.g., Steinberg, *Other Criteria*, pp. 85–90; Danto, *The Madonna of the Future*, pp. 273–78; Dempsey, *Art in the Modern Era*, p. 206.

65 Schimmel, *Robert Rauschenberg Combines*.

66 Danto, *The Madonna of the Future*, p. 278.

67 Hulten, *Jean Tinguely*, p. 28.

68 Arnason, *History of Modern Art*, p. 510.

69 Arnason, *History of Modern Art*, p. 516; Hunter, Jacobus, and Wheeler, *Modern Art*, p. 360.

70 Arnason, *History of Modern Art*, p. 516.

71 Celant, *Piero Manzoni*, p. 132.

72 Chernow, *Christo and Jeanne-Claude*, p. 50.

73 Arnason, *History of Modern Art*, pp. 513–14; Galenson, *Artistic Capital*, p. 129.

74 Chernow, *Christo and Jeanne-Claude*, p. 80.

75 Arnason, *History of Modern Art*, p. 465.

76 Crispolti and Meessen, *Lucio Fontana*, pp. 146–47.

77 *OED*, 6:1097; Kelley, *Childsplay*, p. 1.

78 Kaprow, *Essays on the Blurring of Art and Life*, p. xxvii.

79 Kaprow, *Essays on the Blurring of Art and Life*, p. xxvii–xxviii.

80 Kaprow, *Essays on the Blurring of Art and Life*, p. xxviii.

81 Kaprow, *Essays on the Blurring of Art and Life*, p. 15–26.

82 Hunter, Jacobus, and Wheeler, *Modern Art*, p. 314.

83 Kaprow, *Essays on the Blurring of Art and Life*, p. 61; Hunter, Jacobus, and Wheeler, *Modern Art*, p. 314.

84 *OED*, 6:614; Dempsey, *Art in the Modern Era*, p. 257.

85 Arnason, *History of Modern Art*, p. 594.
86 *OED Additions Series*, 1:11; Stiles and Selz, *Theories and Documents of Contemporary Art*, pp. 385–86.
87 Stiles and Selz, *Theories and Documents of Contemporary Art*, p. 386.
88 Smith, *Pete Townshend*, pp. 14–15.
89 Arnason, *History of Modern Art*, p. 510; Hunter, Jacobus, and Wheeler, *Modern Art*, p. 330.
90 Charlet, *Yves Klein*, p. 170.
91 Arnason, *History of Modern Art*, p. 510.
92 Stich, *Yves Klein*, p. 198.
93 Klein, *Le Dépassement de la problématique de l'art et d'autres écrits*, p. 295.
94 Van der Marck, *Arman*, pp. 59–63.
95 Arnason, *History of Modern Art*, p. 513.
96 Arnason, *History of Modern Art*, p. 511.
97 Van der Marck, *Arman*, pp. 63–72.
98 Arnason, *History of Modern Art*, p. 452; Baldaccini-Puigsegur, *César*, p. 115.
99 Mathey, *Trois sculpteurs*, unpaginated.
100 Arnason, *History of Modern Art*, p. 511.
101 Perlein, *Niki de Saint Phalle*, p. 32
102 Perlein, *Niki de Saint Phalle*, p. 33.
103 Ashbery, *Reported Sightings*, p. 146; Perlein, *Niki de Saint Phalle*, pp. 106, 112.
104 Arnason, *History of Modern Art*, p. 515; Hunter, Jacobus, and Wheeler, *Modern Art*, p. 368.
105 Celant, *Piero Manzoni*, p. 32.
106 Buck, *Moving Targets 2*, pp. 19–22; Button, *The Turner Prize*, pp. 44–48.
107 *OED*, 15:930.
108 Madoff, *Pop Art*, pp. 228–33.
109 Arnason, *History of Modern Art*, p. 698.
110 Richter, *The Daily Practice of Painting*, pp. 22, 33–34.
111 *OED*, 15:627; Stiles and Selz, *Theories and Documents of Contemporary Art*, pp. 811–12.
112 *OED Additions Series*, 2:167; Dempsey, *Art in the Modern Era*, p. 247.
113 Perry and Wood, *Themes in Contemporary Art*, p. 202.
114 *OED*, 11:544.
115 Dempsey, *Art in the Modern Era*, p. 222.
116 Schneeman, *More than Meat Joy*, pp. 9–11.
117 Arnason, *History of Modern Art*, p. 614; Hunter, Jacobus, and Wheeler, *Modern Art*, p. 372; Smithson, *The Collected Writings*, p. 116.
118 Smithson, *The Collected Writings*, p. 68.
119 Arnason, *History of Modern Art*, p. 614.
120 Smithson, *The Collected Writings*, p. 104.
121 Arnason, *History of Modern Art*, p. 552; Garrels, *Sol LeWitt*, p. 37.
122 Zevi, *Sol LeWitt Critical Texts*, pp. 91, 95.
123 Lifson, *Samaras*, p. 43.
124 Levin, *Lucas Samaras*, pp. 23, 83; Lifson, *Samaras*, pp. 13–14.

125 Arnason, *History of Modern Art*, pp. 494–95.
126 Gruen, *The Artist Observed*, p. 235.
127 Arnason, *History of Modern Art*, pp. 481–82.
128 Livingstone, *David Hockney*, pp. 235–38.
129 Detterer, *Art Recollection*, pp. 118–19.
130 Lindsay and Vergo, *Kandinsky*, p. 152.

Chapter 7

1 Schapiro, *The Unity of Picasso's Art*, p. 1.
2 Campbell, "Plotting Polke," p. 19.
3 Danto, *Unnatural Wonders*, p. 182.
4 Schapiro, *The Unity of Picasso's Style*, p. 5.
5 Campbell, "Plotting Polke," p. 19.
6 Danto, *Unnatural Wonders*, p. 182.
7 Galenson, *Painting Outside the Lines*, p. 51.
8 E.g., see Hamilton, *Painting and Sculpture in Europe*, p. 237.
9 Berger, *Selected Essays*, pp. 72, 82, 84.
10 Thistlewood, *Sigmar Polke*, pp. 46–49.
11 Barr, *Picasso*, p. 202.
12 Richter, *The Daily Practice of Painting*, p. 173.
13 Golding, *Cubism*, p. 60.
14 Richter, *The Daily Practice of Painting*, pp. 78, 30, 130.
15 Richter, *The Daily Practice of Painting*, p. 115.
16 Schjeldahl, *Let's See*, p. 144.
17 Henkels, *Mondrian*, p. 203.
18 Schlemmer, *The Letters and Diaries of Oskar Schlemmer*, p. 102.
19 McCully, *A Picasso Anthology*, pp. 146–48.
20 Thistlewood, *Sigmar Polke*, p. 2.
21 Sanouillet and Peterson, *The Writings of Marcel Duchamp*, p. 157.
22 Lindsay and Vergo, *Kandinsky*, p. 52.
23 Fry, *A Roger Fry Reader*, p. 115.
24 McCully, *A Picasso Anthology*, p. 145.
25 McCully, *A Picasso Anthology*, p. 157.
26 McCully, *A Picasso Anthology*, p. 170.
27 Berger, *The Success and Failure of Picasso*, pp. 35–36.
28 Cabanne, *Pablo Picasso*, p. 272.
29 Schapiro, *The Unity of Picasso's Art*, p. 2.
30 Schapiro, *The Unity of Picasso's Art*, p. 29.
31 Flam, *Matisse and Picasso*, p. 122.
32 Schapiro, *The Unity of Picasso's Art*, p. 7.
33 Flam, *Matisse and Picasso*, p. 125.
34 Sylvester, *About Modern Art*, p. 30.
35 Barr, *Picasso*, pp. 270–71.
36 Rewald, *Paul Cézanne Letters*, pp. 293–94.
37 Brassaï, *Conversations with Picasso*, p. 107.
38 Barr, *Picasso*, p. 270.

39   Apollinaire, *The Cubist Painters*, p. 73.
40   McEvilley, *The Triumph of Anti-Art*, p. 105.
41   Kuenzli and Naumann, *Marcel Duchamp*, pp. 32–33.
42   Coplans, *Provocations*, p. 64.
43   Masheck, *Marcel Duchamp in Perspective*, p. 43.
44   McEvilley, *The Triumph of Anti-Art*, pp. 20, 28.
45   Cabanne, *Dialogues with Marcel Duchamp*, p. 37.
46   Camfield, *Francis Picabia*, p. 4.
47   Camfield, *Francis Picabia*, p. xvii.
48   Sanouillet and Peterson, *The Writings of Marcel Duchamp*, pp. 156–57.
49   Camfield, *Francis Picabia*, p. xvi.
50   Camfield, *Francis Picabia*, p. xvi.
51   Camfield, *Francis Picabia*, p. xvi.
52   Camfield, *Francis Picabia*, p. xv.
53   Camfield, *Francis Picabia*, p. 188.
54   Felix, *Francis Picabia*, p. 12.
55   Camfield, *Francis Picabia*, p. 16.
56   Jouffroy, *Picabia*, p. 7.
57   Penrose, *Man Ray*, pp. 58, 173.
58   Man Ray, *Self Portrait*, p. 8.
59   Man Ray, *Self Portrait*, p. 299.
60   Sanouillet and Peterson, *The Writings of Marcel Duchamp*, p. 152.
61   See Table 3.2.
62   Rosenberg, *Art on the Edge*, p. 68.
63   Morphet, *Richard Hamilton*, p. 8.
64   Morphet, *Richard Hamilton*, pp. 16–18.
65   Hamilton, *Collected Words*, p. 109.
66   Stangos, *Concepts of Modern Art*, p. 230.
67   Sylvester, *About Modern Art*, pp. 283, 286.
68   Tomkins, *Duchamp*, pp. 402–03, 436.
69   Hamilton, *Collected Words*, pp. 174, 238.
70   Steinberg, *Other Criteria*, p. 90.
71   Rosenberg, *Art and Other Serious Matters*, p. 245.
72   Tomkins, *Off the Wall*, pp. 87, 134.
73   Galenson, "Was Jackson Pollock the Greatest Modern American Painter?" p. 119.
74   Tomkins, *Off the Wall*, new ed., p. xiv; Mattison, *Robert Rauschenberg*, p. 5.
75   Tomkins, *Off the Wall*, p. 235.
76   Galenson, *Painting Outside the Lines*, pp. 141–44.
77   Danto, *The Madonna of the Future*, p. 273.
78   Cork, *New Spirit, New Sculpture, New Money*, p. 253.
79   Bourdon, *Warhol*, p. 10.
80   Sklar, *Film*, p. 487.
81   Lim, *The Village Voice Film Guide*, pp. 64–65.
82   Andrew, *The Film Handbook*, p. 305.
83   Galenson, *Painting Outside the Lines*, p. 188.

84 Livingstone, *David Hockney*, p. 41.
85 Stiles and Selz, *Theories and Documents of Contemporary Art*, p. 228.
86 Livingstone, *David Hockney*, p. 43.
87 Restany, *Uriburu*, pp. 61–67.
88 Restany, *Uriburu*, pp. 158, 167.
89 Molina, *Nicolas Garcia Uriburu*, p. 11.
90 Restany, *Uriburu*, pp. 236.
91 Schjeldahl, *The "7 Days" Art Columns*, p. 198.
92 Van Bruggen, *Bruce Nauman*, p. 14.
93 Morgan, *Bruce Nauman*, p. 191.
94 Morgan, *Bruce Nauman*, p. 239.
95 Morgan, *Bruce Nauman*, p. 92.
96 Morgan, *Bruce Nauman*, p. 270.
97 Morgan, *Bruce Nauman*, p. 209.
98 Schjeldahl, *Let's See*, p. 111.
99 Buck, *Moving Targets 2*, p. 29.
100 Saltz, *Seeing Out Loud*, p. 219.
101 Buck, *Moving Targets 2*, p. 28.
102 Hirst and Burn, *On the Way to Work*, p. 32.
103 Kenner, *The Poetry of Ezra Pound*, p. 73.
104 Stauffer, *A Short History of American Poetry*, p. 259.
105 Deming, *James Joyce*, 2: 747.
106 O'Brien, *James Joyce*, p. 97.
107 Courthion, *Le Visage de Matisse*, pp. 92–93.
108 Eagleton, *The English Novel*, p. 288.
109 E.g., see Mendelson, *Pynchon*, pp. 56, 172; Pearce, *Critical Essays on Thomas Pynchon*, p. 170; Stonehill, *The Self-Conscious Novel*, p. 146.
110 Stonehill, *The Self-Conscious Novel*, p. 149; Mendelson, *Pynchon*, p. 193.
111 Mendelson, *Pynchon*, p. 167.
112 Revill, *The Roaring Silence*, p. 5.
113 Pritchett, *The Music of John Cage*.
114 Gann, *American Music in the Twentieth Century*, p. 127.
115 Kostelanetz, *Writings About John Cage*, p. 128.
116 Revill, *The Roaring Silence*, p. 13.
117 Nicholls, *The Cambridge Companion to John Cage*, p. ix.
118 Rockwell, *All American Music*, pp. 50–51.
119 Farber, *Negative Space*, p. 259.
120 Wollen, *Paris Hollywood*, pp. 80–81, 77.
121 Godard, *Godard on Godard*, p. 171.
122 Mast, *A Short History of the Movies*, p. 356.
123 Mast, *A Short History of the Movies*, p. 351.
124 Brunette, *Shoot the Piano Player*, p. 152.
125 Brunette, *Shoot the Piano Player*, p. 252.
126 Brunette, *Shoot the Piano Player*, p. 135.
127 Goldstein, *I'll Be Your Mirror*, p. 17.
128 E.g., see Van de Wetering, *Rembrandt*, pp. 162–69; Jensen, "Anticipating Artistic Behavior," pp. 137–53.

129 Brassaï, *Conversations with Picasso*, p. 69.
130 Richter, *The Daily Practice of Painting*, pp. 92–93.

Chapter 8

1   Hamilton, *Manet and his Critics*, p. 106.
2   Hamilton, *Manet and his Critics*, p. 45.
3   Hamilton, *Manet and his Critics*, pp. 71–73.
4   Hamilton, *Manet and his Critics*, p. 75.
5   Hamilton, *Manet and his Critics*, pp. 85–90.
6   Brombert, *Edouard Manet*, pp. 170–71.
7   Brombert, *Edouard Manet*, p. 167.
8   Richardson, *A Life of Picasso*, 2:83.
9   Cabanne, *Dialogues with Marcel Duchamp*, p. 95.
10 Cabanne, *Dialogues with Marcel Duchamp*, pp. 25–26.
11 Cabanne, *Dialogues with Marcel Duchamp*, p. 31.
12 Cabanne, *Dialogues with Marcel Duchamp*, p. 32.
13 Cabanne, *Dialogues with Marcel Duchamp*, p. 89.
14 Kuh, *The Artist's Voice*, pp. 89–90.
15 Sanouillet and Peterson, *The Writings of Marcel Duchamp*, p. 125.
16 Kuh, *The Artist's Voice*, p. 90.
17 Sanouillet and Peterson, *The Writings of Marcel Duchamp*, p. 141.
18 Tomkins, *Duchamp*, pp. 180–82.
19 Cabanne, *Dialogues with Marcel Duchamp*, p. 55.
20 Masheck, *Marcel Duchamp in Perspective*, p. 71.
21 Masheck, *Marcel Duchamp in Perspective*, pp. 71–72.
22 Rosenberg, *Art on the Edge*, p. 17.
23 Masheck, *Marcel Duchamp in Perspective*, p. 115.
24 Shattuck, *The Innocent Eye*, p. 288.
25 Meyer, *Brushes with History*, p. 423.
26 Danto, *Embodied Meanings*, pp. 213–14.
27 Rosenberg, *Art on the Edge*, pp. 18, 15.
28 Goldsmith, *I'll be Your Mirror*, p. 91.
29 Thistlewood, *Joseph Beuys*, p. 32.
30 Sandler, *Art of the Postmodern Era*, p. 88.
31 Stachelhaus, *Joseph Beuys*, p. 136.
32 Stiles and Selz, *Theories and Documents of Contemporary Art*, pp. 582–83, 633.
33 Ray, *Joseph Beuys*, p. 57.
34 Stachelhaus, *Joseph Beuys*, p. 125.
35 Adriani, Konnertz, and Thomas, *Joseph Beuys*, pp. 130, 274–75.
36 Thistlewood, *Joseph Beuys*, p. 32.
37 Ray, *Joseph Beuys*, pp. 200–01.
38 Stachelhaus, *Joseph Beuys*, p. 65; Rorimer, *New Art in the 60s and 70s*, p. 29.
39 Thistlewood, *Joseph Beuys*, p. 23.
40 Tomkins, *Duchamp*, p. 460.

41 Rosenberg, *Art on the Edge*, p. 98.
42 Varnedoe, *Pictures of Nothing*, p. 201.
43 Cresap, *Pop Trickster Fool*, pp. 110, 112.
44 Collings, *It Hurts*, p. 13.
45 Goldsmith, *I'll be Your Mirror*, p. 17.
46 Cresap, *Pop Trickster Fool*, p. 71.
47 Goldsmith, *I'll be Your Mirror*, pp. 87, 90.
48 Geldzahler, *Making It New*, pp. 250–51.
49 McEvilley, *The Triumph of Anti-Art*, p. 73.
50 Ashbery, *Reported Sightings*, p. 139.
51 Canaday, *Culture Gulch*, pp. 84–87.
52 Stich, *Yves Klein*, p. 133.
53 McEvilley, *The Triumph of Anti-Art*, pp. 64–65; Klein, *Le dépassement de la problématique de l'art et autres ecrits*, pp. 80–97.
54 Stich, *Yves Klein*, pp. 133–40.
55 Stich, *Yves Klein*, pp. 155–56.
56 Galenson, *Artistic Capital*, p. 78.
57 Stich, *Yves Klein*, p. 251.
58 Battcock, *Minimal Art*, pp. 300–01.
59 McEvilley, *The Triumph of Anti-Art*, p. 55.
60 Wood, *Varieties of Modernism*, p. 293.
61 Celant, *Piero Manzoni*, p. 15.
62 Celant, *Piero Manzoni*, p. 223.
63 Celant, *Piero Manzoni*, pp. 45, 201–05.
64 Cork, *Breaking Down the Barriers*, p. 520.
65 Bazile, *Manzoni*.
66 Bazile, *Manzoni*, p. 11.
67 Carrubba, *Piero Manzoni*, p. 16.
68 Button, *The Turner Prize*, p. 44.
69 Buck, *Moving Targets 2*, p. 20.
70 Collings, *Blimey!*, pp. 36–38
71 Buck, *Moving Targets 2*, p. 20
72 Sylvester, *About Modern Art*, pp. 315–16.
73 Gilbert and George, *The Words of Gilbert & George*, p. 149.
74 Sylvester, *London Recordings*, p. 149.
75 Gilbert and George, *The Words of Gilbert & George*, pp. 127, 154.
76 Sylvester, *London Recordings*, p.161.
77 Buck, *Moving Targets 2*, p. 20.
78 Stallabrass, *High Art Lite*, p. 47.
79 Hirst and Burn, *On the Way to Work*, p. 55.
80 Schjeldahl, *The "7 Days" Art Columns*, p. 81.
81 Danto, *Unnatural Wonders*, pp. 286–87.
82 Sylvester, *Interviews with American Artists*, pp. 347–49.
83 Haden-Guest, *True Colors*, p. 156.
84 Koons, *The Jeff Koons Handbook*, pp. 56, 78.
85 Haden-Guest, *True Colors*, p. 151.
86 Koons, *The Jeff Koons Handbook*, pp. 31, 33, 82, 120.

87 Sandler, *Art of the Postmodern Era*, p. 494.
88 Schjeldahl, *The "7 Days" Art Columns*, p. 83.
89 Danto, *Unnatural Wonders*, pp. 287–88.
90 Wright, *Writers on Artists*, p. 47.
91 Hirst and Burn, *On the Way to Work*, p. 60.
92 Schjeldahl, *The "7 Days" Art Columns*, p. 82.
93 Cottington, *Modern Art*, p. 93.
94 E.g., see Galenson, "Do the Young British Artists Rule?" pp. 182–83.
95 Stallabrass, *High Art Lite*, p. 36.
96 Stallabrass, *High Art Lite*, p. 37.
97 Wright, *Writers on Artists*, p. 214.
98 Collings, *Art Crazy Nation*, p. 168.
99 Cottington, *Modern Art*, pp. 93–94.
100 Button, *The Turner Prize*, p. 112.
101 Button, *The Turner Prize*, p. 112.
102 Button, *The Turner Prize*, p. 112.
103 Saltz, *Seeing Out Loud*, p. 220.
104 Brewster, "Why young, new money could fuel a bubble in hot, hip art."
105 Thomas and Vogel, "A New Prince of Wall Street Uses His Riches to Buy Art."
106 O'Hagan, "Hirst's diamond creation is art's costliest work ever."
107 Buck, *Moving Targets 2*, p. 26.
108 Stallabrass, *High Art Lite*, pp. 20–21.
109 Hirst and Burn, *On the Way to Work*, pp. 60–61, 72.
110 Danto, *Unnatural Wonders*, p. 53; Danto, *The Madonna of the Future*, p. 394.
111 Buck, *Moving Targets 2*, p. 27.
112 Collings, *Art Crazy Nation*, p. 172.
113 Sylvester, *About Modern Art*, p. 316.
114 Buck, *Moving Targets 2*, p. 28.
115 Cabanne, *Dialogues with Marcel Duchamp*, p. 89.
116 Rosenberg, *Art on the Edge*, p. 21.
117 Sanouillet and Peterson, *The Writings of Marcel Duchamp*, pp. 139–40.
118 Ades, Cox, and Hopkins, *Marcel Duchamp*, p. 205.
119 Sanouillet and Peterson, *The Writings of Marcel Duchamp*, p. 139.

Chapter 9

1 Valéry, *Degas, Manet, Morisot*, pp. 19–20.
2 The two editions differ slightly in content, so the quotations in the following discussions are drawn from both versions, as indicated in the footnotes.
3 Gilson, *Peinture et Réalité*, p. 43. This and subsequent translations are mine.
4 Gilson, *Painting and Reality*, pp. 29–30.
5 Gilson, *Painting and Reality*, p. 38.
6 Gilson, *Painting and Reality*, p. 85.
7 Gilson, *Peinture et Réalité*, p. 78.
8 Gilson, *Painting and Reality*, p. 86.

9   Gilson, *Painting and Reality*, pp. ix–x.
10 E.g., Nakamura, *Rubens and his Workshop*; Brown, Kelch, and van Thiel, *Rembrandt*.
11 Filipczak, *Picturing Art in Antwerp*, p. 82; also see Nakamura, *Rubens and his Workshop*, pp. 97–118.
12 Nakamura, *Rubens and his Workshop*, p. 119.
13 Alpers, *Rembrandt's Enterprise*, p. 102.
14 Alpers, *Rembrandt's Enterprise*, p. 101.
15 Brown, Kelch, and van Thiel, *Rembrandt*, p. 83.
16 Alpers, *Rembrandt's Enterprise*, p. 21.
17 Brown, Kelch, and van Thiel, *Rembrandt*, p. 21.
18 Alpers, *Rembrandt's Enterprise*, pp. 59–60. Also see Bomford et al., *Art in the Making*, p. 34.
19 Brown, Kelch, and van Thiel, *Rembrandt*, p. 83; Alpers, *Rembrandt's Enterprise*, p. 60.
20 Alpers, *Rembrandt's Enterprise*, p. 59.
21 Alpers, *Rembrandt's Enterprise*, p. 59.
22 The conceptual architect Walter Gropius made detailed plans for his buildings, and typically delegated responsibility for the execution of construction to assistants. The experimental Frank Lloyd Wright emphatically rejected this practice. For discussion see Galenson, "The Greatest Architects of the Twentieth Century."
23 On Raphael, Leonardo, and Michelangelo, see Jensen, "Anticipating Artistic Behavior," pp. 137–153, and Galenson, *Old Masters and Young Geniuses*, chap. 5.
24 Van de Wetering, *Rembrandt*, pp. 6, 82.
25 Van de Wetering, *Rembrandt*, pp. 82–84.
26 Filipczak, *Picturing Art in Antwerp*, p. 82.
27 Huelsenbeck, *The Dada Almanac*, p. 95.
28 Passuth, *Moholy-Nagy*, pp. 31–32.
29 Passuth, *Moholy-Nagy*, pp. 33, 394.
30 Hunter, Jacobus, and Wheeler, *Modern Art*, pp. 245–246.
31 Gilot and Lake, *Life with Picasso*, pp. 220–221.
32 Stich, *Yves Klein*, pp. 173–177.
33 Klein, *Le dépassement de la problématique de l'art et autres ecrits*, p. 296.
34 Galenson, *Artistic Capital*, pp. 68–72.
35 Tomkins, Off the Wall, p. 71; Gann, *American Music in the Twentieth Century*, pp. 127, 139.
36 Tomkins, *Off the Wall*, p. 269.
37 Tomkins, *Off the Wall*, p. 269.
38 Garrels, *The Work of Andy Warhol*, p. 86.
39 Bockris, *Warhol*, pp. 150–155.
40 Goldsmith, *I'll Be Your Mirror*, pp. 17–18.
41 Goldsmith, *I'll Be Your Mirror*, p. 48.
42 Goldsmith, *I'll Be Your Mirror*, pp. 119, 99, 297.
43 Bockris, *Warhol*, p. 164.
44 Bockris, *Warhol*, p. 170.

45   Goldsmith, *I'll Be Your Mirror*, pp. 297–298.
46   Goldsmith, *I'll Be Your Mirror*, p. 192.
47   Zevi, *Sol LeWitt Critical Texts*, p. 78.
48   Zevi, *Sol LeWitt Critical Texts*, p. 90.
49   Zevi, *Sol LeWitt Critical Texts*, p. 95.
50   Garrels, *Sol LeWitt*, pp. 38, 90.
51   Garrels, *Sol LeWitt*, p. 90.
52   Schjeldahl, *The "7 Days" Art Columns*, p. 81; Danto, *Unnatural Wonders*, p. 286.
53   Sylvester, *Interviews with American Artists*, pp. 347–351.
54   Saltz, *Seeing Out Loud*, p. 220; Brewster, "Why young, new money could fuel a bubble in hot, hip art."
55   Hirst and Burn, *On the Way to Work*, p. 19.
56   Hirst and Burn, *On the Way to Work*, p. 85.
57   Sanouillet and Peterson, *The Writings of Marcel Duchamp*, p. 142.
58   Hirst and Burn, *On the Way to Work*, p. 90.
59   Hirst and Burn, *On the Way to Work*, p. 81.
60   Button, *The Turner Prize*, p. 116.
61   Gilson, *Painting and Reality*, p. 34.
62   E.g., see Chaps. 6 and 7, this text.
63   Gilson, *Painting and Reality*, p. 31.
64   Galenson, *Old Masters and Young Geniuses*, p. 103.
65   Gilson, *Painting and Reality*, p. 31.
66   Temkin, *Contemporary Voices*, p. 58.

Chapter 10

1   Vasari, *Vasari's Lives of the Artist*, p. 232.
2   Pope-Hennessy, *Raphael*, pp. 217–21.
3   Gombrich, *Gombrich on the Renaissance*, 1:68.
4   Woollett and van Suchtelen, *Rubens and Brueghel*, pp. 2–36.
5   On the process of making the joint paintings, see Woollett and van Suchtelen, *Rubens and Brueghel*, pp. 215–48. On Rubens' conceptual practice of a division of labor within his studio in general, see Alpers, *Rembrandt's Enterprise*, p. 101.
6   The textbooks surveyed in chronological order, are the following: Ruskin, *History in Art*; Cornell, *Art*; Hartt, *Art*; Sproccati, *A Guide to Art*; Strickland, *The Annotated Mona Lisa*; Adams, *A History of Western Art*; Fleming, *Arts and Ideas*; Gombrich, *The Story of Art*; Stokstad, *Art History*; Wilkins, Schultz, and Linduff, *Art Past, Art Present*; Gebhardt, *The History of Art*; Gilbert, *Living With Art*; Kemp, *The Oxford History of Western Art*; Honour and Fleming, *The Visual Arts*; Johnson, *Art*; Cumming, *Art*; Walther, *Masterpieces of Western Art*; Davis et al., *Janson's History of Art*.
7   For a catalogue with many examples of these works, see McCabe, *Artistic Collaboration in the Twentieth Century*.
8   Breton, *Surrealism and Painting*, pp. 288–90.
9   McCabe, *Artistic Collaboration in the Twentieth Century*, pp. 74–75.

10 Jonquet, *Gilbert and George*, p. 58.
11 Sylvester, *About Modern Art*, p. 518.
12 Sylvester, *London Recordings*, p. 162.
13 Violette and Obrist, *The Words of Gilbert & George*, p. 195.
14 Sylvester, *London Recordings*, p. 149.
15 .Sylvester, *London Recordings*, p. 149.
16 Violette and Obrist, *The Words of Gilbert & George*, p. 257.
17 Sylvester, *London Recordings*, pp. 147–48.
18 E.g., see Tusa, *The Janus Aspect*, p. 108.
19 Jonquet, *Gilbert & George*, pp. 65–67.
20 Violette and Obrist, *The Words of Gilbert & George*, pp. 132, 168, 190.
21 Violette and Obrist, *The Words of Gilbert & George*, p. 192.
22 Violette and Obrist, *The Words of Gilbert & George*, p. 168.
23 Sylvester, *About Modern Art*, p. 316.
24 Buck, *Moving Targets 2*, p. 20; Hirst and Burn, *On the Way to Work*, p. 55.
25 Buck, *Moving Targets 2*, p. 128.
26 Buck, *Moving Targets 2*, pp. 47–48.
27 Grunenberg, "Attraction-Repulsion Machines," in Chapman and Chapman, *Bad Art for Bad People*, p. 12.
28 Button, *The Turner Prize*, p. 190; Chapman and Chapman, *Insult to Injury*; Turner, "Great Deeds Against Dead Artists," in Chapman and Chapman, *Bad Art for Bad People*, p. 52.
29 Turner, "Great Deeds Against Dead Artists," p. 52.
30 Chapman and Chapman, *Bad Art for Bad People*, p. 122.
31 Gilot and Lake, *Life With Picasso*, p. 77.
32 McCully, *A Picasso Anthology*, p. 64.
33 Tomkins, *Off the Wall*, p. 118.
34 Johns, *Writings, Sketchbook Notes, Interviews*, pp. 280–81.
35 Tomkins, *Off the Wall*, p. 118.
36 Tomkins, "Everything in Sight," p. 76.
37 Violette and Obrist, *The Words of Gilbert & George*, p. 256.
38 Tate Modern, *Gilbert & George Major Exhibition*, not paginated.
39 Lange, *Bernd and Hilla Becher*, p. 187.
40 Chapman and Chapman, *Bad Art for Bad People*, p. 122.

Chapter 11

1 Matthews, "The Painter's Presence."
2 Varnedoe and Gopnik, *High and Low*, p. 23.
3 Brassaï, *Conversations with Picasso*, p. 93; Danchev, *Georges Braque*, p. 113.
4 Cottington, *Cubism and Its Histories*, pp. 122–31.
5 Golding, *Cubism*, rev. ed., pp. 92–93.
6 Golding, *Cubism*, rev. ed., pp. 93–95.
7 Varnedoe and Gopnik, *High and Low*, p. 40; Richardson, *A Life of Picasso*, 2:222.
8 Varnedoe and Gopnik, *High and Low*, pp. 27–32.

9 Varnedoe and Gopnik, *High and Low*, pp. 23, 39.

10 Kahnweiler, *The Rise of Cubism*, pp. 12–15.

11 Barr, *Picasso*, p. 270.

12 Varnedoe and Gopnik, *High and Low*, pp. 47–49.

13 Crone and Moos, *Kazimir Malevich*, p. 107.

14 Varnedoe and Gopnik, *High and Low*, pp. 54–55.

15 Sanouillet and Peterson, *The Writings of Marcel Duchamp*, p. 125.

16 Cabanne, *Dialogues with Marcel Duchamp*, p. 37.

17 Marquis, *Marcel Duchamp*, p. 99.

18 Tomkins, *Duchamp*, pp. 81–83.

19 Kuh, *The Artist's Voice*, p. 83.

20 De Duve, *Pictorial Nominalism*, p. 41.

21 Sanouillet and Peterson, *The Writings of Marcel Duchamp*, p. 141.

22 Tomkins, *Duchamp*, p. 221.

23 Varnedoe and Gopnik, *High and Low*, pp. 77–78.

24 Sims, *Stuart Davis*, pp. 148–51, 174–75; Varnedoe and Gopnik, *High and Low*, pp. 294–97.

25 Sims, *Stuart Davis*, p. 151.

26 Rubin, *Dada, Surrealism, and Their Heritage*, p. 94.

27 Ernst, *Beyond Painting*, p. 14.

28 Rubin, *Dada, Surrealism, and Their Heritage*, p. 50.

29 Russell, *Max Ernst*, pp. 64–66; Bradley, *Surrealism*, p. 28.

30 Rubin, *Dada, Surrealism, and Their Heritage*, pp. 42–46.

31 Camfied, *Francis Picabia*, pp. 59–62.

32 Elderfield, *Kurt Schwitters*, p. 85.

33 Foster, Krauss, Bois, and Buchloh, *Art Since 1900*, p. 214.

34 Sylvester, *Magritte*, p. 212.

35 Gablik, *Magritte*, p. 14.

36 Gablik, *Magritte*, p. 9.

37 Hamilton, *Collected Words*, pp. 42–43.

38 Johns, *Writings, Sketchbook Notes, Interviews*, p. 82.

39 Johns, *Writings, Sketchbook Notes, Interviews*, p. 136.

40 Sylvester, *Interviews with American Artists*, p. 163.

41 Madoff, *Pop Art*, p. 170.

42 Varnedoe and Gopnik, *High and Low*, p. 335.

43 Foster, Krauss, Bois, and Buchloh, *Art Since 1900*, p. 549; Hunter, Jacobus, and Wheeler, *Modern Art*, p. 364.

44 Stiles and Selz, *Theories and Documents of Contemporary Art*, p. 871.

45 Hunter, Jacobus, and Wheeler, *Modern Art*, p. 365.

46 Galenson, *Artistic Capital*, p. 129.

47 Kosuth, *Art After Philosophy and After*, p. 50.

48 Kosuth, *Art After Philosophy and After*, pp. 91, 180, 20.

49 Kosuth, *Art After Philosophy and After*, pp. 22, xv.

50 Ruscha, *Leave Any Information at the Signal*, pp. 150, 225, 253, 254, 281, 298.

51 Schjeldahl, *The "7 Days" Art Columns*, p. 76.

52 Morgan, *Bruce Nauman*, p. 166.

53 Danto, *The Madonna of the Future*, p. 140.
54 Morgan, *Bruce Nauman*, p. 269.
55 Danto, *Unnatural Wonders*, p. 64.
56 Weintraub, *Art on the Edge and Over*, pp. 194, 196.
57 Auping, *Jenny Holzer*, p. 73.
58 Auping, *Jenny Holzer*, p. 11.
59 Siegel, *Artwords 2*, p. 294.
60 Siegel, *Artwords 2*, p. 289.
61 Auping, *Jenny Holzer*, p. 95.
62 O'Doherty, *Inside the White Cube*, p. 64.

Chapter 12

1 Tojner, *Munch In His Own Words*, p. 183.
2 White and Buvelot, *Rembrandt by Himself*, p. 10.
3 Müller-Westermann, *Munch by Himself*, p. 15.
4 Alpers estimated that Rembrandt depicted himself "approximately fifty times in paint, twenty in etching, and about ten times in surviving drawings"; *Rembrandt's Enterprise*, p. 120. Adding the higher figure for each medium from van de Wetering's and Alpers' estimates – 50 paintings, 31 etchings, and 10 drawings – yields a total of 91.
5 White and Buvelot, *Rembrandt by Himself*, pp. 86, 229; Müller-Westermann, *Munch by Himself*, pp. 19, 176. Other artists have produced self-portraits at rates much higher than either Rembrandt or Munch for shorter periods. Vincent van Gogh, for example, painted all of his 43 self-portraits during the last five years of his life, and 26 of these were executed during the two years he spent in Paris; Erpel, *Van Gogh Self-Portraits*.
6 Alpers' high estimate of 50 self-portraits divided by Bailey's low estimate of 270 total paintings would yield 18.5 percent, which would appear to be an upper bound; Alpers, *Rembrandt's Enterprise*, p. 120; Bailey, *Responses to Rembrandt*, p. 10. For evidence on the distribution of subjects of seventeenth-century Dutch paintings, see e.g., Montias, *Artists and Artisans in Delft*, pp. 238–46.
7 Phillips, *The Confessional Poets*, p. 15.
8 Williamson, *Introspection and Contemporary Poetry*, pp. 1, 8.
9 Phillips, *The Confessional Poets*, pp. xi, 1, 17.
10 Elliott, *The Literary Persona*, pp. 16–21.
11 Phillips, *The Confessional Poets*, pp. 4–5.
12 Simpson, *A Revolution in Taste*, p. xviii.
13 Trilling, *Sincerity and Authenticity*, p. 8.
14 Trilling, *Sincerity and Authenticity*, pp. 8–9.
15 Elliot, *The Literary Persona*, p. 53.
16 Lowell, *Collected Prose*, pp. 246–47.
17 Elliott, *The Literary Persona*, p. 58.
18 Elliott, *The Literary Persona*, p. 55.
19 Lowell, *Collected Prose*, p. 122.
20 Van Gogh, *The Complete Letters of Vincent van Gogh*, 2:605.

21 Schapiro, *Vincent van Gogh*, p. 12.
22 Hamilton, *Painting and Sculpture in Europe*, p. 94.
23 Schapiro, *Vincent van Gogh*, p. 12.
24 Van Gogh, *The Complete Letters of Vincent van Gogh*, 3:420.
25 Van Gogh, *The Complete Letters*, 2:416, 534.
26 Graetz, *The Symbolic Language of Vincent van Gogh*, pp. 39–41.
27 Simmel, *The Reach of Mind*, pp. 205–07.
28 Van Gogh, *Complete Letters*, 3:470.
29 Van Gogh, *Complete Letters*, 2:119.
30 Schapiro, *Vincent van Gogh*, p. 12.
31 Hamilton, *Painting and Sculpture in Europe*, p. 95.
32 Tojner, *Munch in His Own Words*, p. 135.
33 Heller, *Edvard Munch*, p. 62.
34 Tojner, *Munch in His Own Words*, p. 149.
35 Prideaux, *Edvard Munch*, p. 82; Tojner, *Munch in His Own Words*, p. 143.
36 Rosenblum, *Edvard Munch*, p. 11.
37 Prideaux, *Edvard Munch*, p. 83.
38 Tojner, *Munch in His Own Words*, p. 135.
39 Heller, *Edvard Munch*, p. 65.
40 Heller, *Munch*, p. 82.
41 Heller, *Edvard Munch*, pp. 78–80.
42 Tojner, *Munch in His Own Words*, p. 134.
43 Prideaux, *Edvard Munch*, p. 170.
44 Dexter and Barson, *Frida Kahlo*, p. 31.
45 Herrera, *Frida*, p. 74.
46 Herrera, *Frida*, pp. 74–75.
47 Dexter and Barson, *Frida Kahlo*, p. 32.
48 Ankori, *Imaging Her Selves*, p. 10.
49 Dexter and Barson, *Frida Kahlo*, p. 31.
50 Ankori, *Imaging Her Selves*, p. 6.
51 Herrera, *Frida*, p. 97.
52 Herrera, *Frida*, p. 151.
53 Dexter and Barson, *Frida Kahlo*, p. 77; Herrera, *Frida*, p. 120.
54 E.g., see Herrera, *Frida*, pp. 197–214.
55 E.g., see Dexter and Barson, *Frida Kahlo*, pp. 55–78.
56 Herrera, *Frida*, p. 258.
57 Herrera, *Frida*, p. 410.
58 Farr and Martino, *Francis Bacon*, p. 25.
59 Sylvester, *Interviews with Francis Bacon*, p. 70.
60 Sylvester, *Interviews with Francis Bacon*, p. 82.
61 Sylvester, *Interviews with Francis Bacon*, p. 198.
62 Peppiatt, *Francis Bacon*, p. 97.
63 Sylvester, *Interviews with Francis Bacon*, pp. 16–17.
64 Russell, *Francis Bacon*, p. 53.
65 Peppiatt, *Francis Bacon*, pp. 183–84.
66 Russell, *Francis Bacon*, p. 124.
67 Peppiatt, *Francis Bacon*, p. 207.

68 Sylvester, *Interviews with Francis Bacon*, p. 68.
69 Rose, *Francis Bacon.*
70 Sylvester, *Interviews with Francis Bacon*, p. 73.
71 Sylvester, *Interviews with Francis Bacon*, pp. 130, 174.
72 Russell, *Francis Bacon*, p. 178.
73 Peppiatt, *Francis Bacon*, p. 208.
74 Peppiatt, *Francis Bacon*, pp. 250–52.
75 Russell, *Francis Bacon*, p. 182.
76 Bourgeois, *Destruction of the Father, Reconstruction of the Father*, p. 313.
77 Acocella, *Twenty-Eight Artists and Two Saints*, pp. 412–13; Bourgeois, *Destruction of the Father, Reconstruction of the Father*, pp. 133–35, 283.
78 Bourgeois, *Destruction of the Father, Reconstruction of the Father*, p. 101.
79 Bourgeois, *Destruction of the Father, Reconstruction of the Father*, p. 81.
80 Bourgeois, *Destruction of the Father, Reconstruction of the Father*, p. 277.
81 Bourgeois, *Destruction of the Father, Reconstruction of the Father*, p. 285.
82 Bourgeois, *Destruction of the Father, Reconstruction of the Father*, p. 162.
83 Bourgeois, *Destruction of the Father, Reconstruction of the Father*, p. 168.
84 Bourgeois, *Destruction of the Father, Reconstruction of the Father*, p. 269.
85 Bourgeois, *Destruction of the Father, Reconstruction of the Father*, p. 257.
86 Bourgeois, *Destruction of the Father, Reconstruction of the Father*, p. 247.
87 Bourgeois, *Destruction of the Father, Reconstruction of the Father*, p. 261.
88 Ray, *Joseph Beuys*, p. 177.
89 Ray, *Joseph Beuys*, pp. 185–86.
90 Tisdall, *Joseph Beuys*, pp. 16–17.
91 Ray, *Joseph Beuys*, pp. 202–03.
92 Ray, *Joseph Beuys*, p. 9.
93 E.g., Stachelhaus, *Joseph Beuys*, pp. 21–22; Hunter, Jacobus, and Wheeler, *Modern Art*, p. 366; Honour and Fleming, *The Visual Arts*, p. 872.
94 Thistlewood, *Joseph Beuys*, pp. 3, 7.
95 Stachelhaus, *Joseph Beuys*, pp. 112–17.
96 Thistlewood, *Joseph Beuys*, p. 35.
97 Thistlewood, *Joseph Beuys*, p. 182.
98 Morgan, *Bruce Nauman*, p. 242.
99 Lewallen, *A Rose Has No Teeth*, p. 16.
100 Galenson, *Artistic Capital*, pp. 128, 132.
101 For discussion and illustrations, see Lewallen, *A Rose Has No Teeth.*
102 Morgan, *Bruce Nauman*, p. 309.
103 Morgan, *Bruce Nauman*, p.241.
104 Morgan, *Bruce Nauman*, p. 262.
105 Morgan, *Bruce Nauman*, pp. 93–94.
106 Kesten, *The Portraits Speak*, p. 337.
107 Kesten, *The Portraits Speak*, pp. 343–44.
108 Heartney, *After the Revolution*, p. 173.
109 Siegel, *Artwords 2*, p. 275.
110 Stiles and Selz, *Theories and Documents of Contemporary Art*, p. 791.
111 Siegel, *Artwords 2*, p. 282.
112 Sherman, *Untitled Film Stills*, p. 10.

113 Betty van Garrel, *Cindy Sherman*, p. 25.
114 Schjeldahl, *The Hydrogen Jukebox*, p. 115.
115 Sherman, *Untitled Film Stills*, p. 10.
116 Brown, *Tracey Emin*, p. 50.
117 Stallabrass, *High Art Lite*, p. 36.
118 Merck and Townsend, *The Art of Tracey Emin*, p. 40.
119 Virginia Button, *The Turner Prize*, p. 152.
120 Merck and Townsend, *The Art of Tracey Emin*, p. 142.
121 Merck and Townsend, *The Art of Tracey Emin*, p. 36.
122 Brown, *Tracey Emin*, pp. 15–16.
123 Brown, *Tracey Emin*, p. 16.
124 Stallabrass, *High Art Lite*, p. 37.
125 Wright, *Writers on Artists*, p. 214.
126 Brown, *Tracey Emin*, p. 33.
127 Brown, *Tracey Emin*, pp. 50–53.
128 Merck and Townsend, *The Art of Tracey Emin*, pp. 112–14.
129 Brown, *Tracey Emin*, p. 12.
130 Stallabrass, *High Art Lite*, p. 43.
131 Merck and Townsend, *The Art of Tracey Emin*, p. 133.
132 Wright, *Writers on Artists*, p. 213.
133 Stallabrass, *High Art Lite*, p. 43.
134 Van Gogh, *The Complete Letters*, 3:37.
135 Sylvester, *Interviews with Francis Bacon*, p. 172; Brown, *Tracey Emin*, p. 92.
136 Van Gogh, *The Complete Letters*, 1:364.
137 Van Gogh, *The Complete Letters*, 3:399–400.
138 Van Gogh, *The Complete Letters*, 3:201.

Chapter 13

1 Schapiro, *Modern Art*, p. 195.
2 Rosenberg, *Art on the Edge*, p. 39.
3 Greenberg, *The Collected Essays and Criticism*, 1:188–89.
4 Bois, Joosten, Rudenstine, and Janssen, *Piet Mondrian*, p. xix; also see p. 295.
5 Cooper and Spronk, *Mondrian*, p. 49.
6 Seuphor, *Piet Mondrian*, p. 181.
7 Messer, *Piet Mondrian*, pp. 81–82.
8 Holty, "Mondrian in New York," p. 21.
9 Cooper and Spronk, *Mondrian*, p. 67.
10 Cooper and Spronk, *Mondrian*, p. 118.
11 More recently, the scholars Simon Schama and Rosalind Krauss have also considered Mondrian's work to be conceptual; Cooper and Spronk, *Mondrian*, pp. 8–9.
12 Lindsay and Vergo, *Kandinsky*, p. 481.
13 Lindsay and Vergo, *Kandinsky*, p. 363.
14 Lindsay and Vergo, *Kandinsky*, pp. 369–70.

15 Lindsay and Vergo, *Kandinsky*, p. 370.
16 Lindsay and Vergo, *Kandinsky*, p. 393.
17 Lindsay and Vergo, *Kandinsky*, pp. 372–73.
18 Lindsay and Vergo, *Kandinsky*, p. 799.
19 Lindsay and Vergo, *Kandinsky*, p. 827.
20 Barnett, *Kandinsky at the Guggenheim*, pp. 29–30.
21 Bowness, *Modern European Art*, p. 133.
22 Grohmann, *Wassily Kandinsky*, p. 145.
23 Sylvester, *About Modern Art*, p. 79.
24 Janssen and Joosten, *Mondrian 1892–1914*, p. 196.
25 Bois, Joosten, Rudenstine, and Janssen, *Piet Mondrian*, p. 162.
26 Seuphor, *Mondrian*, p. 198.
27 Janssen and Joosten, *Mondrian 1892–1914*, p. 24.
28 Sylvester, *About Modern Art*, p. 434.
29 Bois, Joosten, Rudenstine, and Janssen, *Piet Mondrian*, p. 295.
30 Cooper and Spronk, *Mondrian*, p. 114.
31 Cooper and Spronk, *Mondrian*, p. 67.
32 Janssen and Joosten, *Mondrian 1892–1914*, p. 40.
33 Messer, *Piet Mondrian*, pp. 79, 82.
34 Malevich, *Essays on Art*, 1:24.
35 Malevich, *Essays on Art*, 1:94.
36 Malevich, *Essays on Art*, 1:100–01.
37 Malevich, *Essays on Art*, 1:121.
38 Milner, *Kazimir Malevich and the Art of Geometry*, pp. 80–81.
39 Zhadova, *Malevich*, p. 53.
40 Kemp, *The Oxford History of Western Art*, p. 414.
41 Malevich, *Essays on Art*, 1:19, 38, 41.
42 Golding, *Visions of the Modern*, p. 178.
43 Golding, *Paths to the Absolute*, pp. 82–83.
44 Blotkamp, *Mondrian*, pp. 14–15.
45 Malevich, *Essays*, 1:49, 83.
46 Schapiro, *Modern Art*, p. 218.
47 Galenson, *Artistic Capital*, chap. 4.
48 Newman, *Selected Writings and Interviews*, p. 173.
49 Breslin, *Mark Rothko*, p. 193.
50 Karmel, *Jackson Pollock*, p. 21.
51 Karmel, *Jackson Pollock*, p. 18.
52 Karmel, *Jackson Pollock*, p. 18.
53 Breslin, *Mark Rothko*, pp. 239–40.
54 Sylvester, *Interviews With American Artists*, p. 57.
55 Rosenberg, *The Tradition of the New*, p. 25.
56 De Kooning, *The Spirit of Abstract Expressionism*, p. 228.
57 Breslin, *Mark Rothko*, pp. 317, 469.
58 Carmean and Rathbone, *American Art at Mid-Century*, pp. 133–39.
59 Newman, *Selected Writings and Interviews*, p. 240.
60 Terenzio, *The Collected Writings of Robert Motherwell*, p. 3.
61 Friedman, *Jackson Pollock*, p. 183.

62 Kuthy, *Pierre Soulages*, pp. 22–24. The translations are mine.
63 E.g., see Galenson, *Artistic Capital*, chaps. 3–4.
64 Guilbaut, *How New York Stole the Idea of Modern Art*, p. 1; Seitz, *Abstract Expressionist Painting in America*, p. 165.
65 Breslin, *Mark Rothko*, p. 431.
66 Rodman, *Conversations with Artists*, p. 91.
67 Sylvester, *About Modern Art*, pp. 229–30.
68 Kirk Varnedoe, *Pictures of Nothing*, p. 29.
69 Rose, *Frankenthaler*, p. 29.
70 Seitz, *Art in the Age of Aquarius*, pp. 36–39.
71 Sandler, *The New York School*, pp. 69–87.
72 Garrels, *Plane Image*, pp. 21, 26.
73 Kimmelman, *Portraits*, p. 198.
74 Garrels, *Plane Image*, p. 23.
75 Goldsmith, *I'll Be Your Mirror*, p. 17.
76 De Antonio and Tuchman, *Painters Painting*, p. 87.
77 Tomkins, *Off the Wall*, pp. 96–97.
78 Rosenberg, *Art and Other Serious Matters*, p. 245.
79 Sandler, *The New York School*, pp. 180–83.
80 De Antonio and Tuchman, *Painters Painting*, p. 94.
81 Stich, *Yves Klein*, p. 68.
82 Stich, *Yves Klein*, p. 68.
83 Klein, *Le dépassement de la problématique de l'art et autres écrits*, pp. 295–96.
84 Johns, *Writings, Sketchbook Notes, Interviews*, p. 256.
85 Varnedoe, *Pictures of Nothing*, pp. 226–27.
86 Goldsmith, *I'll Be Your Mirror*, p. 18; Cresap, *Pop Trickster Fool*, p. 71.
87 Varnedoe, *Pictures of Nothing*, p. 203; Bourdon, *Warhol*, pp. 365–72.
88 Krauss, "Warhol's Abstract Spectacle," p. 126.
89 Bourdon, *Warhol*, p. 372.
90 Varnedoe, *Pictures of Nothing*, pp. 203–04.
91 Bourdon, *Warhol*, pp. 393–94.
92 Varnedoe, *Pictures of Nothing*, p. 204; Bourdon, *Warhol*, p. 394.
93 Coplans, *Roy Lichtenstein*, pp. 44–45, 89.
94 Sylvester, *About Modern Art*, p. 233.
95 Varnedoe, *Pictures of Nothing*, p. 194.
96 Rubin, *Frank Stella*, pp. 8–13.
97 Battcock, *Minimal Art*, pp. 157–61.
98 Rubin, *Frank Stella*, p. 32.
99 Galenson, *Artistic Capital*, p. 54.
100 Rosenberg, *The De-Definition of Art*, pp. 121–31.
101 De Antonio and Tuchman, *Painters Painting*, p. 140.
102 Dempsey, *Art in the Modern Era*, pp. 232–37.
103 Zweite, *Gerhard Richter*, pp. 50–54.
104 Richter, The Daily Practice of Painting, p. 264.
105 Zweite, *Gerhard Richter*, pp. 48–91.
106 Varnedoe, *Pictures of Nothing*, pp. 214–16.

107 Varnedoe, *Pictures of Nothing*, p. 237.
108 Danto, *Unnatural Wonders*, p. 187.
109 Hess, *Willem de Kooning*, p. 74; Greenberg, *The Collected Essays and Criticism*, 4:124.

Chapter 14

1 Kandinsky and Marc, *The "Blaue Reiter" Almanac*, p. 251.
2 Greenberg, *Late Writings*, p. 15.
3 Newman, *Selected Writings and Interviews*, p. 80.
4 Danto, *After the End of Art*, pp. 28–30.
5 Apollonio, *Futurist Manifestos*, p. 22.
6 Apollonio, *Futurist Manifestos*, pp. 24–31.
7 Hamilton, *Painting and Sculpture in Europe*, p. 280.
8 Perloff, *The Futurist Moment*, pp. 82–85.
9 Golding, *Paths to the Absolute*, p. 53.
10 Apollonio, *Futurist Manifestos*, p. 7.
11 Perloff, *The Futurist Moment*, p. 90.
12 Malevich, *Essays on Art*, 1:19–41; Golding, *Paths to the Absolute*, p. 60.
13 Perloff, *The Futurist Moment*, pp. 111, 114, 217.
14 Rewald, *The History of Impressionism*, p. 458.
15 Apollinaire, *Apollinaire on Art*, p. 267.
16 Van Gogh, *The Complete Letters of Vincent van Gogh*, 2:295.
17 Schapiro, *Vincent van Gogh*, p. 13; also see Roskill, *Van Gogh, Gauguin and the Impressionist Circle*, pp. 41–42.
18 Van Gogh, *The Complete Letters of Vincent van Gogh*, 2:515.
19 Schapiro, *Vincent van Gogh*, p. 13.
20 Roskill, *Van Gogh, Gauguin, and the Impressionist Circle*, p. 53
21 Van Gogh, *The Complete Letters of Vincent van Gogh*, 3:6.
22 Fry, *Cézanne*, p. 33.
23 Fry, *Cézanne*, pp. 33–34.
24 Doran, *Conversations with Cézanne*, p. 150; Rewald, *Paul Cézanne*, pp. 188–89; Cézanne, *Letters*, p. 320.
25 Pissarro, *Letters to His Son Lucien*, p. 36.
26 Apollinaire, *Apollinaire on Art*, p. 270.
27 Gilot and Lake, *Life with Picasso*, p. 77.
28 McCully, *A Picasso Anthology*, p. 64.
29 Cooper, *The Cubist Epoch*, pp. 11–12.
30 Perloff, *The Futurist Moment*, p. 46.
31 Golding, *Cubism*, revised ed., p. 60.
32 Cooper, *The Cubist Epoch*, chaps. 2–3.
33 Perloff, *The Futurist Moment*, p. 45.
34 Hamilton, *Painting and Sculpture in Europe*, p. 287; Galenson, "Toward Abstraction," p. 101.
35 Hamilton, *Painting and Sculpture in Europe*, p. 288.
36 Apollonio, *Futurist Manifestos*, p. 45.
37 Severini, *The Life of a Painter*, p. 110.

38 Severini, *The Life of a Painter*, p. 111.

39 Apollonio, *Futurist Manifestos*, p. 51; Severini, *The Life of a Painter*, p. 111.

40 Apollinaire, *Apollinaire on Art*, pp. 320–21.

41 Ester Coen, *Umberto Boccioni*, p. 204.

42 Chap. 3, above.

43 Kandinsky and Marc, *The "Blaue Reiter" Almanac*, p. 252.

44 Gordon, *Ernst Ludwig Kirchner*, p. 20.

45 Gordon, *Ernst Ludwig Kirchner*, pp. 48–54.

46 Selz, *German Expressionist Painting*, pp. 81–82.

47 Jensen, "Van Gogh *als Erzieher*."

48 Hamilton, *Painting and Sculpture in Europe*, pp. 215–16.

49 Kandinsky and Marc, *The "Blaue Reiter" Almanac*, p. 153.

50 Kandinsky, *Complete Writings on Art*, p. 796.

51 Kandsinky and Marc, *The "Blaue Reiter" Almanac*, pp. 69, 187.

52 Kandinsky and Marc, *The "Blaue Reiter" Almanac*, p. 251.

53 Malevich, *Essays on Art*, 1:68.

54 Milner, *Kazimir Malevich and the Art of Geometry*, pp. 1–2.

55 Golding, *Paths to the Absolute*, p. 55.

56 Milner, *Kazimir Malevich and the Art of Geometry*, pp. 2, 8–9, 21, 41.

57 Golding, *Visions of the Modern*, p. 173.

58 Milner, *Kazimir Malevich and the Art of Geometry*, pp. 81, 108.

59 Golding, *Visions of the Modern*, pp. 171–77.

60 Milner, *Vladimir Tatlin and the Russian Avant-Garde*, p. 80.

61 Milner, *Vladimir Tatlin and the Russian Avant-Garde*, pp. 59–61.

62 Perloff, *The Futurist Moment*, p. 67.

63 Milner, *Vladimir Tatlin and the Russian Avant-Garde*, p. 76; Richardson, *A Life of Picasso*, 2:256.

64 Hamilton, *Painting and Sculpture in Europe*, p. 316.

65 Milner, *Vladimir Tatlin and the Russian Avant-Garde*, pp. 82–83; Perloff, *The Futurist Moment*, pp. 69–71; Hamilton, *Painting and Sculpture in Europe*, pp. 315–16.

66 Richter, *Dada*, p. 9.

67 Richter, *Dada*, p. 25.

68 Richter, *Dada*, p. 48.

69 Richter, *Dada*, p. 37.

70 Richter, *Dada*, p. 48.

71 Elger, *Dadaism*, p. 11.

72 Richter, *Dada*, pp. 11–12.

73 Ball, *Flight Out of Time*, p. 50.

74 Ball, *Flight Out of Time*, pp. 51–52.

75 Elger, *Dadaism*, p. 11.

76 Ball, *Flight Out of Time*, pp. 56–57.

77 Richter, *Dada*, p. 49.

78 Richter, *Dada*, p. 57.

79 Rubin, *Dada, Surrealism, and Their Heritage*, p. 12.

80 Lavin, *Cut With the Kitchen Knife*, p. 219.

81 Richter, *Dada*, p. 33.

82 Elger, *Dadaism*, p. 8.
83 Richter, *Dada*, p. 102.
84 Richter, *Dada*, chap. 2.
85 Rubin, *Dada, Surrealism, and Their Heritage*, p. 41; Richter, *Dada*, p. 51.
86 Hamilton, *Painting and Sculpture in Europe*, p. 378.
87 Richter, *Dada*, pp. 217–19.
88 Hamilton, *Painting and Sculpture in Europe*, p. 388.
89 Lippard, *Dadas on Art*, p. 35.
90 Motherwell, *The Dada Painters and Poets*, p. xxi and passim.
91 Lippard, *Dadas on Art*, p. 96; Motherwell, *Dada Painters and Poets*, pp. 102, 127; also see Elger, *Dadaism*, p. 22.
92 Richter, *Dada*, p. 164.
93 Barr, *Fantastic Art, Dada, Surrealism*.
94 Richter, *Dada*, pp. 11–12.
95 Richter, *Dada*, pp. 31–32; Elger, *Dadaism*, pp. 10–11.
96 Richter, *Dada*, pp. 116–17; Ades, *Photomontage*, pp. 19–20.
97 Lippard, *Dadas on Art*, p. 24.
98 Elger, *Dadaism*, p. 10.
99 Harrison and Wood, *Art in Theory*, p. 457.
100 Richter, *Dada*, p. 194.
101 Breton, *Manifestoes of Surrealism*, p. 26.
102 Breton, *Manifestoes of Surrealism*, p. 27.
103 Hamilton, *Painting and Sculpture in Europe*, p. 391.
104 Rubin, *Dada, Surrealism, and Their Heritage*, p. 128.
105 Karmel, *Jackson Pollock*, p. 15.
106 Greenberg, *The Collected Essays and Criticism*, 2:87.
107 Greenberg, *Collected Essays and Criticism*, 2:215.
108 Newman, *Selected Writings and Interviews*, p. 150.
109 Breslin, *Mark Rothko*, p. 232.
110 Sylvester, *Interviews With American Artists*, p. 30.
111 Breslin, *Mark Rothko*, pp. 47–54, 539.
112 Sylvester, *Interviews with American Artists*, p. 30; Motherwell, *The Writings of Robert Motherwell*, p. 339.
113 Motherwell, *Writings of Robert Motherwell*, p. 334.
114 Rothko, *Writings on Art*, p. 149.
115 Motherwell, *The Collected Writings of Robert Motherwell*, pp. 158–59.
116 Motherwell, *Collected Writings of Robert Motherwell*, p. 165; Newman, *Selected Writings and Interviews*, p. 152; Rosenberg, *Arshile Gorky*, p. 113; Ashton, *The New York School*, p. 124.
117 Motherwell, *Collected Writings of Robert Motherwell*, pp. 161–66.
118 Alloway, *William Baziotes*, p. 41.
119 Breslin, *Mark Rothko*, pp. 257–58.
120 Motherwell, *Writings of Robert Motherwell*, p. 8.
121 Seitz, *Abstract Expressionist Painting in America*, pp. 165–66.
122 Galenson, "The New York School versus the School of Paris," pp. 141–53.
123 E.g., see Sandler, The *New York School*, p. ix; Galenson, "Was Jackson Pollock the Greatest Modern American Painter?" pp. 117–28.

124 Motherwell, *Collected Writings of Robert Motherwell*, pp. 294–95; Motherwell, *The Writings of Robert Motherwell*, p. 79.
125 Madoff, *Pop Art*, p. 106.
126 Madoff, *Pop Art*, pp. 32, 41.
127 Goldstein, *I'll Be Your Mirror*, p. 9; Madoff, *Pop Art*, p. 198.
128 Madoff, *Pop Art*, pp. 105–106.
129 Russell and Gablik, *Pop Art Redefined*, p. 115.
130 Madoff, *Pop Art*, p. 109.
131 Thistlewood, *Sigmar Polke*, p. 34.
132 Richter, *The Daily Practice of Painting*, pp. 22–23.
133 Richter, *The Daily Practice of Painting*, pp. 16, 24.
134 Richter, *The Daily Practice of Painting*, p. 16.
135 E.g., Richter, *The Daily Practice of Painting*, p. 138.
136 E.g., see Perry and Wood, *Themes in Contemporary Art*, pp. 99–131.
137 Danto, *The Abuse of Beauty*, p. 6.
138 Alloway, *American Pop Art*, p. 47; Lippard, *Pop Art*, pp. 32, 82–87.
139 Sylvester, *About Modern Art*, p. 384.
140 LeWitt, *Critical Texts*, p. 78.
141 LeWitt, *Critical Texts*, p. 84.
142 Kosuth, *Art After Philosophy and After*, p. 139.
143 Lippard, *Six Years*, p. xiv. Also see Wollen, *Paris Manhattan*, p. 29.
144 Wollen, *Paris Manhattan*, pp. 15–16.
145 LeWitt, *Critical Texts*, pp. 78, 88.
146 Kosuth, *Art After Philosophy and After*, pp. 3, 22.
147 Lippard, *Six Years*, pp. 42–43.
148 Lippard, *Six Years*, p. 64.
149 Alberro and Norvell, *Recording Conceptual Art*, pp. 38–39.
150 McShine, *Information*, p. 138.
151 McShine, *Information*, p. 140.
152 Alberro and Norvell, *Recording Conceptual Art*, p. 53.
153 Lippard, *Six Years*, p. 263.
154 Hirst and Burn, *On the Way to Work*, p. 165.
155 Adams, *Sensation*, pp. 16–17.
156 Cork, *Breaking Down the Barriers*, pp. 121–28.
157 Adams, *Sensation*, pp. 8–9.
158 Collings, *It Hurts*, p. 33.
159 Hughes and van Tuyl, *Blast to Freeze*, p. 293.
160 Millard, *The Tastemakers*, pp. 18–21.
161 Buck, *Moving Targets 2*, p. 142.
162 Danto, *The Madonna of the Future*, p. 393.
163 Hirst and Burn, *On the Way to Work*, p. 100.
164 Stallabrass, *High Art Lite*, p. 9.
165 Temkin, *Contemporary Voices*, p. 58.
166 Merck and Townsend, *The Art of Tracey Emin*, p. 8.
167 Merck and Townsend, *The Art of Tracey Emin*, p. 76; Collings, *Sarah Lucas*, p. 44–46; Buck, *Moving Targets 2*, p. 41; Mullins, *Rachel Whiteread*, p. 72–73.

168 Collings, *It Hurts*, p. 33.
169 Millard, *The Tastemakers*, p. 65.
170 Hirst and Burn, *On the Way to Work*, pp. 170, 223.
171 Millard, *The Tastemakers*, p. 22.
172 Stallabrass, *High Art Lite*, p. 18.
173 Chap. 8, above.
174 Saltz, *Seeing Out Loud*, p. 200.
175 Galenson, "Do the Young British Artists Rule?" pp. 175–84.
176 Hoban, *Basquiat*, p. 13.
177 Smith, *Nine Lives*, pp. 37–77.
178 Smith, *Nine Lives*, pp. 63, 65.
179 For example Wang's work is not discussed even in as comprehensive a survey of western art history as Arnason, *History of Modern Art*.
180 Goldwater, *Primitivism in Modern Painting*.
181 Viso, *Ana Mendieta*, pp. 36, 63.
182 Button, *The Turner Prize*, pp. 80–82.
183 Hunter, Jacobus, and Wheeler, *Modern Art*, pp. 432–33.
184 Marshall, *Jean-Michel Basquiat*, p. 30; Mercer, *Exiles, Diasporas and Strangers*, pp. 134–35.
185 Chiappini, *Jean-Michel Basquiat*, p. 119.
186 Shonibare, *Double Dutch*, p. 46.
187 Button, *The Turner Prize*, pp. 144–46; Buck, *Moving Targets 2*, pp. 83–85.
188 Zinnes, *Ezra Pound and the Visual Arts*, p. 4.

Chapter 15

1 Keller, "Painting by the Numbers."
2 Alberti, *On Painting*, p. 64.
3 Wittkower and Wittkower, *Born Under Saturn*, pp. 9–11; Condivi, *The Life of Michelangelo*, p. 9.
4 Wittkower and Wittkower, *Born Under Saturn*, pp. 24–26.
5 Wittkower and Wittkower, *Born Under Saturn*, pp. 14, 23.
6 Alberti, *On Painting*, p. 64.
7 Chastel, *The Genius of Leonardo da Vinci*, p. 199.
8 Wittkower and Wittkower, *Born Under Saturn*, p. 93.
9 Wittkower and Wittkower, *Born Under Saturn*, pp. 15, 24, 93–94.
10 Wittkower and Wittkower, *Born Under Saturn*, pp. 263, 269–70.
11 White and White, *Canvases and Careers*, p. 13.
12 Siegel and Mattick, *Art Works*, p. 18.
13 Van Gogh, *Complete Letters of Vincent van Gogh*, 3:543.
14 Galenson and Jensen, "Careers and Canvases."
15 Jensen, *Marketing Modernism in Fin-de-Siècle Europe*, p. 18.
16 Jensen, *Marketing Modernism in Fin-de-Siècle Europe*, pp. 18–19.
17 Woolf, *Roger Fry*, p. 159.
18 Richardson, *A Life of Picasso*, 1:199, 201; Fitzgerald, *Making Modernism*, pp. 3, 19, 27, 29, 34–36, 65, 83–84, 88; Penrose, *Picasso*, p. 205.
19 Miró, *Selected Writings and Interviews*, p. 71.

20 Kahnweiler, *My Galleries and Painters*, p. 91. Michael Fitzgerald reflected that "To most readers, this goal is probably not much of a secret, since many people follow the same dream – to be financially secure but unrestricted by social expectations. But it does appear to be a secret in regard to the history of avant-garde art, because of the widespread assumption that these artists' rejection of established conventions (aesthetic and otherwise) must involve an opposition to the systems of consumption that generate wealth and fame in our culture"; *Making Modernism*, p. 4.

21 Fitzgerald, *Making Modernism*, p. 268.

22 Greenberg, *The Collected Essays and Criticism*, 3:160.

23 Gottlieb, "The Artist and the Public," p. 267.

24 Newman, *Selected Writings and Interviews*, p. 305.

25 Greenberg, *Collected Essays and Criticism*, 2:170.

26 Rosenberg, *The Tradition of the New*, p. 267.

27 Breslin, *Mark Rothko*, pp. 340–41.

28 Schapiro, *Modern Art*, pp. 224–26.

29 Warhol, *THE Philosophy of Andy Warhol*, p. 135.

30 Galenson, *Artistic Capital*, p. 50.

31 Bourdon, *Warhol*, pp. 104–08; Bockris, *Warhol*, p. 151.

32 Warhol and Hackett, *POPism*, p. 22.

33 Bourdon, *Warhol*, p. 108.

34 Varnedoe, *Pictures of Nothing*, p. 207.

35 Goldsmith, *I'll Be Your Mirror*, p. 88.

36 Warhol and Hackett, *POPism*, p. 26.

37 Bourdon, *Warhol*, p. 350.

38 Warhol, *THE Philosophy of Andy Warhol*, p. 178.

39 Warhol, *THE Philosophy of Andy Warhol*, p. 92.

40 Warhol, *THE Philosophy of Andy Warhol*, p. 130.

41 Bourdon, *Warhol*, p. 327; Warhol, *THE Philosophy of Andy Warhol*, p. 92.

42 Schjeldahl, *The Hydrogen Jukebox*, p. 47; Hughes, *Nothing If Not Critical*, p. 256.

43 Goldsmith, *I'll Be your Mirror*, p. 387.

44 Bourdon, *Warhol*, pp. 40–43; Bockris, *Warhol*, p. 151.

45 Bourdon, *Warhol*, p. 397.

46 Warhol and Hackett, *POPism*, pp. 14–15.

47 Warhol and Hackett, *POPism*, p. 398.

48 Rosenberg, *Art on the Edge*, p. 102.

49 Madoff, *Pop Art*, pp. 397, 404–06.

50 Madoff, *Pop Art*, p. 213.

51 Brilliant, "Park Avenue Art Gallery."

52 Stiles and Selz, *Theories and Documents of Contemporary Art*, p. 726.

53 Stiles and Selz, *Theories and Documents of Contemporary Art*, p. 840.

54 Lippard, *Six Years*, p. 263.

55 Sylvester, *Interviews with American Artists*, p. 334.

56 Koons, *The Jeff Koons Handbook*, pp. 33, 37, 12.

57 Sylvester, *Interviews With American Artists*, p. 337.

58 Sylvester, *Interviews With American Artists*, pp. 343–45.

59 Haden-Guest, *True Colors*, p. 151.
60 Wright, *Writers on Artists*, pp. 47–48.
61 Koons, "Statement."
62 Hirst and Burn, *On the Way to Work*, pp. 16, 63, 84.
63 Hirst and Burn, *On the Way to Work*, pp. 30, 153.
64 Matthew Collings, *Blimey!*, pp. 21–22; Stallabrass, *High Art Lite*, pp. 53–54.
65 Stallabrass, *High Art Lite*, p. 81.
66 E.g., see Riding, "Alas, Poor Art Market."
67 *New York Times*, "Dumping the Shark."
68 Hirst and Burn, *On the Way to Work*, pp. 60, 84.
69 Bourdieu, *The Field of Cultural Production*, p. 79.
70 Hughes, *Nothing If Not Critical*, p. 237.
71 Leonhardt, "The Science of Pricing Great Works of Art."
72 Salmans, "The Fine Art of Yale."
73 Schjeldahl, *The "7 Days" Art Columns*, pp. 88–93.
74 Bowness, *The Conditions of Success*, pp. 9–11.
75 Barr, *Defining Modern Art*, p. 73.
76 Galenson, *Old Masters and Young Geniuses*, pp. 67–70.
77 Galenson, *Old Masters and Young Geniuses*, pp. 71–73.
78 Stolwijk, *Vincent's Choice*, pp. 119–20.
79 E.g., see Galenson, *Artistic Capital*, chaps. 5–6.

Chapter 16

1 Gilot and Lake, *Life With Picasso*, p. 75.
2 Johns, *Writings, Sketchbook Notes, Interviews*, p. 19.
3 Schjeldahl, *Let's See*, pp. 182–183.
4 Robins, *The Pluralist Era*, p. 1.
5 Fineberg, *Art Since 1940*, p. 365.
6 Danto, *After the End of Art*, p. xiii.
7 Foster, Krauss, Bois, and Buchloch, *Art Since 1900*, p. 679.
8 Haden-Guest, *True Colors*, p. 151.
9 Jensen, "Anticipating Artistic Behavior," pp. 137–153.
10 Galenson, *Painting Outside the Lines*, chap. 6.
11 Galenson and Jensen, "Careers and Canvases," pp. 137–66.
12 Galenson and Jensen, "Careers and Canvases," pp. 155–158.
13 Apollinaire, *Apollinaire on Art*, p. 75.
14 For a listing, see Chap. 15, above.
15 Goldstein, *I'll Be Your Mirror*, p. 17.
16 Schapiro, *The Unity of Picasso's Art*, p. 1.
17 Campbell, "Plotting Polke," p. 19.
18 Danto, *Unnatural Wonders*, p. 182.
19 McEvilley, *The Triumph of Anti-Art*, p. 105.
20 Sanouillet and Peterson, *The Writings of Marcel Duchamp*, p. 156.
21 Schjeldahl, *Let's See*, p. 111.
22 Van Bruggen, *Bruce Nauman*, p. 14.
23 Richter, *The Daily Practice of Painting*, pp. 92–93.

24 Sylvester, *About Modern Art*, p. 30; Sanouillet and Peterson, *The Writings of Marcel Duchamp*, p. 157.

25 Barr, *Picasso*, p. 271.

26 Cabanne, *Dialogues with Marcel Duchamp*, p. 48.

27 McEvilley, *The Triumph of Anti-Art*, p. 28.

28 Camfield, *Francis Picabia*, p. xvi.

29 Richter, *Dada*, p. 48.

30 Kimmelman, *Portraits*, p. 198; Bourgeois, *Destruction of the Father, Reconstruction of the Father*, p. 218.

31 Richter, *The Daily Practice of Painting*, p. 115.

32 Brassai, *Conversations with Picasso*, p. 69.

33 Schjeldahl, *Let's See*, p. 222.

34 Golding, *Cubism*, revised ed., pp. 103, 105.

35 Chap. 7, above.

36 Danto, *Art After the End of Art*, p. 170.

37 E.g., see Galenson, "The Reappearing Masterpiece," pp. 178–88; and Galenson, "One-Hit Wonders," pp. 101–117.

38 Archer, *Art Since 1960*, p. 183.

39 See Chap. 5, above.

40 Schjeldahl, *Let's See*, p. 9.

41 Galenson, "The Reappearing Masterpiece," pp. 183–84.

42 See Chap. 7, above.

43 See Chap. 5, above.

44 See Chap. 10, above.

45 Galenson, "Do the Young British Artists Rule?" pp. 175–84.

46 Tomkins, *Post- to Neo-*, p. 242.

47 Also see Danto, *The Abuse of Beauty*, p. 123: "These traditional genres [painting and sculpture] play a decreasingly central role in the contemporary system of the arts."

48 Golding, *Cubism*, revised ed., p. 60.

49 Tomkins, *Lives of the Artists*, p. xi.

50 Danto, *Unnatural Wonders*, p. 99.

51 Tomkins, *The Bride and the Bachelors*, p. 236.

52 Wall caption, Room 27, Tate Britain, London, March, 2008. Also see Wilson, "Out of Control," pp. 3–9.

53 Johns, *Writings, Sketchbook Notes, Interviews*, pp. 93–94.

54 Motherwell, "Introduction," in Cabanne, *Dialogues with Marcel Duchamp*, p. 12.

55 McEvilley, *The Triumph of Anti-Art*, p. 24.

56 Higgins, "Work of art that inspired a movement . . . a urinal."

57 Higgins, "Work of art that inspired a movement . . . a urinal"; Tomkins, *Off the Wall*, p. 125.

58 Stiles and Selz, *Theories and Documents of Contemporary Life*, p. 321.

59 Danto, *The Madonna of the Future*, pp. 273–78.

60 Greenberg, *Late Writings*, p. 10; Perloff, *The Futurist Moment*, p. 52; Masheck, *Marcel Duchamp in Perspective*, p. 11.

61 Motherwell, *The Dada Painters and Poets*, p. 235; Taylor, *Collage*, p. 38.

62 Wescher, *Collage*, pp. 199–200.
63 Motherwell, *Dada Painters and Poets*, pp. 36–37.
64 Rosenberg, *Art on the Edge*, p. 176.
65 Mattison, *Robert Rauschenberg*, pp. 57–64; Schimmel, *Robert Rauschenberg Combines*, pp. 14–26, 211–12.
66 Kaprow, *Essays on the Blurring of Art and Life*, pp. 11, 63.
67 Tomkins, *Lives of the Artists*, pp. 13–14.
68 Bell, *Since Cézanne*, pp. 11, 83.
69 Bell, *Since Cézanne*, p. 2; Doran, *Conversations with Cézanne*, p. 39.
70 Flam, *Matisse on Art*, p. 124; Brassaï, *Conversations with Picasso*, p. 107.
71 Schapiro, *Worldview in Painting – Art and Society*, p. 144.
72 Detterer, *Art Recollection*, p. 117.
73 Hamilton, *Painting and Sculpture in Europe*, p. 15.
74 Danto, *Beyond the Brillo Box*, pp. 4, 8.

Bibliography

Acocella, Joan. *Twenty-Eight Artists and Two Saints*. New York: Pantheon Books, 2006.

Adams, Brooke, et al. *Sensation: Young British Artists from the Saatchi Collection*. London: Thames and Hudson, 1997.

Adams, Laurie. *A History of Western Art*. New York: Harry N. Abrams, 1994.

Ades, Dawn. *Photomontage*. London: Thames and Hudson, 1986.

Ades, Dawn, Neil Cox, and David Hopkins. *Marcel Duchamp*. New York: Thames and Hudson, 1999.

Adriani, Götz, Winfried Konnertz, and Karin Thomas. *Joseph Beuys: Life and Works*. Woodbury, NY: Barron's, 1979.

Alberro, Alexander and Patricia Norvell, eds. *Recording Conceptual Art*. Berkeley: University of California Press, 2001.

Alberti, Leon Battista. *On Painting*. London: Penguin, 1991.

Alloway, Lawrence. *William Baziotes*. New York: Solomon R. Guggenheim Museum, 1965.

Alloway, Lawrence. *American Pop Art*. New York: Macmillan, 1974.

Alpers, Svetlana. *Rembrandt's Enterprise*. Chicago: University of Chicago Press, 1988.

Andrew, Geoff. *The Film Handbook*. Boston: G.K. Hall, 1990.

Andrews, Richard. *Art Into Life*. New York: Rizzoli, 1990.

Ankori, Gannit. *Imaging Her Selves*. Westport, CT: Greenwood Press, 2002.

Apollinaire, Guillaume. *Apollinaire on Art*. Boston: MFA Publications, 2001.

Apollinaire, Guillaume. *The Cubist Painters*. Berkeley: University of California Press, 2004.

Apollonio, Umbro, ed. *Futurist Manifestos*. New York: Viking Press, 1973.

Archer, Michael. *Art Since 1960*, 2nd ed. London: Thames and Hudson, 2002.

Arnason, H. H. *History of Modern Art*, 5th ed. Upper Saddle River, NJ: Prentice Hall, 2004.

Arnheim, Rudolf. *The Genesis of a Painting: Picasso's Guernica*. Berkeley: University of California Press, 1962.

Ashbery, John. *Reported Sightings*. New York: Alfred A. Knopf, 1989.

Ashton, Dore, ed. *The New York School*. Berkeley: University of California Press, 1992.

Ashton, Dore, ed. *The Writings of Robert Motherwell*. Berkeley: University of California Press, 2007.

Auping, Michael. *Jenny Holzer*. New York: Universe, 1992.

Bailey, Anthony. *Responses to Rembrandt*. New York: Timken Publishers, 1994.

Baldaccini-Puigsegur, Anna. *César*. Paris: Images en Manoeuvres Editions, 2002.

Baldwin, Neil. *Man Ray*. New York: Clarkson Potter, 1988.

Ball, Hugo. *Flight Out of Time: A Dada Diary*. New York: Viking Press, 1974.

Barnett, Vivian. *Kandinsky at the Guggenheim*. New York: Abbeville Press, 1983.

Barr, Alfred H. Jr., ed. *Fantastic Art, Dada, Surrealism*. New York: Museum of Modern Art, 1936.

Barr, Alfred H. Jr. *Picasso*. New York: Museum of Modern Art, 1946.

Barr, Alfred H. Jr. *Matisse: His Art and His Public*. New York: Museum of Modern Art, 1966.

Barr, Alfred H. Jr. *Defining Modern Art*. New York: Harry N. Abrams, 1986.

Battcock, Gregory, ed. *Minimal Art*. Berkeley: University of California Press, 1995.

Baudelaire, Charles. *Art in Paris, 1845–1862*. London: Phaidon Press, 1965.

Baudelaire, Charles. *The Painter of Modern Life and Other Essays*. New York: Da Capo Press, 1986.

Bazile, Bernard. *Manzoni*. Villeurbanne: Institut d'art contemporain, 2004.

Berger, John. *The Success and Failure of Picasso*. New York: Vintage Books, 1993.

Berger, John. *Selected Essays*. New York: Vintage Books, 2001.

Bell, Clive. *Since Cézanne*. New York: Harcourt, Brace and Company, 1922.

Blesh, Rudi. *Modern Art USA*. New York: Alfred A. Knopf, 1956.

Blotkamp, Carel. *Mondrian: The Art of Destruction*. New York: Harry N. Abrams, 1995.

Bockris, Victor. *Warhol*. New York: Da Capo Press, 1997.

Bois, Yve-Alain, Joop Joosten, Angelica Rudenstine, and Hans Janssen. *Piet Mondrian*. Boston: Little, Brown, 1995.

Bomford, David, et al. *Art in the Making: Rembrandt*. London: National Gallery, 2006.

Bourdieu, Pierre. *The Field of Cultural Production*. New York: Columbia University Press, 1993.

Bourdon, David. *Warhol*. New York: Harry N. Abrams, 1989.

Bourgeois, Louise. *Destruction of the Father, Reconstruction of the Father*. Cambridge: MIT Press, 1998.

Bowness, Alan. *Modern European Art*. New York: Thames and Hudson, 1995.

Bowness, Alan. *The Conditions of Success: How the Modern Artist Rises to Fame*. New York: Thames and Hudson, 1990.

Bradley, Fiona. *Surrealism*. London: Tate Gallery Publishing, 1997.

Brassaï, *Conversations with Picasso*. Chicago: University of Chicago Press, 1999.

Breslin, James. *Mark Rothko*. Chicago: University of Chicago Press, 1993.

Breton, André. *Manifestoes of Surrealism*. Ann Arbor: University of Michigan Press, 1972.

Breton, André. *Surrealism and Painting*. Boston: MFA Publications, 2002.

Brewster, Deborah. "Why young, new money could fuel a bubble in hot, hip art," *Financial Times* (November 12/13, 2005): 7.

Brilliant, Alan. "Park Avenue Art Gallery," unpublished manuscript, Bryan, TX, 2005.

Brombert, Beth. *Edouard Manet*. Chicago: University of Chicago Press, 1997.

Brown, Christopher, Jan Kelch, and Pieter van Thiel, eds. *Rembrandt: The Master and His Workshop*. New Haven: Yale University Press, 1991.

Brown, Neal. *Tracey Emin*. London: Tate Publishing, 2006.

Brunette, Peter, ed. *Shoot the Piano Player*. New Brunswick, NJ: Rutgers University Press, 1993.

Buck, Louisa. *Moving Targets 2: A User's Guide to British Art Now*. London: Tate Publishing, 2000.

Button, Virginia. *The Turner Prize: Twenty Years*. London: Tate Publishing, 2003.

Cabanne, Pierre. *Pablo Picasso*. New York: William Morrow, 1977.

Cabanne, Pierre. *Dialogues with Marcel Duchamp*. New York: Da Capo Press, 1987.

Calder, Alexander. *Calder*. New York: Pantheon, 1966.

Camfield, William. *Francis Picabia*. Princeton: Princeton University Press, 1979.

Campbell, David. "Plotting Polke," in David Thistlewood, ed., *Sigmar Polke*. Liverpool: Liverpool University Press, 1996, pp. 19–40.

Canaday, John. *Culture Gulch*. New York: Farrar, Straus and Giroux, 1969.

Carmean, E. A. and Eliza Rathbone. *American Art at Mid-Century*. Washington, D.C.: National Gallery of Art, 1978.

Carrubba, Salvatore. *Piero Manzoni*. Milan: Fondazione Mudima, 1997.

Celant, Germano. *Piero Manzoni*. Milan: Edizioni Charta, 1998.

Cézanne, Paul. *Letters*. New York: Da Capo Press, 1995.

Chadwick, Whitney, ed. *Mirror Images*. Cambridge: MIT Press, 1998.

Chapman, Jake and Dinos. *Insult to Injury*. Gottingen: Steidlmack, 2003.

Charlet, N. *Yves Klein*. Paris: Adam Biro, 2000.

Chastel, André. *The Genius of Leonardo da Vinci*. New York: Orion Press, 1961.

Chernow, Burt. *Christo and Jeanne-Claude*. New York: Saint Martin's Press, 2002.

Chiappini, Rudy, ed. *Jean-Michel Basquiat*. Milan: Skira, 2005.

Chipp, Herschel. *Picasso's Guernica*. Berkeley: University of California Press, 1988.

Coen, Ester. *Umberto Boccioni*. New York: Metropolitan Museum of Art, 1988.

Collings, Matthew. *Blimey!: From Bohemia to Britpop*. Cambridge: 21 Publishing Ltd, 1997.

Collings, Matthew. *It Hurts: New York Art from Warhol to Now*. London: 21 Publishing, 1998.

Collings, Matthew. *Art Crazy Nation*. London: 21 Publishing, 2001.

Collings, Matthew. *Sarah Lucas*. London: Tate Publishing, 2002.

Condivi, Ascanio. *The Life of Michelangelo*, 2nd ed. University Park: Pennsylvania State University Press, 1999.

Cooper, Douglas. *The Cubist Epoch*. London: Phaidon Press, 1970.

Cooper, Harry and Ron Spronk. *Mondrian: The Transatlantic Paintings*. New Haven: Yale University Press, 2001.

Coplans, John, ed. *Roy Lichtenstein*. New York: Praeger, 1972.

Coplans, John. *Andy Warhol*. New York: New York Graphic Society, 1978.

Coplans, John. *Provocations*. London: London Projects, 1996.

Cork, Richard. *Breaking Down the Barriers*. New Haven: Yale University Press, 2003.

Cork, Richard. *New Spirit, New Sculpture, New Money*. New Haven: Yale University Press, 2003.

Cornell, Sara. *Art*. Englewood Cliffs: Prentice-Hall, 1983.

Courthion, Pierre. *Le Visage de Matisse*. Lausanne: Marguerat, 1942.

Courthion, Pierre and Pierre Cailler. *Portrait of Manet*. New York: Roy Publishers, 1960.

Cottington, David. *Cubism and Its Histories*. Manchester: Manchester University Press, 2004.

Cottington, David. *Modern Art*. Oxford: Oxford University Press, 2005.

Cresap, Kelly. *Pop Trickster Fool*. Urbana: University of Illinois Press, 2004.

Crispolti, Enrico and Olivier Meessen. *Lucio Fontana*. Saint Paul de Vence: Galerie Pascal Retelet, 2000.

Crone, Rainer and David Moos. *Kazimir Malevich*. Chicago: University of Chicago Press, 1991.

Cumming, Robert. *Art*. London: DK Publishing, 2005.

Dabrowski, Magdalena. "The Russian Contribution to Modernism: 'Construction' as Realization of Innovative Aesthetic Concepts of the Russian Avant-Garde." unpublished Ph.D. dissertation, New York University. 1990.

Danchev, Alex. *Georges Braque*. New York: Arcade Publishing, 2005.

Danto, Arthur. *Beyond the Brillo Box*. Berkeley: University of California Press, 1992

Danto, Arthur. *Embodied Meanings*. New York: Farrar, Straus and Giroux, 1994.

Danto, Arthur. *After the End of Art*. Princeton: Princeton University Press, 1997.

Danto, Arthur. *The Madonna of the Future*. Berkeley: University of California Press, 2000.

Danto, Arthur. *The Abuse of Beauty*. Chicago: Open Court, 2003.

Danto, Arthur. *Unnatural Wonders*. New York: Farrar, Straus, and Giroux, 2005.

Davis, Penelope, et al. *Janson's History of Art*, 7th ed. Upper Saddle River, NJ: Pearson Prentice Hall, 2007.

De Antonio, Emile and Mitch Tuchman. *Painters Painting*. New York: Abbeville Press, 1984.

de Duve, Thierry. *Pictorial Nominalism*. Minneapolis: University of Minnesota Press, 1991.

de Duve, Thierry. *Kant after Duchamp*. Cambridge: MIT Press, 1996.

de Kooning, Elaine. *The Spirit of Abstract Expressionism*. New York: George Braziller, 1994.

Deming, Robert, ed. *James Joyce: The Critical Heritage*, Vol. 2. New York: Barnes and Noble, 1970.

Dempsey, Amy. *Art in the Modern Era*. New York: Harry N. Abrams, 2002.

Detterer, Gabriele, ed. *Art Recollection*. Florence: Danilo Montanari, 1997.

Dexter, Emma and Tanya Barson, eds. *Frida Kahlo*. London: Tate Publishing, 2005.

Doran, Michael, ed. *Conversations with Cézanne*. Berkeley: University of California Press, 2001.

Drohojowska-Philp, Hunter. *Full Bloom*. New York: W. W. Norton, 2004.

Eagleton, Terry. *The English Novel*. Oxford: Blackwell, 2005.

Eggum, Arne. *Munch and Photography*. New Haven: Yale University Press, 1989.

Elderfield, John. *Kurt Schwitters*. London: Thames and Hudson, 1985.

Elger, Dietmar. *Dadaism*. Cologne: Taschen, 2006.

Elliott, Robert. *The Literary Persona*. Chicago: University of Chicago Press, 1982.

Ernst, Max. *Beyond Painting*. New York: Wittenborn, Schultz, 1948.

Erpel, Fritz. *Van Gogh Self-Portraits*. Oxford: Bruno Cassirer, 1964.

Evans, David and Sylvia Gohl. *Photomontage: A Political Weapon*. London: Gordon Fraser, 1986.

Farber, Manny. *Negative Space*, expanded ed. New York: Da Capo Press, 1998.

Farr, Dennis and Massimo Martino, eds. *Francis Bacon*. New York: Harry N. Abrams, 1999.

Felix, Zdenek, ed. *Francis Picabia*. Ostfildern: Hatje, 1998.

Filipczak, Zirka. *Picturing Art in Antwerp, 1550–1700*. Princeton: Princeton University Press, 1987.

Fineberg, Jonathan. *Art Since 1940*, 2nd ed. New York: Harry N. Abrams, 2000.

Fitzgerald, Michael. *Making Modernism*. Berkeley: University of California Press, 1996.

Flam, Jack. *Matisse*. Ithaca: Cornell University Press. 1986.

Flam, Jack. *Matisse on Art*, revised ed. Berkeley: University of California Press, 1995.

Flam, Jack, ed. *Robert Smithson: The Collected Writings*. Berkeley: University of California Press, 1996.

Flam, Jack. *Matisse and Picasso*. Cambridge, MA: Westview, 2004.

Fleming, William. *Arts and Ideas*, 9th ed. Fort Worth: Harcourt Brace, 1995.

Foster, Hal, Rosalind Krauss, Yve-Alain Bois, and Benjamin Buchloh. *Art Since 1900*. New York: Thames and Hudson, 2004.

Friedman, B. H. *Jackson Pollock*. New York: Da Capo Press, 1995.

Fry, Roger. *Last Lectures*. Boston: Beacon Press, 1962.

Fry, Roger. *Cézanne*. Chicago: University of Chicago Press, 1989.

Fry, Roger. *A Roger Fry Reader*. Chicago: University of Chicago Press, 1996.

Gabler, Neal. *Life the Movie*. New York: Alfred A. Knopf, 1998.

Gablik, Suzi. *Magritte*. New York: Thames and Hudson, 1985.

Gablik, Suzi. *Conversations Before the End of Time*. New York: Thames and Hudson, 1995.

Galenson, David. *Painting outside the Lines: Patterns of Creativity in Modern Art*. Cambridge: Harvard University Press, 2001.

Galenson, David. "The New York School versus the School of Paris: Who Really Made the Most Important Art After World War II?" *Historical Methods,* 35, No. 4 (2002): 141–53.

Galenson, David. "Was Jackson Pollock the Greatest Modern American Painter?: A Quantitative Investigation," *Historical Methods,* 35, No. 3 (2002): 117–28.

Galenson, David. "One-Hit Wonders: Why Some of the Most Important Works of Modern Art Are Not by Important Artists," *Historical Methods,* 38, No. 3 (2005): 101–17.

Galenson, David. "Who Are the Greatest Living Artists? The View from the Auction Market," NBER Working Paper 11644 (2005).

Galenson, David. "Anticipating Artistic Success: Lessons from History." *World Economics,* 6, No. 2 (2005): 11–26.

Galenson, David. "Do the Young British Artists Rule?" *World Economics,* 7, No. 1 (2006): 175–84.

Galenson, David. "Toward Abstraction: Ranking European Painters of the Early Twentieth Century," *Historical Methods,* 39, No. 3 (2006): 99–111.

Galenson, David. *Artistic Capital.* London: Routledge, 2006.

Galenson, David. *Old Masters and Young Geniuses.* Princeton: Princeton University Press, 2006.

Galenson, David. "The Greatest Architects of the Twentieth Century: Goals, Methods, and Life Cycles." NBER Working Paper 14182 (2008).

Galenson, David., and Robert Jensen. "Careers and Canvases: The Rise of the Market for Modern Art in the Nineteenth Century." *Van Gogh Studies* 1 (2007):137–66.

Galenson, David., and Bruce A. Weinberg. "Age and the Quality of Work," *Journal of Political Economy.* 108, No. 4 (2000): 761–77.

Gann, Kyle. *American Music in the Twentieth Century.* New York: Schirmer Books, 1997.

Garrels, Gary. ed. *The Work of Andy Warhol.* Seattle: Bay Press, 1989.

Garrels, Gary, ed. *Sol LeWitt: A Retrospective.* New Haven: Yale University Press, 2000.

Garrels, Gary. *Plane Image: A Brice Marden Retrospective.* New York: Museum of Modern Art, 2006.

Gauguin, Paul. *The Writings of a Savage.* New York: Da Capo Press, 1996.

Gebhardt, Volker. *The History of Art.* New York: Barron's, 1998.

Geist, Sidney. *Brancusi.* New York: Grossman Publishers, 1968.

Geist, Sidney. *Constantin Brancusi, 1876–1957: A Retrospective Exhibition.* New York: Solomon R. Guggenheim Museum, 1969.

Geist, Sidney. *Brancusi/The Kiss.* New York: Harper and Row, 1978.

Geldzahler, Henry. *Making It New.* San Diego: Harcourt Brace, 1996.

Gersh-Nesic, Beth. *The Early Criticism of André Salmon.* New York: Garland, 1991.

Gilbert and George. *The Words of Gilbert & George.* London: Violette Editions, 1997.

Gilbert, Rita. *Living With Art,* 5th ed. Boston: McGraw Hill, 1998.

Gilot, Françoise and Carlton Lake. *Life With Picasso*. New York: Anchor Books, 1989.

Gilson, Étienne. *Painting and Reality*. London: Routledge and Kegan Paul, 1958.

Gilson, Étienne. *Peinture et Réalité*. Paris: Librairie Philosophique, 1958.

Giry, Marcel. *Fauvism*. New York: Alpine Fine Arts, 1982.

Godard, Jean-Luc. *Godard on Godard*. New York: Da Capo Press, 1972.

Golding, John. *Cubism*. London: Faber and Faber, 1959.

Golding, John. *Cubism: A History and an Analysis, 1907–1914*, revised ed. Boston: Boston Book and Art Shop, 1968.

Golding, John. *Boccioni's "Unique Forms of Continuity in Space."* Newcastle: University of Newcastle upon Tyne, 1972.

Golding, John. *Visions of the Modern*. Berkeley: University of California Press, 1994.

Golding, John. *Paths to the Absolute*. Princeton: Princeton University Press, 2000.

Goldsmith, Kenneth, ed. *I'll Be Your Mirror: The Selected Andy Warhol Interviews*. New York: Carroll and Graf, 2004.

Goldwater, Robert. *Primitivism in Modern Painting*. New York: Harper and Brothers, 1938.

Gombrich, E. H. *Gombrich on the Renaissance*, Vol. 1, 4th ed. London: Phaidon Press, 1985.

Gombrich, E. H. *The Story of Art*, 16th ed. London: Phaidon, 1995.

Gombrich, Ernst. *Preference for the Primitive*. London: Phaidon, 2002.

Goodrich, Lloyd and Doris Bry. *Georgia O'Keeffe*. New York: Whitney Museum, 1970.

Gordon, Donald. *Ernst Ludwig Kirchner*. Cambridge: Harvard University Press, 1968.

Gottlieb, Adolph. "The Artist and the Public," *Art in America*, 42, No. 4 (1954): 267–71.

Graetz, H. R. *The Symbolic Language of Vincent van Gogh*. New York: McGraw Hill, 1963.

Greenberg, Clement. *The Collected Essays and Criticism*, Vol. 2. Chicago: University of Chicago Press, 1986.

Greenberg, Clement. *The Collected Essays and Criticism*. Vols. 3–4. Chicago: University of Chicago Press, 1993.

Greenberg, Clement. *Late Writings*. Minneapolis: University of Minneapolis Press, 2003.

Grohmann, Will. *Wassily Kandinsky*. New York: Harry N. Abrams, 1958.

Gruen, John. *The Artist Observed*. Chicago: A Cappella Books, 1991.

Grunenberg, Christoph. "Attraction-Repulsion Machines: The Art of Jake and Dinos Chapman," in Jake and Dinos Chapman, *Bad Art for Bad People*. London: Tate Publishing, 2006.

Guilbaut, Serge. *How New York Stole the Idea of Modern Art*. Chicago: University of Chicago Press, 1983.

Haden-Guest, Andy. *True Colors*. New York: Atlantic Monthly Press, 1996.

Hamilton, George Heard. *Manet and His Critics*. New Haven: Yale University Press, 1954.

Hamilton, George Heard. *Painting and Sculpture in Europe, 1880–1940.* Harmondsworth: Penguin, 1972.
Hamilton, Richard. *Collected Words, 1953–1982.* London: Thames and Hudson, 1982.
Hancock, Jane and Stefanie Poley. *Arp,* 1886–1966. Cambridge: Cambridge University Press, 1987.
Harrison, Charles and Paul Wood, eds. *Art in Theory, 1900–2000,* new ed. Oxford: Blackwell, 2003.
Hartley, Marsden. *On Art.* New York: Horizon Press, 1982.
Hartt, Frederick. *Art,* 3rd ed. Englewood Cliffs: Prentice-Hall, 1989.
Heartney, Eleanor, et al. *After the Revolution.* Munich: Prestel, 2007.
Heilbrun, James, and Charles Gray. *The Economics of Art and Culture.* 2nd ed. Cambridge: Cambridge University Press, 2001.
Heller, Nancy. *Women Artists,* 3rd ed. New York: Abbeville Press, 1997.
Heller, Reinhold. *Edvard Munch: The Scream.* New York: Viking Press, 1973.
Heller, Reinhold. *Munch.* Chicago: University of Chicago Press, 1984.
Henkels, Herbert. *Mondrian.* Tokyo: Tokyo Shimbun, 1987.
Henkels, Herbert. *Mondrian: From Figuration to Abstraction.* The Hague: Gemeentemuseum, 1987.
Herrera, Hayden. *Frida: A Biography of Frida Kahlo.* New York: Harper and Row, 1983.
Hess, Thomas. *Willem de Kooning.* New York: Museum of Modern Art, 1968.
Higgins, Charlotte. "Work of art that inspired a movement...a urinal," *Guardian* (Dec. 2, 2004).
Hirst, Damien, and Gordon Burn. *On the Way to Work.* New York: Universe Publishing, 2002.
Hoban, Phoebe. *Basquiat.* New York: Viking, 1998.
Holty, Carl. "Mondrian in New York: A Memoir," *Arts,* 31, No. 10 (1957).
Honour, Hugh and John Fleming. *The Visual Arts,* 6th ed. New York: Harry N. Abrams, 2002.
Huelsenbeck, Richard, ed. *The Dada Almanac.* London: Atlas Press, 1993.
Hughes, Henry Meyric and Gijs van Tuyl, eds. *Blast to Freeze: British Art in the 20th Century.* Wolfsburg, Germany: Kunstmuseum Wolfsburg, 2002.
Hughes, Robert. *Nothing If Not Critical.* New York: Penguin, 1990.
Hughes, Robert. *The Shock of the New.* New York: Afred A. Knopf, 1991.
Hulten, Pontus. *Jean Tinguely.* New York: Abbeville Press, 1987.
Hunter, Sam, John Jacobus, and Daniel Wheeler, *Modern Art,* 3rd ed. New York: Vendome Press, 2004.
Janssen, Hans and Joop Joosten. *Mondrian 1892–1914: The Path to Abstraction.* Zwolle: Waanders Publishers, 2002.
Jensen, Robert. *Marketing Modernism in Fin-de-Siècle Europe.* Princeton: Princeton University Press, 1994.
Jensen, Robert. "Anticipating Artistic Behavior: New Research Tools for Art Historians," *Historical Methods,* 37, No. 3 (2004): 137–53.
Jensen, Robert. "Van Gogh *als Erzieher:* Early Chapters in the Globalization of Conceptual Art," unpublished paper, University of Kentucky, 2007.

Johns, Jasper. *Writings, Sketchbook Notes, Interviews*. New York: Museum of Modern Art, 1996.

Johnson, Paul. *Art*. New York: Harper Collins, 2003.

Jonquet, François. *Gilbert and George*. London: Phaidon Press, 2004.

Jouffroy, Alain. *Picabia*. New York: Assouline, 2002.

Kahnweiler, Daniel-Henry. *The Rise of Cubism*. New York: Wittenborn, Schultz, 1949.

Kahnweiler, Daniel-Henry. *My Galleries and Painters*. Boston: MFA Publications, 2003.

Kandinsky, Wassily. *Complete Writings on Art*. New York: Da Capo Press, 1994.

Kandinsky, Wassily, and Franz Marc, eds. *The "Blaue Reiter" Almanac*. New York: Viking Press, 1974.

Kaprow, Allan. *Assemblage, Environments and Happenings*. New York: Harry N. Abrams, 1966.

Kaprow, Allan. *Essays on the Blurring of Art and Life*, expanded ed. Berkeley: University of California Press, 2003.

Karmel, Pepe, ed. *Jackson Pollock*. New York: Museum of Modern Art, 1999.

Keller, Julia. "Painting by the Numbers," *Chicago Tribune* (April 25, 2002).

Kelley, Jeff. *Childsplay: The Art of Allan Kaprow*. Berkeley: University of California Press, 2004.

Kemp, Martin, ed. *The Oxford History of Western Art*. Oxford: Oxford University Press, 2000.

Kenner, Hugh. *The Poetry of Ezra Pound*. Lincoln: University of Nebraska Press, 1985.

Kesten, Joanne, ed. *The Portraits Speak*. New York: A.R.T. Press, 1997.

Kimmelman, Michael. *Portraits*. New York: Modern Library, 1999.

Klein, Yves. *Le Dépassement de la problématique de l'art et autres écrits*. Paris: Ecole nationale supérieure des beaux-arts, 2003.

Koons, Jeff. *The Jeff Koons Handbook*. New York: Rizzoli, 1992.

Koons, Jeff. "Statement." American Federation of Arts Conference, *Art Matters*, New York, 2005.

Kostelanetz, Richard. ed. *Writings About John Cage*. Ann Arbor: University of Michigan Press, 1993.

Kosuth, Joseph. *Art After Philosophy and After*. Cambridge: MIT Press, 1991.

Krauss, Rosalind. *Cindy Sherman, 1975–1993*. New York: Rizzoli, 1993.

Krauss, Rosalind. "Warhol's Abstract Spectacle," in Yve-Alain Bois, et al., *Abstraction, Gesture, Ecriture*. Zurich: Alesco, 19993

Kubler, George. *The Shape of Time*. New Haven: Yale University Press, 1962.

Kuenzli, Rudolf and Francis Naumann, eds. *Marcel Duchamp*. Cambridge: MIT Press, 1989.

Kuh, Katharine. *The Artist's Voice*. New York: Harper and Row, 1962.

Kuthy, Sandor. *Pierre Soulages*. Berne: Musée des beaux-arts, 1999.

Lange, Susanne. *Bernd and Hilla Becher*. Cambridge: MIT Press, 2007.

Lavin, Maud. *Cut With the Kitchen Knife: The Weimar Photomontages of Hannah Höch*. New Haven: Yale University Press, 1993.

Leonhardt, David. "The Science of Pricing Great Works of Art," *New York Times* (November 15, 2006).

Lewallen, Constance. *A Rose Has No Teeth: Bruce Nauman in the 1960s*. Berkeley: University of California Press, 2007.

Lewis, David. *Constantin Brancusi*. London: Alec Tiranti, 1957.

LeWitt, Sol. *Critical Texts*. Rome: Editrice Inonia, 1994.

Levin, Kim. *Lucas Samaras*. New York: Harry N. Abrams, 1975.

Levin, Kim. *Beyond Modernism*. New York: Harper and Row, 1988.

Lifson, Ben. *Samaras*. New York: Aperture Foundation, 1987.

Lim, Dennis, ed. *The Village Voice Film Guide*. Hoboken, NJ: John Wiley and Sons, 2007.

Lindsay, Kenneth and Peter Vergo, eds. *Kandinsky*. New York: Da Capo Press, 1994.

Lippard, Lucy, ed. *Pop Art*. New York: Frederick A. Praeger, 1996.

Lippard, Lucy. *Changing*. New York: E. P. Dutton, 1971.

Lippard, Lucy. *Eva Hesse*. New York: Da Capo Press, 1992.

Lippard, Lucy. *Six Years: The dematerialization of the art object from 1966 to 1972*. Berkeley: University of California Press, 1997.

Lippard, Lucy, ed. *Dadas on Art*. Mineola, NY: Dover Publications, 2007.

Livingstone, Marco. *Pop Art*. New York: Harry N. Abrams, 1990.

Livingstone, Marco. *David Hockney*. London: Thames and Hudson, 1996.

Lodder, Christina. *Russian Constructivism*. New Haven: Yale University Press, 1983.

Loran, Erle. *Cézanne's Composition*. Berkeley: University of California Press, 2006.

Lowell, Robert. *Collected Prose*. New York: Farrar, Straus and Giroux, 1987.

Lynes, Barbara Buhler. *O'Keeffe, Stieglitz and the Critics, 1916–1929*. Chicago: University of Chicago Press, 1989.

Lynes, Russell. *Good Old Modern*. New York: Atheneum, 1973.

Madoff, Steven, ed. *Pop Art*. Berkeley: University of California Press, 1997.

Malevich, K. S. *Essays on Art, 1915–1933*. Vol. 1. London: Rapp and Whiting, 1968.

Man Ray. *Self Portrait*. Boston: Little, Brown, 1998.

Marquis, Alice Goldfarb. *Marcel Duchamp*. Boston: MFA Publications, 2002.

Marshall, Richard, ed. *Jean-Michel Basquiat*. New York: Whitney Museum, 1992.

Masheck, Joseph, ed. *Marcel Duchamp in Perspective*. New York: Da Capo Press, 2002.

Mast, Gerald. *A Short History of the Movies*, 4th ed. New York: Macmillan, 1986.

Mathey, François. *Trois sculpteurs*. Paris: Musée des arts décoratifs, 1965.

Matthews, Louisa. "The Painter's Presence: Signatures in Venetian Renaissance Pictures," *Art Bulletin*, 30, No. 4 (December 1998): 616–48.

Mattison, Robert. *Robert Rauschenberg*. New Haven: Yale University Press, 2003.

McCabe, Cynthia. *Artistic Collaboration in the Twentieth Century*. Washington, D.C.: Smithsonian Institution Press, 1984.

McCully, Marilyn, ed. *A Picasso Anthology*. Princeton: Princeton University Press, 1982.

McEvilley, Thomas. *The Triumph of Anti-Art*. Kingston, NY: McPherson and Company, 2005.

McShine, Kynaston, ed. *Information*. New York: Museum of Modern Art, 1970.

McShine, Kynaston, ed. *Andy Warhol: A Retrospective*. New York: Museum of Modern Art, 1989.

Mendelson, Edward, ed. *Pynchon*. Englewood Cliffs: Prentice-Hall, 1978.

Mercer, Kobena, ed. *Exiles, Diasporas and Strangers*. London: Iniva, 2008.

Merck, Mandy and Chris Townsend, ed. *The Art of Tracey Emin*. London: Thames and Hudson, 2002.

Messer, Thomas. *Piet Mondrian*. New York: Solomon R. Guggenheim Museum, 1971.

Messinger, Lisa Mintz. *Georgia O'Keeffe*. London: Thames and Hudson, 2001.

Meyer, Karl. *The Art Museum*. New York: William Morrow and Company, 1974.

Meyer, Peter, ed. *Brushes with History*. New York: Nation Books, 2001.

Millard, Rosie. *The Tastemakers: U.K. Art Now*. London: Scribner, 2002.

Milner, John. *Vladimir Tatlin and the Russian Avant-Garde*. New Haven: Yale University Press, 1983.

Milner, John. *Kazimir Malevich and the Art of Geometry*. New Haven: Yale University Press, 1996.

Miró, Joan. *Selected Writings and Interviews*. New York: Da Capo Press, 1992.

Molina, Joaquin. *Nicolas Garcia Uriburu*. Buenos Aires: Nexos, 2002.

Montias, John Michael. *Artists and Artisans in Delft*. Princeton: Princeton University Press, 1982.

Moore, Henry. *Henry Moore: Writings and Conversations*. Berkeley: University of California Press, 2002.

Morgan, Robert, ed. *Bruce Nauman*. Baltimore: Johns Hopkins University Press, 2002.

Morphet, Richard. *Richard Hamilton*. London: Tate Gallery, 1970.

Motherwell, Robert, ed. *The Dada Painters and Poets: An Anthology*, 2nd ed. Cambridge: Harvard University Press, 1981.

Motherwell, Robert. "Introduction," in Pierre Cabanne, *Dialogues with Marcel Duchamp*. New York: Da Capo Press, 1987, pp. 7–12.

Motherwell, Robert. *The Collected Writings of Robert Motherwell*. New York: Oxford University Press, 1992.

Müller-Westermann, Iris. *Munch by Himself*. London: Royal Academy of Arts, 2005.

Mullins, Charlotte. *Rachel Whiteread*. London: Tate Publishing, 2004.

Nakamura, Toshiharu, ed. *Rubens and His Workshop*. Tokyo: National Museum of Western Art, 1994.

Nairne, Sandy. *State of the Art*. London: Chatto and Windus, 1987.

Nemser, Cindy. *Art Talk: Conversations with 15 Women Artists*. New York: Harper Collins, 1995.

Newman, Barnett. *Selected Writings and Interviews*. Berkeley: University of California Press, 1992.

New York Times, editorial. "Dumping the Shark" (July 20, 2007).

Nicholls, David, ed. The Cambridge Companion to John Cage. Cambridge: Cambridge University Press, 2002.

Nixon, Mignon, ed. Eva Hesse. Cambridge: MIT Press, 2002.

O'Brien, Edna. James Joyce. New York: Penguin, 1999.

O'Doherty, Brian. Inside the White Cube. Santa Monica: The Lapis Press, 1986.

O'Hagan, Sean. "Hirst's diamond creation is art's costliest work ever," The Observer (May 21, 2006).

Oxford English Dictionary, 2nd ed., Vols. 1–20. Oxford: Clarendon Press, 1991.

Oxford English Dictionary Additions Series, Vols. 1–2. Oxford: Clarendon Press, 1993.

Passuth, Krisztina. Moholy-Nagy. New York: Thames and Hudson, 1987.

Pearce, Richard, ed. Critical Essays on Thomas Pynchon. Boston: G.K. Hall, 1981

Penrose, Roland. Man Ray. Boston: New York Graphic Society, 1975.

Penrose, Roland. Picasso, 3rd ed. Berkeley: University of California Press, 1981.

Peppiatt, Michael. Francis Bacon. London: Weidenfeld and Nicolson, 1996.

Perlein, Gilbert, ed. Niki de Saint Phalle. Nice: Musée d'art modern et d'art contemporain, 2002.

Perloff, Marjorie. The Futurist Moment. Chicago: University of Chicago Press, 1986.

Perry, Gill and Paul Wood, eds. Themes in Contemporary Art. New Haven: Yale University Press, 2004.

Phillips, Robert. The Confessional Poets. Carbondale: Southern Illinois University Press, 1973.

Pissarro, Camille. Letters to His Son Lucien. New York: Da Capo Press, 1995.

Planck, Max. Scientific Autobiography and Other Papers. New York: Greenwood Press, 1968.

Polsky, Richard. Art Market Guide, 1995–96 Season. New York: D. A. P., 1995.

Pope-Hennessy, John. Raphael. New York: Harper and Row, 1970.

Porter, Fairfield. Art In Its Own Terms. New York: Taplinger Publishing Co., 1979.

Prather, Marla. Claes Oldenburg: An Anthology. New York: Guggenheim Museum, 1995.

Pratt, Alan, ed. The Critical Response to Andy Warhol. Westport, Ct: Greenwood Press, 1997.

Prideaux, Sue. Edvard Munch. New Haven: Yale University Press, 2005.

Pritchett, James. The Music of John Cage. Cambridge: Cambridge University Press, 1993.

Ray, Gene, ed. Joseph Beuys. New York: Distributed Art Publishers, 2001.

Restany, Pierre. Uriburu. Milan: Electa, 2001.

Rewald, John. Paul Cézanne. New York: Simon and Schuster, 1948.

Rewald, John. The History of Impressionism, revised ed. New York: Museum of Modern Art, 1961.

Rewald, John, ed. Paul Cézanne Letters. New York: Da Capo Press, 1995.

Revill, David. The Roaring Silence. New York: Arcade Publishing, 1992.

Richardson, John. A Life of Picasso, Vol. 1. New York: Random House, 1991.

Richardson, John. *A Life of Picasso*, Vol. 2. New York: Random House, 1996.

Richter, Gerhard. *The Daily Practice of Painting*. Cambridge: MIT Press, 1995.

Richter, Hans. *Dada: Art and Anti-Art*. London: Thames and Hudson, 1965.

Riding, Alan. "Alas, Poor Art Market: A Multimillion-Dollar Head Case," *New York Times* (June 13, 2007).

Robins, Corinne. *The Pluralist Era: American Art 1968–1981*. New York: Harper and Row, 1984.

Rockwell, John. *All American Music*. New York: Alfred A. Knopf, 1983.

Rodman, Selden. *Conversations with Artists*. New York: Capricorn Books, 1961.

Rorimer, Anne. *New Art in the 60s and 70s*. London: Thames and Hudson, 2001.

Rose, Andrea. *Francis Bacon*. Edinburgh: National Galleries of Scotland, 2005.

Rose, Barbara. *Frankenthaler*. New York: Harry N. Abrams, 1971.

Rosen, Randy and Catherine Brawer, eds. *Making Their Mark: Women Artists Move into the Mainstream, 1970–85*. New York: Abbeville Press, 1988.

Rosenberg, Harold. *Arshile Gorky*. New York: Sheep Meadow Press, 1962.

Rosenberg, Harold. *Discovering the Present*. Chicago: University of Chicago Press, 1973.

Rosenberg, Harold. *Art on the Edge*. Chicago: University of Chicago Press, 1983.

Rosenberg, Harold. *The De-Definition of Art*. Chicago: University of Chicago Press, 1983.

Rosenberg, Harold. *Art and Other Serious Matters*. Chicago: University of Chicago Press, 1985.

Rosenberg, Harold. *The Tradition of the New*. New York: Da Capo Press, 1994.

Rosenblum, Robert, et al. *Edvard Munch*. Washington: National Gallery of Art, 1978.

Roskill, Mark. *Van Gogh, Gauguin and the Impressionist Circle*. Greenwich, Conn.: New York Graphic Society, 1970.

Rothko, Mark. *Writings on Art*. New Haven: Yale University Press, 2006.

Rubin, William. *Dada, Surrealism, and Their Heritage*. New York: Museum of Modern Art, 1968.

Rubin, William. *Frank Stella*. New York: Museum of Modern Art, 1970.

Rubin, William. ed. *Pablo Picasso: A Retrospective*. New York: Museum of Modern Art, 1980.

Rubin, William. *"Primitivism" in 20th Century Art*. Vol. 1. New York: Museum of Modern Art, 1984.

Rubin, William, Hélène Seckel, and Judith Cousins. *Les Demoiselles d'Avignon*. New York: Museum of Modern Art, 1994.

Ruscha, Ed. *Leave Any Information at the Signal*. Cambridge: MIT Press, 2002.

Ruskin, Ariane. *History in Art*. New York: Franklin Watts, 1974.

Russell, John. *Max Ernst*. New York: Harry N. Abrams, 1967.

Russell, John. *The Meanings of Modern Art*. New York: Museum of Modern Art, 1981.

Russell, John. *Francis Bacon*, revised ed. New York: Thames and Hudson, 1993.

Russell, John and Suzi Gablik, eds. *Pop Art Redefined*. New York: Frederick A. Praeger, 1969.

Salmans, Sandra. "The Fine Art of Yale," *New York Times* (April 24, 2005).

Saltz, Jerry. *Seeing Out Loud*. Great Barrington, MA: The Figures, 2003.

Sandler, Irving. *The New York School*. New York: Harper and Row, 1978.
Sandler, Irving. *Art of the Postmodern Era*. New York: Harper Collins, 1996.
Sanouillet, Michel and Elmer Peterson, eds., *The Writings of Marcel Duchamp*. New York: Da Capo Press, 1989.
Schapiro, Meyer. *Modern Art: 19th and 20th Centuries*. New York: George Braziller, 1982.
Schapiro, Meyer. *Vincent van Gogh*. New York: Harry N. Abrams, 1994.
Schapiro, Meyer. *Worldview in Painting – Art and Society*. New York: George Braziller, 1999.
Schapiro, Meyer. *The Unity of Picasso's Art*. New York: George Braziller, 2000.
Schneeman, Carolee. *More than Meat Joy*. New Paltz, NY: Documentext, 1979.
Schimmel, Paul. *Robert Rauschenberg Combines*. Los Angeles: Museum of Contemporary Art, 2005.
Schjeldahl, Peter. *The "7 Days" Art Columns, 1988–1990*. Great Barrington, MA: The Figures, 1990.
Schjeldahl, Peter. *The Hydrogen Jukebox*. Berkeley: University of California Press, 1991.
Schjeldahl, Peter. *Let's See*. New York: Thames and Hudson, 2008.
Schjeldahl, Peter and Lisa Phillips. *Cindy Sherman*. New York: Whitney Museum, 1987.
Schlemmer, Tut, ed. *The Letters and Diaries of Oskar Schlemmer*. Middletown, CT: Wesleyan University Press, 1972.
Schubert, Karsten. *The Curator's Egg*. London: One-Off Press, 2000.
Seitz, William. *The Art of Assemblage*. New York: Museum of Modern Art, 1961.
Seitz, William. *Abstract Expressionist Painting in America*. Cambridge: Harvard University Press, 1983.
Seitz, William. *Art in the Age of Aquarius, 1955–1970*. Washington: Smithsonian Institution Press, 1992.
Selz, Peter. *The Work of Jean Dubuffet*. New York: Museum of Modern Art, 1962.
Selz, Peter. *German Expressionist Painting*. Berkeley: University of California Press, 1974.
Seuphor, Michel. *Piet Mondrian*. New York: Harry N. Abrams, 1956.
Severini, Gino. *The Life of a Painter*. Princeton: Princeton University Press, 1995.
Shattuck, Roger. *The Innocent Eye*. Boston: MFA Publications, 2003.
Sherman, Cindy. *Untitled Film Stills*. New York: Rizzoli, 1990.
Sherman, Cindy. *The Complete "Untitled Film Stills."* New York: Museum of Modern Art, 2003.
Shonibare, Yinka. *Double Dutch*. Rotterdam: NAi Publishers, 2004.
Sickert, Walter. *The Complete Writings on Art*. Oxford: Oxford University Press, 2000.
Siegel, Jeanne, ed. *Artwords 2: Discourse on the Early 80s*. Ann Arbor: UMI Research Press, 1988.
Siegel, Katy and Paul Mattick. *Art Works: Money*. New York: Thames and Hudson, 2004.
Simmel, Marianne, ed. *The Reach of Mind*. New York: Springer Publishing, 1968.
Simpson, Louis. *A Revolution in Taste*. New York: Macmillan, 1978.

Sims, Lowery, ed. *Stuart Davis*. New York: Metropolitan Museum of Art, 1991.

Sklar, Robert. *Film*. New York: Harry N. Abrams, 1993.

Slatkin, Wendy. *The Voices of Women Artists*. Englewood Cliffs, NJ: Prentice Hall, 1993.

Solomon, Deborah. "Frank Stella's Expressionist Phase," *New York Times Magazine* (May 4, 2003).

Smith, Karen. *Nine Lives: The Birth of Avant-Garde Art in New China*. Zurich: Scalo Verlag, 2005.

Smith, Larry. *Pete Townshend*. Westport, Conn.: Praeger, 1999.

Smithson, Robert. *The Collected Writings*. Berkeley: University of California Press, 1996.

Sproccati, Sandro. *A Guide to Art*. New York: Harry N. Abrams, 1992.

Spurling, Hilary. *The Unknown Matisse*. New York: Alfred Knopf, 1998.

Stachelhaus, Heiner. *Joseph Beuys*. New York: Abbeville Press, 1991.

Stallabrass, Julian. *High Art Lite*. London: Verso, 1999.

Stallabrass, Julian. *High Art Lite*, revised ed. London: Verso, 2006.

Stangos, Nikos, ed. *Concepts of Modern Art*, 3rd ed. New York: Thames and Hudson, 1994.

Stauffer, Donald. *A Short History of American Poetry*. New York: E. P. Dutton, 1974.

Steinberg, Leo. *Other Criteria*. London: Oxford University Press, 1972.

Stich, Sidra. *Yves Klein*. Stuttgart: Cantz Verlag, 1994.

Stiles, Kristine and Peter Selz, eds., *Theories and Documents of Contemporary Art*. Berkeley: University of California Press, 1996.

Stokstad, Marilyn. *Art History*. New York: Harry N. Abrams, 1995.

Stolwijk, Chris, ed. *Vincent's Choice: Van Gogh's Musée Imaginaire*. Amsterdam: Van Gogh Museum, 2003.

Stonehill, Brian. *The Self-Conscious Novel: Artifice in Fiction from Joyce to Pynchon*. Philadelphia: University of Pennsylvania Press, 1988.

Storr, Robert. *Chuck Close*. New York: Museum of Modern Art, 1998.

Strickland, Carol. *The Annotated Mona Lisa*. Kansas City: Andrews and McMeel, 1992.

Sylvester, David. *Magritte*. Antwerp: Mercatorfonds, 1992.

Sylvester, David. *About Modern Art*. New York: Henry Holt, 1997.

Sylvester, David. *Interviews with Francis Bacon*. New York: Thames and Hudson, 1999.

Sylvester, David. *About Modern Art*, 2nd ed. New Haven: Yale University Press, 2001.

Sylvester, David. *Interviews with American Artists*. New Haven: Yale University Press, 2001.

Sylvester, David. *London Recordings*. London: Chatto and Windus, 2003.

Tate Modern. *Gilbert & George Major Exhibition*. London: Tate Modern, 2007.

Taylor, Brandon. *Collage*. London: Thames and Hudson, 2004.

Temkin, Ann. *Contemporary Voices*. New York: Museum of Modern Art, 2005.

Terenzio, Stephanie, ed. *The Collected Writings of Robert Motherwell*. New York: Oxford University Press, 1992.

Thistlewood, David, ed. *Joseph Beuys*. Liverpool: Liverpool University Press, 1995.

Thistlewood, David, ed. *Sigmar Polke*. Liverpool: Liverpool University Press, 1996.

Thomas, Landon and Carol Vogel. "A New Prince of Wall Street Uses His Riches to Buy Art," *New York Times* (March 3, 2005): A1.

Tisdall, Caroline. *Joseph Beuys*. New York: Solomon R. Guggenheim Museum, 1979.

Tojner, Paul Erik. *Munch In His Own Words*. Munich: Prestel, 2001.

Tomkins, Calvin. *The Bride and the Bachelors*. New York: Viking Press, 1965.

Tomkins, Calvin. *Off the Wall*. Harmondsworth: Penguin, 1981.

Tomkins, Calvin. *Post- to Neo-: The Art World of the 1980s*. New York: Penguin, 1989.

Tomkins, Calvin. *Duchamp*. New York: Henry Holt and Company, 1996.

Tomkins, Calvin. *Off the Wall*, new ed. New York: Picador, 2005.

Tomkins, Calvin. "Everything in Sight: Robert Rauschenberg's New Life." *New Yorker* (May 23, 2005): 68–77.

Tomkins, Calvin. *Lives of the Artists*. New York: Henry Holt. 2008.

Trilling, Lionel. *Sincerity and Authenticity*. Cambridge: Harvard University Press, 1972.

Tucker, Anne Wilkes. *Brassaï*. New York: Harry N. Abrams. 1999.

Turner, Christopher. "Great Deeds Against Dead Artists," in Jake and Dinos Chapman, *Bad Art for Bad People*. London: Tate Publishing, 2006.

Tusa, John. *The Janus Aspect*. London: Methuen, 2006.

Valéry, Paul. *Degas, Manet, Morisot*. Princeton: Princeton University Press, 1960.

van Bruggen, Coosje. *Bruce Nauman*. New York: Rizzoli, 1988.

van de Wetering, Ernst. *Rembrandt*. Berkeley: University of California Press, 2000.

Van Der Marck, Jan. *Arman*. New York: Abbeville Press, 1984.

van Garrel, Betty, ed. *Cindy Sherman*. Rotterdam: Museum Boijmans Van Beuningen, 1996.

van Gogh, Vincent. *The Complete Letters of Vincent van Gogh*, 2nd ed., Vols. 1–3. Greenwich, Ct.: New York Graphic Society, 1959.

Varnedoe, Kirk. *Jackson Pollock*. New York: Museum of Modern Art, 1998.

Varnedoe, Kirk. *Pictures of Nothing*. Princeton: Princeton University Press, 2006.

Varnedoe, Kirk, and Adam Gopnik. *High and Low*. New York: Museum of Modern Art, 1990.

Vasari, Giorgio. *Vasari's Lives of the Artists*. New York: Simon and Schuster, 1946.

Violette, Robert and Hans-Ulrich Obrist, eds. *The Words of Gilbert & George*. New York: Violette Editions, 1997.

Viso, Olga. *Ana Mendieta*. Washington, DC: Hirschhorn Museum, 2004.

Wagner, Anne Middleton. *Three Artists (Three Women)*. Berkeley: University of California Press, 1996.

Walker, John. *Art and Celebrity*. London: Pluto Press, 2003.

Warhol, Andy. *THE Philosophy of Andy Warhol*. San Diego: Harcourt Brace and Company, 1975.

Warhol, Andy and Pat Hackett. *POPism: The Warhol Sixties*. Orlando: Harcourt, 1980.

Walther, Ingo, ed. *Masterpieces of Western Art*. Cologne: Taschen, 2005.

Weintraub, Linda. *Art on the Edge and Over*. Litchfield, CT: Art Insights, 1996.

Wescher, Herta. *Collage*. New York: Harry N. Abrams, 1968.

White, Christopher and Quentin Buvelot. *Rembrandt by Himself*. London: National Gallery Publications, 1999.

White, Harrison and Cynthia. *Canvases and Careers*. Chicago: University of Chicago Press, 1993.

Wilkins, David, Bernard Schultz, and Katheryn Linduff. *Art Past, Art Present*, 3rd ed. New York: Harry N. Abrams, 1997.

Williamson, Alan. *Introspection and Contemporary Poetry*. Cambridge: Harvard University Press, 1984.

Wilson, Andrew. "Out of Control," *Art Monthly*, 177 (1994): 3–9.

Wittkower, Margot, and Rudolf Wittkower. *Born Under Saturn*. New York: New York Review Books, 2007.

Wittkower, Rudolf. *Sculpture: Processes and Principles*. New York: Harper and Row, 1977.

Wollen, Peter. *Paris Hollywood*. London: Verso, 2002.

Wollen, Peter. *Paris Manhattan*. London: Verso, 2004.

Wood, Paul, ed. *Varieties of Modernism*. New Haven: Yale University Press, 2004.

Woolf, Virginia. *Roger Fry: A Biography*. San Diego: Harcourt Brace Jovanovich, 1976.

Woollett, Anne and Ariane van Suchtelen. *Rubens and Brueghel: A Working Friendship*. Los Angeles: Getty Publications, 2006.

Wright, Karen, ed. *Writers on Artists*. New York: DK Publishing, 2001.

Wullschlager, Jackie. "Rachel Whiteread," *Financial Times* (Jan. 20/21, 2007): W3.

Wye, Deborah. *Louise Bourgeois*. New York: Museum of Modern Art, 1982.

Zevi, Adachiara, ed. *Sol LeWitt Critical Texts*. Rome: Editrice Inonia, 1994.

Zhadova, Larissa. *Malevich*. London: Thames and Hudson, 1982.

Zinnes, Harriet, ed. *Ezra Pound and the Visual Arts*. New York: New Directions Books, 1980.

Zurcher, Bernard. *Georges Braque*. New York: Rizzoli, 1988.

Zweite, Armin. *Gerhard Richter*. New York: Distributed Art Publishers, 2005.

Index

121; exquisite corpse, Breton's invention of, 119, 201; found objects, Breton's invention of, 120–21; frottage, Ernst's invention of, 118–19; "genre," meaning of, 113; happening, Kaprow's invention of, 124, 357–58; installations, invention of, 128–29; introduced in the 1910s, 114–18; introduced in the 1920s, 118–19; introduced in the 1930s, 119–21; introduced in the 1940s, 121; introduced in the 1950s, 121–25; introduced in the 1960s, 125–30; introduced in the 1970s, 130; introduced in the 1980s, 130; involuntary sculptures, Brassaï's invention of, 120; joiners, Hockney's invention of, 130; light-space modulator, Moholy-Nagy's invention of, 119–20; living sculptures, Manzoni's invention of, 127, 171; merz, Schwitters's invention of, 117; meta-matics, Tinguely's invention of, 123; mobiles, Calder's invention of, 120; non-site, Smithson's invention of, 129; papier collé, Braque's invention of, 114–15, 350; papier déchiré, Arp's invention of, 117; performance, invention of, 129; photograms, Moholy-Nagy's invention of, 118; photomontage, Dada artists' invention of, 117–18, 300; photopainting, Richter's invention of, 128; photo-transformation, Samaras's invention of, 130; poubelles, Arman's invention of, 126; proliferation of in the twentieth century, 112, 132–34, 349–50; proun, Lissitzky's invention of, 118; puzzle of post-1960s drop-off in creation of, 133; rayograms, Man Ray's invention of, 118, 147; readymades, Duchamp's invention of, 68–69, 115–16, 163, 350 (*see also* readymades); shot-reliefs, de Saint Phalle's invention of, 127; skoobs, Latham's invention of, 128; soft sculpture, Oldenburg's invention of, 128; spatial concepts, Fontana's invention of, 121; stabiles, Calder's invention of, 120; tagli, Fontana's invention of, 123–24; video, Vostell and Paik's invention of, 125; wall drawings, LeWitt's invention of, 129–30, 193–94; wrapped projects, Javacheff's invention of, 123

artistic importance/success: limited potential for achieving in contemporary art world, 59–60, 353–54; manufacture of, 4–5; measuring, 15–16, 30–31, 62–63; peer recognition as key to establishing, 5–6; speed of attaining, change in, 6–7

artistic tricksters: attacks on Manet and Picasso as, 159–60; Beuys, 166–67; as conceptual innovators producing a type of conceptual art, 182; Duchamp as the prototype, 161–66, 181–83; Emin, 177–78; Gilbert and George, 173–75; Hirst, 178–80; Klein, 169–71; Koons, 175–77; Manzoni, 171–73; model of in the twentieth-century, 160–61, 180–83; public persona as part of a constructed, 317; Warhol, 167–69

artists: artistic success, as key judges of, 4–6; best years in careers of the greatest twentieth-century, 81–87; as celebrities, 26–29; changing behavior of, the shift beginning in the late nineteenth century and, 360–63; co-authorship by (*see* co-authorship of art); collaborations between (*see* collaborations); experimental and conceptual innovators, distinction between (*see* innovators, conceptual distinguished from experimental); generational conflicts between (*see* generational conflicts); greatest of the twentieth century, ranking of, 31–33, 59–60; importance of based on impact as innovator on other artists, 4–6; innovative in a competitive art market, rewards for, 22–23; labor of/production of art by (*see* production of art); language, use of in works (*see* language); location of, significance of, 278–79 (*see also* artistic centers; globalization of art); market conditions and production of art by, relationship of, 17–23 (*see also* economics of art, the); photography, use of, 23–25 (*see also* photography); self-portraiture and personal visual art by (*see* personal visual art); speed at which avant-garde are recognized, 6–7; stylistic versatility among (*see* stylistic versatility); as tricksters (*see* artistic tricksters); women (*see* women artists)